Financial Exposure

Elise J. Bean

Financial Exposure

Carl Levin's Senate Investigations into Finance and Tax Abuse

palgrave
macmillan

Elise J. Bean
Levin Center at Wayne Law
Wayne State University Law School
Detroit, MI, USA

ISBN 978-3-319-94387-9   ISBN 978-3-319-94388-6   (eBook)
https://doi.org/10.1007/978-3-319-94388-6

Library of Congress Control Number: 2018947171

Cover design by Ran Shauli
Cover image credit: US Senate

This Palgrave Macmillan imprint is published by the registered company Springer Nature Switzerland AG
The registered company address is: Gewerbestrasse 11, 6330 Cham, Switzerland

For the brave, hard-working public servants
who fight for good government every day

Foreword

Elise Bean has written a richly textured and highly readable chronicle about the power of congressional oversight and how—when done as an objective, bipartisan search for truth—it can enhance public policy and lead to real reforms.

Her story is based on her staff leadership role on the Senate's Permanent Subcommittee on Investigations for 15 years. She describes with gusto the grinding work of that subcommittee staff—how they dug deeply into events and helped provide grist for the legislative mill.

The book dramatically recounts that the PSI investigations achieved their goals and their legislative impact because PSI's Democratic and Republican leadership trusted each other to jointly search for the facts wherever the search might lead them, and because those leaders gave clear, unambiguous direction to their staffs to work together as a bipartisan team, from sharing all witness interviews to sharing all documents.

In a heartwarming way, Elise describes how the staffs welcomed that direction and found highly rewarding work in a mutual commitment to discovering the facts as a team, a commitment so different from the many places on Capitol Hill where information is looked at through partisan filters.

The book is also a reassuring reminder of the power of facts, and how facts can be "stubborn things." Facts have also become increasingly "fragile things," making Elise's account, dramatizing how powerful facts can be when honestly pursued and presented, a reassuring tonic for our times.

Congressional oversight, when pursued on a bipartisan basis, has long served as an essential check on the executive branch and on misconduct in the private sector. Elise's book provides the best insider account I know of showing how oversight is an essential legislative function at the heart of efforts by persons of all political persuasions to improve our communities. Her account should give us confidence that fact-driven, in-depth, bipartisan oversight, as so presciently envisioned by the Constitution, can continue to be an effective defender of our national values.

Former U.S. Senator from Michigan, USA   Carl Levin

Prologue

This improbable tale defies conventional wisdom about Congress as a grid-locked, inept, and partisan black hole. It is a story about congressional oversight investigations that exposed wrongdoing, built bipartisan trust, and served as an instrument of positive change, despite widespread distemper in Washington.

The part I played was as a congressional investigator, a job that had never crossed my mind when thinking about a career. I lucked into the oversight world with no notion of the challenges and sheer hard work ahead of me. From the beginning, the job gripped me, stretched me, made me both more cynical and more idealistic. It led me to a deep commitment to Congress, as diabolically frustrating and disillusioning as that institution can be.

My journey began when I was hired by Senator Carl Levin from Michigan. I didn't know it then, but he was the public servant everyone imagines when thinking of how Congress ought to work. He was tough and shrewd, with the integrity, smarts, and stamina to take on any opponent. His signature image was of a disheveled, avuncular everyman, piercing blue eyes peering calmly over half-rim glasses perched on the end of his nose, refusing to avert his eyes from what he saw. His level gaze, Midwestern decency, and willingness to combat wrongdoing even in the face of long odds inspired the oversight adventures narrated here.

The Levin investigative crew was also right out of central casting—fearless, brilliant, and unrelenting. Folks dedicated to public service despite all the jokes about government and Congress, all the frustrations, and all the disrespect. Colleagues willing to confront powerful interests backed by the biggest lobbyists, law firms, and public relations specialists in town, putting in endless hours to make up for our small numbers and limited resources. And, like many investigators, we relished the battle.

This book focuses on 15 years, from 1999 to 2014, when Senator Levin served in leadership positions on the U.S. Senate Permanent Subcommittee on Investigations, also known as PSI. PSI has been the premier investigative body in the Senate for decades, with special tools, traditions, and know-how to carry out high-profile investigations. During my time there, I learned how to squeeze the facts out of opponents, overcome dirty tricks, feed the media, take the political heat, and make the case for change.

In addition, because Senator Levin's favorite investigative topic was financial chicanery, I learned more than I ever wanted to about money laundering, offshore gimmicks, tax dodging, accounting skullduggery, and derivatives double-dealing. Our investigations ranged from wrongdoing that fueled crime, produced billion-dollar losses, or cheated average families, to dishonest practices that led to widescale economic mayhem like the 2008 financial crisis. We followed the money, unraveled the facts, and disclosed troubling practices to policymakers and the public. And we did it while drinking Manhattans with our Republican colleagues.

The Levin years taught me how simply bearing witness to the facts can spark change, how conducting a good-faith investigation can turn a political competitor into an ally, and how congressional oversight can contribute to the common good. It is an education worth sharing.

More than that, it convinced me that constructive congressional oversight lies at the core of our democratic system of checks and balances. At its best, it can stop abuses, expose wrongdoing, and compel reforms. It can build a factual foundation for a shared understanding of a complex problem and lead to consensus on what to do about it. It offers a bipartisan mechanism to cure some of what ails us.

That's not to say all congressional oversight plays a positive role. Many of the norms driving high-quality oversight have broken down, leading to congressional investigations that are unfair, dishonest, and counterproductive. Rather than bemoan those bad examples, this book focuses on what congressional oversight can be, should be, and, at times, has been.

This book is intended as a resource for all those brave souls who haven't given up on good government, who believe that fair-minded congressional investigations are possible and valuable, and who want to practice the art of fact-based, nonpartisan, high-quality oversight. It is dedicated to those who, like me, see congressional oversight as a precious heritage that merits more attention, appreciation, and nurturing by our elected officials, policymakers, academics, the American public, and world community.

I would like to thank everyone who assisted in the writing of this book, including Senator Levin; the folks who lived the PSI investigations; the agency personnel, investigative reporters, and public interest advocates who contributed to PSI's work; and the Senate legal counsel and historian's offices—everyone who took the time to help inform this history of PSI. I would also like to thank the nonprofit Levin Center at Wayne Law for banging the drum on the importance of congressional oversight and doing the hard work needed to strengthen fact-based, bipartisan, in-depth congressional investigations. More thanks are due to Linda Gustitus, public servant extraordinaire and valued friend, who was a never-ending source of insight and encouragement. Thanks also to Steve Blakely who managed to diplomatically improve my prose. Above all, my gratitude goes to my husband Paul Carver and our sons Jacob and Joey, who put up with me without complaint and made it possible for me to complete this manuscript.

Detroit, MI, USA   Elise J. Bean

Contents

List of Figures

List of Figures

1

Entering the Oversight World

"The scope of [Congress'] power of inquiry … is as penetrating and far-reaching as the potential power to enact and appropriate under the Constitution."
Eastland v. U.S. Servicemen's Fund, *421 U.S. 491, 504, n. 15 (1975)*

The date was Friday, December 12, 2014, and it was time to celebrate. We gathered in the stately hearing room that witnessed so many of the hearings held by the U.S. Senate Permanent Subcommittee on Investigations, also known as PSI. Wood-paneled walls, blue carpeting, and massive doors with shiny brass fittings provided the setting. The lofty ceiling, soaring some 15 feet overhead, featured elegant art deco insets with the 12 signs of the zodiac hovering above the expanding crowd.

We'd decorated the perimeter of the room with a dozen poster boards showcasing past PSI investigations—photographs of witnesses, investigators, and Senators; newspaper articles; copies of key exhibits and colorful hearing charts. As folks trickled in, they surveyed the images, chuckled, and reminisced. Some grabbed our semi-official PSI cocktail—Manhattans made from whiskey and vermouth—sipping as they circulated the room.

The unfolding gala was a celebration of the Levin era on PSI. For 15 years stretching back to 1999, Senator Carl Levin had held the Democratic leadership post on the subcommittee. In January 2015, he was retiring.

During his tenure, he'd worked with four PSI Republican partners: Senator Susan Collins from Maine; Senator Norm Coleman from Minnesota; Senator Tom Coburn from Oklahoma; and Senator John McCain from Arizona.

© The Author(s) 2018
E. J. Bean, *Financial Exposure*, https://doi.org/10.1007/978-3-319-94388-6_1

Invitations had been sent to staff at all four Senate offices, along with the Levin crew. The result was that rarest of Washington scenes: a truly bipartisan assembly of friends and colleagues.

Those joining the celebration were past and present denizens of PSI—folks who'd been on the payroll as legal counsel or investigators, and those who'd provided unpaid help including law students, college interns, and agency personnel who'd worked for PSI on a temporary basis. Invitations also went to a kaleidoscope of House and Senate offices on both sides of the aisle. The well-wishers included a few academics, lawyers, and investigative reporters who'd been invited or heard about the party and snuck in. All around the room, as the numbers swelled, din deepened, and air warmed, folks grinned, greeted old friends, and shook hands with PSI alumni.

When the crowd reached its peak, we clinked glasses for attention and let loose a flood of stories from the Democratic and Republican staff directors who'd served on PSI during the Levin years. Taking turns, we recalled investigative highlights from hard-hitting inquiries into money laundering, abusive tax shelters, the financial crisis, secret offshore bank accounts, credit card misconduct, and corporate misdeeds.

Together, over the years, PSI had faced down corrupt bankers, arrogant executives, and sleazy lawyers. We'd confronted tax dodgers of all stripes, from billionaires to multinationals. We'd interviewed crooks in prison, North Korean representatives, and tax haven operatives. We'd protected whistleblowers, championed victims, and defended honest government employees battling abuses. We'd stood up to dirty tricks, assaults on PSI's bipartisanship, and attacks on our bosses.

Investigators are generally a cynical bunch, but as each story of PSI's past exploits was recounted, the emotion in the room cranked up a notch. Everyone present knew that during the Levin years, unlike so much that disappointed in Congress and in Washington, PSI had functioned the way government should—it had conducted its inquiries on a bipartisan basis, pursued the facts honestly, and treated its targets fairly. At the same time, it had exposed monumental wrongdoing, named names, and won reforms. Pride in PSI's legacy ricocheted around the room with centrifugal force.

At the crescendo of that good feeling, we turned the spotlight on a surprised colleague, Mary Robertson, who'd served as the PSI clerk for 39 years and was retiring along with Senator Levin. Mary had been a hurricane of work, our institutional memory, and a stern guardian of PSI's bipartisan traditions. When we honored her as the "heart and soul" of PSI, the crowd roared its approval (Image 1.1).

Image 1.1   December 2014 PSI farewell party. Source: U.S. Senate

As the party slowly wound down, bidding farewell to the investigative community we'd built was bittersweet. Fifteen years of all-out effort had produced complex relationships tinged with affection, tough times, jokes, disagreements, successes, and respect. I savored every moment, reminiscing with participants from every period of PSI's past. I couldn't help but think back on how the journey to that point had begun.

*   *   *

I first joined the Levin team in 1985, leaving behind a job working for the U.S. Department of Justice as a trial attorney in the civil fraud division. I'd been looking for a post on Capitol Hill for months, and Senator Levin was exactly the type of lawmaker I wanted to work for, an up-and-coming legislator admired in Democratic circles as smart, active, and diligent.

Senator Levin was first elected to the Senate in 1978. Then head of the Detroit City Council, he'd entered the Senate race as a long-shot underdog, but unexpectedly defeated the incumbent, Senator Robert P. Griffin, a member of the Republican leadership. In 1984, Senator Levin won re-election to a second term, defeating another attractive Republican candidate, astronaut Jack Lousma, by a vote margin of 51.8%. It was close, but a win was a win, and it gave him six more years in office.

I was so nervous during my job interview with him that the only thing I remember is twice mentioning I'd attended the University of Michigan Law School, my lone tie to his home state. After the second time, Senator Levin gazed mildly at me over his half-rim glasses and said, "University of Michigan—I got it." I turned bright red. But at the end of the interview, he offered me the job, and I heard a heavenly choir singing hallelujah in my head as I accepted.

Shaping American Politics

I was hired to be a Levin investigator on the Subcommittee on Oversight of Government Management. At the time, I wasn't altogether sure what I'd signed up for. To get a better sense of what it meant, I did some research into past landmark congressional investigations. It was like reviewing a pageant of American history.

I learned that the Pujo Committee hearings of 1912 and 1913—named after Congressman Arsene Pujo of Louisiana who led them—exposed how a handful of major Wall Street banks had acquired control over vast commercial enterprises including railroads, oil companies, insurance firms, and shipping and mining ventures.[1] The hearings showed how the banks had acquired company shares in so-called money trusts and engaged in stock trades that contributed to chaotic stock prices and financial panics. The hearings set the stage for later enactment of stronger antitrust laws and new constraints on banks.

The Pecora hearings during the 1930s—named after Senate Banking chief counsel Ferdinand Pecora who led the questioning—exposed the role banks played in the 1929 stock crash. They showed how the banks had packaged and sold worthless securities, favored the wealthy and powerful with stock deals unavailable to the general public, and took control of major corporations, at the same time many wealthy bankers were paying no tax.[2] The hearings led to a slew of new laws that, among other measures, regulated U.S. stock sales and stock exchanges.

In the 1950s, hearings led by Senator Joe McCarthy fanned the flames of the "Red Scare," the fear that Communists had secretly infiltrated the U.S. government. Together with other anti-Communist hearings, his efforts helped shape U.S. foreign policy, the U.S. military's approach to the Cold War, Hollywood, and more. The McCarthy hearings were conducted in such an unfair manner, however, that they eventually triggered a backlash not only against the senator, but against congressional oversight in general. I would learn more about that later.

In the 1970s, the Watergate hearings burst onto the national scene, exposing White House dirty tricks, including break-ins into the offices of political opponents and secret campaign contributions.[3] A few years later, the Church Committee—named after Senator Frank Church who led the inquiry—shook the nation again by exposing even dirtier tricks at the Central Intelligence Agency, including plans to assassinate world leaders and covert operations that subjected unsuspecting U.S. military personnel and other Americans to mind-altering drugs.[4]

Each of those congressional oversight investigations left marks on the American psyche, demonstrating the power Congress had to expose abuses, shake up the nation, and change how the United States operated. That was the world I was about to enter. I couldn't wait.

Joining the Levin Oversight Team

I reported for my first day of work in November 1985, climbing the stairs to the fourth floor of the Hart Senate Office Building. My immediate supervisor was Linda Gustitus, Senator Levin's subcommittee staff director and chief counsel. She welcomed me and provided a quick history of the subcommittee which had been designed especially for Senator Levin. She explained that when he was first elected in 1978, Democrats were the majority party in the Senate, and Senator Abe Ribicoff of Connecticut was chairman of the Governmental Affairs Committee. To attract Senator Levin to his committee, Senator Ribicoff offered to create a small subcommittee with a jurisdictional mandate to his liking. Senator Levin requested one that could investigate waste, fraud, abuse, and mismanagement affecting the federal government, and the Subcommittee on Oversight of Government Management—the OGM Subcommittee—was born.

Senator Levin hired the staff for the new subcommittee. In many Senate committees, the full committee chair controls hiring decisions on both the full committee and subcommittee levels. But the Governmental Affairs Committee was different. By tradition, the full committee chair hired the full committee staff, but gave each subcommittee chair the authority to hire and fire their own staff. I was to learn that hiring staff represented real power in the Senate, because it enabled the hiring senator to get things done.

I also learned what a big impact every election had on the composition, staffing, and funding of congressional committees. The Senate and House each supported about two dozen committees, most of which had multiple subcommittees. Each committee and subcommittee operated under dual leadership provided by the two major political parties, the Democrats and Republicans. The few members of Congress who were independent from both parties still caucused with one side or the other for purposes of committee assignments, thereby helping determine which qualified as the majority party.

The majority party—meaning the party whose elected members comprised at least 50% of the House or Senate—controlled selection of the committee chairs, while the minority party selected the "ranking minority members." The chairs generally controlled the committee agenda, while the ranking members led the minority party's activities on each body.

The partisan divide in Congress not only determined who set the agenda, but also committee membership numbers and budgets. In the Senate, the number of senators assigned to each committee and subcommittee reflected the numerical split between the two parties in the full Senate. In other words, if the Senate was made up of 60 Republicans and 40 Democrats, each committee and subcommittee had a 60–40 split in its membership, with Republican senators outnumbering their counterparts. In addition, during the 1970s and 1980s, the majority party in the Senate typically controlled two-thirds of the committee budget, while the minority party controlled only one-third, a funding difference of two-to-one.

When I was hired, the Democrats were the minority party, but Senator Levin still had the budget to hire a tiny staff. His OGM employees numbered three, of whom I was the third. Linda was our fearless leader, and my co-worker was Allie Giles, a young woman who'd worked on the senator's personal staff. All three of us were tucked into a small suite of rooms across the hall from our Republican counterparts, who occupied a slightly larger space with slightly more staff.

The Republican offices also housed the OGM Subcommittee "clerk," Frankie de Vergie, who handled administrative duties like the budget, office equipment, travel arrangements, and archiving as well as hearings and hearing records. I learned that virtually all Senate committees and subcommittees shared administrative staff between the two parties, each paying half their salaries to provide nonpartisan assistance. OGM's star clerk was a cheerful workaholic who taught me critical lessons about how the Senate operated.

During my OGM years, the majority party in the Senate flipped twice, in 1987 and 1995, with dramatic consequences for our budget and operations. In 1987, when the Democrats regained majority status in the Senate, the Levin OGM budget doubled, and our staff swelled to ten employees. In 1995, when the Democrats lost majority status, the Levin OGM budget was cut in half and our staff shrank to just two—Linda and me. The erratic size of our budget and staff exacted a human and political toll that I'd been oblivious to when, before law school, I'd worked for a Democratic House member, Congressman Joe Moakley from Massachusetts.

In later years, when the split between Republican and Democratic senators began hovering around the 50% mark, the parties gradually abandoned the one-third/two-thirds budget division as an unfair reflection of political reality. Instead, the budget allocation began to reflect more closely the numerical difference between the parties. If the Senate had a 52–48 split between the parties, it led to a 52–48% split in committee funds. It took years, however, before that sensible approach took hold in the Senate. In the House, the two-to-one budget split between the parties still reins.

Learning from Linda

In the meantime, I was just happy to have a job on Capitol Hill, even in the minority. I was ready to learn the basics of congressional oversight—how to investigate, organize a hearing, and use investigative results to fight for change.

Linda took me under her wing and taught me what to do, step by step. She sent me on errands all over Capitol Hill, so I would learn the Capitol's byzantine architecture. She had me get charts from the Service Department, bills from the bill clerk, and advice from the Senate Parliamentarian. She sent me to the office of the Official Reporters of Debates to review Senator Levin's floor remarks, and to the Senate recording studio to watch him do radio shows. She had me prepare hearing exhibits, floor statements, and press releases. She took me to endless meetings with Senator Levin so I could see how he operated and what he wanted from staff.

Linda also gave me a frightening amount of responsibility to conduct investigations, essentially assigning me a topic, allowing me to develop an investigative plan, and then monitoring the actions I took to gather information and develop findings. Throughout the process, she provided investigative guidance and encouragement, seesawing between giving me room to develop and saving me from my missteps. Linda showed me how to write a memo to the boss, how to request documents and prepare for an interview, and how to stand up to agency intransigence. She explained the intricacies of drafting legislation, the etiquette involved with going on the Senate floor, and the unspoken rules for negotiating with the House. She steeped me in Senate procedure, practice, and tradition. And she did it with humor and patience.

Another stroke of fortune: I found myself on a committee with a strong bipartisan tradition. Republicans and Democrats on the Governmental Affairs Committee routinely worked together. Essentially, everyone was against government waste, fraud, and abuse, so it was relatively easy for senators to find common ground to combat problems and design reforms.

On the OGM Subcommittee, Senator Levin's Republican counterpart was Senator Bill Cohen from Maine, a smart, elegant, and hard-working senator eager to tackle government mismanagement. They collaborated on a wide range of issues, including requiring more government contracts to undergo competitive bidding, combating unfair Social Security disability terminations, requiring lobbyists to disclose more information about their work, and improving federal regulations by increasing the use of negotiated rulemaking.[5]

The senators, who traded the chair and ranking minority posts twice, were unfailingly courteous with each other. They designed their hearings jointly and often co-sponsored each other's legislation. If the senator chairing a hearing had to leave for a vote, he routinely gave the gavel to the ranking minority member until his return. The minority member was routinely allowed to initiate his own investigations and hold a hearing on the results. Once a year, he could also hold a field hearing in his home state.

On a staff level, Linda's counterpart was Susan Collins, who was then Senator Cohen's subcommittee staff director. Susan had the trust and respect of her boss and was hard-working, courteous, and fair to the Democrats. Later, Susan returned to Maine and, after Senator Cohen retired in 1997, won election as a senator in her own right. She ended up working with Senator Levin on the PSI and, a few years after that, chairing the full Governmental Affairs Committee. But that was unsuspected territory during our OGM years.

Learning Oversight

In the meantime, Linda threw me into oversight. My assignments included investigating subcontractor kickbacks in the U.S. defense industry; pollution and oil spills affecting the Great Lakes; unsafe laboratory practices in U.S. chemical and biological warfare research projects; mismanagement of federal programs designed to protect U.S. business from unfair foreign trading; and safety and environmental problems plaguing oil tankers carrying fuel world-wide for the Department of Defense. Each investigation took six months to a year to complete. Most resulted in a hearing and report.[6]

Due to limited funding and staff resources, I did much of the work on my own, under Linda's watchful eye. I sometimes had help from a college intern or law clerk, but they typically returned to school after a semester. Sometimes we had on staff a federal agency employee—called a "detailee"—who was paid by their agency to work for Congress for a year to gain Hill experience. While they provided tremendous assistance, detailees typically had never worked for Congress or conducted an investigation. Which meant I had to supervise their work, a delicate task since most were older and more experienced than me. Linda helped me figure it out.

Each of the investigations I worked on uncovered complex legal and adminis-trative issues, surprising fact patterns, and problems needing resolution. Each riv-eted my attention with stories of abuse, dysfunctional programs, incompetence, mismanagement, and sometimes a brave whistleblower fighting internally to improve government operations. While we found problems everywhere, we also identified ways to clamp down on abuses and improve government programs. And we found many hard-working, good-hearted government employees willing to make changes to their operations or programs, a lift that kept me going.

Learning the Law and the Rules

During my 11 years on the OGM Subcommittee, I became seeped in the law, rules, and practices governing congressional oversight investigations. I learned there were some clear rules about what was allowed and what wasn't, and those rules had a real impact on the investigative work, though their contours and significance took years to really sink in.

I learned, first, that Congress' authority to investigate was rooted in the Constitution. Article One created Congress. My Capitol Hill friends liked to point out that the Constitution set up Congress before the president and executive branch (Article Two) and the judiciary (Article Three), showing who was top dog in the minds of the Framers.

Article One bestowed a long list of "powers" on Congress, including the power to legislate, raise revenue, and provide for the country's common defense and general welfare. At the end of that list, Section Eight of Article One stated that Congress had the power to "make all Laws which shall be necessary and proper for carrying into Execution the foregoing Powers, and all other Powers vested by this Constitution in the Government of the United States."

The Supreme Court invoked that "Necessary and Proper" clause when it held that the Constitution authorized Congress to conduct oversight investigations, even though the power to investigate was never spelled out explicitly in the text. The key Supreme Court case was *McGrain v. Daugherty*, which arose out of the Teapot Dome scandal of the 1920s.[7] The scandal involved oil leases on federal land sold to businessmen who'd provided financial benefits to the Secretary of the Interior Albert Fall. The scandal acquired its name from a Wyoming oil reserve that featured a rock formation shaped like a teapot.

As part of an extended investigation into the scandal, the U.S. Senate formed a select committee to investigate the failure of the Justice Department, under Attorney General Harry Daugherty, to prosecute the wrongdoing. The select committee issued a subpoena to the attorney general's brother, Ohio banker Mally Daugherty, for oral testimony. When the brother refused to comply, the Senate Sergeant at Arms took him into custody. He sued, challenging the Senate's authority to investigate, issue subpoenas, and punish noncompliance with imprisonment.

His legal challenge went all the way to the Supreme Court which, in an 8–0 decision, upheld Congress' right both to investigate and enforce its subpoenas. The Supreme Court found that "the power of inquiry—with process to enforce it—is an essential and appropriate auxiliary to the legislative function." In upholding the Senate's right to compel testimony, the Court wrote:

A legislative body cannot legislate wisely or effectively in the absence of information respecting the conditions which the legislation is intended to affect or change; and where the legislative body does not itself possess the requisite information— which not infrequently is true—recourse must be had to others who do possess it. Experience has taught that mere requests for such information often are unavailing, and also that information which is volunteered is not always accurate or complete; so some means of compulsion are essential to obtain what is needed.

The Supreme Court was careful to note that Congress' authority to investigate was not limitless. It had to be "in aid of the legislative function." The Court prohibited Congress, for example, from inquiring into the "private affairs" of individuals without a legislative purpose. Nor could Congress take on the judicial branch's role of adjudicating specific disputes, or the executive branch's role of prosecuting wrongdoers.[8] Instead, Congress had to design its investigations to inform and guide its legislative duties.

The Supreme Court dismissed a claim that the Senate's inquiry was invalid because it had essentially put the Attorney General on trial, which was a "judicial function." The Court stated that the investigation provided "no warrant for thinking the Senate was attempting … to try the Attorney General … for any crime or wrongdoing. Nor do we think it is a valid objection to the investigation that it might possibly disclose crimes or wrongdoing on his part." The Supreme Court ruled instead that a congressional inquiry could proceed even if it disclosed wrongdoing that might merit law enforcement or court proceedings, so long as it was founded upon a legislative function.

The 1927 Supreme Court case made it crystal clear that Congress possessed inherent authority under the Constitution to conduct investigations tied to a legislative purpose. While Congress had no authority to prosecute crimes or resolve specific disputes, the Supreme Court confirmed Congress' broad authority to engage in fact-finding to support its legislative function. It also made clear that Congress could use the federal courts to enforce congressional subpoenas compelling testimony or documents. While later cases added nuance and detail, the broad principles laid out in *McGrain v. Daugherty* provided an unshakable foundation for congressional oversight over the ensuing decades.

Compelling Information

My congressional education also led me deep into the laws and rules controlling when Congress could compel information, a key issue in every investigation. I learned that Congress had enacted statutes that explicitly granted the

Senate and House the right to conduct inquiries, issue subpoenas, and compel compliance with their information requests.[9] Equally important, the courts had given Congress the ability to brand anyone who defied a congressional subpoena as a wrongdoer in "contempt" of Congress. The Supreme Court held that Congress possessed inherent authority to hold such persons in contempt reasoning that, otherwise, Congress would be "exposed to every indignity and interruption that rudeness, caprice or even conspiracy may mediate against it."[10] Not only that, the Supreme Court ruled that Congress could force an individual accused of contempt to appear before the House or Senate, undergo a trial, and upon conviction, to be imprisoned at a place of Congress' choosing.[11] Strong stuff.

Over time, Congress moved away from conducting its own contempt trials and enacted criminal and civil contempt statutes, enabling it to use federal courts and prisons to compel compliance with its subpoenas.[12] The criminal contempt statute authorized Congress to send a convicted person to "a common jail" for up to one year. To invoke the statute, the offended committee and house of Congress each had to vote to hold the individual in contempt and then send the case to a federal judge to order the person's imprisonment.[13] The Senate also enacted civil contempt statutes authorizing the Senate to file civil suits to enforce its subpoenas. In such suits, the federal district court could order defiant individuals to be imprisoned or pay a civil fine, in order to compel their cooperation with the Senate or punish ongoing contempt.

I also learned that, to show respect and deference to a co-equal branch of government, the courts made it fairly easy for Congress to prevail in a contempt proceeding, setting standards that made it hard for targets to defy a congressional subpoena.

First, the courts held that a subpoena recipient could not ask a judge to prospectively overrule or invalidate a subpoena. Instead, the recipient had to refuse to comply, get cited for contempt by Congress, and then raise objections during the contempt proceedings.[14] Not a comfortable legal posture for the person challenging Congress.

Second, when gauging the validity of a congressional subpoena, the courts typically used a three-part test, promulgated by the Supreme Court, whose minimal requirements seemed to favor Congress. The key case involved a hearing witness whom the House had voted to hold in contempt for refusing to answer a question about whether he was a member of the Communist Party. The Supreme Court sided with the House, holding that the witness had to answer the question, because the House Committee's inquiry had met three basic criteria: (1) it involved matters that the committee was "authorized" by Congress to investigate; (2) the investigation had "a valid legislative purpose"; and (3) the requested information was "pertinent to the subject matter of the investigation."[15] The three-part test, which required a relatively minimal showing, made it easy for lower courts to enforce congressional subpoenas.

Jurisdiction

The first prong of the test focused on congressional authority to investigate a particular subject matter. To evaluate that issue, the court looked to the "jurisdiction" assigned to the committee or subcommittee making the information request.

Committee jurisdictions were routinely disclosed at the beginning of each new Congress. Since the U.S. Congress first convened in 1789, each subsequent "Congress" has had a duration of two years, with each component year referred to as a "session." For example, the Congress first employing me was the 99th Congress. Its first session was in 1985; its second session was in 1986. The two-year period corresponded with the terms of the members of the House of Representatives, all of whom had to be re-elected every two years. Each time the House members were elected, they constituted an entirely new body and started a new Congress. In contrast, in the Senate, only one-third of its members faced election every two years. That meant, unlike the House, the Senate had a continuous existence. Nevertheless, the Senate used the same two-year timeframe as the House to identify each Congress.

At the beginning of each new Congress, the House adopted a set of rules and resolutions to govern its operation. The Senate, as a continuing body, didn't have to adopt new rules, but could choose to amend its rules at the start of a new Congress or at some other time. The House and Senate rules, as well as resolutions passed by each body at the beginning of a new Congress, were used to assign subject matter jurisdiction to each of their standing, select, joint, and ad hoc committees. The jurisdictional assignments were typically broad and often overlapped.

The committee names were indicative of their jurisdictions such as the Committee on Agriculture or Select Committee on Intelligence. Over time, many of their names and jurisdictions changed to adapt to new issues and needs. For example, the committee where I worked would undergo four name changes over the span of 100 years. From 1921 to 1952, it was known as the Committee on Expenditures in the Executive Departments. In 1952, its name changed to the Committee on Government Operations. In 1977, the name changed again to the Committee on Governmental Affairs. In 2005, it would change once more to the Committee on Homeland Security and Governmental Affairs.[16]

When I was hired in 1985, the Committee on Governmental Affairs served as the Senate's chief investigative body, and its assigned jurisdiction was one of the most sweeping in the Senate. It included the authority to investigate "the efficiency, economy, and effectiveness" of all federal agencies, including any instance of fraud, mismanagement, corruption, or unethical practice; all instances of waste, extravagance, or "improper expenditure of Government funds"; any corporate or individual "noncompliance" with a federal regulation or law; all "organized criminal activity" that crossed state lines; and "all other aspects of crime and lawlessness," including "investment fraud schemes, commodity and security fraud, computer fraud, and the use of offshore banking and corporate facilities to carry out criminal objectives."[17] Whoa.

Despite that already mind-blowingly broad mandate, in 2005, when the committee name changed to the Committee on Homeland Security and Governmental Affairs, the Senate added a raft of new homeland security issues to the committee's plate. The result was that jurisdiction wasn't much of a limiting factor for subpoenas issued by our committee or its subcommittees.

Legislative Purpose and Pertinence

The final two prongs of the courts' three-part test to evaluate congressional subpoenas were equally easy to meet. They required Congress to show that a subpoena was tied to "a valid legislative purpose" and was "pertinent to the subject under inquiry." The courts interpreted both requirements broadly. For example, the courts ruled that the phrase, "valid legislative purpose," justified subpoenas aimed at determining whether a law was working or a new law was needed, whether appropriated funds were being spent wisely or should be spent otherwise, whether federal agency actions or presidential orders were acceptable, whether nominations of federal office should be approved, and a host of other matters tied to Congress' legislative functions. The courts gave Congress a lot of leeway.

The courts also made it easy for Congress to show that a subpoena was "pertinent" to an investigation. As one court explained in upholding a congressional subpoena:

A legislative inquiry may be as broad, as searching, and as exhaustive as is necessary to make effective the constitutional powers of Congress. ... A judicial inquiry relates to a case, and the evidence to be admissible must be measured by the narrow limits of the pleadings. A legislative inquiry anticipates all possible cases which may arise thereunder and the evidence admissible must be responsive to the scope of the inquiry which generally is very broad.[18]

The courts further broadened the standard by holding that a congressional inquiry could evolve over time to encompass new subjects, and that a congressional "subpoena was to be enforced 'unless the district court determines that there is no reasonable possibility that the category of materials the Government seeks will produce information relevant to the general subject of the ... investigation.'"[19] The Supreme Court instructed that a congressional subpoena should be upheld even if investigators end up searching "some 'blind alleys' or "non-productive enterprises." It stated: "To be a valid legislative inquiry there need be no predicable end result."[20]

With that type of direction from the high court, lower courts were generally unreceptive to claims that a congressional subpoena should be invalidated because it was overbroad. The courts followed Supreme Court precedent holding that, when it came to policy-oriented inquiries, Congress had discretion to explore the facts, related issues, and even remote connections.

There was one big exception to that broad approach—when Congress subpoenaed information from the president or executive branch. Several Supreme Court cases had held that, unlike a private individual or entity, the president had certain executive privileges that could limit the information obtainable by Congress. Figuring out the bounds of those executive privileges was an ongoing source of conflict between the executive and legislative branches.

Lying and Obstructing

One more critical set of legal issues in congressional oversight involved the federal statutes that prohibited lying to Congress or obstructing its investigations. I learned that the prohibition against lying to Congress was very broad. It wasn't limited to hearings where a witness swore an oath to tell the truth and risked a perjury charge for material misstatements.[21] It also applied to statements made during the course of any authorized "investigation or review" by Congress, which meant it applied to statements made to a member or congressional staffer during a deposition, interview, telephone call, letter, or email exchange. The key criminal statute, 18 U.S.C. § 1001, stated that anyone who "knowingly and willfully ... falsifies, conceals, or covers up ... a material fact" or "makes any materially false, fictitious, or fraudulent statement," or makes or uses "any false writing" in a matter within the jurisdiction of Congress could be fined or imprisoned for up to five years.

The obstruction statute, 18 U.S.C. § 1505, was equally tough. The law made it a crime for anyone to "corruptly" or through the use of "any threatening letter or communication" to "influence, obstruct, or impede" a congressional inquiry. Persons who violated the statute could be fined or imprisoned for up to five years.

Pretty stern stuff. While it was relatively rare for someone to be prosecuted for lying to or obstructing Congress, it wasn't an empty threat. In fact, several years later, in connection with a Levin investigation into the 2001 collapse of Enron Corporation, a corporate executive would be convicted of lying to the Senate and jailed for three years. I learned that a credible threat of criminal prosecution for false statements played a frequent and critical role in getting to the truth.

A final source of oversight restrictions and practices involved specific rules issued by Congress itself. In each Congress, the Senate and House issued rules governing the circumstances under which their respective committees could conduct an inquiry, issue a subpoena, or hold a hearing.[22] In addition, most committees issued their own supplementary set of rules governing their operations. Some subcommittees did the same, including PSI. I was to learn that those rules also had a real impact on how investigations played out.

Learning What Not to Do

During my OGM tenure, while I participated in many compelling investigations, one stood out. It was the highest profile investigation undertaken by the Governmental Affairs Committee while I was there, and it swept up the whole committee for an entire year.

The investigation arose out of the 1996 campaign won by President Bill Clinton and Vice President Al Gore over Republican challengers Senator Bob Dole and his running mate Congressman Jack Kemp. It was a hard-fought election that led to angry recriminations and allegations of wrongdoing by both sides. Questions included whether foreign money had influenced the outcome, whether the White House had broken any laws by selling political access to big campaign contributors, and whether loopholes in federal campaign finance laws were allowing campaign contributions to corrupt American politics.

The Republicans were then the majority party in the Senate, and in December 1996, Senate Majority Leader Trent Lott announced the Governmental Affairs Committee would conduct a special investigation into the 1996 campaign. The committee chair was Senator Fred Thompson, a Tennessee Republican who'd been a staff lawyer during the Watergate inquiry.

In January 1997, under Senator Thompson's leadership, the committee approved a bipartisan description of the scope of the inquiry, authorizing an investigation "into illegal or improper fundraising and spending practices in the 1996 Federal election campaigns."[23] After three months of bickering, the full Senate passed a supporting resolution in March 1997 and imposed a one-year deadline to complete the inquiry.[24]

The investigation concluded on time in March 1998. Along the way, the committee hired more than 50 new staffers, set up a special room to secure about 1.5 million pages of documents, issued 427 subpoenas, conducted 200 depositions and another 200 interviews, held 32 days of hearings over three months, took testimony from 72 witnesses, and wrote a six-volume, 9575-page report with findings and recommendations.[25] The investigation was fast-paced, wide-ranging, and riven with partisan disagreements. It dominated my life for the entire year. And it taught me lesson after lesson about how not to conduct congressional oversight.

In Washington, the common wisdom is never to allow a crisis to go to waste, but to use it to analyze and fix real problems. Public outcry about the 1996 election campaign provided a rare opportunity to clean up the sewer system that the U.S. campaign finance system had become. But to do that, the parties needed to work together, admit the stink permeated both sides of the aisle, and develop bipartisan solutions. The problem with the Governmental Affairs investigation was that, while the committee Republicans were happy to point out all the problems on the Democratic side, they refused to admit that similar problems afflicted their party.

The refusal to acknowledge a bipartisan problem played out in every aspect of the investigation. Multiple witnesses with information about Democratic fundraising practices were brought in for questioning, but requests to interrogate their Republican counterparts were largely ignored. Not one witness from the Republican National Committee (RNC) or Dole campaign was called to testify at a committee hearing. The 32 days of hearings examined Democratic fundraising misconduct in detail, while the three days of hearings promised to examine similar problems on the Republican side never materialized.

The GOP's "see-no-evil" approach, as Senator Levin labeled it at one point, didn't actually protect the Republicans from criticism. Despite a lack of interviews and hearing opportunities, the committee Democrats repeatedly released evidence of Republican fundraising misconduct that paralleled Democratic misdeeds. When the Republicans denounced President Clinton for letting big contributors stay overnight in the White House's Lincoln bedroom, the Democrats produced invitations from President George H.W. Bush enabling big contributors to meet Cabinet members in the White House's Indian Treaty Room. When the Republicans ridiculed Al Gore for attending a fundraiser in a Buddhist temple, the Democrats castigated President Bush for taking $500,000 from a Japanese businessman, Michael Kojima, who'd been labeled a "deadbeat dad" for failing to pay child support. When the Republicans showed Chinese money being bundled by Democratic contributor John Huang, Democrats traced Hong Kong money flowing to the RNC through a conduit called the National Policy Forum.

The investigation's tit-for-tat dynamic poisoned committee relationships. Instead of everyone agreeing on the facts underlying the campaign finance problems and pushing for a bipartisan solution, the two sides got increasingly angry at each other for criticizing their counterparts and not themselves. Republicans charged Democrats with trying to deflect attention from President Clinton's misdeeds, while Democrats slammed Republicans for trying to hide their party's own wrongdoing. The inquiry produced a dysfunctional stalemate instead of a joint effort to solve a mutual problem. The infighting also disgusted the media and the public.

Perhaps the lowest point in the investigation from an institutional perspective came when the committee abandoned efforts to enforce document subpoenas it'd sent to politically powerful organizations on both sides of the aisle. Neither side would support the other's enforcement effort. When a committee throws up its hands on enforcing its own subpoenas, it weakens Congress as a whole by enabling investigative subjects to thumb their noses at congressional requests.

Another low point was the committee's final report. The two sides didn't even attempt to draft a joint product. Instead, each wrote its own report. The final result was over 9000 pages of divergent depictions of what happened during the 1996 presidential campaign. I wonder how many people—other than those of us involved in the drafting—ever read the whole thing.

Despite the disastrous Senate investigation, it had one positive outcome. The awful facts it compiled contributed to a growing public demand to reform the U.S. campaign finance system. It took another five years, but in 2002, Senator John McCain, a Republican from Arizona, and Senator Russ Feingold, a Democrat from Wisconsin, won enactment of the landmark Bipartisan Campaign Reform Act, also known as the McCain-Feingold Act. It tackled a wide range of campaign finance problems, many of which had been documented in the Senate investigation.

For a while, the McCain-Feingold Act halted a host of ugly practices in U.S. campaign finance. But few reforms endure where money in politics is concerned. As Supreme Court decisions weakened many of the McCain-Feingold restrictions, Congress failed to respond with new legislation, leading to another surge in campaign finance abuses. When allegations of foreign influence over the U.S. presidential election erupted in 2016, it demonstrated the ongoing need for congressional oversight in the electoral arena.

Mastering the Basics

In the Levin camp, the campaign finance investigation produced bitter regret that the 1996 campaign crisis had not led to a truly bipartisan inquiry. The crucible of that failed investigation was painful, but it also helped crystalize my views about congressional oversight.

By the investigation's end in 1998, I felt I finally had a good grasp of the oversight process. It was no longer a mysterious, amorphous subject, but one composed of distinct phases:

- Designing the investigation;
- Getting the facts through research, document requests, and interviews;
- Writing up the investigative results;
- Holding a hearing; and
- Pushing to fix the identified problems.

I was also convinced that bipartisan investigations led to more thorough, accurate, and credible fact-finding as well as to higher-quality, longer-lasting policy reforms.

But perhaps more important than the investigative techniques were the lessons I had soaked up about Congress itself. I had learned that, in many ways, Congress was a closed world, insular, with its own traditions, unwritten rules, and sensitivities. At the same time, Congress was exposed to and buffeted by multiple outside forces including constituents, lobbyists, and the public, expressing a cacophony of differing points of view. I had begun to understand that the 100 senators and 435 House members were, first and foremost, singular individuals with strengths, weaknesses, and interests, operating in an ever-shifting network of political pressures and alliances. Each member of Congress decided on how to devote their time and energy; the puzzle was figuring out how to enlist them into a common endeavor.

I found myself fascinated with the whole complicated process. While the rest of the country was becoming increasingly disillusioned with Congress, I found I'd become a full-fledged congressional junkie whose knees got weak when I gazed at the statue of Freedom on top of the Capitol dome. I found I'd become fiercely devoted to Congress as an institution. While most congressional staff left the Hill after a few years, I found I didn't want to leave; working for Congress had become my chosen career.

I also realized that I'd been able to maintain my positive feelings about Congress, because I had landed a job in oversight working for an outstanding senator. The thing about oversight, when done well, is that it's worthwhile and fun, even in an otherwise dysfunctional Congress. When everyone else is banging their heads against the wall trying to pass legislation that can't get passed, oversight investigators can continue to do valuable work. They dig out the facts, interview victims and wrongdoers, analyze problems, and try to discover what might make things better. And isn't that why many people go to Washington in the first place—to analyze and fix problems hurting the country?

Even in troubled times, when solutions require a political consensus that isn't possible at the moment, an oversight investigation can prime the pump by educating policymakers and the public about a problem and what can be done about it. Then when a crisis hits, all that analysis and work on possible solutions will be ready—to make sure the crisis doesn't go to waste.

What I didn't realize in 1998 was that, while OGM had been a remarkable adventure in its own right and produced terrific oversight, it was only a warm-up for what was coming.

Notes

1. For more information on the Pujo Committee investigation, see *Congress Investigates: A Critical and Documentary History*, editors Roger A. Bruns, David L. Hostetter, and Raymond W. Smock (Facts on File 2011) (hereinafter *"Congress Investigates"*), Volumes 1–2, at 417–459; "Money Trust Investigation: Financial and Monetary Conditions in the United States," House Committee on Banking and Currency subcommittee (5/16/1912), HRG-1912-BCU-0017, Y4.B22/1:M74/2-1, http://bit.ly/2ASceSc (first of multiple hearing days).
2. For more information on the Pecora investigation, see *Congress Investigates*, at 500–539; "Stock Exchange Practices," Senate Committee on Banking and Currency, S. Hrg. 73-1455 (6/6/1934), http://bit.ly/2hKZVDt (report and associated hearings from January 1933 to May 1934).
3. For more information on the Watergate investigation, see *Congress Investigates*, at 886–926.
4. For more information on the Church Committee investigation, see *Congress Investigates*, at 927–967; "Final Report of the Select Committee to Study Governmental Operations with Respect to Intelligence Activities, United States Senate together with Additional, Supplemental, and Separate Views," S. Rpt. 94-755 (4/26/1976), https://archive.org/details/finalreportofsel01unit.
5. See, for example, the Competition in Contracting Act of 1984, P.L. 98-369 (S. 2127); Social Security Disability Reform Act of 1984, P.L. 98-460 (S. 476); Anti-Kickback Enforcement Act of 1986, P.L. 99-634 (S. 2250);

Computer Matching and Privacy Protection Act of 1988, P.L. 100-503 (S. 496); Negotiated Rulemaking Act of 1990, P.L. 101-648 (S. 303); Lobbying Disclosure Act of 1995, P.L. 104-65 (S. 349).

6. See, for example, the following hearings and reports from investigations conducted by the Subcommittee on Oversight of Government Management: "Department of Defense Subcontractor Kickbacks," S. Hrg. 99-810 (2/27/1986), http://bit.ly/2jEncHL; "Wedtech: A Review of Federal Procurement Decisions," S. Prt. 100-108 (5/1988), http://bit.ly/2Cwa9Q8; "Department of Defense Safety Programs for Chemical and Biological Warfare Research," S. Hrg. 100-902 (7/27–28/1988), http://bit.ly/2itP2mx; "Oversight of Oil Spill Protections for the Great Lakes," S. Hrg. 101-354 (9/6/1989), http://bit.ly/2yWWFbk; "Lax Federal Enforcement of the Antidumping and Countervailing Duty Program," S. Prt. 102-52 (10/1991), http://bit.ly/2zPXVAu; "Navy's Mismanagement of the Sealift Tanker Program," S. Hrg. 103-1044 (10/12/1994), http://bit.ly/2zPYNVJ.

7. 273 U.S. 135 (1927). For more information on the Teapot Dome scandal, see *Congress Investigates*, at 460–499.

8. See also *Watkins v. United States*, 354 U.S. 178 (1957).

9. See U.S. Code, Title 2, "The Congress."

10. *Anderson v. Dunn*, 19 U.S. 204 (1821).

11. The Supreme Court has upheld Congress' right to use imprisonment to induce a subpoena recipient to produce requested information or impose punishment for noncompliance. The Court has limited the term of imprisonment by stating it may not exceed the term of the Congress that authorized it. See, for example, "Congress's Contempt Power and the Enforcement of Congressional Subpoenas: Law, History, Practice, and Procedure," Report No. RL34097, Congressional Research Service (5/12/2017), at 8, 10–11 (hereinafter "CRS Report on Congress's Contempt Power").

12. See 2 U.S.C. § 192 (authorizing Congress to find a person who was summoned as a "witness" before a house of Congress, but refused to appear, answer questions, or produce requested papers, guilty of a criminal misdemeanor, and subject to a monetary fine or imprisonment for up to one year); 2 U.S.C. §§ 288b(b) and 288d, 28 U.S.C. § 1365 (authorizing the Senate to file civil contempt lawsuits in federal district court); CRS Report on Congress's Contempt Power, at 20–25. In place of the Senate's civil contempt statutes, the House requires adoption of a House resolution each time a House committee seeks to enforce a subpoena through civil contempt proceedings. Id. at 25–30. The last time Congress conducted its own trial on contempt charges, outside of a federal court, was in 1935. Id., at 12.

13. If voting is successful and a contempt citation is "certified" by the Senate President or House Speaker, the law states it becomes the "duty" of a federal prosecutor "to bring the matter before the grand jury for its action."

14. *Eastland v. U.S. Servicemen's Fund*, 421 U.S. 491, 503–507 (1975).

15. *Wilkinson v. United States*, 365 U.S. 399, 408–409 (1961).

16. The number, names, and jurisdictions of its subcommittees also underwent repeated alteration.

17. The Governmental Affairs Committee's jurisdiction was set forth in the Senate's standing committee rules and the committee's funding resolution. See, for example, Senate Rule XXV-1(k) and S. Res. 85, both in force during the 99th Congress.

18. *Townsend v. United States*, 95 F.2d 352, 361 (D.C. Cir.), cert. denied, 303 U.S. 665 (1938).

19. *Senate Select Committee on Ethics v. Packwood*, 845 F. Supp. 17, 20–21 (D.D.C. 1994), stay pending appeal denied, 510 U.S. 1319 (1994).

20. *Eastland v. U.S. Servicemen's Fund*, 421 U.S. 491, 503–507 (1975). See also *Watkins v. United States*, 354 U.S. 178, 187 (1957) (The investigative power of Congress "encompasses inquiries concerning the administration of existing laws as well as proposed or possibly needed statutes. It includes surveys of defects in our social, economic or political system for the purpose of enabling Congress to remedy them. It comprehends probes into departments of the Federal Government to expose corruption, inefficiency or waste.").

21. 18 U.S.C. § 1621.

22. In the 99th Congress, Senate Rule XXVI provided the standing procedural rules for how Senate committees operated, while the same function was performed for House committees by House Rule XI.2(m)(1).

23. "Investigation of Illegal or Improper Activities in Connection with 1996 Federal Election Campaigns," Report, Volumes 1–6, U.S. Senate Committee on Governmental Affairs, Rept. 105-167 (3/10/1998) (hereinafter "1996 Campaign Report"), Volume 1, at 11–12, http://bit.ly/2hKgO0W et seq. (6 parts). See also related hearings at http://bit.ly/2zQ0bHF et seq. (10 parts).

24. Senate Resolution 39 (3/11/1997).

25. 1996 Campaign Report, Volume 1, at 14–15.

2

Landing at PSI

"While the conventional assumption is that the strength of legislative bodies lies in the power to legislate, a respectable tradition has long argued that it lies as much or more in the power to investigate."
Arthur M. Schlesinger Jr., Congress Investigates: A Critical and Documentary History, *Volume 1, at xxi (Facts on File 2011)*

What followed next was 15 years of big-league investigations by the U.S. Senate Permanent Subcommittee on Investigations, known to insiders as PSI. PSI has long been seen as the Senate's premier investigative panel with decades of bipartisan, hard-hitting, high-quality oversight inquiries.

PSI originated as a temporary investigative committee, led by then Senator Harry Truman, to examine war profiteering during World War II. It later became a "permanent" subcommittee and built a formidable reputation taking on Nazi war criminals, political corruption, and organized crime. In 1954, it faltered when, for two years, Senator Joe McCarthy conducted a series of investigations so offensive they corroded the PSI brand. After his departure, PSI slowly rebuilt its credibility with high-profile investigations into labor racketeering, the mafia, drug trafficking, and white-collar crime. PSI also examined such matters as the U.S. race riots in the 1960s, gasoline shortages in the 1970s, and money laundering in the 1980s.

Senator Levin claimed his PSI leadership spot in 1999. For the rest of his Senate career, he used his position on PSI to conduct one high-stakes inquiry after another. He exposed tax cheats hiding money offshore, credit card companies abusing American families, money launderers misusing U.S. financial

© The Author(s) 2018
E. J. Bean, *Financial Exposure*, https://doi.org/10.1007/978-3-319-94388-6_2

institutions, Wall Street banks generating the financial crisis that devastated middle America, multinational corporations gaming the tax system, and more. His investigations targeted some of the most powerful corporations in America, including Apple, Citibank, Enron, and Goldman Sachs, as well as tax-cheating billionaires, corrupt foreign dictators, and bankers behaving badly.

Through it all, Senator Levin burnished PSI's reputation for fact-based, bipartisan inquiries that not only exposed wrongdoing, but also pushed for policy reforms. As one opponent quipped during the Levin era: "PSI stands for pretty scary investigations."[1]

Distilling the Levin Principles

I was lucky enough to have a front-row seat during the whole of the Levin years on PSI, first as a Levin investigator and later as his staff director and chief counsel. Over time, as one investigation rolled into the next, the Levin PSI team built up a set of principles that guided our oversight efforts. They functioned as informal supplements to our official committee and subcommittee rules. What follows is a distillation of a dozen of what I think of as the key Levin Principles for delivering high-quality congressional oversight.

The Levin Principles

1. *Apply the Two-Year Rule.* Given limited resources, the Levin PSI team could conduct only a few investigations each year, so selecting our investigative topics was a crucial first step. While many factors were weighed, one important one was whether the subject was worth two years of intensive effort out of our lives, because that would be the minimum amount of time involved. We found that evaluating an investigative topic in terms of the time taken from our own lives helped focus the mind.
2. *Conduct Original Research.* Our second principle was to use PSI resources to conduct research that hadn't been done before. Too many congressional inquiries consist of little more than asking experts to describe prior research. Senator Levin didn't want a regurgitation of what was already known. He wanted new information.
3. *Focus on the Facts.* Third, Levin inquiries focused on compiling factual information. The world is a complicated place, and problems worth

investigating typically have layers of complexity. A good investigation has to dig through those layers to figure out what happened and why. Reaching bipartisan agreement on the key facts underlying important issues is usually a difficult process. Once accomplished, however, bipartisan factual findings provide a solid foundation for informed public policy.

4. *Use Case Studies*. Every Levin investigation used case studies to investigate and analyze targeted problems. Too many congressional investigations allow witnesses to spout generalities and platitudes when asked about an issue. We learned those generalities rarely reflected how things really worked. Detailed case studies, on the other hand, typically exposed the true nature of the problems in question.

5. *Be Relentlessly Bipartisan*. One of the most important Levin principles was to conduct investigations that were relentlessly bipartisan. All documents were shared. Key interviews had both sides present. Interview questions were shared beforehand. Everyone was encouraged to ask as many questions as it took to reach consensus on the facts. Our bottom line was that investigators with political differences had to investigate together, reviewing the same evidence at the same time, if they were ever to agree on the facts. More, we learned that investigators with different viewpoints produced more thorough, accurate, and credible fact-finding.

6. *Take the Time*. Another key lesson was that bipartisan investigations required time to succeed. Two weeks wasn't enough. Neither was two months. Enabling investigators to build sufficient bipartisan trust to come to agreement on a complex set of facts typically took a year. That was the cold, hard truth, even in inquiries that proceeded at the grueling pace of most PSI investigations. To succeed, we had to take the time.

7. *Listen to All Sides*. Still another key principle was that investigators had to listen to all parties. Our rule was not to go public with negative information about anyone unless we first gave them an opportunity to present their side of the story. The resulting investigation took longer, but it afforded everyone a fair shot and produced a more accurate and complete picture of the facts.

8. *Maintain Confidentiality*. Another critical principle was confidentiality. Confidential investigations enabled our investigators to follow the facts wherever they led and to change their minds about what was important and why. Confidentiality allowed the investigative team to drop witnesses, reverse directions, and develop new leads without having to justify each step in public, expose innocent parties to public scrutiny, or publicly spar with opponents seeking to disrupt the inquiry. The PSI team wasn't always successful at preventing leaks, sometimes because our targets used

leaks to try to spin information to their advantage. But we did our best to keep our investigations quiet until we were ready to go public.

9. *Write It Up*. The next key Levin principle was to write up the investigative results. Hearings can produce a truncated, even distorted picture of an inquiry. To prevent that outcome, almost all Levin investigations included a detailed report, complete with footnotes identifying the source of every fact in the text. Writing the report was often the toughest part of the investigation, necessitating months of agonizing work. But the pain was counterbalanced by the benefits—capturing months or years of work with accuracy, getting clear bipartisan agreement on the facts, and providing context to understand the issues and events. We had many rules about how PSI reports were organized, footnoted, and reviewed. We usually made explicit factual findings and recommendations. We also typically shared key parts of the report with the targets 24 hours before its release, to alert them to our findings and provide an opportunity to identify any errors. The final result was a bipartisan product that informed the public about a complex problem and possible solutions, an educational undertaking which we saw as PSI's single most important function.

10. *Use Hearings to Effect Change*. In addition to a report, Senator Levin almost always held a hearing on the results of an investigation. The hearing wasn't intended simply to trumpet the findings. It was also designed to effect change. One key step was to give the witnesses ample notice of the hearing so they could prepare for it. Human nature being what it is, we knew many witnesses would use the time to come up with solutions that could be announced at the hearing. That meant the resulting hearing could expose not only an important problem, but also what could be done about it, including commitments for future action.

11. *Take on the Tough Guys*. Perhaps the most satisfying aspect of the Levin approach was his commitment to taking on the tough guys—the big institutions, the CEOs, the bullies no one else had faced down. Names were named in our reports, and wrongdoers typically hauled in for a public hearing. The goal was not to berate the witnesses, but to hold them accountable for their actions. Forced to confront their own actions, a number of the tough guys chose to acknowledge wrongdoing and announce changes in policy or practice.

12. *Tackle the Problems*. The final Levin principle was that every investigation had to tackle the problems identified. Too often, congressional inquiries stop after exposing problems or make only a faint-hearted effort to right the wrongs uncovered. In contrast, Senator Levin saw tackling the identified problems as an essential part of the investigative

process. Our rule of thumb was to spend at least two years trying to fix the problems, using the report recommendations as a road map. We referred wrongdoers to law enforcement and pushed for reforms through legislation, regulations, and better policies and practices in both the public and private sectors.

These dozen principles evolved over time, arising from our mistakes as well as our successes. While we never reduced them to writing, we often discussed how we should handle various issues to ensure we were conducting our investigations in a consistent, effective, and fair way. We consciously worked to develop standard practices to guide our actions. The Levin Principles served us well.

The remainder of this book recounts how the Levin Principles played out in actual PSI investigations over time. But before diving into those specific inquiries is the series of events that led to Senator Levin's landing his leadership slot at PSI in the first place.

Jumping to PSI

Senator Levin's move from the Oversight of Government Management Subcommittee to the Permanent Subcommittee on Investigations came in two stages.

The first was in 1997, when Senator Fred Thompson, then Republican chair of the full Governmental Affairs Committee, decided to commandeer key portions of OGM's jurisdiction, including contract and ethics issues, for handling at the full committee level. After reducing OGM's jurisdiction, he also clipped its budget. Since Senator Levin was by then an OGM fixture, having held OGM leadership posts for 18 years, no one thought he'd jump ship from the subcommittee designed for him. But with less money and jurisdiction, that's just what he did.

When the 105th Congress convened in January 1997, Senator Levin invoked his seniority to become ranking minority member on a new Subcommittee on Proliferation, Federal Services, and the District of Columbia. Linda and I promptly moved to the new subcommittee's offices.

The subcommittee chair was Senator Thad Cochran from Mississippi, an active, intelligent Republican senator with a courteous staff. While our first year on the subcommittee was consumed by the campaign finance investigation described earlier, the next year we began investigating the export of so-called "dual use" technologies suitable for both military and non-military use. The issue had arisen because dual use computers were being exported to China, raising national security concerns on both sides of the aisle.

The Cochran-Levin partnership was cut short, however, because, in 1997, Senator John Glenn, a Democrat from Ohio, announced he was retiring from the Senate at the end of 1998. At the time, he was the ranking Democrat on both the full Governmental Affairs Committee and on PSI. His retirement meant both slots would open.

As the next most senior Democrat on the committee, Senator Levin could step into Senator Glenn's shoes and claim both leadership posts. But there was a complicating factor. A few months after the Glenn announcement, Senator Sam Nunn, ranking Democrat on the Senate Armed Services Committee, announced that he, too, was retiring, which meant Senator Levin would be the most senior Democrat on that committee as well.

The Armed Services Committee was one of the most powerful in the Senate, overseeing U.S. military operations around the world and defense spending involving hundreds of billions of dollars. Leading it was a once-in-a-lifetime opportunity. But under Democratic Party rules, Senator Levin couldn't lead two full committees at the same time. If he took the ranking minority member post on Armed Services, he couldn't hold the same position on Governmental Affairs; he would have to choose between the two committees.

After weeks of deliberation, Senator Levin took the leadership post on the Armed Services Committee, bypassing that position on the Governmental Affairs Committee. He took the ranking slot on the PSI subcommittee instead. Linda and I prepared to jump a second time.

Tracing PSI's Origins and History

Relinquishing the leadership post on the full Governmental Affairs Committee was a hard decision, but PSI was an exceptional consolation prize. Excited to join such a celebrated Senate institution, I took some time to delve into its origins and history. I learned to my surprise that PSI's past was more checkered than I thought.

Its history began in 1941, when the Senate established a temporary investigative body called the Committee to Investigate the National Defense Program.[2] Chaired by Senator Harry Truman, it soon became known as the Truman Committee. Senator Truman used it to traverse the United States rooting out instances of war profiteering, waste, fraud, and abuse during World War II. His investigations became famous for exposing waste and wrongdoing in U.S. defense operations, recommending reforms, and taking a responsible, bipartisan approach to oversight.[3] His work helped propel his selection as vice president by President Franklin Roosevelt in 1944. After President Roosevelt's death the following year, Vice President Truman assumed the presidency.

The Truman Committee continued to battle defense-related misconduct for several years after Senator Truman left. When it completed its work in 1948, among other accomplishments, it was credited with producing an overhaul of the military contracting system estimated to have saved the Defense Department $250 million; increasing production of aluminum, steel, and other metals needed in the war effort; and reorganizing the Navy's Bureau of Ships. Altogether, it had held 450 public hearings and 300 executive sessions, while issuing 50 reports.[4]

Upon completing its work, the Truman Committee became subject to the Legislative Reorganization Act of 1946, which required Congress' standing committees to conduct oversight investigations and withdrew authorization for its many temporary investigative committees.[5] Out of respect for the Truman Committee, however, Senator George Aiken, chair of the then-named Committee on Expenditures in the Executive Departments, did not disband the committee, but merged it with a subcommittee.[6] The renamed "Subcommittee on Investigations" was assigned a broad jurisdiction allowing it to investigate "the operation of the executive branch of the Government at all levels to determine its economy and efficiency,"[7] including, as the full committee later put it, instances of "fraud, malfeasance, collusion, corrupt or unethical practices and waste and extravagance in transactions, contracts, and activities."[8]

During its first year, the new subcommittee was chaired by Senator Homer Ferguson, a Michigan Republican who'd served on the Truman Committee and also served as head of the Senate Republican Policy Committee. During his one-year tenure, he held two high-profile hearings. The first examined issues related to two suspected Soviet spies, Elizabeth Bentley and William Remington, who were called to testify.[9] The second examined actions taken by the American military related to a Nazi war criminal, Ilse Koch known as the Beast of Buchenwald, whose sentence of life imprisonment had been mysteriously shortened to four years.[10] The two hearings provided an auspicious start for the new investigative subcommittee.

The subcommittee's next chair was Senator Clyde R. Hoey of North Carolina, who held the post from 1949 to 1952. His best-known investigation exposed the so-called Five Percenters, Washington lobbyists who helped clients obtain federal contracts in exchange for 5% of the contract profits. Emblematic of the crass corruption going on was the disclosure that some Five Percenter lobbyists were supplying some government officials with expensive "deep freezers" for storing food.[11] Another Hoey hearing that attracted attention examined the illegal "sale" of rural postal jobs by the Mississippi Democratic Party, featuring testimony from persons who had "purchased" their posts.[12]

Around the same time, a new ad hoc Senate investigative committee began an inquiry that would eventually lead to an expansion of PSI's jurisdiction. Formed in 1950, the Special Committee to Investigate Organized Crime in Interstate Commerce was chaired by Senator Estes Kefauver of Tennessee.[13] Known as the Kefauver Committee, it held hearings across the country, exposing wrongdoing by organized crime and taking testimony from notorious mobsters as well as "bookies, pimps, and gangland enforcers." Many of its hearings were televised, attracting the first huge television audiences to Senate hearings. The committee probed local organized crime syndicates across the United States and documented "shocking corruption in local government" allowing the syndicates to operate, leading to "numerous local indictments."[14] After issuing several reports, the committee disbanded. Later, its mandate to investigate organized crime affecting interstate commerce was transferred to the Subcommittee on Investigations.[15]

Sometime around 1952, the subcommittee underwent a second name change, becoming the "Permanent" Subcommittee on Investigations, to distinguish it from the Senate's many temporary committees that were formed to conduct a single investigation and then disappear. The new name signaled that PSI was intended to remain in existence from Congress to Congress, building its expertise in conducting oversight investigations.

Surviving McCarthy

Despite the impressive first five years of the Subcommittee on Investigations, once it became "Permanent," PSI's reputation took a nosedive. Its first chair became its most infamous: Senator Joe McCarthy of Wisconsin, who held sway over PSI for only 2 years from 1953 to 1954, but engaged in a litany of investigative abuses so offensive they still reverberate more than 60 years later.[16] Paradoxically, Senator McCarthy's misdeeds also served as a catalyst for rule changes that caused PSI to evolve into one of the most bipartisan operations in Congress today.

Senator McCarthy began his political career as a Democrat, but later switched to the Republican Party. He won his first election as a circuit judge in 1937, at age 29. In 1942, he enlisted in the U.S. Marine Corps to fight in World War II. In 1945, he returned home and re-entered politics. In 1946, in a Republican primary, he unexpectedly defeated respected Wisconsin Senator Robert La Follette Jr. and went on to win the general election for Senate.

His first four years as a U.S. senator were relatively quiet, but in 1950, in a Lincoln Day speech in Wheeling, West Virginia, Senator McCarthy claimed to have a list of 205 Communists working in the State Department under President Truman. The Red Scare was on.

Over the next two years, Senator McCarthy became a leading voice in the anti-Communist movement then sweeping the country, easily winning re-election in 1952. His re-election was part of a wave of Republican victories that helped Republicans regain the Senate majority for only the second time in 20 years, on a razor-thin margin of 48–47 plus one Republican-leaning independent. As a member of the majority party, Senator McCarthy won a spot as chair of the newly named Permanent Subcommittee on Investigations. He immediately launched a PSI investigation into alleged Communist influence on the U.S. government, even though the newly elected President Dwight Eisenhower was a member of his own party.

During the course of his controversial investigation, Senator McCarthy held 161 hearings behind closed doors and interrogated nearly 500 individuals, including well-known figures such as Aaron Copland, Dashiell Hammett, and Langston Hughes, along with government employees, labor organizers, and Army officers. The closed-door hearing transcripts, released by PSI in 2003, disclosed that Senator McCarthy browbeat witnesses, grilled them about their political beliefs, families, and past associations, and threatened them with imprisonment—sometimes for holding unpopular views and sometimes for resisting the government's authority to probe their personal lives.[17]

Senator McCarthy also held public hearings, many televised, pursuing allegations of Communist subversion of U.S. agencies, including the State Department, Army Signal Corps, and Government Printing Office. In April 1954, he held a 35-day series of hearings on alleged Communist infiltration of the U.S. Army before a television audience estimated at 20 million.[18] Due to the blatant unfairness of the proceedings, which included Senator McCarthy badgering and berating witnesses, the hearings undercut much of his public support. It was in one of those televised hearings that a witness, Joseph Nye Welch, famously asked the senator: "Have you no sense of decency, sir? At long last, have you left no sense of decency?"[19]

Senator McCarthy's two-year tenure as PSI chair was marked by rocky relations with the subcommittee's other members, due among other reasons to his failure to share information, outrageous conduct, appearing inebriated at some hearings, and abrasive staff. At the time, he controlled the hiring of all subcommittee personnel. His majority staff director, Roy Cohn, was just 26 years old and widely disliked. Perhaps his most famous hire was Robert Kennedy, an ardent anti-Communist who joined the PSI staff in 1953, at about the same age as Cohn. Cohen and Kennedy apparently acquired a quick distaste for each other and ultimately engaged in a fist fight that led to Kennedy's quitting the subcommittee.[20]

In July 1953, the three Democrats on PSI, Senators John McClellan of Arkansas, Henry ("Scoop") Jackson of Washington, and Stuart Symington of Missouri, resigned en masse and refused to attend future hearings.

Their resignations failed, however, to deter Senator McCarthy who barreled ahead with more closed-door and public hearings.

One constraint on his conduct was a string of unexpected deaths that kept Republican control over the U.S. Senate on a knife's edge. During the course of the 83rd Congress from 1953 through 1954, nine senators died in office and were replaced by individuals who either extended the Republicans' one-seat margin or left the Senate equally divided with an independent deciding the status of the majority party.[21] For example, in July 1953, the same month the three Democrats resigned from PSI, Republican Senate Majority Leader Robert A. Taft died in office, leaving Republicans with two open seats, a 46–47 split between the parties, and a wavering independent. Senator Taft was later replaced by a Democrat.

Given the uncertain circumstances, to ensure approval of PSI's budget in 1954, Senator McCarthy needed his Democratic counterparts to support his budget request. The Democrats conditioned their support upon his giving them authority to hire their own staff. Having little choice, Senator McCarthy agreed. In response, the Democrats supported the PSI budget request and hired Robert Kennedy as PSI's first minority counsel.[22]

On July 30, 1954, Republican Senator Ralph Flanders of Vermont filed a Senate resolution seeking censure of Senator McCarthy's increasingly offensive conduct, and the Senate formed a special committee to examine the charges.[23] Senator McCarthy attacked the committee, calling it an "unwitting handmaiden" of Communism. In November, elections returned the Democrats to majority status in the Senate by a one-vote margin of 48–47.[24] The results meant that, in the next Congress, Senator McCarthy would lose the PSI chair, though he'd remain senior Republican on the subcommittee. In December 1954, by a vote of 67–22, the Senate approved a resolution censuring Senator McCarthy for conduct "contrary to senatorial traditions." After the censure, his influence collapsed. Senator McCarthy died three years later, on May 2, 1957, at age 48, of ailments triggered by alcoholism.[25]

In the 84th Congress, in response to Senator McCarthy's malfeasance, the members of PSI amended the subcommittee's rules to reinstate a more bipartisan approach and prevent investigative abuses. Among other changes, the new rules required a quorum of members to be present to hold a hearing, barred confidential testimony unless authorized by a subcommittee majority, and enabled a unanimous subcommittee minority to block a public hearing unless supported by a full committee vote. The new rules also gave both parties full access to all information in the subcommittee's possession and confirmed the minority's right to hire staff.[26]

The McCarthy years represented the nadir of PSI's influence and respect. "McCarthyism" has since become synonymous with abusive investigations—excessive secrecy, unsubstantiated accusations, the bullying of witnesses, inadequate due process, and disrespect for individuals holding unpopular views. While the McCarthy years ravaged PSI's reputation, they also revived and gave new urgency to the earlier Truman approach, with its emphasis on responsible, bipartisan oversight. In the end, the McCarthy years appear to have burned into the consciousness of every PSI leader the need to conduct responsible investigations.

Rebuilding PSI

Rebuilding PSI after the McCarthy debacle took time. Luckily, his immediate successor was Senator John McClellan of Arkansas who would turn out to be PSI's longest sitting chair, holding the subcommittee's helm for the next 18 years, from 1955 to 1972. During his tenure, Senator McClellan restored PSI's reputation for responsible investigations and strengthened its staff expertise, while also increasing the subcommittee's jurisdictional reach.

A key part of his work, from 1957 to 1961, came from chairing a separate temporary investigative committee, the Select Committee on Improper Activities in the Labor or Management Field, which was formed after PSI uncovered troubling information warranting an in-depth investigation.[27] Including senators from PSI and the Committee on Labor and Public Welfare, the select committee launched an inquiry into the extent to which organized crime and criminal practices were influencing labor unions, including issues related to labor racketeering. For the next three years, the select committee operated out of PSI offices and shared PSI personnel, including Robert Kennedy who acted as chief counsel for both bodies. Senator McClellan led both PSI and the new select committee.

Over three years, the select committee held 270 days of hearings, took testimony from over 1500 witnesses, and served over 8000 subpoenas, including taking testimony from Jimmy Hoffa, head of the Teamsters labor union.[28] At its height, it had over 100 staffers located in PSI's Washington office as well as in field offices across the country. Upon its dissolution, the select committee's files and jurisdiction were transferred to PSI, which gained new authority to investigate criminal activity affecting labor-management relations. In addition, the investigation contributed to enactment of the Labor-Management Reporting and Disclosure Act of 1959, also known as the Landrum-Griffin Act, to curb labor union misconduct.

Senator McClellan also delved more deeply into issues associated with organized crime. Following up on the Kefauver hearings, he held a famous series of PSI hearings in 1963 known as the "Valachi Hearings."[29] They featured a low-level mobster, Joseph Valachi, who provided firsthand testimony about organized crime activities in the United States. He testified about the Mafia's leadership structure, recruitment and induction practices, alleged code of conduct, and crimes. The hearings encouraged the Department of Justice, then led by Attorney General Robert Kennedy—whose interest in organized crime deepened during his stint at PSI—to set up the first Organized Crime Strike Force. The Justice Department also increased federal organized crime investigations and installed new information-sharing procedures with other law enforcement agencies. In addition, based in part on PSI's work, Congress enacted the Racketeer Influenced and Corrupt Organizations (RICO) provisions of the Crime Control Act of 1970.

Senator McClellan conducted investigations into a wide range of other issues as well. They included key causes of the 1967 riots in U.S. cities, commodities and mortgage fraud involving Texas financier Billie Sol Estes, contract problems at the Department of Defense, narcotics trafficking, and securities and banking fraud.[30] Hearings on a labor leader's alleged misuse of $4 million in union benefit funds contributed to eventual enactment of the 1974 Employee Retirement Income Security Act (ERISA).[31] By the time Senator McClellan left office, PSI had regained its stature as Congress' premier investigative body.

Senator McClellan was followed by a succession of strong PSI leaders who continued the subcommittee's effective oversight and bipartisan traditions. Henry "Scoop" Jackson of Washington State held the post for five years, from 1973 to 1978, working closely with his Republican counterpart, Senator Charles "Chuck" Percy of Illinois. Together, they held hearings on both majority and minority-led inquiries. They also oversaw a further expansion of PSI's jurisdiction when, in 1973, the National Security Subcommittee was folded into PSI along with its jurisdiction over national security issues, technology transfer, and international organizations; and in 1974, when energy resources and shortages were added to PSI's palette.[32] The Jackson-Percy investigations included inquiries into U.S. energy shortages after the Arab-Israeli war; federal drug busts of questionable effectiveness; and misconduct associated with the hearing aid industry, arson-for-hire crimes, and illegal insurance schemes.[33]

After the Jackson-Percy era came the Roth-Nunn era. Beginning in 1978 and continuing for 17 years until 1996, PSI was led by Senator William Roth, a Republican from Delaware, and Senator Sam Nunn, a Democrat from

Georgia, who traded the chair and ranking positions on PSI three times. Like their predecessors, they worked closely together. They took turns initiating investigations, resulting in both majority and minority-led hearings and reports. Their inquiries included examinations of money laundering, pension fraud, offshore banking and tax evasion, commodity investment and illegal currency frauds, defense procurement problems, insurance fraud, student loan abuses, health care fraud, and corruption in professional boxing.[34] Among other accomplishments, their work spurred passage of the Money Laundering Control Act of 1986, the first statute in the world to make money laundering a crime.

In addition, during his tenure as PSI chair in the 1980s, Senator Roth strengthened the bipartisan nature of the subcommittee's rules, elevating the role of the minority in setting the subcommittee's agenda. For example, new rules explicitly gave the minority unilateral authority to initiate its own pre- liminary inquiries. They also provided that an official PSI investigation— whether majority or minority led—had to be approved by both the majority and minority parties to proceed.[35] Those rule changes further cemented the bipartisan nature of PSI investigations.

In 1997, Senator Susan Collins, a Republican from Maine, became the first woman to chair PSI, holding that post for four years until 2001. Senator John Glenn was her initial ranking member followed by Senator Levin in 1999. During her tenure, Senator Collins turned the PSI spotlight on matters affect- ing Americans in their day-to-day lives, conducting investigations into such matters as mortgage fraud, phony credentials obtained through the Internet, deceptive sweepstakes promotions, day-trading of securities, securities fraud on the Internet, and fraudulent schemes that crossed international borders.[36]

Senator Collins had already led PSI for two years when Senator Levin became the subcommittee's ranking Democrat. In 2001, they would trade the subcommittee's chair and ranking positions as their respective parties traded majority status in the Senate. Like their predecessors, Senators Collins and Levin would establish a strong working partnership and become a powerful investigative team.

Confronting Mice and Flies

But that was in the future. In January 1999, at the start of the 106th Congress when Senator Levin took his initial leadership post on PSI, the first order of business for Linda and me was to pick up stakes and move to PSI's offices. For me, it was a culture shock.

In all my years on the Levin team, I'd worked out of fairly modern offices on the upper floors of the bright and airy Hart Senate Office Building. I had a small office with a door, a large sunny window, modular furniture, and well-functioning office equipment.

PSI was different. The PSI office suite was located in Russell, the oldest of the three Senate office buildings. A dimly lit, massive hallway with a downward sloping floor led to the offices, which were nominally on the first floor, but actually sat below ground level.

That became clear upon opening the door to the office suite. The wall opposite the door was lined with multiple, tall windows that let in light, but instead of opening onto a street scene, showed a gray concrete wall that stretched across the entire expanse of windows, about three feet from the window panes. The wall made it clear that the suite of rooms was far below ground. It was only by looking straight up that you could see a thin strip of blue sky. Cars driving on the street produced a thrum of vibration above head-level.

In addition to their subterranean feel, the offices looked like a set out of a 1950s movie. The ceilings were some 15 feet high; the walls were heavy and thick; the floor was a solid slab; and the windows had wooden sashes, wavy glass, and blinds yellowed with age. The carpeting was a threadbare, years-old red weave.

Our suite consisted of three massive, interconnected rooms, the back two of which were linked by an odd side hallway interrupted by five stairs. While the middle room of the three was unobstructed, the rooms on each side had been subdivided into smaller offices using thin, dark wooden paneling hung with hollow doors. Despite a height of about 10 feet, the paneling came nowhere close to the towering ceilings, which meant that all the subdivided offices shared the same empty space above them. Voices echoed across the rooms, with no sound-proofing to stop anyone from hearing everyone else's conversations.

The three rooms—each of which seemed to need fumigating—were filled with a haphazard collection of scuffed-up desks, industrial gray filing cabinets, and lamps with yellow, stained lampshades. The copying machine was ancient. Mousetraps testified to late-night visitors. A few massive black flies lazily buzzed around the rooms. Adding to the charm was an intermittent low roar from what turned out to be a poorly functioning air-flow system that failed to reduce the large temperature differences between the rooms.

When I first walked into the offices, I was so taken aback I couldn't say a word. When Linda arrived, however, she breezed in, apparently unfazed. She set up shop in the second of the three rooms and gave me my pick of the subdivided offices in the first room. I selected the one closest to her door. While it was significantly larger than my old office, the negatives included the concrete-walled view, the open-air ceiling, and a broken-down desk.

When the Senate Russell Building first opened in 1909, it was seen as a statement of the United States' power and wealth, and money was spent on elegant furniture, awe-inspiring windows, and majestic architectural spaces, not to mention marble staircases and floors. But that was then. By 1999, taxpayers showed their disregard for Congress by starving it for funds and expecting government workers to work in shabby, poorly equipped offices.

I had long ago accepted that elegance wasn't part of the package in government service and found I could work just about anywhere. But there was shabby, and then there was dilapidated. With the PSI offices falling into the latter category, I decided to invest some time and energy into modestly improving our work environment.

I kicked off the effort using a high-tech dolly lent by our prior clerk, Frankie, to go hall shopping. During the first months of a new Congress, as multiple offices changed hands, the hallways became filled with unneeded office furniture marked "return to stock." Buzzing through the corridors, I quickly located some decent-looking furnishings and swapped them for our sad specimens. The only furniture I couldn't manage was the big disaster of a desk sitting in my office. As I contemplated its marred surfaces and broken drawers, I realized I'd been passing the office of the official furniture movers, right down the hall from us.

Early the next morning, doughnuts in tow, I introduced myself to our new neighbors. I mentioned that I understood one of the movers was married to a woman in Senator Levin's mailroom; heads nodded. Then I asked if they could help me move into my office an available desk sitting in a nearby hallway. They knew and I knew that they were not supposed to help me—they were supposed to work on specific offices in a specific sequence. But the guys gave me a big smile and said sure, if they could do it quickly. Ten minutes later, they had the new desk in my office and my old desk out in the hallway, marked for storage.

By the end of my hall-shopping spree, while our offices would never be called attractive, they looked, functioned, and smelled a lot better. My jangling nerves soothed. Over the years, the window views never improved, the room temperatures never evened out, and the huge black flies continued to make sporadic wavering flights through the office. And yet, over time, the PSI offices felt more and more welcoming, providing a hard-boiled, squalid charm that in the end, for me, added to the PSI magic.

Building the Levin Team

Moving to PSI's offices was a big change. Another was staffing up. Most of the Levin investigative staff had moved on when the Democrats lost majority status in 1996. Linda and I were the only holdovers. We had to build a new team.

In 1999, the Democrats were still the minority party in the Senate, but because the PSI budget was bigger than at our prior subcommittee, Linda had the funds to hire one new staffer. Her pick was Bob Roach, who ended up spending the next 15 years with us and was the best investigator I've ever worked with.

Bob was already a PSI employee, having been hired by Senator Glenn. He was a few years older than I—in his mid-forties—medium height, wiry, with black hair in a short military cut, glasses, and a ready grin. His intensity was palpable, as was his sense of humor and good cheer. Before PSI, Bob had worked for several House members known for effective oversight, including Congressmen John Dingell from Michigan and Mike Synar from Oklahoma.

I was to learn that Bob was an investigator's investigator, relishing the chase after facts and documents, delighting in the battles against powerful interests, and astonishing in his ability to unravel the most complicated schemes. But I didn't know all that when we first began working together. Instead, we had to overcome a rocky beginning to build what became a rock-solid partnership. As the years went by, Bob not only burnished his reputation as a fearsome investigator, he became central to the ethical compass and intangible fighting spirit of PSI.

Another new partner in 1999 was the PSI clerk, Mary Robertson. Subcommittee clerks handle administrative duties for both sides of the aisle, so she worked for both Senator Collins and Senator Levin, with her salary split between the two.

I learned that Mary was one of two long-time clerks in PSI's history. The first, Ruth Young Watt, had held the job for 31 years from 1948 to 1979, followed by three short-timers.[37] Mary had begun her PSI career working for Ruth as a 1973 summer intern, later became a full-time assistant clerk, and then outlasted the short-timers to become chief clerk in 1987. Her tenure had already encompassed six of PSI's leaders: Senators Jackson, Percy, Roth, Nunn, Collins, and Glenn. By the time we got there, Mary had already seen over two decades of PSI investigative effort and knew how everything was supposed to work.

Mary was my age—in her early forties—with brown hair, a solid frame, and endless energy. Her grasp of issues was immediate, and she had no time for incompetence, delay, or deception. She ended up spending a total of 39 years at PSI, including all 15 years of the Levin era. But it wasn't just her longevity that made Mary indispensable. What mattered was that she set impossibly high standards, met them, encouraged others to do the same, and acted with such integrity that she became the subcommittee's institutional memory, as well as an honest broker who kept PSI humming on a bipartisan basis.

In 2001, Linda added another investigator to our team, Laura Stuber, who also became a long-term PSI staffer. Laura came from Senator Levin's personal staff. She was younger than me—in her early thirties—slim, cheerful, and generally unflappable. She'd worked previously as a prosecutor in Kansas. She was self-directed, completed tasks promptly, and could whip a team of inexperienced investigators into shape, convincing them to work long hours and produce results that amazed even themselves. Over the years, she became an expert on money laundering investigations, gathering evidence that produced some of our most powerful hearings.

We five made up the core of the Levin PSI team—Linda as staff director and chief counsel, me as her deputy, Bob as chief investigator, Laura as our investigative counsel, and Mary as our clerk. A few years later, in 2003, Linda was promoted to chief of staff in Senator Levin's personal office, and I took her position as PSI staff director. Two years after that, Linda retired. The rest of us stayed with PSI pretty much until Senator Levin retired in 2015. We all agreed that working at PSI was a wild, intoxicating ride, the best job any of us ever had.

Along the way, we were joined by other stellar staffers. Dan Berkovitz, our expert on energy and commodity issues, joined us in 2001, and stayed six years. Zack Schram, our utility infielder and outstanding negotiator, joined us in 2004 and gave us nine years as subcommittee counsel. Ross Kirschner, who did stints as an intern, law clerk, and legal counsel, gave us two short but brilliant years. Dan Goshorn, who could dissect the most complicated puzzles thrown his way, stayed five years while also supplying us with delicious home-made pies. David Katz and Allison Murphy, who joined us as legal counsel in 2009, gave us five years at the height of our work, injecting a new supply of energy, expertise, and humor. Around the same time, Adam Henderson became our computer expert, helping us access millions of pages of documents.

Senator Levin always attracted the best and brightest in staff. At the same time, the subcommittee work was never easy, in part because the Levin PSI staff was never big enough. At our peak, we totaled only ten paid staffers. Often we had fewer. Not nearly enough to tackle all the scandals and abuses Senator Levin wanted to investigate. So we were constantly overworked.

The upside of our small staff was our agility and lack of bureaucracy. We could make decisions quickly and adapt nimbly to changing circumstances. We also supplemented our ranks with an unceasing flow of volunteer law clerks, college interns, fellows, and detailees. And we pushed ourselves at a punishing pace to get things done.

In addition, we worked with outstanding Republican colleagues who were another key to the subcommittee's success. During the Levin years, we worked with four Republican senators who, together, covered the waterfront in terms of Republican philosophies and leadership styles. But each was dedicated to effective oversight, willing to operate in a bipartisan manner, and adept at taking political heat.

Their Republican staffs often began wary of working with the Levin crew, but ultimately—despite missteps and mix-ups—became not only our colleagues, but our friends. They included Lee Blalack, Claire Barnard, and Kim Corthell with Senator Collins; Ray Shepherd, Mark Greenblatt, Mark Nelson, Steve Groves, Leland Erickson, Jay Jennings, and Mike Flowers with Senator Coleman; Chris Barkley, Keith Ashdown, and Andy Dockham with Senator Coburn; and Henry Kerner, Stephanie Hall, and Mike Lueptow with Senator McCain. Our Republican counterparts kept us on our toes, helped us avoid mistakes, and played key roles in making PSI work.

Working with Senator Levin

And then there was Senator Levin, one of the little-known giants of the U.S. Senate. He was made for oversight. He was scary smart, had an immense capacity for hard work, and a passion for honest fact-finding which he viewed as essential to informed policymaking. He also displayed the discipline, drive, and intellect needed to master difficult subjects and plow through extensive materials. He seemed to have a boundless capacity to confront complex problems, abusive conduct, and injustice, approaching them with a quiet optimism that something could be done to make things better. He never gave up a fight, even when it took years to make progress.

Senator Levin believed in bipartisanship, respected his Republican colleagues, and had the negotiating skills and patience that made joint investigations work. He viewed compromise as an honorable way for people with diverse views to work together. Still another critical attribute: he was willing to take on powerful interests.

Best of all from an investigator's perspective, Senator Levin knew how to make the most of a Senate hearing. The staff knew that if they got him the goods, he'd use their work to pack a wallop in public settings. He had a knack for asking tough questions without being unfair or offensive, and could explain complicated issues in an understandable way. He was also the best listener I ever encountered; he heard what witnesses actually said and followed up with questions that clarified the facts and exposed attempts to skirt the truth. He didn't allow bullies or cagey witnesses to twist the record. Most important of all, he paid attention to detail and remembered those details when it counted—a talent that some critics portrayed as a weakness, because it got him down in the weeds, but was, in fact, his greatest strength, because it's in the weeds where facts emerge, not only to explain problems and hold individuals accountable, but also to produce workable solutions that cross political divides.

On a day-to-day level, it was clear Senator Levin loved the Senate as an institution and enjoyed being a senator. In the office, he was energetic and engaged, juggling multiple tasks without complaint. He was a willing participant in endless rounds of meetings with senators, officials, dignitaries, and constituents, preparing carefully and using each occasion to learn and persuade. He took pleasure in talking to the press, even when cornered in a hallway.

With staff, he was accessible and collaborative, but also demanding. He prized hard work, setting a personal example that started early in the morning, extended late into the night, and included weekends. He expected the same of staff. He favored teams working together on difficult issues and held multiple staff meetings per day. He read everything staff gave him, asked searching questions, and listened to the answers. He valued staff insights and advice, and often used them to develop plans to advance his policy goals. He then asked staff to carry out those plans, giving senior staff significant authority and discretion to act, and displaying profound trust in their judgment. For Senate staff, Senator Levin's respect for their professionalism and reliance on their work was about as good as it gets in Washington.

In addition, Senator Levin was a warm, funny, and compassionate boss. His smile was infectious, his eyes twinkled, and he excelled at telling jokes. He could be a delightful conversationalist, witty, informed, and full of wise counsel. Bring in a baby or toddler to the office, and the Senator dropped everything to try to make the child laugh. He cherished his wife, three daughters, and extended family. He adored his grandchildren. He liked lunching with the interns. He kept packages of cookies in his desk and offered them during meetings.

Of course, he wasn't perfect. At times his demands on staff were unreasonable, piling long hours on top of long hours. He sometimes edited drafts so heavily, producing version after version of the same document marked up with nearly illegible scrawls, that we despaired of ever getting a final product. At other times, he wanted to know so many facts that it became counterproductive, eating up time and resources better spent elsewhere. For example, he once was booked on a flight to Europe with a stopover in Iceland, and staff was frantically preparing for the trip. He interrupted to ask if the airplane was refueling in Iceland. When a puzzled staffer asked why he wanted that information, he said he was curious.

While occasionally frustrating, it was also clear his imperfections paled in comparison to the strengths he brought to the Senate; he was a man working flat out to do the best he could for his country. In a Senate debilitated by high employee turnover, Senator Levin became known for his stable staff, many of whom stayed with him for decades. It was his close collaboration with PSI staff that, in part, enabled Senator Levin to produce his remarkable investigative legacy.

The following chapters recount that legacy, detailing the key investigations undertaken during the Levin years on PSI. They include inquiries into money laundering, financial wrongdoing, offshore tax abuse, and bank misconduct. The subject matter reflects Senator Levin's concerns as well as staff recommendations, bipartisan considerations, and prominent topics of the day. Earlier investigations also begat follow-up inquiries, as Senator Levin gradually built up a body of work. While the following chapters do not describe all the inquiries Senator Levin undertook, they cover the major ones, highlighting the key issues, investigative work, and policy reforms that went into each oversight effort.

During the Levin era at PSI, the Senate and Congress as a whole grew more partisan, more dysfunctional, and less effective. Despite the deterioration around it, PSI managed to create an island of sanity, bipartisanship, and mutual respect where we could conduct meaningful oversight. Under Senator Levin's leadership, we worked hard to uphold PSI's traditions and enhance its reputation for high-quality, bipartisan investigations. At the same time, we had a lot of fun. Here's how we did it.

Notes

1. "Corporate World Won't Miss Levin," *Politico*, Kelsey Snell (9/11/2014), http://politi.co/2hCzWdH.
2. Senate Resolution 71, 87 Congressional Record 1615 (1941), introduced by Senator Truman, reprinted in *The Truman Committee: A Study in Congressional Responsibility*, Donald H. Riddle (Rutgers University Press 1964) (hereinafter "*The Truman Committee*"), at 179.
3. See, for example, *The Truman Committee*, at vii (Truman Committee "was not only extremely successful, but it was also one of the most responsible investigating committees in recent history"); *Congress Investigates*, at 636–667 (Truman Committee's "record of responsible, restrained investigation established an admirable standard"); *The Power to Probe: A Study of Congressional Investigations*, James Hamilton (Random House 1976), at 9 (Truman Committee was "one of the country's most effective investigating panels"); *Congressional Investigations and Oversight*, Lance Cole and Stanley M. Brand (Carolina Academic Press 2011) (hereinafter "Cole and Brand"), at 41 (Truman Committee was "one of the most productive investigating committees in [the Senate's] entire history").

4. "The Impact of the Senate Permanent Subcommittee on Investigations on Federal Policy," *Georgia Law Review*, Volume 21, at 17, 20–21 (Special Issue 1986), Senator Sam Nunn (hereinafter "1986 Nunn Law Review article"); Cole and Brand, at 42.
5. Legislative Reorganization Act of 1946, P.L. 79-601, 60 Stat. 812, Section 136 ("To assist the Congress in appraising the administration of the laws and in developing such amendments or related legislation as it may deem necessary, each standing committee of the Senate and the House shall exercise continuous watchfulness of the execution by administrative agencies concerned of any laws, the subject matter of which is within the jurisdiction of such committee …") (S. 2177); see also "Record of the 79th Congress (Second Session)," CQ Researcher, section on "Modernization of Government," (undated), http://library.cqpress.com/cqresearcher/document.php?id=cqresrre1946080300.
6. The Truman Committee was merged with the Surplus Property Disposal Subcommittee chaired by former Truman Committee member Senator Homer Ferguson of Michigan. The new subcommittee was given custody of the Truman Committee's files and records. See Senate Oral History of Ruth Young Watt, Interview No. 2, at 51–52, http://bit.ly/2j4tIDL; 1986 Nunn Law Review article, at 21–22; "History of the Senate Permanent Subcommittee on Investigations of the Committee of Governmental Affairs," prepared by PSI (6/1996), at 1 (hereinafter "1996 PSI History").
7. "First Annual Report of the Investigations Subcommittee of the Committee on Expenditures in the Executive Departments," S. Rpt. 5 (1/17/1949), at 2 (hereinafter "1949 Annual Report"), http://bit.ly/2zSF7hL.
8. "The Organization of Congress: Some Problems of Committee Jurisdiction," Committee on Expenditures in the Executive Departments," S. Rpt. 51 (7/1951), at 34.
9. See "Export Policy and Loyalty," Part 1 (7/30/1948), http://bit.ly/2AaPcJM.
10. See "Conduct of Ilse Koch War Crimes Trial," Part 5 (9/28 and 12/8–9/1948), at 995, http://bit.ly/2zOnqm8; 1949 Annual Report, at 7.
11. See "The 5-Percenter Investigation," S. Rpt. 1232 (1/18/1950), at 401, http://bit.ly/2zfS200; 2004 GAC Activities Report, at 118; 1986 Nunn Law Review article, at 22.
12. See "Activities of the Mississippi Democratic Committee," (April 9–11, 26, and May 2, 5, 10, 1951), at 81, http://bit.ly/2Ac6d6L and http://bit.ly/2hItsNV.
13. For more information about the Kefauver Committee, see *Congress Investigates*, at 715–756; "Guide to the Records of the U.S. Senate in the National Archives of the United States," Chapter 18, "Records of Senate Select Committees, 1789–1988," prepared by the National Archives (hereinafter "Records of Senate Select Committees"), ¶¶ 18.133–18.144, http://bit.ly/2j4hniQ.
14. *The Power to Probe*, at 10.

15. This addition to the subcommittee's jurisdiction occurred in 1961. 1996 PSI History, at 1.
16. The information in this section is largely based upon *Congress Investigates*, at 808–848.
17. See, for example, "Executive Sessions of the Senate Permanent Subcommittee on Investigations of the Committee on Government Operations," Part 1, S. Prt. 107-84 (1953) (hereinafter "McCarthy Executive Sessions"), http://bit.ly/2mDEOo3.
18. See, for example, "Special Senate Investigation on Charges and Countercharges Involving Secretary of the Army Robert T. Stevens, John G. Adams, H. Struve Hensel and Senator Joe McCarthy, Roy M. Cohen, and Francis P. Carr" (1954), http://bit.ly/2AR9eWk.
19. Mr. Welch was outside legal counsel for the U.S. Army and testified on June 9, 1954. After Senator McCarthy described Fred Fisher, a young lawyer in Mr. Welch's law firm, as a law school member of the National Lawyers Guild, which Senator McCarthy described as the "legal arm of the Communist Party," Mr. Welch said:

   > Until this moment, Senator, I think I have never really gauged your cruelty or your recklessness. Fred Fisher is a young man who went to the Harvard Law School and came into my firm and is starting what looks to be a brilliant career with us. ... Little did I dream you could be so reckless and so cruel as to do an injury to that lad. It is, I regret to say, equally true that I fear he shall always bear a scar needlessly inflicted by you. ... Let us not assassinate this lad further, Senator. You've done enough. Have you no sense of decency, sir? At long last, have you left no sense of decency?

   For a recording of his testimony, see "American Rhetoric: Top 100 Speeches," "McCarthy-Welch Exchange," http://bit.ly/1NSGNcP.
20. See, for example, McCarthy Executive Sessions, introduction, at XVII.
21. See, for example, "Membership Changes of 83rd Congress (1953–55)," U.S. Senate, http://bit.ly/2is2s2m.
22. PSI still has the desk—one of 100 specially designed for Senate offices in the Russell Building—that PSI lore says Robert Kennedy used during his PSI tenure. After a departing Republican staffer bequeathed it to me, I used it until the day I retired.
23. See *United States Senate Election, Expulsion and Censure Cases, 1793–1990*, U.S. Senate Historical Office (1995), at 404–407, http://bit.ly/2AaQkgu; Senate Resolution 301 (12/2/1954).
24. See, for example, "Membership Changes of 83rd Congress (1953–55)," U.S. Senate, http://bit.ly/2is2s2m.
25. See *A Conspiracy So Immense: The World of Joe McCarthy*, David Oshinsky (The Free Press 1983), at 502–505.
26. See McCarthy Executive Sessions, introduction, at XXVIII.

27. Records of Senate Select Committees, ¶¶ 18.165–18.171; 1986 Nunn Law Review article, at 26–29; 1996 PSI History, at 1; *Congress Investigates*, at 849–885; "Investigation of Improper Activities in the Labor or Management Field—Index to Hearings" (1959), http://bit.ly/2jE0JKB.
28. See, for example, "Gambling and Organized Crime," Part 1 (8/22–25/1961), http://bit.ly/2j66M79; "James R. Hoffa and Continued Underworld Control of New York Teamster Local 239," (1/10–12 and 24–25/1961), http://bit.ly/2jGj5uQ.
29. See, for example, 1986 Nunn Law Review article, at 30–33; "Organized Crime and Illicit Traffic in Narcotics," Part 1 (9/25 and 27, and 10/1–2, 8–9/1963), http://bit.ly/2yUUyF4.
30. See, for example, "Riots, Civil and Criminal Disorders," Part 1 (11/1–3 and 6/1967), http://bit.ly/2zPva6L; "Department of Agriculture Handling of Pooled Cotton Allotments of Billie Sol Estes," Part 1 (6/27–29 and 7/5/1962), http://bit.ly/2yYgTS5; "TFX Contract Investigation," Part 1 (2/26–28 and 3/5–6/1963), http://bit.ly/2AcZBVw; and "Organized Crime—Stolen Securities," Part 1 (6/8–10 and 16/1971), http://bit.ly/2zREEfV.
31. See, for example, "Diversion of Union Welfare-Pension Funds of Allied Trades Council and Teamsters 815," (6/29 and 7/20–22/1965), http://bit.ly/2hLUC6y; "The Employee Retirement Income Security Act of 1974: The First Decade," Senate Special Committee on Aging, S. Prt. 98-221 (8/1984), at 10–12, http://bit.ly/2AbwlOL (tracing McClelland hearings' contribution to ERISA).
32. 1996 PSI History, at 1–2.
33. See "Current Energy Shortages Oversight Series-Conflicting Information on Fuel Shortages," Part 1 (12/14/1973), http://bit.ly/2zNXKpB; "Federal Drug Enforcement," Part 1 (6/9–11/1975), http://bit.ly/2zdpKmZ; "Hearing Aid Industry," (4/1–2/1976), http://bit.ly/2mDbDl3; "Arson-for-Hire," (8/23–24 and 9/13–14/1978), http://bit.ly/2zQTGVi; "Severance Pay-Life Insurance Plans Adopted by Local Unions," (3/21/1977), http://bit.ly/2mEhFlA; "Labor Union Insurance," Part 1 (10/10–12 and 17–19/1977), http://bit.ly/2zQ4FOx.
34. "Activities of the Committee on Governmental Affairs," Report by Governmental Affairs Committee, S. Rpt. 108-421 (12/7/2004) (hereinafter "2004 GAC Activities Report"), at 120, http://bit.ly/2zg37hE; 1986 Nunn Law Review article, at 37–55.
35. See PSI Rule No. 1.
36. 2004 GAC Activities Report, at 120–121.
37. Myra Crase was PSI chief clerk from 1979 to 1980, Katherine Bidden from 1981 to 1985, and Carla Martin from 1985 to 1986.

3

Combating Money Laundering: Round One

"There is no power on earth that can tear away the veil behind which powerful and audacious and unscrupulous groups operate save the sovereign legislative power armed with the right of subpoena and search."
Senator Hugo Black (D-Alabama), *"Inside a Senate Investigation,"* 1936
Harper's Magazine ©

Duffle bags of cash. Corrupt dictators and their money-grubbing relatives. Sleazy offshore banks. Shell companies. Drug money. Terrorist finance. Bankers, lawyers, and accountants awash in wrongdoing. We saw it all in our investigations into money laundering.

Laundering money involves taking dirty cash—the proceeds of crime—and hiding its illicit origins. Buy a house with $1 million in drug money, sell it, and, voila, the cash appears to be the legitimate proceeds of a real estate sale. Deposit a bribe in a bank account, transfer it to another account disguised as a payment in a business deal, and its criminal taint fades.

Senator Levin's first two PSI investigations delved deep into the issue of money laundering using case studies involving private banking and correspondent banking; his later hearings dug even deeper. They exposed outrageous misconduct at multiple U.S. banks, disclosed how U.S. professionals were facilitating the movement of suspect funds, and highlighted glaring weaknesses in U.S. laws and financial regulation.

Over the years, the Levin oversight efforts drove legislative and regulatory changes that not only fortified U.S. anti-money laundering efforts but also

© The Author(s) 2018
E. J. Bean, *Financial Exposure*, https://doi.org/10.1007/978-3-319-94388-6_3

forced the cleanup of a number of financial institutions. By the time Senator Levin left office in 2015, it was a whole lot harder to launder dirty money than when he started.

Zeroing in on Dirty Money

When Senator Levin joined PSI in 1999, the Democrats were the minority party in the Senate. In most committees, the majority party alone sets the committee agenda. But PSI was an exception; it had special rules and a long history supporting minority-led inquiries. So once at PSI, Senator Levin was eager to launch his own investigation. Out of respect for the PSI chair Senator Susan Collins, he also wanted to select a topic that was clearly within PSI's jurisdiction, would attract bipartisan support, and could enhance PSI's reputation.

When Senator Levin proposed money laundering as his first official investigation, Senator Collins welcomed the inquiry. Her staff director, Lee Blalack, a smart, hard-working, wise-cracking lawyer, asked Claire Barnard of the Collins staff to work with us.[1]

Zeroing in on money laundering proved to be an inspired choice. An earlier PSI chair, Republican Senator Bill Roth, had already conducted several money laundering hearings, so there was solid precedent and a bipartisan foundation for the inquiry. In addition, a brewing scandal provided a perfect case study. The key allegation was that Raul Salinas, brother to the then President of Mexico, had laundered substantial sums through U.S. and Swiss banks, culminating in a 1998 Swiss court order requiring the forfeiture of $114 million determined by the court to be related to drug trafficking.[2] One of the named U.S. banks was Citicorp.

When Linda first alerted Senator Levin to the Salinas scandal, he'd asked PSI's then ranking Democrat Senator John Glenn to join him in asking the General Accounting Office to look into the facts. The General Accounting Office—later renamed the Government Accountability Office but consistently known by the initials "GAO"—is an independent agency that works for Congress. Established in 1921, GAO's mission is to respond to House and Senate requests for investigations. Called Congress' "watchdog," GAO produces hundreds of reports and audits per year and frequently testifies before Congress. While its work is often slow-moving, its results are generally seen as reliable and nonpartisan. GAO readily accepted the request to look into the Salinas facts and accelerated its efforts once Senator Levin acquired a PSI leadership position and made money laundering the focus of his first PSI inquiry.

As GAO intensified its efforts, Bob and I began learning everything we could about money laundering. For me, one of the attractions of oversight was learning new things, so I dug in with a will. We started by researching money laundering crimes, U.S. anti-money laundering laws and regulations, international anti-money laundering standards, and what was known about the Salinas case. Since Mr. Salinas opened accounts at Citigroup's so-called private bank, we delved into that as well. In the end, we framed the entire investigation as an examination of the extent to which U.S. private banking was vulnerable to money laundering.

Investigating Private Banking

Prior to the PSI investigation, I knew next to nothing about the private banking industry. I soon learned "private banks" were financial institutions—or operating divisions within financial institutions—that catered solely to very wealthy individuals. Private banks typically had three defining characteristics. They imposed a minimum amount of deposits for a client to be admitted into the private bank, often $1 million or more; they assigned a bank employee—typically called a private banker or relationship manager—to act as the client's personal liaison within the bank; and they provided clients with a host of confidential banking services, which frequently included opening offshore accounts. We also learned that most major U.S. banks had private banking divisions whose clients included powerful foreign officials and their relatives.

Our research also uncovered longstanding concerns that some foreign officials were using their U.S. private banking accounts to launder suspect cash, including the proceeds of bribery, drug trafficking, and other crimes. The 1994 conviction of a U.S. private banker who helped launder drug proceeds had been an early wake-up call.[3] We learned that the Federal Reserve had become so concerned that it had initiated an in-depth investigation into the problem and, in 1997, issued guidance on recommended anti-money laundering controls at private banks.[4] Bob and I decided it was time to get a briefing from the Federal Reserve.

Federal Reserve

In response to our request, a team of Federal Reserve staffers met with PSI's bipartisan staff about the Fed's 1997 guidance. We learned it was part of a three-year effort by the Federal Reserve Bank of New York (FRBNY) to reduce private banking vulnerabilities to money laundering. The effort had included FRBNY anti-money laundering (AML) audits of 40 private banking operations in the New York area in 1996, including Citigroup. In 1997, the FRBNY had conducted follow-up reviews at four financial institutions with AML deficiencies, a group which again included Citigroup. In 1998, the FRBNY conducted one last follow-up inspection—ding, ding, ding if you guessed that the lone bank was Citigroup.

When we reported back to Linda, she decided we needed to know more. We sent a formal document request seeking copies of, not only the FRBNY's three audit reports for Citigroup's private bank, but also the underlying workpapers. The most powerful and secretive of U.S. bank regulators, the Federal Reserve initially refused to provide any written materials. We informed Senator Levin who authorized us to ask the PSI majority if they would support issuing a subpoena to the Federal Reserve. After Senator Collins signaled she would, and we informed the Federal Reserve, it ultimately consented to allowing us to review the requested documents onsite at its Washington headquarters.

It took several weeks for the documents to be collected and shipped from New York to Washington. When they arrived in March 1999, Linda asked me to review them. For the next two weeks, that's all I did. I reported early to work, loaded up my backpack with pens, paper, and lunch, and took a 20-minute trek straight down Capitol Hill, walking past the Capitol, Smithsonian museums, and Washington Monument, to the Federal Reserve's classic marble edifice sitting across the street from the Lincoln Memorial. After passing through security, I was ushered into an empty room with a long table, leather-backed chairs, and dim lighting. Stacks of folders awaited me. I spent each day in the uninterrupted quiet reviewing the materials.

From years of document review, I knew to organize the material into groups, put the documents within each group into chronological order, and prepare a list of the documents by type, date, author, number of pages, and subject matter. After completing that initial inventory, my next steps were to identify the most important documents, review them, and copy down the key passages and data verbatim. Essentially, it came down to taking notes eight hours a day, at breakneck speed, rolling through the documents as fast as possible.

Speed was critical not only because of the volume of documents to be reviewed, but also because I'd learned that you never knew when someone who provided documents might try to take them back. So I put my head down and worked flat out. Back then, no one used laptops to take notes, so I wrote everything out longhand on yellow legal pads. Luckily, I was a champion notetaker with good penmanship, which was why Linda liked to assign me to document review.

The days flew by, because the Federal Reserve documents were dynamite. The Fed's AML audits of Citigroup's private bank contained harsh assessments of what the bank examiners had found. Memos noted that the private bank's Swiss headquarters received the "worst possible audit rating" from Citigroup's own AML auditors in 1995; that poor audit scores were "not taken seriously" within the private bank; and that the private bank's AML "practice lag[ged] behind the pack" of its peers. The examiners wrote that, at Citigroup's private bank, the "control environment is weaker, and risk tolerance is greater"; and "the corporate culture ... did not foster 'a climate of integrity, ethical conduct and prudent risk taking' by U.S. standards." One memo attributed the private bank's ongoing AML problems "in part to the fact that senior management responsible for these problems [were] still in charge."

The negative assessments explained why the FRBNY had ended up conducting three consecutive AML reviews of Citigroup's private bank. The first uncovered outrageously bad conditions; the follow-up found little improvement; and it was only after the third review that the Fed was satisfied Citigroup had begun to clean up its act.

At the end of each day, I walked the 20 minutes back to PSI and briefed Linda, Bob, and the majority staff on what I'd found. We agreed the Fed materials, which included Citigroup's own audits, provided powerful evidence of the private bank's AML deficiencies. The documents also made it clear that the private bank's AML problems extended far beyond the Salinas case. We decided to take a deeper dive into three other accounts mentioned in the documents. Each involved a foreign head of state or close relative who'd moved millions of dollars in suspect funds through Citigroup's private bank.

Prison Interview

The Fed documents weren't the only early break we got in the investigation. During our research, we also came across newspaper articles reporting that a Citigroup private banker, Carlos Gomez, had recently been convicted of stealing from clients and sent to federal prison.[5] A Citigroup private banker in prison? We decided to pay him a visit.

Our first step was to check the Bureau of Prisons (BOP) website to find him in the federal prisoner locator system. The BOP data named a Miami prison, but when we called, the prison said he wasn't there. Stumped, we tracked down his lawyer who explained his client was incarcerated at an upstate New York prison that was supposed to have sent him on to Florida where he had relatives, but never did. Later on, we had the chilly realization that it was only because we'd inquired into his status that BOP realized he'd been misplaced in the system and ultimately transferred him to Florida.

In the meantime, in February 1999, I joined Bob and Wes Phillips from the Collins staff on a flight to New York where we rented a car for the drive north to Otisville Federal Correctional Institute. The prison was a grim, concrete structure in a cheerless rural area. We were taken to a linoleum-tiled room with cinder block walls, cheap chairs, and a table. When Mr. Gomez walked in, we saw a relatively young man with a quiet demeanor, reserved voice, and an air of determination to survive his new surroundings. We politely explained that we were looking for information about Citibank's private bank. He spoke with us for the next three hours.

Our standard operating procedure before an interview was to write out our questions beforehand, both to map our strategy and ensure we covered all the issues. So we had pages of typed questions ready, all of which the prisoner answered calmly and in detail. He told us how the private bank was organized; estimated the number of private bank employees, accounts, and assets; described individual private bankers, their supervisors, and senior leaders; explained the typical paperwork, reviews, and meetings associated with private bank accounts; discussed the extent to which private bankers knew their clients; explained the available client services; and described the private bank's AML practices. On top of that, he provided specific details about the Salinas account and the role of the key private banker, Amy Elliott, and her supervisors. He indicated, while he hadn't personally handled the Salinas account, since Amy Elliott was his boss, he had observed events associated with the account throughout his employment.

It was a torrent of information. That one interview equipped us with detailed, inside information about both the private bank and Salinas account. It was a lesson in how prisoners, when treated with courtesy and asked wide-ranging questions, can help advance an investigation. When we thanked Mr. Gomez for his help, he murmured that we had gotten him out of kitchen duty, and he'd be willing to speak with us again. But he'd already provided what we needed.

Studying Citigroup

The prison interview, coupled with the Federal Reserve documents, enabled us to draft document requests to Citigroup seeking specific types of information about, not only the Salinas account, but also three other accounts we'd targeted for review. Those accounts had been opened for Omar Bongo, longstanding dictator of Gabon, a small country in West Africa; Asif Ali Zardari, husband of Benazir Bhutto, former Prime Minister of Pakistan; and Mohammed, Ibrahim, and Abba Abacha, sons of General Sani Abacha, the recently deceased ruler of Nigeria.

Citigroup initially responded to our subpoena by offering to turn over documents it had already supplied to several criminal probes, but balked at producing new materials. When it became clear in meetings, however, that we had detailed information about the inner workings of the private bank, the bank grew increasingly nervous about stiffing us. Eventually, Citigroup provided documents from virtually all the categories we'd specified.

The documents arrived in hard copy form, about 2000 pages to a box, ultimately totaling a couple dozen boxes. We stacked them on top of file cabinets and against the wall around the office. Bob and I went through every page. The documents were in no discernable order. We joked that after Citibank had compiled the documents, someone must have thrown them down a stairwell before packing the disordered collection into the boxes sent to us. Multiple copies of the same documents also appeared again and again throughout the boxes. But if that was meant to slow us down, it didn't work. We methodically picked out what we called the "hot docs" and assembled them into an organized set of files.

The next step was to conduct interviews. Over several months, we conducted nearly 100. We spoke with the Citibank private bankers who handled the four accounts serving as our case studies, their supervisors, compliance officers, and auditors, as well as senior officials in the private bank and Citibank as a whole. We also interviewed other private banks that were involved in some of the money transfers as well as other private bankers and private bank clients. On top of that, we interviewed federal bank and securities regulators, law enforcement personnel in Mexico, France, and elsewhere, as well as banking and money laundering experts.

Since it was our first money laundering investigation, we had a lot to learn. We also knew we had to get the facts right, since the stakes involved a global bank, multiple foreign leaders, millions of dollars, and Senator Levin's reputation on PSI. So we checked and doublechecked.

The interviews produced critical information. The key Citigroup private bankers involved with the four case studies, Amy Elliot, Alain Ober, Christopher Rogers, and Mike Matthews, were poised, sophisticated bankers. They answered questions quietly, volunteering nothing. Step by step, we asked them to explain how the accounts were opened, the measures they took to get to know their clients, why they ignored evidence of client involvement with corruption or worse, and why the bank helped their clients form offshore corporations, open accounts that didn't use the clients' names, and move suspect funds. We asked similar questions of their immediate supervisors and even more senior Citigroup officials who determined bank policy.

Three of the most interesting interviews were with the former head of the private bank, Hubertus Rukavina; the man who replaced him, Shaukat Aziz; and Citigroup's chief executive John Reed. In his interview, Mr. Rukavina, a well-dressed Swiss national who spoke in clipped tones, came off as arrogant and secretive. He'd been in charge of the private bank's Swiss headquarters when awarded the lowest rating by Citicorp auditors; he explained it away as due to differing Swiss and U.S. standards. When asked about a telephone call in which he suggested moving Salinas money from London to Switzerland to take advantage of stronger Swiss secrecy laws, he shrugged off the question. Imagination could not have conjured up a better example of a glib private banker speaking softly about handling funds for the wealthy and powerful.

In his interview, Mr. Aziz came off as the opposite—as he was, no doubt, intended to—an upright senior manager, distressed by his bank's missteps and intent on cleaning up the mess. To our relief, internal bank emails and memos indicated it was more than an act; they portrayed a man taking decisive action to close suspect accounts despite staff protests over losing accounts.

The interview with CEO John Reed was our last and the culmination of months of investigatory work. At the time, Mr. Reed was one of the leading bankers in the United States, well respected and influential. Because of the number of people attending his interview—minority and majority staff as well as multiple Citigroup lawyers and banking personnel—we moved to a large utilitarian room near our offices. Well over a dozen people took seats.

As in our prior interviews, we'd written out our questions ahead of time and shared them with the majority staff to make sure everyone's issues were covered. Linda had assigned me to take the lead in the questioning. We followed our standard practice of asking questions all morning, taking a short break before working through lunch, and finishing up around 5:00 or 6:00 p.m. Mr. Reed's manner throughout the day was precise, direct, forthcoming, and polite. He answered all of our questions with virtually no input from his lawyers or other bank personnel. He was well-prepared and had an impressive command of the facts.

By the time we spoke with him, we had a thick book of disturbing Citigroup emails and memos suggesting the private bank knew or should have known it was dealing with suspect funds. To his credit, Mr. Reed didn't dispute the facts or try to wish them away. He acknowledged the problems and said Citigroup needed to clean house. He pointed out that the bank had not broken any laws—even if its private bankers had known that some deposits were the product of foreign corruption, U.S. anti-money laundering laws did not prohibit Citigroup from accepting those funds—but he also said that the bank was wrong to have taken the money.

He noted that although the case studies involved millions of dollars, the funds comprised a tiny percentage of Citigroup's assets and weren't worth tarnishing the bank's reputation. He described plans to beef up the private bank's AML controls. Accounts were being closed, private bankers reprimanded, and new policies installed against accepting suspect foreign funds.

The Reed interview essentially validated our investigative findings. It also signaled that the bank intended to put an end to much of the misconduct we'd uncovered. It was a heady feeling to have brought important facts to the attention of the senior-most decisionmaker in one of the largest banks in the United States, and to have been told the bank would stop acting as a global banker for corrupt foreign officials and their relatives.

At the same time, promises made during a private interview weren't binding in the same way as public testimony in a Senate hearing, and our aims went beyond cleaning up a single bank. We wanted to send a wake-up call to the private banking industry as a whole.

Writing It Up

By the time the interviews concluded, we had the low down on money laundering problems at private banks generally as well as what happened with the four accounts at Citigroup. But the facts were so sprawling and complex that we had to write them up. Otherwise, much of what we'd learned would be lost. Linda asked me to do the first draft, launching what was to become my niche contribution to the Levin PSI squad—writing reports.

The report went through multiple drafts, ending up about 65 pages long. Linda and Bob, and then Senator Levin, went through it line by line, making countless changes. Our Republican colleagues reviewed the revised text and made still more changes. We didn't complain. The high stakes meant we had to get the law and the facts right; no errors allowed.

The final version provided background on U.S. AML laws and the private banking industry, as well as the Federal Reserve's three-year AML review. We were careful to abide by our agreement with the Fed, which allowed us to quote from its examination materials, but not release any of the actual documents. Our report described the factors that made private banks particularly susceptible to money laundering, pointing to powerful clients with private bankers who acted as their inside advocates and operated within a culture of secrecy. The report also went through each of the four case studies, describing the facts and issues raised.

We issued the final version as a Levin staff report. Although we'd worked closely with the Collins staff throughout the investigation, it didn't occur to us to issue a joint report. The final version also lacked an executive summary, findings of fact, and recommendations, all of which became standard elements in later Levin reports. Still, our first PSI report covered a lot of ground, and the details of the four case studies were both compelling and damning.

When all the facts were laid out together, what struck me the most was how Citigroup had actively helped its private bank clients deposit, hide, and move millions of dollars in suspect funds. To me, the facts didn't show a passive financial institution misused by unsuspected wrongdoers; instead, the facts disclosed a cynical Citigroup acting with eyes wide-open and very dirty hands.

Salinas Accounts

The Salinas case was perhaps the most blatant example.[6] Amy Elliott, who headed up Mexican accounts for Citigroup's private bank in New York, was Mr. Salinas' private banker. At his request, Ms. Elliott opened private bank accounts for him at Citigroup's private bank branches in New York, London, and Switzerland—but not Mexico—and accepted funds that eventually approached $100 million.

Only one of the accounts, in New York, actually named Mr. Salinas. The rest did not. Instead, Citigroup's Cayman affiliate, Cititrust, selected a Cayman shell corporation named Trocca Ltd. to serve as his accountholder. Cititrust did not mention Mr. Salinas in Trocca's paperwork, even though the company was controlled by him. Instead, Cititrust used Citicorp-owned shell entities to serve as Trocca's shareholders, directors, and officers. A year later, Cititrust formed a trust, known only as Trust No. PT-5242, to function Trocca's sole shareholder.

At one point, Mr. Salinas apparently expressed concern that he was depositing millions of dollars into Trocca accounts without any written evidence that he owned or controlled the company, and requested a letter from the bank declaring he was Trocca's "beneficial owner." Cititrust supplied the letter. Later, Cititrust formed a second offshore shell company for Mr. Salinas called Birchwood Ltd. In addition, Citicorp opened a Swiss private bank account for him under the code name "Bonaparte," a word used simply to mask his ownership role.

In addition to opening accounts that did not bear his name, Ms. Elliott instituted strict secrecy rules regarding how the Salinas accounts were to operate. She required Citicorp personnel to refer to Mr. Salinas in bank records as

"Confidential Client #2" or "CC-2," and took steps to ensure no one outside of Cititrust and a small circle of senior private bank personnel knew that Mr. Salinas stood behind Trocca.

The private bank didn't stop there. Citigroup concocted a scheme that essentially hid Mr. Salinas' transfer of tens of millions of dollars out of Mexico into his foreign bank accounts, and made it extremely difficult to trace the cash back to him. The scheme worked like this.

Over the course of several months, Mr. Salinas' then fiance and later wife, Paulina Castanon, used cash provided by Mr. Salinas to obtain cashier's checks from several large banks in Mexico. Each cashier's check named a Mexican bank as the payor and Citibank as the recipient; none mentioned Mr. Salinas. Ms. Castanon brought the cashier's checks to Citigroup's flagship bank in Mexico City and gave them to a bank manager to whom she'd been introduced by Ms. Elliott as Patricia Rios, which were Ms. Castanon's middle names. Ms. Elliott made no mention of her full name or her connection to Mr. Salinas.

Following Ms. Elliott's instructions, as each cashier's check came in, the bank manager deposited it into Citigroup's general account—known as a "concentration account" since it concentrated deposits from multiple sources into one place—and wire transferred the funds from Mexico to Citigroup's general account in New York, to the attention of Ms. Elliott. The wire transfer made no mention of Ms. Rios, Mr. Salinas, or any account number. Once the funds arrived and were flagged for her, Ms. Elliott wired the funds to Citigroup's private bank branches in London or Switzerland, for deposit into accounts belonging to Trocca. Bank personnel who deposited the funds into the Trocca accounts—and later the Bonaparte account—were not told who was behind them. This method was used to transfer over $87 million out of Mexico to London and Switzerland, while leaving few clues as to the origin of the funds.

On top of all that, Citigroup made a secret $3 million loan to Mr. Salinas, again through his Trocca accounts.

The scheme went bust in 1995. The first shoe fell in February, when Raul Salinas was arrested in Mexico on suspicion of murdering his brother-in-law, a prominent Mexican politician. The second came in November, when his then wife, Paulina Salinas, was arrested while making a cash withdrawal from Banque Pictet in Switzerland, where she and Mr. Salinas had an $84 million account under a false name.

As word of her arrest leaked out to the news, telephone calls among Citigroup personnel in New York, London, and Switzerland discussed how the bank should react. Because London requires its banks to record their bankers' telephone conversations, we were able to acquire transcripts of those calls. In them, the bankers disclosed that the Salinas account in New York held about $200,000; the Trocca account in Switzerland held about $22 million; and the Trocca account in London held about $78 million. The bank loan of $3 million was also outstanding.

In one recorded conversation, the private bank head, Hubertus Rukavina, asked whether they should immediately move the $78 million out of London to Switzerland which had stronger secrecy laws. The head of Citigroup's Swiss affiliate Confidas nixed the idea in a later call, since the wire transfer and London bank records would leave paper trails. So the funds were left in the London account. But the bank still tried to conceal them. In November 1995, when Citigroup filed a report with U.S. law enforcement on the Salinas matter, it disclosed the Salinas account in New York, but not the Trocca accounts in London or Switzerland.

As the facts unfolded, it became impossible to view Citigroup private bank as an innocent bystander misused by Mr. Salinas. Instead, they showed Citigroup contributing to the wrong-doing by actively helping Mr. Salinas spirit nearly $100 million out of Mexico and hide the funds abroad. After his arrest, Citigroup continued to conceal his funds, rather than disclose them to law enforcement. U.S. and Swiss authorities later discovered and froze the Trocca accounts.[7]

Bongo Accounts

The facts were equally damaging with respect to a second set of Citigroup private banking accounts involving Omar Bongo, longtime dictator of Gabon, an African country notorious for rampant corruption.[8]

The account came to our attention through the Federal Reserve audits of Citigroup. The Fed examiners had selected accounts for a closer review, including one opened in the name of a Bahamas corporation called Tendin Investments Ltd. It turned out Tendin had been formed by Cititrust and assigned to President Bongo in 1985.

Tendin was part of a much larger Citigroup relationship with President Bongo. Begun in 1970, it had become a complex network of consumer and private banking accounts at Citigroup branches in Bahrain, Gabon, Jersey, London, Luxembourg, New York, Paris, and Switzerland. Most of the New York accounts carried the Tendin name; some in Paris bore the name of a second Bongo-related shell company called Leontine Ltd. In addition, in 1995, the Citigroup private bank in New York opened an account for him under the name "OS"—perhaps standing for "offshore"—which was simply the title of the account and not a legal entity. From 1985 to 1999, the funds moving through the Bongo private banking accounts exceeded $130 million.

In addition to providing President Bongo with shell corporations, secret accounts, and wire transfers to transport his funds across international lines, Citigroup private bank invested his funds and significantly increased his holdings. It also supplied him with millions of dollars in loans, some of which may have helped finance his re-election campaigns.

Citigroup issued the loans from 1989 to 1996, under a complex arrangement that used his offshore deposits as collateral to secure the lending, but also structured the loans in a way that hid their offshore connection. Essentially, Citigroup loaned the money by allowing President Bongo's personal accounts at Citibank Gabon to incur multi-million-dollar overdrafts, which were immediately covered by transfers from Bongo-related accounts in Paris, which were, in turn, covered by transfers from offshore accounts belonging to Tendin. This three-step process avoided direct transfers from the Tendin offshore accounts into the president's Gabon accounts, minimizing the chance that Gabon bank personnel would learn of his offshore corporation. The private bank loans peaked in 1994 at about $50 million.

The Citigroup private banker responsible for the Bongo accounts was Alain Ober, the only private banker in New York specializing in clients from Africa. He managed about 100 clients of which the Bongo relationship was the largest. Mr. Ober told PSI that he reviewed the account at least once per year with the Western Hemisphere Division head in New York, Edward Montero, but Mr. Montero said he was unfamiliar with the account. Another Citigroup private banker handling the Bongo account was Christopher Rogers, who was then located in Paris and also specialized in handling clients from Africa.

One of the wildest fact patterns associated with the Bongo accounts arose in 1996, when during one of the private bank audits, the Federal Reserve asked Citigroup to explain the source of the funds in the Tendin accounts. Internal bank documents showed the private bankers scrambling to come up with an explanation. The Bongo bank profile at the time simply stated: "Head of State for over 25 Years—Source of Wealth/business Background: Self-made as a result of position. Country is oil producer." Referring to President Bongo as "self-made" meant family money couldn't explain his wealth. The money at Citigroup appeared after he took office.

The New York private banker, Mr. Ober, sent an email to his Paris colleague, Mr. Rogers, asking for help:

[T]he Federal Examiners are auditing the Tendin Account. …You may remember that this account was opened in 1985 at [the private bank in New York] with $52MM coming from a time deposit at Citibank Bahrain …. Bill indicated that the $52MM were accumulated over several years at the Branch at the time you were there. Neither Bill nor myself ever asked our client where this money came from. My guess, as well as Bill's is that … the French Government/French oil companies (ELF) made 'donations' to him (very much like we give to PACS in the US!). … [D]o you remember specifically where [the monies] came from …?

Mr. Rogers responded: "Gabon resembles a Gulf Emirate in that Oil … accounts for 95 pct of revenues for a population of less than 1 million. It is clear therefore that Tendin Investments draws most of its wealth from oil, but we have no way of being more specific." The bankers concluded that the Bongo funds were definitely oil-related and speculated they came from "donations"—whatever that meant—from the French government or French oil companies.

Those vague explanations weren't enough to satisfy the Fed which asked the bank's primary regulator—the Office of the Comptroller of the Currency or OCC—to take over the inquiry. An OCC bank examiner then began to press the private bank to document the origins of the tens of millions of dollars in the Bongo accounts.

In 1997, Citigroup's private bank manufactured an explanation. After Mr. Rogers met with a "senior Gabonese civil servant" and sent an email to his colleagues about the meeting, Mr. Ober prepared a one-page memorandum to the file and gave a copy to the OCC with the bank's explanation of the source of funds in the Bongo accounts. The memo stated that certain funds from the 1995 Gabon budget were made available "to be used at the discretion of our client," listing four Gabon budget categories "representing 8.5% of the Budget" or $111 million. The memo said "[w]e can assume the same level of allocations exist" in the 1996 and 1997 budgets. In other words, Citigroup told the OCC that about $111 million per year in Gabon government funds were being given to President Bongo to be spent at his discretion, and that his discretion extended so far as to allow him to deposit the funds into his personal offshore accounts.

It was an audacious explanation. But it was apparently good enough for the OCC examiner who considered the matter closed, since the explanation accounted for the millions in the Bongo accounts. At the time, identifying government funds as the source of the Bongo funds had apparently failed to raise red flags related to corruption, embezzlement, or other illicit conduct. As the OCC examiner later explained to us, he thought President Bongo had carte blanche authority over Gabon's revenues. Essentially, he viewed the president as a type of king with absolute authority over the country's wealth as opposed to an elected official bound by law. He also admitted, as did Mr. Ober, that no attempt was made by the OCC or Citigroup to verify the information provided about the Gabon budget.

We did attempt to verify it. We spoke with Gabon budget experts at the International Monetary Fund (IMF) and reviewed information from Gabon budget experts at the World Bank supplied to the Library of Congress at our request. The budget experts were unanimous in rejecting the assertion that the 1995, 1996, or 1997 Gabon budgets allocated $111 million or a similar annual amount to President Bongo. They said no recent Gabon budget had authorized the president to make personal use of government funds. In addition, they pointed out that the monies in the four specified Gabon budget categories had paid for actual expenses. They said any assertion that a Gabon budget created a $111 million set-aside for the president was inaccurate, implausible, and plainly contrary to Gabon's budget policy and actual spending.

The IMF also noted that, in 1997 and 1998, the Gabon government had engaged in over $62 million of "extrabudgetary expenditures" not specified in its enacted budgets. The IMF informed us that, as a result, it had stopped authorizing loan disbursements to Gabon while an independent accounting of those expenditures took place, and that no further loans were being disbursed to the country until the budget questions were resolved.

The IMF and World Bank information flatly contradicted the Citigroup memorandum. Yet it also appeared to be true that a senior Gabon official had told a Citigroup official that government money was a major source of the Bongo funds. Not only that, but Citigroup later disclosed a wire transfer showing a 1996 Tendin deposit of $1.9 million transferred directly from the Gabon treasury. The private bank had accepted those funds apparently without any bank official questioning the transfer. In light of that wire transfer, the Gabon official, and the earlier Ober email referring to payoffs by the French government, identifying government money as a primary source of the Bongo funds was, indeed, plausible. President Bongo was, in fact, a self-made man in a country rife with oil corruption.

In addition, an ongoing criminal probe by a French magistrate, Eva Joly, was then investigating allegations that a French oil company, Elf Aquitaine, and its subsidiary Elf Gabon, had paid bribes to Gabon officials. In 1997, the leading French newspaper, *Le Monde*, carried multiple articles about President Bongo's possible role in the scandal, including one headlined, "Omar Bongo Could be Implicated in the Elf Affair." In one court proceeding in Switzerland in which prosecutors sought to seize millions of dollars in two Swiss bank accounts allegedly used to pay bribes, allegations linked the accounts to President Bongo whom a Swiss prosecutor described in open court as "the head of an association of criminals."

Citigroup documents showed the private bank was fully aware of the corruption allegations. Documents associated with the private bank's annual review of its public figure accounts included this notation for President Bongo: "Newspaper reports 4/1997 claim he [President Bongo] accepted bribes from ELF-Aquitaine."

The bribery allegations and French investigation did not, however, cause Citigroup to close the Bongo accounts. Nor did it close them after the Federal Reserve and OCC inquiries, despite its scramble to explain where the money came from. Worse yet, no U.S. bank regulator called for closing the accounts. Perhaps that was because, at the time, it wasn't against the law for U.S. banks to knowingly accept corruption proceeds as bank deposits, so long as the corrupt acts took place outside U.S. borders. But illegal or not, the Bongo facts still stunk.

Zardari and Abacha Accounts

Our investigation uncovered similarly unsettling facts related to two other Citigroup private bank accounts we targeted for review.

One set of accounts was opened in 1994 at Citigroup's private bank headquarters in Switzerland in the name of three offshore shell corporations controlled by Asif Ali Zardari, husband of the former Prime Minister of Pakistan, Benazir Bhutto.[9] Mr. Zardari had an unsavory reputation. Among other incidents, he had been incarcerated in Pakistan in 1990 and 1991 on corruption charges that were eventually dropped. Citigroup CEO John Reed told PSI he'd been personally warned about Mr. Zardari, and was surprised their Swiss private bank had accepted him as a client, saying the private banker who opened the account must have been "an idiot."

Another surprise came when Mr. Zardari's wife, Benazir Bhutto, showed up at PSI offices one day in 2006, unannounced and on her own, to defend her husband. She simply walked through the door and asked to speak to the staff director. Linda, with me in tow, invited Ms. Bhutto into her office where Ms. Bhutto casually sat down on a leather sofa and listened to what we had to say. After we showed her documents indicating that her husband was the beneficial owner of the Swiss accounts which included $10 million in deposits associated with kickbacks, she promised to send us materials establishing otherwise. But she never did.

Bank documents showed that, altogether, more than $40 million had flowed through the three Zardari accounts in Switzerland, with no information on the source of the funds. After Mr. Zardari was arrested in Pakistan in November 1996, Citigroup closed all three accounts. In 1998, both Mr. Zardari and Ms. Bhutto were indicted in Switzerland on charges of money laundering and in Pakistan on charges of corruption. In 1999, both were convicted in Pakistan of taking bribes, but Mr. Zardari and Ms. Bhutto denounced the convictions as politically motivated. In internal bank documents, Mr. Reed described Citigroup's association with Mr. Zardari as "a mistake" and "[m]ore reason than ever to rework our Private Bank."

The fourth and final set of accounts we examined was opened by the sons of General Sani Abacha, the military dictator who ruled Nigeria from 1993 until his sudden death in 1998, allegedly from a heart attack suffered while with two prostitutes, although some claim the prostitutes poisoned him.[10] Throughout his tenure, General Abacha was widely condemned for running one of the most corrupt and brutal regimes in Africa. Shortly after his death, his wife was stopped at a Nigerian airport with 38 suitcases stuffed with foreign currency, while a son was caught transporting $100 million in cash. The Nigerian government reportedly recovered about $750 million from Abacha family members through those and other seizures, a staggering amount nevertheless rumored to be a fraction of the $5 billion allegedly stolen from the country.

General Abacha's sons, Mohammed and Ibrahim, and later Abba, opened Citigroup private bank accounts in London in 1988, and in New York in 1992, all prior to their father's ascension to the presidency. Bank documents show, over ten years, the accounts saw deposits totaling more than $110 million, with large sums occasionally running through the accounts. In addition to allowing those fleeting deposits, the private bank performed its usual services for the sons, creating an offshore shell corporation for them, Morgan Procurement, as well as opening special name accounts, Chinquinto, Gelsobella, and Navarrio, that concealed the sons' account ownership. The key Citigroup private bankers, Michael Mathews in London and Alain Ober in New York, asked no questions when odd millions suddenly hurtled through the accounts.

When General Abacha unexpectedly died in June 1998, the Nigerian government began searching for stolen government funds in Abacha accounts. In September 1998, the Abacha sons made an urgent request to Citigroup to transfer $39 million from their private bank account in London to another bank. At the time, the funds were invested in a time deposit that, under normal circumstances, would impose a hefty financial penalty if cashed early. But Citigroup raced to the rescue, allowing the sons to take a $39 million overdraft on their London account so they could move the funds immediately, without financial penalty. When the time deposit matured a few weeks later, the bank repaid the overdraft. It was a nifty example of Citibank's customer service. A few months later, a London court froze the Abacha accounts in a civil suit.

The Abacha and Zardari accounts showed once again that Citigroup private bank was acting not as a passive victim of wrongdoing but as an active participant in depositing, concealing, and shifting suspect funds for shady clients.

Equally sobering was the reality that the four case studies represented only a fraction of Citigroup's private bank accounts, which included hundreds opened for foreign officials and their relatives. Bob suggested a new investigative theory which he called "the unitary theory of evil"—it postulated that, if you looked hard enough during those years, you might find Citibank as the financier behind many of the big-time corrupt dictators around the globe.

Going Public

Senator Levin decided it was time to go public with our findings. At his request, in November 1999, Senator Collins held two days of hearings on the private banking investigation and released the Levin report. The first day featured five Citigroup representatives: two of the private bankers who handled the suspect accounts, their immediate superiors, and Citigroup CEO John Reed. It closed with GAO describing how Citigroup had facilitated the transfer of the Salinas millions out of Mexico while obscuring the audit trail. The second day featured U.S. bank regulators, money laundering experts, and a private banker convicted of laundering drug proceeds.

Senators Collins and Levin knew the facts cold and were ready to disclose them to the public. A powerful tag team, they delivered a one-two punch that prevented the witnesses from dodging the issues.

Perhaps most riveting was the Collins-Levin questioning of Amy Elliott, the Citigroup private banker who'd handled the Salinas account. Ms. Elliot calmly rationalized both opening the Salinas account and helping secretly wire tens of millions of dollars out of Mexico. She claimed she'd reasonably assumed his funds were legitimate since Mr. Salinas came from a wealthy family, and claimed she took reasonable measures to protect his privacy. At times, Ms. Elliott testified as if she were a victim rather than a perpetrator of wrongdoing. But the senators didn't let her get away with it, forcing Ms. Elliott to admit the shortcuts she took, the questions she didn't ask, and the irregular and deceptive system she'd set up to move the Salinas millions offshore, complete with false names, shell companies, and unattributed wire transfers.

The November hearings marked the high point of our first PSI investigation. We'd taken nearly a year to gather documents, conduct interviews, and write up the results. While the Levin side had borne the brunt of the investigative work, we'd involved the Collins staff every step of the way and worked with them to reach consensus on the facts. Our combined efforts paid off with hearings that were rich in detail, featured witnesses directly involved in the wrongdoing, and bank regulators who were forced to take public note of the sordid goings on at a major U.S. bank. The media coverage was extensive, as reporters described the outrageous facts and quoted the many damning documents. The bipartisan nature of the inquiry also attracted notice.

Most of all, the investigation documented with undisputed facts how private banks were servicing corrupt foreign leaders and their relatives with multi-million-dollar secret accounts. It disclosed the pressures on U.S. private bankers to look the other way so they didn't lose those accounts. It showed how U.S. banks could, and in some cases did, facilitate corruption and other misconduct. It also exposed glaring weaknesses in U.S. AML laws and bank regulation.

Tackling the Problem

One ironclad Levin rule was that no investigation was complete until an attempt was made to fix the problems uncovered, so our final step in the investigation was an all-out effort to clamp down on the money laundering problems in private banking.

First, we exercised oversight of the house-cleaning already underway at Citigroup. We held meetings every few months for more than a year to get updates on the private bank's actions, which included closing the accounts we'd investigated as well as many other public figure accounts. To our amazement, Mr. Reed also produced a video of the Citigroup bankers getting grilled at the Senate hearing and apparently required all Citigroup private bankers to watch it, warning them not to put themselves or the bank in that position again. Second was overseeing ongoing efforts by the Federal Reserve and OCC to crackdown on AML deficiencies at other private banks. We held periodic meetings to track those efforts as well.

Third, Senator Levin directed us to draft legislation to strengthen U.S. AML laws. After consulting with prosecutors and other experts, we got a bill ready. On November 10, 1999, Senator Levin introduced the Money Laundering Abatement Act with Senator Arlen Specter, a Republican from Pennsylvania.[11] The bipartisan bill was referred to the Senate Banking Committee, then chaired by Senator Phil Gramm, a Republican from Texas. Unfortunately, since Texas banks were recipients of huge amounts of suspect money from

Mexico and elsewhere, the Texas Bankers Association wasn't interested in requiring Texas banks to ask where that money came from. Senator Gramm responded to our bill with a deafening silence.

Deciphering Correspondent Banking

Despite the legislative deep freeze, the 1999 investigation was otherwise so successful that Senator Levin decided to launch a second money laundering investigation. After reading news reports about a scandal in which Russian banks moved more than $7 billion in suspect funds through correspondent accounts at the Bank of New York, he directed PSI to focus on money laundering through U.S. correspondent banks. Linda again assigned the investigation to Bob and me. It ended up taking even longer than the private banking inquiry—more than a year to complete. It also took us to a whole new level of understanding of the offshore banking world and the gimmicks bad guys used to move ill-gotten gains through U.S. banks.

Correspondent banking sounds complicated, but the concept is simple—it refers to banking services provided by one bank to another bank. Any account opened for a bank is called a correspondent account. The bank supplying the account is called the correspondent bank; the bank using the account is called the respondent. As we began to dig into the facts, we learned that correspondent accounts were a fundamental building block of the international banking system, enabling banks and their clients to conduct business worldwide.[12]

A bank typically opens an account at another bank so that it can conduct business for its customers in a jurisdiction where the bank has no physical presence. Suppose, for example, that a foreign bank wanted to provide its clients with banking services in the United States, but didn't want to spend money opening its own U.S. branch. The foreign bank could, instead, simply open an account at a U.S. bank and use that bank's services for its own clients.

We spent the next year learning the ins and outs of how foreign banks actually used their U.S. accounts. We focused, in particular, on little known, high-risk banks. What we found was that U.S. banks hardly thought twice before opening an account for another bank, even if it was an offshore bank with no physical presence anywhere, operated in a secrecy jurisdiction known for sleaze, and used its U.S. account to engage in dubious transactions. The U.S. banks' general attitude was that a bank was a bank, and all licensed banks—even high-risk offshore banks—were legitimate customers. That see-no-evil attitude came to an abrupt end after Senator Levin publicized the results of the PSI correspondent banking investigation.

Getting Started

Figuring out how to investigate correspondent banking required some creativity. We decided to take a two-pronged approach—survey U.S. banks to get information about their correspondent clients, and pick out some high-risk offshore banks to explore abusive accounts.

To conduct the survey, we sent questionnaires to 20 banks of various sizes, including 10 U.S. banks and 10 foreign banks operating in the United States. With some prodding, all 20 responded. The survey results showed great variance among the banks. The U.S. bank with the most correspondent accounts had about 3800, while the foreign bank with the most had 12,000. The U.S. bank with the most correspondent accounts processed nearly 1 million wire transfers per day involving over $1 trillion, while the bank with the fewest accounts processed wire transfers totaling about $114 million per day. We also learned that, in mid-1999, the top five U.S. bank holding companies held correspondent account balances exceeding $17 billion. The bottom line: correspondent banking was big business at some banks.

The survey also disclosed the types of services being provided by U.S. correspondent banks. They typically included savings and checking accounts, wire transfers, foreign exchange, check clearing and settlement services, trade-related services, and investments. Some correspondent banks also provided loans or lines of credit. In addition, the survey disclosed that half of the surveyed banks were perfectly willing to open an account for an offshore bank, while a third would do the same for an offshore shell bank with no physical presence in any country. Those numbers indicated that high-risk foreign banks had a lot of U.S. choices.

While the survey provided a useful overview of U.S. correspondent banks, developing case studies of offshore banks abusing their U.S. correspondent accounts was more tricky. Since offshore banks thrive on secrecy and operated beyond our subpoena authority, investigating them stumped us at first. Then Bob had the brilliant idea of asking the Justice Department to provide us with closed cases in which offshore banks handled criminal proceeds in their U.S. accounts. That way we could focus on offshore banks already determined by Justice to be bad news.

While Justice was infamous among congressional investigators for refusing to provide information on open cases, it was happy to cooperate on closed cases. Justice quickly sent us a couple dozen recent, successful criminal prosecutions in which drug money, fraud proceeds, or other illicit funds were run through an offshore bank's U.S. accounts. It was an embarrassment of riches, allowing us to choose among a vivid array of fact patterns.

As we dug into the details, we learned that some of the cases involved shell banks with no physical presence anywhere. Others involved small banks with a single physical office. Most held a so-called "offshore" or "B" license that prohibited the bank from doing business inside the country where it was licensed, and restricted it to doing business outside the country's borders. In other words, after protecting its own citizens, the licensing jurisdictions had unleashed the bank on the rest of the world. Virtually all of the banks seemed to have few employees of their own and to function primarily through the correspondent accounts they'd opened at U.S. banks.

We learned, for example, that the U.S. banks provided monthly statements that enabled the offshore banks to easily track their clients' deposits and withdrawals. The U.S. banks also typically placed the offshore banks' deposits in overnight or timed investments that generated decent returns, while simultaneously giving the offshore banks access to a supply of U.S. dollars which many might otherwise be unable to get. In addition, the U.S. banks gave the offshore banks ready access to U.S. wire transfer systems to send or receive funds globally.

We found that U.S. banks servicing high-risk offshore banks often failed to effectively screen them or monitor their account activity. Instead, the U.S. banks typically gave the offshore banks unfettered use of their U.S. accounts. The U.S. banks told PSI that they'd assumed a licensed bank would act lawfully. It was a lousy assumption.

Getting Documents and Conducting Interviews

Once we identified interesting offshore banks involved in criminal wrongdoing, our next step was to identify their U.S. correspondents, which varied from major U.S. banks to small U.S. branch offices of foreign banks. In some cases, we got the correspondent banks' names from court records, but we soon found an easier way—using the Bankers Almanac. The Almanac was an online service offering basic information about almost every bank in the world, including the bank's address, size, and officers. It also usually named the banks' correspondents, which most banks publicized so other banks could figure out how to wire them money.

Once we identified an offshore bank's U.S. correspondents, we sent each U.S. bank a subpoena asking for documents related to the key U.S. accounts. Because U.S. banks routinely get subpoenas for bank records—from law enforcement, creditors, and civil litigants—they readily responded.

We discovered that the U.S. banks often had mother-loads of useful information about their offshore bank clients. The material included account

opening documents in which the offshore bank disclosed its owners and officers; monthly statements listing transactions; wire transfer records; and sometimes U.S. bank memos analyzing specific issues. If the offshore bank requested
a line of credit, the U.S. bank typically also had a credit analysis detailing the
offshore bank's assets, business activities, and reputation.

Our subpoenas elicited a deluge of documents, which led to marathon
review sessions. Every set of correspondent bank records contained dozens of
leads to other banks as well as data on the offshore bank's ownership, personnel, operations, and transactions. To manage the inquiry, Bob and I divided
up the offshore banks between us and formed overlapping teams of detailees,
law clerks, interns, and fellows to help us sort through the documents for each
bank. After several months of analysis, we'd identified over a dozen offshore
banks with eye-popping misconduct and suspect transactions. We were ready
for interviews.

We did most of the interviews in the United States. One set of interviews
focused on the U.S. banks, asking how the U.S. bank handled its correspondent accounts generally as well as the specific offshore banks we'd targeted. A
second set of interviews questioned individuals who'd used the targeted offshore banks to commit crimes, been prosecuted by the Justice Department,
and were willing to talk. A third set involved the offshore banks themselves,
and a fourth set targeted key bank regulators, both here and abroad.

Hanover Bank

One remarkable early interview involved William H. Koop, a portly New
Jersey man in his 60s who had retired from a career of selling swimming pools
and started a second career selling fraudulent financial investments to elderly
investors across the country. Because he'd already pled guilty to fraud and
agreed to cooperate as part of his plea, he submitted to a day-long interview
with us explaining how he had made use of Hanover Bank, an offshore shell
bank licensed in Antigua-Barbuda.

The interview took place in New Jersey where the federal prosecutor who
handled the fraud case instructed Mr. Koop to be helpful. What his story
boiled down to was, after promising high investment returns to various groups
of elderly investors, he'd convinced hundreds of them to wire money to Harris
Bank International in New York. At Mr. Koop's instruction, Harris Bank
credited the funds to a correspondent account for Standard Bank Jersey, a
bank located on an island off the U.K. coast. That bank, in turn, credited the
funds to a correspondent account for Hanover Bank in Antigua. Mr. Koop

told us, and the wire transfer records confirmed, that the defrauded investors wired a total of almost $5 million to Hanover Bank. Mr. Koop claimed that he never saw the money again.

To find out what happened to the money, Mr. Koop suggested we talk to his Hanover Bank contact, Terrence S. Wingrove. Mr. Wingrove was a British citizen who was then incarcerated at Wormwood Scrubs Prison in London fighting extradition to the United States on money laundering charges associated with the Koop fraud.

Bob and I got permission to interview Mr. Wingrove in prison. Although "The Scrubs" had a dire reputation, it didn't live up to the grim reality of U.S. prisons. Located in the outskirts of London, it was reachable by subway. The prison's façade included stone portraits of Queen Victoria and Prince Albert. The 100-year-old doorways were so short we had to stoop to get through them, and the walls were robin egg blue. A slow-moving, overweight guard led us to an interview room, huge keys from a Dickens novel hanging from a key chain under his gut.

Mr. Wingrove was a wiry elderly man who could have played Fagin in Oliver Twist. We were apparently his first visitors in months. We asked one question, and he was off to the races, telling us in a thick Cockney accent about Hanover Bank. He said he had no ownership interest in the bank, but did have an account where he'd deposited the $5 million. He confirmed that the funds had come from multiple wire transfers sent by third parties across the United States with whom he had no direct contact, but understood were investors working with Mr. Koop.

He also confirmed that the wire transfers had moved through a chain of correspondent accounts, from Harris Bank International through Standard Bank Jersey to Hanover Bank, which then credited the funds to his account. He said he used the same correspondent bank chain to wire the funds out of Hanover Bank to other accounts he controlled around the world and invest in artwork and antiques, as he'd arranged with Mr. Koop. He claimed he was an international art dealer and strenuously denied being part of the Koop fraud or laundering ill-gotten gains.

We took our leave hours later. As we left, we heard a prison guard call out in a high squeaky voice, "Mr. Wingrove, you missed your tea. Would you like your tea?" I shook my head thinking of the federal prison he was battling to avoid.

Back at PSI offices, we telephoned Tony Fitzpatrick, whom Mr. Wingrove and Antiguan bank records named as Hanover Bank's owner. We asked if we could interview him in Ireland by phone, and to our surprise he agreed. We speculated that he realized his bank depended on its U.S. correspondent account to operate, so he had to do whatever he could to preserve access to that account. We set up a time and conducted an interview that lasted several hours.

Speaking in a melodious Irish accent, Mr. Fitzpatrick told us he'd run Hanover Bank from its inception, even though his name did not appear on the bank's licensing application or incorporation papers and only surfaced a year after the bank began operation. He explained that he'd used a British banker and Antiguan resident as the bank's initial nominal owners, to make it easier to obtain a license. He said he'd provided all of the financial backing from the start.

Mr. Fitzpatrick confirmed that Hanover Bank had no physical presence anywhere and no employee other than himself. He explained that he kept the bank's records at his residence in Ireland, and could operate it from there or anywhere else he traveled. He joked that he was "no banker," admitted the bank did not follow standard banking procedures, and confirmed it had never been examined by a regulator. He said the bank kept 100% of its funds in its correspondent account and conducted all incoming and outgoing wire transfers through that account.

Mr. Fitzpatrick explained that, over the years, Hanover had opened accounts for only a handful of clients so that when he received, for example, multiple wire transfers from unknown parties across the United States, he knew they were to be deposited into the Wingrove account. He confirmed that, at Mr. Wingrove's direction, Hanover Bank had then arranged for the transfer of those funds to other accounts around the world. Mr. Fitzpatrick also admitted what our research had already uncovered, that the few clients holding Hanover Bank accounts had all run into trouble with the law. He told us he'd been trying to sell the bank for several years.

When we later contacted Harris Bank International in New York, it claimed it had no idea Hanover Bank was using its services, since its client, Standard Bank Jersey, had never mentioned the offshore shell bank. When we contacted Standard Bank Jersey, a subsidiary of the larger Standard Bank of South Africa, the bank declined to speak with us.

British Trade and Commerce Bank

A second memorable interview came when Bob, Claire from the Collins staff, and I flew to Dominica, a small Caribbean island nation, to interview British Trade and Commerce Bank (BTCB) about its U.S. correspondent accounts. Since BTCB was suspected of handling millions of dollars in illicit funds, while also ripping off local residents, the U.S. State Department had advised us not to stay overnight on the island. Accordingly, we flew in early in the morning to Dominica's only airport, which was a good two-hour drive from the capital city, Roseau. We took an airport van to the capital, passing through acres of tropical rainforest which, I mused, could easily hide all of our bodies without a trace.

BTCB was located in a small, unattractive concrete building in a Roseau business district with little commercial activity. I remember a scrawny dog slouching down the middle of one street. At the bank, we were taken to a basement conference room with a faint dank smell. The bank president showed up a few minutes later in tennis whites and aviator sunglasses as if he were on his way to a tennis match. It was a bizarre getup.

When he took off his sunglasses, he looked so sickly that we asked if he was okay. He smiled weakly and said he was suffering from a bout of dengue fever, but was ready to answer our questions. In response to our looks of concern, he said not to worry, dengue fever wasn't contagious; it came from mosquito bites. For the next two hours, as we conducted the interview, we were repeatedly bitten by mosquitos, including steel-jawed critters that got me right through my stockings. Luckily, no one got sick.

The documents we'd reviewed indicated that, when it opened its doors in 1997, BTCB was a tiny bank in a secrecy jurisdiction known for weak AML controls. Nevertheless, within three years, BTCB had opened accounts at several U.S. banks and moved more than $85 million through them, including millions of dollars associated with money laundering, financial frauds, illegal Internet gambling, and possibly drug trafficking. BTCB's president worked hard to explain away all of the problems, but none of it was convincing. It was mind-blowing to think of all the millions of suspect dollars that had sped through the accounts of that small, smelly bank.

We flew out of Dominica the same day we arrived. Our outbound trip lingers in my memory, not as the conclusion of a visit to a tropical paradise, but as an escape from an island buzzing with mosquitos and bank corruption.

419 Scams

Back in the United States, we spoke with a number of bank regulators and prosecutors. One prosecutor opened our eyes to how some foreign criminals were deliberately using U.S. correspondent accounts to rip off average Americans. His favorite example involved Nigerian "419" scams, so-called because they violated section 419 of Nigeria's legal code. In a typical scenario, the prosecutor explained, a Nigerian fraudster used emails or phone calls to convince an American victim to wire cash to a local U.S. bank, for credit to the account of a Nigerian bank, for further credit to the fraudster's account. The fraudster then disappeared.

When victims tried to retrieve their funds from the local bank, they ran into a legal brick wall. The prosecutor explained that fraudulent funds deposited into a regular U.S. bank account could be frozen and seized. But funds deposited in a Nigerian bank's U.S. correspondent account were deemed to belong to the Nigerian bank, and could not be frozen without evidence that the Nigerian bank itself was part of the scam. Given that daunting legal hurdle, most U.S. victims couldn't recover their funds, even though they sat in a U.S. bank. He urged us to change the law to allow funds in correspondent accounts to be frozen the same way as funds in other accounts.

Writing It Up

By the end of our interviews, we had detailed information about how offshore banks were misusing U.S. bank accounts to facilitate the deposit and transfer of illicit funds. As far as we knew, no one else had ever collected the same information in the same depth about the offshore banking world, and we were excited to convey what we had learned.

Linda directed us to write up ten case studies. We were taken aback, because writing up that many case studies was no small task. In our prior investigation, our report had examined four accounts at a single bank, Citigroup. The new task was to write up ten offshore banks, each of which had accounts at one or more U.S. correspondent banks. That meant we would be taking on, not one financial institution, but dozens. Moreover, each case study required describing a set of complex facts amid offshore secrecy laws that made double-checking the facts very difficult. We also expected blowback from offshore government and bank officials, not to mention U.S. bank regulators, who would be embarrassed by our findings. As a result, the pressure to get the facts right was even more intense than in our first inquiry.

We pressed ahead. Each case study was written up by a different PSI team, depending upon who knew the most about the relevant offshore bank. To standardize the sections, Linda set up a template for us to follow, which required descriptions of the offshore bank at issue, its correspondent accounts, AML controls, regulators, and misuse of its U.S. correspondent accounts. The template required detailed information about the bank's formation, ownership, and services, as well as how it obtained its correspondent accounts and what due diligence review had been performed by the U.S. banks. Given the variability of the correspondent bank records and our inability to subpoena the offshore banks directly, getting all the specified information about each bank was back-breaking work.

Another problem was that we all worked at different speeds with different writing styles. In the future, as the fastest writer on the crew, I typically cranked out the first draft, while Bob, our best editor, caught errors and strengthened the analysis. But that writing partnership had yet to form. Back then, we were still learning how to mesh our efforts with uneven results.

The final report was over 400 pages, six times longer than the private banking report. It was jam-packed with details. To make it readable, we added an executive summary, factual findings and recommendations, and a chart summarizing the ten case studies.

The report disclosed that virtually every U.S. bank examined, from Chase Manhattan to Bank of America, First Union, and Citigroup, had opened correspondent accounts for high-risk offshore banks with minimal screening and monitoring. The case studies detailed how the offshore banks had misused their U.S. accounts to move billions of suspect dollars, including funds associated with drug trafficking, financial fraud, or illegal gambling. In some cases, the offshore bank itself seemed to have engaged in criminal conduct; in others, the offshore bank seemed not to care whether its clients had done so. All of the offshore banks had limited staff and resources, and relied instead on their U.S. correspondents to take deposits, record transactions, change currencies, and move funds. Their U.S. accounts had provided an open gateway into the U.S. financial system for criminals and money launderers.

The case studies included four shell banks formed in Antigua, the Bahamas, or Cayman Islands. As far as we knew, shell banks had never before been profiled with the level of detail we were able to provide, exposing in particular how they used their U.S. accounts to transfer illicit proceeds. We showed how the absence of a physical office and local employees meant regulators had no place to go to inspect a shell bank's records, observe bank operations, or seize suspect funds. Shell banks instead benefited from a shifting, shadowy existence, often operating from the offices of a related company, residence, or undisclosed location. The report attempted to show why it was time to shut the door on U.S. correspondent accounts for those high-risk banks.

Senator Levin released the report in February 2001. As with our first report, although the investigation had been conducted in close cooperation with our Republican colleagues, we issued it solely as a minority staff report. Its release generated a stack of media stories that paved the way for related hearings at the beginning of March.

Conducting the Hearings

In March 2001, Senator Collins chaired three days of hearings on the Levin-led inquiry into correspondent banking and money laundering. After multiple preparatory sessions, Senators Collins and Levin had become experts on the intricacies of correspondent banking and delivered the same one-two punch as in the private banking hearings.

The first day focused on how offshore banks and correspondent accounts worked. The opening witness was a U.S. citizen and former offshore bank owner, John Mathewson, who'd pled guilty to U.S. charges of conspiracy to commit money laundering and tax evasion. To avoid prison, he'd turned over the entirety of his offshore bank's records, a first for U.S. law enforcement. He'd then spent several years testifying against his former clients.

Mr. Mathewson characterized his offshore bank, Guardian Bank and Trust, as a "run-of-the-mill" operation in the Cayman Islands. He described how the bank had charged most clients $8000 to set up a shell corporation and open an account in the name of that corporation, noting that no one would pay $8000 for an account they could open for free in the United States, unless they were paying for secrecy. He said his bank also charged a $100 fee for wire transfers that cost $10 in the United States, an amount made possible only by clients willing to pay for secret funding transfers. He also flashed a credit card bearing the name of an offshore company. He explained that, for another fee, he provided his clients with credit cards in the name of their shell companies and advised them to sign their names illegibly on the back. His clients then used those credit cards to access their offshore funds while in the United States.

Mr. Mathewson testified that 95% of his 2000 bank clients were U.S. citizens, and he guessed 100% were engaged in tax evasion. He stated that the Achilles' heel of his bank and the offshore banking community as a whole was their total dependence upon correspondent banks to do business. He said the offshore banks could not operate without them. He also said that taking control of the correspondent banking process to screen out high-risk banks was how jurisdictions like the United States could stop the offshore abuses, if they had the political will.

Two U.S. banks, Bank of America and JPMorgan Chase, testified next. The senators grilled them about opening accounts for two Antiguan banks we'd profiled, American International Bank and Swiss American Bank, both of which dealt in dirty money. The Levin-Collins team questioned the U.S. banks about why they'd provided those offshore banks with access to the U.S. financial system despite shady reputations and suspect transactions. At one point, Senator Levin surprised the U.S. banks by disclosing that, although both had closed accounts for one of the offshore banks, American International Bank (AIB), they had unknowingly continued doing business with AIB, since AIB was a correspondent client of another offshore bank with a correspondent account at each of the two U.S. banks.

Bank of America and JPMorgan Chase admitted they had not done enough to protect the U.S. financial system from high-risk banks, and described how, in response to our investigation, they were revamping their correspondent banking controls.

The second day of hearings focused on the issue of shell banks, using M.A. Bank and Federal Bank as examples. M.A. Bank was licensed in the Cayman Islands, while Federal Bank was licensed in the Bahamas. Neither had its own physical office anywhere, but both offered banking services in Argentina, despite having no banking license there. Neither bank had ever been examined by any bank regulator. Both had managed, however, to open Citibank accounts in New York, helped by high-level Argentine connections. Both banks kept virtually all of their funds in their Citibank accounts which, records showed, had processed billions of dollars.

Citi records showed M.A. Bank was owned by three former senior Argentine officials and operated through the offices of a related Argentine company, Mercado Abierto, a securities firm. Other records showed M.A. Bank had violated standard banking practice by opening accounts in fictitious names, accepting deposits from unknown parties, disbursing large amounts of cash to unknown individuals, and manufacturing fake withdrawal slips upon request. Altogether, M.A. Bank had moved over $1.8 billion through its Citibank account, including $7.7 million in illegal drug money sent to the account as part of a U.S. sting operation.

Federal Bank turned out to be a secret offshore affiliate of Banco Republica, a large Argentine bank that'd collapsed the prior year amid reports of insider loans, insufficient capital, and sudden withdrawals, causing a regional fiscal crisis. Federal Bank was secretly owned by Grupo Moneta, a group of companies associated with Raul Moneta, an Argentine billionaire. Grupo Moneta was also an investment partner of Citigroup Argentina. When Citibank Argentina first opened the Federal Bank account, it was told the bank was owned by the Moneta Group and was affiliated with Banco Republica, and had numerous records to that effect. But when asked by Argentina's Central Bank about Federal Bank's ownership, Citibank Argentina had claimed it had no relevant records. Moreover, despite reports of bribe money and suspicious transactions, Citibank had allowed Federal Bank to move more than $4.5 billion through its New York account. After PSI began investigating that New York account, Citibank suddenly closed it.

The key hearing witnesses were three Citigroup officials, including the head of Citibank Argentina and the banker who'd handled the Federal Bank account. The most riveting exchange came when Senator Levin confronted them about misleading Argentina's Central Bank regarding Federal Bank's ownership. The bankers claimed they thought the Central Bank wanted official proof of Federal Bank's ownership, which they didn't have. Senator Levin countered by reading the Central Bank's letter requesting "all information" related to Federal Bank, especially information on "the identity of its shareholders." He also quoted a key Citibank document that laid out Federal Bank's ownership. He asked why Citigroup had not honestly answered the Central Bank's inquiry. The bankers admitted they should have provided the information.

Then it was Senator Collins's turn. She started by asking why, after Citigroup received a U.S. seizure warrant for $7.7 million in drug money deposited into the M.A. Bank account, Citigroup waited a year and a half before launching a review of that account. The bankers blamed a breakdown in communications between the New York and Argentine offices. Senator Collins didn't buy it. She also walked through the outrageous examples of M.A. Bank's poor AML controls, deposit, and withdrawal procedures. When asked how M.A. Bank came to use those procedures, the bankers had no response.

Citigroup was the only major U.S. bank to admit to a policy of accepting offshore shell banks as correspondent clients. The hearing repeatedly highlighted the secrecy and inaccessibility that defines shell banks, hammering home why offshore shell banks—the bottom feeders in the global banking industry—had no place in the U.S. financial system.

The third and final day of hearings took testimony about a fraud victim whose money was deposited into the U.S. correspondent account of an offshore bank. The witness explained that the offshore bank was essentially immune to legal discovery due to offshore secrecy laws, and was also immune to seizure procedures unless the victim could somehow prove the offshore bank was involved in the fraud. The witness called for reform of the relevant U.S. laws.

The final witnesses represented the U.S. Treasury and Justice Departments. Senators Collins and Levin pressed both agencies about the money laundering going on through U.S. correspondent accounts and how they planned to protect the U.S. financial system.

Attacking the Problem

Press coverage of the correspondent bank hearings was extensive, detailing the misuse of U.S. correspondent accounts and questioning why the misconduct was allowed. Exposing the problem was satisfying, but fixing it was going to be a much taller order.

We concentrated first on the offshore banks we'd profiled. Within months, the U.S. banks closed every one of their accounts. In addition, most of the offshore jurisdictions yanked their bank licenses. The Caymans and Bahamas went farther by halting the licensing of all new shell banks, and informing the 120-plus shell banks already licensed that they had to open physical offices or close down. That unexpected announcement shook the offshore world.

Next was getting U.S. banks to review their correspondent portfolios to identify and evaluate the high-risk banks. We also pressed the U.S. banks to institutionalize the principle that some foreign banks were riskier than others, and to include a risk analysis in their initial due diligence and ongoing monitoring procedures. We also leaned on the bank regulators to mandate risk-based due diligence and monitoring procedures for all correspondent accounts.

Finally, at Senator Levin's direction, we expanded his private banking bill to address money laundering through U.S. correspondent accounts. On August 3, 2001, Senator Levin introduced his revised Money Laundering Abatement Act with an impressive bipartisan group that included Senators Grassley, Sarbanes, Kyl, Bill Nelson, DeWine, Durbin, Stabenow, and Kerry.[13] New provisions included a prohibition on U.S. banks opening accounts for shell banks, a requirement that U.S. banks conduct extra due diligence before opening an account for an offshore bank, and making foreign banks' U.S. correspondent accounts subject to the same freeze-and-seize rules that applied to other U.S. accounts.

The bill was referred to the same Senate Banking Committee that deep sixed our private banking bill two years earlier. But the result this time was very different, due primarily to the tragic events that unfolded soon after.

Winning a Legislative Battle

Five weeks after Senator Levin introduced his revised AML bill, the United States was hit by the 9/11 terrorist attack. A month later, the Senate suffered an anthrax attack. Our first PSI legislative victory arose out of the bitter aftermath of both events.

On the morning of September 11, 2001, I was sitting at my desk working away when my husband telephoned and barked to turn on the television. As soon as I did, I saw one of the World Trade Center's twin towers burning; slow-motion footage showed how an airplane had rammed into the side of the building. My first impression was that a small plane had somehow lost control. But as I watched, a second airplane rammed the second tower. I suddenly realized I was watching acts of terrorism. As the commentary reached a fever pitch, I learned that the two airplanes had been full-sized jetliners, hijacked with the passengers onboard, and deliberately crashed into the buildings. Everyone in the office gathered around the television, transfixed by the unfolding events. Plane crashes at the Pentagon and in Pennsylvania were also described.

Suddenly, a massive boom shook the marble foundations of the Russell Building. Some claimed later it was a sonic boom caused by military aircraft crossing the Capitol; at the time it felt like another attack. Within minutes, Capitol Hill police began pacing the hallways shouting for everyone to evacuate. Back then, the Senate had no public area loudspeakers or evacuation procedures; it was all ad hoc. In response, Bob snorted and closed his door, but the rest of us joined an eerily silent crowd in the hallway as scores of congressional staffers—calmly, with no signs of panic—loped quietly toward the exits.

We burst out of the building into a gorgeous, sunny day. Hundreds of staffers were milling around, a few senators among them. Cell phone service was down so no one could call their offices. A massive traffic jam built up as hundreds of cars tried to leave. The chaos showed how completely unprepared Congress was to respond to a major act of terrorism.

Over the next few weeks, the 9/11 attack, with its 3000 dead, consumed Capitol Hill. Nothing else mattered. Hearings were held daily as facts were pieced together. Outrage built over how the U.S. banking system had been used to further the attack. In a Senate Banking hearing two weeks after the attack, Senator Levin provided the following testimony:

> According to press reports, the 19 terrorists identified by the FBI used cash, checks, credit cards and wire transfers involving U.S. banks in States such as Florida, New York, and Pennsylvania. We have seen the photograph of 2 terrorists using a U.S. bank's ATM. …The fact that these terrorists used U.S. financial institutions to accomplish their ends is not to conclude that any U.S. bank or credit card company did anything wrong; these terrorists may have met every requirement for credentials and credit histories, false though such information may prove to be. But the evidence is clear that terrorists are using our own financial institutions against us, and we need to understand our vulnerabilities and take new measures to protect ourselves from similar abuses down the road.[14]

Enacting stronger AML measures seemed possible for the first time in years due not only to the terrorist attack, but also to a major change in the Senate. A few months earlier, in June 2001, Senator Jim Jeffords from Vermont had switched his political affiliation from Republican to Independent, and begun caucusing with the Democrats. His action caused the Democrats to become the majority party in the Senate—by a 50–49 split—for the first time since 1994. As a result, Senator Levin had become PSI chair, and Senator Paul Sarbanes from Maryland chaired the Banking Committee, replacing Senator Phil Gramm. Where Senator Gramm had buried our AML bill, Senator Sarbanes had cosponsored it. As a result, he identified the Levin bill as a starting point for legislative action, but didn't stop there. He added an AML expert to the Banking Committee staff, Steven Kroll, and directed him to further strengthen the bill.

Working with Senators Kerry, Grassley, and others, the resulting Sarbanes bill added a host of measures to the Levin reforms. Immediately opposed by the Texas Bankers Association, others also began lobbying against the bill behind closed doors. Perhaps most shameless was Citigroup which, after hiring the former head of the Federal Reserve's AML program, Rick Small, used him to lobby against a proposed ban on opening accounts for offshore shell banks. When a Washington Post article exposed Citigroup's lobbying effort, however, the bank quietly took Rick off the job, and opposition to the shell bank ban faded.[15]

On October 4, the Banking Committee passed the amended AML bill on a unanimous vote of 21–0.[16] Even Senator Gramm voted for it. At the urging of Senators Sarbanes, Grassley, Levin, and others, the bill was folded into a larger anti-terrorism bill taking form in the Senate, S. 1510, later known as the Patriot Act.

On October 11, the Senate passed S. 1510 by a vote of 96–1, with the AML provisions included as Title III.[17] The next day, the House passed its own anti-terrorism bill, H.R. 2975, but without an AML title, perhaps because the House Majority Leader was Dick Armey, a Republican from Texas whose bankers continued to oppose stiffer AML requirements. Negotiations over the two anti-terrorism bills commenced immediately.

Anthrax Attack

In the midst of those negotiations, terrorism struck again. On Monday, October 15, an aide to Senate Majority Leader Tom Daschle opened a letter filled with deadly anthrax spores which immediately infected the Daschle office in the Hart Building. It was later discovered that someone—no one has ever named who—sent anthrax-filled letters to both Senator Daschle and Senator Patrick Leahy, the Judiciary Committee chair. A frantic review of Senate mail caught the Leahy letter before it was opened.

Law enforcement determined that the Senate letters were linked to earlier anthrax incidents in which letters containing the same anthrax strain had been sent to multiple media outlets. Those letters had contaminated several postal service centers, and at least 22 individuals were diagnosed with anthrax infections, of whom 5 died.

The Senate anthrax attack rattled Congress and dislocated staff. On October 16, the Senate closed its office buildings and tested hundreds for anthrax exposure. On October 17, the House also closed. The House buildings soon re-opened, but the Senate buildings remained closed, undergoing testing to evaluate the extent of the contamination. Eventually, two of the Senate buildings re-opened and took in staff from the still closed Hart Building. Later still, a specialized cleaning firm removed contaminated materials from the Daschle office and used chlorine dioxide gas to fumigate the Hart Building.[18] Since the Hart, Dirksen, and Russell buildings are connected by underground passageways, the process left PSI hallways smelling like a swimming pool. Many Senate staffers stayed home during the acute disinfection process. But congressional leadership refused to hit the pause button on the Patriot Act.

The anthrax attack also re-energized the House. On October 17, the same day the House buildings closed, the House passed its own strong AML bill, H.R. 3004. Afterward, Senate leadership insisted that the Patriot Act include an AML title, since AML bills had passed both bodies. The House leadership gave in. But the House leaders refused to hold a formal conference on the two anti-terrorism bills, choosing instead to write a new bill, H.R. 3291, to be presented to both chambers. Congress scrambled to reach agreement on the new bill.

Sarbanes Magic

Amid mounting pressure to finalize the Patriot Act, Senator Sarbanes hosted negotiations over the AML title in his hideaway office in the Capitol. His office was tucked away on an upper floor in a back corridor. The rooms were small but elegant; extra chairs were brought in for the negotiations. I was able to attend, because Senator Sarbanes had invited Senator Levin to send a PSI staffer. It quickly became clear that Steve Kroll and I were the only ones present with detailed knowledge of federal AML laws and regulations.

The final negotiating session took place the evening of Tuesday, October 23. The Patriot Act was scheduled for a House floor vote the next day. The Sarbanes hideaway was packed with about 50 Senate and House staffers, as well as representatives from the White House, Justice, Treasury, and other agencies. Senator Sarbanes was the only member of Congress present. The sole computer was the laptop of a representative from the Senate Legislative Counsel's office, Laura Ayoud, responsible for ensuring legislative technicalities were met.

Most of the issues had already been ironed out in staff negotiations. The function of the final meeting was to reach official House and Senate agreement on Title III. The staff marched through the provisions, adding a few measures from the House AML bill to strengthen laws on counterfeiting and bulk cash seizures. I stayed quiet.

Around midnight, Linda Lord, a formidable senior counsel with Senator Gramm, began talking about one more small addition to the bill to ensure that the privacy of bank clients would be respected. I saw her writing out a sentence or two that, for the first time, would create a broad statutory right to banking privacy. No such statutory right then existed, and years earlier the Supreme Court had refused to recognize banking privacy rights on Constitutional grounds.[19]

As Linda Lord continued her effort, I straightened, my face distraught. I took a big breath to register an objection when Senator Sarbanes suddenly began speaking. Heads swiveled his way. I don't know whether he'd seen my distress or just decided enough was enough. He interrupted Linda, saying that the hour was late and there was no time to open up a new issue. When he paused, Linda Lord tried again, explaining she had a simple addition to the bill. Senator Sarbanes interrupted her again and spoke over her until she stopped talking. With Senator Gramm absent, she knew she could not insist and subsided with a look of grim frustration. She had come close to sneaking in a major change in U.S. banking law, but it was not to be.

Senator Sarbanes thanked everybody and directed his staff to have the final version of Title III ready at 7:00 a.m. He looked directly at me and gave a small nod. I was still holding my breath. His decisive action had moved the AML title to closure. It was a magical moment.

When the 50-plus staffers reassembled in the Sarbanes hideaway at 7:00 a.m., they had to wait until the groggy Banking staff stumbled in with the bill text in hand, having encountered maddening overnight printing problems. After everyone signed off, the Banking staff dashed off to a meeting where the Patriot Act's final components were being assembled. A few hours later, the House passed the bill. The Senate passed it the next day. President Bush signed it into law on Friday, October 26, 2001, six weeks after the 9/11 attack.

As others have warned, it takes a strong stomach to observe lawmaking. I pondered the importance of having a bill ready when opportunity knocks, knowing the law inside out, and having a Senate champion present during negotiations. In our case, the end result was landmark legislation that greatly strengthened U.S. anti-money laundering laws. Among other provisions, the new law banned U.S. banks from opening accounts for shell banks; required enhanced due diligence before opening accounts for private banking clients or offshore banks; required all types of U.S. financial institutions to establish AML programs; made foreign corruption a U.S. money laundering offense; and made correspondent accounts subject to the seizure of funds.[20] It addressed virtually every one of the problems identified in our three-year money laundering investigation. It was an oversight triumph.

Notes

1. The information in this section is based upon "Private Banking and Money Laundering: A Case Study of Opportunities and Vulnerabilities," S. Hrg. 106-428 (11/9–10/1999) (hereinafter "Private Banking Hearing"), including the minority staff report, at 872–939 (hereafter "Private Banking Report"), https://www.gpo.gov/fdsys/pkg/CHRG-106shrg61699/pdf/CHRG-106shrg61699.pdf.
2. See, for example, "Swiss Government Confiscates US$114 Million in Raul Salinas de Gortari's Bank Accounts," The Free Library, 1998, Latin American Data Base/Latin American Institute (7/4/2016), http://bit.ly/2hHWehG; "Swiss Recount Key Drug Role of Salinas Kin," *New York Times*, Tim Golden (9/19/1998), http://nyti.ms/2mClE1X.
3. *United States v. Giraldi*, 86 F.3d 1368 (5th Cir. 1996), http://bit.ly/2hHWihq.
4. "Sound Risk Management Practices Governing Private Banking Activities," Federal Reserve Bank of New York (1997) (providing private banks "with guidance regarding the basic controls necessary to minimize reputational and legal risk and to deter illicit activities, such as money laundering"), https://www.newyorkfed.org/banking/circulars/10962.html.
5. See, for example, "55-Month Jail Term in Citibank Fraud," *New York Times* (7/28/1998), http://nyti.ms/2mClZSh.
6. The information on the Salinas account is based upon the Private Banking Hearing, including the Private Banking Report, at 889–901.
7. Litigation over the frozen funds continued for the next decade. In 2008, Switzerland returned about $74 million to Mexico and additional funds to other parties. See, for example, "Salinas Funds Finally Head Back to Mexico," Swiss Info (6/18/2008), http://bit.ly/2hLWwEe. In 2013, a Mexican court held that, while it could not explain how Raul Salinas had accumulated his wealth, prosecutors had failed to establish that he had obtained certain properties and monies by abusing his position, and acquitted him of charges of "illegal enrichment." The ruling was upheld on appeal. See, for example, "Mexican Ex-President Salinas's Brother Acquitted," *Wall Street Journal*, Jose de Cordoba (12/16/2014), http://on.wsj.com/2mDttVe.
8. The information on the Bongo account is based upon the Private Banking Hearing, including the Private Banking Report, at 910–924.
9. The information on the Zardari account is based upon the Private Banking Hearing, including the Private Banking Report, at 902–909.
10. The information on the Abacha account is based upon the Private Banking Hearing, including the Private Banking Report, at 925–934.
11. S. 1920 (106th Congress).
12. The information on correspondent banking is based upon the five-volume PSI hearing record, "Role of U.S. Correspondent Banking in International Money Laundering," S. Hrg. 107-84 (March 1, 2, 6, 2001) (hereinafter "PSI

Correspondent Banking Hearing"), and accompanying report, "Correspondent Banking: A Gateway for Money Laundering," Volume I, at 273–691 (hereinafter "Correspondent Banking Report"), https://www.gpo.gov/fdsys/pkg/CHRG-107shrg71166/pdf/CHRG-107shrg71166.pdf (Volume 1); https://www.gpo.gov/fdsys/pkg/CHRG-107shrg73779/pdf/CHRG-107shrg73779.pdf (Volume 2); https://www.gpo.gov/fdsys/pkg/CHRG-107shrg73780/pdf/CHRG-107shrg73780.pdf (Volume 3); https://www.gpo.gov/fdsys/pkg/CHRG-107shrg73781/pdf/CHRG-107shrg73781.pdf (Volume 4); https://www.gpo.gov/fdsys/pkg/CHRG-107shrg74037/pdf/CHRG-107shrg74037.pdf (Volume 5).

13. S. 1371 addressed both private banking and correspondent banking deficiencies.

14. "The Administration's National Money Laundering Strategy for 2001," Senate Committee on Banking, Housing and Urban Affairs, S. Hrg. 107-641 (9/26/2001), at 66 (prepared statement by Senator Levin), see also 4–6 (testimony of Senator Levin), https://www.gpo.gov/fdsys/pkg/CHRG-107shrg81577/pdf/CHRG-107shrg81577.pdf.

15. "Banks Seek to Alter Bill," *Washington Post*, Kathleen Day (10/11/2001), http://wapo.st/2ATyElU.

16. "Money Laundering Limits Moves Through Senate Panel," *Congressional Quarterly*, Suzanne Dougherty (10/4/2001).

17. Information about S. 1510, and companion House bill H.R. 3162, can be found in the floor statement of Senator Patrick Leahy and others in connection with final approval of the Patriot Act. See, for example, Congressional Record (10/25/2001), at S10990-S11060.

18. The Senate anthrax cleanup took three months, included seven buildings, and cost $27 million. See "Capitol Hill Anthrax Incident" GAO, Report No. GAO-03-686 (6/2003), at 2–3, 8, http://www.gao.gov/new.items/d03686.pdf.

19. See *United States v. Miller*, 425 U.S. 435 (1976).

20. The new Title III contained a long list of provisions to strengthen U.S. AML laws.

4

Taking on Enron and Its Bankers

"The Enron fraud is the story of synergistic corruption. … When a company commits fraud, they have to commit a little more fraud the next quarter to make up for last quarter, and then more and more each quarter until it gets too out of hand to contain."
Enron: The Smartest Guys in the Room, *Alex Gibney, film director (2005)* ©

On December 2, 2001, Enron Corporation, the seventh largest company in the United States suddenly collapsed into bankruptcy.[1] An energy company that won prize after prize for innovative business practices, boasted its executives were the "smartest guys in the room," and claimed $100 billion in gross revenues, was suddenly almost worthless. Its failure kneecapped thousands of Enron employees who lost their jobs, their health care, their savings, and their pensions. It disrupted companies around the world who'd transacted business with Enron and suddenly became involuntary creditors with little prospect of recovery. It triggered a wholesale plunge in dot.com company stock prices and widespread distrust of the U.S. stock market. The Enron implosion convulsed the public, corporate America, and the U.S. economy.

On the day Enron collapsed, Senator Levin had been PSI chair for just six months. He was still savoring his anti-money laundering legislative victory six weeks earlier. He'd just begun considering proposals for a new PSI investigation, all of which vanished amid the Enron shock waves. On January 2, 2002, Senator Levin held a press conference to announce that PSI's next investigative target was Enron. His Republican partner, Senator Collins, was fully supportive.

© The Author(s) 2018
E. J. Bean, *Financial Exposure*, https://doi.org/10.1007/978-3-319-94388-6_4

Over the next year, on a bipartisan basis, PSI collected and reviewed over two million pages of documents, conducted more than 100 interviews, held four days of hearings, and issued two Enron-related reports. Its investigation exposed the role played by the Enron board of directors in the company's misdeeds, the role played by U.S. financial institutions in concealing Enron's massive debt, and the role played by Enron itself in using structured finance to cook its books and dodge taxes.

The investigation was powered by a strong Levin-Collins collaboration that documented Enron's accounting deceptions, corporate scams, and executive pay abuses. PSI's investigative work would provide not only a detailed explanation of Enron's misconduct but also a factual foundation supporting the enactment of the Sarbanes-Oxley Act of 2002, imposing new accounting and corporate controls to curb abuses.

Unfortunately, even after Enron's bankruptcy, its accounting firm's downfall, the jailing of its executives, and widespread condemnation of its actions, too many U.S. businesses appear to continue to copy Enron's discredited business model. Too many U.S. businesses still try to profit from complex financial gimmicks instead of real products and services. Too many dabble in accounting deceptions, structured finance rackets, executive pay excesses, commodity price manipulation, offshore schemes, and tax scams—an ongoing disservice to corporate America.

Designing the Investigation

When PSI announced its investigation into Enron, it wasn't alone. Multiple committees in both the House and Senate announced their own Enron investigations. And those came on top of multiple law enforcement inquiries. While congressional leadership could have pressured the committees to coordinate, in light of widespread public outrage at the company, no one really tried. When it came to Enron, it was a free-for-all.

In the face of the ensuing investigative frenzy, our first issue in response to Senator Levin's announcement was deciding on PSI's focus—how it would design its inquiry in the face of all the competing inquiries. Senator Levin directed us to brainstorm about the best approach.

Linda, Bob, and I, called on to lead the PSI effort, worried away at the problem. We were wary about taking on Enron as a whole—it was too large, federal prosecutors were already crawling all over the company, and it was in bankruptcy. With our small staff, we had to take a more narrow focus. We also wanted to concentrate on issues with ongoing relevance, even after Enron closed down.

Linda had the ingenious idea of focusing our initial document request on the information given to Enron's board of directors. That approach would allow us to ask for a confined set of documents that would nevertheless address the company's major activities while putting the spotlight on Enron's board members—to see what the company's top brass knew and did.

Bob advocated taking an in-depth look at Enron's bankers. We all agreed that Enron couldn't have operated the way it did without massive credit lines, and a burning question was what its bankers knew, advised, and did to help Enron carry out its schemes.

A third area of inquiry piquing Senator Levin's interest involved Enron's use of special purpose entities, offshore corporations, and complex structured finance arrangements to carry out its operations. No one really knew how Enron had used those devices and whether its actions had violated any securities, accounting, commodities, or tax laws.

We decided to pursue all three avenues, framing each as a factual inquiry— what happened, how it happened, and who knew what when. We had learned from long experience that the best investigations involved answering open-ended factual questions, not postulating conclusions and then trying to prove them.

When we presented our proposals to Senator Levin, he directed us to proceed, as did Senator Collins. Senator Levin also told us to follow the facts wherever they led, and not to worry about being first out of the box with hearings. He said he'd rather dig deep than go first, to ensure we really understood the complexities of what happened and got the facts right. By turning us loose without any instruction on where we had to end up or when, he gave us the freedom to undertake a flexible, fact-based investigation.

Staffing Up

Investigating a major corporation is never an easy task, and the usual problems were compounded by a company as aggressive, secretive, and complicated as Enron. We knew we couldn't get the job done with just the three of us. To beef up our ranks, Senator Levin lent us Joe Bryan, a Levin staffer who was a gifted investigator. He also lent us his banking and securities expert, Tim Henseler, a whip-smart staffer who was funny and hard-working to boot. In addition, Linda scraped up the funds to hire a new PSI staffer for a year: Jamie Duckman, a young accountant who had become disillusioned after a year at a big accounting firm and wanted to use his forensic skills to combat wrongdoing. He would end up excavating Enron's unorthodox accounting, while tutoring us on complex accounting concepts.

That got us up to six, but then we learned Linda was leaving PSI to become chief of staff in Senator Levin's personal office. Although Linda would continue to help from her new post, we knew she'd be slammed with work. Losing her full-time involvement was a blow.

Linda appointed me acting staff director in her place, but that didn't fix our staffing problem. Instead, it left us to staff up the only other way we could, with agency detailees, academic fellows, and volunteer law clerks and interns.

We quickly picked up five professionals. Edna Falk Curtin was a GAO detailee with financial expertise and actual investigative experience—a real catch. Stephanie Segal volunteered while waiting for a security clearance for a Treasury Department job. Luckily, the clearance process took months, enabling us to take full advantage of her financial skills. Jerry Feierstein was a seasoned State Department detailee used to high pressured, complex demands. Roseanne Woodroff was an accountant from the Commerce Department Inspector General's office. Clark Cohen was a physicist on a year-long Hill fellowship sponsored by the American Association for the Advancement of Science. He turned out to be a hidden gem, analyzing Enron's complex transactions as if they were physics problems, chasing dollars like electrons until he figured out all the moving parts. We rounded out the team with a slew of interns and law clerks, including Ross Kirschner who would eventually join PSI as paid staff.

One immediate issue was where to house all our newbies. We ended up cramming in desks everywhere we could, including housing four detailees in Linda's old office. Bursting at the seams, we still had enough work to keep everyone laboring at full speed.

Bob and I were well aware of the dangers of investigating with inexperienced staff; we'd done it many times, sidestepping problems through careful supervision. Still, it was the first time we were overseeing a group that significantly outnumbered the permanent staff.

We started out with the usual warnings. First, confidentiality—we explained that a lot of people, from Enron to news outlets to rival committees, would like to know what PSI was up to. It was of the utmost importance that no one discussed the investigation outside the office—with spouses, parents, roommates, or buddies. We told them to use that Washington phrase with special cache—sorry, but I can't discuss it. We also told them to be wary of lawyers and journalists on the phone pretending to be friends of ours while fishing for information. We told them we didn't have any friends we'd want them to chat with.

We also told them about the importance of the investigation, how our limited resources made their ranks critical to the subcommittee's success, and how they needed to protect PSI's and Senator Levin's reputation. We asked them to check with us before doing anything an outsider could see. We told them that the bottom line was that PSI could never get the facts wrong. Period. And it was up to them, in part, to make sure that bottom line was never crossed.

Our motley crew of financial analysts, diplomats, a physicist, and baby-faced do-gooders faced an enormous task. But through sheer hard work and determination, they evolved into a crack investigative team that got the job done.

Our Republican colleagues also played a critical role. Senator Collins' staff director by then was Kim Corthell who assigned herself and several staffers to the investigation. Claire Barnard, who'd worked with us on money laundering, was eager to dig in. Jim Pittrizzi, a GAO detailee with the Collins staff, turned out to be, not only a workaholic, but a talented investigator who could follow the money through a maze of documents. Later, we got help from Gary Brown, a securities law expert working for Senator Fred Thompson, then ranking Republican on the full committee. Gary ended up playing a key role in the investigation.

The Republican staff gave us a shot in the arm in terms of energy, expertise, and investigative muscle. With them, our investigative squad had expanded to almost 20. We finally had enough people for all the work. We began meeting every week to enable everyone to keep up with each other's rapid progress.

Issuing Subpoenas

As we got ready to dive into the Enron vortex, PSI had one big advantage over other congressional committees—its unilateral subpoena authority. To issue a subpoena, most committees had to reach agreement among their members, sometimes by taking a formal vote. In contrast, the House and Senate had each designated one investigative body where subpoenas were easy to issue, under the unilateral authority of the chair alone. In the House, it was the Government Operations Committee. In the Senate, it was PSI.

That meant Senator Levin, as PSI chair, had the authority to issue any subpoena, in either a majority or minority investigation, without getting anyone else's consent. Before issuing the subpoena, PSI rules required him to submit the text to the full committee chair and ranking minority member and wait 48 hours, but that was only a notice requirement. While the waiting period gave the full committee leadership time to try to persuade PSI to withhold a subpoena or change its terms, it did not empower them to stop the subpoena from going out.

By eliminating red tape and political hurdles, unilateral subpoena authority enabled a congressional investigation to move quickly and decisively. PSI made regular use of its streamlined subpoena authority and had vast experience in drafting, serving, and getting compliance with its document requests. At the same time, given subcommittee abuses under Senator McCarthy, PSI had a longstanding tradition of exercising its subpoena authority in a bipartisan manner. That meant, even though PSI rules didn't require it, every subpoena was shared with the minority party, and before it went out, bipartisan agreement was reached on its content. That was how Senator Levin operated.

We spent the first two months of the Enron investigation churning out subpoenas. Drafting them required hours of painstaking work. Since we insisted on reviewing every single document we requested, we worked hard to design requests that produced a manageable number of highly useful documents and a minimal amount of useless filler. We also customized each request to suit the different recipients and different types of materials. In a Herculean effort, by the end of the first month, we got out a total of 50 subpoenas targeting Enron; its accounting firm, Arthur Andersen; its senior executives and board members; and its primary banks.

Other committees also issued document requests. Enron got hit with so many that, to manage them, it agreed to provide one set of documents to the Commerce Committee. The committee then shared the 41 boxes it received with other Senate offices. PSI staffers spent hours in the Commerce Committee's document room, copying tens of thousands of pages.

Arthur Andersen's response to the avalanche of document requests was to invite congressional staff, law enforcement, and others to a warehouse containing millions of pages of Enron-related documents. While the number of documents and ready access sounded promising, Andersen tempered our enthusiasm by issuing a statement in mid-January 2002, admitting "individuals" at the firm had, in prior months, destroyed "a significant but undetermined number" of Enron-related documents.

Andersen's document destruction spree ultimately sparked a federal criminal investigation and an indictment that led to the firm's demise. But that was in the future. In the meantime, we sent our two accounting experts, Roseanne and Jamie, to Anderson's Houston warehouse for a week. By the end of the week, they'd reviewed 75 boxes of material and shipped us tens of thousands of pages with information about Enron's financial gymnastics.

As the documents began pouring in, our next logistical nightmare was where to store them. After extended negotiations, the Senate Rules Committee finally gave us a storage room in Suite 6, located in the basement of the Dirksen building, usually reserved for new Senators awaiting permanent offices. We filled the assigned room with hundreds of boxes, stacking them nearly to the ceiling and layering them in rows until all that was left was a narrow corridor from the door. By the end, we'd accumulated over 800 boxes with over 2 million pages.

We numbered each box and carefully indexed its contents so that we knew what documents were where. We also set up a system for retrieving and reviewing the material, requiring staff to get through a certain number of boxes per week. Each staffer had to sign out their boxes so we could track who had what. All day long, using cheap folding dollies, our interns wheeled boxes back and forth between various storage rooms and PSI offices as staff methodically churned through the pages.

Besides their sheer mass, the Enron documents were grueling to review. Many were peppered with abbreviations, acronyms, mysterious charts, and financial jargon. Before we could decipher what they meant, we had to bring in experts to teach us about structured finance, energy swaps, asset sales, and prepays, as well as related accounting, securities, and swaps rules. It was a punishing education in Wall Street machinations.

We divided the staff into teams specializing in particular topics. Joe and I took the lead on the Enron board. Bob and Tim took the lead on the financial institutions. Jamie and Roseanne, working with Bob and me, focused on Andersen. Jerry, Clark, and others analyzed specific Enron transactions carrying such fanciful names as Whitewing, Yosemite, or Raptors.

While PSI was still climbing the learning curve, other committees began holding hearings. Some examined the harms caused by Enron's collapse. Others seemed designed solely to enable members of Congress to blast Enron executives for the mayhem they'd caused. Still others castigated federal regulators for not preventing Enron's misdeeds. But hardly any explained the details of those misdeeds. We dug deeper into the documents and began to piece together the specifics of what had happened.

A Whirlwind of Interviewing

In the spring of 2002, we moved from document analysis to interviews. The first step was scheduling the interviews—a logistical ordeal given our small staff, the many moving targets, and the unending games used to avoid locking in specific dates.

Bob took on the Enron lawyers and didn't give ground until employee interview dates were set. He did it, in part, by announcing that PSI staff would fly to Houston for a two-week period to conduct interviews on Enron's home turf. Bob also confronted Arthur Andersen, successfully scheduling a round of interviews in Washington. At the same time, Joe hammered out the Board member interviews with their legal counsel, establishing a demanding two-week schedule of D.C. meetings. On top of that, we scheduled a raft of one-off interviews with a variety of Enron business associates, lenders, accountants, and hangers-on. The end result was a nonstop interview whirlwind that literally took months to complete.

Enron

First up was Enron. Six PSI staffers made the trek to Houston. The Collins staffers were Kim, Pittrizzi, and Claire; the Levin staffers were Bob, Ross, and Tim (Image 4.1).

After two weeks, the interview team returned exhausted, but with new insights. They described a tough slog. Many Enron employees had responded "I don't remember" to multiple questions. Mid- and senior-level employees claimed not to recall the details of even major transactions and couldn't

Image 4.1 PSI team at Enron's Houston headquarters in 2002. Source: Private photograph used with permission

explain what was meant in company documents, emails, and charts, even if they'd authored them. Bob joked, "When I showed one woman a photograph of her kids, she claimed she couldn't recall who they were."

The law firm representing the Enron employees was Swidler Berlin. The PSI team said the Swidler Berlin lawyers seemed unprepared and unmoved by their clients' amnesia. One lawyer had pressed for completion of an interview in time to attend a baseball game that evening.

Later, when we were ready to speak with the senior-most tier of Enron executives, CEO Ken Lay, President Jeffrey Skilling, and Chief Financial Officer Andy Fastow asserted their Fifth Amendment rights against self-incrimination due to pending criminal investigations, and denied all interviews. So we never spoke with them at all.

Despite Enron's minimal cooperation, we saw it as important that we'd given its employees an opportunity to tell their side of the story. Giving targets a chance to say their piece—even if they choose not to—is critical to a fair inquiry and never a waste of time.

Arthur Andersen

Our interviews with Enron's accountants at Arthur Andersen were more productive. Only one Andersen employee, the head of the engagement team for Enron, David Duncan, was facing an active criminal probe and asserted his Fifth Amendment right not to answer questions. The rest submitted to interviews.

The Andersen interviews took place in PSI's conference room. Better looking than the rest of our office, it had a long, imposing wooden table and 12 matching chairs. A few feet further out from the table, lining three of the room's four walls, was an assortment of additional chairs and a red leather sofa. The fourth wall consisted of a ten-foot tall glass-paneled bookcase with bound volumes of PSI hearings. Across from the bookcase, a tall window let in natural light, although an outside concrete wall three feet from the window pane blocked the street view. A few green plants occupied the window well. Two inexpensive copies of famous oil paintings, supplied for free by the Smithsonian, decorated the walls.

We spent countless hours in that conference room. Typically, the individual being interviewed sat next to legal counsel in the middle of the long side of the table farthest from the door. Additional lawyers and representatives sat nearby at the table or in the chairs lining the walls, often creating an entourage that numbered as many as ten individuals. The key Levin and Collins staffers sat across the table from the interview subject, with additional PSI staff occupying the remaining seats at the table and some of the chairs along the walls. Depending upon the importance of the interview, PSI also might have as many as ten people in the room.

During interviews, we always designated one PSI staffer to lead the questioning. We'd found that using a lead questioner increased the efficiency of the interview and reduced confusion. Before key interviews, we also circulated a list of questions to both Republican and Democratic staffs to ensure that everyone's issues were addressed and to make it easier for folks to wait patiently for their topics to be raised. During the interviews, staffers from both sides of the aisle could chime in with questions to clarify the facts and ensure everyone understood what was being said. To facilitate questions about documents, we supplied both the interview subject and key PSI staffers with notebooks containing copies of documents that might come up.

Most of the interviews were not recorded, primarily because we'd found that people spoke more freely and provided more information in a less formal setting. We used stenographers only when individuals refused to cooperate, and we were forced to subpoena them for a sworn deposition. Our preference was to seek information in a more relaxed setting and take notes on what was said. We generally asked everyone present from PSI to take notes, since we'd found that different people heard and recorded different things, and more than one set of notes increased the accuracy of the conversation record. In addition, we encouraged everyone to adopt a polite tone in their questions, having found that a courteous approach usually elicited more information. A few interviews turned contentious or even hostile when sensitive topics were addressed. In a very few, we had to caution the interview subject that, even without being sworn, it was a violation of law to lie to Congress.

During the Andersen interviews in the PSI conference room, Bob generally led the questioning. In response to his inquiries, all of the accountants readily described Enron as using complex, aggressive accounting. They explained that Enron employed its own cadre of accountants who continually pressed Andersen to approve the accounting results they wanted. When shown copies of Andersen's 1999 and 2000 annual risk assessments categorizing Enron as a "maximum" risk client due to the "accounting and financial reporting risk" it took, "form over substance transactions," and "management pressures" related to "aggressive earnings targets," the Andersen accountants confirmed the accuracy of those descriptions. One Andersen attorney stated it would be "ridiculous" to characterize Enron as engaged in mainstream accounting.

In several interviews, we asked about Andersen presentations to the Enron Board's Audit Committee in 1999, noting written materials indicating that Enron used high-risk accounting practices. One document contained a handwritten notation stating that the head of the Andersen team, David Duncan, had told the Audit Committee that some Enron accounting practices "push[ed] limits" and were "at the edge" of acceptable practice. Tom Bauer, an Andersen accountant who attended that Audit Committee meeting, confirmed Mr. Duncan had conveyed that information to the committee members. He and his colleagues admitted Andersen also told the Audit Committee that Andersen had signed off on all of Enron's financial statements.

In response to questions, the Andersen accountants discussed providing both consulting and auditing services to Enron. They admitted Andersen sometimes audited its own work, including risky transactions that its consultants had helped design or approve. They also acknowledged that Enron was one of Andersen's largest clients, paying consulting and auditing fees that, in 2000 alone, added up to nearly $50 million.

In some interviews, we noted that, in its financial statements, Enron had reported gross revenues of $40 billion in 1999, and the very next year, in 2000, gross revenues of $100 billion. We asked whether that astounding jump in revenues had raised any eyebrows at Andersen or led to any inquiries into the numbers. None of the Andersen accountants remembered any questions asked or actions taken.

The PSI team spent hours marching the Andersen accountants through specific Enron transactions, including those involving Whitewing, LJM, prepays, Yosemite, Nigerian barges, and the Raptors, to ensure we understood how the transactions had been structured, what the accounting issues were, and what had happened.

We went into excruciating detail, for example, about Whitewing, a shell entity formed by Enron. Enron had caused Whitewing to purchase $2.4 billion in poorly performing Enron assets, booked Whitewing's purchases as "sales" income, and then claimed it had "monetized" the assets. Enron included the Whitewing sales income in the revenues Enron reported publicly, to boost its bottom line. Enron removed from its balance sheet the poorly performing assets "sold" to Whitewing. Two years later, Enron "deconsolidated" Whitewing altogether, so that its problematic finances no longer appeared anywhere in Enron's financial statements.

At the same time Enron was using Whitewing to buff up its books, the Andersen accountants confirmed that, behind the scenes, Enron was issuing guarantees for the bank loans Whitewing took out to "buy" Enron's troubled assets. The accountants explained that Enron had secured those guarantees, in part, by pledging $1.4 billion in Enron stock. In other words, Enron had used its own stock to guarantee bank loans to Whitewing to buy weak Enron assets that Enron knew were losing value. The accountants confirmed that, by doing so, Enron had taken on a large contingent liability—the risk of a Whitewing loan default—that didn't appear on Enron's financials. The end result was that Whitewing had made Enron's finances look better than they really were by generating "sales" income for substandard Enron assets, while also hiding Enron's billion-dollar-plus liability for the debt Whitewing was taking on to cook Enron's books.

We also went through the "LJM partnerships," three private equity funds formed by Enron's chief financial officer Andy Fastow and named by him using the initials of his wife and children. Like Whitewing, the LJM partnerships conducted business exclusively with Enron and mostly purchased troubled Enron assets. But instead of taking out bank loans to make the purchases, Mr. Fastow managed to convince investors like insurance companies and other banks to supply funds to his partnerships to finance the transactions. Marketing materials showed that he did so, in part, by touting his insider status at Enron, a status suggesting he would have nonpublic information about what assets would make good investments for LJM.

Mr. Fastow used the invested funds to buy poorly performing assets from Enron and move them off the company's balance sheet. He also reported earning significant profits from the transactions, a mystery it took a while to unravel. We learned that one of his tactics was for LJM to "buy" the assets from Enron on the covert understanding that Enron would later repurchase them at a higher price. Under Generally Accepted Accounting Rules, that type of buy-back arrangement didn't qualify as a true "sale," and the "sales" income from the LJM purchases never should have been added to Enron's revenues.

We asked several Andersen accountants about an email exchange discussing whether Andersen should have supported formation of the LJM partnerships in the first place. A senior Andersen executive had written to Enron team leader David Duncan: "Setting aside the accounting, idea of a venture entity managed by CFO [the chief financial officer] is terrible from a business point of view. Conflicts galore. Why would any director in his or her right mind ever approve such a scheme?" Mr. Duncan replied he "couldn't agree more," and Andersen wouldn't go along with the scheme unless Mr. Fastow got support from both Enron senior management and the Enron Board.[2] In their interviews, several Andersen accountants confirmed the firm's misgivings about the whole LJM venture, but also confirmed that when the Enron Board and senior management signed off on the LJM arrangement, Andersen did, too.

Several Andersen interviews focused on the Raptors, structured finance entities that supposedly functioned as "hedges" to offset losses from certain risky Enron investments. Andersen personnel confirmed the Raptor entities had been formed at Enron's direction, had little capital of their own, and were secretly backed with Enron's own stock, which meant Enron was essentially hedging its own risks. The accountants also confirmed LJM had played a key role in the Raptor transactions by providing and then withdrawing the Raptors' initial funding of $30 million each. They confirmed Enron had paid LJM a hefty $10 million profit per Raptor simply for putting up the initial cash. It was another instance of LJM profiting from junk assets.

We asked Andersen to explain how it had initially approved the Raptor accounting and then reversed course and disallowed it after the transactions became public. We also asked how Andersen had reacted to an Enron employee, Sherron Watkins, who had contacted the firm about the Raptors, later calling them an "accounting scandal" ready to implode. None of the explanations offered by the accountants for supporting the Raptor transactions made sense; the only convincing explanation was the $1.3 million payment Anderson had received from Enron to help design the Raptors and approve their deceptive accounting. When the Raptors later failed, and Enron disclosed a multi-million dollar liability for their losses, investor shock at the size of the loss, the convoluted transactions, and the secret Enron liability had triggered widespread sales of Enron stock, contributing to Enron's ultimate collapse.

As our understanding of these and other Enron transactions deepened, we began to see how they had been used to create fictional financial results. As Senator Levin later described them, the transactions had been used "to make debt look like equity, to make loans look like sales, to make poorly performing assets look like money makers, and to make Enron-controlled entities look like legitimate third parties."

Still another episode examined during the Andersen interviews involved a successful effort by Enron to eliminate from the Andersen audit team a senior partner, Carl Bass, who had raised questions about its accounting practices and delayed approval of some transactions. At Enron's urging, Mr. Bass had been reassigned to another client. The Andersen accountants had little to say about Mr. Bass' transfer, shrugging and looking down when asked for details.

By the time the interviews concluded, it was clear to us that Andersen had facilitated Enron's deceptive accounting by signing off on questionable transactions, allowing high-risk accounting practices, and enabling the company's Audit Committee to go along with financial statements that disguised Enron's debt, hid losses, overvalued assets, inflated earnings, and downplayed risk. Andersen had played a critical role in helping Enron cook its books and make its finances appear better than they really were.

Enron Board Members

While Bob and crew were plowing through the Enron management and Andersen employee interviews, Joe and I took the lead in interviewing the Enron board members.

Enron had 15 board members, many of whom were big shots with good reputations in their fields. The board chairman was Enron's CEO Ken Lay. Enron's president, Jeff Skilling, was another board member. Leaving aside those two company executives, we interviewed 13 other former or sitting Enron board members. They included John Duncan, founder of Gulf and Western Industries and head of the Enron board's Executive Committee; Robert Jaedicke, dean emeritus of Stanford Business School, an accounting expert and head of the board's Audit Committee; Herbert ("Pug") Winokur, an investment expert and head of the board's Finance Committee; Wendy Gramm, former head of the Commodity Futures Trading Commission and wife of Texas Senator Phil Gramm; Dr. Charles LeMaistre, director of a famous Texas cancer center and head of the board's Compensation Committee; and Norman Blake, a finance expert, former General Electric board member, and interim board chair after Ken Lay stepped down.

Each of the outside directors was paid over $300,000 a year for serving on the Enron board, compensation well above average for U.S. corporate board members. Many had been Enron board members for years. A number had lucrative work arrangements or relationships with Enron in addition to serving on the board. Prior to our interviews, none of the board members had been interviewed by the Justice Department, FBI, or SEC.

Because the PSI conference room was hosting the Andersen interviews, we conducted the board member interviews in an office that normally housed Levin interns. Located down the hall from PSI, the office sat in a short side hallway that ended in a loading dock. The main windowless room was dominated by four mismatched tables shoved together in the center. Mismatched chairs circled them. Along the walls were worn-out desks and stacked boxes. The room's seediness was due largely to its hosting a constant stream of students who were hard on the furniture. The upside was that we'd been able to clear the room of occupants, allowing us to hold nonstop interviews for two weeks.

The interviews lasted three to six hours each. Joe led the questioning. Linda, a Collins staffer, and I were also present. The interviews followed the same general script. We methodically went through a series of board minutes and materials identifying various issues, and asked what the board member understood and why no one had objected to transactions that were high-risk, misleading, or tainted by conflicts of interest. One key goal was finding out whether the board members had been witting or unwitting facilitators of Enron's misconduct.

From beginning to end, through words, tone, and body language, the board members sent the message that they bore no blame for Enron's demise. They acted as if they were innocent bystanders, shocked by developments, instead of well-paid corporate insiders charged with monitoring Enron's actions, overseeing management, and protecting Enron's shareholders.

We ran each of the board members through a long list of issues. In each interview, for example, we asked about structured finance transactions approved by the board to move poorly performing Enron assets off its balance sheet to related entities, making Enron's finances look better than they were. While generally familiar with the transactions, most board members could not recall any details other than to note both Andersen and Enron's legal counsel, Vinson & Elkins, had signed off on Enron's financials. Many described the transactions as part of an Enron "asset light" strategy seeking to "monetize" company assets by "selling" them to affiliates.

In each interview, we asked about the board's allowing Enron to conduct extensive, undisclosed, off-the-books activities and incur large, off-the-books liabilities that later contributed to the company's collapse. We highlighted reports to the board that, in 2000, almost 50% of Enron's assets, worth $27 billion, were off-balance sheet and parked at affiliates; that, in 2001, 64% of Enron's assets were troubled or not performing; and that, in 2001, its international assets were overvalued on its books by $2.3 billion. We also noted Enron's recent announcement that it might have to write down its assets by $24 billion. In response to our questions, while some board members squirmed, all defended their actions by again pointing to Andersen and Vinson & Elkins as having approved Enron's financial statements.

Another topic was the board's approval of three conflict of interest waivers that enabled Enron's chief financial officer Andy Fastow to set up the LJM partnerships and conduct business with Enron. The board members reluctantly admitted that none had previously seen or approved similar conflict of interest waivers. They also said they'd been unaware of LJM's private report to its investors that its Enron deals were very profitable, with a 69% rate of return, apparently at Enron's direct expense. Some board members asserted that the board set up LJM oversight procedures that, had they been followed, would have prevented any unfair dealing.

One electric moment came when, during his interview, Dr. LeMaistre, head of the Enron Compensation Committee, reached into a jacket pocket, unfolded a document he'd brought with him, and handed it to us—the original copy of his handwritten notes from a phone call in which he'd asked Andy Fastow about how much income he had personally earned from the LJM partnerships. His handwriting indicated Mr. Fastow said $23 million from "LJM I" and $22 million from "LJM II," after which he'd written the word "incredible."

After a stunned moment of silence following disclosure of the document, Joe and Linda turned to the Enron Board's legal counsel and asked why the document hadn't been produced to PSI earlier. He blinked and said he thought it had. Without that interview, the document might never have made it to PSI. In our hearings, it helped show the moment when the board realized that Mr. Fastow was profiting at Enron's expense, but then failed to take strong action in response.

Still another topic brought up in each interview was board approval of the Raptor transactions, which supposedly "hedged" some of Enron's risky transactions. The board had authorized Enron to back the Raptors with Enron's own stock, resulting in Enron's essentially hedging its own risks. We asked about reports given to the board tracking the Raptors' rapid losses and Enron's exploding contingent liability for them. Like clockwork, most board members pointed the finger of blame at Andersen for approving the transactions. When we asked about Andersen's taking back its approval of the Raptor accounting, several board members expressed outrage at the firm's reversing its position.

With members of the board's Audit Committee, we asked detailed questions about the Andersen presentation informing them that Enron was engaged in "high" risk accounting that "push[ed] limits" and were "at the edge" of acceptable accounting practice. None of the Audit Committee members recalled Andersen's using those words. Most even denied Enron used high-risk accounting, instead describing its accounting practices as "innovative" or "leading edge," noting still again that Andersen had routinely signed off on Enron's finances.

Finally, we confronted members of the Compensation Committee about paying Enron's CEO Ken Lay $140 million in 2000, as the company was struggling, and then giving him a $4 million line of credit using company funds, later increased to $7.5 million. Records showed that, starting in 2000, Mr. Lay had drawn down the entire line of credit once per month, then every two weeks, and then, on occasion, several days in a row. The result: over a one-year period from October 2000 to October 2001, Mr. Lay tapped the credit line for about $77 million in loans, at a time when the company was suffering from a feeble cash flow.

The cherry on top came when Mr. Lay repaid the loans using Enron stock. Paying with Enron stock meant he never replaced the cash taken from company coffers. Mr. Lay also claimed that, because he used stock to repay the loans, he hadn't engaged in stock "sales" and so didn't have to complete SEC forms tracking stock sales by corporate insiders. His failure to file the SEC forms meant Enron investors didn't know until too late to protect themselves that, during 2000 and 2001, Enron's CEO had reduced his Enron stock holdings by $77 million.

When asked about Ken Lay's compensation and insider loans, the board's Compensation Committee members defended their actions, saying the company's philosophy was to reward extraordinary effort with extraordinary pay. That analysis didn't exactly resonate given Enron's bankruptcy, but the board members didn't seem to appreciate the irony. The Compensation Committee members all claimed to have been unaware of what one board member described as Mr. Lay's "ATM approach" to his credit line. The committee members also denied any responsibility to track his use of that credit line. When we asked who else at Enron could have curbed the CEO's irresponsible cash withdrawals, we were met with shrugs, stares, or silence.

By the end of the two weeks, we had a solid grasp of the individual board members, how the board functioned, and what the board had been told. It was clear that most of the board members were sophisticated, high-powered captains of industry, well versed in complex accounting, financial, and securities issues. Given the board's meeting minutes and materials, we no longer bought the claim that they'd been duped by Enron's management. While there were times where the board appeared to have been misinformed, the evidence showed it had been given plenty of information about what Enron was up to and had explicitly approved the company's operating with high-risk accounting, off-the-books transactions, conflicts of interest, and lavish executive pay, only to have it all blow up in the board's face.

JPMorgan and Citigroup

As the board interviews drew to a close, Bob and Tim turned to the next group of interviews which targeted Enron's bankers. They were the toughest lot of all—a bunch of hard-boiled New York bankers who viewed Congress—and PSI—as generally incapable of understanding high finance. Enron had done business with many of the largest financial institutions on Wall Street. After studying the documents, we decided to zero in on three for interviews:

JPMorgan Chase, Citigroup, and Merrill Lynch. We also narrowed our focus to two types of transactions: prepays and asset sales.

Prepays are common business arrangements in which a company is paid in advance to deliver a service or product at a later date. The prepays conducted by Enron, however, with the help of JPMorgan and Citigroup, turned out to be sham transactions in which huge cash payments were made to look like energy trades, but actually functioned as massive bank loans never declared on Enron's books as debt.

We had already worked out the scam from analyzing (with the help of experts) a massive number of Enron and Andersen documents, interviewing the Andersen accountants, and talking to financial regulators. It worked like this.

First, each bank set up an offshore shell corporation it secretly controlled. JPMorgan paid for the formation of Mahonia Ltd. in Jersey, a notorious offshore jurisdiction, and arranged for Mahonia to be owned on paper by a so-called charitable trust, Eastmoss, which the bank also controlled. Citigroup did much the same, forming Delta Energy Corp. in the Caymans Islands and arranging for it to be owned by a "charitable" trust called Grand Commodities Corporation. Neither shell entity had any employees, offices, or business activities apart from transactions undertaken at the direction of the bank that formed it. The banks also provided the legal advice, paperwork, and financial support necessary for the shell entities to participate in the prepays.

Next, Enron and the banks orchestrated a series of purported energy trades among themselves and the offshore companies. The relevant bank started off by sending a lump sum (the loan destined for Enron) to the offshore entity it controlled in exchange for a contract promising future delivery of a fixed amount of oil or natural gas. The offshore company then entered into an identical transaction with Enron, essentially serving as a pass through for the cash. Enron deposited the funds in its bank account and used the money as it would have used a bank loan. Enron repaid the funds over time, with interest, by sending the promised oil or natural gas to the offshore company which, in turn, passed it to the bank.

To ensure repayment of the entire lump sum plus interest according to an agreed schedule and to protect the bank from losing money due to fluctuations over time in the value of the delivered oil or gas, Enron also entered into a financial "swap" agreement with the bank. In the swap agreement, Enron promised to pay a fixed price for the energy commodities in return for the bank paying a floating price. The net effect was to cancel out any price risk attached to the energy trades among the three parties. And to make it even easier for the bank, Enron itself often served as the purchaser of the oil or gas supplied to the bank. The end result was that the bank received cash, oil, and natural gas shipments from Enron in quantities whose combined value was equal to the bank's original lump sum cash payment plus interest.

Why go to all that trouble to disguise bank loans as energy trades? Our experts explained it this way. Think of a business that tells investors it has $1 million in revenues. Those revenues send a very different signal to investors and financial analysts, and require different accounting treatment, depending upon whether they represent profits from business activity versus loan proceeds that have to be repaid. Cash from business activity is recorded on company financials as "cash flow from operations," while loan proceeds are recorded as "cash flow from financing."

Investors and financial analysts obviously prefer revenues that come from business activity, rather than debt. Money from business activity signals a healthy enterprise. In contrast, money from increased debt raises cash flow issues, financing costs, and repayment risks.

Enron wanted to minimize its reported debt, not only to attract investors but also to convince financial analysts to support or boost its credit rating and stock price. By 2000, Enron's credit rating was on the lowest rung for an "investment grade" company; any lower would re-categorize Enron as below-investment grade, narrow its investor pool, increase its financing costs, and possibly trigger debt repayments. So sustaining or improving its credit rating was hugely important to the company. In addition, higher stock prices meant, among other benefits, better payoffs for the stock and stock options held by Enron executives.

Our experts also explained—and an Andersen memo informed Enron—that to book the cash generated from Enron's prepays as "cash flow from operations," Generally Accepted Accounting Rules required the prepays to meet four criteria. The trading parties had to be independent; their trades could not be linked; the trades had to incur some degree of price risk; and the trades needed to have a legitimate business reason other than producing an accounting result. Enron's prepays flunked all four criteria.

The documents contained abundant evidence that the offshore companies and banks were linked, and their energy trades were orchestrated, risk-free, and designed solely to achieve an accounting result. The documents also demonstrated that the key players were wise to the accounting scam. In one internal presentation, for example, an Enron employee wrote: "Why Does Enron Enter into Prepays? Off balance sheet financing (i.e., generate cash without increasing debt load)." In an email, a JPMorgan banker wrote: "Enron loves these deals as they are able to hide funded debt from their equity analysts because they (at the very least) book it as deferred rev[enue] or (better yet) bury it in their trading liabilities." An email from a Citigroup banker stated: "E[nron] gets money that gives them c[ash]flow but does not show up on books as big D Debt." Even Andersen's auditors knew what was going on: "Enron is continuing to pursue various structures to get cash in the door without accounting for it as debt."

We calculated from the documents that, at a minimum over a six-year period from 1995 through 2001, Enron had executed prepays involving more than $8 billion. Of those, JPMorgan Chase had participated in 12 prepays involving more than $3.7 billion, while Citigroup had participated in 14 involving more than $4.8 billion. Nine other banks had also participated in Enron prepays involving more than $1 billion, but we didn't have the staff to run them all down. So we concentrated on the big two.

As the banks began to realize how much we knew about Enron's prepays and how revealing the documents were, the bankers became increasingly wary. No one was prepared to acknowledge that the actions taken by JPMorgan and Citigroup had helped Enron hide debt to the tune of $8 billion. Head-shaking denials came even when the bankers were shown emails containing pointed descriptions of what was going on. Even when shown diagrams from Enron or the banks proving the prepay trades were orchestrated and price risk eliminated. Even when shown an Enron memo indicating that, despite treating prepays as trading income on its books, Enron was treating them as loans on its tax returns in order to deduct the interest. Even when confronted by the banks' own marketing materials pitching prepays to other corporations as a "balance sheet 'friendly'" way to disguise debt.

Merrill Lynch

As the JPMorgan and Citigroup interviews wound down, we began a new series with Merrill Lynch. The interviews probed a range of questionable transactions between Merrill and Enron, but the one that stood out was a 1999 deal in which Merrill Lynch paid Enron millions of dollars for three barges outfitted as floating power stations moored off the coast of Nigeria. Besides the issue of how Merrill Lynch justified such an outlandish purchase, multiple documents suggested the asset "sale" was little more than an accounting scam.

The facts turned out to be relatively straightforward. Enron bought the Nigerian barges in 1999. After unsuccessful efforts to re-sell them and with a view toward a fast-approaching deadline for its year-end financials, Enron "sold" the barges in mid-December to Merrill Lynch for $28 million. Merrill put up only $7 million of the purchase price and used a $21 million "loan" from Enron to pay the rest. Enron immediately booked $12 million in "sales" income in its 1999 financial statement. That phony income enabled the Enron African Division to meet its financial targets for the year and pay bigger bonuses to its executives.[3]

The income was phony, because contemporaneous documents showed Merrill Lynch had "bought" the barges as a favor to Enron and, in the words of a later indictment, to solidify its status as a "friend of Enron" entitled to an "increased slice of the lucrative deals that Enron dispensed to financial institutions."[4] At the same time, wary about getting stuck with lousy assets, Merrill Lynch did the deal only after obtaining Enron's oral agreement that if Merrill couldn't unload the barges in six months, Enron would buy them back at an agreed-upon profit equal to 15% of Merrill's $7 million cash payment.

Big problem: Generally Accepted Accounting Rules were quite clear that if a company promised to buy back an asset later, the asset "sale" wasn't final, and the seller couldn't book the sales income. So Enron and Merrill omitted any reference to the buy-back arrangement in the written sales contract. At the same time, the oral agreement was described in multiple Enron, Merrill, and LJM memos and emails. Not only that, when Merrill Lynch was unable to sell the barges after six months, it invoked the oral agreement to sell them back to Enron. In response, Enron arranged for LJM to purchase the barges at the agreed-upon price.

Tim and Bob interviewed half a dozen Merrill Lynch executives about the barge deal, highlighting the incriminating documents. Some admitted the existence of the oral agreement to buy back the barges, saying Merrill Lynch would not have participated in the deal without the oral guarantee. Others denied it. Tim and Bob worked their way up the executive chain, finally asking to speak with the most senior executive involved in the deal, Dan Bayly, head of Merrill's Global Investment Banking division. A key document stated that Mr. Bayly was going to confirm the buy-back guarantee with Andy Fastow at Enron just before the deal closed. Unlike other Merrill executives, however, Mr. Bayly's legal counsel continually dodged PSI's interview request, claiming a scheduling conflict each time a date was suggested.

The Nigerian barges were a blatant example of the phony asset sales that Enron used to inflate its revenues, and Merrill Lynch exemplified the role that too many financial institutions had played in helping Enron "monetize" its assets. Enron could not have executed the Nigerian barge accounting deception without a financial institution like Merrill Lynch providing the millions of dollars and cover needed to make it work.

By the end of the interviews, it was clear the big banks had helped Enron cook it books by hiding Enron's growing debt, helping it generate phony income, and otherwise facilitating Enron's accounting deceptions. We were ready to go public with our findings.

Throwing the First Two Strikes

Senator Levin approved two rounds of hearings. The first examined the role of Enron's board of directors in allowing Enron to run wild. The second looked at the role of the financial institutions in facilitating Enron's deceptive accounting.

Role of the Board of Directors

The board of directors hearing took place in May 2002. Two panels provided testimony. The first consisted of five Enron board members; the second heard from three experts on corporate governance.

Senators Levin and Collins opened the hearing by confronting the Enron board members with evidence showing that they had been informed of and allowed Enron to engage in high-risk accounting, extensive off-the-books activities, conflict of interest waivers for the LJM partnerships, and excessive executive pay. In a replay of their interviews, the board members refused to acknowledge any misjudgment or accept any blame for Enron's collapse. One particularly sharp exchange came when Senator Levin confronted board members about giving the CEO a multi-million-dollar line of credit which Ken Lay used to take $77 million in cash out of the company while it was experiencing cash flow problems, then repaying the loans with Enron stock. No director would admit Mr. Lay had "abused" the credit line or the company.

In contrast, the experts panel seemed aghast at the Enron board's poor oversight. They disagreed with the board's allowing Andersen to audit its own consulting work, calling the practice "terrible" and "horrible." They disapproved of the board's allowing Enron to engage in high-risk accounting, describing the decision as hard to imagine, "scary," and "a giant red flag." They also criticized board members for accepting fees and work from Enron in addition to their board compensation, explaining how the practice undercut their independence and calling it "absolutely wrong."

Three months later, in July 2002, we issued a bipartisan report summarizing the Enron board of directors' investigation. The first factual finding was that the Enron board had failed to safeguard Enron shareholders and contributed to the company's collapse by "allowing Enron to engage in high risk accounting, inappropriate conflict of interest transactions, extensive undisclosed off-the-books activities, and excessive executive compensation." The report recommended that U.S. corporate boards clean up their act, and that the SEC strengthen requirements for both corporate boards and companies' external auditors.

Role of the Financial Institutions

Our second set of hearings, in July 2002, focused on the roles played by the three financial institutions in Enron's prepays and the Nigerian barge transaction. Testimony was taken on two days, a week apart.

The stakes were much higher in the second round of hearings. In addition to Enron, we were taking on JPMorgan, Citigroup, and Merrill Lynch, and accusing them of facilitating Enron's accounting deceptions. The banks were indignantly denying everything. The media wanted to know if we had the goods to back up our assertions.

The first day of the hearings, July 23, 2002, focused solely on the prepays. Senator Levin decided to open the hearing with a panel of PSI investigators who could lay out what we'd found. To keep it simple, he settled on a two-person bipartisan panel: Bob who'd led the Levin prepay investigative team; and Gary Brown who was a Republican securities law expert on Senator Thompson staff, had helped dissect the Enron transactions, and had a good way of explaining complex issues. Instead of a report, Bob and Gary prepared joint testimony with bipartisan findings.

In the weeks leading up to the hearing, we labored over Bob and Gary's prepared statement which ended up 50 pages long with five appendices.[5] We developed multiple charts summarizing the prepays and Enron's finances, and selected over 100 documents for release at the hearing. We met with multiple accounting, securities, and credit rating experts to go over our analysis and numbers. We also worked with Senator Levin on his opening statement and questions. In between, we dealt with a barrage of questions from congressional staff, the banks, hearing witnesses, and the media.

Night after night, we worked past midnight. On the night before the hearing, we were stumbling from weariness and intensity. I left around 1:00 a.m. Around 2:00 a.m., since the subway had closed, Bob asked Clark Cohen, our physicist fellow and the only staffer left at that hour with a car, if he could borrow the car to get home, take a shower, put on a suit, and drive back. Clark tossed him the keys. As Bob told the story later, the next thing he knew, he woke up a few blocks from his house, having crashed into a curb-high median. Bob backed off the median curb, with two flat tires. He drove the car the rest of the way to his house, ruining the wheel rims. He changed, got in his own car, and drove back to the Hill.

The hearing began at 9:30 am. From Bob's calm and polished delivery, no one would have suspected his having experienced a car crash in the wee hours. He laid out the prepay accounting scam and answered questions from multiple senators. He was smooth, articulate, and sharp. Gary was equally impressive, handling difficult securities inquiries with aplomb. They did the subcommittee proud.

The second panel heard from an accounting expert who was a former SEC chief accountant, Lynn Turner, and representatives from the two major credit rating agencies, Moody's and Standard & Poor's. Given how complicated the prepay topic was, we had the experts panel go early so they could explain the accounting issues and their implications.

All three panelists were highly critical of Enron and the banks for engaging in deceptive accounting. The credit rating agencies testified that they'd been unaware of the prepays when evaluating Enron's financials and, had they known, would have downgraded its credit rating due to the increased debt. S&P also validated a chart we'd prepared showing, if the prepays had been treated as debt on Enron's 2000 financial statement, its debt level would have jumped from $10 billion to $14 billion, a 40% increase, and its cash flow from operations would have fallen from $3.2 billion to $1.7 billion, a drop of nearly 50%. They testified those were dramatic changes and, by omitting that key information, Enron's financial statements had misled investors and analysts. They also criticized Citigroup for selling bonds to investors from an Enron structured finance deal known as Yosemite, without alerting investors to Enron's true level of debt.

The rest of the hearing was a volley of questions and answers between the senators and the bankers who'd devised and executed the prepays. As the day wore on and senators left for other appointments, the PSI team boiled down to Senator Levin and Senator Pete Fitzgerald, a Republican from Illinois, to get out the facts.

First up was a panel of JPMorgan bankers. For two hours, they denied that JPMorgan controlled Mahonia, despite document after document showing that the bank had directed the formation of the offshore company, paid the lawyers who were its part-time directors and officers, determined what trades it would do, and provided its financing. The bankers also denied that the prepays functioned as loans, even after admitting the trades were orchestrated and moved money from the bank through the offshore shell to Enron and back again.

At one point, Senator Levin asked one of the JPMorgan bankers if he would describe the prepays as a "circular deal." "I don't know if I'd call that a circular deal," the banker sniffed. Senator Levin gazed at him: "Do you want to hear yourself?" He signaled our clerk, Mary, who pressed a button and replayed for the audience a recording of the banker talking to colleagues on the telephone about an Enron prepay. The banker said: "This is a circular deal that goes right back to them." A second participant in the conversation—another witness—added: "Yeah, it's totally a financing." The witnesses' shock at hearing their own voices explain the scam was palpable. It was a devastating moment. Bob, who had suggested the question and use of the recording, sat back in grim satisfaction.

After the JPMorgan panel concluded, the hearing recessed for 20 minutes to allow the senators to cast votes on the Senate floor. Our crew milled around in the back room, gulping down stale food to refuel. An intern reported that an unhappy group of Citigroup lawyers and witnesses, huddled in the hallway, were speaking in hushed, urgent tones.

The hearing reconvened with a Citigroup panel of four bankers. Citigroup took a different tack than JPMorgan. It didn't fight the facts; it admitted them and said the bank's actions were typical in structured financing arrangements. It also said the bank bore no responsibility to police the accounting used by Enron to book the transactions. Citigroup admitted, for example, that it had formed Delta, that Delta was an offshore shell entity, and that Citigroup directed its trading activities and paid its bills. It said that was typical of structured finance transactions and, despite its level of control, the accounting rules allowed Delta to be treated as an independent entity. It also admitted that the prepay trades had been coordinated, had no price risk, and were designed to allow Enron to treat the financing provided by the bank as cash flow from operations.

When Senator Levin took Citigroup through the criteria necessary for a prepay to be treated as cash flow from operations rather than cash flow from financing, the bankers acted as if Enron must have found a loophole around the requirements, since Andersen had signed off on the transactions. When Senator Levin asked whether Citigroup's own accountant had signed off on the arrangement, the bankers insisted the bank had reasonably relied on Andersen's judgment. When he pointed out that the bank had started pitching prepays to other companies as a way to avoid reporting debt—wholly apart from Enron—the bankers seemed to offer a collective shrug. When Senator Levin asked if Citigroup had a responsibility not to be part of an accounting deception, one banker responded that the bank needed to follow the rules, but also added: "it depends on what the definition of a deception is." That got a low gasp from PSI staff.

Senator Levin and Senator Fitzgerald pounded on the fact that Citigroup, after accruing $2.4 billion in debt from extending multiple prepays to Enron, eliminated that debt by selling Yosemite bonds to investors without providing key information. Citigroup didn't disclose, for example, that Yosemite funds would be used to repay Citigroup and finance added prepays, and that Enron's cash flow from operations included billions of dollars that came from debt rather than real business activity. Citigroup rejected any suggestion that it had deceived investors.

The hearing finished at 7:30 p.m., ten hours after it began. We were exhausted but satisfied that the facts had gotten out. I barely made it home before conking out.

Extensive media coverage of the hearing blasted the banks. We knew we'd made our case when the Wall Street Journal—no fan of Senator Levin—printed an editorial excoriating JPMorgan and Citigroup for enabling Enron's accounting deceptions, declaring the "banks deserve the beating they're now getting."[6]

Nigerian Barges

One week later, we were back. The July 30, 2002, hearing focused on Merrill Lynch's role in a number of shady transactions with Enron, all of which stunk, but none more so than the Nigerian barge deal.

The hearing started off with the two Merrill Lynch executives in charge of the Enron relationship asserting their Fifth Amendment rights against self-incrimination and declining to answer questions. Both had participated in all-day PSI interviews, but later learned they were subjects in an ongoing federal criminal probe. Both were excused from the hearing.

Dan Bayly, the most senior Merrill executive involved in the Nigerian barge deal, was scheduled to testify next. Knowing we'd bring up the fact that he had dodged a subcommittee interview, his legal counsel had telephoned Bob around 9:00 p.m. the night before the hearing and announced Mr. Bayly was finally available for a short interview. Bob informed the senator. Fed up with the gameplaying and brinksmanship, Senator Levin decided enough was enough. At his direction and after consulting with our Republican colleagues, Bob informed the attorney that it was too late for an interview, Mr. Bayly's hearing appearance was canceled, and PSI would instead take Mr. Bayly's deposition immediately following the hearing's conclusion.

So that left one executive, the former head of Merrill Lynch's Global Debt Markets Division—who had not been personally involved in any of the transactions at issue—to bear the brunt of the questions.

Senator Levin began by reading one document after another describing Enron's oral agreement to buy back the Nigerian barges in six months at a 15% profit. He read, for example, a Merrill memo stating that Enron had assured the company "we will be taken out of our investment within 6 months," and "Dan Bayly will have a conference call with senior management of Enron confirming this commitment to guarantee the Merrill Lynch take out within 6 months." Senator Levin also quoted an email and draft letter at the six-month mark in which Merrill Lynch called on Enron to buy back the barges at the agreed price, which Enron then did through LJM. In response, the witness asserted what he'd been told—that there was no oral agreement to buy back the barges.

Senator Collins asked him about a handwritten note from the head of Merrill's structured finance division warning of reputation risk if Merrill Lynch were to "aid and abet Enron income statement manipulation." The witness responded that his company must have received assurances that resolved that issue, since it subsequently approved the transaction. Senators Lieberman, Durbin, and Fitzgerald asked equally tough questions about the barges and other troubling transactions, leaving the witness floundering.

He was put out of his misery when the hearing ended at 1:00 p.m. At Senator Levin's direction, Bob and crew then withdrew to another room and began what became a three-hour deposition of Dan Bayly. It produced a powerful transcript later reviewed by federal prosecutors.

Two months after the hearing, the Department of Justice indicted Mr. Bayly and other Merrill employees in connection with the Nigerian barge transaction, while simultaneously announcing a nonprosecution agreement with Merrill Lynch, which got off with accepting responsibility for its employees' misconduct and agreeing to institute reforms.[7] Merrill also paid the SEC $80 million to settle civil charges related to its Enron dealings.[8]

A Texas jury convicted four Merrill Lynch executives, including Mr. Bayly, of fraud and conspiracy in connection with the phony Nigerian barge deal.[9] In addition, an Enron executive, Dan Boyle, was convicted, in part for lying to PSI.[10] Our own Tim Henseler testified at the Boyle trial. Three years later, in 2006, several of the convictions, including that of Mr. Bayly, were overturned by the Fifth Circuit Court of Appeals on the ground that the Merrill executives hadn't defrauded their firm, but did exactly what Merrill wanted. The Boyle conviction, however, was neither appealed nor overturned.

Throwing Strike Three

Our two Enron hearings, examining the role of the board and the financial institutions, had exposed wide-ranging corporate misconduct, but Senator Levin wasn't done. His third hearing zeroed in on how Enron had used structured finance, not only to cook its books but also to dodge taxes.

Months earlier, Senator Levin had asked us how Enron was finding the money to pay taxes on all the phony income it was claiming from fake asset sales and disguised loans. We told him that part of the answer was that Enron hadn't paid any federal income taxes in four of its last five years, despite claiming large profits. We let him know that the Senate Finance Committee was already conducting a detailed investigation into Enron's tax practices.

We also told him that one way Enron had gotten out of paying taxes was by making liberal use of a legal tax dodge involving stock options. Enron was infamous for giving huge stock option grants to its executives. In his last year, for example, Enron CEO Ken Lay received stock options worth $123 million. Lou Pai, head of Enron Energy Services, had earlier sold stock from his options for $270 million. Enron claimed tax deductions for all of those stock option profits as if the company had paid the executives, even though the executives had, in fact, sold their options to third parties in the marketplace and Enron had not recorded any stock option compensation expense on its books. For years, Senator Levin had worked to change the tax treatment of stock options so that corporations could deduct only the stock option expenses actually shown on their books, but Congress hadn't made the change. Which meant Enron could legally deduct all of the stock option profits claimed by its executives (even though it never booked the amounts as expenses) and use those deductions to lower its taxable income.

Senator Levin used Enron to condemn again the nonsensical stock option tax loophole,[11] but that wasn't the subject of his third and final Enron hearing. Instead, his focus was on showing how Enron used structured finance to dodge taxes. He used Slapshot to explain.

Investigating Slapshot

One day during the prepay interviews, Bob finished questioning an Enron employee earlier than expected. Rather than call it a day, he took the opportunity to ask about a transaction that had only recently appeared on our radar screens: Slapshot. The executive's evasive answers caused us to intensify our inquiry into the deal. We eventually learned that Slapshot was one of four interconnected structured finance transactions that Enron had used, not only to inflate its income but also to dodge millions of dollars in taxes.[12]

The scam was as complicated as anything we'd come across, but we were able to locate documents that provided a roadmap to the whole sordid deal. It was part of a new Enron business venture involving pulp and paper assets, and took place over a six-month period from December 2000 to June 2001. All four transactions were financed by JPMorgan or Citigroup which, in exchange, had received substantial fees or favorable consideration in other Enron business dealings. The evidence showed that Enron could not have completed any of the transactions without the millions of dollars in financing provided by the two banks.

As in earlier deals, the transactions included sleight of hand accounting by Enron to keep debt off its balance sheet and manufacture income from phony asset sales, all to pump up its financial results in 2000 and 2001. The first three transactions, known as Fishtail, Bacchus, and Sundance, involved a series of inter-related asset sales to special purpose entities and joint ventures, complete with inflated asset values, hidden Enron guarantees, and sham third party investments. Senior Citigroup managers had strongly objected to participating in one of the transactions, warning: "The GAAP accounting is aggressive and a franchise risk to us if there is publicity." Citigroup executives decided to plow ahead anyway.

The fourth and final transaction, Slapshot, took place on June 22, 2001. It involved combining a sham $1 billion loan with a valid $375 million loan from a bank consortium, using a convoluted set of phony structured finance transactions. The transactions had been concocted by JPMorgan as a way to provide Enron with $65 million in financial statement benefits and $60 million in Canadian tax benefits. Enron paid JPMorgan $5 million for the scam.

The key to the scam was JPMorgan and Citigroup's agreeing to generate two separate $1 billion overdrafts on certain Enron bank accounts. JPMorgan required Enron to deposit the $1 billion overdraft from Citigroup in an escrow account under JPMorgan's control before it released the second billion-dollar overdraft. Once it had the $1 billion from Citigroup in hand, JPMorgan ran its own $1 billion through multiple accounts, briefly commingled the money with funds from the valid $375 million loan, and created a paper trail suggesting Enron had really taken out a $1.4 billion loan (the $375 million loan plus $1.039 billion from JPMorgan). At day's end, Enron used the $1 billion supplied by JPMorgan to repay the Citigroup overdraft, while JPMorgan used the $1 billion held in escrow to satisfy the overdraft it had extended. Despite its recovering the $1 billion, JPMorgan continued to claim Enron had taken out a $1.4 billion loan.

Afterward, Enron made a series of $22 million loan payments. While the $22 million was actually a repayment of principal and interest on the $375 million loan, Enron pretended it was solely an interest payment on the $1.4 billion "loan." Enron did so, because Canadian tax law, like U.S. tax law, allowed companies to take tax deductions for interest payments on a loan, but not for repaying loan principal. By characterizing each $22 million payment as a payment of interest, Enron claimed it could deduct the whole amount from its Canadian taxes.

The Slapshot materials included a detailed diagram and action plan showing how the transaction was to be carried out, step-by-step. The diagram alone radiated sleaze (Image 4.2).

When we first walked through the transaction with Senator Levin, we described Slapshot as a circular deal, but he corrected us. He noted that it was not a situation where the same $1 billion in overdraft money circulated through all the accounts. Instead, it was a case in which Enron gave $1 billion to the bank to be placed into an escrow account, in response to which the bank used a different $1 billion to create the fake $1.4 billion loan. Fake because the bank had received the $1 billion from Enron before "loaning" out the second $1 billion. Senator Levin reduced the transaction to a simple hand motion—the left hand bringing in the $1 billion from Enron while the right hand released the separate $1 billion to Enron for use in the phony loan. His fidelity to the facts was a powerful reminder of his drive for accuracy.

PSI exposed the Slapshot scam, along with the three related transactions, in a December 2002 hearing. Four panels testified. The first panel featured Citigroup, the second JPMorgan, the third a financial expert, and the fourth federal regulators.

What I remember most from the hearing is Senator Levin going through the transaction—the "slapshot" that sent $1 billion speeding around selected accounts—and asking how JPMorgan could design and execute such a deceptive loan transaction. The JPMorgan banker who designed Slapshot had a puzzled, panicked look on his face. He testified that the loan wasn't a deception, since the bank had actually executed the loan paperwork. When Senator Levin pointed out that the paperwork didn't create a real loan, since JPMorgan had received $1 billion from Enron before providing the $1 billion overdraft, the banker just repeated that the paperwork had been executed. He was so immersed in the paper world of structured finance that he was unable to respond to the point that, in the real world, the $1 billion JPMorgan used to trigger the Slapshot was not really an extension of credit at all.

Senator Collins exposed similar deceptions in the transactions involving Citigroup. Using the bank's own documents, she forced Citigroup's bankers to confront the fact that Citigroup had based its participation in the Fishtail,

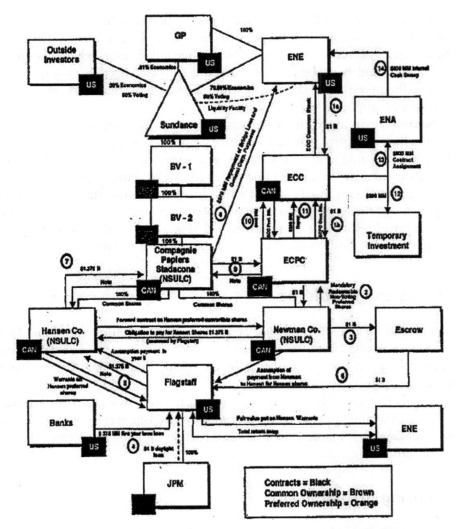

Source: Diagram of the Slapshot transaction, Bates ECa000195943, Hearing Exhibit 337.

Image 4.2   JPMorgan Slapshot diagram. Source: 2002 Senate Hearing Exhibit 337

Bacchus, and Sundance transactions on verbal guarantees and unwritten side agreements with Enron that contradicted the very accounting Enron used to inflate its earnings and cash flow on its financial statements.

The final panel consisted of federal banking and securities regulators. Senator Levin opened by noting that the SEC didn't normally regulate banks, and the banking regulators didn't normally regulate accounting practices, so there was a regulatory and enforcement gap when it came to banks that facilitated deceptive accounting. He pointed out how both agencies—as well as the banks and securities firms they oversaw—depended upon reliable financial statements, and how the regulators needed to band together to stop banks from selling products and entering into transactions designed to corrupt the accuracy of corporate financial reports.

Senator Levin urged the regulators to prohibit U.S. financial institutions from selling deceptive structured finance products that aided and abetted dishonest accounting and from knowingly or recklessly participating in deceptive structured transactions. He also urged the banking regulators to treat such conduct as an unsafe and unsound banking practice that could trigger regulatory enforcement actions. In addition, he urged the regulators to conduct a broad review of existing structured finance transactions at U.S. banks to root out the abusive ones. The regulators appeared receptive to his pleas.

Fixing the Problems

By the end of January 2003, our active Enron investigation was done. In a year of unceasing effort, we had laid bare dozens of Enron's financial scams, while taking on the smartest guys in the room. And we had done it with bipartisan flair.

The final stage of the investigation was to try to fix the problems exposed by Enron's wrongdoing. At first, progress was swift. But over time, key reforms were weakened or ignored, an ill-advised backpedaling by regulators that factored into the financial crisis of 2008.

Enforcing Accountability

One satisfying development was a series of criminal prosecutions and civil lawsuits holding the wrongdoers accountable. A highlight was the 2006 criminal conviction of Enron President Jeff Skilling on fraud and insider trading charges. He was sentenced to 24 years in prison, a sentence later reduced by 10 years in exchange for his surrendering $42 million and the right to appeal his conviction. Enron CEO Ken Lay was also convicted on fraud charges, but died of a heart attack before sentencing. Other Enron executives, including Andy Fastow, pled guilty to a variety of charges, and a number went to prison.

Arthur Andersen was also prosecuted and, after a jury trial, found guilty of obstruction of justice stemming from its destruction of numerous

Enron-related documents. The document destruction had been ordered by Andersen's Enron team leader David Duncan and by Andersen lawyer Nancy Temple. The firm's indictment was filed in March 2002; its conviction came just three months later in June. Because the SEC cannot accept audits from a convicted felon, Andersen surrendered its CPA license in August 2002, and went out of business. While the firm's corrupt culture and unreliable audits warranted its demise, many innocent partners and employees suffered from its fall. Three years later, in 2005, the Supreme Court reversed the firm's conviction, ruling that the jury instructions had failed to make clear that the evidence had to prove Andersen knew it was engaged in wrongdoing, but the firm had already disappeared.[13]

After the Supreme Court's ruling, David Duncan, who had pled guilty to obstruction of justice and testified against Andersen at trial, withdrew his guilty plea. He never went to jail. In 2008, without admitting guilt or paying a fine, he settled SEC civil charges that he had violated U.S. securities laws by approving Enron's deceptive financial statements.[14] He was permanently barred from appearing before the SEC.

Another set of prosecutions involved issues that we'd examined only briefly in this investigation but would revisit later, Enron's online energy trading activities and secret manipulation of energy prices in the California energy market.

In addition, Enron's directors were hit with a class action lawsuit which they settled for $168 million.[15] Of that amount, $155 million was paid by Enron's insurance policies and $13 million came out of the pockets of ten former directors. Since corporate directors rarely pay a penny out of pocket, some trumpeted the civil settlement as a meaningful punishment of culpable directors; others noted that the ten directors had collectively sold Enron stock worth $250 million and dismissed the settlement payment as paltry.[16]

Enron itself was never convicted of a crime. Instead, its bankruptcy slowly took the company apart. Multiple civil suits dragged on for years, dividing up Enron assets in partial satisfaction of losses by its investors, pensioners, and creditors.[17]

Structured Finance Reform

A second cleanup effort involved stopping the deceptive structured finance that underlay so much of Enron's misconduct. After the Enron hearings, the SEC and banking regulators started out strong. In 2004, they proposed tough new interagency guidance condemning complex structured finance transactions designed to corrupt financial statements or abet tax evasion.[18] The agencies immediately began enforcing the proposed guidance, including by treating violations as unsafe and unsound banking practices. Among other actions, they put a complete halt to bank sales of "balance sheet friendly" prepays.

Three years later, however, in 2007, the regulators issued a final version of the guidance that was dramatically weaker.[19] It removed stern warnings against abuses, recordkeeping requirements, and preventive measures that were to be taken by management, legal counsel, and board members. The financial industry had somehow snuck in and convinced the regulators to gut the guidance; at the same time, a new wave of structured finance abuses was gathering speed, infecting markets, and rushing toward the devastating mortgage market crash of 2008.

Sarbanes-Oxley Act

The most important changes sparked by the Enron scandal came when Congress enacted the Sarbanes-Oxley Act.[20] Signed into law in July 2002, it put into place landmark reforms to stop Enron-style accounting and corporate abuses.

The law was a reaction to not only Enron, but also a raft of other accounting scandals that scarred 2002. They included World Com, whose $11 billion accounting fraud and bankruptcy dwarfed Enron's downfall; Adelphia, the sixth-largest U.S. cable television company whose books were secretly manipulated by its founders; Healthsouth, a healthcare company whose earnings were overstated by $1.4 billion; and Tyco, a $36 billion behemoth whose reputation was shattered by accounting frauds, inflated earnings, and a tawdry CEO notorious for buying a $6000 shower curtain. Those serial corporate scandals kept Wall Street in a continual state of shock and disarray, and added critical mass to post-Enron efforts in Congress to stiffen the law.

Senator Paul Sarbanes, Democratic chair of the Senate Banking Committee, and Rep. Michael Oxley, Republican chair of the House Financial Services Committee, championed the bill. The result was the bicameral and bipartisan Sarbanes-Oxley Act, also known as SOX.

SOX imposed numerous needed reforms. First, it ended the hoary tradition of the accounting profession being allowed to self-regulate rather than submit to government oversight. It established the Public Company Accounting Oversight Board (PCAOB) to police accounting firms that audit public companies. The PCAOB was charged with registering auditors of U.S. corporations, issuing auditing standards, ensuring compliance, and imposing penalties for misconduct. It was a revolution in the accounting world, brought on by years of auditing malpractice.

Second, the law imposed new controls on accounting firms and publicly traded corporations to clamp down on abuses. Accounting firms were barred from providing consulting services to the companies they audited without explicit board approval—a big thumbs down on auditing their own work. Corporate CEOs and CFOs were required to personally certify each financial statement issued by their company, indicating it fairly presented the company's financial condition. Financial statements were required to report all material off-balance-sheet transactions and obligations. Board audit committees were given authority to hire and fire the company auditor and charged with reviewing accounting complaints.

The law's most controversial provision turned out to be Section 404. It required publicly traded corporations to implement internal controls to ensure accurate financial reporting, and required auditors to attest to the controls' effectiveness every year. The provision produced howls of protest from companies caterwauling about how burdensome it was. Really? Isn't establishing internal controls to ensure accurate financial reporting about as basic as it gets?

My favorite provision in the law was Section 402 banning insider corporate loans. I was sitting in the staff area on the Senate floor watching the bill debate when Senator Schumer offered his amendment to prohibit publicly traded corporations from giving company-financed loans to executives and directors.[21] He said his amendment had been cleared by both parties and was supported by President Bush. It immediately passed by voice vote. I nearly fell off my chair.

Giving executives company loans on absurdly favorable terms was an entrenched practice. Forgiving those loans was another form of executive pay. Outrageous examples included not only Enron's $77 million in loans to Ken Lay, but also $400 million in loans given to Worldcom's CEO, and $100 million in loans given to Tyco executives and subsequently forgiven by the company. In one fell swoop, the Schumer amendment prohibited those practices. When shell-shocked executives later tried to narrow the ban, Senators Levin and Collins wrote a letter urging the SEC not to weaken the prohibition. For once, the good guys prevailed. Today, virtually no publicly traded company gives company-financed loans to executives or directors.

Of course, the good guys didn't prevail on everything. Lobbyists weakened many SOX protections. They convinced Congress to issue so many exemptions to Section 404 that, today, almost no publicly traded companies are required to conduct annual audits of their internal controls ensuring accurate financial results. The accounting industry ganged up on the PCAOB to block many of its efforts to strengthen accounting controls. But at least the PCAOB still exists. Not only that, but other countries set up similar oversight bodies for their accountants. CEOs and CFOs still have to certify their financial statements, and auditors still generally can't combine auditing with other consulting services. Overall, SOX still packs a punch.

PSI's role in documenting Enron's abuses helped policymakers and the public understand in a deeper way what had happened at the company. It also provided factual support for new, concrete measures to prevent the type of corporate misconduct that bankrupts companies, devastates workers, cheats investors, and undermines confidence in American business. It was a grim victory in congressional oversight.

Notes

1. The information in this chapter is based upon the following reports and hearing records produced by PSI: "The Role of the Board of Directors in Enron's Collapse," S. Hrg. 107-511 (5/7/2002) (hereinafter "PSI Enron Board Hearing"), https://www.gpo.gov/fdsys/pkg/CHRG-107shrg80300/pdf/CHRG-107shrg80300.pdf; "The Role of the Board of Directors in Enron's Collapse," S. Prt. 107-70 (7/8/2002) (hereinafter "PSI Enron Board Report"), https://www.gpo.gov/fdsys/pkg/CPRT-107SPRT80393/pdf/CPRT-107SPRT80393.pdf; "The Role of the Financial Institutions in Enron's Collapse," S. Hrg. 107-618 (7/23, 30/2002), Volumes 1–2 (hereinafter "PSI Financial Institution Hearing"), https://www.gpo.gov/fdsys/pkg/CHRG-107shrg81313/pdf/CHRG-107shrg81313.pdf (Volume 1) and https://www.gpo.gov/fdsys/pkg/CHRG-107shrg83050/pdf/CHRG-107shrg83050.pdf (Volume 2); "Oversight of Investment Banks' Response to the Lessons of Enron," S. Hrg. 107-871 (12/11/2002), Volumes I–II, https://www.gpo.gov/fdsys/pkg/CHRG-107shrg83485/pdf/CHRG-107shrg83485.pdf (Volume 1) and https://www.gpo.gov/fdsys/pkg/CHRG-107shrg86375/pdf/CHRG-107shrg86375.pdf (Volume II); "Fishtail, Bacchus, Sundance, and Slapshot: Four Enron Transactions Funded and Facilitated by U.S. Financial Institutions," S. Prt. 107-82 (1/2/2003) (also reprinted in the 12/11/2002 hearing record), https://www.gpo.gov/fdsys/pkg/CPRT-107SPRT83559/pdf/CPRT-107SPRT83559.pdf.
2. See PSI Enron Board Report, at 24, citing Hearing Exhibit, at 55, "Defendant Andersen Exhibit 763," from *U.S v. Arthur Andersen*, Case No. H-02-0121 (USCD SD Texas).
3. See *United States v. Bayly*, Case No. H-03-363 (USCD SD Texas, Houston), Third Superseding Indictment (7/22/2004) (hereinafter "Bayly Case"), ¶ 11, at 3–4; *United States v. Brown*, 459 F.3d. 509 (5th Cir. 2006).
4. Bayly Case, ¶ 11, at 3–4.
5. PSI Financial Institutions Hearing, at 215–264.

6. "Enron's Enablers," *Wall Street Journal* editorial (7/29/2002), http://on.wsj. com/2ARvuiT.

7. See "Three Top Former Merrill Lynch Executives Charged with Conspiracy, Obstruction of Justice, Perjury in Enron Investigation," Department of Justice Press Release (9/17/2003), http://www.justice.gov/archive/opa/ pr/2003/September/03_crm_510.htm; letter agreement between Justice Department and Merrill Lynch (9/17/2003), http://www.justice.gov/archive/ opa/pr/2003/September/enronagree.pdf.

8. See "SEC Charges Merrill Lynch, Four Merrill Lynch Executives with Aiding and Abetting Enron Accounting Fraud," SEC Press Release No. 2003-32 (3/17/2003), https://www.sec.gov/news/press/2003-32.htm.

9. See *United States v. Brown*, 459 F.3d. 509 (5th Cir. 2006).

10. Id. While other Merrill and Enron executives also made false statements to PSI, they did so while in Washington, DC, outside the reach of the Texas prosecutor. In contrast, Mr. Boyle participated in his interview by telephone from Texas.

11. For more information about the stock option tax loophole, see "Executive Stock Options: Should the Internal Revenue Service and Stockholders Be Given Different Information?" Permanent Subcommittee on Investigations, S. Hrg. 110-141 (6/5/2007), https://www.gpo.gov/fdsys/pkg/CHRG-110 shrg36611/pdf/CHRG-110shrg36611.pdf.

12. The information in this section is based upon "Fishtail, Bacchus, Sundance, and Slapshot: Four Enron Transactions Funded and Facilitated by U.S. Financial Institutions," S. Prt. 107-82 (1/2/2003), at 4, https://www. gpo.gov/fdsys/pkg/CPRT-107SPRT83559/pdf/CPRT-107SPRT83559.pdf.

13. See *Arthur Andersen LLP v. United States*, 544 U.S. 696 (2005).

14. See "Commission Files Settled Action against Former Arthur Andersen Partner in Connection with the Audits of Enron's Financial Statements," SEC Litigation Release No. 20441 (1/28/2008), https://www.sec.gov/litigation/ litreleases/2008/lr20441.htm.

15. See, for example, "UC Reaches $168-Million Settlement with Enron Directors in Securities Fraud Case," University of California Press Release (1/12/2005), http://bit.ly/2iuCbjV.

16. See, for example, "What's $13 Million among Friends?" Opinion Editorial by Harvard Professor Lucian Bebchuk, *New York Times* (1/17/2005), http://nyti. ms/2j4YmwH.

17. For a discussion of some of the more than 140 civil lawsuits involving Enron, see "Enron: Navigating the Civil Side of the Corporate Case of the Century," Diane M. Sumoski, http://bit.ly/2AZqTM3.

18. "Interagency Statement on Sound Practices Concerning Complex Structured Finance Activities," 69 Fed. Reg. 97 (5/19/2004), at 28980. This interagency statement built upon earlier guidance issued by the SEC in 2003. "Guidance on the Potential Liability of Financial Institutions for Securities Law Violations

Arising from Deceptive Structured Finance Products and Transactions," Prepared by Annette Nazareth, Director, SEC Division of Market Regulation (12/4/2003), http://www.federalreserve.gov/boarddocs/srletters/2004/sr0407a1.pdf.

19. "Interagency Statement on Sound Practices Concerning Elevated Risk Complex Structured Finance Activities," Federal Reserve Supervisory Letter No. SR 07-5 (4/17/2007), http://www.federalreserve.gov/boarddocs/srletters/2007/SR0705.htm.

20. Sarbanes-Oxley Act of 2002, P.L. 107-204 (7/30/2002).

21. Senate Amendment 4295, offered by Senators Schumer and Feinstein to S. 2673, the Senate precursor to the Sarbanes-Oxley Act, H.R. 3763.

5

Stopping Abusive Tax Shelters

"Crimes like terrorism or murder or fraud or embezzlement produce instant
recognition of the immorality involved. But abusive tax shelters are MEGOs—
that means 'my eyes glaze over.' Those who cook up these concoctions count on their
complexity to escape scrutiny and public ire."
Senator Carl Levin, KPMG hearing (Nov. 18, 2003)

The new year, post-Enron, brought many changes. The 2002 November elections relegated the Democrats back to minority status in the Senate. That meant when the 108th Congress convened in late January 2003, Senator Levin would lose his post as PSI chair and return to ranking minority member. Linda was on track to retire at the same time after which, at Senator Levin's request, I would become official staff director of his PSI team. In another development, Senator Fred Thompson announced his retirement, which meant Senator Collins would move up to take his spot chairing the full committee, leaving PSI behind. Her slot would eventually be filled by Senator Norman Coleman, a Republican from Minnesota.

As Senator Levin prepared to relinquish his PSI chairmanship, he decided to initiate one new investigation that would take him deeper into the world of tax dodging. The issue would grip his attention for the next decade, leading him to hold hearing after hearing on tax schemes used by profitable corporations and wealthy individuals to cheat Uncle Sam.

When asked why he took up the fight against big-time tax dodging, Senator Levin attributed his interest partly to his father who was proud to pay his taxes. He said his father-in-law was the same way, so grateful to the United States for taking him in as an immigrant and giving him a shot at the American

© The Author(s) 2018
E. J. Bean, *Financial Exposure*, https://doi.org/10.1007/978-3-319-94388-6_5

dream that, when he died, he donated $10,000 in his will to the U.S. treasury. Senator Levin thought everyone should pay their fair share to support their country. He was personally offended by freeloaders who dumped their tax burden onto the backs of honest taxpayers, making them feel like chumps for honoring their civic obligations.

His first full-blown tax inquiry after Enron focused on how major accounting firms were devising, mass-marketing, and hawking abusive tax shelters to anyone who would buy. His next, in 2006, exposed how U.S. taxpayers were using offshore tax havens to hide assets and dodge U.S. taxes. Two years after that, in 2008, he showed how banks located in offshore tax havens were facilitating U.S. tax evasion by providing U.S. clients with secret bank accounts. Each of those investigations broke new ground detailing how America's business elite—bankers, attorneys, accountants, investment advisers, and tax professionals—fueled abusive tax practices.

This chapter and the next explore that sequence of tax investigations. Senator Levin used them to help shut down dozens of outrageous tax schemes, spur the collection of billions of dollars in unpaid tax, and spark enactment of new laws to expose hidden offshore accounts.

Mass-Marketing Tax Shelters

In contrast to our money laundering and Enron inquiries where we had to invent ways to dig out the facts, our first in-depth tax-related investigation grew out of evidence freely transmitted to us by a whistleblower.

The whistleblower worked in the Tax Services Practice at KPMG, one of the biggest accounting firms in the world. After watching the Enron prepay hearing on television, he reached out to PSI about a similarly misleading accounting scheme that his firm was promoting.

In late 2002, Bob Roach and Jamie Duckman from the Levin staff and Claire Barnard from the Collins staff flew to meet with him. As he laid out the scheme's details and answered a set of wide-ranging questions, Bob realized that the bigger story was not KPMG's deceptive accounting product, but the fact that KPMG was deliberately manufacturing and mass-marketing dozens of high-cost tax shelters to multiple taxpayers across the country.

When Bob conveyed what we'd learned to Senator Levin, the senator directed us to launch an all-out inquiry into how KPMG and other accounting firms were cranking out abusive tax shelters, who was buying them, and how extensive the practice was. It was the type of open-ended factual inquiry that made for a great investigation.

Working with Whistleblowers

Our first step was to go back to the KPMG whistleblower. Working with whistleblowers and other informants can be tricky. Many are disgruntled employees who've been harassed, demoted, or fired by their employer. Many have an axe to grind. So we always handled them with kid gloves, testing everything they said for bias, exaggeration, or incorrect information. At the same time, whistleblowers with the guts to approach a Senate investigative subcommittee typically had something to say worth listening to. So we also listened.

The KPMG whistleblower who'd approached us hadn't been demoted or fired, but said he'd become increasingly disgusted with his firm's generating tax shelters disguised as phony business deals with even phonier tax benefits. Over time, he linked us up with other KPMG insiders holding similar views. After they established procedures to protect their identities, one of them sent us an electronic list of what appeared to be KPMG's entire roster of tax shelter clients, complete with each client's name, the "tax product" they purchased, the KPMG partner who'd sold the shelter, and its price tag. It was a vast catalogue of tax shelter shenanigans.

With incoming information so hot it burned our fingers, we took careful measures to protect our sources. We knew that, no matter how hard we tried, we couldn't protect the KPMG insiders from retaliation once their identities were blown, so our number one priority was to ensure no one got their names from us. To minimize possible disclosure, we limited the lead whistleblower's interactions to a very few staffers, and allowed only one staffer from the minority and one from the majority to know his real identity. We never wrote down or spoke his name, referring to him instead as Confidential Source No. 1 or CS-1. We never even learned the names of the other KPMG insiders.

We also warned the insiders against giving us documents to which they were not entitled, recommending that they get legal advice about providing us with any documents at all. They apparently consulted a lawyer and made a decision to send us what they did.

Battling for Information

Our next step was to draft a subpoena for not only KPMG, but also Ernst & Young, another big accounting firm in the news for selling abusive tax shelters. Linda, Bob, and I drafted and got the subpoenas out the door in early January 2003, before Senator Levin lost his chairmanship and Linda retired.

We knew that if we didn't act then, it would be months before the incoming PSI chair would get up to speed on our inquiry and approve document requests. So we issued the subpoenas and waited for the responses.

In the meantime, we received an ongoing stream of information from our KPMG sources about the firm's tax shelter products and buyers. We also began educating ourselves on tax shelters in general, examining their history, fiscal impact, and how Uncle Sam was fighting back.

About a month after sending the subpoenas, we began receiving limited documents from Ernst & Young, but almost nothing from KPMG. Getting documents via subpoena is rarely a simple process. In virtually all of our investigations, subpoena requests became a test of wills and stamina, infused with drama. Senator Levin never seemed to fully grasp how hard it was. He acted as if all we had to do was present a valid subpoena, wait a reasonable period of time, and then collect the requested documents. If only.

What really happened, even with parties acting in good faith, was that a subpoena kicked off a set of negotiations to determine what documents should be produced. The two sides first had to agree on the nature of the documents being requested. Every company and agency had its own lingo and way of doing things—the records they generated, who got copies, and who kept copies. The request's wording had to be translated into the documents actually held by the subpoena recipient. Issues of scope and interpretation had to be hashed out. Emails, telephone records, instant messages, and other materials required added negotiations to clarify coverage.

To short-circuit some of those issues, we usually held preliminary discussions with parties we expected to subpoena so we could learn the nature of the parties' records and the terms used. But in the case of KPMG, our KPMG sources had already helped us design our document requests to target the most useful information.

For subpoenas that requested a large number of documents—as the KPMG subpoena did—the next issue was prioritizing which groups of documents should be produced first. Without giving up on our broader requests, we often agreed to a much smaller, initial document production so we could review the subset of documents, figure out what was useful, and identify the priority documents. Still another issue was getting a "privilege log," meaning a list of any documents being withheld from production under a claim of legal privilege.

We typically engaged in multiple discussions with a subpoenaed party's legal counsel over the documents we wanted and when they would be produced. Counsel typically asked for 30–60 days to conduct a good faith search, review the documents for possible privilege, redact nonresponsive or privileged content, add identifying numbers to track the pages being produced, and provide copies in electronic or physical format. To me, 30–60 days was a reasonable amount of time in most cases, even though I knew, when we told Senator Levin when the documents would arrive, he would typically shake his head and urge us to move faster.

In the case of KPMG, the problem wasn't that the firm needed time to make a good faith document production. And it wasn't confusion over the requests; the KPMG insider information had enabled us to get very specific about the documents we wanted. The problem was that KPMG didn't want to produce the documents at all.

KPMG's attitude was clear from the start. Whenever we sent a subpoena, we deliberately structured it to begin with clear and easy document requests before moving on to more difficult ones. That format facilitated the inevitable negotiations over the subpoena—moving from easier to harder categories of documents.

The first request in the KPMG subpoena asked for the tax division's organizational charts and telephone directories for certain years. KPMG failed to produce either. When confronted, the general counsel claimed, for example, that KPMG didn't have a telephone directory; it kept all of its employees' telephone numbers electronically with no physical document. Bob replied that the firm could satisfy the request by printing off the computer screens containing the telephone numbers. But KPMG continued to insist that it couldn't produce any telephone directory at all.

After nearly four months, the total number of documents KPMG had produced fit into two boxes. It was time to get serious. Luckily, by April 2003, it looked like we could do just that.

The new PSI chair, Senator Coleman, had finished hiring his investigative staff who were itching to get down to business. His staff director was Ray Shepherd, an experienced investigator from the House. He was a strong supporter of Congress as an institution, admired PSI's status as the Senate's premier investigative body, and was ready to defend its prerogatives. In addition, the Coleman staffer he'd assigned to the inquiry, Leland Erickson, had confirmed our complaint that KPMG had failed to produce even run-of-the-mill documents.

Ray met with Senator Coleman and got his approval to support the Levin document request. Senator Coleman gave his backing even though the inquiry had been initiated by Senator Levin in his last days as PSI chair, and KPMG was rumored to be pushing Senator Coleman to quash the subpoena and end the Levin-led inquiry. Instead, Ray directed us to set up a meeting.

The result was a two-hour, knock-down, drag-out confrontation with KPMG. We went through the subpoena line by line, noting KPMG's failure to produce most of the requested documents. Bob demanded that KPMG's lawyers identify the legal authority for withholding them. Ray told KPMG there was no excuse for the delay and demanded immediate compliance with the PSI subpoena. Our aggressive, bipartisan stance seemed to unsettle KPMG, but not enough to break the logjam. KPMG continued to produce virtually nothing.

Benefiting from a Leak

That changed on April 22, 2003, when the Wall Street Journal published an article disclosing that both KPMG and Ernst & Young had received document requests from PSI for information about abusive tax shelters.[1] Since our investigation had not been publicly known up until then, the article was seen as big news.

The press report was a surprise to us, since we had not breathed a word outside of PSI about the inquiry. It was flat out against our rules to break the confidentiality of an investigation, and we had no reason to believe Senator Coleman wanted anyone to know someone was defying a PSI subpoena. We never did find out who leaked the story, but my personal guess was that one of the KPMG insiders got fed up with the firm's stonewalling and contacted the press.

In any event, the news apparently exploded inside KPMG, and a partners' meeting was called in response. We later learned that some partners participating by conference call had put the call on speakerphone so others could listen in. Apparently, the KPMG brass had told virtually no one in the firm about the months-old Senate subpoena, and many partners were shocked and angry at having been kept in the dark. The partners demanded that the firm cooperate with the Senate. Within days, documents started pouring in.

By the end, we received over 235 boxes and several electronic compact disks from KPMG with hundreds of thousands of pages of documents.[2] They included memos, emails, letters, tax product descriptions, marketing material, and transactional documents. Together, they pulled back the curtain on KPMG's extensive, sordid entanglement with abusive tax shelters.

Investigating KPMG

Abusive tax shelters provide taxpayers with significant tax benefits never intended by the tax code. They typically have no economic substance or business purpose other than to reduce the user's taxes. Most are designed as complex business transactions that generate tax benefits, such as substantial paper losses that can be used to offset—or "shelter"—real income from taxes.

In the past, most tax shelters had been concocted by shady, fly-by-night firms. What had changed was that the world's premier accounting firms—$4 billion behemoths like KPMG—had entered the field, ramping up both the number and complexity of the tax gimmicks and systematically hawking them to anyone who would buy. Not only that, other professional businesses like banks, law firms, and investment advisors had gotten into the game. Alliances had formed to develop the infrastructure needed to design, market, and implement hundreds of abusive tax shelters. Tax shelters had become big business.

Documenting the exact role of the accounting firms in the tax shelter industry wasn't, however, easy. The four biggest accounting companies were private firms rather than publicly traded corporations, so there were no SEC filings to review. Few outsiders knew how the firms were organized or run. Frequent campaign contributions and aggressive lobbying had also built up their political influence. The Big Four were secretive and powerful.

At the same time, some of their conduct was so outrageous that the IRS and Justice Department had begun probing their tax activities. In 2002 and 2003, to settle DOJ charges that they'd violated rules requiring tax shelter promoters to register certain tax strategies with the IRS and maintain lists of participants, PricewaterhouseCoopers and Ernst & Young had paid fines and agreed to start following the rules.[3] KPMG, in contrast, was continuing to fight the IRS and DOJ every step of the way, denying it was a tax shelter promoter, rebuffing their information requests, and making law enforcement work for every shred of evidence.

KPMG may have thought it could do the same to PSI, but the insiders had already enabled us to leapfrog the firm's initial barriers. The documents they'd disclosed to us were staggering: evidence that KPMG's Tax Services Practice had developed over 500 "tax products" to sell to clients for lucrative fees. KPMG was marinating in money from its tax shelter racket.

The evidence suggested the racket was less than ten years old. The documents indicated that, in the late 1990s, the KPMG Tax Services Practice had undergone a fundamental change in direction, moving from providing individualized tax advice to clients who asked for help minimizing their taxes on legitimate business transactions to developing generic tax products that could be peddled across the country to clients who'd never sought them. Here's how it happened.

In 1997, the Tax Services Practice established a "Tax Innovation Center" with about a dozen employees. Each year after that, the Center had set a firm-wide numerical goal for new "tax products" and pressured KPMG tax partners to submit proposals to its "Tax Services Idea Bank." The Center then identified the proposals with the greatest revenue potential plus "speed to market," and assigned them to "National Development Champions." Those champions developed the proposals into generic tax products and asked KPMG's senior tax experts to sign off on the new products as compliant with the tax code.

Once approved for sale, each tax product was assigned to a "National Deployment Champion" charged with designing a marketing campaign. One sales tactic was to pressure KPMG tax partners to market the shelters to their existing clients. In the case of one shelter, we found an email exhorting tax partners to "SELL, SELL, SELL!!" Another warned: "Look at the last partner scorecard. Unlike golf, a low number is not a good thing. … A lot of us need to put more revenue on the board." Still another urged senior tax partners to "temporarily defer non-revenue producing activities" and concentrate for the "next 5 months" on meeting the office's revenue goals for the year. The email stated: "We are dealing with ruthless execution—hand to hand combat—blocking and tackling. Whatever the mixed metaphor, let's just do it."

In some cases, the tax partners pressured KPMG's audit partners to help sell tax products to the companies they audited, a conflict of interest since those same audit partners would later be required to determine whether the products met tax code requirements. Most surprising of all, we discovered a KPMG telemarketing "call center" in Fort Wayne, Indiana making cold calls to businesses across the country to sell KPMG tax products.

To understand at a deeper level what was going on, we decided to dig into the details of four specific tax shelters marketed by KPMG and known by the acronyms BLIPS, OPIS, FLIP, and SC2.[4] We learned that each had been constructed to look like a legitimate business investment, but actually involved phony partnerships, fake loans to shell companies from banks that never actually disbursed the funds, or investment activity that involved no real risk. The objective of most of the tax shelters was to generate millions of dollars in fake losses, which clients could then use to offset real income and thereby dodge paying taxes on their earnings.

The PSI team located emails from KPMG tax professionals reviewing and, in some cases, raising objections to the four transactions and pointing out flaws that risked a court invalidating the products. In response, some senior tax professionals made changes or pressed the skeptics to drop their objections; in others, higher-ups simply approved the products for sale anyway.

Bob uncovered one key piece of evidence that helped prove the tax shelters were a lot of hooey. He found that, in BLIPS, KPMG's fees were linked to the size of the loss generated by the tax product. In other words, the bigger the loss, the more the customer paid KPMG. What legitimate business investment based its fee on the size of the losses it produced?

We also found a memo discussing OPIS in which one KPMG partner seemed to advise breaking the law on tax shelter registrations. The federal tax code explicitly required tax shelter promoters to register their tax strategies with the IRS. But in the 1998 memo, a KPMG tax partner dispassionately analyzed the maximum amount of fines that the IRS might impose on the firm if it failed to register OPIS. The memo calculated that the maximum fine, $31,000, was far outweighed by the likely profits, $360,000, from KPMG's selling the shelter. The memo also noted that "the tax community at large continues to avoid registration of all products," which meant KPMG would be at a "severe competitive disadvantage" if it were to register its tax products with the IRS. The memo concluded that, even if OPIS qualified as a tax shelter legally required to be registered with the IRS, KPMG should not register it. And KPMG didn't register OPIS. In fact, for five years from 1998 to 2003, KPMG failed to register with the IRS a single one of its 500 tax products.

KPMG's tax shelter business didn't stop with designing and selling its tax products; the firm also actively implemented them. Because the shelters were so complex, clients needed help carrying out the required transactions. KPMG helped by identifying banks, investment advisors, and lawyers to execute the transactions; arranging favorable tax opinion letters; facilitating purported loans; preparing transactional documents; preparing tax returns; and offering other administrative services. It was a one-stop tax shelter service provider.

It was a lucrative line of business. We determined that, from 1997 to 2001, KPMG sold the four tax products we'd examined to more than 350 taxpayers for more than $124 million. And those revenues represented just a sliver of the 496 other tax products in KPMG's catalogue.

In addition to lining up KPMG documents illustrating the firm's abusive practices, we interviewed multiple KPMG tax professionals about the four tax products, including some who'd registered objections to them. But rather than admit the firm had been selling abusive tax shelters, almost all insisted they'd been marketing legitimate investment products.

One of our last interviews was with Jeffery Stein, a KPMG partner who'd held senior positions in the Tax Services Practice before becoming Deputy Chairman of the whole firm. Documents and interviews suggested he'd been a leader in the firm's decision to mass-market generic tax products. Bob led the questioning, in response to which Mr. Stein turned in one of the more brazen performances I'd witnessed.

First, he flat out denied that KPMG was a tax shelter promoter, despite the many documents indicating otherwise. In addition, at one point, Bob showed him a three-page email in which Mr. Stein described the flaws in one of the KPMG tax products, explained how a tax partner had devised a replacement product, and recommended that partner for a big bonus. When Bob asked him to explain the flaws in the earlier tax product, Mr. Stein coolly responded that he didn't really understand anything he had written in the email; he said he'd simply relied on information supplied to him by the tax partner seeking the bonus. He claimed he knew little to nothing about any of the tax products KPMG sold, and so could not answer our questions. His disdainful gaze made me think that he viewed our inquiry as a waste of his valuable time.

After completing the interviews, we wrote up the investigation's results in a 130-page staff report. As with our earlier reports, we coordinated closely with our Republican colleagues, running the text by them to see if they agreed with our characterizations. Leland offered many helpful suggestions which we incorporated. Senator Levin approved the final version and, as was our practice back then, issued it as a minority staff report.

Going Public

At Senator Levin's request and to show his support for the investigation, Senator Coleman scheduled two days of hearings, on a Tuesday and Thursday, November 18 and 20, 2003. On the Friday before the hearings, we held a press briefing in which we released the report to reporters and explained what we'd found. Due to the tax shelters' complexity, the press briefing took two hours. Senators Coleman and Levin spoke for the first 15 minutes or so and took questions on the record. After they left, we spoke on background to the reporters, describing the details of how the four tax shelters worked, how KPMG had developed, marketed, and implemented them, and the incriminating documents we'd discovered. Both Levin and Coleman staffers presented information, demonstrating the inquiry's bipartisan nature.

We distributed the report on an embargoed basis, meaning that all of the reporters who took a copy agreed not to publish an article with the information until the embargo ended that evening. The embargo period gave the reporters time to review the report, analyze the facts, and talk to KPMG and others, without having to rush out an article to beat their competitors. The end result was longer, more detailed, and more varied articles. The reporters loved that, and so did we. It also meant we got multiple days of press coverage—articles from the press briefing came out on Sunday and Monday, while articles based on the hearings appeared the rest of the week.

The pre-hearing press coverage was highly critical of KPMG's tax shelter activities. The hearing generated additional fireworks, with Senators Levin and Coleman taking a strong, bipartisan stance against the mass marketing of tax shelters by U.S. accounting firms and asking KPMG tough questions about its actions.

The first day took testimony from three panels: a group of tax shelter experts, a set of KPMG partners who handled the four targeted tax shelters, and a group of senior tax decisionmakers from not only KPMG but also Ernst & Young and PricewaterhouseCoopers (PwC).

The second panel got the toughest questions. One witness was a senior KPMG tax partner, Jeffrey Eischeid, who led the "Personal Financial Planning" group that administered FLIP, OPIS, and BLIPS. When asked if those tax products were designed primarily as tax reduction strategies, Mr. Eischeid denied it, testifying they were primarily investment products that also had attractive "tax attributes." Senator Levin responded with nearly a dozen documents describing them as tax reduction strategies. First, he quoted documents from the banks and investment firms working with KPMG. Mr. Eischeid protested that he was not responsible for what other firms said. Next, Senator Levin quoted documents produced by KPMG itself, including presentations made by KPMG personnel to other, cooperating firms. Mr. Eischeid responded that he was not responsible for how others at KPMG described the tax products.

Senator Levin then quoted documents authored by Mr. Eischeid himself, including one describing BLIPS as used to generate losses and another describing it as part of a portfolio of products "designed to mitigate an individual's income tax as well as estate and gift tax burdens." When confronted with his own documents, Mr. Eischeid mumbled, "Senator, I don't know how to change my answer to—." Senator Levin interrupted: "[T]ry an honest answer."

My favorite line of questioning came at the end of the day with Richard H. Smith, Jr., then head of KPMG's Tax Services Practice. He testified that KPMG had cleaned up its act and no longer offered aggressive tax strategies. Senator Levin asked him a simple question: whether over the prior five years, KPMG had encouraged the sale of its tax products to potential clients. Mr. Smith responded warily. He apparently realized if he said yes, it might portray KPMG as a tax shelter promoter with a responsibility to register its tax products with the IRS, a status the firm had been denying for more than a year. So he tried not to answer the question.

First he said KPMG, of course, offered tax advice to its clients and encouraged its professionals to serve their clients. When Senator Levin repeated his question—whether KPMG had encouraged the sale of its tax products to potential clients—Mr. Smith squirmed and rattled out the following:

In a number of different components of our business, we talk to our clients in many different ways, over the telephone and in writing, in meetings face-to-face, and we do encourage our tax professionals to meet with our clients and talk to them about the complexities of the tax code and to talk about their business and the things they ought to be thinking about from a tax perspective, yes.

The audience burst into laughter.

Senator Levin asked: "Is 'yes' the answer to my question?" Mr. Smith hemmed and hawed. That's when Senator Levin let him have it:

No, I am sorry. See, you come here and you are asking us to believe that you have basically changed your ways, things are done differently there now for various reasons. And, frankly, I am skeptical. And one of the reasons which makes me skeptical is I cannot get a straight answer out of you to a very direct question, whether or not KPMG encouraged the sale or acceptance of its tax products to potential clients. There is a mass of evidence that you did, but I cannot get you to say, 'Yes, one of the things we did was encourage the sale or acceptance of our tax products to potential clients.' … Even though it is obviously true. It is as clear as the nose on your face that it is true.

He asked his question again. Mr. Smith finally gave a short, clear answer: "Yes."

Senator Levin had taken nearly 15 minutes to get KPMG to admit it had encouraged the sale of its tax products. It was a question at the heart of whether KPMG had acted as a tax shelter promoter, and Senator Levin had refused to let the witness off the hook. Most Senators don't have the patience or discipline to ask the same question multiple times. Senator Levin demonstrated the value of taking the time to do so, not only to get a clear answer but also to show how cagey, even slippery, KPMG was. In addition, as he explained to me later, repeating the same point multiple times was the best way he knew to get listeners to focus on an issue. He said, "Until I say it three times, no one hears it." It was a lesson I didn't forget.

The second day of hearings featured some of the professional firms that worked with KPMG on its tax shelters. The witnesses included two law firms that wrote "independent" tax opinions supporting the tax shelters while secretly working with KPMG on the content; two banks that pretended to lend millions of dollars to shell entities as part of the transactions, while actually depositing the loan proceeds into accounts they controlled; and two investment advisory firms that had participated in rigged securities trades with no real risk. One of the lawyers, Raymond

Ruble, asserted his Fifth Amendment right against self-incrimination and was excused, but the rest were subjected to intense questioning that exposed the entire kabuki dance.

The final witness panel consisted of senior officials from three federal agencies: the IRS, Federal Reserve, and Public Company Accounting Oversight Board. All three decried what they'd heard and promised to clamp down on U.S. firms facilitating abusive tax shelters.

The hearings produced new rounds of incendiary press accounts describing the tax shelter industry. Senator Coleman got so fired up that he instructed Leland to write up the tax shelters devised by Ernst & Young and PwC, combine it with the KPMG tax shelters already described in the Levin report, and issue a follow-up bipartisan report showing how tax shelter wrongdoing had infected multiple accounting firms. He also convinced Senator Collins, the full committee chair, to hold a vote making it an official committee report. The whole process took two years, with the final official, bipartisan report issued in April 2005.[5]

Curbing Abusive Tax Shelters

Having exposed the tax shelter racket at the accounting firms, our next step was to try to stop it. The first thing we did, when the IRS and DOJ asked for the documents underlying our report, was to tie them up with a bow and turn them over. We also met with their investigators and prosecutors to explain what we'd learned and answer questions.

Two years later, in August 2005, DOJ announced criminal proceedings against KPMG, six of its tax partners, two bankers, and an outside lawyer, for designing, selling, and executing fraudulent tax shelters. A contrite KPMG signed a deferred prosecution agreement, admitted to engaging in criminal tax fraud, and paid a then-record $456 million fine. The DOJ press release stated: "In the largest criminal tax case ever filed, KPMG has admitted that it engaged in a fraud that generated at least $11 billion dollars in phony tax losses which, according to court papers, cost the United States at least $2.5 billion dollars in evaded taxes."[6]

A few months later, DOJ amended the indictment to add nine more KPMG tax partners and another financial advisor, for a total of 19 defendants.[7] While DOJ and the IRS had begun investigating KPMG long before we got started, it was clear our hearings had provided new information and momentum in their ongoing effort to take on those powerful adversaries.

As fate would have it, however, KPMG's tax leadership, including Jeffrey Stein, got off on a technicality. KPMG had a long history of voluntarily paying the legal fees incurred by its employees as a result of doing their jobs, including employees accused of crimes. But in the tax shelter case, when faced with multiple indictments, strong evidence of wrongdoing, and huge legal bills from attorneys going all out to defend that wrongdoing, KPMG announced a cap on the reimbursable legal fees of $400,000 per partner and an end to the payment of all fees in the event of an indictment or an employee's decision to stop cooperating with the government.

While most criminal defendants would have swooned at getting a $400,000 defense fund, KPMG's tax partners were outraged. They went to court and won. In an 80-page opinion, Judge Lewis Kaplan found that DOJ had pressured KPMG to limit its fees and, in so doing, violated the defendants' Constitutional rights to legal counsel, due process, and fair treatment.[8] To deter and punish DOJ's actions, the judge let all the KPMG tax partners walk. The Second Circuit Court of Appeals upheld his decision.[9] The result was that, while others later went to jail for their part in the massive tax shelter fraud, the KPMG masterminds got off scot free.

In the meantime, under its deferred prosecution agreement, KPMG cleaned house. It jettisoned virtually all the tax professionals and tax products involved in its tax shelter fiasco. Ernst & Young and PwC did the same. Over the following years, multiple E&Y tax partners were convicted of or pled guilty to tax crimes. In 2013, E&Y itself entered into a deferred prosecution agreement with DOJ, admitting it had sold illegal tax shelter products to about 200 clients dodging about $2 billion in taxes, and paid a fine of $123 million.[10] Other prosecutions targeted lawyers, bankers, and investment advisors involved in the schemes. The ultimate outcome: the accounting sector largely abandoned the tax shelter mass-marketing business.

The firms' exit from the tax shelter industry did not, however, shield them from the wrath of former clients. For years after, clients filed suit against the accounting firms for selling them illegal tax shelters leading to tax assessments, interest, and penalties. Years of paying settlements and legal fees in connection with those civil suits served as an added deterrent to the accounting firms peddling abusive tax shelters.

To further encourage an exodus from the tax shelter industry, Senator Levin ordered the staff to draft new legislation. In March 2004, he and Senator Coleman introduced the Tax Shelter and Tax Haven Reform Act, S. 2210. Key provisions sought to increase penalties on tax shelter promoters;

end tax benefits for transactions with no economic substance; restrict legal opinions supporting tax shelters; and cut off tax benefits and increase disclosures for transactions involving tax havens.

The Levin-Coleman bill was referred to the Senate Finance Committee which was already working on its own anti-tax shelter legislation which actually made it to the Senate floor. During the bill debate, the committee declined to include any Levin-Coleman provisions other than a narrow amendment to strengthen the bill's tax shelter promoter penalties.[11] A weakened version of those penalties made it into law later in 2004.[12]

In 2005, in the new 109th Congress, Senators Levin and Coleman reintroduced the bill as S. 1565 and added a new cosponsor, then Senator Barack Obama. While the Levin-Coleman-Obama bill didn't get very far, the three senators won a partial victory when the Public Company Accounting Oversight Board, which oversees the accounting industry, approved new conflict of interest limitations on the tax shelter services that accounting firms could provide to their audit clients.[13] That 2005 accounting reform arose straight out of PSI's work.

Another sign of progress was the IRS' collection of more than $3.7 billion in back taxes, interest, and penalties in connection with a set of fraudulent tax shelters that had been marketed by both KPMG and E&Y. IRS Commissioner Mark Everson handed out an award to the Coleman and Levin staffs for assisting in that tax shelter battle. At the time, we joked that if PSI could have collected just a 1% finder's fee, it could have funded a bigger staff and done a lot more to stop tax shelter abuses (Image 5.1).

Image 5.1 The 2005 IRS award: Bob Roach, Ray Shepherd, IRS Commissioner Mark Everson, Elise Bean and Leland Erickson. Source: IRS

Going Offshore

Our successful investigation into the accounting industry's tax shelter activities only whetted Senator Levin's appetite for the battle against tax dodging. He soon issued us a new challenge—to find out how tax professionals at home and abroad were using offshore tax havens to help U.S. taxpayers dodge taxes. He knew that we were already familiar with the offshore world from our money laundering investigations; he wanted to know if the financial institutions and offshore professionals facilitating money laundering were also assisting U.S. tax dodgers.

It was a good question. To get the answer, we decided the best course was to investigate actual instances of offshore tax abuse. Digging into specific case studies would help us get past the stereotypes, platitudes, and conventional wisdom to find out what was really going on. We started researching news reports and court cases, and asking offshore tax experts for worthwhile examples. As the investigation gained steam, Bob and I began adding staff, including Laura Stuber, Zack Schram, Julie Davis, a securities expert in the Levin personal office, and John McDougal, an IRS detailee with vast expertise in offshore tax issues. The Coleman staff, led by Mark Nelson and Leland Erickson, added still more energy and expertise.

In the end, we wrote up six case studies.[14] All six had wild facts, but two were particularly stunning in the depth of their offshore deceptions and brazen tax cheating. Both involved U.S. billionaires, multiple offshore shell entities, and an armada of bankers, lawyers, accountants, investment advisors, and trust and corporate service providers who facilitated the tax schemes. One of the case studies featured a pair of American brothers, the other an offshore tax shelter known as POINT. Together, the two case studies exposed the secrecy, duplicity, and abusive practices at the heart of offshore tax dodging.

The Wyly Offshore Network

The first case study featured Sam and Charles Wyly, two American success stories. Born into poverty and raised during the Great Depression, the brothers had become self-made billionaires with multiple profitable businesses. Their enterprises included three publicly traded companies, Sterling Software and Sterling Commerce, both focused on computer software, and Michael's Stores, an arts and crafts retail chain. The brothers were also major-league tax cheats.

The Levin inquiry was triggered by SEC reports filed by the Wylys in April 2005, disclosing publicly for the first time that a substantial number of Michael Stores shares were held in the name of offshore companies affiliated with the Wylys. The filings offered the first public clue to what would turn out to be an extensive network of 58 offshore trusts and corporations under the secret control of the Wyly brothers. PSI's investigation exposed not only that network, but also how the brothers had used it to produce over $700 million in concealed, untaxed gains for their families and businesses, while circumventing a host of U.S. tax, securities, and money laundering safeguards.

Investigating the Wylys

Sam and Charles Wyly were wealthy, prominent citizens of Texas, politically connected and litigious. When the Levin team contacted the Wylys' legal counsel with questions about the offshore entities described in the SEC filings, the brothers let the majority staff know they weren't pleased. Despite that stance, to his credit, Senator Coleman never wavered in his support for the Levin-led inquiry.

We eventually sent a series of document requests to the Wylys. To avoid being subpoenaed, the Wylys provided the requested materials voluntarily. A small Texas "family office" that handled the family's finances and investments became a key source of emails, financial reports, and other records.

We obtained additional documents from the U.S. banks and securities firms that maintained accounts for the Wyly-related offshore entities. Account statements, wire transfers, and other records helped us not only follow the money, but also identify more Wyly-related entities and accounts, as well as the individuals directing the financial activity. The list of Wyly-related offshore entities eventually topped out at 19 trusts and 39 corporations bearing a kaleidoscope of fanciful names like Bulldog Trust, Elegance Ltd., and Yurta Faf LLC.

One of the first things we noticed from the documents was that virtually all of the accounts were serviced by the same U.S. securities broker. We also noticed that most of the account signatories were employees of a handful of small companies located in the Isle of Man, an offshore secrecy jurisdiction. The Isle of Man companies specialized in administering offshore trusts and corporations; we learned they were the trustees of the Wyly-related trusts. Also named in the documents was a person working for a Wyly-related office in the Cayman Islands.

The documentation opened another window as well. It disclosed transfers of funds to and from a dozen businesses that also turned out to be under Wyly control, including two hedge funds called Maverick and Ranger, a private equity firm called First Dallas, an energy company called Green Mountain Energy Resources, and an offshore insurance company called Scottish Re. Other money transfers led to Wyly-related corporations that held U.S. real estate and other assets used by Wyly family members. Still others led to a mysterious company called Security Capital Ltd., with accounts at Queensgate Bank in the Cayman Islands.

One by one, we contacted the financial institutions, Isle of Man companies, businesses, and individuals named in the documents, and began piecing together the Wyly offshore empire. Altogether, we issued 40 subpoenas and document requests, and collected about 1.5 million pages from multiple sources. In all our inquiries, we made clear we were interested solely in the Wylys' offshore activities, not their domestic arrangements. While we were unable to subpoena any offshore entity directly—our subpoena authority did not reach beyond U.S. borders—numerous offshore communications popped up in the U.S. materials we were able to acquire.

To analyze the flood of information coming in, we formed small, overlapping teams and assigned them to specific entities or issues. The teams sorted and analyzed the documents, and developed lists and chronologies. Weekly meetings enabled the teams to update each other. Bit by bit, we built up a detailed composite picture of the Wylys' offshore activities.

Conducting Interviews

After months of document analysis, we initiated several rounds of interviews. One early meeting was with the Wylys' lead attorney, Bill Brewer, a principal of Bickel & Brewer, a Dallas law firm known for aggressive litigation. Mr. Brewer walked into our conference room the first time decked out in classic Texas fashion, including elegant cowboy boots. We learned later that he was born and raised in New York, but had recast himself as a Lone Star State enthusiast.

In response to our request for a detailed briefing, Mr. Brewer arrived at our conference room trailing several associates, one of whom carried a small projector. Mr. Brewer asked if he could take down a painting to display projections on the wall. We dimmed the lights, the projector started hissing, and in a thick Texas drawl, Mr. Brewer began recounting the Wyly brothers' football victories in high school and college, complete with photos. He then described their storied business careers. Not a word about their offshore activities. His presentation went on for about 45 minutes. Our investigators, on both sides of the aisle, listened in stony silence.

When the lights went up and Mr. Brewer sat back, Bob broke the silence by launching into a series of detailed questions about the Wylys' offshore network. The attorneys seemed taken aback by how much we knew. Mr. Brewer replied to most of the questions with long-winded answers that said little of substance. By meeting's end, the Wyly legal team had managed to stave off our questions without advancing our fact-finding, but we also sent them a message. The investigation was serious, bipartisan, and progressing.

Over the next couple of months, we interviewed multiple former and current Wyly employees. One of the most important was Michael French who'd worked for years as the Wyly family attorney, as an executive in several of their businesses, and as a so-called trust protector who oversaw their offshore trusts. Although he parted ways from the Wylys on less than amiable terms, Mr. French was very aware of and diligent about his legal obligations to his former clients. He and his counsel repeatedly declined to answer certain questions, citing his legal and ethical constraints. In response, we began focusing our questions on his administrative work related to the offshore trusts and corporations, steering clear of matters involving legal advice. Mr. French and his counsel appreciated that approach and, over time, as we fashioned questions they viewed as acceptable, Mr. French provided critical information.

Mr. French disclosed that he'd been present when the Wylys first launched their offshore effort, supervised formation of the offshore trusts and corporations, and helped select the Isle of Man trustees. We knew from the trust agreements that the Wyly trust protector could hire and fire the trustees at will, and confirmed that the Isle of Man companies served at the pleasure of Mr. French and, through him, the Wylys. We also learned that the Wylys, through Mr. French, had been intimately involved with the day-to-day activities of the offshore entities, using Mr. French as their liaison to the Isle of Man trustees.

When Mr. French left the Wylys, his trust protector duties were taken up by a Canadian citizen living in the Cayman Islands, Michelle Boucher. Ms. Boucher headed a Wyly-related Cayman corporation with the geographically misleading name of the Irish Trust Company. It essentially functioned as the Wylys' offshore family office. We were never able to interview Ms. Boucher directly, since she was beyond our subpoena authority and the Wylys declined to direct her to talk to us, but we read hundreds of her emails, which appeared in many of the email chains produced to PSI. They showed that Ms. Boucher, in her role as Wyly trust protector, regularly communicated with the Wylys, their employees and agents, and the Isle of Man trustees.

In contrast to the inaccessible Ms. Boucher, we were able to interview several employees of the official Wyly family office in Texas. The longtime head of that office was Sharyl Robertson who'd served as the Wyly family's chief financial officer and produced multiple financial reports for the brothers, including on their offshore holdings. She also acted as a secondary trust protector for the Wylys, filling in for Mr. French or Ms. Boucher when needed. Keeley Hennington was Ms. Robertson's administrative right hand, and eventually replaced her when Ms. Robertson became chief financial officer for the Wyly's first hedge fund, Maverick.

Another key interview was with Louis Schaufele, the Wylys' longtime securities broker. Mr. Schaufele, who lived in Dallas, handled dozens of accounts opened in the names of Wyly-related offshore entities. Over the years, he took those accounts with him as he changed jobs and moved from Credit Suisse First Boston to Lehman Brothers and then to Bank of America. We learned that the accounts he opened were not actually bank accounts, but securities accounts. While those accounts were designed to conduct security transactions, the documents showed they also routinely held and transferred substantial funds, functioning in effect as bank accounts as well as securities accounts for the offshore entities.

We tried to interview the Isle of Man companies that administered the Wylys' offshore trusts and corporations: IFG International, Lorne House, Trident Trust, and Wychwood Trust. But all four firms declined to speak with us about anything of substance, citing their country's secrecy laws. While we weren't surprised, we thought it important to have given them a chance to tell us whatever they wanted. We also met with the Isle of Man's financial regulators to clarify our understanding of Isle of Man law and the companies' standing and operations.

Finally, we asked to interview Sam and Charles Wyly, but both asserted their Fifth Amendment rights under the Constitution not to answer any questions.

Moving Millions Offshore

The document analysis and interviews took months to complete but, when done, produced a detailed picture of the Wylys' offshore activities. While the details were complex, the basic storyline was not. In a sentence, the Wylys moved millions of dollars worth of stock options offshore, paying virtually no U.S. tax; used the stock options to generate at least $700 million in untaxed offshore money; and then spent those offshore dollars on themselves, their families, and their businesses, while again paying virtually no U.S. tax.

The Wylys' ability to establish, operate, and benefit from an extensive offshore network of trusts and corporations—avoiding detection until they self-disclosed some of the companies more than a decade later—was due in large part to the many professionals who'd guided their actions. The case study provided a powerful example of how bankers, lawyers, brokers, and other tax and financial professionals facilitate offshore abuses by America's wealthiest.

The Wyly offshore story began in 1992, when with the assistance of tax attorneys David Tedder and Michael Chatzky, the Wylys used an elaborate process to transfer offshore about three million stock options and warrants worth an estimated $42 million. Two more offshore transfers followed over the next ten years, for a total of 17 million stock options and warrants worth an estimated $190 million.

The brothers had obtained their stock options and warrants as compensation for services at their U.S. publicly traded corporations. Ostensibly, the Wylys transferred the stock options and warrants to the offshore entities in exchange for annuity contracts in which the offshore entities promised to make millions of dollars in fixed annuity payments to the brothers starting about ten years later. The Wylys entered into those contracts even though the offshore entities were shell operations with no employees, no offices, no investment track record, and no assets other than the stock options and warrants given to them. On its face, handing over multi-million-dollar assets to such ill-equipped entities made no investment sense.

But it did make sense in the context of a tax deferral scheme. The Wylys' tax advisers told the brothers, because the offshore entities made no immediate payment for the stock options or warrants, the brothers didn't have to pay any tax on those assets, even though they represented compensation worth millions of dollars. The advisers counseled that the tax could be deferred until the annuity payments began years later. The tax advisers also told the Wylys they had no legal obligation to report any income earned by the allegedly independent offshore entities.

In reality, however, the offshore entities were anything but independent from the Wylys. Hundreds of emails, faxes, and other documents showed that, from day one, the Wylys had exercised near constant control over every entity in their offshore empire, directing their spending, investments, and other actions. If the extent of their control had been known, the offshore entities' income could have been immediately attributed to the brothers as taxable income, but their controlling role was concealed instead for years.

The documents showed that, to exercise control, the Wylys typically communicated their offshore instructions to one of their trust protectors—Michael French, Michelle Boucher, or Sharyl Robertson—via email, a telephone call, or a meeting. The trust protector then recast the instructions as "recommendations" and communicated them in writing or by telephone to the relevant

Isle of Man trustee. The trustee then allegedly made a final decision on whether to act on the recommendations, considering its fiduciary obligation to protect the trust assets.

What we learned from both the documents and interviews, however, was that in 13 years the trustees had never failed to take an action "recommended" by the Wylys nor had they ever initiated an action on their own.[15] The whole thing was a sham. The trustees didn't run the offshore trusts and corporations; the Wylys did.

Using the Offshore Funds

The documents also showed how the Wylys turned the $190 million in stock options and warrants into more than $700 million in gains. The evidence made it clear that it was the Wylys—not the Isle of Man trustees—who had the business acumen to more than triple the value of their offshore holdings. The Wylys then spent the funds on themselves, their families, and businesses.

The documents showed, for example, how the Wylys directed the offshore entities to exercise the options and warrants they'd been given, acquire the underlying stock, and use that stock to make money. In some cases, the Wylys instructed a trust or corporation to sell the stock and reinvest the cash; in others they directed the trust or corporation to pledge the stock as collateral for a loan or use it in a complex financial deal such as an equity swap or variable prepaid forward. On a few occasions, the Wylys appeared to direct stock trades while in possession of material nonpublic information about the relevant publicly traded corporations, raising insider trading concerns. Throughout, the Wylys failed to file any forms with the SEC disclosing the offshore entities' significant stock holdings and relationship to the Wylys.

The Wylys also instructed the offshore trusts and corporations on how to invest their stock profits, including in Wyly-related businesses such as the Maverick and Ranger hedge funds, First Dallas fund, Green Mountain Energy company, and Scottish Re insurance firm. We traced about $600 million in untaxed offshore funds invested in Wyly-related business ventures.

Other documents disclosed how the Wylys used another $85 million in offshore funds to purchase U.S. real estate for themselves and their families. A Texas law firm, Meadows Owens, designed a U.S. management trust that enabled the Wylys' offshore entities to pay 99% of the U.S. real estate acquisition and operating costs without disclosing the funds' offshore origin.

That arrangement was used to purchase, for example, a 244-acre ranch outside Aspen, Colorado for Sam Wyly and his family for about $11.3 million.[16] Meadows Owens created a three-tier ownership structure. The immediate owners of record for the ranch were two U.S. limited liability companies (LLCs) formed in Colorado. They were owned, in turn, by a U.S. management trust. That trust had two trustees, Sam Wyly and a newly formed Isle of Man shell company. Trust documents showed that Mr. Wyly held a 1% "trust share" in the U.S. management trust, while the offshore company held the remaining 99%. Both trustees were given "full and complete Usage" of all trust property. To buy the ranch, Mr. Wyly contributed about $110,000 to the U.S. management trust, while the offshore shell company—using funds provided by other Wyly-related offshore entities—supplied more than $11.2 million. The U.S. management trust then transferred the funds—concealing the offshore origin of 99% of the money—to the Colorado LLCs to make the purchase.

Over the next decade, Mr. Wyly and his six children designed and built six homes on the ranch. By 2004, internal documents showed Mr. Wyly had supplied about $434,000 of the cost, while the offshore company supplied more than $43 million. Again, those funds were first paid to the U.S. management trust which then forwarded the money to the Colorado LLCs which paid the bills. Using that multi-step process continued to conceal the LLCs' use of offshore funds to pay the expenses. The ranch's multiple homes, maintained almost entirely with offshore dollars, served as the personal residences of Wyly family members when skiing in Colorado.

The Wylys didn't stop with real estate. They also directed various offshore entities to spend still another $30 million in offshore dollars on lavish furnishings and artwork decorating their homes or on jewelry worn by family members.[17] Examples included a $937,500 portrait of Ben Franklin, a $162,000 bureau cabinet, a $622,000 ruby, and a $759,000 emerald necklace, all of which were selected, held, and used by individual Wyly family members. Another $870,000 paid for 20 family portraits. When asked about those portraits, the Wyly legal counsel claimed they were artwork "investments" made by the offshore trusts. Right. In reality, the offshore dollars spent on family portraits, jewels, antiques, and other artwork gracing the Wyly homes were more proof of the Wylys' absolute control over their offshore wealth.

One final twist also deserves mention. It involves the mysterious company called Security Capital Ltd.[18] Security Capital turned out to be a Cayman corporation formed by Queensgate Bank and Trust, a Cayman company that presented itself as a bank and provided accounts for multiple Wyly-related offshore entities. Security Capital Ltd. was owned by a supposedly charitable trust, Security Capital Trust, which was also formed by Queensgate and was officially owned by no one. Neither the trust nor corporation had any employees or physical presence of its own; both were shell operations run by Queensgate employees. And Security Capital served only one function—as a gateway for Wyly offshore funds into the United States.

It worked like this. When the Wylys wanted to use some of their offshore funds, they sometimes instructed an offshore entity to wire cash to Security Capital's account at Queensgate and characterize the funds as a "loan." Over five years, eight Wyly-related offshore entities sent millions of dollars in alleged "loans" to Security Capital. Upon receiving a slug of offshore cash, Security Capital immediately issued a "loan" in the same amount to one of the Wylys or a Wyly-related business venture, as directed by Wyly personnel. Funneling the "loans" through a company with an impressive-sounding name like "Security Capital" helped disguise the fact that Wyly-related offshore entities were sending untaxed offshore cash to the Wylys in the United States.

Over five years, Security Capital issued ten pass-through "loans" to the Wylys, their children, or businesses totaling $140 million. Although all were substantial in size, ranging from $1.5 million to $56 million, some of the "loans" were unsecured, had low interest rates, or did not require repayment of the principle for years. On top of that, when the Wylys repaid the "loans" with "interest," they sent the money back offshore while simultaneously generating tax deductions for their "interest" payments. Security Capital turned out to be just another brazen offshore scam—one that generated phony tax deductions while allowing the Wylys to secretly access their hidden offshore cash—all made possible with the help of Queensgate.

By the time we concluded our investigation, we'd mapped the most extensive and intricate offshore network we'd ever seen. It was a startling showing by the Texas duo.

Going Public

We wrote up the Wyly case history in a joint Levin-Coleman staff report. It followed by a year the Coleman-Levin report we'd issued on tax shelter promoters. Our work on that earlier report made it a natural for us to team up again on a joint report describing not just the Wylys, but all six of the case studies we'd compiled during our offshore tax investigation. The report title said it all: "Tax Haven Abuses: The Enablers, The Tools and Secrecy."[19]

The final report was 450 pages long, with 100 pages on the Wyly case study alone. Since we knew the Wylys' lawyers would pounce on any mistakes, we were careful to build the text around the many incriminating documents we'd unearthed, quoting from them at length with only a few sentences of explanation before and after. While none of the documents was a smoking gun in and of itself, together the documents told an ugly story of offshore deceit, complete with hidden accounts, offshore shell companies, multi-million-dollar transfers, and multiple tax maneuvers. It felt good to expose the Wylys' misconduct using their own words.

As had become our practice, we held a two-hour joint press briefing on the day before the hearing to explain to the media what we'd found. We distributed embargoed copies of the report so that the media could digest the facts. Senators Levin and Coleman opened the briefing with a summary of the six case studies and our findings and recommendations. After they left, the staff went through the report in detail and answered reporters' questions.

The hearing took place on a Tuesday. Sam and Charles Wyly should have been center stage, but were noticeably absent. In response to a PSI letter asking them to testify, their legal counsel stated that the Wylys were asserting their Fifth Amendment rights and did not plan to appear at the hearing. When other witnesses took that tack, we typically issued a subpoena requiring their appearance, not only to forestall arguments that they never had a chance to make their case in public, but also to provide a last ditch opportunity for them to reconsider and testify. But in the case of the Wylys, Senator Coleman made a different decision. In our fifteen years on PSI, the Wylys were the only oversight subjects permitted to assert their Fifth Amendment rights without making a personal appearance at a PSI hearing.

In their absence, the key Wyly witness became Michael French. Under questioning, he confirmed that the Wylys were behind the formation of all 58 of the Wyly-related offshore trusts and corporations and had actively directed their activities. At one point, Senator Levin paraded in a series of charts filled with quotations from Wyly emails and other documents directing the offshore entities to act. Mr. French testified that he had communicated those instructions to the offshore trustees in the guise of "recommendations," all of which were carried out.

The hearing also heard from Louis Schaufele, the Bank of America securities broker who handled the accounts opened by the offshore entities. He admitted knowing that the Wylys were behind the accounts, yet treated the accounts as owned by foreign account holders whose account information did not have to be reported on 1099 forms to the IRS. He also admitted that when another broker processing securities transactions for Bank of America had pressed him for information about the account holders, Mr. Schaufele and Bank of America had refused to provide specifics, despite the 2001 Patriot Act requiring securities firms to know their customers.

Holding the Wylys Accountable

After the hearing, it took time, but the facts uncovered in the Wyly investigation slowly began to produce policy changes and enforcement actions. In 2010, a full four years after the hearing, Senator Levin won enactment of legislation ending the ability of U.S. taxpayers to use offshore trusts to purchase U.S. real estate, jewelry, furnishings, and artwork without paying taxes on the funds spent on their behalf.[20]

In 2014, eight years after our hearing, the SEC won a civil trial against the Wylys.[21] The jury found the Wylys liable on nine counts of civil securities fraud stemming from hiding their ownership of stock in their publicly-traded corporations by holding that stock in the name of offshore entities. Based upon the jury's verdict and other evidence, the court determined that the Wylys had engaged in the ruse primarily to evade U.S. taxes.[22] The court ruled that the Wylys had to disgorge the profits generated by their securities fraud and, in response to an SEC request, measured their illicit profits using a rough approximation of the taxes the Wylys had failed to pay.[23] The final judgment ordered the two Wylys to pay disgorgement and interest that, together, totaled about $300 million.[24]

The Wylys were outraged, not only by the jury verdict, but also by the size of the dollar judgment. Despite Sam Wyly's having been listed in *Forbes* magazine for years as one of the 400 richest Americans with an estimated net worth of around $1 billion[25]—an amount that didn't include his hidden offshore wealth—the Wylys decided to try to get out of paying the $300 million judgment by declaring bankruptcy.

That legal tactic backfired, however, when the IRS stepped in and asserted a tax claim in bankruptcy court. The IRS requested payment of back taxes and interest on the Wylys' undeclared stock option compensation and offshore income stretching all the way back to when the brothers first went offshore in 1992. In addition, the IRS requested, and the bankruptcy court agreed, that all factual issues settled in the SEC case could not be re-litigated.[26] Relying on those factual findings and other evidence, the bankruptcy court held the Wylys had committed tax fraud and owed the IRS $1.1 billion.[27] The Wylys immediately vowed to contest the ruling.

It had taken ten years, but by 2016, the PSI investigation of the Wylys had produced a series of positive policy outcomes. They included stronger statutory safeguards against abusive tax practices by offshore trusts, case law establishing that corporate executives who use offshore entities to hide stock ownership are guilty of securities fraud, and solid proof that wealthy and powerful individuals who hide money offshore can incur severe tax consequences. Not bad.

The POINT Tax Shelter

The Wyly case study was a doozy, but a second case study developed during the same 2006 offshore tax investigation was every bit as brazen. It involved an off-shore tax shelter known as the Personally Optimized INvestment Transaction or "POINT." POINT was used by a handful of wealthy U.S. taxpayers to generate fake stock losses to offset otherwise taxable capital gains of more than $2 billion, dodging taxes totaling nearly $400 million.[28] Brainchild of a Seattle securities firm known as the Quellos Group, it offered another striking illustration of the offshore gimmicks designed by tax professionals to facilitate U.S. tax evasion.[29]

Investigating POINT

Quellos, the Seattle securities firm that dreamed up POINT, had already crossed swords with PSI for participating in some of the illegal KPMG tax shelters we'd examined back in 2003. As part of that inquiry, we'd tangled with Quellos CEO Jeff Greenstein who'd testified at our hearing. We hadn't been impressed with his or his company's ethics back then, and suspected the POINT tax shelter wouldn't turn out much better.

We dove into the facts by subpoenaing documents from various partici-pants. They included Quellos; HSBC, a major bank that issued loans in con-nection with several POINT transactions; and six U.S. clients who purchased the tax strategy. We amassed the usual load of documents and set up teams to go through them.

POINT turned out to be enormously complicated. After several months of document analysis, we began interviews to learn more. First up was a week-long trip to Seattle to talk to multiple Quellos executives involved with design-ing, promoting, and executing the POINT transactions. Bob Roach from the Levin staff and Leland Erickson from the Coleman staff made the trip. The interviews were long and difficult, but produced a lot of information.

Next we interviewed several bankers who'd worked with Quellos and helped finance the POINT transactions. We also interviewed two tax attor-neys who'd backed the strategy. Lewis Steinberg, a big-time tax attorney from the firm of Cravath, Swain, & Moore, had worked directly with Quellos on the design of the tax shelter and issued an opinion letter stating POINT complied with the tax code. A second supportive tax opinion letter came from John Barrie of Bryan Cave, another large law firm. As reputable tax lawyers, their opinion letters had apparently been viewed by Quellos as key to selling the strategy to prospective clients.

We also interviewed two U.S. billionaires who'd purchased the tax shelter, Haim Saban and Robert Wood Johnson IV, both of whom traveled to our conference room in Washington to answer questions. During his interview, Mr. Saban, who'd earned his initial wealth from marketing the popular action figures the Mighty Morphin Power Rangers, explained that he had sold his interest in the Fox Family Channel to Disney for a $1.5 billion profit. His longtime tax attorney had then advised him that he could effectively avoid paying any tax on that profit by engaging in a POINT transaction that would generate losses to offset his gains.

Mr. Saban told us that his tax adviser had attempted to explain POINT to him, but it was too complex for him to follow. Mr. Saban said he'd instead asked his attorney two questions: whether the arrangement was "kosher," and whether a reputable law firm would say so in writing. After being told yes, Mr. Saban said he purchased the tax shelter for about $50 million.

During his interview, Woody Johnson explained he'd sold a large block of stock in his family's company, Johnson & Johnson, to finance his purchase of the Jets football team. His profits totaled about $143 million. To avoid paying tax on his stock gain, he'd engaged in a POINT transaction that allegedly generated stock losses to offset his gain. He said that he, too, paid Quellos a multi-million-dollar fee to purchase and execute the POINT transaction.

Finally, we contacted the European American Investment Group—Euram—a financial services provider involved with the POINT transactions. Euram was headquartered abroad, operated in major financial capitals around the world, and employed professionals formerly with top banks and firms.[30] The Euram employees who handled POINT lived outside of the United States and so were beyond our subpoena power. While Euram declined to make them available for an interview, the firm did agree to allow them to answer written questions. Eventually, Euram sent us an email with explosive information about how phony POINT really was.

Learning the Scam

Together, the interviews and documents laid bare how POINT worked. At the heart of the scam were two shell companies, Jackstones and Barnville, formed in the Isle of Man and capitalized with less than £2, or about $5, each. Since neither company had employees or a physical presence, we were unable to discover how to contact them. More, no one would tell us who owned the companies. The Isle of Man agents responsible for forming the companies explained that the country's secrecy laws barred them from disclosing ownership information. All of the other players that dealt with the two companies, including Quellos, HSBC, and the tax lawyers, claimed not to know who was behind them.

When we examined the shell companies' activities, we found a collection of twisted derivatives, phantom partnerships, and financing gimmicks that supposedly had produced a stock portfolio worth in excess of $9 billion. The portfolio's ridiculous size didn't pass the laugh test. When asked how companies with less than $5 in capital each generated a stock portfolio worth $9 billion, Quellos executives produced stacks of documents filled with legal jargon and talked a mile a minute about complex derivatives. But no one at PSI bought the Quellos snake oil that the firm had discovered how to use swaps and hedges to produce something out of nothing.

The story came down to the assertion that the two Isle of Man companies created their stock portfolio simply by exchanging contracts with each other. Under the contracts, Jackstones—which owned no stock—"sold" shares to Barnville in exchange for a specified amount of cash—which Barnville did not actually have. At the same time, Barnville "loaned" the stock—which it had not actually received—back to Jackstones in exchange for a specified amount of cash collateral to secure the "loan"—cash which Jackstones did not actually possess. Because the two transactions were undertaken simultaneously, Quellos claimed that the obligations to pay each other equal amounts of stock and cash were offset. The result was a stock portfolio that allegedly popped into existence even though no stock or cash had actually changed hands.

The baloney didn't stop there. The portfolio that sprang into existence from the tandem Jackstones-Barnville contracts named stocks that had been selected by Quellos to represent overvalued companies whose stock prices were likely to fall. And many did fall. Quellos then allocated the paper losses to partnerships formed with POINT clients, including Mr. Saban and Mr. Johnson, who used the losses to offset their real capital gains. Picking up a trick from KPMG's tax shelters, Quellos assessed its fees according to the size of the losses generated. In other words, the bigger the stock loss produced, the bigger the fee owed to Quellos.

While POINT's phony features had been hinted at in various documents, the killer proof came in an email from Euram which claimed that everyone knew or was supposed to know that the POINT shell companies never actually purchased any stock or exchanged actual cash. The email, sent by the head of the Euram Structured Products Group in response to written questions from PSI, stated in part:

> It was always the case that the portfolio of securities traded by and between Barnville and Jackstones was of a purely contractual book-entry nature. This was

understood by all concerned given the dollar values of the portfolios in question. The sale and purchase of the securities were accomplished through contractual commitments ... which gave rise to legal obligations which were recorded in the entities' respective books and records. ... Because the transactions were conducted in this manner ... no physical transfer of shares were made. No transactions took place over any exchange and no cash transfers passed between bank accounts of the two companies. ... Euram obtained assurances from Quellos that the book-entry nature of these transactions had been known by the counsel with whom they developed the strategy and that it would be disclosed to any client advisor and opinion provider involved in any subsequent implementation.[31]

No cash, no stocks, no trades. The POINT stock portfolio involved, instead, "book entry" transactions supposedly "understood by all concerned."

But all concerned did not admit to that understanding. Mr. Saban and Mr. Johnson claimed they had no idea that their stock losses came from transactions that didn't involve real stock sales. The two tax attorneys whose opinion letters supported POINT also claimed ignorance. So did the key bank, HSBC. Everyone was shocked, just shocked, that the offshore companies didn't actually have any cash or stocks. Quellos, which loudly objected to our relying on Euram's email without interviewing Euram's executives, didn't actually dispute the facts.

Going Public

We wrote up the POINT case study in the same 450-page Levin-Coleman staff report that included the Wyly case. As with our other reports, the Coleman staff offered extensive comments on the text, which we largely accepted. Senator Levin also reviewed and edited the draft. Along the way, he requested, and we provided copies of key documents cited in the report, so he could track what happened. By the end of the report review process, he had the facts down cold.

Despite intense pushback from Quellos, Senator Coleman scheduled a hearing for the first day of August 2006. The hearing featured both the POINT and Wyly case studies. We held our usual press briefing the day before the hearing and described all six of the case histories we'd developed in the offshore tax investigation. We provided the reporters with embargoed copies of the report to give them time to review the information, ask questions, and write their articles.

Due to its complexity, we worked extra hard to explain the POINT tax shelter. As part of that effort, we developed a chart depicting the details of how it worked.

Senator Levin viewed charts as critical to communicating information about complex subjects. I'm not sure he ever held a hearing without at least one chart. He was also very demanding about their design and wording. He wanted each chart to make an immediate visual statement on a major point in the hearing, while also presenting key factual information. It wasn't unusual for us to bring him numerous drafts of various charts, each of which Senator Levin patiently reviewed and revised, explaining what he wanted.

When the Senate Service Department that produced our hearing charts saw us coming, to its credit, no one actually hid. The crew instead took a breath, smiled, and repeatedly churned out multiple versions of the same chart without complaint, perhaps because we brought them treats after hearings to thank them for their diligence.

We expected the typical lengthy process on our POINT chart, but for once, that's not what happened. Working with an intern who was a graphics whiz, Bob produced a chart that mapped out the POINT tax shelter in all its dishonesty. Colorful boxes depicted the entities and phony linkages used to turn $9 billion of nothing into multi-billion-dollar stock losses. As soon as he saw the chart, Senator Levin smiled. It immediately conveyed an unmistakable message—the POINT tax shelter was an unholy concoction. One look and the viewer knew it was no good (Image 5.2).

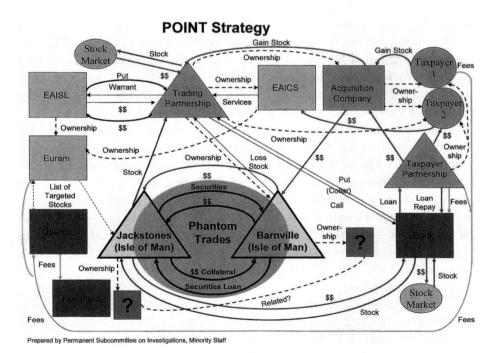

Image 5.2 Point Strategy chart. Source: 2006 Senate Hearing Exhibit 6

When the media articles appeared the next morning, it was clear the reporters had digested POINT's essential features and saw it as a deceptive tax dodge for the wealthy.

Holding the Hearing

In the hearing the next day, it was tough to tell whether the POINT or Wyly case study proved to be the more dramatic example of offshore tax abuse.

The POINT-related witnesses seemed to vie with each other over who knew the least and could disassociate themselves the most from the tax strategy. Quellos, architect of the scam, and HSBC, the financier, both claimed they didn't know who owned the shell companies controlling the POINT transactions and didn't realize they had no real assets. Quellos and HSBC took that tack despite their legal obligation to know their customers. The lawyers who issued the favorable POINT opinion letters—one of whom made $125,000 in fees and the other $1.3 million—claimed to have been unaware of the fake stock trades, the purported $9 billion stock portfolio, and the shell company owners. It was a parade of denials and failures to inquire.

In contrast, one fact became very clear. Under questioning, Quellos CEO Jeff Greenstein admitted his firm's fees were tied to the size of the losses POINT generated for its clients. The greater the loss, the greater the Quellos fee. Senator Levin asserted that the fee calculation said it all—it proved POINT was intended to produce losses for its buyers, not investment profits.

The standout witness at the hearing was Mr. Saban. He didn't invoke his Fifth Amendment rights like the Wylys. He didn't beat around the bush or duck the facts. He testified that POINT had been sold to him as a tax avoidance strategy, not an investment. He admitted he'd paid nearly $50 million to avoid paying a dime in taxes on profits of $1.5 billion. He said he'd relied on his tax advisor's representation that POINT was legal, but wasn't proud of his actions—that the United States had given him so much, he should have given back. After the hearing, he settled his federal tax bill, wrote a nine-figure check, and got right with Uncle Sam. Woody Johnson also paid the taxes he'd dodged.

The last hearing panel was perhaps the most dispiriting. It consisted of four tax lawyers—the two who'd issued the favorable POINT opinions and the two who'd facilitated the Wyly offshore scam. The POINT lawyers came from prominent firms that charged top dollar for tax advice; the Wyly lawyers came from smaller firms offering tax services. While the two big-firm lawyers wore expensive suits, spoke softly, and strained to differentiate themselves from the two tax practitioners sporting cheaper threads, to me all four spoke the same language of tax avoidance, transactional complexity, and offshore maneuvering. To me, all four radiated tax sleaze. It was a sad commentary on the legal profession's role in too many tax matters today.

The hearing lasted five hours, from about 9:00 a.m. to 2:00 p.m. That sounds like a long time, but it wasn't. We'd wanted separate witness panels for the Wyly and POINT case studies, but to save time at Senator Coleman's request, we combined the Wyly and POINT witnesses on the same panels. The result was a somewhat confusing dialogue as senators switched back and forth between the two case studies when questioning each panel. Some witnesses ended up undergoing intense questioning, while others escaped attention. It showed that complex case studies required separate panels if each set of facts was to be clearly presented and probed.

Holding Wrongdoers Accountable

Like the Wyly hearing, it took time for the POINT repercussions to play out. But play out they did, with key POINT participants eventually held accountable for their actions.

One set of repercussions unfolded after Mr. Saban learned that his longtime tax adviser, Matthew Krane, had taken a kickback from Quellos to recommend using the POINT tax shelter. By the time of the hearing, Mr. Krane had left the country. But by 2009, Mr. Krane was back in the United States, jailed on charges of defrauding Mr. Saban and laundering the proceeds of his crime.[32] In 2011, he pled guilty to evading taxes on a $36 million kickback from Quellos and trying to obtain a passport under a false name.[33] He was sentenced to 32 months in prison, paid $23 million in back taxes, and returned $18 million to Mr. Saban.

Mr. Krane wasn't the only one whose misdeeds led to imprisonment. In 2009, the Justice Department indicted the two top Quellos executives involved with POINT.[34] Unlike the KPMG tax shelter masterminds, neither got off on a technicality. In 2010, Quellos CEO Jeff Greenstein and lead tax attorney Charles Wilk pleaded guilty, paid fines totaling $7.4 million, and received prison sentences exceeding four years each.[35] Needless to say, POINT was never used again.

Tackling Offshore Tax Abuse

Our 2006 investigation—which extended beyond the Wyly and POINT case studies—laid bare a thriving industry of financial professionals, at home and abroad, making a living by facilitating tax evasion through offshore jurisdictions. As Senator Levin said at the hearing, those offshore secrecy jurisdictions had, in effect, "declared economic war on U.S. taxpayers by giving tax dodgers the means to avoid their tax bills and leave them for others to pay."

To fight back, we strengthened the Levin-Coleman-Obama tax shelter bill from the prior Congress. The three senators introduced the newly named "Stop Tax Haven Abuse Act" in 2007.[36] Among other provisions, it authorized the Treasury Department to take special measures against jurisdictions and financial institutions that impeded U.S. tax enforcement; imposed new requirements on U.S. taxpayers who did business in 34 named tax havens; and enabled U.S. authorities to presume that offshore entities were controlled by the U.S. taxpayer who formed them, sent them assets, or benefited from their actions, unless the taxpayer proved otherwise.

The next year, in 2008, the same three senators introduced a second bill focused on the problem of U.S. shell corporations.[37] We'd learned during the course of multiple PSI investigations that U.S. corporations were being used to perpetrate not only tax crimes but also money laundering, terrorism, drug trafficking, financial fraud, and other wrongdoings.

The bill tackled the issue by trying to clean up our own backyard. We'd learned that the United States formed nearly two million corporations per year—more than the rest of the world put together—but never even asked who was behind them. Instead, every year, states like Delaware, Wyoming, and Nevada churned out U.S. shell companies with hidden owners, some of which inevitably ended up involved with wrongdoing. The Levin-Coleman-Obama bill required the 50 states, each time they formed a U.S. corporation, to get the names of the true owners behind it and penalized any false information provided on the "beneficial owners."

Both bills represented our best efforts to come up with creative, cost-effective ways to curb offshore tax abuse. The first bill went to the Senate Finance Committee and the second to the Homeland Security and Government Affairs Committee. But neither took any action.

Together, the KPMG, Wyly, and POINT investigations drove home some uncomfortable truths. They demonstrated that tax evasion by the wealthiest among us was rampant in the United States, and was being facilitated by some of our top business professionals. The tax dodging was undermining public trust in the U.S. tax system, and forcing honest taxpayers to pick up the tab for those who could afford high-priced help to cheat Uncle Sam. Those somber facts did not, however, deter Senator Levin; they energized him. He was just getting started.

Notes

1. "Senate Panel Seeks Documents on Accountants' Tax Shelters," *Wall Street Journal*, Cassell Bryan-Low (4/22/2003), http://on.wsj.com/2hBblWw. The article did not mention the subpoenas we'd sent to KPMG and Ernst & Young, only document requests, suggesting the leak came from someone with limited knowledge of the PSI investigation.
2. The information in this section is based on the following PSI reports and hearings: "U.S. Tax Shelter Industry: The Role of Accountants, Lawyers, and Financial Professionals; Four KPMG Case Studies: FLIP, OPIS, BLIPS, and SC2," S. Prt. 108-34 (11/18 & 20/2003); "U.S. Tax Shelter Industry: The Role of Accountants, Lawyers, and Financial Professionals," S. Hrg. 108-473, Volumes 1–4 (11/18, 20/2003), https://www.gpo.gov/fdsys/pkg/CHRG-108shrg91043/pdf/CHRG-108shrg91043.pdf (Volume 1); "The Role of Professional Firms in the U.S. Tax Shelter Industry," S. Rept. 109-54 (4/13/2005) (hereinafter "2005 Tax Shelter Committee Report").
3. See, for example, IRS News Release No. IR-2003-84 (7/2/2003) (IRS Settlement with E&Y); "Pricewaterhouse and I.R.S. Settle Tax Shelter Dispute," *New York Times*, David Cay Johnston (6/28/2002), http://nyti.ms/2zUec52.
4. BLIPS is an abbreviation for Bond Linked Issue Premium Structure. OPIS stands for Offshore Portfolio Investment Strategy. FLIP stands for Foreign Leveraged Investment Program. SC2 stands for S-Corporation Charitable Contribution Strategy.
5. 2005 Tax Shelter Committee Report.
6. "KPMG to Pay $456 Million for Criminal Violations in Relation to Largest-Ever Tax Shelter Fraud Case," Department of Justice Press Release (8/29/2005), https://www.justice.gov/archive/opa/pr/2005/August/05_ag_433.html.
7. See "Superseding Indictment of 19 Individuals Filed in KPMG Criminal Tax Fraud Case," Department of Justice Press Release (10/17/2005), http://www.justice.gov/archive/opa/pr/2005/October/05_tax_547.html.
8. *United States v. Stein*, Case No. S1 05 Crim. 0888 (LAK) (District Court SDNY), Opinion (6/26/2006), at 4–6.
9. *United States v. Stein*, 541 F.3d 130 (2nd Cir. 2008).

10. "Manhattan U.S. Attorney Announces Agreement With Ernst & Young LLP To Pay $123 Million To Resolve Federal Tax Shelter Fraud Investigation," Department of Justice Press Release (3/1/2013), http://www.justice.gov/usao-sdny/pr/manhattan-us-attorney-announces-agreement-ernst-young-llp-pay-123-million-resolve.

11. Levin-Coleman Amendment No. 3120 to S. 1637.

12. See Section 818 of H.R. 4520, American Jobs Creation Act of 2004, enacted as Public Law 108-357 (10/22/2004) and codified at 26 U.S.C. 6700.

13. 2005 PCAOB Rule on Auditor Independence and Tax Services, https://pcaobus.org/Rulemaking/Docket017/2004-12-14_Release_2004-015.pdf (proposed rule) and https://pcaobus.org/Rulemaking/Docket017/2005-07-26_Release_2005-014.pdf (final rule); comment letter filed by Senator Levin (2/24/2005), https://pcaobus.org/Rulemaking/Docket017/794_Carl_Levin.pdf.

14. Information about the six case studies is based upon "Tax Haven Abuses: The Enablers, The Tools and Secrecy," S. Hrg. 109-797 (8/1/2006), Volumes 1–4 (hereinafter "Tax Haven Abuses Hearing"), https://www.gpo.gov/fdsys/pkg/CHRG-109shrg29760/pdf/CHRG-109shrg29760.pdf (Volume 1), https://www.gpo.gov/fdsys/pkg/CHRG-109shrg33413/pdf/CHRG-109shrg33413.pdf (Volume 2), https://www.gpo.gov/fdsys/pkg/CHRG-109shrg33414/pdf/CHRG-109shrg33414.pdf (Volume 3), and https://www.gpo.gov/fdsys/pkg/CHRG-109shrg33415/pdf/CHRG-109shrg33415.pdf (Volume 4).

15. A federal court later came to the same factual conclusion. See *SEC v. Wyly*, Case No. 1:10-CV-5760-SAS (District Court SDNY), Opinion and Order (9/25/2014), at 23.

16. For more information on the Wyly ranch, see Tax Haven Abuses Hearing, at 496–502, 508–514.

17. For more information on the Wyly-related jewelry, furnishings, and artwork, see Tax Haven Abuses Hearing, at 518–529.

18. For more information on Security Capital, see Tax Haven Abuses Hearing, at 440–454.

19. See Tax Haven Abuses Hearing, at 161–620.

20. See Hiring Incentives to Restore Employment (HIRE) Act, P.L. 111-147, §533.

21. See *SEC v. Wyly*, Case No. 1:10-CV-5760-SAS (SDNY); "Statement on Jury's Verdict in Case against the Wylys," SEC Press Release, http://www.sec.gov/News/PublicStmt/Detail/PublicStmt/1370541799330. Charles Wyly died in a car accident in 2011, so at the time of trial, the defendants were Sam Wyly and the Charles Wyly estate. See *SEC v. Wyly*, Case No. 1:10-CV-5760-SAS (SDNY), Opinion and Order (1/27/2012) (allowing disgorgement action to proceed against Charles Wyly estate).

22. See, for example, *In Re Sam Wyly*, Case No. 14-35043-BJH (Chap. 11) (NDTX Bankruptcy Court), Memorandum Opinion and Order (8/25/2015),

at 7 ("The District Court ultimately concluded that the purpose of the securities fraud was 'to maintain the secrecy of the offshore system and preserve their tax benefits.'").

23. *SEC v. Wyly*, Case No. 1:10-CV-5760-SAS (SDNY), Opinion and Order (9/25/2014).

24. Id., Final Judgment (2/26/2015), http://bit.ly/2zf61n8.

25. See, for example, "Forbes 400," *Forbes* (2006) (ranking Sam Wyly at 354 in the list with an estimated net worth of $1.1 billion), http://bit.ly/292O1KS; and "Forbes 400," *Forbes* (2011) (dropping Sam Wyly from Forbes 400 list after noting his rank of 385 in 2010), http://bit.ly/2itlCor.

26. *In Re Sam Wyly*, Case No. 14-35043-BJH (Chap. 11) (NDTX Bankruptcy Court), Memorandum Opinion and Order (8/25/2015).

27. Id., Memorandum Opinion (5/10/2016), at 419 (finding tax fraud); unpublished opinion (6/27/2016); "Sam Wyly Tax Bill Totals $1.1B In Fraud Case," *Law360*, Jess Davis (6/27/2016), http://bit.ly/2AaW5Lg.

28. See *United States v. Greenstein, Wilk, and Krane*, Case No. CR08-0296 RSM (USDC WDWA), Superseding Indictment (6/4/2009) (hereinafter "Greenstein Indictment"), at ¶14.

29. The information is based upon the Tax Haven Abuses Hearing, at 230–296.

30. Id., at 237. A later indictment of Jeffrey Greenstein disclosed that he and other Quellos principals were Euram shareholders. See Greenstein Indictment, at ¶8.

31. Id., at 243–244.

32. See Greenstein Indictment.

33. See "Los Angeles Lawyer Sentenced for Tax Evasion and Passport Fraud in Connection with Quellos Tax Shelter Scheme," Department of Justice Press Release (6/10/2011), http://www.justice.gov/archive/usao/waw/press/2011/jun/krane.html.

34. See Greenstein Indictment.

35. See "Former Quellos Executives Plead Guilty in Offshore Tax Shelter Scam Involving More Than $9.6 Billion in Phony Stock Sales," Department of Justice Press Release (9/13/2010), http://www.justice.gov/archive/usao/waw/press/2010/sep/quellos.html.

36. Tax Haven Abuse Act, S. 681, 110th Congress (2/17/2007).

37. Incorporation Transparency and Law Enforcement Assistance Act, S. 2956, 110th Congress (5/1/2008).

6

Battling Tax Haven Banks

"In case of an interrogation by any authority: protect the banking secrecy."
UBS, US International Training, at 5 (9/26/2006), 2009 Senate Hearing
Exhibit 1d

Our first forays into the world of high-stakes tax dodging focused on tax shelters and tax professionals using offshore secrecy jurisdictions to help the wealthy cheat on their taxes. Our next zeroed in on the role of tax haven banks. Meaning banks that operate in jurisdictions with strong secrecy laws and minimal taxes. Banks that offer secret offshore accounts for U.S. clients to stash cash and assets hidden from Uncle Sam. Banks regulated by jurisdictions with little or no compunction about facilitating tax evasion that robbed other countries of needed revenue.

Our first hearing on tax haven banks, in 2008, showed how they used offshore secrecy to hide misconduct by not only their clients, but also themselves. Dirty tricks included slipping private bankers into the United States to recruit and service U.S. clients; opening accounts in the names of shell entities; concealing money transfers; ignoring disclosure obligations; and thwarting subpoenas and extradition requests to punish wrongdoers.

PSI exposed the billions of dollars being hidden in offshore accounts, contributing to a worldwide backlash against banks trafficking in tax dodging. A 2009 hearing added fuel to the fire with additional evidence. In 2010, Congress enacted landmark legislation to force foreign banks to disclose accounts opened for U.S. clients. The international community created a

© The Author(s) 2018
E. J. Bean, *Financial Exposure*, https://doi.org/10.1007/978-3-319-94388-6_6

parallel global system a few years later. In 2014, a third PSI hearing acknowledged the progress made in the battle against tax haven banks, but also showed how far the world still had to go.

Getting Explosive Information on LGT and UBS

Like our investigation into KPMG, our inquiry into tax haven banks was sparked by bank insiders who found us instead of the other way around.[1] In 2007, two unrelated informants from two different offshore banks walked through our door and dropped explosive information into our laps. Why us? Presumably because PSI's earlier investigations had shown we were willing to challenge abusive offshore tax practices and take on powerful interests.

The first came from Liechtenstein, a tiny European country then known for some of the dirtiest banking in the world. Heinrich Kieber was a slight man, in his 40s, with dark hair, large brown eyes, thick eyebrows, black-rimmed glasses, and stubble on his chin. He told us he was an information technology specialist who'd been hired by LGT Bank and Trust—owned by Liechtenstein's royal family—to convert it into a paperless operation. To do so, he'd been given full access to LGT's records. While reviewing those records, he indicated he'd been appalled to find LGT was helping the wealthy and corrupt hide assets and evade taxes.

After he left the bank, Mr. Kieber visited a number of tax authorities around the world and informed them he had copies of records of Liechtenstein accounts opened by their citizens. He reportedly sold LGT account records naming hundreds of Germans to the German government for more than 5 million euros.[2] He reportedly also provided records to tax authorities in Australia, France, Italy, the United Kingdom, and elsewhere for undisclosed sums.

Mr. Kieber also traveled to the United States. While the IRS does not, as a policy matter, pay money upfront for taxpayer information, if the IRS later determines that the information led to its collecting unpaid taxes, it will pay a percentage of the recovered tax to the information source. Mr. Kieber apparently was willing to wait. After his IRS meeting, Mr. Kieber also paid PSI a visit, accompanied by a lawyer we knew and respected, Jack Blum, an offshore expert.

Mr. Kieber and Mr. Blum met in our conference room with Bob Roach from the Levin staff and Mike Flowers from the Coleman staff. Mr. Kieber explained his situation and handed over about 12,000 pages of documents related to LGT accounts opened by Americans. For free. No strings attached. Without us even asking. He also offered to answer questions.

The unexpected treasure trove of offshore documents was a thunderbolt in our office. A quick peek showed it included memos, letters, legal papers, and other documents related to numerous accounts. While we wanted to dive right in, a pending investigation meant we had to wait. The stack of documents was hidden in a corner of Bob's office for later review.

A few months later, the second bank insider walked through our door. Bradley Birkenfeld was a ginger-haired American, in his 40s, with a high forehead and square jaw. Born in Boston, a surgeon's son, he'd gone to graduate school in Switzerland. Unlike our first insider, Mr. Birkenfeld had spent years as a private banker in the wealth management business opening accounts for high net-worth individuals. He'd worked first for Credit Suisse, then Barclays, then UBS. UBS, whose initials once stood for Union Bank of Switzerland, was that country's largest bank and one of the largest in the world. It specialized in serving the very wealthy.

Mr. Birkenfeld told us he'd worked in Switzerland at UBS from 2001 to 2005, when according to him, he'd resigned from the bank over policy differences. He informed us that he'd traveled to the United States to meet with the Justice Department, IRS, and others to discuss troubling practices at UBS. He indicated that he would like to convey the same information to PSI, but could not do so voluntarily. He asked that we issue him a subpoena and interview him under oath in a deposition. It was an unusual, but intriguing request.

Given our intense investigative schedule, finding time for a lengthy deposition was no snap. But offers like his didn't occur every day, so we made the time.

On October 4, 2007, we issued a friendly subpoena to Mr. Birkenfeld. A week later, on October 11, Bob and Laura Stuber from our crew, and Mike Flowers from the Coleman staff, deposed him for several hours. Mr. Birkenfeld had an explosive story about UBS misdeeds, with limited documentation to back up his claims. He recommended that we request additional documents from UBS, describing with particularity what we should ask for. We thanked him for the information but, again, set it aside due to other investigative demands.

In February 2008, as we began wrapping up other work, the media suddenly erupted with news of tax authorities around the world moving against tax dodgers with hidden accounts at LGT. Germany led the way with a raid on several hundred individuals, even televising a perp walk by a leading corporate executive.[3] Not to be left out, on February 26, 2008, the IRS announced it, too, was investigating U.S. taxpayers with Liechtenstein accounts. The IRS press release also disclosed that the United States, Australia, Canada, France, Italy, New Zealand, Sweden, and United Kingdom were "working together following revelations that the Liechtenstein accounts [were] being used for tax avoidance and evasion."[4] The LGT scandal had gone global.

In light of the LGT developments and the white-hot LGT and UBS documents burning a hole through the floor in his office, Bob proposed a new investigation into how tax haven banks handle offshore accounts for U.S. clients. As soon as he said it, we were sold. It was a factual inquiry that promised to be both newsworthy and key to understanding how tax haven banks facilitated offshore tax abuse. We proposed the inquiry to Senators Levin and Coleman who gave us an immediate go-ahead.

Investigating LGT

Our first task was tackling the LGT documents, since they provided explicit and detailed information about offshore accounts opened for U.S. taxpayers. It wasn't nearly as easy or straightforward as we thought it would be.

The first problem was that most of the documents were in German. And not standard German, but Liechtenstein German riddled with technical and not-so-technical banking and legal terms. The second problem was the LGT documents were poorly organized—it was hard to tell which documents applied to which accounts. Still another problem was our unfamiliarity with Liechtenstein banking practices, including opening accounts in the name of "foundations," a certain type of legal entity not found in U.S. law. Those and other hurdles didn't deter us—they just made us hungrier to figure things out.

We reached out to staff and lucked out in finding several who knew German. We asked them to categorize the documents by account, and figure out which accounts had the most money and most interesting facts. We soon identified a couple dozen worth pursuing.

To brush up on Liechtenstein, we contacted the Law Library of Congress, which maintains a top-notch legal team with expertise in international law. A Liechtenstein specialist, Edith Palmer, provided us with basic information about the country and also translated some key documents. We located other Liechtenstein legal experts as well who provided us with more briefings and more translations. The documents turned out to be filled with blunt assessments and raw data about LGT's clients, perfect for an investigation.

Next, we started tracking down the LGT accountholders who spanned the country from Florida to New York to California. We made initial contact by telephone. No one was happy to hear from us, but since most were already in negotiations with the IRS—which we assumed had the same documents we did—they simply directed us to their legal counsel.

We set up meetings with the accountholders' lawyers. We usually brought a set of LGT documents to each meeting, demonstrating how much we already knew and how strong the written evidence was. We indicated that we also wanted to understand the facts from the accountholder's view, and invited the lawyer to clarify or challenge anything in the documents.

In most cases, we also sent a subpoena to the accountholder, not only to obtain documents supporting the LGT materials we already had, but also to update the accounts since the LGT documents were generally several years old. Almost all of the accountholders responded with some additional account-related documents, including recent correspondence with the IRS about unpaid taxes. When contacted for follow-up interviews, however, almost all invoked their Fifth Amendment rights against self-incrimination and declined to speak with us. Even so, the added documents and information provided by their legal counsel generally confirmed the authenticity of the LGT documents and the existence of their secret accounts.

A few lawyers offered hard luck stories about clients who learned of their LGT accounts after inheriting them from relatives who died. They claimed the relatives had hidden the funds from corrupt government officials, never withdrew the money, and never told anyone taxes had to be paid on the interest. While a few of those presentations were persuasive, most rang hollow. We finally settled on seven accounts oozing with secrecy, deception, and indicia of tax evasion.

Marsh Accounts

One of those accounts belonged to a Florida resident in the construction business, James Albright Marsh, who'd recently passed away.[5] The LGT documents showed that, over a period of 20 years, he'd formed four Liechtenstein foundations and opened accounts for them at five Liechtenstein banks. LGT had created two of the foundations and maintained accounts for both in Liechtenstein.

Mr. Marsh had supplied the foundation accounts with millions of dollars in cash, which he apparently snuck into Liechtenstein during several trips there. By 2007, his accounts held assets with a combined value exceeding $49 million. While his three sons had claimed in an IRS submission they didn't know they were account beneficiaries until after their father's death, the LGT documents indicated otherwise. They showed one son had signed a letter of wishes related to a foundation as early as 1985; another had traveled to Liechtenstein with his father in 2000; and in 2004, two sons, then aged 50 and 43, had agreed in writing to serve as "protectors" for the two LGT-formed foundations.

The documents also showed LGT was an active partner in concealing the Marsh accounts from U.S. authorities. Among other steps, LGT never disclosed the accounts in filings with the IRS; never sent mail to Mr. Marsh in Florida; instructed the Marshes to use the code, "Friends of J.N.," to "get in touch" with LGT personnel; and created foundation documents that maximized secrecy. For example, the foundation documents authorized LGT, through a "Foundation Council" composed of LGT personnel, to transfer the Marsh foundations to another country if pressed for information about them—a so-called flee clause. The documents also allowed the Foundation Council to refuse to provide information about the foundations, even to the beneficiaries, if the Council concluded disclosing the information might be "detrimental to the Foundation or the members of the Class of Beneficiaries." The documents also contained the bald statement that "any legal facts and aspects of the Foundation must not be drawn to the attention of outside parties, especially foreign authorities." The result: if the IRS or a U.S. court were to have ordered Mr. Marsh to obtain information from LGT about his own foundations, LGT could have legally refused to provide it.

It was clear from the foundation documents that the secrecy provisions had been dreamed up and put in place by LGT. Mr. Marsh then sat back and watched as LGT invested his untaxed cash and grew his wealth. The Marshes' legal counsel informed us that the family was negotiating with the IRS to resolve tax liabilities associated with the once hidden accounts.

Wu Accounts

A second set of LGT accounts involved a New Yorker named William S. Wu.[6] The documents showed LGT had established two Liechtenstein foundations for him in 1996 and 2006, and opened LGT accounts in their names. Three months after forming the first foundation, Mr. Wu pretended to sell his New York residence to a company in Hong Kong. That company, first formed in the British Virgin Islands, was owned by a Bahamian company which, in turn, was owned by Mr. Wu's Liechtenstein foundation. In other words, using a chain of shell entities, he had essentially sold his house to himself. He then paid "rent" to the Hong Kong company, moving more of his money offshore without alerting U.S. authorities.

LGT documents showed that LGT personnel knew about the whole arrangement and never expressed any concern about it, despite the multi-jurisdictional contortions—a New York house owned by a BVI company (with a Hong Kong address), owned by a Bahamas company, owned by a Liechtenstein foundation, founded by a New Yorker—a cross-border structure with no apparent purpose other than concealment.

LGT had also assisted Mr. Wu with withdrawing money from his foundation accounts without attracting U.S. notice. To facilitate a withdrawal in 2002, for example, LGT gave Mr. Wu a $100,000 cashier's check that was financed with his funds but, on its face, named only LGT as the payor. The check was made "[p]ayable at any branch of HSBC Bank USA," enabling Mr. Wu to withdraw his money from any HSBC bank in the United States in a way almost impossible to trace back to his Liechtenstein accounts.

In 2006, his LGT account assets exceeded $4.5 million. Mr. Wu's legal counsel indicated he was then negotiating with the IRS over the taxes owed on his undeclared income.

Greenfield Accounts

Two other New Yorkers, Harvey and Steven Greenfield, father and son involved in the toy manufacturing business, were also secret accountholders at LGT.[7] What made their story interesting was a 2001 meeting with LGT's top brass.

At the time, the Greenfields were considering what to do with $30 million at a Bank of Bermuda branch in Hong Kong in an account that was being closed. Three LGT bankers set up the 2001 meeting primarily to make a sales pitch for transferring the $30 million to LGT. The meeting lasted five hours and included an appearance by Prince Philipp von und zu Liechtenstein, chairman of the board of the LGT Group and brother to the reigning sovereign of Liechtenstein. An internal LGT memorandum summarized the meeting, in part, as follows:

> The Bank of Bermuda has indicated to the client that it would like to end the business relationship with him as a U.S. citizen. Due to these circumstances, the client is now on the search for a safe haven for his offshore assets. ... There follows a long discussion about the banking location Liechtenstein, the banking privacy law as well as the security and stability, that Liechtenstein ... can guarantee its clients. The Bank ... indicated strong interest in receiving the U.S. $30 million. ... The clients are very careful and eager to dissolve the Trust with the Bank of Bermuda leaving behind as few traces as possible.[8]

In short, while the Bank of Bermuda was closing the Greenfield account for unspecified reasons, LGT was happy to pick it up. LGT and Prince Philipp cited Liechtenstein's "banking privacy law" as a selling point to attract the cash and leave behind as "few traces as possible."

The Greenfields' legal counsel told PSI that his clients were then negotiating with the IRS and Justice Department over tax liability issues related to their Liechtenstein accounts.

Lowy Accounts

The biggest LGT account we examined involved a $68 million Liechtenstein foundation established by members of the Lowy family.[9] We'd never heard of the Lowys prior to the LGT inquiry, but by the end concluded that they'd concocted one of the more inventive, intricate, and deceptive schemes for hiding offshore assets that we'd ever seen.

The family patriarch, Frank Lowy, was an Australian billionaire who'd made his fortune as head of the Westfield Group, one of the world's leading developers of shopping malls. His three sons, David, Peter, and Steven, held senior positions in the Westfield organization. Peter Lowy, head of Westfield's U.S. operations, was variously described to us as the richest man in Los Angeles or in all of California, depending upon whom we asked.

The LGT documents indicated the Lowys were longtime LGT clients and, by 1998, one of LGT's largest clients. The particular account we were interested in had been opened in the name of the Luperla Foundation, a Lowy-related entity created by LGT in 1996, after speaking with the Lowys and one of their lawyers, Joshua Gelbard, a resident of Israel.

Internal LGT memoranda were crystal clear that the Luperla Foundation had been formed by Frank Lowy solely to benefit himself and his three sons. The memoranda also indicated Frank Lowy had explicitly informed LGT that he had experienced multiple run-ins with Australian tax authorities and did not want to have to testify in an Australian court about the Luperla assets.

Rather than express concern about concealing assets from tax authorities, LGT took several measures to accommodate Mr. Lowy. LGT allowed the Luperla Foundation agreement to be signed, for example, not by the Lowys, but by their lawyer, Mr. Gelbard, who was the only person named in the papers. In addition, the official foundation documents never named the Lowys as foundation beneficiaries. Instead, they incorporated a complex mechanism to identify the foundation's future beneficiaries, stating the beneficiaries would be named by the last corporation in which Beverly Park Corporation, a U.S. company formed in Delaware, held stock.

Beverly Park Corporation, we learned, operated under a complex ownership chain that ended up with the Frank Lowy Family Trust. Beverly Park's president was Peter Lowy, who was also one of its three directors.

The beneficiary provision in the Luperla documents was both unusual and clever. It meant that the Luperla Foundation had no existing beneficiaries so, when asked, the Lowys could truthfully deny having that status. At the same time, the Lowys secretly controlled the mechanism for naming the future beneficiaries. Meanwhile, internal LGT documents were explicit that, no matter what the foundation documents said, Mr. Lowy and his sons were to be treated as the Luperla Foundation's existing beneficiaries.

The LGT documents also disclosed how LGT actively helped the Lowys transfer assets into a new account under cover of extreme secrecy. LGT avoided direct transfers into the account using wire transfers from outside the bank. Instead, LGT acquired a shell company in the British Virgin Islands called Sewell Services Ltd. and opened an account for it at the LGT bank.

Assets intended for the Lowy foundation were then transferred directly into the Sewell account. After they were safely inside the bank, the assets were transferred internally from the Sewell account to the Luperla account. Those inside-the-bank transfers, called "journaling," were a way to move assets into or out of accounts without using wire transfers or other documents that could be subpoenaed from outside parties. Instead, the inside transfers were executed through simple "book entries" under the bank's sole control.

LGT used Sewell—which it called a "transfer company"—to move cash and assets to and from the Luperla account with no outside trace of the Sewell-Luperla link behind the bank's walls. LGT used the same device for other accounts as well, and it worked like a charm.

Money and assets accumulated in the Luperla account for several years. But all offshore money eventually moves on, and in 2001, it was Luperla's turn. For unspecified reasons, the Lowys decided to liquidate Luperla and move its $68 million from LGT to a Swiss bank. Prior to liquidation, however, the foundation had to name a beneficiary since, under the foundation agreement, only a beneficiary could direct final disposition of the foundation's assets.

Multiple LGT documents recounted the painstaking process used by LGT to verify Luperla's beneficiary and liquidate its assets. One LGT memo memorialized a telephone conversation with David Lowy in which LGT explained the extensive documentation it required. It was also David Lowy who apparently informed LGT that a new Beverly Park subsidiary had been acquired in the British Virgin Islands, Lonas Ltd., to name Luperla's beneficiary.

A later LGT memo recounted LGT's receipt of documents confirming that Beverly Park had, in fact, acquired Lonas, that Lonas was its latest subsidiary, and that Beverly Park held its lone share of stock. Other documents showed Lonas had appointed Mr. Gelbard, the Lowy family attorney, as its sole director, and Mr. Gelbard had issued a directive describing what should be done with the $68 million. The memo stated that, even after receiving the Gelbard directive, LGT telephoned David Lowy a second time and recorded the conversation to confirm the "accuracy" of the Gelbard instructions. Three days later, LGT telephoned David Lowy yet again, to get his verbal consent before actually wiring the $68 million, in two tranches, from LGT Bank to Bank Jacob Safra in Geneva, Switzerland.

The three phone calls to David Lowy were additional proof that LGT viewed the Lowys as its true clients and the true decisionmakers behind Luperla, Beverly Park, and Lonas. They also showed how careful LGT was to document the facts before sending the $68 million to bank accounts that apparently did not name the Lowys as accountholders.

When we quizzed the Lowys' Washington counsel about what happened to the $68 million sent to Switzerland in 2001, we were told the Lowys never touched the money but, instead, distributed the funds a few years ago "for charitable purposes in Israel." And no, the Lowys did not wish to provide the charities' names, the donation amounts, or donation dates; we'd have to take their word for it. When we asked about a 2007 IRS submission in which Beverly Park claimed to have "no records demonstrating ownership of stock in any other entity, including Lonas"—a statement directly contradicting the LGT documents stating Beverly Park, in fact, owned Lonas stock—the Lowys declined to elaborate.

Interviewing LGT

In addition to interviewing LGT accountholders, we asked LGT itself to meet with us. We explained that we wanted to lay out what we knew and hear whatever LGT would like to tell us so that we had an accurate picture of the facts. LGT was at first dismissive but, when we persisted, offered to send a representative to a meeting in Washington, provided that we would promise not to serve that representative with a subpoena. We agreed.

The meeting took place in our conference room. We laid out the documents we had and the accounts we'd investigated. We held nothing back. When we then asked LGT to confirm certain information, its representative—a bland, middle-aged executive who headed LGT's compliance office—said LGT could not discuss client-specific information. He also informed us that Liechtenstein had issued an arrest warrant for the person who'd stolen the LGT account documentation.[10] It wasn't a very productive exchange from our point of view, but afterward we felt we had done all we could to get LGT's perspective.

We also met with representatives from the Liechtenstein government, including the head of their financial intelligence unit, Rene Bruelhart, to alert them to our investigation. Mr. Bruelhart, who looked like he'd just stepped off the ski slopes, was slim, dark-haired, charming, and fluent in English. He was familiar with Liechtenstein's laws, banks, and banking practices. Somehow, he convinced us that he was sincerely interested in addressing our concerns, while also protecting Liechtenstein and encouraging its banks to clean up their practices and portfolios.

By the time we completed the interviews, we viewed the evidence as overwhelming that LGT had deliberately helped U.S. clients hide funds from Uncle Sam.

Investigating UBS

At the same time we were bearing down on LGT, an overlapping set of PSI investigators were pressing UBS for information. Since we'd already received a lot of UBS details from Bradley Birkenfeld, our first step was to request a meeting with the bank to let it know what we had and our intent to investigate further.

By the time we contacted the bank, UBS was already in tense negotiations with both the IRS and Justice Department, so it apparently viewed us as just the latest to pile on. In our initial meeting, the bank's legal counsel was cold and correct. We let him know we would be sending a subpoena for documents. He responded that the documents we wanted were primarily in Switzerland and beyond our authority to obtain. We replied, because the U.S. branch of UBS was not a separate corporation but part of the parent corporation, our subpoena could reach through the branch office to the motherland. The legal counsel sniffed his disagreement.

The PSI subpoena requested specific categories of documents, relying on information supplied by the bank and Mr. Birkenfeld. While waiting for UBS' response, we also set up a meeting with the Swiss Embassy to inform it of our inquiry. The Embassy's representative, Eric Hess, met in the conference room with me and Mike Flowers from the Coleman staff.

The Swiss diplomat struck me as even colder and more disdainful of the subcommittee than the UBS lawyer. He began the meeting by declaring that Switzerland had no bank secrecy laws. I replied that was good to know and asked when we could get the names of U.S. clients with Swiss accounts. He reacted with a stiff smile that seemed more an exercise in baring his teeth than displaying his diplomatic skills. Mr. Hess informed us that tax evasion was not a crime in Switzerland and suggested it wouldn't be such a problem in the United States if we had more reasonable tax laws. The conversation went downhill from there. It became clear that the Swiss government wasn't going to help our inquiry or take any action to discipline UBS.

Over the next few weeks, we worked to substantiate some of the information supplied by Mr. Birkenfeld about UBS. One of his claims was that UBS had regularly sent private bankers from Switzerland to the United States to recruit new clients and service existing ones. He estimated that "around 25 people in Geneva, 50 people in Zurich, and five to ten in Lugano" made multiple U.S. trips per year, calling them a "formidable force." In other words, it wasn't a case of U.S. taxpayers traveling to Switzerland to open accounts; UBS was secretly sending Swiss bankers onto U.S. soil to target U.S. clients and convince them to hide money abroad.

To evaluate that claim, we asked the Department of Homeland Security for entry and exit data for travelers from Switzerland to the United States from 2001 to 2008. Sure enough, the data disclosed over 300 visits by 20 UBS Swiss "client advisors," sometimes using visas that said they were visiting the United States for pleasure rather than business. The entries placed the bankers at several locations predicted by Mr. Birkenfeld—in Miami in time to attend the Art Basel Show, in cities hosting yachting events that included a UBS-sponsored yachting team, and in still other cities where golf or tennis tournaments attracted wealthy fans. According to Mr. Birkenfeld, UBS paid the travel and event costs so that its Swiss bankers could mingle with affluent guests, quietly hand out their business cards, and set up appointments.

We also initiated a detailed inquiry into the one UBS client we knew had a hidden Swiss account—Igor Olenicoff. Mr. Olenicoff was a Russian-born U.S. citizen and billionaire real estate developer who lived in California. From 2001 to 2005, he'd been a client of Mr. Birkenfeld and a Liechtenstein trust officer, Mario Staggl, who together helped him open multiple bank accounts in the names of offshore companies at UBS in Switzerland and Neue Bank in Liechtenstein. His assets had peaked in 2005 at $200 million.

Mr. Birkenfeld indicated during his PSI deposition that Mr. Olenicoff was his largest client. He explained that they'd communicated in person and by telephone, fax, and email, and he'd advised Mr. Olenicoff on how to avoid disclosure of his offshore assets to the IRS. When Mr. Birkenfeld left UBS in 2005, he convinced Mr. Olenicoff to transfer his UBS holdings to Neue Bank in Liechtenstein, where Mr. Birkenfeld and Mr. Staggl could continue to advise him.

We later learned that federal prosecutors had been pursuing Mr. Olenicoff for years on suspicion of massive tax evasion. In the fall of 2007, Mr. Olenicoff pled guilty to one criminal count of filing a false income tax return for failing to disclose his offshore accounts.[11] Under the plea agreement, he paid back taxes, interest, and penalties totaling $52 million, but avoided any prison time, receiving instead two years of probation and some community service. After seeing press reports about the case, we contacted the court, prosecutor, and Mr. Olenicoff's lawyer, and got copies of documents related to his accounts.

2008 Surprise

In May 2008, the unexpected happened. Mr. Birkenfeld was arrested upon arriving at a Boston airport and charged with conspiring with Mr. Olenicoff to evade U.S. taxes on the $200 million hidden in his offshore accounts.

We learned later that Mr. Birkenfeld's relationship with the Justice Department had taken a nosedive after federal prosecutors learned he was Mr. Olenicoff's private banker. While Mr. Birkenfeld had disclosed that fact during his PSI deposition, he'd apparently not informed the prosecutors until after they'd concluded the Olenicoff plea agreement. Had Justice known of the relationship earlier and realized it could use Mr. Birkenfeld to testify against Mr. Olenicoff at trial, prosecutors presumably could have negotiated a tougher plea deal than the one that let Mr. Olenicoff walk free after paying back taxes. The prosecutors were apparently outraged at what they saw as Mr. Birkenfeld's deliberate delay in disclosing his Olenicoff connection.

The next month, June 2008, Mr. Birkenfeld pled guilty to conspiring with Mr. Olenicoff, Mario Staggl, and others to defraud the IRS out of millions of dollars in unpaid taxes on the Olenicoff assets. As part of his plea agreement, Mr. Birkenfeld signed an extensive statement of facts and turned over multiple documents, some of which were filed in court and made publicly available for the first time. Mr. Birkenfeld admitted, among other matters, that he and others had:

> advised U.S. clients to place cash and valuables in Swiss safety deposit boxes[;] … advised the clients to misrepresent the receipt of funds from the Swiss bank account in the United States as loans from the bank; destroy all off-shore banking records existing in the United States; utilize Swiss bank credit cards that they claimed could not be discovered by U.S. authorities; and file false U.S. individual income tax returns.[12]

In perhaps his most notorious disclosure, Mr. Birkenfeld admitted smuggling diamonds for a UBS client into the United States by hiding them in a tube of toothpaste.

The criminal pleadings also stated that Mr. Birkenfeld's actions were part of a larger pattern of misconduct by UBS. The bank was estimated to hold $20 billion in Swiss accounts for U.S. clients who'd never disclosed the accounts to the IRS, and obtained account-related revenues in the neighborhood of $200 million per year. Together, the indictment, factual statement, and admission of wrongdoing made it clear that Mr. Birkenfeld was not a whistleblower with clean hands—he had been involved in criminal misconduct for years.[13]

Prying Information from UBS

After the Birkenfeld guilty plea, with its new facts and documents, we redoubled our efforts to pry information out of UBS. We pressed the bank for specific data on the number of Swiss accounts opened for U.S. clients but never declared to the IRS; the total amount of funds involved; and how many accounts were opened in the name of offshore corporations, trusts, or Liechtenstein foundations. We also wanted to know how many Swiss bankers were involved, and whether it was true that they had routinely traveled to the United States to secretly service existing clients and recruit new ones.

UBS finally coughed up a few statistics, most of which we later learned understated its misconduct. The most important was its statement that the bank had opened an estimated 19,000 undeclared Swiss accounts with about $18 billion in assets. The bank also admitted to selecting a firm to which it referred U.S. clients seeking to set up shell entities to disguise their account ownership. By then, we were ready to wrap up the investigation.

Writing It Up

We wrote up the LGT and UBS case studies in a 130-page Levin-Coleman report. The LGT example provided the specifics on how U.S. clients used tax haven banks to hide and access their offshore assets. The UBS example provided the big numbers—$18 billion and 19,000 undeclared accounts—illustrating the scope of the problem.

To further hammer home what was going on, our report opened with a single powerful fact: "Each year, the United States loses an estimated $100 billion in tax revenues due to offshore tax abuses."[14] An attention-getting number, we supplied a long footnote citing a variety of academic and other sources to ensure the $100 billion estimate stood up to scrutiny. The figure clearly resonated with reporters, policymakers, and the public, all of whom were trying to understand and quantify the harm connected to offshore tax abuse. The frequency with which the $100 billion figure was cited in the following years taught me the importance and power of using a simple, bottom-line numerical estimate to elevate an issue.

Our tax haven bank report also brought home another important lesson—the value of allowing targets to review a report before it goes public. For years, our standard operating procedure had been to provide a copy of our report to investigative subjects 24 hours before making it public. We didn't provide a copy to everyone mentioned in the report—only parties who were a focus of the investigation and portrayed in a negative light. In addition, we didn't give the entire report to anyone. Instead, we provided each party with only those portions of the report that mentioned them. No one got the executive summary.

We provided the 24-hour review period, not only because fairness dictated giving targets a chance to see what was said about them before the press did, but also because it helped ensure the report's accuracy. As we explained to everyone given an early excerpt, we were not giving the report to them to approve the text or argue for a change in the findings; instead, we were providing a courtesy copy so they could digest the information prior to public disclosure. In addition, we said if they found a factual error and could demonstrate its inaccuracy with documents or other information, we would correct the text before the report went public.

Lawyers who regularly worked with PSI knew of our deep commitment to the facts, and took full advantage of the opportunity to spot errors. Some firms literally lined up lawyers at the start of the 24-hour review period and, as soon as they got the text, divided up the pages and footnotes among the attorneys to fact-check every word, date, and name. Because we performed our own exhaustive fact-checking prior to release, most reviews uncovered only a few minor matters easily corrected. It was rare for anyone to find an error of significance. But it did happen.

The tax haven bank report provided the most spectacular example during the Levin era. To make a long story short, in the course of researching the U.S. clients with LGT accounts, a law clerk found information on the Internet indicating that a family member was a former federal prisoner with a felony record. The information included details of the crime and an arrest photo. We'd referenced that information in a single sentence in the report with a footnote.

The party who received that report section immediately asked us to strike the sentence. Their lawyer explained that the family member had run into the same problem before—he and the prisoner had the same name and age, were from the same state, and even looked alike, but were not the same person. The lawyer had documents to prove it. We deleted the sentence from the report, and no one outside PSI was the wiser. After our law clerk stopped shaking at having almost mislabeled someone a criminal, and we stopped shaking at having almost released misinformation to the public, we all swore undying allegiance to the 24-hour review.

The next day, we held our usual press briefing and handed out the report. Due to scheduling issues, the press briefing was two days before the hearings, but we set the embargo for the night before the hearings to ensure the articles came out on the morning that the hearings began.

Going Public

The tax haven bank hearings took place on July 17 and 25, 2008. In his opening statement the first day, Senator Levin blasted tax havens whose "twin hallmarks are secrecy and tax avoidance," condemning them for conducting "economic warfare against the United States and against honest, hard-working American taxpayers." Senator Coleman was equally strong, charging tax haven banks with actively facilitating U.S. tax evasion, including LGT and UBS which, he stated, "didn't just facilitate this misconduct; they orchestrated it."

At several points during the hearing, Senator Levin used a chart entitled, "Tax Haven Bank Secrecy Tricks." It included a long list of sleazy banking practices we'd uncovered at LGT or UBS. The list included using code names to hide client identities; opening accounts in the name of shell companies; providing bankers visiting the United States with counter-surveillance training to evade U.S. customs, tax, and law enforcement efforts; and funneling money through so-called transfer companies to hide the true parties behind wire transfers (Image 6.1).

My favorite was an LGT instruction telling its personnel to use public pay phones when calling clients so the calls couldn't be traced back to LGT. Even more surreal was an instruction that came after Italian tax authorities began tracing calls using the Liechtenstein area code; LGT told personnel to use only telephone booths outside of Liechtenstein. The hearing exhibit encapsulated the financial firms' indefensible practices.

We began the hearing with two witnesses, the IRS Commissioner and a senior Justice Department official, who characterized offshore tax evasion as a serious problem and described their many battles to obtain information from tax haven banks.

Tax Haven Bank Secrecy Tricks

- **Code Names for Clients**
- **Pay Phones, not Business Phones**
- **Foreign Area Codes**
- **Undeclared Accounts**
- **Encrypted Computers**
- **Transfer Companies to Cover Tracks**
- **Foreign Shell Companies**
- **Fake Charitable Trusts**
- **Straw Man Settlors**
- **Captive Trustees**
- **Anonymous Wire Transfers**
- **Disguised Business Trips**
- **Counter-Surveillance Training**
- **Foreign Credit Cards**
- **Hold Mail**
- **Shred Files**

Prepared by the U.S. Senate Permanent Subcommittee on Investigations, July 2008.

Image 6.1   Tax Haven Bank Secrecy Tricks chart. Source: 2008 Senate Hearing Exhibit 104

We wanted LGT to testify next, but it had declined our request. Since it was outside of our subpoena authority, we couldn't compel its attendance. Instead, we presented testimony from the LGT whistleblower, Heinrich Kieber. Including him in the hearing had been tricky. At the time, Liechtenstein had an outstanding warrant for his arrest for disclosing "company business secrets for use abroad and for data theft."[15] In addition, an unnamed party had offered a $7 million reward on the Internet for information leading to his capture.[16]

Mr. Kieber told us that, in response, he'd entered a witness protection program and been given a new name and identity. Since we couldn't bring him to the hearing without endangering his new status, we arranged instead for a 20-minute pre-recorded videotape of him making a statement and answering questions from Bob Roach and Mike Flowers. Mr. Kieber spoke from an undisclosed location, his face cloaked in shadow.

We played the videotape on a huge TV screen set up at the front of the hearing room. We'd worried that no one would listen to the tape, given Mr. Kieber's heavy accent and the monotone gray outline of his head, but the 200 plus people in the hearing room seemed mesmerized by his testimony. You could hear a pin drop while he spoke.

Mr. Kieber testified about how he had been hired by LGT to turn it into a paperless office; the disturbing information he'd come across, including evidence of LGT's helping corrupt government officials, criminals, and tax evaders hide and transfer funds; and his decision to keep copies of the account documents and release them to other governments. It was a powerful and unrelenting condemnation of Liechtenstein's leading financial firm. By skipping the hearing, LGT gave up its chance to respond.

The next witness panel consisted of two U.S. taxpayers, Shannon Marsh and William Wu, who were associated with LGT accounts described in our report. Both asserted their Fifth Amendment rights not to answer questions and were excused.

Senator Levin announced that two additional individuals, Steven Greenfield and Peter Lowy, had also been scheduled to testify about LGT accounts, but Mr. Greenfield had defied a Senate subpoena by failing to appear, and Mr. Lowy had dodged his subpoena by leaving town. Senator Levin announced that Mr. Lowy had already agreed to appear at a second day of hearings on July 25, and a decision would be made soon on a legal response to Mr. Greenfield. Senator Coleman expressed his support for Senator Levin's announcement.

The tax haven bank hearing was the first in years in which witnesses had actually defied PSI's right to compel attendance. Both senators had already resolved to pursue legal action against Mr. Greenfield. They knew if the subcommittee let him off the hook, others would follow, and they were determined to protect PSI's authority. But Mr. Greenfield, like Mr. Lowy, decided not to test PSI's mettle and agreed to appear the following week.

Last up at the hearing was UBS. To examine the bank's conduct, Senator Levin called first on Martin Liechti, a senior UBS official who was based in Switzerland and headed the bank's wealth management group for North and South America. A few months earlier, during a visit to Florida, Mr. Liechti had been unexpectedly detained by the Justice Department as a material witness in the UBS matter. He'd ended up cooling his heels in Florida for several months, with rumors flying about whether he was cooperating with U.S. authorities.

Given his U.S. presence and first-hand knowledge of Swiss accounts opened for U.S. clients, we asked Justice to allow him to travel with a Justice official to Washington to testify at our hearing. Justice agreed, and we were hopeful Mr. Liechti would provide new insights. Instead, despite being a foreign citizen, he claimed a Constitutional right not to answer PSI's questions. Rather than contest his Constitutional standing, Senator Levin excused him.

All the Fifth Amendment assertions were making this hearing one of our shortest. We were down to our final witness, another UBS representative. In preparation for the hearing, we'd informed UBS that PSI was ready to subpoena the most senior UBS official in the United States to testify, but we urged the bank to consider sending instead a bank official from Switzerland. After all, the conduct we were concerned about had emanated from Switzerland, and we didn't think the U.S. bankers should have to answer for their Swiss colleagues.

UBS obliged by sending Mark Branson, a Swiss national who was chief financial officer of UBS' global wealth management and business banking group, and a member of its managing board. Mr. Branson looked the part— reserved, attractive, with a trustworthy demeanor, quiet voice, and perfect English. We'd never spoken with him before the hearing and had no idea what he would say. He proceeded to floor us.

After introducing himself, Mr. Branson essentially admitted everything, apologized, and promised to end the bank's misconduct:

> I have now had the chance to review your Subcommittee's staff report. I am here to make absolutely clear that UBS genuinely regrets any compliance failures that may have occurred. We will take responsibility for them. We will not seek to minimize them. On behalf of UBS, I am apologizing. I am committing to you that we will take the actions necessary to see that this does not happen again.
>
> First, we have decided to exit entirely the business in question. That means UBS will no longer provide offshore banking or securities services to U.S. residents through our bank branches. … Second, we are working with the U.S. Government to identify those names of U.S. clients who may have engaged in tax fraud. … We will fully support and assist that process.

I nearly fell off my chair. UBS had never given us any indication that the bank would acknowledge wrongdoing at the hearing. I scribbled "Wow!" on a note and passed it to Senator Levin. We looked at each other without our expressions changing, knowing we were on television. If ever there was a moment proving the value of congressional oversight, that was it. We had called out a Swiss bank for helping U.S. tax cheats and received a public apology. More, we had struck a blow against the walls of Swiss secrecy and were told they were coming down.

Press coverage of the hearing was worldwide. The combination of our report, the documents, Kieber videotape, and UBS' acknowledgement of wrongdoing, pledge to stop offering undisclosed offshore accounts to U.S. taxpayers, and promise to start turning over U.S. client names, was an earthquake in the offshore world. Expressions of shock reverberated around the globe at the first cracks in Swiss secrecy.

Grilling Two More Accountholders

A week later, we completed the tax haven bank hearing record by holding a one-day follow-up. The witnesses were limited to Steven Greenfield and Peter Lowy, who had chosen not to show up the week before. While both men would have played a small part in the larger story told that day, by appearing later, they attracted increased scrutiny. Senator Levin detailed their LGT accounts, for example, before asking them questions.

Mr. Greenfield responded by asserting his Fifth Amendment right against self-incrimination and apologizing for not appearing earlier. He left the panel promptly.

In contrast, Mr. Lowy's lawyer tried to intervene on behalf of his client. That may have been because his client had a lot to lose. Particularly damning for Mr. Lowy was Hearing Exhibit 36. That exhibit was an LGT memo describing a 1997 meeting in Los Angeles on forming a new Liechtenstein structure for the Lowy family. Attendees were two LGT bankers, Frank Lowy, and sons David and Peter. The memo put Peter Lowy smack in the middle of the effort to establish a new foundation, stating: "The meeting concerned determining the investment strategy for … around US $54.2 million, and simultaneous discussion or determination of the transfer to a new structure." Another problem was the resulting Luperla Foundation agreement which relied on a U.S. corporation controlled by Peter Lowy as the mechanism for identifying the foundation's future beneficiaries.

The evidence suggested that Peter Lowy not only knew what was going on, but was apparently willing to allow a U.S. corporation under his control to be used to further the offshore scheme. Also working against him was his fast footwork in 2008, in which he'd departed the country knowing PSI planned to serve him with a subpoena for the July 17 hearing, leaving his high-profile attorney, Bob Bennett, to make excuses for him.[17]

At the July 25 hearing, in response to Senator Levin's questions, Mr. Lowy quietly asserted his Fifth Amendment right against self-incrimination. Mr. Bennett then piped up, asking permission to make a correction to the record, apparently related to Mr. Lowy's leaving the country after having been informed about a possible subpoena. Senator Levin replied that Mr. Bennett could make a written submission after the hearing, but could not testify in the place of his client.

Mr. Bennett responded: "That is fine. I will deal with it outside this room." Senator Levin replied: "We have already had you folks talk to the press instead of talking to us, so we are not the least bit surprised that you will do it outside this room. But we are not going to have you take the place of your client." The conflict between the two ended when Senator Levin gaveled the hearing to a close.

After their heated exchange, Mr. Lowy's failure to testify seemed anti-climactic. That may have been, in fact, the point of the exchange. Caught on tape in an elevator after the hearing, Mr. Bennett told his client: "[t]his will be the story," implying that his clash with Senator Levin, rather than Mr. Lowy's refusal to testify, would be the media focus.[18] But if that was the plan, it didn't work. Media in the United States, Australia, and elsewhere described the Lowys' Liechtenstein maneuvers in detail.[19]

Taking Criminal Action Against UBS

Seven months later, on February 18, 2009, the Justice Department made history by taking criminal action against UBS. In a formal deferred prosecution agreement between the United States and UBS settling the criminal charges, UBS admitted to engaging in a conspiracy to defraud the United States out of millions of dollars in tax revenue, agreed to pay a penalty of $780 million, promised not to open any more Swiss accounts for U.S. persons without notifying the IRS, and immediately turned over 250–300 U.S. client names.[20] It was a huge U.S. victory over the world's biggest tax haven bank.

And Justice wasn't done. It made clear that the client names turned over in connection with the criminal case weren't sufficient. The deferred prosecution agreement memorialized the parties' understanding that Justice, on behalf of the IRS, would continue to seek court enforcement of a so-called John Doe summons served on UBS to obtain the name of every U.S. client with a Swiss account that hadn't been disclosed to the IRS. The agreement stated that UBS had agreed, if it lost the John Doe case, to turn over all of the client names or risk having the United States re-open the criminal case with UBS' admissions of wrongdoing on the record.

On top of that, Justice filed in court additional incriminating documents, making them public for the first time. One was a 2004 UBS internal report on the Swiss accounts opened by U.S. clients. Among other information, it disclosed that the U.S. "account relationships" in Switzerland totaled—not the 19,000 disclosed by UBS in July—but 52,000. When we saw that number, our jaws dropped—52,000 U.S. taxpayers with undisclosed UBS Swiss accounts was more dramatic than anything we'd expected.

UBS' capitulation to U.S. authorities—its admission of wrongdoing, penalty payment, and disclosure of client names—sent another tremor through the offshore world, still reeling from the PSI hearing marking the fall of what had once been impenetrable Swiss bank secrecy.

At the subcommittee, we saw the UBS case as added proof that our investigations were no impediment to criminal proceedings. Just the opposite. My experience over the years was that PSI hearings aided, rather than impeded, parallel criminal cases by providing prosecutors with additional evidence, a brighter spotlight on wrongdoing, and more heft to the prosecutors' efforts to take on a powerful adversary.

2009 Hearing

Two weeks after the UBS criminal case went public, on March 4, 2009, PSI held its third tax haven bank hearing.[21] Senator Levin held it in part to highlight the new evidence released in the UBS criminal case and include in the hearing record the more accurate (and dramatic) facts. He noted during the hearing, for example, that new UBS documents showed the bank had 52,000—not 19,000—U.S. client account relationships in Switzerland, and its Swiss bankers had paid thousands—not hundreds—of client visits to the United States per year, including 3800 visits in 2004 alone. He also highlighted a newly disclosed 2006 UBS counter-surveillance training packet for UBS bankers traveling abroad. One instruction stated: "In case of an interrogation by any authority: protect the banking secrecy ... wait for assistance of a UBS lawyer."[22] That instruction, "protect the banking secrecy," said it all.

The hearing also took updates from three witnesses: the IRS, Justice Department, and UBS. During the hearing, Senator Levin expressed support for the Justice Department's ongoing effort to use the John Doe summons civil proceeding to obtain the names of U.S. taxpayers with undeclared UBS accounts in Switzerland. He also presented evidence showing that alternative methods for getting those names—such as the U.S.-Swiss tax treaty—rarely worked. He noted that a U.S. treaty request in the UBS case had led a Swiss court to rule that just 12 names out of 52,000 could be disclosed. He pointed out, even then, the 12 U.S. clients had been allowed to appeal the ruling, which meant their names still hadn't actually been turned over. Senator Levin charged that, "[t]oo many countries [were] using our treaties as a shield to deny us tax information instead of using those treaties as a sword to expose tax cheats as was intended."

Post-Hearing Shock Waves

Shock waves from the PSI tax haven bank hearings and the UBS prosecution began rippling outward with surprising results. It became difficult to keep up with the rush of events.

First, in late 2008, a tidal wave of U.S. taxpayers began contacting the IRS to settle tax liabilities related to secret offshore accounts.[23] Many had Swiss accounts at UBS; others had accounts at LGT or other offshore banks. To handle the incoming flood, in late March 2009, the IRS announced a new Offshore Voluntary Disclosure Program. The program offered streamlined procedures, reduced civil penalties, and a reduced likelihood of criminal prosecution if taxpayers disclosed their offshore accounts before the IRS got their names some other way. By October 2009, when the first phase of the program ended, over 15,000 U.S. taxpayers with accounts in more than 60 countries had turned themselves in to the IRS.[24]

Another set of dramatic developments took place outside of the United States. In October 2008, 17 countries led by France and Germany tasked the Organization for Economic Cooperation and Development (OECD) with issuing a revised "blacklist" of uncooperative tax havens that would be subject to international sanctions.[25] To avoid inclusion on the list, countries that had long refused to exchange bank account information in tax matters reversed course and began announcing they would adopt the international information exchange standards earlier developed by the OECD. The OECD standards required countries to exchange account information on a case-by-case basis in tax matters, in response to a specific request by a treaty partner, without invoking domestic secrecy laws.

Liechtenstein led the way by endorsing the OECD standards for the first time and, in December 2008, signing a revised tax information exchange agreement with the United States incorporating the OECD standards.[26] Three months later, Switzerland announced it, too, would re-negotiate its tax treaty with the United States to incorporate the OECD standards.[27]

On April 2, 2009, after months of behind-the-scenes negotiations, the OECD published a new tax haven list with three categories—a "white" list of countries in substantial compliance with OECD information exchange standards, a "gray" list of countries that had pledged compliance but not yet achieved it, and a "black" list of just four countries still refusing to adopt the standards.[28] Five days later, all four countries, Costa Rica, Malaysia, Philippines, and Uruguay, bowed to international pressure and agreed to adopt the OECD standards. In addition, four OECD members, Austria,

Belgium, Luxembourg, and Switzerland, dropped longstanding objections to the OECD's information exchange standards, thereby producing unanimous support for them within the OECD.[29]

Against that backdrop of swelling international support for information exchange in tax matters, in August 2009, Justice announced settlement of the John Doe summons case against UBS.[30] Even though the litigation involved a single, private sector bank, the Swiss government had stepped in to negotiate the settlement and fought to limit the disclosure of U.S. client names. Under the final settlement, Justice announced that UBS would ultimately turn over only about 4500 U.S. client names to U.S. authorities. While we were disappointed by the outcome—4500 was less than 10% of the outstanding 52,000 UBS Swiss accounts—the media portrayed the agreement as another cataclysmic blow against bank secrecy.

The next month, September 2009, Switzerland signed a revised tax treaty with the United States allowing greater access to Swiss bank information in tax cases, using the OECD standards.[31] Even though the revised treaty applied only to future, not past, tax matters, the media portrayed the agreement as pounding still another nail in the coffin of Swiss bank secrecy.

By the end of 2009, over 90 jurisdictions had endorsed the OECD's information exchange standards. According to the OECD, it had witnessed more progress on its tax transparency efforts in that single year than it had over the prior decade.[32]

Enacting FATCA

The changes didn't stop there. In 2010, an even more momentous reform emerged: the Foreign Account Tax Compliance Act or FATCA.

FATCA—the acronym always made me think of "FATCAT"—had two primary authors, Congressman Charlie Rangel, then chair of the House Committee on Ways and Means, and Senator Max Baucus, then chair of the Senate Committee on Finance. Their two committees oversaw the tax laws in Congress. Both had been under mounting pressure to take action against hidden offshore accounts, as exposed in the Levin-led hearings. While Senator Levin had introduced a bill to address the problem, neither committee liked his approach, which involved developing a list of tax havens and imposing extra requirements on U.S. taxpayers who opened accounts or formed legal entities in those jurisdictions. Countries had immediately begun lobbying Ways and Means and Finance against being listed as a tax haven and against the Levin bill altogether. The committee staffs were getting pummeled.

So the Rangel-Baucus bill took a different approach—one that was more comprehensive and hard-hitting than anything we had proposed. Instead of focusing on tax havens, the Rangel-Baucus bill applied worldwide; instead of imposing procedural restrictions on U.S. taxpayers, it mandated account disclosures by foreign firms. The key provision required all non-U.S. financial institutions worldwide to make annual disclosures to the IRS of every account opened by a U.S. person or pay a 30% excise tax on their U.S. earnings. Ka-boom!

The bill applied its new disclosure mandate not only to banks but also to securities firms, hedge funds, and a host of other financial firms. It defined "U.S. persons" broadly to include not only U.S. citizens and residents but also the companies, partnerships, and other entities they formed or controlled. In addition, since U.S. treasury bonds were a safe investment held by nearly all financial institutions worldwide, the bill made virtually all of those institutions subject to the 30% tax on their earnings unless they disclosed their U.S. client accounts. In short, the bill was a powershot, with broad coverage and a meaningful, enforceable penalty.

John Buckley of the Rangel staff first contacted us about the bill and asked if Senator Levin would like to cosponsor it. At first, we were dazzled by its scope, but after taking a few deep breaths, we began pressing for it to add key provisions from the Levin bill. While the bill sponsors accepted a few, they rejected the provisions that mattered the most to Senator Levin. In the end, he didn't cosponsor the Rangel-Baucus bill, even though he supported the legislation.

The Rangel-Baucus team wasn't bothered by Senator Levin's decision not to cosponsor the bill; it may have even made their job easier. They quickly scheduled a House hearing and, soon after, slipped a revised version of FATCA into the HIRE Act, a jobs bill on a fast track to enactment. The end result: FATCA became law about five months after it was introduced.[33] Given the bill's worldwide sweep, we were amazed by the quick legislative win.

Later we learned that one reason the bill moved so quickly was its quiet backing by the powerful U.S. banking industry. Banks in the United States already had to disclose all of their U.S. client accounts to the IRS. They had watched in frustration as increasing numbers of rich Americans moved their money offshore to tax haven banks with no equivalent disclosure obligation. Because U.S. banks couldn't compete against offshore banks offering secret accounts, they supported their foreign competitors facing the same disclosure requirements they had. So behind the scenes, U.S. banks were cheering on FATCA's enactment.

In contrast, most foreign banks had little or no notice of FATCA until after it became law. When they realized its impact on bank secrecy, many erupted in protest, but were unable to overcome the U.S. bank lobby or public anger with offshore tax abuse. They were stuck with the U.S. law. And if they wanted to keep investing in U.S. treasuries without paying the 30% excise tax, they were stuck with having to disclose their U.S. client accounts.

It took six years—until 2016—for governments and banks around the globe to create the infrastructure needed to meet the law's annual disclosure requirement. Along the way, many countries demanded that the United States reciprocate by compelling U.S. banks to disclose any accounts opened by their nationals. The United States acquiesced, adopting over the vigorous objection of some U.S. banks a regulation requiring U.S. banks to disclose to the IRS all accounts opened by non-U.S. persons.[34] That regulation set the stage for annual, automatic exchanges of account information between the United States and its partner countries.

There's more. FATCA quickly became a catalyst for international information exchanges unrelated to the United States. Once other countries realized how automatic information exchanges could be used to combat secret accounts and tax evasion, and that an automatic information exchange infrastructure was being put into place at banks around the world to meet FATCA's requirements, jurisdictions began to call for FATCA-like arrangements between themselves, unrelated to the United States.

Their efforts culminated in a 2010 amendment to the OECD's Convention on Mutual Administrative Assistance in Tax Matters, endorsed by over 90 countries, authorizing automatic cross-border information exchanges in tax matters.[35] It went beyond the 2009 OECD standard which facilitated information exchanges on a case-by-case basis in response to treaty requests; instead, the new agreement facilitated annual information exchanges on an automated basis. Over 90 countries also signed a Common Reporting Standard and a Multilateral Competent Authority Agreement to begin automatic information exchanges by 2017.[36]

While Senator Levin did not author FATCA or its progeny, given the direct connection between FATCA and his tax haven bank hearings, some view Senator Levin's oversight efforts as the spark that fueled the international revolution in bank account transparency and information exchange.

Taking on Credit Suisse Five Years Later

Senator Levin's battle against tax haven banks didn't end, however, with adoption of FATCA. In his last year at PSI, he held one more hearing spotlighting tax haven bank misdeeds.[37] It exposed a huge gulf between what was being said and what was really happening on the ground.

The genesis of the hearing was, after the 2008 UBS scandal broke, when we asked other Swiss banks if they were engaged in similar misconduct. Credit Suisse, Switzerland's second largest bank, privately admitted it was, but claimed it would close or disclose to the IRS all of its undeclared U.S. client accounts in Switzerland. Since we'd already made our point with UBS, we figured we'd let sleeping dogs lie while Credit Suisse and the other Swiss banks cleaned up their act.

Fast forward three years to 2011. That's when the Justice Department indicted seven Credit Suisse bankers for aiding and abetting U.S. tax evasion. It was also when whispers reached us that Credit Suisse still had thousands of undeclared U.S. client accounts open in Switzerland. Surprised, we decided to check.

Credit Suisse grudgingly agreed to a meeting. Participants on our side included Bob, Allison Murphy, and me, as well as Henry Kerner, Stephanie Hall, and Mike Lueptow from the staff of Senator John McCain, then PSI's ranking Republican. The meeting had a bad feeling from the get-go. Credit Suisse wouldn't provide even basic information about its U.S. client accounts in Switzerland, offering only vague responses to our questions. Not a good sign.

We decided to launch a full-blown investigation—subpoenas, interviews, the works. Because we were juggling several other inquiries, however, it proceeded slowly. Eventually, we put Allison Murphy in charge and through sheer relentless exertion as well as unexpected cooperation from some bank insiders, she got the information we needed. We learned Credit Suisse had been holding back on the extent of its U.S. client business. At its height, the bank had over 22,000 undisclosed Swiss accounts with U.S. clients holding up to $12 billion in assets. Not as big as UBS, but still a huge portfolio compared to other offshore banks we'd reviewed.

We also learned that, like UBS, Credit Suisse had repeatedly sent Swiss bankers into the United States to recruit new clients and service existing ones. In addition, the bank had opened a Zurich airport branch to make it easy for foreigners to fly in, conduct their banking business, and depart. Almost 10,000 of its U.S. client accounts were located at the Zurich airport branch. Another 2000 were housed in a small private Swiss bank, Clariden Leu, which Credit Suisse had quietly purchased and allowed to operate with few controls.

We confirmed that Credit Suisse had used many of the same secrecy tricks as UBS and LGT, including client code names, accounts opened in the name of shell entities, and clandestine interactions with U.S. clients. A former U.S. client located by Allison told us about a posh hotel breakfast where a Credit Suisse banker had passed him his bank statement slipped in between the pages of a *Sports Illustrated* magazine. He also described visiting Credit Suisse's Zurich headquarters, riding a remotely controlled elevator with no floor buttons, meeting a banker in a bare room with white walls, and being assured his bank documents would be shredded—all to highlight the bank's secrecy and willingness to conceal his assets.

Confirming that Credit Suisse's banking practices had been as sleazy as those at UBS was jarring, but not a big surprise. What we hadn't expected was that, after being told by PSI the jig was up and promising to change its ways, Credit Suisse took years to actually close the offending Swiss accounts—five years, in fact, using so-called Exit Projects that stretched out from 2008 to 2013. Many U.S. client accounts in Switzerland had finally closed only after the Credit Suisse bankers were indicted, and PSI began nosing around.

That wasn't the only bad news. When we looked more broadly, we found that the Justice Department effort to prosecute U.S. tax cheats with offshore accounts—an effort marked by bold, innovative, and effective legal actions under the Bush administration—had stalled under the Obama administration. Under the Department's number two official, Deputy Attorney General Jim Cole, U.S. prosecutors had generally stopped using U.S. courts and U.S. tools to go after U.S. tax cheats in Switzerland. Instead, U.S. prosecutors had generally limited themselves to making requests for information in Swiss courts using the U.S.-Swiss treaty process.

Past evidence had shown the treaty process was both glacial and ineffective. Even if the Swiss government agreed to disclose account information under the treaty, its laws enabled the targets of the treaty requests to file their own objections in Swiss court. The cases forced the United States to ask a Swiss court to order a Swiss bank to disclose accountholder names and information to the U.S. government, setting up the kind of frontal assault on Swiss secrecy traditions that was bound to fail, even when limited to U.S. accountholders. And fail it did.

We learned that, after years of effort, of the 22,000 U.S. client accounts in Switzerland that Credit Suisse admitted were never disclosed to the IRS, the Justice Department had managed to get accountholder names for just 238. That's 238 out of 22,000: a success rate of 1%. For the other 99% of accounts, Justice still had no names at all.

Justice responded to our dismay at its track record by highlighting a new program it set up in 2013 to negotiate non-prosecution agreements with Swiss banks suspected of providing undeclared accounts to U.S. clients.[38]

Justice said 106 Swiss banks had already signed up to the program, which required the banks not only to pay fines and stop opening secret accounts but also disclose account details. When we asked why those account details didn't include the U.S. accountholder names, DOJ representatives sighed at our harping on the same issue.

We explained that, to Senator Levin, it was unconscionable for Justice to wipe out the Swiss banks' criminal liability for helping U.S. taxpayers evade taxes without also requiring disclosure of the U.S. client names needed to collect the unpaid taxes. Justice officials huffed that we just didn't understand how good a deal they had struck with the Swiss, insisting they'd created a process that would, eventually and indirectly, produce the accountholder names we wanted. While we agreed that might happen, we couldn't understand why Justice hadn't taken a harder line and insisted on getting the names directly from the banks with less delay and hassle.

A second sour realization was how hard the Swiss government was still fighting to preserve secrecy for Swiss accountholders, including U.S. clients. We'd heard Credit Suisse and other Swiss banks were ready to turn over relevant client names to the United States, but the Swiss government wouldn't allow it. Its refusal to permit its banks to cooperate spoke louder than all the Swiss rhetoric claiming the country had become a fan of greater transparency, would no longer use its secrecy laws to facilitate tax evasion, and was disinfecting its banking sector.

Going Public Again

By early 2014, we'd written up the investigation's results in a 200-page Levin-McCain report that exposed not only what Credit Suisse had done but also what the Justice Department had failed to do. We handed out the report at a press briefing the day before the hearing. Senator Levin gaveled in the hearing on February 26, 2014, the first hearing of his last year in the Senate. PSI heard from two panels of witnesses.

The first panel consisted of four high-ranking Credit Suisse officials, including CEO Brady Dougan. Mr. Dougan acknowledged the bank's past wrongdoing and expressed "regret" for its actions, but also blamed any violations of U.S. law on a "small group" of Swiss bankers who hid their "bad conduct" from the bank. No one bought that last line, however, given the tens of thousands of undeclared accounts, billions of dollars in assets, years of U.S. travel paid for by Credit Suisse, and massive profits made by the bank. In fact, in a statement issued the day after the hearing, the Swiss Association of Bank

Employees described Credit Suisse's efforts to blame rogue employees for the bank's misconduct as "hardly credible," stating that the facilitation of tax evasion had "long been the banks' business model and was well-known."[39]

The second hearing panel consisted of two senior Justice officials, Deputy Attorney General Jim Cole and Assistant Attorney General in charge of the Tax Division Kathryn Keneally. Both vigorously disputed criticism of their enforcement strategy as slow and ineffective. When asked why they'd stopped using John Doe summons to get U.S. client names, they said the treaty process took precedence. When asked why they'd secured only 238 Credit Suisse accountholder names out of 22,000 under the treaty, they said they were on track to obtain more. When asked why Justice never tried to extradite the seven Credit Suisse bankers indicted in 2011, they said the Swiss never granted extradition requests so it was pointless to try. When asked why Credit Suisse itself hadn't been indicted, despite the evidence in 2011, they urged patience. When asked why so few other tax haven banks had been prosecuted, they claimed to have information they were not at liberty to disclose and asked the subcommittee to trust its handling of the cases.

The hearing received extensive press coverage. Three months later, in May 2014, the Justice Department announced Credit Suisse had agreed to plead guilty to aiding and abetting U.S. tax evasion and pay a fine of $2.6 billion.[40] Senator Levin welcomed the huge penalty, but couldn't help noting what still hadn't happened: "This guilty plea strikes an important blow against tax evasion through bank secrecy. But it is a mystery to me why the U.S. government didn't require as part of the agreement that the bank cough up some of the names of the U.S. clients with secret Swiss bank accounts."[41]

At the end of 2014, the Justice Department announced criminal charges against another bank that opened secret offshore accounts for U.S. clients, Bank Leumi of Israel. In a deferred prosecution agreement, the bank not only admitted facilitating U.S. tax evasion and paid $400 million in fines, but also turned over 1500 U.S. client names.[42] Since then, through its Swiss bank settlement program, the Justice Department is rumored to be obtaining a steady stream of U.S. accountholder names, though public prosecutions remain scarce.

Handling the Battle Aftermath

Senator Levin's tax haven bank battle spanned five years. The UBS and Credit Suisse hearings were bookends around his all-out effort.

Those five years saw real progress. By mid-2014, over 45,000 U.S. taxpayers had come clean through the IRS Offshore Voluntary Disclosure Program, disclosing tens of thousands of offshore accounts and paying back taxes and penalties exceeding $6.5 billion.[43] By 2017, those numbers swelled to 100,000 taxpayers and $10 billion. In addition, Congress enacted FATCA, compelling financial institutions around the world to disclose offshore accounts opened by U.S. persons. The OECD, using FATCA as a model, won support for a parallel global agreement enabling tax authorities worldwide to exchange automated information on accounts opened by their nationals. Tax haven governments and banks around the globe had changed their rhetoric, claiming they would no longer use secrecy laws to facilitate tax evasion. In short, by the time Senator Levin left office, it had gotten a whole lot harder to open a secret offshore account.

At the same time, bank secrecy was far from vanquished. Both FATCA and the OECD agreements contained gaping loopholes allowing offshore accounts to be opened without triggering disclosure requirements. Some offshore banks continued to secretly service wealthy clients dodging taxes. Switzerland and other tax haven jurisdictions continued to resist key transparency measures. Senator Rand Paul and Congressman Mark Meadows continued to attack FATCA and Senate ratification of stronger tax disclosure treaties. In short, while the Levin investigations exposed massive wrongdoing and inspired new laws and practices, it is clear that the war to end tax haven secrecy and tax haven bank abuses will take years longer to win.

Notes

1. Information about LGT Bank and UBS is based upon "Tax Haven Banks and U.S. Tax Compliance," S.Hrg. 110-614 (7/17 and 25/2008) (hereinafter "Tax Haven Bank Hearing Record"), https://www.gpo.gov/fdsys/pkg/CHRG-110shrg44127/pdf/CHRG-110shrg44127.pdf.
2. See, for example, "Tax Scandal in Germany Fans Complaints of Inequity," *New York Times*, Carter Dougherty and Mark Landler (2/18/2008), http://nyti.ms/2mGyzQw.
3. Id.
4. "IRS and Tax Treaty Partners Target Liechtenstein Accounts," IRS Press Release No. IR-2008-26 (2/26/2008), https://www.irs.gov/newsroom/irs-and-tax-treaty-partners-target-liechtenstein-accounts.
5. For more information about the Marsh accounts, see Tax Haven Bank Hearing Record, at 81–82, 122–128.

6. For more information about the Wu accounts, see Tax Haven Bank Hearing Record, at 82, 128–135.

7. For more information about the Greenfield accounts, see Tax Haven Bank Hearing Record, at 83–84, 144–147.

8. Id., at 84.

9. For more information about the Lowy accounts, see Tax Haven Bank Hearing Record, at 82–83, 135–144.

10. For a copy of the international arrest warrant, see Id., at 222.

11. *United States v. Olenicoff*, Case No. 8:07-CR-00227-CJC (USDC CD Calif.), Plea Agreement for Defendant Igor M. Olenicoff (12/10/2007). See also "Stay Out of Jail for $52 Million?" *Forbes*, William P. Barrett and Janet Novack (12/12/2007), http://bit.ly/1dRoZZG.

12. "Banker Pleads Guilty to Helping American Real Estate Developer Evade Income Tax on $200 Million," U.S. Attorney's Office for the Southern District of Florida Press Release (6/19/2008), http://www.usdoj.gov/usao/fls/PressReleases/080619-01.html; *United States v. Birkenfeld*, Case No. 08-CR-60099-ZLOCH (USDC SD Fla.), Statement of Facts (6/19/2008), at 3–4.

13. Mr. Birkenfeld was sentenced in August 2009. In preparation for the sentencing, his legal counsel requested and PSI provided a one-page letter stating that Mr. Birkenfeld had provided accurate information that was of assistance in the PSI investigation. He was ultimately sentenced to 40 months in prison. In 2012, the IRS awarded Mr. Birkenfeld $104 million for supplying information that led, among other results, to the recovery of $780 million from UBS. Mr. Birkenfeld was released from prison that same year.

14. Tax Haven Bank Hearing Record, at 77.

15. Id., at 31.

16. See, for example, "Mystery Site Puts $7-million Bounty on Man Wanted in Theft of Canadians' Bank Data," *The Globe and Mail*, Greg McArthur (6/11/2008), https://tgam.ca/2mIhYvM.

17. Tax Haven Bank Hearing Record, at 708–709 (August 8, 2008 letter from PSI to Mr. Bennett regarding Peter Lowy's actions).

18. "Super-Rich Tax Cheats," American News Project (7/25/2008), https://www.youtube.com/watch?v=noU5dRoPIX4.

19. After the hearing, representatives of Peter Lowy occasionally contacted PSI, urging it as late as 2014 to issue a statement indicating it had been mistaken about his role in the Liechtenstein scandal, and that he was not involved in tax avoidance. However, in light of the unchallenged Liechtenstein documents providing contemporaneous evidence that Mr. Lowy was a knowing and willing participant in the formation and dissolution of the $68 million Luperla Foundation, PSI declined the requests to provide a retraction.

20. *United States v. UBS*, Case No. 09-60033-CR-Cohn (SDFL), Deferred Prosecution Agreement (2/18/2009). See also "UBS Enters into Deferred

Prosecution Agreement," Justice Department Press Release (2/18/2009), https://www.justice.gov/opa/pr/ubs-enters-deferred-prosecution-agreement.

21. "Tax Haven Banks and U.S. Tax Compliance: Obtaining the Names of U.S. Clients with Swiss Accounts," S. Hrg. 111-30 (3/4/2009), https://www.gpo.gov/fdsys/pkg/CHRG-111shrg49492/pdf/CHRG-111shrg49492.pdf.

22. Id., Exhibit 13, "US International Training," UBS Document, (9/26/2006), "Lessons Learned," at 231.

23. See, for example, "UBS Clients Seek Amnesty on U.S. Taxes," *Wall Street Journal*, Carrick Mollenkamp and Evan Perez (11/24/2008), http://on.wsj.com/2hCLpdg.

24. See "IRS Reminds Taxpayers that the August 31 Deadline Is Fast Approaching for the Second Special Voluntary Disclosure Initiative of Offshore Accounts," IRS Press Release No. IR-2011-84 (8/8/2011), https://www.irs.gov/newsroom/irs-reminds-taxpayers-that-the-aug-31-deadline-is-fast-approaching-for-the-second-special-voluntary-disclosure-initiative-of-offshore-accounts.

25. See, for example, "France, Germany Led Charge for New Tax Havens Blacklist," AFP (10/21/2008), http://nws.mx/2zVPHEZ.

26. See "U.S., Liechtenstein Sign Tax Information Exchange Agreement," Department of Treasury Press Release No. HP-1320 (12/8/2008), https://www.treasury.gov/press-center/press-releases/Pages/hp1320.aspx. Five years later, in 2013, LGT's affiliated bank entered into a Non-Prosecution Agreement with the United States and paid a penalty of over $23 million. See "Manhattan U.S. Attorney Announces Agreement with Liechtenstein Bank to Pay $23.8 Million to Resolve Criminal Tax Investigation," U.S. Attorney for the Southern District of New York press release (7/30/2013), http://www.justice.gov/usao-sdny/pr/manhattan-us-attorney-announces-agreement-liechtenstein-bank-pay-238-million-resolve. In the Non-Prosecution Agreement, the bank admitted, among other matters, that by 2006, it held over 900 undeclared Liechtenstein accounts containing more than $340 million for U.S. clients, and that the bank had assisted a significant number of its U.S. clients to evade their U.S. tax obligations. As part of the agreement, the bank turned over more than 200 client files to U.S. authorities.

27. "Switzerland to Adopt OECD Standard on Administrative Assistance in Fiscal Matters," Swiss Government Press Release (3/13/2009), www.news.admin.ch/message/?lang=en&msg-id=25863. The next month, Switzerland announced its intention to agree to a revised tax treaty with the United States, incorporating the OECD standards. See, for example, "U.S., Switzerland Begin Negotiations to Bolster Tax Information Exchange," U.S. Treasury Department Press Release No. TG-85 (4/7/2009), www.treas.gov/press/releases/tg85.htm.

28. See OECD chart entitled, "A Progress Report on the Jurisdictions Surveyed by the OECD Global Forum in Implementing the Internationally Agreed Tax Standard," (4/2/2009), http://www.oecd.org/ctp/42497950.pdf.

29. See "Promoting Transparency and Exchange of Information for Tax Purposes," OECD Report (1/19/2010), at ¶ 9, http://www.oecd.org/newsroom/4443 1965.pdf.

30. "U.S. Discloses Terms of Agreement with Swiss Government Regarding UBS," U.S. Justice Department Press Release (8/19/2009), https://www.justice.gov/opa/pr/us-discloses-terms-agreement-swiss-government-regarding-ubs.

31. 2009 Protocol to 1996 Switzerland-U.S. Income Tax Convention, https://www.congress.gov/treaty-document/112th-congress/1/document-text. The protocol will take effect when it is ratified by the U.S. Senate. Due to Senator Rand Paul's opposition, the Senate has never taken a vote to ratify the protocol. As of 2017, eight years after the Swiss agreed to provide greater disclosures related to U.S. tax matters, the new protocol has yet to take effect.

32. "Promoting Transparency and Exchange of Information for Tax Purposes," OECD Report (1/19/2010), at ¶ 4, http://www.oecd.org/newsroom/44431965.pdf.

33. FATCA was introduced as H.R. 3933 on October 27, 2009; examined in a House hearing on November 5, 2009; and enacted into law on March 18, 2010, as Title V(A) of the Hiring Incentives to Restore Employment (HIRE) Act, P.L. 111-47.

34. See "Guidance on Reporting Interest Paid to Nonresident Aliens," Treasury Department and IRS, 26 CFR §§1.6049-4(b) (5) and 1.6049-8, as revised by TD 9584 (4/17/2012), requiring the reporting of such interest as of January 1, 2013.

35. See "Convention on Mutual Administrative Assistance in Tax Matters," OECD Website, http://bit.ly/2Abebg9.

36. OECD Automatic Exchange Portal, "About Automatic Exchange," "A Brief History of AEOI," http://www.oecd.org/tax/automatic-exchange/about-automatic-exchange/.

37. "Offshore Tax Evasion: The Effort to Collect Unpaid Taxes on Billions in Hidden Offshore Accounts," S. Hrg. 113-397 (2/26/2014), Volumes 1–2, https://www.gpo.gov/fdsys/pkg/CHRG-113shrg88276/pdf/CHRG-113shrg88276.pdf (Volume 1); and https://www.gpo.gov/fdsys/pkg/CHRG-113shrg89751/pdf/CHRG-113shrg89751.pdf (Volume 2).

38. See "United States and Switzerland Issue Joint Statement Regarding Tax Evasion Investigations," Justice Department Press Release (8/29/2013), http://www.justice.gov/opa/pr/2013/August/13-tax-975.html.

39. "Dougan's Reign Tested as Credit Suisse Tax Charge Looms," *Bloomberg*, Elisa Martinuzzi, Max Abelson and Elena Logutenkova (5/11/2014), https://bloom.bg/2zMTSFg.

40. *United States v. Credit Suisse*, Case No. 1:14-CR-188 (USDC ED Va.), Information (5/19/2014).

41. "Levin Statement on Credit Suisse Pleading Guilty to Aiding U.S. Tax Evasion," (5/19/2014).

42. See "Bank Leumi Admits to Assisting U.S. Taxpayers in Hiding Assets in Offshore Bank Accounts," Justice Department Press Release (12/22/2014), http://www.justice.gov/opa/pr/bank-leumi-admits-assisting-us-taxpayers-hiding-assets-offshore-bank-accounts. For another example, see "Acting Manhattan U.S. Attorney Announces Agreement with Swiss Asset Management Firm to Resolve Criminal Tax Investigation," Justice Department Press Release (8/15/2017), https://www.justice.gov/opa/pr/acting-manhattan-us-attorney-announces-agreement-swiss-asset-management-firm-resolve-criminal (describing non-prosecution agreement with Swiss asset manager, Prime Partners, promising disclosure of estimated 175 client names of U.S. persons helped to evade U.S. taxes).

43. "IRS Offshore Voluntary Disclosure Efforts Produce $6.5 Billion; 45,000 Taxpayers Participate," IRS Press Release No. FS-2014-6 (6/2014), https://www.irs.gov/uac/Newsroom/IRS-Offshore-Voluntary-Disclosure-Efforts-Produce-$6.5-Billion;-45,000-Taxpayers-Participate.

7

Crossing Party Lines

"Coming together is a beginning; keeping together is progress; working together is success."
Henry Ford

Introduction

The investigations I know best are the ones led by the Levin team. But another important part of our work on PSI involved supporting investigations led by our Republican counterparts. During his 15 years on the subcommittee, Senator Levin partnered with four Republicans: Senator Susan Collins from Maine, Senator Norm Coleman from Minnesota, Senator Tom Coburn from Oklahoma, and Senator John McCain from Arizona. Whether serving with them in the majority or minority, Senator Levin urged us to support the investigations of our Republican colleagues in the same way we'd want them to support ours.

Supporting an investigation is different than leading it. On PSI, leading an investigation meant formulating the objectives of the inquiry, developing the investigative plan, drafting the subpoenas, reviewing the documents, leading the interviews, writing the first draft of the report, fact-checking and footnoting the text, designing the hearing, selecting the hearing exhibits, handling the press, and proposing a follow-up plan. It meant shouldering the bulk of the work.

Supporting an investigation was a much easier gig, although doing it well required attention, anticipation, and negotiating skills. The inherent tension was to support the inquiry, while also representing Senator Levin's

© The Author(s) 2018
E. J. Bean, *Financial Exposure*, https://doi.org/10.1007/978-3-319-94388-6_7

interests. Representing his interests involved a host of intangibles, including ensuring the inquiry was fact-based and even-handed, issues important to him were addressed, written products were framed in a way he could support, and the hearing examined issues in a fair and interesting way. It also meant protecting PSI as an institution, enforcing its information requests, avoiding setting bad precedents, and presenting a united front against those trying to foil an inquiry. In addition, we continuously sought to build goodwill with our colleagues during their investigations in hopes they would repay the favor in ours.

A significant issue in all of the investigations involved policy differences between Democrats and Republicans. PSI's leaders simply didn't see eye to eye on some policy matters. So working together required sensitivity, accommodation, compromise, and creative solutions to bridge the divides. When consensus wasn't possible, we expressed regret over the specific short-term disagreement, while reaffirming support for the long-term relationship. At times, some investigations felt like an obstacle course in which a primary objective was surviving the inquiry with our bipartisan relationship intact.

Weighing In

Over time, to minimize conflict and maximize chances for a joint effort, I learned to pay careful attention to key investigative inflection points that tended to set the course of an inquiry. Finding common ground at those points often paved the way for a bipartisan effort.

One of the most important inflection points was the initial framing of the investigation. Investigative options generated a constant buzz at PSI; ideas materialized from press articles, reports, whistleblowers, constituents, other Senate offices, and, of course, the boss. If our Republican colleagues began to coalesce around a particular inquiry, it was typical for them to chat with us about it, often seeking advice from Bob on how to tackle the problem. Bob and I encouraged our colleagues to think big, reciting the internal adage that "PSI was made to hunt lions, not rabbits." In addition, we always urged framing an inquiry in terms of answering a complex factual question, while realizing it might take up to a year to get an answer.

When our Republican colleagues settled on a specific proposal, we set up a meeting with Senator Levin to discuss it. Generally, he took the position that both sides of the aisle had the right to investigate anything within PSI's broad mandate. At the same time, he disliked inquiries into highly partisan issues that could undermine PSI's bipartisan well-being. Those two competing principles shaped his reaction to most investigative proposals. In addition, because he'd been in the Senate for so many years, Senator Levin had developed an uncanny ability to see around corners—how an investigation might unfold, what danger points might arise, and what could be done to sidestep problems before they tripped us up. He often provided cautionary notes or advice that helped shape a successful effort. In addition, at times, he identified specific issues that he wanted to examine as part of a proposed investigation. By the end of the meeting, we usually had his approval and helpful guidance or a clear sense of what was needed for him to get comfortable with signing off on a new GOP inquiry.

A second key inflection point involved the initial document requests. Because we wanted every investigation to be bipartisan, we carefully reviewed the GOP's document requests to make sure they were ones we could vigorously support. That meant they had to be targeted, well drafted, and likely to produce a manageable volume of documents; we simply couldn't fight for unreasonable demands. At the same time, we tried to use the drafting process to build goodwill with our GOP colleagues, often by providing copies of previous PSI subpoenas, strengthening or clarifying draft language, or suggesting third party document requests that might be useful. If necessary, we negotiated to reduce a problematic document request, working to convince our colleagues that we really did support their inquiry but thought a more modest request was necessary for Senator Levin's support. For large or sensitive document requests, we met with Senator Levin to make sure he was okay with the wording and would be willing to fight for the documents if needed. Sometimes he required more changes before signing off.

Once we were comfortable with the framing of the investigation and document requests, we tended to step back and watch the evidence unfold. We usually did not engage in document review—the Republican staff took the lead on that. They also chose the interview subjects and took the lead on questions. We typically chimed in during interviews only occasionally, having had an opportunity to include our concerns in the interview questions circulated beforehand. Throughout this phase of the investigation, we tried to remain alert to new opportunities to build goodwill with our Republican counterparts by making creative suggestions to advance the investigation, advising on how to proceed under PSI rules, or helping tackle any problems.

We also usually participated actively in any meetings with outside legal counsel. Typically, the key PSI staffers set up a bipartisan staff meeting beforehand to develop joint positions on likely issues, so we could present a united front in discussions with outside counsel. We followed that procedure even when the outside counsel came from a Democratic administration or friendly organization, because our institutional loyalty went first to PSI. In addition, PSI policy was to insist on outside counsel meeting with both Republican and Democratic staff at the same time and to decline meetings where only one side of the aisle was welcome. We'd found meetings targeting only one party were often designed to divide the two sides. They also frequently caused confusion or conflict since meetings geared to a single party often conveyed skewed, partial, or disputed facts. So PSI policy was to require joint meetings.

Telephone calls raised similar issues. On occasion, some agency or company counsel insisted on calling the Levin staff to convey information or requests related to a GOP-led investigation. We were wary about taking those calls since, again, the usual objective was to try to play the Democrats off the Republicans. After a few stiff conversations and referrals to our GOP counterparts, those calls usually dwindled to instances where outside counsel was really trying to accommodate the GOP and seeking advice on how to proceed.

A third key inflection point came when the investigation progressed to the stage where staff began working on a written product. In GOP-led inquiries, the Republican staff always wrote the first draft and then sought our comments. We always read the drafts with care and offered detailed edits, dedicating significant time and resources to the review process. Our goals were to help ensure accuracy, encourage an approach our boss could support, and produce a polished product that burnished PSI's reputation. Once the staffs went as far as they could to produce a joint product, Senator Levin typically conducted his own review and offered additional edits. We met with him to discuss his concerns and conveyed the key points to our GOP colleagues. On a few occasions, contentious issues were resolved in a meeting between the two senators, with staff present to record the outcome.

The two PSI staffs worked hard to produce written products that both sides could support. Even when unsuccessful, our joint drafting process produced an improved end product; ensured both sides were familiar with the reasoning, conclusions, and recommendations of the other; and often enabled the side that didn't sign on to nevertheless describe the opposite party's work in positive terms. When done well, the process also built bipartisan trust as colleagues realized each side valued the advice of the other and would listen to that advice even if the other side was unable to join the final product.

Most investigations culminated with a public hearing. By that stage, both sides were familiar with the investigative findings and issues. The Republican staff typically suggested the hearing panels, witnesses, key issues, and key documents. We offered comments and suggestions, again trying to build goodwill while also fashioning an approach that would appeal to our boss. In addition, the staffs almost always drafted a joint press release that included quotes from both senators. We then met with Senator Levin to present the proposed hearing and press release, conveyed any concerns he had to our counterparts, and negotiated the final details.

A week or so before a hearing, the GOP staff typically disclosed its general media strategy. They took the lead in contacting reporters, while we often assisted with a few press calls of our own. If the Republicans held a press briefing, we attended on a staff level. If his schedule permitted and he was welcome, Senator Levin also attended, following the lead of his Republican partner. At the hearing itself, Senator Levin always cleared his schedule to be present for the entire proceeding and used his opening statement and questions to help create a positive bipartisan environment and assist in establishing the facts.

PSI's bipartisan approach to hearings stood in stark contrast to many other congressional committees. We regularly heard stories of committees where the majority staff concealed the witness list and issues from the minority staff until a few days before the hearing, then sprang the information on the other side, and only grudgingly allowed the minority staff to scramble and locate one witness of its own. The resulting hearing often suffered from a lack of coordination, negative staff interactions, and competing or disjointed objectives. Instead of being the culmination of a bipartisan process in which consensus was built around the facts, the hearing became a painful and unproductive battle over what the key facts were. Luckily, in the 15 years I was on PSI, due to our collaborative process, we never experienced that type of hearing.

The final component of the investigation—the follow-up—was also, in many cases, a bipartisan effort. For example, we typically joined our GOP colleagues in submitting post-hearing questions to witnesses, sending referral letters to agencies requesting additional investigative or enforcement actions, or meeting with key parties on post-hearing reforms. In addition, if his Republican partner drafted legislation, Senator Levin often cosponsored it.

By weighing in on GOP investigations from beginning to end, providing what we hoped were helpful contributions to their document requests, interviews, meetings with opposing counsel, reports, hearings, media, and post-hearing reforms, we tried to model the bipartisan support we wanted our Republican counterparts to provide in Levin-led investigations. Over time, our efforts seemed to generate a lot of reciprocal goodwill.

Building Bipartisan Ties

While most of the Levin staff got involved with PSI's Republican investigations at some stage, especially during hearing prep, on a day-to-day-basis, due to limited staff, we typically assigned a single Levin staffer to each GOP-led inquiry. That person had lead responsibility to represent Senator Levin's interests during an often year-long effort. Our liaison often spent 50–100% of their time on the GOP-led investigation.

Our best liaisons were committed to bipartisanship, respected people with different points of view, and were at ease working on their own. They displayed tact, courtesy, and the ability to talk about issues in ways that didn't offend Republican staffers. They also were mature enough not to take offense at partisan jokes or thoughtless phrasing. Most important of all was their ability to sense where an investigation was headed, what political or investigative problems might arise, and when other Levin staff needed to be alerted to an issue or brought in to solve a problem before it hit critical mass. That normally required an experienced investigator.

Some Levin staffers were reluctant liaisons, viewing the task as akin to tiptoeing through a minefield. Others enjoyed swimming in GOP waters. They felt good about conducting joint investigations, enjoyed crossing party lines, and were confidant in their ability to sense and deal with trouble. Those folks were key to our GOP goodwill efforts.

We supported our liaisons by providing a work environment that valued bipartisan interactions and put a premium on bipartisan trust. PSI was unusual that way. In much of Washington, having colleagues—much less friends—on the other side of the aisle could be seen as odd, suspect, or even traitorous. But PSI's longstanding bipartisan traditions, operations, and social activities gave staffs on both sides of the aisle a chance to transcend Washington's usual atmosphere of distrust and suspicion.

PSI's rules and standard operating procedures also helped by requiring a lot of routine bipartisan interaction—approving each other's investigations, sharing documents, conducting joint interviews, and working together on reports, hearings, and press releases. In addition, PSI tradition favored frequent, informal staff communications to provide investigation updates, hash out issues, and prepare for meetings with outsiders. PSI's fluid lines of communication sometimes surprised new staffers, especially those who'd worked in the House where information was often closely held and crossed party lines at the last minute, if at all. In contrast, at PSI, information was shared across party lines on a daily basis.

Contributing to that free flow of information was the physical layout of PSI's offices. The Republican and Democratic staffs worked in adjoining offices stretching out on opposite sides of our public reception area. No one had to exit PSI territory and walk through the public hallways to reach a counterpart's desk; PSI staffers could walk straight through the offices from end to end, passing the reception area in the middle to reach the other side. Behind the reception area sat the clerk's office, where Mary held court on administrative matters, offering still another venue for bipartisan chit-chat on a daily basis.

In addition, PSI habit was for staff on one side to physically walk to the other side for quick staff meetings. We'd found that in-person meetings built bipartisan ties quicker than phone calls or emails. For some Levin staffers, it initially felt hard—mentally and physically tough—to walk through the door into GOP territory, worrying they might be unwelcome, but it got easier with repetition. PSI etiquette also called for visitors to announce their presence as they walked in, to preclude unintended eavesdropping. We explicitly encouraged our staffers to walk over and talk with their counterparts on a daily basis, in addition to exchanging emails and telephone calls, so everyone would get to know each other better.

Drinking Manhattans

Complementing PSI's culture of in-person staff meetings was a set of PSI social traditions that also helped break down walls between the two parties. The most important involved Manhattans, a whiskey and vermouth drink that most PSI staffers (including me) had never tried before joining the sub-committee. A running argument was whether Harry Truman, Joe McCarthy, or Linda Gustitus started it,[1] but throughout the Levin era, Manhattans were PSI's official beverage. Every two to three weeks, work stopped around 5:30 or 6:00 p.m., and PSI staff from both sides gathered in the conference room for a few drinks. Bob was in charge of mixing the Manhattans which usually packed quite a punch. With money in hand from senior staffers, interns also picked up snacks and other beverages.

As folks gathered around the conference room table, no discussion of work was allowed. Instead, topics ran from movies, kids, and significant others to jokes and PSI lore. Bob was our secret weapon—gregarious, full of great stories, sometimes hilarious—he was always a hit with the GOP crew. And they usually had a Bob counterpart, someone with new jokes and stories that invigorated the cross-party banter. For 15 years, PSI hosted a rolling series of low-key cocktail parties fueled by investigators spinning funny stories. The social hours relaxed the ranks and helped them discover they could actually enjoy each other's company.

We also used other social occasions to build bipartisan ties. For Halloween, I played pumpkin fairy and put a tiny pumpkin on everyone's desk in both sets of offices. In Levinland, staff were expected to celebrate their birthdays by bringing in treats for everyone else; that led to donuts, cupcakes, and homemade pies being shared on both sides of the aisle. We also held a steady stream of thank-you parties when interns, law clerks, or detailees finished their PSI tours.

Still another social tradition was marking the end of a big PSI hearing by gathering afterward for a bipartisan dinner at an inexpensive local restaurant, often joined by Senator Levin and his wife. During dinner, the hearing was dissected; funny or poignant moments during the investigation were recalled; toasts were drunk. Senator Levin often picked up the tab for everyone. In later years, at the end of an investigation, we also arranged for the Senate photographer to take a photo of the investigative team, staffers gathered in a bipartisan group, faces beaming, with Senator Levin in the middle. We handed out copies on both sides of the aisle, often with a handwritten, personalized thank you at the bottom from Senator Levin (Image 7.1).

It was a conscious decision on our part to use the commemorative photos, Manhattans, parties, and other joint activities to strengthen PSI's social fabric, staff spirit, and bipartisan ties. We worked hard at it, and despite occasional missteps, misunderstandings, and miscommunications, we largely succeeded in creating a bipartisan safe-zone within PSI's walls.

At the same time, we were aiming for more than bipartisan ties within PSI ranks; our real goal was building bipartisan trust. For that, we learned there was no substitute for time. It usually took a year before a new set of Republican colleagues began to believe that the Levin staff took its own rhetoric seriously—that we really did see bipartisan investigations as more thorough, thoughtful, accurate, and credible. It took that long for them to see that we really would fight for their investigative rights and try to improve their investigative results. And it took that long for them to see that we wanted them to help strengthen Levin-led investigations in the same way.

It was no surprise it took time for our Republican colleagues to adapt to PSI's bipartisan microclimate, which was so different from much of the rest of Congress. But adapt they did, and with only a few exceptions, seemed to be as relieved as we were to have a place where people with different views were allowed to find common ground and work together to solve problems.

Supporting GOP Investigations

Examples help illustrate what cross-party investigative support meant at PSI. During the Levin era, we participated in a wide variety of inquiries led by our Republican partners. The four Republican Senators whose staffs we collaborated with each had different interests, skills, and styles. But all four conducted some crackerjack investigations. What follows is a sample of some of the best Republican-led PSI investigations in which the Levin team played a supporting role.

Image 7.1   2014 Credit Suisse investigation team. Source: U.S. Senate

Supporting Senator Collins

Senator Collins, the first woman to chair PSI chair, was an avid and talented investigator whose hearing questions were both sharp and penetrating. She led PSI for two years before Senator Levin took the senior Democrat slot in 1999. Her investigations covered such varied topics as securities fraud on the Internet, day trading, mortgage flipping, and phony Internet credentials. But of all the investigations she conducted while partnering with Senator Levin, the clear favorite among the Levin crew involved sweepstakes abuses.[2]

Sweepstakes are a marketing tool used by direct mail companies to promote the sale of magazines and other merchandise by offering mail recipients a chance to win prizes—sometimes large dollar prizes—through a chance drawing. In 1998, companies sent over one billion sweepstakes mailings across the country producing nearly $1 billion in magazine revenues. Those same sweepstakes mailings also generated thousands of consumer complaints per year.

The first Senate hearing on the subject, in September 1998, was held by the Subcommittee on International Security, Proliferation, and Federal Services, chaired by Senator Thad Cochran from Mississippi. The hearing was held at the request of Senator Levin who was then the subcommittee's ranking Democrat and led its sweepstakes inquiry.[3] It exposed a host of deceptive sweepstakes practices as well as problems confronting the U.S. Postal Service and state Attorneys General trying to stop the abuses. It also prompted Senator Collins to launch a similar PSI inquiry into deceptive mailings, culminating in two days of hearings in March 1999, the first PSI hearings attended by Senator Levin in his new role as PSI's ranking Democrat.

The PSI sweepstakes hearings elicited dramatic testimony. On the first day, elderly contestants and their children described multiple deceptive marketing practices in connection with sweepstakes mailings, including misleading suggestions that the recipients were likely to win a prize and that purchases increased their chances of winning when they didn't. Maryland's Attorney General testified how some companies used small type that was difficult for elderly consumers to see or used mailings that mimicked government documents and seemed to "guarantee" winning if an entry was returned. Other mailings asked consumers to call a number to claim their winnings, then imposed a fee or required a purchase to get a prize. Purchasing sweepstakes merchandise led some companies to target the purchasers with still more mailings.

Evidence at the hearing also showed that some contestants, mostly elderly, had spent tens of thousands of dollars on merchandise in an effort to win the sweepstakes, cluttering their homes with tchotchkes and depleting their savings. Some retirees overspent so dramatically, they were forced to re-enter the job market. Witnesses also testified about how difficult it was to remove their names or the names of family members from sweepstakes mailing lists. Some companies made it hard to find the correct address or took months to stop the mailings, if they did at all. In addition, the hearings showed that the Postal Service did not have subpoena authority to investigate deceptive mailings, could not impose nationwide orders to stop abusive mailings, and had limited authority to impose fines for misconduct.

The second day of hearings took testimony from executives at four leading sweepstakes companies, Publishers Clearing House, American Family Enterprises, Time, and The Reader's Digest Association. Senators Collins and Levin grilled all four about abusive marketing practices. In July 1999, PSI held a third day of hearings focused on smaller sweepstakes companies engaging in similar deceptive practices.

Senator Collins chaired the PSI sweepstakes hearings, provided forceful opening statements, and led the questioning of witnesses. Senator Levin, who'd been an active partner in the investigation from start to finish, provided her with energetic support. His then staff director, Linda Gustitus, had worked with the Collins staff led by Tim Shea, to obtain documents, conduct interviews, and locate witnesses. She'd helped force the sweepstakes companies to acknowledge shortfalls and helped law enforcement and the Postal Service identify new tools to uncover and stop misconduct. By the time of the hearings, Senator Levin was able to use PSI's investigative work to detail the abusive practices in his opening statements and pose tough questions to witnesses. He and Senator Collins were a powerful team.

PSI's satisfaction with the sweepstakes investigation increased when legislative and enforcement actions quickly followed. In less than a year, Congress enacted a bill that was introduced by Senator Collins and cosponsored by Senator Levin to clamp down on sweepstakes abuses.[4] Among other measures, it required mailings to specify the odds of winning a prize, disclose contest rules, and state that no purchase was necessary or would improve the chances of winning. The law prohibited mailings made to look like government documents. It also strengthened the Postal Service's authority to investigate, stop, and penalize deceptive mailings. In addition, it required sweepstakes companies to adopt reasonable procedures to enable persons who personally or through a guardian made a written request to get off their mailing lists.

Multiple enforcement actions also tamped down the abuses, with the most visible actions taken against Publishers Clearing House (PCH). In 2000, without admitting wrongdoing, PCH paid $18 million to settle complaints in 23 states and the District of Columbia that it had misled consumers. In 2001, PCH paid another $34 million to settle consumer complaints in 26 states.

The Levin staff valued the sweepstakes investigation, because it helped stop unfair marketing tactics that hurt thousands—perhaps tens of thousands—of families. While we knew sweepstakes abuses required continual vigilance to protect consumers, it felt good to have given law enforcement and the Postal Service better tools to stop the wrongdoing and to have publicly warned sweepstakes companies to stop taking advantage of the elderly.

The sweepstakes investigation was just one of many Collins-led investigations that Senator Levin supported. Senator Collins returned the favor by supporting Levin-led inquiries into money laundering and Enron's collapse. Their investigative partnership continued for four years until, in 2003, Senator Collins was elevated to chair of our full committee.

Supporting Senator Coleman

After Senator Collins ascended to the full committee in 2003, Senator Norm Coleman from Minnesota took her place as PSI chair. He was then a newly elected Senator, having previously served as a big city mayor and, before that, as a senior state prosecutor. Despite his freshman status, the Republican leadership had awarded him PSI's chairmanship, apparently assuming his prosecutorial skills would carry him through. And they did. But it took a while before Senator Coleman and his staff got fully in sync with PSI traditions.

First, it took several months for Senator Coleman to assemble his subcommittee staff. Then, once they were in place, he held seven hearings the first year (compared to one on the Levin side). Holding frequent hearings is grueling work. It not only places non-stop logistical demands on staff to identify and prepare witnesses, book their travel and hotel, and crank out the paperwork needed for each hearing, it also drastically limits the time available for the staff to engage in their own investigative efforts. About all they can do is conduct quick research projects while vetting experts to speak on the flavor of the month.

Luckily, over time, Senator Coleman warmed up to the PSI tradition of conducting fewer, longer-term investigations generating original research to examine complex problems. By the end of his six-year term on PSI, Senator Coleman had led multiple in-depth investigations into a variety of topics, including unfair credit counseling practices, Medicare fraud, unsafe pharmaceutical sales over the Internet, and nuclear terrorism threats posed by shipping containers. Three noteworthy examples of his investigations follow.

Oil-for-Food Corruption Scandal

The most dramatic and sustained investigative effort of the Coleman years focused on misconduct associated with the United Nations Oil-for-Food Program. During the inquiry, which stretched from 2004 to 2006, Senator Coleman chaired four hearings and released multiple reports. It was a wide-ranging examination of corruption on an international scale.[5]

The U.N. Oil-for-Food (OFF) Program was created in response to criticisms of U.N. sanctions imposed on Iraq after it invaded Kuwait. The economic sanctions had been designed to prevent Saddam Hussein from rebuilding Iraq's military and acquiring weapons of mass destruction. Critics charged that the sanctions were also denying food and other necessities to ordinary Iraqi citizens. To mitigate the impact on Iraqi families, the OFF Program allowed Iraq to sell its oil, deposit the proceeds in a U.N.-controlled bank account, and use the funds to buy food, medicine, and humanitarian goods, but not weapons. The OFF Program was perceived as highly successful for several years. But in January 2004, a Middle Eastern newspaper published a list of persons alleged to have received Iraqi oil "allocations" under the OFF Program and, in return, paid the Hussein regime illegal "surcharges" or kickbacks that enabled the regime to buy military arms. A worldwide outcry erupted over the apparent corruption of the U.N. program.

The Coleman staff, led by Steve Groves and Mark Greenblatt, threw themselves into the investigation, digging deep for facts. To obtain documents, they requested or subpoenaed materials from multiple sources, including a cache of documents seized by the U.S. military from Iraq's state-owned oil corporation. They obtained a copy of the list of persons who supposedly received Iraqi oil "allocations"—meaning contract options to buy oil—and then paid surcharges to the Hussein regime. It looked like a kickback ledger. The Coleman staff hired a translator to begin translating the ledger details as well as other Iraqi documents.

The staff also obtained documents from the U.S. State Department, United Nations, and oil industry participants, and opened lines of communication with the U.N.'s own committee of inquiry into the scandal. In addition, they arranged a slew of interviews. The Coleman staff even arranged, with Senator Levin's support, a two-week trip to Iraq in which PSI staffers lodged in an abandoned Iraqi palace in Baghdad's Green Zone and interviewed detained Iraqi prisoners, including senior officials from the Hussein regime.

Dan Berkovitz was the Levin liaison to the Coleman investigation and spent nearly 100% of his time on the inquiry. He studied the documents, traveled with the Coleman staff to Iraq, and played a supporting role in their interviews and data analysis. At Senator Levin's direction, Dan focused on the part played by U.S. firms. He learned that, from 2000 to 2002, when Iraq collected about $228 million in kickbacks, U.S. firms imported about half of Iraq's oil and paid about $118 million of those kickbacks. He even developed a case study detailing how one U.S. firm, Bayoil, became the largest U.S. importer of Iraqi oil and apparently paid $37 million in kickbacks to the Hussein regime, yet attracted virtually no U.S. government oversight.

Dan also compiled data showing that the $228 million in kickbacks were dwarfed by an estimated $8 billion in illicit Iraqi oil sales to neighboring countries including Jordan, Turkey, Syria, and Egypt, in direct violation of U.N. sanctions. To illustrate what happened, he developed a case study of the largest single illicit sale of Iraqi oil transported by ship out of Iraq during the sanctions period: a 2003 shipment of over seven million barrels using seven oil tankers through the Khor al-Amaya port in southern Iraq. Using emails, cables, and other documents, he established that the U.S. military knew about the Khor al-Amaya shipments, took no action to stop them, and instead allowed Jordan to supply Iraq with $53 million in hard currency. Dan also compiled evidence showing that, despite the corruption, U.N. sanctions had, in fact, helped prevent Iraq from acquiring weapons of mass destruction. Dan and I summarized the information he'd uncovered in two Levin reports released in connection with the Coleman-led hearings.[6] Both reports supplemented information disclosed by the broader Coleman investigation.

Senator Coleman held four hearings on the OFF scandal. The first, in November 2004, showcased evidence demonstrating how the Hussein regime had exploited and manipulated the OFF Program, obtaining hundreds of millions of dollars in kickbacks and billions of dollars in illicit oil sales in violation of U.N. sanctions.[7] The second hearing, in February 2005, criticized the ineffective oversight exercised by the United Nations and by the inspection companies it had hired to monitor Iraqi oil sales.

The third hearing, in May 2005, presented case studies, laid out in three bipartisan staff reports, detailing how Iraq had curried political support for itself and against the U.N. sanctions by secretly awarding oil allocations to foreign politicians, naming British Member of Parliament George Galloway, French Interior Minister Charles Pasqua, Russian politician Vladimir Zhirinovsky, and the Russian Presidential Council.[8] Iraqi documents and interviews indicated that the recipients had added a per-barrel sales commission before re-selling their oil allocations to commercial firms. It was a gutsy hearing in which Senator Coleman, with Senator Levin's support, essentially took on multiple foreign politicians.

Only one of the named politicians chose to appear at the hearing: George Galloway from the U.K. Parliament. One of PSI's more colorful witnesses, Mr. Galloway loudly proclaimed his innocence and denied ever received any Iraqi oil allocations. While Senators Coleman and Levin responded calmly to his rhetorical onslaught, they never managed to shake his flat denials.

Afterward, in response to Mr. Galloway's testimony, the Coleman staff re-examined the evidence of his involvement with the OFF Program. They identified a Jordanian businessman, Fawaz Zureikat, who'd acted as an intermediary between Mr. Galloway and the Hussein regime. They located additional Iraqi documents, bank account statements, and wire transfers indicating that Mr. Zureikat had sold the Galloway oil allocations for a profit, paid surcharges to the Hussein regime, and wired hundreds of thousands of dollars to accounts held by Mr. Galloway's wife and a Galloway-related charity. After laying out the additional evidence, a Coleman report concluded Mr. Galloway had made false or misleading statements at the May hearing.[9]

The fourth and final OFF hearing, in October 2005, focused on U.N. reforms needed to prevent the corruption of future U.N. sanctions programs.[10]

In the years following the PSI investigation, a variety of legal actions were taken to penalize corruption of the OFF Program. U.S. prosecutors indicted the OFF Program head, Benon Sevan, for taking $160,000 in bribes, but he dodged trial by fleeing to his home country, Cyprus, which does not cooperate with U.S. extradition requests.[11] The United States had more success prosecuting Bayoil and its owner, both of whom were convicted of paying kickbacks to Iraq, as were several other Americans and U.S. firms.[12] Charles Pasqua was indicted in France on OFF corruption charges, amid several other corruption cases. In 2013, a French appeals court reinstated OFF charges that had been dismissed by a lower court, but Mr. Pasqua died before any trial took place.[13] As for George Galloway, the U.K. Charity Commission found that his charity had improperly accepted $376,000 in suspect funds linked to OFF oil sales, after which he was briefly suspended from the U.K. Parliament, but he was never indicted.[14]

The OFF investigation was a difficult, multi-layered investigation with complex domestic and international dimensions. The U.N. sanctions imposed on Iraq were alternately hailed as the world's most successful international sanctions program and condemned for their susceptibility to corruption. In the United States, Republicans and Democrats split over the effectiveness of the Iraq sanctions, the OFF Program, and the United Nations as a whole. The Coleman and Levin staffs resisted partisan pressures to portray their investigation as a referendum on the United Nations itself, focusing instead on the facts and on how to protect future U.N. sanctions from corruption. Amid all the cross-pressures, we were able to reach consensus on most, though not all aspects of the inquiry. More importantly, the two sides grew to respect each other's dedication to honest fact-finding and finally emerged from the investigation with stronger bipartisan trust than when we began.

UNDP and North Korea

A few years later, in 2007, a second U.N. program caught Senator Coleman's attention when a scandal erupted over the United Nations Development Program (UNDP) in North Korea. In response to outcries over possible impropriety and mismanagement, the UNDP had taken the highly unusual step of suspending its operations and withdrawing UNDP personnel from North Korea. Senator Coleman, with the support of Senator Levin who was, by then, PSI chair, opened an investigation to find out what happened.[15]

The UNDP is one of the world's principal humanitarian agencies, battling natural disasters, health threats, and poverty, while encouraging economic development in over 160 countries. In the United States, the North Korean scandal generated intense partisan disagreement over the UNDP's value, management, and missteps, with U.N. critics and supporters falling on opposite sides of the divide.

The PSI investigation, led by Mark Greenblatt and Mike Flowers on the Coleman staff, was long and complex, but what I remember most was an issue involving North Korea's abuse of a UNDP bank account set up at a North Korean bank to fund UNDP activities. The Coleman staff managed to get copies of wire transfer records showing $2.7 million in highly suspicious funding transfers over a six-month period from the UNDP bank account to North Korean diplomatic missions around the world. In interviews, U.N. and State Department personnel denied all knowledge of the wire transfers. It looked as if North Korea had quietly hijacked the UNDP account to send wire transfers under the U.N.'s name and avoid U.S. scrutiny of banks doing business with the rogue regime.

A few weeks before the hearing, during a bipartisan staff discussion of the bank account issue, I asked if we'd ever tried to contact North Korea to get its side of the story. Our liaison to the Coleman investigation, Zack Schram, offered to try to reach the government by email. He quickly found an Internet address for the Democratic People's Republic of North Korea and sent off a polite email message. Within a few hours, to our amazement, he got a response. We followed with a formal letter from Senators Coleman and Levin notifying the North Korean government of the upcoming hearing and requesting a meeting to discuss the PSI investigation. A few days later, an email arrived accepting the offer to meet.

North Korean diplomats were allowed to function in the United States within only a limited geographical area adjacent to the United Nations headquarters in New York City. Representatives from the North Korean U.N. Mission were willing to meet with us there. After first obtaining security briefings from both the Senate and State Department, Mike Flowers from the Coleman staff and Zack Schram from our staff hopped a train to New York.

When they returned, Mike and Zack described a surreal meeting at a dilapidated hotel near U.N. headquarters. They met in the hotel lobby with two North Korean representatives who spoke fluent English. In their 20s or 30s, both seemed well informed about the U.S. Congress. During the ensuing discussion, everyone ordered coffee or tea. Mike and Zack described the upcoming hearing and the issues related to the wire transfers. With respect to the hearing, the North Korean representatives asked whether they would be able to watch the proceedings on television on C-SPAN 3. When shown copies of the wire transfer documents, the two promised to convey our questions to their government.

A second meeting took place a month later, in mid-January. (By then, the hearing had been postponed.) At the same hotel, the same two North Korean representatives met with Mike and Zack, and confirmed that North Korea had used the UNDP bank account for its own transactions, explaining that their government had otherwise found it difficult to transmit funds abroad to its diplomatic missions. They noted that the entire $2.7 million came from North Korea and did not include any UNDP funds, a fact the United Nations later confirmed.

The lesson we took away from that surprisingly frank and cordial exchange was how important it was to contact all investigative targets. North Korea's admissions eliminated all uncertainty about what had happened, and we no longer had to hedge our finding that North Korea had engaged in deceptive financial transactions in which it secretly misused the UNDP bank account to transmit its own funds abroad. At the same time, the absence of any expressions of concern by North Korea about its conduct suggested that cultural differences were at work, and its officials may not have realized how the West would view its actions. To prevent future problems, one obvious solution was for the UNDP to strengthen its bank account controls to ensure that only UNDP personnel could authorize wire transfers.

On January 24, 2008, PSI held a hearing and released a bipartisan staff report on a range of management and operational deficiencies affecting UNDP activities in North Korea. North Korea's misuse of the UNDP bank account was one small, but revealing part of that larger story. On a deeper level, the hearing examined a range of complex issues that arose when important humanitarian work was undermined by a repressive regime, including questions about when that work should be stopped if the regime won't cooperate.

I like to think that our hearing cut through some of the partisan bluster about the UNDP's activities in North Korea and encouraged everyone— including the North Koreans—to take a breath and re-examine the facts. It took another year, but in January 2009, North Korea finally agreed to accept stronger U.N. controls over the UNDP's in-country operations, after which the UNDP agreed to resume its humanitarian aid.

Federal Contractors Who Don't Pay Their Taxes

The final example of a Coleman investigation is a lot less flashy than the first two but, to me, stands as a shining example of how bipartisan oversight can improve government operations.

The issue was federal contractors who don't pay their taxes—companies that did business with the U.S. government, got paid with taxpayer dollars, but then failed to pay the taxes they themselves owed.[16] Dodging taxes is never acceptable, but doing it while simultaneously pocketing taxpayer dollars was the type of raw hypocrisy that offended both sides of the aisle. Our shared outrage grew when we learned that tens of thousands of profitable federal contractors owed billions of dollars in unpaid taxes.

The Coleman investigation was led by his staffer Jay Jennings who sustained the effort for five years from 2004 to 2009. I served as the Levin liaison supporting his work. A former investigator at the Government Accountability Office (GAO), Jay knew that the U.S. government already had a system, known as the Federal Tax Levy Program, to try to catch contractor tax cheats. Under that program, the IRS periodically sent the U.S. Treasury a list of tax delinquents which the Treasury then checked against the lists provided by other federal agencies of the contractors scheduled to receive federal payments. If a contractor's name appeared on the IRS list as owing taxes, the Treasury was supposed to divert a portion of the upcoming federal payment to reduce the contractor's tax debt.

Jay also knew that the tax levy program was riddled with technical and policy problems, including incomplete agency lists of contractors receiving payments, contractors using invalid taxpayer identification numbers, and IRS notice and procedural requirements that delayed the tax levies. The goal of the investigation was to expose the problems, fix the glitches, and stop dishonest businesses from collecting taxpayer dollars while ignoring their own tax obligations.

To conduct the investigation, Jay reached out to a GAO team with the technical expertise to analyze the tax levy program. The GAO team agreed to set up data protocols to assess, for specified federal agencies, the number of their contractors on the IRS list of tax delinquents, the amount of taxes owed, whether their federal payments had been levied, and the amount of levies actually collected. In addition, the GAO team agreed to profile a sample of the tax-delinquent businesses to evaluate their tax practices. In other words, GAO committed to doing the bulk of the investigative work needed to tackle the issue.

The first hearing, in 2004, featured a GAO report determining that 27,000 contractors doing work for the Department of Defense (DOD) had unpaid taxes totaling nearly $3 billion. In a profile of 47 of those DOD contractors, GAO found that all had engaged in abusive or potentially criminal tax activities, most often by failing to remit payroll taxes owed to the IRS. One example was a contractor who was awarded over $60 million in DOD contracts yet had delinquent payroll taxes dating back to 1994.

Similar hearings followed. In 2005, for example, a PSI hearing featured a GAO report showing that 33,000 contractors doing business with civilian federal agencies had unpaid taxes totaling $3.3 billion. GAO profiled 50 of those contractors and, again, found all had engaged in abusive or potentially criminal tax activities. Examples included company owners who'd spent money earmarked for payroll taxes on gambling, million-dollar homes, and luxury cars.

In response to the PSI investigation, in 2004, the federal government formed a task force to strengthen the tax levy program. It drew on personnel from the Treasury, IRS, DOD, and other agencies, and included capable employees willing to drive reforms. Over the next three years, Jay and I met repeatedly with that task force to identify practical ways to improve the levy program, strengthen interagency cooperation, and track the changes being made.

The task force devised multiple technical improvements to the program. One example: it increased the DOD payment systems using automated procedures to screen contractor payments, moving from one to all 16 DOD payment systems. As a result, tax levy collections from DOD contractors increased 25-fold, from $680,000 in 2003 to $17.25 million in 2005.

In 2007, Jay took the investigation in a new direction, identifying agencies that had failed to install any payment screening procedures to trigger tax levies.[17] His first big catch was the U.S. Postal Service which quickly admitted fault and agreed to start sending contractor payments through the tax levy screening process. A more substantial prize was the Medicare and Medicaid programs that sent over $400 billion in federal payments to health care providers each year, but did not screen any of those payments for possible tax levies. Not only that, but the Centers for Medicare & Medicaid Services (CMM) informed us that the CMM director didn't view the tax levy program as part of her responsibilities and didn't plan to implement it.

PSI held two hearings in 2007 focused on Medicare and Medicaid. The first disclosed that more than 21,000 Medicare health care providers, including doctors and medical laboratories, owed more than $1.3 billion in unpaid taxes, while the second found that more than 30,000 Medicaid health care providers owed more than $1 billion in taxes. At both hearings, Senators Coleman and Levin confronted the CMM director with the agency's abject failure to implement the tax levy program. They forced her to acknowledge that, at least when it came to Medicare, CMM was violating the law.

Even after the pounding CMM took during the two hearings, however, it was far from clear that the agency would comply with the law. So Senator Coleman introduced and Senator Levin cosponsored a bill to impose legally enforceable deadlines on CMM to develop tax levy procedures for Medicare payments.[18] That same year, the Coleman-Levin bill was enacted into law as part of a 2008 Medicare reform bill. It was only then that CMM changed its tune and agreed to start screening Medicare payments for tax debt and possible imposition of tax levies.

The results were immediate. In 2010 alone, Medicare-related tax levies raised $45 million, increasing the total amount of tax levies collected from federal contractors to $115 million.[19] It was the first time the total had exceeded the $100 million mark.

The Coleman effort spurred other actions as well. In 2008, in reaction to PSI's work, the Federal Acquisition Regulation Council amended government-wide procurement regulations to require persons bidding on federal contracts to disclose, as part of the criteria determining whether they were "responsible" contractors, whether they had unpaid taxes exceeding $3000. Contractors with unpaid tax debt over the threshold could be deemed ineligible to bid on upcoming contracts and even barred from federal contracts for a period of years.[20] Senators Coleman and Levin welcomed the new rule, which made it more likely that federal agencies would stop issuing new contracts to tax-delinquent contractors.

To me, the Coleman investigation exemplified how congressional oversight can improve government operations while building goodwill across party lines and across government. The PSI hearings created an environment that made it possible for multiple agencies to harness their collective expertise to improve a complex cross-agency program. When an uncooperative agency refused to screen billions of taxpayer dollars in Medicare payments, a Coleman-Levin bill compelled the agency to act. Tax levy collections increased and set the stage for new government-wide standards penalizing federal contractors that failed to meet their federal tax obligations. That's the way oversight ought to work.

Senator Coleman spent six years at PSI, the longest of Senator Levin's four Republican partners. In 2009, their partnership came to an end when Senator Coleman lost his Senate re-election bid by 312 votes out of over three million cast. While we supported the Democratic victory which helped Democrats retake the Senate majority, it was bittersweet—we'd become close to the Coleman investigative team and were sorry to see the staff broken up and dispersed.

Supporting Senator Coburn

After Senator Coleman's loss, PSI acquired a new ranking Republican, Senator Tom Coburn, a medical doctor and former House member from Oklahoma. Because he was very conservative, some Democrats warned that PSI's bipartisan traditions wouldn't survive his arrival. Those predictions were wrong. Senator Coburn turned out to be not only a strong supporter of bipartisan investigations, but a champion of fact-based, in-depth oversight. Like Senator Levin, he was willing to take on powerful interests and understood the importance of taking the time needed to conduct bipartisan investigations. He was a terrific PSI partner.

Senator Coburn spent four years as PSI's ranking Republican from 2008 to 2012. His first act upon arrival was to replace most of the Coleman staff, which surprised and dismayed us by essentially erasing the relationship we had built up so carefully. But over the following months, Senator Coburn assembled an outstanding team of investigators who were ready and willing to work on a bipartisan basis. The first two years of the Coburn team were dominated by Levin-led investigations into commodity speculation and the financial crisis, described later in this book, but after that, his team began to concentrate on Senator Coburn's priorities. Once they did, the Coburn staff conducted serious inquiries with important results. My two favorites follow.

Social Security Disability Fraud

One of Senator Coburn's PSI priorities was an in-depth examination of fraud and mismanagement problems affecting federal disability payment programs. Designed to help disabled Americans live independently, the two key federal programs were huge and growing, paying benefits that, in 2009 alone, totaled $160 billion.

As a practicing physician, Senator Coburn was personally familiar with the process used to gauge when an individual was disabled, and was concerned about fraudsters abusing the criteria, program mismanagement awarding benefits to individuals who were not truly disabled, and rapidly multiplying awards bankrupting the disability trust funds. I and others on the Levin staff began the investigation skeptical about how much fraud or mismanagement was really going on and more worried about lengthy backlogs in awarding disability benefits. But over time, as the Coburn staff dug into the facts and laid out the evidence, we, too, became convinced that fraud and mismanagement were serious problems requiring agency attention and action.

The two key programs examined by the Coburn investigation were the Social Security Disability Insurance program which provides benefits to disabled individuals who can no longer work, and the Supplemental Security Income program which, in part, supports disabled persons and their families based upon financial need. Both are administered by the Social Security Administration (SSA). The Coburn investigative team was led by Chris Barkley and Andy Dockham, who devoted countless hours to detailed document review and in-depth fact-finding.

Conn Investigation

Senator Coburn's work led to three sets of hearings on Social Security disability issues, but the part of his investigation that really won us over was his inquiry into the actions of Eric Conn, an aptly-named Kentucky lawyer whose rural law firm was dedicated to obtaining disability benefits for claimants, not only in Kentucky but across the country.[21] Along the way, the Conn law firm became one of the largest recipients in the country of attorney fees from SSA, pulling in millions of taxpayer dollars each year for representing disability applicants. Rumors abounded that the Conn success had been built on fraudulent practices and improper relationships with SSA administrative law judges.

The Conn investigation was sparked by a 2011 Wall Street Journal article spotlighting an SSA administrative law judge, David B. Daugherty, who processed more disability cases per year than almost any other SSA judge nationwide and, in 2011, ordered benefits to be paid in over 90% of his cases compared to the SSA average of 60%.[22] The article noted that the judge's statistics arose, in large part, from approving benefits for individuals represented by Mr. Conn and speculated about an improper relationship between the two. The article also noted that the disability appeals office where Judge Daugherty worked in Huntington, West Virginia, had won SSA awards and bonuses for processing so many cases, due primarily to the judge's efforts.

Eric Conn turned out to be quite a character. Instead of waiting for clients to contact him, he ran a major advertising campaign seeking disability claimants. The campaign included billboards; television, radio, and online commercials; and women known as "Conn's hotties" who wore t-shirts with his law firm's phone number.[23] He referred to himself as "Mr. Social Security," and named his website "Mr.SocialSecurity.com." Despite his rural location, by 2011, he had built one of the largest and most lucrative disability practices in the country.

The Coburn crew, led by Chris and Andy, decided to take a field trip to get a closer look at both the Huntington SSA office and the Conn law firm. Accompanying them on the 7-hour drive was our liaison to the investigation, Mary McKoy, a Census Bureau detailee assigned to our staff for a year. When the three PSI staffers returned, they described 48 hours of eye-opening fact-finding.

They first visited the SSA Office of Disability Adjudication and Review located in Huntington, West Virginia. It served as the agency's regional hub and hearing location for many Conn clients. It also operated a satellite office in Prestonsburg, Kentucky. The PSI crew met and handed out business cards to a number of SSA officials. Next, they visited the site of the Conn law firm. It operated out of several trailers around a small office building in a 500-person town, Stanville, Kentucky. In front sat a huge replica of the statue of Abraham Lincoln from the Lincoln Memorial, designed as a tourist attraction and draw for clients. The team learned that the firm employed about 40 individuals and was managed by Mr. Conn's mother who kept the books. Cameras located throughout the complex recorded everyone's moves.

That evening, at their hotel, the PSI staff began receiving a stream of surreptitious visits from SSA and Conn law firm employees who wanted to talk. Word of PSI's presence in town had apparently spread like wildfire. The employees quietly told one story after another about troubling conduct they'd witnessed involving SSA disability benefit awards and possible fraud, providing both detailed information and documents. It seemed as if the whole town had been waiting for someone to show up after the Wall Street Journal article to get the full story.

Convinced there was a problem worth investigating, Senator Coburn opened a formal PSI inquiry supported by Senator Levin and issued document requests to SSA, Eric Conn, the Conn law firm, several SSA administrative law judges, and others. While waiting for the documents, his staff continued to collect information from the insiders at SSA and the law firm. On a tip, the Coburn crew tracked down a former Conn law firm employee who'd moved away. The former employee agreed to meet in a dingy fast food restaurant and later led the staff to an even dingier self-storage unit containing boxes of Conn and Conn law firm documents. Asked why the documents had been kept, the former employee shrugged and smiled that someone was bound to want them one day. The Coburn staffers carted the boxes back to Washington.

Piecing together evidence from multiple sources, the Coburn staff slowly built up a picture of the facts, which were later disclosed in a report and hearing. The tale began with the Conn law firm, which solicited clients whose disability benefit applications had been turned down by SSA, submitted appeals on their behalf, and collected attorney fees from SSA for each client representation—fees which, in 2010 alone, added up to nearly $4 million.

Judge Daugherty was their favored judge. Circumventing SSA rules requiring cases to be randomly assigned to its administrative law judges, Judge Daugherty used a variety of tactics to assign Conn cases to himself. Then, once a month, he telephoned the Conn law firm with a list of the cases he planned to decide over the next 30 days and specified what additional evidence should be provided in each case.

Within days, the Conn firm arranged for the named clients to see certain doctors to generate the specified paperwork. Mr. Conn had instructed his staff to identify doctors with troubled pasts, including malpractice problems, revoked medicine licenses, or suspended hospital privileges, because "he could get them to do whatever he wanted, and they were cheaper to work with." Over time, the firm had developed a small cadre of preferred doctors. The clients either traveled to those doctors' offices or met them at the Conn law firm. The doctors almost invariably concluded the claimants were disabled, signing medical forms prepared by the Conn law firm. The law firm paid the doctors inflated fees of between $350 and $650 per patient, later subtracting the fees from the claimants' disability benefit awards.

The Coburn staff decided to collect and analyze the medical forms submitted by the Conn law firm to SSA. They discovered that many of the forms contained identical medical data, even though the forms named different patients. A closer analysis determined that there were ten versions of the key forms, and that each version detailed a particular set of medical conditions that could give rise to a disability finding. The Coburn staff discovered that the Conn law firm had given the same ten versions of the forms over and over to the doctors, attributing identical medical conditions to multiple clients. The doctors had signed the forms without making any changes, determining over and over that the described individuals were disabled.

The Conn firm submitted the signed forms to Judge Daugherty who scheduled the claimants' hearings. While most SSA hearings lasted at least an hour, Judge Daugherty sometimes scheduled the Conn cases in 15-minute segments, running through as many as 20 cases in a single day. Some sessions lasted less than five minutes. In other cases, the judge skipped the hearing altogether and decided the Conn cases "on the record."

The impact on the Conn cases was dramatic. Most Conn clients received a decision on a claim within 30 days of a hearing request, even though the average wait time nationally and at the Huntington office was one year. Not only that, in almost every case, Judge Daugherty overturned the agency denial of benefits and found in favor of the Conn client, often citing the recently submitted medical forms as key evidence. In 2010, he overturned agency denials and awarded disability benefits in 99.7% of the cases he reviewed, compared to the average overturn rate for all SSA judges of 60%.

After hearing from multiple sources that Judge Daugherty might have been on the take, we decided to take a look at his bank records. It wasn't hard to figure out which bank he used, since there were so few in town. PSI subpoenas quickly produced records for accounts opened by the judge and his adult daughter. They showed that, from 2003 to 2011, the judge's bank accounts recorded irregular monthly cash deposits in amounts varying from $400 to $5000 per month. Similar cash deposits appeared on some bank account records for the judge's daughter, in particular from 2007 to 2008, when she ran unsuccessfully for election as a local magistrate. When asked about the cash deposits, which totaled $96,000 altogether, the judge refused to explain the origin of the funds.

The suspect evidence didn't end there. We learned about dozens of Conn law firm computers that had been physically destroyed when tossed into a bonfire; a warehouse of Conn case files which had been shredded; an unknown number of emails deleted by Judge Daugherty; personal shredders suddenly purchased by the SSA Huntington office; law firm receipts for multiple so-called burn phones; SSA judges who'd retired out of state when questions began to be asked; and multiple complaints that had been buried by Huntington Chief Judge Charles Andrus. There was even an SSA employee who'd been suspected of reporting misconduct to U.S. authorities and then was secretly videotaped and criticized by Mr. Conn and Chief Judge Andrus in a joint attempt to discredit her. It was a hornet's nest of deception, obstruction, and misconduct. Which is why it took the Coburn investigation nearly two years to sort it out.

In late 2012, the Coburn staff began drafting a report. Finished in 2013, the final report concluded that the Conn law firm had engaged in "a raft of improper practices" to obtain disability benefits for its clients, including misusing waivers to direct disability claims to the Huntington office, employing suspect doctors willing to conduct cursory medical exams and sign pre-prepared forms, manufacturing false medical forms, and colluding with administrative law judges on practices that improperly favored Conn clients.[24] The report specifically condemned Judge Daugherty's actions, which included improperly assigning Conn cases to himself, secretly informing Mr. Conn of the cases he would decide and the documentation needed to produce favorable results, relying on conclusory medical forms to reverse prior benefit denials, and favoring Conn clients with expedited adjudications.

The report also faulted SSA. It criticized the agency for lax oversight which allowed the suspect conduct to continue for years, and for pressuring SSA judges to resolve cases faster without doublechecking the quality of the decisions. Out of fairness, the report also noted that SSA itself had been pressured by members of Congress to reduce its backlog of unresolved cases. In addition, the report criticized SSA for paying tens of millions of taxpayer dollars in attorney and physician fees to parties engaged in abusive practices, calculating that, from 2001 to 2013, SSA fees paid to the Conn law firm alone exceeded $22 million.

The Senate hearing took place in October 2013. By then, Senator Coburn had left PSI to become ranking Republican on our full committee. But because the hearing was based in large part on work done by PSI, Senator Levin attended the hearing and joined in the bipartisan report issued by the full committee. Senator Tom Carper, the full committee chair, presided over the hearing.

It was a classic oversight hearing exposing corruption, fraud, and improper favoritism in a government program. Senator Coburn opened the hearing by explaining that two years of work had uncovered "how one lawyer, one judge, and a group of doctors financially benefited by working together to manufacture bogus, fraudulent medical evidence to award disability benefits to over 1800 people."

The first panel took testimony from four former Conn law firm and SSA employees who laid out the misconduct each had observed, confirming the evidence in the report. Next up was a panel of three doctors who'd examined disability claimants for the Conn law firm. One asserted his Fifth Amendment right against self-incrimination and was excused. The other two denied wrongdoing, but under questioning admitted routinely signing forms with medical information supplied by the law firm. When Senator Coburn asked one doctor, psychologist Alfred Bradley Adkins, about signing a medical form stating that an 8-year-old had "work related stresses," Dr. Adkins admitted that he hadn't filled out the form himself or noticed the discrepancy. When Senator Levin asked Dr. Adkins, of the more than 560 medical forms he'd signed, how many times he'd changed the medical information typed in by the Conn law firm prior to the medical examination, the doctor admitted the number was "probably zero."

Judge Daugherty was supposed to testify next, but failed to appear. Eric Conn did show up, but asserted his Fifth Amendment right not to answer questions and was excused. The final witness was the former chief judge of the Huntington office, Charles Andrus, who had been demoted from his leadership post by SSA, but continued to decide disability cases. The senators grilled him about his failure to act on complaints about Judge Daugherty, the procedures that led to Judge Daugherty's deciding hundreds of Conn cases, and the sordid Conn-Andrus attempt to discredit the SSA whistleblower.

The 2013 hearing was a knock out. The Conn case gained further notoriety when the investigative television show, *60 Minutes*, featured the scandal.[25] And yet, despite overwhelming evidence of suspect conduct, for years, nothing of significance happened to the perpetrators. SSA failed to initiate any proceedings to bar Mr. Conn or his law firm from appearing before the agency, and he continued to represent disability claimants, even opening a new office in Beverly Hills, California.

Back in 2011, two former Conn employees had filed a civil lawsuit against Mr. Conn and his law firm, alleging the submission to the government of false claims for disability benefits. For five years, no government agency joined the lawsuit, forcing the private litigants to soldier on alone. Then, in 2016, citing evidence from the 2013 PSI hearing on the firm's use of bogus medical forms, the Justice Department suddenly joined the civil lawsuit, the first visible sign that the federal government was willing to try to hold Mr. Conn accountable.[26]

In the meantime, SSA had suspended disability payments to over 1500 Conn clients whose claims had been decided by the Huntington office, initiating a re-evaluation of their eligibility for benefits.[27] In other words, the claimants—who may or may not have been disabled, and who may or may not have realized they were bit players in a years-long scam—began paying the price for the conniving lawyers and doctors who'd facilitated their awards.

Finally, in April 2016, two months after the Justice Department joined the civil false claims lawsuit, the U.S. Attorney for the Eastern District of Kentucky filed an 18-count criminal indictment against Eric Conn, Mr. Daugherty, and Dr. Adkins.[28] The charges included conspiracy to commit Social Security disability fraud and obstruction of justice.

In 2017, Mr. Conn and Mr. Daugherty pleaded guilty to paying and receiving bribes, among other crimes.[29] Mr. Daugherty admitted to accepting more than $609,000 in cash payments to render judgments in more than 3000 cases obligating SSA to pay benefits totaling more than $550 million.[30] Dr. Adkins refused to admit guilt, but was convicted after a jury trial.[31] The wheels of justice had turned slowly, but had at last caught up with the culprits.[32]

300 Case Files

The Conn case history was only one aspect of the extended Social Security disability investigation led by Senator Coburn. Another important though less dramatic phase culminated in a 2012 PSI hearing examining decisions issued by SSA administrative law judges who overruled agency denials of disability benefits and awarded benefits to claimants.[33] The Coburn investigation concluded that some of those SSA judges were issuing poor quality decisions—poor quality not because of incorrect results, but because they were poorly written, reasoned, and supported. To reach that conclusion, the Coburn staff conducted an in-depth review of 300 disability cases, examining not only the written opinions issued by the administrative law judges, but also the underlying agency decisions and medical evidence.

The investigation had a rough start. Senator Coburn's staff originally wanted to review substantially more than 300 cases, drafting an expansive document request that we saw as overly ambitious. We just didn't think the agency could produce or the limited Coburn staff could review such a huge volume of case files in a reasonable period of time. So we engaged in what was, for us, a painful negotiation with the Coburn staff, trying to convince them at an early stage of our relationship that if they reduced their document request to a more manageable number of documents, we would fight for them on a bipartisan basis to get the materials they wanted.

The Coburn staff took a leap of faith and agreed to a radically reduced request—seeking just 100 case files each from three regional offices in counties with varying levels of per capital enrollments in federal disability programs. The three offices were located in West Virginia, Alabama, and Oklahoma, with the first selected to include the prolific Huntington office and the last selected to show Senator Coburn wasn't asking anyone to do anything he wouldn't ask of his own state. The Coburn staff established general criteria to obtain case files that went through different stages in the decision-making process and allowed SSA itself to randomly select the 100 specific cases to be reviewed from each office.

Senator Levin agreed to support the Coburn document request, even though he and we knew SSA would have a fit. And SSA did. When SSA got the Coburn-Levin letter requesting the 300 case files, SSA staff wasted no time calling our liaison to the investigation, Dan Goshorn, and bitterly complaining that it was a nightmare request that would cost the agency huge amounts of money, divert taxpayer dollars from pressing needs, and tie up large numbers of staffers with better things to do. We responded that Congress had the right to evaluate the disability benefits decisionmaking process, and the request was about as reasonable as it was going to get to do a good faith review. SSA continued to protest, first escalating the call to me and then having the SSA Commissioner call Senator Levin, but Senator Levin held firm in his support of Senator Coburn's right to obtain the documents.

In the end, SSA grudgingly complied. To make the job more manageable, we agreed to SSA's producing only files that were stored electronically and skipping any paper files. We also agreed to the redaction of personal identifying information like names and addresses, but not relevant details such as age and health. We also committed to keeping the files confidential.

It took months for all the documents to be produced, and it was clear that the data collection and redaction process took a real toll on SSA resources. But once the 300 case files came in, the Coburn staff buckled down and read every page. Not only read, but studied and analyzed every file, working hard to understand the process, standards, and results. Where the Conn inquiry had been a wild ride, this inquiry was a slow, steady slog.

After months of work, the Coburn staff wrote up their investigative results, producing an internal review of each of the 300 cases as well as a draft report for public release summarizing their analysis and findings. As far as we knew, the Coburn effort was the first ever by an outside party to examine raw Social Security disability case files, trace the initial and subsequent decisions by SSA personnel from start to finish, and use that information to evaluate the quality of the written decisions issued by SSA administrative law judges. It was innovative, difficult, and revealing research.

At the same time, it was the type of research that presented tremendous difficulties for Senator Levin. Unlike Senator Coburn, he had little familiarity with medical decisionmaking and was extremely reluctant to second-guess medical findings in individual cases. In addition, his whole modus operandi was to dig into the details of a case. But when Senator Levin began quizzing us about individual disability cases, asking questions about the maladies, contradictory medical evidence, and medical findings, we were often unable to answer his questions or explain the issues to his satisfaction. Senator Levin was also troubled about whether the overall investigative results were skewed by the Coburn decision to examine ALJ decisions that awarded benefits, but not those that denied benefits.

In some cases, the poor quality of the administrative law judge decisions was obvious—those where medical findings or hearing testimony were misreported or missing, contradictory medical evidence was ignored, or the explanation for overturning an agency denial was absent. Judge Daugherty was the absolute worst. He had won accolades for disposing of over 1000 cases per year when the standard called for deciding between 500 and 700 per year, but he'd reached those numbers by employing numerous inappropriate shortcuts. His tactics included skipping hearings, ignoring a lot of the case file evidence, leaving contradictory evidence unresolved, sometimes cutting and pasting descriptions of medical evidence from the case file directly into his opinions without explaining what it meant, and sometimes writing the phrase "etc., etc., etc." rather than describe the relevant evidence. That type of shoddy work was easy to condemn. But decisions issued by other judges were more difficult to assess, because the Levin team just didn't know enough about medical decisionmaking. It became clear that getting ourselves and Senator Levin comfortable with all 300 cases, while not impossible, would require weeks, if not months, of additional work.

Still another problem was that Senator Levin disagreed with a key Coburn recommendation for stopping the abuses—mandating the participation of an SSA representative in every disability appeals hearing. Senator Levin saw that approach as expensive, time consuming, and one that would turn the proceedings into adversarial adjudications instead of non-adversarial, administrative reviews.

In the end, given the time already spent on the investigation and differences over how to solve the problems, Senator Levin decided not to join the Coburn report, but to support its release and hold a PSI hearing on the issues. He also instructed us to be supportive of the report with the press by describing the enormous amount of work that went into the investigation, the bipartisan nature of the inquiry, and the many important issues uncovered. We knew that his decision not to join the report would be a blow to the Coburn team, and it was hard to convey it. But we did, explaining the problem. By then, they were very familiar with Senator Levin's focus on detail and were able to accept the explanation as sincere. We attended the press briefing in which Senator Coburn released the report and were as supportive of it as we could be while holding true to Senator Levin's concerns.

The hearing took place in September 2012. The key finding in the Coburn report was that more than a quarter of the administrative law judges' decisions reviewed had "failed to properly address insufficient, contradictory, or incomplete evidence." The report noted that its finding corroborated a 2011 internal quality review conducted by SSA itself which found that, on average nationwide, administrative law judge disability decisions contained errors or insufficient information 22% of the time. Problems identified by the Coburn report included superficial hearings; the misuse of expert testimony; and decisions approving disability benefits without citing adequate, objective medical evidence to support the finding, without explaining the medical basis for the decision, without showing how the claimant met the basic listing elements, or at times without taking into account contradictory evidence.

The Coburn report was immediately condemned by some disability advocates who let us know how unhappy they were that Senator Levin had supported the investigation. Part of their worry was that the criticisms would lead to SSA funding cuts that would exacerbate the agency's problems. But what happened instead was that SSA strengthened its training and quality review efforts to improve the ALJ decisionmaking process, and began to focus on the quality as well as the speed of judges' written decisions. SSA even put an upper limit on the number of cases that a judge could decide per year at 1200—100 per month—to discourage judges from racing through cases to earn bonuses. Those policy outcomes were good for everyone.

Senator Coburn's years at PSI came to an end when, like Senator Collins, he was elevated to ranking Republican on the full committee. We continued to work with his staff off and on until, a few years later, health issues led Senator Coburn to leave the Senate a year before his term concluded. When he left office, many of his staffers left the committee's ranks as well. We had come to like and admire the Coburn investigators, and were sad to see them go.

Supporting Senator McCain

Senator Levin's final Republican partner on PSI was Senator John McCain from Arizona. Senator McCain took the post after Senator Coburn was elevated to a leadership position on the full committee. Like Senator Coburn, Senator McCain was an active conservative who enjoyed conducting investigations. He and Senator Levin were already good friends, having spent years together on the Senate Armed Services Committee.

Senator McCain joined PSI in early 2013, around the same time that Senator Levin announced he would be retiring from the Senate in early 2015. That meant their PSI partnership had only a two-year run, and took place at the same time that Senator Levin was working to complete multiple inquiries before leaving office. Senator McCain graciously supported Senator Levin's priorities, which meant his staff had only limited time to initiate their own investigations. Our favorite involved Senator McCain's inquiry into malicious Internet advertising.

Malicious Internet Advertising

In 2013, the McCain staff, led by Jack Thorlin, launched an inquiry into instances in which online advertisements infected the computers of web users with malware that stole or destroyed their personal information, compromised their software, misused their computers, and often rendered them subject to identity theft, bank account raids, or other cybercrimes.[34]

It was a timely inquiry. In 2013, U.S. online advertising revenue had, for the first time, surpassed that of broadcast television, with companies spending nearly $43 billion to reach online consumers. Increased online advertising had brought with it a rise in cybercriminals using mainstream websites to infect consumers' computers with advertisement-based malware or "malvertising." One study estimated that malvertising attacks had more than doubled in 2013, with over 200,000 incidents generating over 12.4 billion malicious ad impressions. Another study found more than half of Internet website publishers had suffered malvertising attacks.

One example of the problem came on December 27, 2013, during the winter holiday season, when cyber criminals hacked into Yahoo's online advertising network and began delivering malware-infected ads to consumers' computers. Cyber criminals had apparently noticed that computer security was weaker around holidays, when key personnel were not at work, and had begun targeting those periods. Without so much as a click, the malware took over computers on the Yahoo network and used them to generate bitcoins. Independent security firms judged that tens of thousands of computers may have been infected in that one incident.

While describing the malware threat was easy, we were to learn that understanding how advertising malware actually worked online was not. Luckily, the Levin liaison to the McCain investigation, Dan Goshorn, was not only a data-driven lawyer, talented investigator, and clear thinker, but also one of the few on our staff with a deep understanding of the Internet. He ended up educating not only us, but some McCain staff on the intricacies of the Internet.

The first task was simply understanding the mechanics of Internet advertising. Surprise number one was learning that consumers' computer systems could be affected by advertising displays that appeared on their computer screens, even if the consumer never clicked on any ad. Another surprise was how many parties were involved in delivering a single ad. The simple display of an online advertisement typically triggered a consumer's interactions with a chain of companies, many of which were completely unknown to the consumer, and each of which could compromise the consumer's privacy and open the door to cybercrime. The investigation found, for example, that visiting just one popular tabloid news website triggered the consumer's interaction with some 352 other web servers.

A third surprise was that, contrary to radio or television ads where the ad content was generally transmitted by the same party that hosted the rest of the broadcast, online host websites usually didn't transmit or control the ads that appeared on their webpages. Instead, the website host commonly sold advertising space on its website through a separate intermediary company, often a well-known technology corporation like Google or Yahoo. When a consumer then visited the host site, the intermediary—often referred to as an ad network—typically instantly contacted other Internet companies which, in turn, instantly collected and analyzed data on the consumer in order to target an appropriate advertisement. The advertisement actually sent to the consumer's computer screen was typically provided by still another party, using a web server that was not under the control of either the ad network or the original host website.

In fact, the host website often did not know and could not predict which advertisements would be delivered to its website users by the intermediary who rented the space. On top of that, most intermediaries had only limited control over the content of the advertisements whose placements they facilitated. The result was that neither the website host nor the ad network necessarily knew or controlled the ultimate advertisers that might be transmitting malware.

Given the complex and unpredictable online advertising outcomes, the investigation also examined what online industries and regulators were doing to try to protect consumers from malvertising, using case studies of actual attacks to gauge what was happening. The ad networks explained that they routinely screened advertisers, scanned individual ads to identify and disable malware, and directed consumers away from high-risk sites, but cybercriminals sometimes found ways to circumvent their safeguards. PSI investigators learned that the industry countermeasures largely depended upon voluntary industry compliance with standards, procedures, and contract provisions that were often incomplete, unreliable, or poorly enforced. Another problem was that companies were not required to inform the public or regulators when an ad network was compromised. Interviews with the Federal Trade Commission (FTC) disclosed that regulators needed new and stronger tools to detect, stop, and penalize malvertising.

In May 2014, PSI held its hearing and released a bipartisan report on the McCain-led investigation. The report explained how online advertising worked, so that others could benefit from PSI's research. It also described examples of malvertising attacks and explained how online advertising's multi-layered vulnerabilities made it difficult for individual industry participants to employ effective countermeasures. The report also highlighted weak industry standards and inadequate regulatory tools, and noted how, as online advertising grew in complexity, it became even more difficult to ascertain who was responsible for specific cases of malicious advertising.

At the hearing, Senators McCain and Levin took testimony and questioned representatives from Yahoo and Google, which ran intermediary ad networks; the Online Trust Alliance, which represented web users; the Digital Advertising Alliance, which served as an industry-based self-regulatory group for online advertisers; and the FTC. Senator McCain framed the key issue as follows:

> Consumers who venture into the online world should not have to know more than cyber criminals about technology and the Internet in order to stay safe. Instead, sophisticated online advertising companies like Google and Yahoo!, whose representatives are here with us today, have a responsibility to help protect consumers from the potentially harmful effects of the advertisements they deliver.

During the hearing, the witnesses acknowledged that malvertising was a growing problem and more needed to be done to stop abuses and protect consumers.

Senator Levin's retirement intervened before we could do much follow-up work on reforms. But the issues swirling around Internet advertising have only deepened since 2014, making the McCain-led inquiry into how the advertising ecosystem works more important than ever. In addition, the McCain inquiry showed how congressional oversight could perform a vital analytical and educational role in a complex matter as well as generate pressure on industry and regulators alike to address key issues. It provided another instance of an investigative topic that transcended political divides and benefited from bipartisan attention and cooperation.

Conclusion

Fifteen years of supporting Republican-led PSI investigations exposed the Levin team to a variety of important issues we never otherwise would have tackled. Crossing party lines to conduct joint investigations also felt good—even with the accommodations and painful compromises sometimes required. Over time, the work generated constant reminders that bipartisanship was a two-way street, and that bipartisan investigations really did encourage oversight results that were more thorough, thoughtful, accurate, and credible. Supporting our Republican colleagues' investigative efforts also became a key contributor to bipartisan good will within our ranks and played a critical, ongoing role in the success of the Levin era on PSI.

Notes

1. The Senate Historian's office informed PSI that both President Truman and Senator McCarthy drank bourbon, which is commonly used as the whiskey in Manhattans, but found no mention of Manhattans in particular.
2. The information in this section is based upon "Deceptive Mailings and Sweepstakes Promotions," S. Hrg. 106-71 (3/9–10/1999), https://www.gpo.gov/fdsys/pkg/CHRG-106shrg57308/pdf/CHRG-106shrg57308.pdf; and "The Hidden Operators of Deceptive Mailings," S. Hrg. 106-181 (7/20/1999), https://www.gpo.gov/fdsys/pkg/CHRG-106shrg59577/pdf/CHRG-106shrg59577.pdf.
3. See "Deceptive Mail Prevention and Enforcement Act, S. 335," Senate Committee on Governmental Affairs, S. Rpt. 106-102 (7/1/1999) (hereinafter "Committee Report"), at 13–14, https://www.gpo.gov/fdsys/pkg/CRPT-106srpt102/pdf/CRPT-106srpt102.pdf.
4. See S. 335, Deceptive Mail Prevention and Enforcement Act, P.L. 106-168, which combined provisions from earlier bills, as discussed in the Committee Report, at 12–13.
5. The information in this section is based upon "How Saddam Hussein Abused the United Nations Oil-For-Food Program," S. Hrg. 108-761 (11/15/2004) (hereinafter "2004 OFF Hearing"), https://www.gpo.gov/fdsys/pkg/CHRG-108shrg97048/pdf/CHRG-108shrg97048.pdf, as well as the related hearings and reports identified below.
6. See "Report on Illegal Surcharges on Oil-for-Food Contracts and Illegal Oil Shipments From Khor al-Amaya," Levin staff report reprinted in "Oil for Influence: How Saddam Used Oil to Reward Politicians Under the United Nations Oil-For-Food Program," S. Hrg. 109-185 (5/17/2005) (hereinafter "May 2005 OFF Hearing"), at 836, https://www.gpo.gov/fdsys/pkg/CHRG-109shrg21438/pdf/CHRG-109shrg21438.pdf; "Supplemental Report on Bayoil Diversions of Iraqi Oil and Related Oversight Failures," Levin staff report reprinted in "Corruption in the United Nations Oil-For-Food Program: Reaching a Consensus on United Nations Reform," S. Hrg. 109-247 (10/31/2005) (hereinafter, "October 2005 OFF Hearing"), at 396, https://www.gpo.gov/fdsys/pkg/CHRG-109shrg24445/pdf/CHRG-109shrg24445.pdf.
7. See 2004 OFF Hearing; "The United Nations' Management and Oversight of the Oil-for-Food Program," S. Hrg. 109-43 (2/15/2005), https://www.gpo.gov/fdsys/pkg/CHRG-109shrg20172/pdf/CHRG-109shrg20172.pdf.
8. May 2005 OFF Hearing, including three bipartisan staff reports: "Report on Oil Allocations Granted to Charles Pasqua and George Galloway," at 84; "Report on Oil Allocations Granted to Vladimir Zhirinovsky," at 180; "Report on Oil Allocations Granted to The Russian Presidential Council," at

459,   https://www.gpo.gov/fdsys/pkg/CHRG-109shrg21438/pdf/CHRG-109shrg21438.pdf.

9. "Report Concerning the Testimony of George Galloway before the Permanent Subcommittee on Investigations," Coleman staff report reprinted in October 2005 OFF Hearing, at 126.

10. October 2005 OFF Hearing.

11. See "U.S. Indicts Former Executive Director of United Nations Oil-For-Food Program, and United States Businessman," U.S. Attorney for the Southern District of New York Press Release (1/16/2007), https://www.justice.gov/archive/usao/nys/pressreleases/January07/sevanindictmentpr.pdf. See also, for example, "U.S. Legislators Want Cyprus to Extradite UN Official," Reuters (2/13/2007), http://reut.rs/2ARKa17.

12. See "Texas Oil Executive and Two Corporations Sentenced on Charges Involving a Scheme to Pay Secret Kickbacks to the Former Government of Saddam Hussein," U.S. Attorney for the Southern District of New York Press Release (3/7/2008), http://www.prnewswire.com/news-releases/texas-oil-executive-and-two-corporations-sentenced-on-charges-involving-a-scheme-to-pay-secret-kickbacks-to-the-former-government-of-saddam-hussein-56859947.html.

13. See, for example, "Total, Pasqua Cleared of Oil-for-Food Corruption Charges," RFI, Sarah Elzas (9/7/2013), http://bit.ly/2zfuwAB; "France's Total Fined 750,000 Euros Over Iraq 'Oil for Food' Graft," AFP, Sylvain Peuchmaurd (2/26/2016), https://yhoo.it/2j4okjW; "Angolagate Accused Found Guilty, Ex-minister Jailed," RFI (10/27/2009), http://bit.ly/2zdPaRt; "Former Minister Pasqua Gets One-year Suspended Sentence," RFI (4/30/2010), http://bit.ly/2yXeTJM.

14. See, for example, "Mariam Appeal," The Charity Commission for England and Wales (6/8/2007); "Galloway Criticised over Appeal," BBC News (6/8/2007), http://bbc.in/2zgZGr5; "Galloway Ejected as MPs Back Suspension," The Guardian, Matthew Tempest and Agencies (7/24/2007), http://bit.ly/2jB6hpp.

15. The information in this section is based on "United Nations Development Program: A Case Study of North Korea," S. Hrg. 110-544 (1/24/2008), https://www.gpo.gov/fdsys/pkg/CHRG-110shrg41447/pdf/CHRG-110shrg41447.pdf.

16. The information in this section is based on "DOD Contractors Who Cheat on Their Taxes and What Should be Done About It," S. Hrg. 108-493 (2/12/2004), https://www.gpo.gov/fdsys/pkg/CHRG-108shrg92689/pdf/CHRG-108shrg92689.pdf; "Civilian Contractors Who Cheat on their Taxes and What Should be Done About It," S. Hrg. 109-189 (6/16/2005), https://www.gpo.gov/fdsys/pkg/CHRG-109shrg22195/pdf/CHRG-109shrg22195.pdf; "GSA Contractors Who Cheat on Their Taxes and What Should be

Done About It," S. Hrg. 109-418 (3/14/2006), https://www.gpo.gov/fdsys/pkg/CHRG-109shrg27750/pdf/CHRG-109shrg27750.pdf; and related hearings below.

17. The information in this section is based on "Medicare Doctors Who Cheat on their Taxes and What Should be Done About It," S. Hrg. 110-77 (3/20/2007), https://www.gpo.gov/fdsys/pkg/CHRG-110shrg36076/pdf/CHRG-110shrg36076.pdf; "Medicaid Providers Who Cheat on Their Taxes and What Should be Done About It," S. Hrg. 110-309 (11/14/2007), https://www.gpo.gov/fdsys/pkg/CHRG-110shrg38991/pdf/CHRG-110shrg38991.pdf.

18. S. 1307, the Medicare Provider Accountability Act, which was incorporated into the Medicare Improvements for Patients and Providers Act of 2008, P.L. 110-275.

19. "Stimulus Contractors Who Cheat on their Taxes: What Happened?" S. Hrg. 112-53 (5/24/2011) (hereinafter "Stimulus Contractors Hearing"), https://www.gpo.gov/fdsys/pkg/CHRG-112shrg67639/pdf/CHRG-112shrg67639.pdf.

20. See Federal Acquisition Regulation §§ 9.104-5 and 52.209-5; explanation of the final rule, "FAR Case 2006-011, Representations and Certifications—Tax Delinquencies," 73 Fed.Reg. 78 (4/22/2008), at 21791 (stating the rule was drafted in response to PSI work). See also Stimulus Contractors Hearing, at 39–40 (noting that a 2010 review by the Office of Management and Budget found contractors with tax delinquencies generally did not receive contracts).

21. The information in this section is based on "Social Security Disability Benefits: Did a Group of Judges, Doctors, and Lawyers Abuse Programs for the Country's Most Vulnerable?," Senate Committee on Homeland Security and Governmental Affairs, S. Hrg. 113-503 (10/7/2013) (hereinafter "2013 Social Security Disability Hearing"), https://www.gpo.gov/fdsys/pkg/CHRG-113shrg85499/pdf/CHRG-113shrg85499.pdf.

22. "Disability-Claim Judge Has Trouble Saying 'No'," *Wall Street Journal*, Damian Paletta (5/19/2011), http://on.wsj.com/2jBHJg7.

23. For an example of a Conn commercial, see https://www.youtube.com/watch?v=zqtL78-H_YI.

24. "How Some Legal, Medical, and Judicial Professionals Abused Social Security Disability Programs for the Country's Most Vulnerable: A Case Study of the Conn Law Firm," report reprinted in the 2013 Social Security Disability Hearing record, at 171.

25. See, for example, "Disability Program Probe Focuses on Attorney, Judge in W.Va.," CBS News (10/8/2013), http://cbsn.ws/1jBfnwv.

26. See *United States v. Conn*, Case No. 7:11-CV-57-157-ART (USDC ED KY), United States' Motion to Partially Intervene For Good Cause (2/9/2016).

27. Id., at 5. See also, for example, "Government Moves to Suspend Disability Payments to Many in Eastern Kentucky, Citing Suspected Fraud," *Lexington Herald Leader*, Bill Estep (5/26/2015), http://bit.ly/1IZkKAn.
28. "Retired Judge, Attorney and Psychologist Indicted in $600 Million Social Security Fraud Scheme," Department of Justice Press Release (4/5/2016), https://www.justice.gov/opa/pr/retired-judge-attorney-and-psychologist-indicted-600-million-social-security-fraud-scheme.
29. "Social Security Disability Lawyer Pleads Guilty for Role in $550 Million Social Security Fraud Scheme," Justice Department Press Release (3/24/2017), https://www.justice.gov/opa/pr/social-security-disability-lawyer-pleads-guilty-role-550-million-social-security-fraud-scheme; "Well-known Disability Lawyer Eric Conn Pleads Guilty in Federal Fraud Case," *Herald-Leader*, Bill Estep (3/24/2017), http://bit.ly/2yObEUW; "Former Administrative Law Judge Pleads Guilty for Role in $550 Million Social Security Disability Fraud Scheme," SSA Office of the Inspector General (5/12/2017), http://oig.ssa.gov/audits-and-investigations/investigations/may12-daugherty-guilty-plea.
30. "Former Administrative Law Judge Pleads Guilty for Role in $550 Million Social Security Disability Fraud Scheme," SSA Office of the Inspector General Press Release (5/12/2017), http://oig.ssa.gov/audits-and-investigations/investigations/may12-daugherty-guilty-plea.
31. "Lexington, Kentucky, Jury Convicts Clinical Psychologist for Role in $600 Million Social Security Disability Fraud Scheme," Justice Department Press Release (6/12/2017), https://www.justice.gov/opa/pr/lexington-kentucky-jury-convicts-clinical-psychologist-role-600-million-social-security.
32. Prior to sentencing, Mr. Conn fled the country, but was recaptured six months later in Honduras and returned to the United States to begin serving a 12-year prison term. "FBI Returning Fugitive Lawyer to Kentucky after Capture," Associated Press, Moises Castillo (12/5/2017), http://bit.ly/2BKwZQZ.
33. The information in this section is based on "Social Security Disability Programs: Improving the Quality of Benefit Award Decisions," S. Hrg. 112-800 (9/13/2012), https://www.gpo.gov/fdsys/pkg/CHRG-112shrg76068/pdf/CHRG-112shrg76068.pdf.
34. The information in this section is based on "Online Advertising and Hidden Hazards to Consumer Security and Data Privacy," S. Hrg. 113-407 (5/14/2014), https://www.gpo.gov/fdsys/pkg/CHRG-113shrg89686/pdf/CHRG-113shrg89686.pdf.

8

Halting Unfair Credit Card Practices

> "Every credit card for a credit card company is like a lottery ticket. They're just waiting to see who's going to maybe stumble a little. ... Those are the ones you hit with the 29% interest rate, the 35% interest rate, the new fees. And then, because of course if you can't pay it, then you get hit with a fee for not paying or for paying late, for going over limit. And the game is afoot. With any luck at all from the credit card company's perspective, these people will become little annuities that will just keep generating profits for the credit card companies for months, for years, maybe forever."
> Then-Harvard Professor Elizabeth Warren (1/2/2009), http://www.pbs.org/now/shows/501/credit-traps.html

Levin-led PSI investigations into issues like money laundering, accounting fraud, and offshore tax abuse fell outside the ambit of most Americans. But one PSI investigation hit much closer to home: stopping unfair credit card practices loading down ordinary working families with unjustified, high-priced debt. Abuses included credit card companies charging interest on credit card debt already paid, hiking interest rates on families who paid on time, manipulating credit card charges to trigger over-the-limit fees, and other predatory practices. By exposing the abuses and championing credit card reform, the Levin oversight effort helped bring relief to hundreds of millions of average Americans.

PSI got into the credit card issue, in part, because Senator Levin himself fell victim to a sneaky practice. In his case, he'd mistakenly paid slightly less than he owed on a credit card account and, the next month, got a bill for the $15 or so he still owed plus about $35 in interest charges. When he inquired how

© The Author(s) 2018
E. J. Bean, *Financial Exposure*, https://doi.org/10.1007/978-3-319-94388-6_8

he could possibly owe $35 of interest on an unpaid balance of $15, he learned for the first time that when he didn't pay 100% of his credit card bill on time, he was charged interest on the full amount of the prior month's balance, even if he'd paid off most of it. In short, the credit card company was collecting interest on debt he'd already paid.

That disclosure made Senator Levin wonder what other shady practices were going on in the credit card industry. In 2005, he directed us to take a closer look. I decided to assign myself lead responsibility for the credit card investigation.

Using GAO

We began the inquiry by asking the Government Accountability Office (GAO) to assemble some key data about common credit cards—identifying, for example, the types of interest rates, fees, and penalties credit card issuers were imposing on cardholders. Over the years, we'd learned that GAO's strongest suit was compiling and analyzing complex data. So we decided to make use of its expertise, both to bridge a gap in available credit card data and construct a solid factual foundation for our own investigation.

Senator Levin was then the ranking minority member on PSI. We asked our Republican buddies whether Senator Coleman, then PSI chair, would like to join the request to GAO, but he declined. That was a disappointment, since GAO assigned a higher priority to bipartisan requests. But undeterred, Senator Levin sent his own request letter to GAO in April 2005.

It took until June for the project to advance through GAO's job queue, but soon after, GAO identified 28 popular credit cards at the six largest credit card issuers for the data collection effort. When GAO asked the issuers for the information, however, it ran into a buzz saw of resistance. The credit card issuers—all major banks—claimed the requested information was proprietary trade data whose public disclosure would damage their businesses, even though the credit card terms were already generally available to prospective cardholders.

GAO came to us with the problem, and we responded that one solution was for PSI to subpoena the banks for the information. When the banks—most of whom knew us from prior investigations—heard PSI might intervene with subpoenas, they began negotiating with GAO on another way forward. The banks proposed submitting the requested information to a mutually-agreed-upon third party who would put the data into a standard format, strip out the bank names, and substitute identifiers like "Credit Card Issuer A" and

"Credit Card 1." The third party could then turn over the scrubbed data to GAO for further analysis. After determining it could still extract useful information from the data and checking with PSI, GAO agreed to the proposal.

Setting up the third party arrangement, waiting for the scrubbed credit card data, and analyzing the resulting information consumed an entire year at GAO. Along the way, GAO provided us with brief status reports. Since we were swamped with other investigations, we were content to wait, encouraging GAO to alert us to any roadblocks.

In the fall of 2006, GAO informed us the work was done, and it was ready to issue a report. Following its standard procedure, the GAO team gave us a copy 30 days before the release date so we could digest the details and prepare a press release.[1] The report turned out to be jam-packed with interesting facts and analysis, but it also ran 125 pages long and was written in such dry prose we worried no one would get through it. We decided to draft a press release to pull out the key nuggets and add explanatory remarks by Senator Levin.

The press release began by noting that the GAO report provided, for the first time in years, detailed data on the interest rates, fees, penalties, and disclosure practices of 28 popular credit cards.[2] It summarized the report's key information along the following lines.

- *Increased Credit Card Use.* U.S. consumers had about 690 million credit cards. The amount charged on them had grown from about $69 billion in 1980 to more than $1.8 trillion in 2005; in 2004, the average U.S. household credit card debt was $5100.
- *Higher Late Fees.* The average 2005 fee for making a late payment was $34, a 115% increase from $13 in 1995. The highest late fee was $39.
- *Hidden Fees.* Some fees weren't disclosed in materials given to cardholders, such as a $5–$15 fee to pay a bill by telephone and a $2–$13 fee to get a copy of a bill.
- *Penalty Interest Rates.* Some credit cards imposed penalty interest rates of over 30% on cardholders who paid late or exceeded a credit limit.
- *Inadequate Fee Disclosure.* Fee disclosures were difficult to understand and often failed to convey to cardholders when late fees would be charged and what actions could trigger penalty interest rates.
- *Increased Profits.* From 1986 to 2004, the average profitability of large credit card banks was more than double that of all commercial banks, and was increasingly due to penalty interest rates and fees.

The press release also disclosed that the credit cards had been issued by Bank of America, Capital One Bank, Chase Bank, Citibank, Discover Financial

Services, and MBNA America Bank which, together, generated 80% of the credit card lending in the United States.

Since Senator Coleman hadn't requested the GAO report, he decided not to go on the press release either. We ran the draft by his staff anyway to make sure they were okay with the wording. They were fine with our issuing the press release in the name of PSI.

Helped by our media alert, when the GAO credit card report went public in October 2006, it was an immediate hit. GAO told us it quickly experienced over 10,000 downloads, the most of any GAO report at the time. It seemed as if the public, policymakers, and media were starved for solid credit card data and feasting on the new figures. At PSI, the GAO report fired up our resolve to dig deeper.

Investigating Credit Card Practices

In November 2006, the month after the GAO report went public, mid-term elections gave Democrats enough new Senate seats to capture a bare majority in the Senate. The narrow electoral victory meant Senator Levin would regain the PSI chair in early 2007. In a strategy session preparing for the new Congress, Senator Levin directed us to put a priority on the credit card investigation to determine if it justified a hearing.

I cleared my calendar and alerted our Coleman colleagues to our elevated focus on credit cards. Tim Terry and Mark Nelson from the Coleman staff, Zack Schram and a volunteer lawyer Alan Kahn from our side, as well as an ever-changing assortment of detailees, law clerks, and interns, powered the inquiry. In our first meeting, we decided to gain a more detailed understanding of how credit cards actually functioned; identify and catalog the practices that raised concerns; and identify case studies to illustrate the problems.

The PSI team began by contacting multiple credit card experts to get their views on potentially unfair credit card practices. We spoke with GAO, consumer groups, federal bank regulators, academics, and others. One of the most helpful was then Harvard Professor Elizabeth Warren who'd been studying credit cards for years and had detailed information about troubling practices. We also interviewed the Fair Issac Corp., developer of the "FICO credit score" used to predict the likelihood of a person's paying off their debts, as well as the three credit bureaus that compiled credit histories on millions of Americans. All four relied heavily on credit card data.

To develop case studies, we posted a request on Senator Levin's website asking the public to send us examples of abuse. That online request generated a steady stream of emails and letters with a wide range of credit card complaints. Our interns processed the information, creating a paper file for each complaint, requesting documentation when appropriate, and building a spreadsheet with key data points. By the end of 2007, they'd logged in over 2000 credit card complaints involving multiple credit card issuers and individuals across the country. Zack led an analysis of the data to identify trends and the most troubling practices.

Many of the cases described traumatic experiences. Senior citizens on fixed incomes socked with massive interest rate hikes that exploded their budgets. Families that used a credit card to pay a large medical bill, got hit with interest rate hikes, and when they couldn't keep up with the payments, got hit again with non-stop over-the-limit and late fees. Individuals who paid off their credit card debt only to be harassed by debt collectors insisting they still owed the money. The negative stories piled up. To try to alleviate the depression that began enveloping our young staff, I allowed each intern to pick out one case per month that we would try to help.

One of those cases involved a woman who'd been working late, drove home in the early hours from her job, and had a car accident on the highway resulting in the death of a prominent citizen. She was convicted of involuntary manslaughter and sent to prison in Arizona for two years, leaving her teenage son home alone. While imprisoned, her credit card debt skyrocketed due to her inability to pay down bills totaling about $8600, compounded by a 29% penalty interest rate and monthly $39 late fee. In addition, once she was in prison, the bank lowered the credit limit on her cards so she also began incurring monthly over-the-limit fees of $39.

She instructed the bank to close both her credit card accounts and asked for a breakdown of the debt in terms of purchases, cash advances, interest, and fees, so she could negotiate a payoff amount. The bank declined to provide the information, even though she was entitled to it by law. A friend who contacted us on her behalf asked us to call the bank. When we did, the bank immediately provided the data, apologizing for not acting sooner. The cardholder then negotiated a settlement and, by refinancing her home, paid off the debt. The bank's refusal to cooperate earlier was one more painful indicator of how little clout average cardholders held.

In addition to speaking with credit cardholders, consumer advocates, regulators, and academics, we worked with half a dozen large credit card issuers to learn more from their point of view. To increase our practical understanding, Bank of America provided a tour of its credit card processing facility in Delaware. The Levin and Coleman staffers who made the trip reported seeing vast conveyor belts of envelopes subjected to sophisticated processing techniques that slit open the envelopes, extracted the contents, directed checks for deposit, and directed other materials to specialists. The staff also learned how credit card issuers handled payments made online, by telephone, or at bank offices, and kept track of the various payment streams. In addition, they learned about the industry's vast call centers and training operations geared to handle a daily torrent of cardholder inquiries.

In addition to the tour, we held intense, day-long meetings in the PSI conference room with each of the big credit card issuers to learn more about their operations. Each bank sent a team of senior personnel with extensive knowledge about how their company functioned. After sending them an advance list with topics of interest, we asked detailed questions about how their credit cards worked, covering interest rates, grace periods, fees, penalties, risk analysis, credit scores, customer service operations, billing disputes, debt collection, customer assistance, settlements, and disclosure practices. The sessions told the companies how serious we were about understanding exactly what was going on. The interviews also drummed into us just how complex credit cards were as financial instruments.

We learned, for example, that credit card issuers imposed a wide range of fees on cardholders including annual fees, late fees, over-the-limit fees, balance transfer fees, and foreign exchange fees. One surprise was a $5–$15 charge to cardholders who paid their bills by telephone, often in an effort to pay on time and avoid late fees and interest rate hikes. The companies rewarded that responsible behavior by charging cardholders a fee to pay their bills, what critics called a "pay to pay fee." We also learned that the financial toll taken by fees was worsened by an industry practice of including the fees in cardholders' credit card balances so that the fees incurred interest charges. In other words, the banks were charging interest not only on the funds lent to cardholders, but also on the fees added to their credit card accounts.

Another topic involved grace periods. We learned that although many consumers thought all credit cards provided a grace period before interest was charged, in fact, most credit cards did not provide a grace period unless the cardholder paid the balance in full each month. If a cardholder owed any balance from a prior month, there was typically no grace period at all for new purchases, which began incurring interest charges from day one. We also learned that the banks sometimes differed in how long a grace period they offered and when it began. Many had due dates that shifted each month depending upon the number of days in the month, sometimes tripping up cardholders and triggering late fees and penalty interest rates. In addition, we found if a cardholder paid off a portion of a monthly balance but not the entire amount owed, every single bank charged interest on the full monthly balance, including the portion paid on time.

We asked a lot of questions about how interest rates were assessed. We learned that banks typically applied multiple interest rates to the same credit card, depending upon the circumstances. For example, they typically used one interest rate for regular purchases, another for cash advances, a third for balance transfers, and, in the case of cardholders who paid late or exceeded a credit limit, a penalty interest rate that could exceed 30%. We also learned that many banks competed for new customers by offering extremely low initial interest rates—what we called "teaser rates"—that, under a variety of triggers, could suddenly escalate. On top of that, many of the interest rates varied over time, often rising and falling with a "prime rate." The combination of multiple interest rates applying to a single account, some of which varied over time, made it nearly impossible for cardholders to predict or track their total finance charges.

Still another level of complexity involved how interest rates were affected by automated risk analyses. We learned that banks used mathematical models that continually calculated the riskiness of their cardholders, using credit scores and other factors. The software programs monitored cardholders on an ongoing basis and, if an individual's risk increased by a specified amount, hiked that person's interest rate to a pre-determined level, even if the cardholder had a perfect history of paying their bills on time. We learned that, in most cases, no human being was involved in hiking the interest rates on tens of thousands of accounts and, sometimes, the reasons why a software program hiked a specific individual's interest rate were unclear, even to the issuer. In addition, we learned that, while the issuers' software was programmed to increase cardholders' interest rates when their risk increased, it was not programmed the other way—to lower their rates when their risk decreased. That as well as the systemic disregard of on-time payment histories seemed to create hidden biases weighted toward imposing higher interest rates.

In our interviews with the banks, we confirmed that all of them worded their credit card contracts to allow unilateral interest rate hikes on their cardholders "at any time for any reason." Cardholders were usually powerless to object and sometimes received little or no notice of an upcoming rate hike. The higher interest rate was typically applied not only to new debt but also to pre-existing debt originally incurred at a lower interest rate. We learned it was the only type of consumer debt where the lender had the right, on a unilateral, retroactive basis, to hike the interest rate on a borrower's loan.

Finally, we examined the disclosures provided to cardholders. Reading the often tiny type was an eye strain, and the boilerplate jargon was often unintelligible even to our finance-trained lawyers. Hours of close reading led us to conclude that the disclosures often left out or buried key information, or contained such ambiguous terms it was impossible to understand exactly how the credit card worked without talking to the credit card issuer. A discussion which PSI could compel, but most cardholders could not.

When we asked the banks why their contracts allowed such unfair practices as unilateral retroactive interest hikes, interest charges on debt already paid, or risk analysis programs that disregarded years of on-time payments, the folks we interviewed typically blinked and said they'd always operated that way. Because no one had ever said they couldn't.

By early 2007, we'd concluded that the credit card industry was, in fact, riddled with unfair practices that not only disadvantaged cardholders, but often condemned them to years of unjustified and expensive credit card debt. We'd also vetted multiple case studies that illustrated the problems. We reported to Senator Levin on what we'd found, highlighting the particularly egregious practices. He decided it was time to go public.

Holding the First Hearing

Senator Levin held two credit card hearings in 2007. The first took place in March. It was the first PSI hearing in the new 110th Congress and the first since Senator Levin had regained the chair. It focused on two fundamental credit card issues: exorbitant penalty interest rates and excessive fees. It also tackled the more complicated issue of banks' charging interest on credit card debt that had already been paid.[3]

We decided to feature a single case study that exemplified the unfair credit card tactics that can trap working families in a downward spiral of debt. It focused on Wesley Wannemacher, a middle-aged Midwestern family man with a medium build and mild demeanor.

Mr. Wannemacher was from Ohio. In 2001, he decided to get married. To help pay for his wedding, he took out a new Chase credit card with a $3000 credit limit. He used the card to pay for expenses mostly related to his wedding, and charged a total of about $3200, exceeding the credit limit by $200. He spent the next six years trying to pay off the debt, averaging payments of about $1000 per year.

Credit card statements authenticated by Chase showed that, during those six years, Mr. Wannemacher was charged about $4900 in interest, $1100 in late fees, and $1500 in over-the-limit fees. His penalty interest rate climbed to 30%. He was hit 47 times with over-the-limit fees, even though he'd exceeded the limit by only $200. He'd made offers to Chase to settle his debt, but each offer had been rejected. At the time of the hearing, he'd paid about $6300 on his $3200 debt, but still owed $4400. With no end in sight.

The Wannemacher case history said it all. Despite paying nearly twice what he'd charged, he still owed thousands of dollars more. He was subjected to a predatory interest rate of 30% that he'd never agreed to. He was charged non-stop over-the-limit fees out of all proportion to the amount by which he'd exceeded the credit limit. The bank charged him "late" fees even when he paid on time, because he didn't pay 100% of the amount owed. The bank rejected his settlement offers and continued to squeeze him for money. At the end of six years, despite payments that added up to more than $6300, he was deeper in debt than when he'd started. It was a rigged game that had pounded Mr. Wannemacher financially for years on end.[4]

Mr. Wannemacher agreed to speak on the hearing's first panel. He turned out to be a dream witness. He described what happened in simple terms using a quiet, measured voice. He calmly explained how hard he'd worked to pay off his debt and how difficult the credit card company had made it. He was every-man struggling to survive predatory credit card practices.

He was followed on the panel by a National Consumer Law Center attorney, Alys Cohen, who testified that Mr. Wannemacher's experience was far from unique. She explained that sky-high credit card interest rates and fees were a growing source of financial hardship for American families. She described a litany of abusive credit card practices, including sudden interest rate hikes with little or no notice, manipulation of credit card charges to trigger over-the-limit violations, and shifting payment due dates that led to late payments followed by late fees and penalty interest rates. She described penalty interest rates triggered by a single instance of exceeding a credit limit or by a payment only one day late. She noted the penalty rates applied not just to future transactions but also to existing balances, constituting a retroactive, unilateral change in the credit card loan terms. Ms. Cohen also criticized the practice of so-called universal default in which banks hiked a cardholder's interest rate, not for conduct that affected the bank, but for conduct reported by and affecting only other creditors.

The second panel heard from chief executive officers leading the credit card operations at three banks with massive credit card portfolios, Chase Bank USA, Bank of America Card Services, and Citi Cards. Senator Levin had insisted on hearing from the CEOs, because he wanted the ultimate decision-makers to answer for what their companies were doing. When some of the CEOs balked, we indicated that Senator Levin was prepared to issue subpoenas to compel their attendance. In response, each CEO agreed to appear "voluntarily."

Chase's credit card CEO Richard Srednicki was faced with defending the outrageous interest rates and fees his company had imposed on a cardholder who'd paid $6300 on a $3200 debt, yet faced $4400 more in charges. Given the damning facts, it wasn't surprising when, five days after learning Mr. Wannemacher would be testifying, the bank informed him that Chase had forgiven his debt, and he was free and clear. But Chase didn't stop there. Two days before the hearing, Chase informed the subcommittee that, due to a review triggered by the Wannemacher case, it had changed its over-the-limit fee policy. Instead of charging non-stop fees for each over-the-limit violation, the bank would, in future, stop after three over-the-limit fees per violation. And the new policy would apply immediately to all 100 million Chase credit card accounts. Whoa.

At the hearing itself, the Chase credit card CEO began his testimony by apologizing to Mr. Wannemacher. He stated that Chase had policies and procedures in place to identify and help credit card customers who had fallen into debt and were finding it difficult to work their way out. The CEO said he regretted those policies and procedures had not been used in the Wannemacher case, which was why the bank had forgiven his debt. Mr. Srednicki also accepted criticism of the bank's over-the-limit practices and announced the bank's change in policy.

He was not the only bank to announce major policy changes at the hearing. Citi Cards' CEO announced that, to better serve its customers, Citi Cards would no longer use "universal default" to impose penalty interest rates for conduct that affected only other creditors. He also announced that Citi Cards would eliminate from its credit card agreements the clause allowing it to raise credit card rates "at any time for any reason." Double whoa.

Gaining Steam for Reform

The PSI hearing provided a remarkable demonstration of the power of oversight—how shining a public spotlight on indefensible conduct could, all by itself without legislation, spark dramatic reform. In response to the facts, the Chase CEO had essentially snapped his fingers, eliminated a back-breaking debt for one individual, and eased future fees for 100 million cardholders. Then Citi Cards' CEO snapped his fingers and eased the rules for another 100 million accounts. Those two reforms alone were staggering. But we also knew, when the spotlight switched off, both CEOs could snap their fingers again and resurrect the prior credit card landscape.

That's why, after the hearing, Senator Levin directed us to develop a bill to put an end to the worst of the credit card abuses we'd identified.

Before beginning that work, however, we took a moment to savor the fact that our March hearing, together with the 2006 GAO report, had generated an enormous amount of press attention to the problem of unfair credit card practices. Mr. Wannemacher had amplified the hearing's impact by talking to the media afterward and even going on camera to discuss his experiences. When asked what he would do in response to his credit card debt's being forgiven, he smiled and said he planned to get his son braces. We couldn't have found a more modest, likeable representative of middle class America struggling with unfair credit card debt.

Over the next two months, we worked on a bill to stop the worst of the abuses. We presented our ideas to Senator Levin whose direction was to design a bill that was short, understandable, and politically palatable, yet effective.

In May 2007, Senator Levin introduced the Stop Unfair Practices in Credit Cards Act, a 13-page bill that addressed the most troubling practices we'd identified.[5] Key provisions prohibited credit card companies from charging interest on debt that had been repaid on time and from retroactively applying increased interest rates to past credit card debt. Other provisions targeted abusive fees, allowing only one over-the-limit fee per credit limit violation, barring pay-to-pay fees altogether, and prohibiting the charging of interest on any fee amount included in a credit card balance. Still another set of provisions sought to require credit card issuers to apply credit card payments first to the credit card balances bearing the highest interest rates and to pay off credit card charges in the order that would minimize finance charges. The most controversial provision proposed that, when a credit card issuer imposed a penalty interest rate on a cardholder, the new interest rate could not exceed the prior rate by more than 7%.

Senator Coleman had put in a strong performance at the credit card hearing, condemning unfair credit card practices and asking tough questions. So we were hopeful he would cosponsor the bill. But as with the GAO request letter, Senator Coleman declined. We weren't sure why. We were also unable to find any other Republican cosponsor. So we turned to Senator Claire McCaskill, a Missouri Democrat who was a member of PSI, had actively participated in the hearing, and was a fierce critic of credit card abuses.

The Levin-McCaskill bill was referred to the Banking Committee, then chaired by Senator Chris Dodd from Connecticut, a long-time champion of credit card reform. He'd held multiple hearings and repeatedly introduced legislation over the years, but hadn't been able to win reforms. One problem was that two of the senior Banking Committee Democrats, Senators Tim Johnson of South Dakota and Tom Carper of Delaware, were from states that hosted large credit card operations; neither was a fan of credit card reform. We hoped the publicity generated by our hearing would convince Senator Dodd to try again anyway. To encourage him, we added Democratic heavyweights to our bill: Senators Patrick Leahy, Dick Durbin, and Ted Kennedy.

Our hopes for Senate action got a boost when the House swung into action. Democratic Congresswoman Carolyn Maloney from New York, chair of the House Financial Services Subcommittee on Financial Institutions and Consumer Credit, held two high-profile hearings on unfair credit card practices in April and June 2007.[6] In July, with the blessing of Financial Services Committee Chair Barney Frank, she convened a closed-door meeting with credit card issuers and consumer advocates to see if they could reach common ground on legislation.[7] At the end of the meeting, Congressman Frank announced to the press that he hoped to move a credit card reform bill through his committee by October.

Preparing a Second Hearing

Barney Frank's announcement was a bombshell. While he didn't actually meet the October timetable, his stated intention to move a bill quickly catapulted credit card reform onto the House agenda. His action also upped the pressure on the Senate. But we knew we needed more than Barney Frank to kickstart Senate action. So Senator Levin decided to hold a second hearing, concentrating on one of the credit card industry's most objectionable practices—imposing unilateral interest rate hikes on cardholders who'd played by the rules and paid their credit card bills on time. He told us to schedule the second hearing before the end of the year.[8]

Because Mr. Wannemacher had been such a hit at our first hearing, we decided to use the same approach in the next one. To identify promising case studies, we combed through our database of 2000 credit card complaints. We identified over a dozen examples of unilateral, retroactive interest rate hikes on cardholders who appeared to have paid all their bills on time. Since hearings that feature victims of wrongdoing typically succeed or fail based upon the strength of the specific examples, we carefully vetted the potential case studies.

Our first step was to contact the cardholders and collect their credit card statements. Most had some, but not all of their statements, so we prepared letters signed by each cardholder giving PSI permission to get their records from the credit card issuer. Next, we contacted the credit card issuers and requested the account documentation, including any mitigating information, so we could get a complete picture of what happened. Based upon the information supplied by the banks, some of which disclosed facts at odds with what we'd been told by cardholders, we dropped some cases and zeroed in on others.

Next, we interviewed the cardholders. Since they were scattered across the country and we didn't have much in the way of travel funds, we conducted the interviews by telephone. Zack Schram and Alan Kahn led the effort. The interviews sought not only to confirm the details of each case, but also to gauge how articulate each cardholder was, how each might function in the glare of a public hearing, and how each might serve as a symbol of the need for credit card reform. It was a high bar.

Over the course of several months, we settled on eight case studies. All eight involved cardholders who'd fully met their credit card obligations, but were hit with whopping interest rate hikes anyway. We decided to write up all eight cases in two-page "fact sheets" that contained a narrative describing what had happened and a chart containing month-by-month financial data showing how the rate increases had impacted the cardholder's finances. We also decided to feature only three of the case studies at the hearing. Experience had taught us that hearings were not good at presenting multiple case studies with complicated facts; three examples were pretty much the maximum that could be digested by a viewing public.

Choosing which of the three case histories to feature at the hearing was difficult. One of the most compelling involved a feisty elderly lady from Alabama who, despite years of on-time payments reducing her credit card debt, had been suddenly slugged with an interest rate hike from 19% to 30% that began burying her in debt. We thought she'd be an attractive witness, in part because she had a lively Southern drawl, a great sense of humor, and resided in the home state of the Banking Committee's ranking Republican, Senator Richard Shelby. When we approached her about testifying, however, she hesitated and finally declined. She suggested without saying so directly that the details were too embarrassing for her to discuss in a public setting, even though she was fine with us publicizing her circumstances in our written materials.

We had better luck with Janet Hard of Freeland, Michigan. She was a 42-year-old nurse, married to a steamfitter, had two children, and exemplified America's working families. It didn't hurt that she was also Senator Levin's constituent. Ms. Hard was surprised when PSI contacted her, but readily agreed to go public. Like Wesley Wannemacher, she was able to describe what happened to her in a calm, straightforward, and earnest way.

Her case was typical of many we'd studied. In 2006, despite a more than two-year history of making all her credit card payments on time and never exceeding the credit limit, Ms. Hard learned Discover Financial Services had suddenly hiked her credit card interest rate from 18% to 24%. Ms. Hard said she'd received no prior notice of the rate hike, detecting it only when she analyzed her bill to figure out why her credit card balance was hardly budging despite her many regular payments. When we asked the bank why it had raised her interest rate, Discover explained that a credit bureau had lowered Ms. Hard's credit score which automatically caused the bank's software to raise her interest rate. Discover did not know what specific event triggered the lower credit score, nor did Ms. Hard. She said she knew of no change in her financial status that would have lowered her credit score. The bank also admitted that, even after Ms. Hard's credit rating dropped—supposedly signifying she was a greater credit risk—Discover had increased the limit on her credit card from $10,000 to $11,000.

Her credit card statements showed that Discover applied the higher 24% rate retroactively to her existing credit card debt of $8300. In response to her ongoing objections, after a year, the bank slightly reduced the rate to 21%. The ongoing damage to her finances was clear. Her records showed that despite making steady $200 payments totaling $2400 from October 2006 to October 2007, while keeping new purchases to a total of less than $100, Ms. Hard's credit card debt had fallen by only $350. When we analyzed why $2400 in payments had reduced her debt by only $350, we learned that the higher interest rates had directed a much larger portion of her payments—$176 out of $200—to finance charges instead of reducing her principal debt. Mrs. Hard told us the slower rate of debt reduction had translated into greater financial hardship for her family. We asked her to be our lead witness at the upcoming hearing, and she agreed.

A second cardholder who agreed to testify was Millard Glasshof of Milwaukee, Wisconsin, a senior citizen on a fixed income. A proud elderly Midwesterner, he explained that, for many years, he had made a $119 monthly payment to Chase to pay off a $5000 debt on a closed credit card account, gradually reducing the amount owed. But in December 2006, Chase suddenly increased his interest rate from 15% to 17%, and then hiked it again to 27%. He said Chase applied the new 27% rate retroactively to his existing debt, which meant, out of his $119 payment, $114 went to pay finance charges and only $5 went to reducing the principal debt. Due to the new penalty interest rate as well as steep fees, Mr. Glasshof testified that, despite paying $1300 over a 12-month period, his credit card debt had not gone down by a single dollar.

We chose as our third hearing witness Bonnie Rushing of Naples, Florida. Ms. Rushing worked as a corporate paralegal and was married to a retired engineer. She agreed to describe her experience with a Bank of America credit card with an interest rate of about 8%. Her credit card statements showed she'd never made a late payment or exceeded the limit on that credit card, and was slowly paying off a debt of about $21,000. In April 2007, despite her history of on-time payments, Bank of America nearly tripled her interest rate from 8% to 23%.

When asked about the tripled rate increase, the bank explained that a credit bureau had lowered Ms. Rushing's credit score which, in turn, caused the bank's software automatically to raise her interest rate to a pre-determined level. When we asked the credit bureau why it had lowered Ms. Rushing's credit score, it explained that it, too, used an automated system to calculate credit scores. When queried, the credit bureau's software generated a boiler-plate explanation that Ms. Rushing's credit score had been lowered because her debt had been too high compared to her credit limit, even though her debt level had not substantially changed in months and had been higher in the past. Ms. Rushing speculated that, perhaps, her credit score was affected when she opened Macy's and J. Jill credit cards to obtain discounted purchases of cosmetics and clothes, even though she'd closed both accounts after paying her bills promptly and in full. The credit bureau couldn't confirm that was why her credit score fell. In the end, no one knew for sure why her credit score had dropped, triggering the higher interest rate.

The 23% interest rate had an immediate impact. Ms. Rushing's monthly finance charge suddenly tripled, jumping from about $150 to $450. Ms. Rushing said she'd received no prior notice of the rate hike. Instead, she'd first learned of it when she received her credit card bill. When she contacted the bank to object, according to Ms. Rushing, the bank told her she had no recourse other than to accept the increased rate, pay off the account with another credit card, or try to negotiate a different interest rate. Ms. Rushing asked to close the account and pay off the existing debt at the prior 8% rate, but was told that wasn't an option. Ms. Rushing closed the account anyway and complained to the Florida Attorney General, AAA which had sponsored the credit card, and PSI. Bank of America eventually agreed to allow her to pay off her debt at the prior 8% rate. Her monthly finance charge dropped back down to $150.

In our view, the three case studies presented dramatic facts that exemplified the unfairness of unilateral, retroactive interest rate hikes on cardholders who had done everything asked of them. We also knew that, to present those facts, we were taking a chance, since we'd never met our witnesses in person and had only spoken with them by telephone. With fingers crossed, we asked all three to fly to Washington on the day before the hearing so that we could meet them, show them the hearing room, and explain what would happen during the proceedings. The subcommittee paid their travel expenses so they could afford to participate.

The limited resources we had to prepare our hearing witnesses stood in stark contrast to the credit card issuers which could afford, not only to fly in their executives, but also pay top-flight lawyers to prep them on how to make their case and answer tough questions.

Holding the Second Hearing

On December 4, 2007, PSI held its second hearing of the year on unfair credit card practices. Like the first hearing, we heard from both credit card-holders and credit card issuers.

The first panel took testimony from the three cardholders, Janet Hard, Millard Glasshof, and Bonnie Rushing. Despite some nerves, each calmly explained what'd happened to them and answered questions. On many committees, members of Congress were given just five minutes each to question witnesses, which wasn't enough time to elicit complicated facts or confront recalcitrant witnesses. PSI was different. PSI practice was to allow the chair and ranking minority member to take 8, 10, and even 15 minutes each in the first round of questioning to draw out the facts, depending upon the agreement reached between them. Other senators could also get more time for witness questions just by requesting it. In addition, PSI practice was to allow multiple rounds of questions so that senators willing to put in the time could ask all the questions they felt necessary to establish the facts. That was one reason PSI hearings ran so long.

At the credit card hearing, Senators Levin, Coleman, and McCaskill questioned the cardholders about what had happened to them, including how none of the three had received prior notice of their rate hikes, how the higher rates had impacted their finances, and how all three had been penalized despite years of on-time payments. Senator Carper from Delaware, who was a member of our committee as well as the Banking Committee, tried to elicit some sympathy for the credit card issuers. At one point, he asked Ms. Rushing whether it was fair in evaluating risk for a credit card issuer to consider the fact that a cardholder was missing payments on other debts. She responded that whether or not that was fair, those facts didn't apply to her; she had paid every one of her bills on time, but her interest rate was hiked anyway.

The second hearing panel heard from senior officials at three credit card banks: Bank of America, Capital One, and Discover Financial Services. All three strongly defended raising the interest rates of their cardholders on a unilateral basis, noting that they issued unsecured loans to millions of card-holders. They explained that they had to rely on automated systems to evaluate the cardholders' risk factors and, if an individual's credit risk increased, needed to be able to quickly raise that person's interest rate. Discover testified that its ability to make risk-based "price adjustments" to cardholders' interest rates was critical to its offering credit to a wide segment of the public and to setting prices that were appropriate for each borrower. Capital One testified that "repricing" credit card interest rates on existing debt was essential to the safe and sound underwriting of open-ended, unsecured credit products and to accommodating changes over time to the economy and to individuals' creditworthiness.

Senators Levin, Coleman, and McCaskill responded with a series of tough questions. They asked how the banks could hike the interest rates of individuals who had complied with all the terms of their credit card agreements; the executives noted the contracts allowed it. The senators asked why the interest rate hikes applied to existing debt instead of just future debt; the executives, again, pointed to the contracts allowing retroactive rate hikes. The senators asked whether hiking an individual's interest rate actually increased their credit risk and made it more likely they would default; the executives denied it. The senators asked why hiking interest rates on cardholders who were already reliably reducing their credit card debts made economic sense; the executives insisted that persons with higher credit risk should pay more, even if those persons had a rock-solid record of on-time payments. Their united front made it clear that, unlike the first hearing which prompted industry-initiated reforms, the banks would continuing imposing unilateral, retroactive rate increases on their cardholders unless and until the law stopped them.

Enacting Reforms

The December 2007 hearing generated a flood of additional media stories about unfair credit card practices. They hit the press around the same time the financial crisis in the mortgage market began rattling the economy. As the crisis worsened in 2008, public anger at the financial industry deepened, weakening the industry's political power. In addition, as more people hit hard times, losing their homes or jobs, abusive credit card practices became increasingly intolerable.

Adding to the tension was the presidential election with contested primaries and multiple close Senate races. Stopping abusive credit card practices began to be seen as a potent issue for voters. The two leading Democratic presidential candidates, Senator Barack Obama and Senator Hillary Clinton, began mentioning credit card abuses on the campaign trail.

In February 2008, the House elevated the issue further when a Maloney-Frank credit card reform bill was introduced.[9] In April, Congresswoman Maloney held a hearing on the bill which, by then, had over 100 cosponsors. Senator Levin was the lead-off witness in recognition of, as Ms. Maloney put it, his leadership in "holding hearings that have shone a light on abusive practices and by introducing the first comprehensive credit card reform bill in this Congress, a mark against which subsequent bills must be measured."[10] The next panel heard from three cardholders who, like our December hearing witnesses, had incurred substantial interest rate increases, despite histories of on-time payments. Next came a panel of federal bank regulators discussing possible regulatory actions to clamp down on abuses. The final panel heard from three credit card bank executives and three consumer advocates.

From our point of view, the most encouraging aspect of the House hearing was that its condemnation of unfair credit card practices was bipartisan. The committee's ranking Republican Spencer Bachus was the first to criticize the credit card industry, followed by a few others. Their criticisms of the credit card industry were muted, but audible and unmistakable. Only one Republican, Jeb Hensarling, vocally opposed the credit card reform bill.

The House hearing again cranked up pressure on the Senate to get moving. Senator Dodd's Banking staff had been talking to us off and on for weeks about introducing a new bill, but their boss had yet to commit to pushing that legislative boulder up the mountain again. On April 30, 2008, two weeks after the House hearing, Senator Dodd held a press conference and announced his intent to introduce a new credit card reform bill. Actually introduced in July, the bill was entitled the Credit Card Accountability Responsibility and Disclosure Act or CARD Act.[11] Senator Levin was the lead cosponsor. Two more cosponsors were the key Democratic presidential contenders, Senators Clinton and Obama. Unfortunately, not a single GOP senator signed on. Also noticeably absent were the Banking Committee Senators Johnson and Carper.

Despite those troubling signs, PSI staffers gave each other high fives over the Dodd-Levin bill. It was chock full of great credit card reforms, and constituted the strongest, most pro-consumer legislation introduced to date. It incorporated almost all of the Levin bill provisions alongside key provisions from prior Dodd bills.

In September 2008, the House passed the Maloney-Frank credit card bill 312-112, a bipartisan margin large enough to overcome a veto by President George W. Bush.[12] The Senate seemed poised to follow when, suddenly, everything changed. That same month, half a dozen Wall Street firms began faltering, and a maelstrom of frightening financial news swept the news. As a full-blown crisis began enveloping the country, credit card reform fell by the wayside.

At the same time, the election season roared ahead. Two months later, in November 2008, the Democrats won big. The country elected Barack Obama the 44th President and gave Democrats a 58-41 majority in the Senate, the party's largest majority in years. After a contested Senate election in Minnesota was resolved in favor of the Democrat and Pennsylvania's Senator Arlen Spector switched parties, the Democratic Senate majority climbed to 60-40. The astounding result was that, for two full years, 2009 and 2010, Democrats controlled the Senate, House, and Presidency, a confluence of political power that hadn't occurred in decades.

The 111th Congress followed, the most productive of my 30 years in the Senate. In February 2009, Senator Dodd re-introduced the Dodd-Levin credit card reform bill and, six weeks later, on March 31, 2009, scheduled a committee vote.[13] Grimly silent, committee Republicans didn't offer any amendments. Instead, at the markup's conclusion, while all Democrats except one voted in favor of the bill, all Republicans plus Senator Carper voted against it. The bill squeaked through committee by a razor thin margin of 12-11.

In a post-markup press release urging Senate action on the committee-approved bill, Senator Levin noted that, due to the financial crisis and subsequent recession, "[m]illions of Americans are facing the worst economic crisis of their lifetime, and their hardship is being compounded by unfair credit card fees and interest charges." Increasingly, credit card reform was seen as an important way to help American families survive the deepening recession.

One month after the Senate committee markup, on April 30, 2009, the full House again passed the Maloney-Frank credit card reform bill, approving an even stronger version than the prior year with an even stronger bipartisan vote of 357 to 70.[14] When the Senate's Democratic leaders signaled their intention to take up the House bill, Senator Shelby, the Banking Committee's ranking Republican, apparently decided it was better to win a few concessions than allow the House bill to move unchallenged through the Senate, and offered to negotiate. Senator Dodd wisely decided he would rather pass the bill on a bipartisan basis than shove through a version with only Democratic votes.

On May 11, 2009, Senators Dodd and Shelby disclosed their compromise. To our relief, while it watered down or eliminated some reforms, it also retained many key provisions. The biggest win for Senator Shelby involved preserving the credit card issuers' ability to impose penalty interest rates on some cardholders. The key provision distinguished between cardholders who'd violated their credit card agreements versus those who'd met their legal obligations. Specifically, if a cardholder paid a bill more than 60 days late, the bill allowed the credit card issuer to impose a unilateral, retroactive penalty interest rate on the cardholder's existing and future debt. The compromise also offered an escape hatch—if the late-paying cardholder made on-time payments at the higher interest rate for six months, the cardholder could regain the prior lower rate. In addition, the bill prohibited issuers from imposing unilateral, retroactive penalty interest rates on any cardholder who paid their bills on time. Period.

While the Dodd-Shelby compromise failed to ban all retroactive interest rate hikes as Senator Levin had urged, it was significantly better than the status quo and apparently paved the way for other credit card reforms to survive. With a sigh for what might have been, Senator Levin threw his support behind the compromise, as did many others. Over the next week, Senators Dodd and Shelby, as bill managers, worked through a crush of floor amendments from both sides of the aisle. On May 19, 2009, the Senate passed a revised credit card reform bill by an overwhelming, bipartisan vote of 90-5.[15]

By coincidence, the vote on final passage of the credit card bill was also the 11,000th vote cast by Senator Levin, a milestone recognized with kind words by both Senate Majority Leader Harry Reid and Minority Leader Mitch McConnell.[16] It was a sweet moment. The next day, the House approved the Senate bill 279-147, and it was on its way to the president.[17]

Levinland was thrilled by the victory. Amid a round of Manhattans, we recalled the 2006 GAO report, our 2007 hearings, and the Levin-McCaskill bill that got the legislative ball rolling. We cheered Representatives Carolyn Maloney and Barney Frank, toasted Senators Dodd and Shelby, and drank to the health of Wesley Wannemacher and Janet Hard. Most of all, we celebrated how Senator Levin's oversight work had generated momentum for a new law that promised to make life easier for hundreds of millions of Americans.

The next day, to our delight, the White House announced it would host a bill signing ceremony.[18] Senator Levin was not only invited but received permission to bring two staffers; he asked yours truly and Zack Schram to accompany him. That same day, we got a call from the White House asking if we could suggest some average Americans to attend the ceremony. Zack gave them the names and stories of the individuals who'd testified at our hearings.

Friday, May 22, 2009, dawned bright and hot. Zack and I drove to the White House with Senator Levin who had somehow snagged a White House parking spot. It was only the second time I'd attended a White House signing ceremony; I was giddy with excitement as we walked across the White House grounds and through the West Wing to the rose garden at the back. Zack and I joined about 100 others on rickety folding chairs, squinting in the sunlight and beaming huge smiles at each other. President Obama spoke briefly, lauding the bipartisan bill.

Members of Congress thronged around the president as he sat at a table signing the bill. Senator Levin and Congresswoman Maloney—in a gorgeous pink suit—were given prime spots in front. After the signing ceremony concluded, Zack and I saw Janet Hard and her husband in the swirling crowd and congratulated them on their part in the years-long credit card reform saga. They seemed as thrilled to be at the White House as we were.

The CARD Act signed into law that sunny day really did crack down on a host of credit card abuses. For the first time, the law prohibited credit card issuers from charging interest on debt that was already paid, a Levin priority. For cardholders who paid their bills on time, the law prohibited unilateral, retroactive interest rate hikes. It also provided that, if a card expired and the issuer wanted to impose a higher rate on a new card, the issuer had to give the cardholder 45 days advance notice, the new rate could apply only to future debt, and the cardholder had the right to cancel the card and pay off existing debt at the old rate.

A second set of measures tackled fee issues. One provision required penalty fee amounts to be "reasonable and proportional" to the violation being penalized. Another prohibited over-the-limit fees unless the cardholder explicitly opted for a card allowing charges in excess of the card's limit, and allowed no more than three fees per violation. While falling short of the total prohibition on pay-to-pay fees in the Levin bill, the bill stopped issuers from imposing fees for making online payments, automated telephone payments, and payments made at a bank branch.

Another set of provisions put an end to a variety of gimmicks that'd caused cardholders to pay late. The law required credit card issuers to send out bills a minimum of 21 days before payment was due, set a cardholder's due date on the same day each month, and allow payments until 5:00 p.m. on that due date. If the due date fell on a weekend or holiday, the law required credit card issuers to allow bill payments until 5:00 p.m. the next business day. The list of reforms, which didn't stop there, was a long one.

In the end, the CARD Act created an interwoven set of consumer protections that, for the first time, shielded hundreds of millions of Americans from a wide range of unfair credit card practices. It was landmark legislation we were proud to have helped enact into law.

Measuring Progress

A few years later, several agencies and groups undertook studies to gauge the real-world impact of the CARD Act.[19] Banks had warned it would produce a parade of horribles, including less available credit, increased borrowing costs, and unhealthy credit card markets. Critics and supporters alike wanted to see how the hype compared to reality.

The most authoritative reviews, in 2013 and 2015, found the law had produced a wealth of positives for consumers, including evidence the new law had reduced late fees, over-the-limit fees, and penalty interest rate hikes, and "significantly enhanced transparency" for cardholders.[20] The 2015 report estimated that, if credit card fees had continued at pre-CARD Act levels from 2011 through 2014, cardholders would have paid added fees totaling $16 billion. The 2015 report also found credit cards had become increasingly affordable, and the credit card market was "growing by every measure." In addition, the report found that credit cards had remained profitable: "Indeed, the credit card business continues to be the most profitable bank lending business, with returns more than four times higher than the average return on assets."

In 2016, I ran into a Bank of America representative at a Washington reception, and we reminisced about the PSI credit card investigation we'd both worked on. I observed that the investigation, while painful at the time, had resulted in legislation that actually ended most of the credit card abuses. He smiled and noted that, even without those abusive practices, his bank's credit card operations were still making money. We were both silent a moment thinking about how Congress had actually improved life for average Americans without hurting the financial sector. Now that's valuable oversight.

Notes

1. "Credit Cards: Increased Complexity in Rates and Fees Heightens Need for More Effective Disclosures to Consumers," GAO, Report No. GAO-06-929 (9/2006), http://www.gao.gov/new.items/d06929.pdf.
2. "Levin Releases GAO Report That Discloses Excessive Credit Card Fees, Unfair Interest Rates, and Disclosure Problems," PSI Press Release (10/11/2006).
3. The information in this section is based on "Credit Card Practices: Fees, Interest Charges, and Grace Periods," S. Hrg. 110-76 (3/7/2007), https://www.gpo.gov/fdsys/pkg/CHRG-110shrg34409/pdf/CHRG-110shrg34409.pdf.
4. Mr. Wannemacher was far from the only cardholder subjected to exorbitant interest rates and excessive fees. Another case we investigated involved a

Maryland resident who, 15 years earlier, exceeded the $2000 limit on her Chase credit card, got hit with a penalty interest rate and fees, and had been making regular payments ever since to pay off the debt. She estimated that she'd paid about $12,000 on a debt not much above $2000, yet still owed about $6600. After PSI's March hearing, she contacted Chase about her case, and the bank forgave her debt.

5. S. 1395, the Stop Unfair Credit Card Practices Act (5/15/2007), https://www.congress.gov/bill/110th-congress/senate-bill/1395.

6. See "Credit Card Practices: Current Consumer and Regulatory Issues," House Financial Services Subcommittee on Financial Institutions and Consumer Credit, Serial No. 110-26 (4/26/2007), https://www.gpo.gov/fdsys/pkg/CHRG-110hhrg36821/pdf/CHRG-110hhrg36821.pdf; "Improving Credit Card Consumer Protection: Recent Industry and Regulatory Initiatives," House Financial Services Subcommittee on Financial Institutions and Consumer Credit, Serial No. 110-36 (6/7/2007), https://www.gpo.gov/fdsys/pkg/CHRG-110hhrg37552/pdf/CHRG-110hhrg37552.pdf. Ms. Maloney held a third hearing in August. "Credit Cards and Older Americans," House Financial Services Subcommittee on Financial Institutions and Consumer Credit, Serial No. 110-56 (8/7/2007), https://www.gpo.gov/fdsys/pkg/CHRG-110hhrg38396/pdf/CHRG-110hhrg38396.pdf.

7. See, for example, "Frank Sets October Goal for Moving Credit Card Legislation," *Congress Daily*, Bill Swindell (7/30/2007).

8. The information in this section is based on "Credit Card Practices: Unfair Interest Rate Increases," S. Hrg. 110-289 (12/4/2007), https://www.gpo.gov/fdsys/pkg/CHRG-110shrg40504/pdf/CHRG-110shrg40504.pdf.

9. H.R. 5244, the Credit Cardholders' Bill of Rights of 2008 (2/7/2008).

10. "H.R. 5244: the Credit Cardholders' Bill of Rights: New Protections for Consumers," House Financial Services Subcommittee on Financial Institutions and Consumer Credit, Serial No. 110-109 (4/17/2008), at 12, https://www.gpo.gov/fdsys/pkg/CHRG-110hhrg42721/pdf/CHRG-110hhrg42721.pdf.

11. S. 3252, Credit Card Accountability Responsibility and Disclosure Act (7/10/2008).

12. House Roll Call Vote No. 623, House approval of H.R. 5244 (9/23/2008).

13. S. 414, Credit Card Accountability Responsibility and Disclosure Act (2/11/2009).

14. House Roll Call Vote No. 228, House approval of H.R. 627 (4/30/2009).

15. Senate Roll Call Vote No. 194, Senate approval of H.R. 627 (5/19/2009).

16. See CR S5572 (5/19/2009).

17. The House approved the bill 361-64 on May 20, 2009. House Roll Call Votes Nos. 276 and 277.

18. H.R. 627, signed into law on May 22, 2009, became Public Law 111-24.

19. See, for example, "A New Equilibrium: After Passage of Landmark Credit Card Reform, Interest Rates and Fees Have Stabilized," PEW Charitable

Trusts (5/10/2011), http://bit.ly/2AaMcgR; "The CARD Act: Has It Made a Difference?" Federal Reserve Bank of St. Louis (Spring 2014), https://www.stlouisfed.org/publications/inside-the-vault/spring-2014/the-card-act; "Regulating Consumer Financial Products: Evidence from Credit Cards," Social Science Research Network, Sumit Agarwal, Souphala Chomsisengphet, Neale Mahoney, and Johannes Stroebel (8/2014), http://papers.ssrn.com/sol3/papers.cfm?abstract_id=2330942.

20. See "Card Act Report: A Review of the Impact of the CARD Act on the Consumer Credit Card Market," CFPB (10/1/2013), http://files.consumerfinance.gov/f/201309_cfpb_card-act-report.pdf; "The Consumer Credit Card Market," CFPB (12/2015), http://files.consumerfinance.gov/f/201512_cfpb_report-the-consumer-credit-card-market.pdf.

9

Deconstructing the Financial Crisis

"I seen my opportunities and I took 'em."
Plunkitt of Tammany Hall, William L. Riordon, at 3 (E.P. Dutton & Co., Inc.,
1963)

In the fall of 2008, the United States suffered a devastating economic collapse, the worst since the stock market crash of 1929. Securities backed by home mortgages lost much of their value, stock markets plummeted, and storied financial firms went under. Millions of Americans lost their jobs, their homes, or both. Estimates placed the financial cost at $15–$20 trillion in lost gross domestic product, including costs associated with bankrupt businesses, foreclosures, homelessness, underwater mortgages, unemployment, and lost savings.[1]

When the financial crisis first grabbed public attention in September 2008, as half a dozen mammoth Wall Street firms suddenly teetered on the edge of economic collapse, Senator Levin was serving as PSI chair. Senator Coleman was then PSI's ranking Republican, but was replaced in January by Senator Coburn. Although Senators Levin and Coburn held very different political views, both put fact-finding before politics and made bipartisanship a priority. As Wall Street's outlook worsened, financial panic deepened, and Congress was forced to take drastic action to save the economy, PSI cleared its decks and launched an all-out, in-depth investigation to find out what had happened.

Investigating the financial crisis turned out to be the longest, toughest inquiry of the Levin era on PSI. The facts were tangled, the players powerful, and the stakes huge. The investigation required over two years of brutal work, racking up over 50 million pages of documents, 150 interviews, four hearings,

© The Author(s) 2018
E. J. Bean, *Financial Exposure*, https://doi.org/10.1007/978-3-319-94388-6_9

and a 750-page report.[2] The resulting Levin-Coburn report provided the only bipartisan analysis of the financial crisis, complete with joint findings of fact and policy recommendations. PSI's hearings not only garnered worldwide attention, they helped break the filibuster blocking Senate consideration of what would become the Dodd-Frank Act, the most extensive set of U.S. financial reforms in a generation.

Climbing the Mountain

In November 2008, our investigative assignment was simple yet infinitely complex: identify the key causes of the financial crisis. The goal was to figure out what had happened in order to prevent it from happening again.

Knowing how hard it was going to be, we staffed up. Because the 2008 election had returned Democrats to a majority in the Senate, we got our first budget increase in years and were able to hire new staff. David Katz, a securities and tax expert who'd worked for several federal agencies, and Allison Murphy, a big firm lawyer with investigatory experience, brought the Levin PSI permanent staff up to ten. Senator Coburn's troops included his staff director Chris Barkley, second in command Keith Ashdown, and lead financial investigator Tony Cotto. All three Coburn staffers would turn out to be terrific partners in the investigation.

We beefed up PSI ranks still further with a raft of detailees, law clerks, and college interns. Hiring them carried the usual risk of relying on persons we didn't know well, a risk we elevated by hiring more free help than we had employees on payroll. Supervising novice investigators was always hard, but doing it when outnumbered was, at times, nerve-racking. But given the mountain of work facing us, we felt we needed to leverage all the resources we could.

To our relief, we were able to enlist detailees with financial expertise from the Securities and Exchange Commission, Department of Justice, Government Accountability Office, and Homeland Security Department. We also brought back a securities expert from our Enron days, Gary Brown, a Republican who agreed to work under a contract barely covering his travel costs. In addition, an ever-evolving roster of law clerks and college interns produced colossal amounts of amazingly good work. The quality of the people willing to devote their time and talents to PSI despite public negativity about government service was a continual comfort.

Once we assembled our investigative crew, our next step was to educate ourselves about the financial instruments at the heart of the crisis. None of us knew much about them, so it was a steep learning curve. Past experience had taught us that experts around the globe, when asked, would make time for Senate investigators. So we identified experts on mortgage-backed securities, credit derivatives, and related fields, and asked them to educate us. Our teachers included longtime SEC staffers, college professors, and industry stalwarts. On one occasion, a leading credit derivatives expert—who lived in Australia—conducted a four-hour seminar for us by telephone that, due to time differences, started at 8:00 p.m. our time and ended at midnight. The grueling sessions were always attended by staffers from both sides of the aisle.

At first it was a hard slog. Even learning the acronyms—MBS, CDOs, CDS—took time. And it wasn't a matter of learning just enough to get a good grade on a test; we had to really understand what was going on at a deep level. At the same time, the whole crew got a buzz from digging deep—we wouldn't have been much good as investigators otherwise.

Every week or so, Senator Levin called in his staff for an update on what we'd learned. Typically, we prepared charts summarizing key information and went over them in sessions that lasted 15–60 minutes, sandwiched between his other appointments. If we couldn't answer his questions, we contacted the experts and reported back. Senator Levin also began reading books and articles on the financial crisis, marking up the text, and, on occasion, scheduling meetings to discuss the marked-up sections.

It took us months of intense effort to get a solid grasp of the U.S. mortgage market and its key financial instruments. But by the time we'd climbed that mountain, we had a pretty good idea of where we needed to go.

Narrowing the Focus

Based upon what we'd learned, after lengthy staff discussions, we recommended that PSI focus its investigation on four key questions, framing them as factual inquiries:

1. Why did the banks turn from low-risk to high-risk mortgages, and how did large numbers of high-risk mortgages enter the U.S. mortgage market?
2. Why did federal regulators fail to stop the flood of high-risk mortgages?
3. Why did credit rating agencies give AAA ultra-safe ratings to mortgage-related securities that included high-risk mortgages?
4. What role was played by the investment banks, and how did they contribute to the crisis?

In keeping with PSI's classic approach to understanding complex issues, we also identified the key case studies we wanted to use to explore each question. To examine the role of banks in high-risk lending, we recommended Washington Mutual. The sixth-largest U.S. bank with over $300 billion in assets, it had been a massive mortgage issuer before becoming the largest bank failure in U.S. history. To examine the role of federal regulators, we recommended the Office of Thrift Supervision. OTS was the primary regulator of thrifts like Washington Mutual, Countrywide, and IndyMac, all of which played outsized roles in the financial crisis.

To examine the role of the credit rating agencies, we proposed focusing on the two largest, Moody's and Standard and Poor's (S&P). Both had issued credit ratings for the bulk of the mortgage-related securities at the heart of the crisis, later downgraded many of those ratings, and along the way reported large profits from their activities. Finally, to examine the role of investment banks, we recommended looking at Goldman Sachs and possibly a second firm. Goldman was rumored to have made billions of dollars building up and then betting against the mortgage market; other investment banks were rumored to have lost billions. We figured both offered important lessons.

We presented our proposals to Senator Levin. After a lot of analysis, he gave us the go-ahead. We then presented the proposal to our Republican colleagues. They checked with Senator Coburn who signaled his support.

The next step was to form four teams to tackle the four issue areas. Since Senator Levin was the chair and had the larger staff, Levin staffers took the lead on each one. Zack Schram headed up high-risk lending; Allison Murphy took on the regulators; David Katz accepted the credit ratings challenge; and Bob Roach took charge of the investment banks. As staff director, I oversaw all four. The Coburn staff used their smaller roster to staff the teams as best they could.

Battling for Documents

The next big task was getting documents. The four PSI teams met to strategize about what to request. First, each team analyzed possible documents at the companies and agencies serving as our case studies. Then they brainstormed about third parties who might have useful materials, including federal and state agencies, litigants suing each other in court, and parties involved with particular financial deals. Accountants were another possibility since, unlike lawyers, they had no attorney-client type privilege barring access to documents, and past investigations had taught us that accountants often kept detailed financial and analytical records.

Next, the PSI teams contacted the companies or agencies serving as their case studies and requested an introductory meeting. Needless to say, no one was happy to hear from us. Everyone lawyered up, and we held a series of meetings in our conference room with legal counsel and representatives from each party.

In line with PSI practice, prior to each meeting, the relevant team leader wrote out a list of the topics to be addressed, usually in bullet points, and circulated it to the team members for review. Since we'd already done a lot of research in selecting the case studies, the list typically identified the key facts and issues we wanted the meeting to address. To facilitate our document requests, the list also sought to elicit such basic information as how the company or agency was organized, key offices and individuals involved in the facts, the types of documents they had, and the terms used to identify those documents.

Everyone who reviewed the list could offer edits to ensure all topics of interest were covered in a good order. PSI practice was to begin a meeting with easier issues and work up to more sensitive ones. Broaching sensitive topics early on could trigger wariness or offense, jeopardizing cooperation. The PSI team leader circulated the final version prior to the meeting so everyone knew what issues would be raised when. Most team members printed a copy of the bullet points, with spaces in between each topic, to take meeting notes directly on the document.

To ensure a useful and efficient meeting, the PSI team leader typically provided a list of topics of interest to opposing counsel and asked for the counsel to be prepared to address them. If the counsel and accompanying individuals showed up at the meeting with insufficient information, the team leader typically scheduled a second meeting.

The PSI teams used the information gleaned from the meetings to draft their document requests. Each request took the form of an attachment that could be appended to either a letter or subpoena. The drafts were circulated on a bipartisan basis for edits. We also compared the requests to identify the best ideas and to standardize their language as much as possible.

Our goal was to fashion requests that produced a manageable number of highly useful documents and a minimal amount of irrelevant material. We also sought to put the easiest requests first and the most complex or controversial requests later to facilitate document negotiations and rolling document productions. Chris Barkley and I signed off on each of the final versions. Most were attached to subpoenas, a few to letters. We then met with Senator Levin to update him on the requests and obtain his signature on the subpoenas.

Once the document requests were approved, the PSI team leaders telephoned legal counsel for the relevant parties to let them know a request was on the way. Most of the lawyers had already obtained client consent for the lawyer to accept a subpoena. We highlighted the due dates and offered to meet to discuss any issues.

Once those document requests went out the door, the PSI teams initiated the same process with respect to third parties thought to have useful materials. Soon, we had over a dozen outstanding requests.

Playing Hardball on Documents

Getting our hands on the documents ran into the usual problems. The subpoena recipients worried that their documents would be used against them and worked hard to limit what they gave us. At the same time, prominent financial institutions didn't want to be seen as obstructing a Senate investigation or risk an actual obstruction charge. Federal agencies like OTS had even less standing or legal basis to refuse an official Senate document request. The four PSI teams engaged in multiple discussions with each party's legal team over the categories and timing of the documents to be produced.

While a variety of document battles involving multiple parties arose during the investigation, Goldman Sachs was the standout. When everyone else had finally begun producing a substantial number of documents, Goldman was still producing a trickle.

Faced with Goldman's intransigence over producing the requested information, Senator Levin called us in and gave us marching orders to take the deposition of Goldman's chief executive officer Lloyd Blankfein. Surprised, we observed that we usually organized our interviews around documents, but had virtually no Blankfein materials and weren't sure what to focus on. Senator Levin gave us a level stare over the half-rim glasses perched on the end of his nose: "Ask him everything you want to know."

With Senator Coburn's support, we contacted Goldman's outside legal counsel to schedule the deposition. We indicated that we were willing to pick a mutually agreeable date in the next week or so, but otherwise would select the date ourselves and send a subpoena requiring Mr. Blankfein's appearance. During the ensuing back and forth, we actually executed the subpoena but, in the end, Mr. Blankfein agreed to appear "voluntarily." We were later told Mr. Blankfein had never provided a deposition before—the PSI one would be his first.

The deposition took place in our conference room. Bob, head of the investment bank team, took the lead and deposed Mr. Blankfein under oath, before a stenographer, for most of the day. Bob asked about every aspect of Goldman's involvement with the mortgage market and financial crisis. Mr. Blankfein answered the questions with a minimal amount of disruption from his lawyers.

After the deposition, we asked Goldman's legal counsel to remain behind for a moment. We indicated that, to get the information we needed, we planned to take a similar deposition of Goldman President Gary Cohn and then work our way through the entire executive suite. We noted that a good faith production of documents was an alternative way to provide much of the information we needed and could shorten or even alleviate the need for some of those interviews.

A few days later, Goldman documents began pouring in. Goldman had clearly decided to switch from the minimum to the maximum. When added to the documents already produced by other parties, the total number of documents in PSI's possession exploded into tens of millions of pages. We began referring to the vast document pool as "the ocean" and told PSI staff to jump in and start swimming as fast as possible.

Swimming in Documents

For the next three months, the entire investigative team did little aside from document review. We'd collected materials from a wide variety of sources, not only from the parties serving as our case studies, but also from agencies with relevant filings, lawsuits seeking damages, former company employees, investors burned by mortgage-related investments, and accountants who handled various deals. The documents included emails, memoranda, board minutes, correspondence, bank examinations, audits, SEC filings, mortgage transactions, due diligence reviews, reports, legal pleadings, and more. All had been entered into a single vast database available for review by all PSI staff.

The four PSI teams met weekly, updating each other on documents of interest, analyzing the complex transactions they'd uncovered, and developing theories as to what had happened, when, and why. Each team produced thick notebooks of key documents, referred to as "hot docs." Each developed chronologies of events and lists of key players.

Fact patterns and themes began to emerge. At Washington Mutual, we located board meeting materials in which senior management explicitly asked the directors to approve a switch from low-risk to high-risk mortgages. The materials gave a single rationale to justify the switch—higher-risk mortgages were more profitable. Higher-risk borrowers could be charged more, and higher-risk loans fetched higher prices on Wall Street, because they were bundled into financial instruments that paid higher returns for the higher risk. Neither the board materials nor any other documents we reviewed cited government requirements on affordable housing or community reinvestment for making the switch—profit alone was cited as the motivating factor. Other documents tracked the bank's actual acquisition of high-risk home loans, explained the mortgage features, identified multiple problem areas, and showed how the bank marketed loans to Wall Street, created its own securities, and permitted high-risk mortgages to be slipped into mortgage pools even when they knew the borrowers were more likely to default.

At OTS, emails and memoranda showed that many examiners were fully aware of the growing number of high-risk mortgages being issued by U.S. financial institutions, had warned their superiors, and had supported tougher restrictions on high-risk practices to no avail. Other materials showed OTS supervisors downplaying the risk, highlighting bank profits and the speed with which banks sold the high-risk loans to Wall Street. Still other materials documented a petty turf battle between OTS and the FDIC over analyzing Washington Mutual's risks, with OTS employees impeding FDIC oversight by denying bank documents and even office space to FDIC examiners. Those documents disclosed an increasingly bitter dispute between OTS and FDIC executives over the need to crack down on the thrift's mounting risk.

At Moody's and S&P, emails, memoranda, and other documents showed credit rating analysts were well aware of the growing tide of high-risk mortgages. Records also depicted a struggle between analysts and supervisors over assigning accurate credit ratings versus the inflated ratings sought by investment banks pushing the deals. Some emails showed supervisors pressuring analysts to take whatever measures were needed to maintain the firm's "market share," including assigning higher credit ratings than might otherwise be warranted.

Still other internal documents chronicled the concerns of analysts tasked with monitoring existing mortgage securities and deciding whether to downgrade their ratings as more mortgages defaulted and the securities lost value. Records also illustrated what happened when both credit rating firms decided, within two days of each other in July 2007, to suddenly downgrade the ratings of hundreds of existing subprime mortgage-backed securities, slashing their resale value and shocking the mortgage market worldwide with the lowered ratings. At the same time, we noted the absence of documents indicating how the two firms decided to execute hundreds of downgrades within two days of each other; neither firm produced a single document explaining that coincidental timing.

At Goldman, documents tracked how the firm purchased billions of dollars of high-risk, poor-quality loans, bundled them into mortgage-backed securities, procured AAA credit ratings for the securities, and sold the securities to investors around the world. Some emails included the abbreviation "ldl"—let's discuss live—to signal when sensitive topics should be discussed orally rather than in email. Other documents showed how, starting in late 2006, Goldman traders noticed high-risk mortgages were beginning to lose value, reported it to their superiors, and then went into high gear betting against—or "shorting"—mortgage-related securities so the firm would make money on the market downturn.

The documents disclosed multiple ways in which Goldman shorted the mortgage market. Some involved so-called synthetic collateral debt obligations (CDOs) that enabled investors to bet on whether a specified group of mortgage-backed securities would gain or lose value. One set of documents for a CDO known as Abacus showed how Goldman had allowed a favored client to influence the CDO's selection of assets, while simultaneously placing a bet they'd lose value. Goldman then advised other clients to bet the Abacus assets would gain value, without disclosing the role of the favored client in selecting the assets. When the asset values later tanked, the favored client walked away with $1 billion that had been invested by the other clients. Still other documents showed how Goldman itself began using its CDOs to secretly bet against clients taking the other side, making money hand over fist when the asset values plummeted.

The document review took months, but produced invaluable, first-hand evidence of the events that led to the financial crisis. We were ready for the next phase.

Conducting Interviews

In the latter half of 2009, we began conducting dozens of interviews. Interviews are critical to picking up nuance, context, and relationships, as well as people, events, and documents that might not otherwise come to light. In addition, PSI practice was to use interviews to gain a better understanding of key documents, since at least some would turn out not to mean what they seemed to.

The four PSI teams each drew up a list of the individuals they wanted to interview in the order they wanted to speak with them. Since we had limited staff, the teams confined themselves to only the most important players. When we presented the interview lists to the parties, battles erupted over scheduling as every firm and agency attempted to push back their interviews. We fought hard for quicker scheduling and a reasonable timeline to complete the work.

Our interview schedule in late 2009 and early 2010 coincided with an unusually snowy Washington winter. We often questioned witnesses watching hours of snow drift past the conference room window, wondering how we'd make it home. We told folks traveling from New York to take the train to Union Station and book a nearby hotel, so they could walk to our offices if necessary. Zack used his Detroit driving skills to rescue staff stranded by snow. We also brought in blankets in case staff got caught by a snowstorm and had to overnight at work.

We ended up conducting over 150 interviews. We followed PSI's standard practice of interviewing lower-level employees first and working our way up the chain-of-command. Most interviews took all day, generally starting at 10:00 a.m. and finishing at 5:00 p.m. or later. The interview lead wrote out the questions beforehand, circulated them, and identified the relevant documents. Interns and law clerks made copies of the key documents and prepared five to seven document notebooks for each interview, a tedious but critical task necessitating hours of work.

We opened most interviews by asking for the interviewee's background and then patiently worked our way through multiple events, transactions, and documents, usually chronologically. We generally took a very polite tone, which we found encouraged cooperation.

We typically asked multiple interviewees the same questions to confirm the facts and get added detail. When given information that conflicted with what others had told us, we slowed down and gave the person being interviewed an opportunity to clarify the facts or identify supporting documents. Sometimes, we began a topic by asking the person to describe in their own words what had happened—occasionally eliciting new information—and then checked the description against the documents. If the documents didn't match, we provided copies, and the interviewee usually corrected their version of events or was left stammering that the documents had gotten it wrong. Occasionally, we had to caution that, under 18 U.S.C. §1001, it was a crime to make a false statement to Congress.

When we got important new information, we slowed down again and asked multiple questions to be sure we understood what was being said. We didn't believe in asking one question, getting a perfect answer, and then moving on. We weren't playing lawyers in a TV drama. Instead, we asked similar questions several ways, not only to make sure we understood but to give the interviewee an opportunity to correct or clarify the facts. The questions also served to lock them into what they were saying in the presence of their lawyers. That made it less likely they would backtrack if asked about the same matter at a public hearing. Slowly, we built up the factual record.

Throughout the process, we never played hide the ball. We laid out the facts and issues that concerned us, and asked the interviewees to educate us on what had really happened and how we should think about it. We asked them to explain complicated transactions from their point of view and were often rewarded by explanations that shed light on key events. We didn't use rhetorical games or surprise questions, because we found they didn't help much when the objective was to find out the facts. In addition, since the facts didn't change, we saw no risk in laying out what we thought had happened and requesting any evidence we'd gotten something wrong. We also continued to follow the practice of asking easy questions first and hard questions later. Many interviewees, after being asked a question that implicated them in wrongdoing, simply shut down.

The interviews were both illuminating and surprising. With Washington Mutual, we realized that the thrift had relied on conventional low-risk loans, until newly hired East Coast executives talked up the high-risk road. With OTS, we saw close up the frustration of some examiners who saw what was happening but couldn't stop it, versus the pandering by some OTS executives who referred to thrifts as their "constituents" and discouraged tough enforcement actions out of concern a thrift might switch to another regulator. With the credit rating agencies, we interviewed financial analysts mortified at how their employers had chased business from investment banks and supported inflated ratings for financial instruments with hidden risks.

With Goldman, we interviewed traders and executives who uniformly insisted, despite a mountain of evidence, that the firm had never bet against the mortgage market or against their own clients. We also heard Goldman bankers refer to investors in its mortgage-related securities as "counterparties," rather than "clients," a revealing switch in terminology. We eventually realized that the traders saw their jobs, not as designing financial products that would succeed, but as engineering and pricing financial instruments with multiple layers of risk that could pay off by either succeeding or failing. We also learned of the existence of brag sheets—"self-reviews" filled out by Goldman traders competing for bonuses—in which the traders boasted of designing complex shorts or making millions or even billions of dollars for the firm off the backs of clients who took their investment advice and then lost big. The brag sheets provided powerful evidence of how the Goldman traders viewed what had been going on within the firm.

Unraveling the complex deals and relationships behind the financial crisis took patience, persistence, and careful attention to detail. In addition, it required being willing to recognize and accept what had really happened as opposed to what you thought had happened. That was sometimes the hardest part.

One example involved Fannie Mae and Freddie Mac. One of the big questions we wanted to answer was why banks had moved from low-risk to high-risk mortgages. One theory was that Fannie and Freddie, the biggest players in the secondary mortgage market, had caused the shift by purchasing higher-risk mortgages and bundling them into the mortgage-backed securities sold to investors. To test that theory, the Coburn staff asked to include in the Washington Mutual subpoena an extensive request for documents related to Fannie and Freddie. We agreed, knowing it was a hot issue for many parties, and waited to see what would emerge.

To the surprise of both sides, the Washington Mutual documents told a fascinating story the exact opposite of what the theory had predicted. It turned out that Washington Mutual was one of the biggest suppliers of mortgages to Fannie. Internal documents showed that the bank itself—without any prompting from Fannie or Freddie—had decided to move from low-risk to high-risk mortgages, because they were more profitable. As it began to pump out more high-risk mortgages, Washington Mutual pressed Fannie to buy more of them on more favorable terms. When Fannie declined, the bank threatened to switch the lion's share of its mortgages to Freddie. When Fannie stood fast, Washington Mutual did just that, after securing Freddie's agreement to buy more of its high-risk mortgages on better terms than Fannie offered. In short, the documents showed it was Washington Mutual who had pressured Fannie and Freddie to buy high-risk mortgages rather than the other way around.

The interviews continued through the first quarter of 2010.

Going Public

In early 2010, more than a year after the investigation began, Senator Levin decided it was time to go public. He informed me that he wanted all four hearings held during the month of April. I protested that we'd never held so many hearings so close in time on such complex subjects and warned Senator Levin that the staff was already exhausted. He replied that the inquiry had gone on long enough, and it was time to let folks know what we'd found.

When I got back to my office, I asked Bob to join me on a walk around the hallways and told him about the hearing schedule. He could see my trepidation as we discussed how to handle four in-depth hearings in a month. When we got back, he dropped me off in my office, returned with a Manhattan and some new hot docs, and told me to trust the staff, that we'd get it done.

The hearing prep involved multiple steps, carefully choreographed. First, we proposed an overall design for the four hearings, suggested the major points to be made, and got signoff from Senator Levin. The design called for featuring the key participants in each case study as witnesses, using them to lay out the facts of what happened. We decided against using academics, public interest groups, or trade associations in order to concentrate on holding accountable the individuals most responsible for the troubling conduct we'd identified. We also agreed that, for once, we wouldn't issue a report before the hearings, but would use the hearings to acquire added information and issue a final report later.

From there, we planned the specifics of each hearing. That included identifying the witnesses, witness panels, documents to be made public, and key issues. After consulting with our Republican staff colleagues, we submitted the proposals to Senator Levin. Once he gave us a thumbs-up, we notified the witnesses well in advance of the hearing dates—often a month or more before—to minimize calendar conflicts. We also drafted witness letters alerting each person to the issues they'd be asked about and the opportunity to submit a written statement. We let those who balked know we'd issue subpoenas to ensure hearing attendance, if necessary.

Because hearings can illuminate only a limited set of facts and issues, each team began working to identify the most important points to make. We directed each team to draft a short background memorandum from Senators Levin and Coburn to PSI's other members, the media, and the public about the hearing. A memo was a long way from a report, but still offered a good way to lay out key information, present joint findings of fact, and demonstrate the investigation's bipartisan nature. In a single, short document, we could convey the narrative we wanted each hearing to communicate. In addition, we asked each team to compile a list of the most significant quotes from key documents, both to highlight the evidence and help others locate the most important materials. We also asked each team to develop hearing charts. Senators Levin and Coburn approved each memo, document quote, and chart before it went out.

Next, we directed each team to designate up to 100 documents as hearing exhibits. We knew 100 was a huge number, but given the complexity of the issues and the expected opposition from hearing witnesses, we figured providing first-hand evidence was the best way to help the media and public judge the facts. Compiling so many documents—locating the best copies, putting them in a good order, tagging them with exhibit numbers, creating a descriptive list, redacting unrelated but sensitive information, making 100 packets for the hearing, and creating an electronic version for the PSI website—was an avalanche of work.

Our next task was to draft three of the most important hearing documents from Senator Levin's perspective: the joint press release, his opening statement, and possible witness questions. Each was key in conveying to the public his views about the facts and their significance. A few days prior to each hearing, we presented him with drafts and then met with him in demanding sessions that involved his going over every issue, every witness, and every document. The sessions, which took place before or after business hours or over the weekend, lasted anywhere from two to four hours. Senator Levin painstakingly analyzed and revised the questions, changing the order, content, and wording until he was satisfied.

Senator Levin typically prepared for hearings with more care than any senator I'd ever heard of, but for the financial crisis hearings, he stepped up his game still more. He did his homework until he knew the facts and documents inside and out. Another critical factor turned out to be his staying power: Senator Levin presided over each hearing for as many hours as it took to build the record and get answers.

Holding Washington Mutual Accountable

The first hearing, on April 13, 2010, featured Washington Mutual. My favorite of the four hearings, it went to the roots of the crisis, tracking the shift to higher-risk, poorer-quality mortgages. It explained how the mortgages began using initial low "teaser" rates to enable "subprime" and even "prime" borrowers to take out loans they couldn't afford, and showed how banks like Washington Mutual had disregarded the default risk, since it quickly sold the loans to Wall Street. The hearing also showcased the increasing use of "stated loans" in which borrowers stated their income, and lenders accepted their statements as true without backup verification. Critics called them "liar loans."

The hearing also disclosed how Washington Mutual had been repeatedly criticized by its auditors and regulators for shoddy lending and securitization practices, high loan default rates, and massive loan fraud, but never improved its operations. It showed how the bank had become a conveyor belt of toxic mortgages and mortgage-backed securities fueling Wall Street. Then, when mass credit rating downgrades suddenly shocked the mortgage market, Washington Mutual got stuck with billions of dollars in unmarketable, poor-quality mortgage securities. The bank's stock price plunged, and depositors began withdrawing billions of dollars from their accounts, creating a quiet run on the bank. In September 2008, the regulators finally had to step in, leading to the largest bank failure in U.S. history.

We held a press briefing the day before the hearing, attended by about 20 reporters. We released a six-page memorandum from Senators Levin and Coburn, summarizing what we'd found, with six joint findings of fact. We also released a list of key document quotes and several charts summarizing the bank's mortgage activity, including $77 billion in subprime mortgage loans and $115 billion in high-risk "Option ARM" loans. We announced that we would release nearly 100 hearing exhibits the next day. We didn't hand out any exhibits at the press briefing itself. Delaying their release gave reporters a concrete reason to show up at the hearing room, even if they'd attended the press briefing the day before. It also made it more likely we'd get two days of media stories—one from the press briefing and one from the hearing itself.

The hearing took testimony from three panels of Washington Mutual executives. The first panel consisted of former chief risk and audit officers who described in chilling detail how the bank favored loan volume and speed over loan quality, accepted borrower income statements without verification, turned a blind eye to rampant loan fraud, and never fixed even blatant problems. The next two panels of senior executives, including CEO Kerry Killinger, tried to defend their actions which, in the end, led to the bank's collapse after 100 years in business.

Senators Levin and Coburn, with assists from Senator Susan Collins from Maine and Senator Ted Kaufman from Delaware, grilled the witnesses for seven hours, confronting them with document after incriminating document. A chart entitled "Washington Mutual Mortgage Practices that Created a Mortgage Time Bomb" listed the bank's shoddy practices. Audit reports laid bare loan fraud rates of 58%, 62%, and 83% at some offices. Executive emails blasted the bank's "horrible" loan performance. Post-hearing media coverage detailed the evidence disclosed at the hearing, showing how a single bank injected into U.S. financial markets a flood of toxic mortgages. The press uniformly criticized Washington Mutual's role in the financial crisis.

Confronting the Regulators at OTS

The second hearing, focused on OTS, came three days later on Friday, April 16. Because it, too, featured Washington Mutual, we scheduled it for the same week, while the first hearing was still resonating with the public. Again, we held a press briefing the day before, attended this time by 20–30 reporters. Again, we released a Levin-Coburn memorandum summarizing what we'd found, this one nine pages long with nine joint findings of fact. Again, we released key document quotes and promised to release nearly 100 exhibits the next day. At this and the other press briefings, Senator Levin spoke on the record for the first 15 minutes or so. Staff followed, off the record, going through the facts, details, and handouts in sessions that typically lasted 90 minutes.

The second hearing took testimony from four panels over five and a half hours. The first featured Treasury and FDIC Inspectors General discussing their new joint report on regulatory shortcomings involving Washington Mutual; it confirmed many of our negative findings on OTS. Next up were four OTS regulators who'd overseen the bank, including former OTS director John Reich. Next were three FDIC regulators who'd tried, despite OTS resistance, to analyze and discipline the bank. The final panel featured Acting OTS head John Bowman and FDIC head Sheila Bair.

During the hearing, Senators Levin, Coburn, and Kaufman took OTS to task over its years-long tolerance of Washington Mutual's shoddy mortgage practices, its infighting with the FDIC, and its failure to take enforcement action against the bank despite over 500 deficiencies identified by OTS examiners. The senators also confronted OTS and the FDIC for issuing weak restrictions on high-risk mortgage practices and failing to recognize the systemic risk caused by allowing U.S. banks to sell billions of dollars of high-risk, poor-quality mortgages that polluted financial markets globally.

Exposing the Credit Rating Agencies

The third hearing, on the credit rating agencies, took place a week later on Friday, April 23, 2010. Our press briefing the day before attracted an even larger crowd of over 40 reporters. Again, we released a Levin-Coburn memorandum, this one eleven pages long with nine joint findings of fact. Again, we released the key document quotes and promised to hand out the actual documents the next day at the hearing. Using the same kinds of materials and approach in each press briefing had made it easier, not only for us to prepare but also for the media to review our work, since the reporters knew what to expect.

The hearing took testimony from three panels of witnesses, all former or current employees of Moody's or S&P. The first panel consisted of three financial analysts who criticized their former employers for elevating market share and profits over accurate ratings, giving in to bank pressure to keep tough analysts off deals, failing to apply more accurate credit rating models to existing ratings, and delaying the rating downgrades. The following two panels heard from executives who'd participated in the ratings process and from the Moody's and S&P CEOs Raymond McDaniel and Kathleen Corbet.

The executives defended their firms, while also admitting, when faced with incriminating documents, that the investment banks had engaged in high-pressure tactics and ratings shopping, that inadequate staff resources had been assigned to track the ratings, and that numerous inflated ratings had required later downgrades.

Senators Levin and Kaufman (Senator Coburn had been pulled away) grilled the Moody's and S&P witnesses for six hours, asking why AAA ratings were awarded to securities laced with high-risk, poor-quality loans from mortgage companies notorious for loan defaults. They confronted the executives about issuing mass rating downgrades to hundreds of subprime mortgage-backed securities at the same time, shocking the markets and causing the collapse of the subprime mortgage market. Senator Levin produced a chart showing that 91% of AAA subprime mortgage-backed securities issued in 2007, and 93% of those issued in 2006, had fallen into junk status. He also cited an email in which, when pressed by a ratings analyst about a deal, a banker wrote back: "IBG-YBG," meaning "I'll be gone, you'll be gone" by the time the loans default, so stop worrying.

Press coverage was, again, extensive, detailing the evidence disclosed during the hearing. Some stories favorably compared the hearing to the Senate's depression-era Pecora hearings which had set the stage for major financial reforms.[3]

Playing Hardball in the Press

At the end of the credit rating hearing, Senator Levin summarized the three financial crisis hearings PSI had held to date and announced the fourth and final hearing would take place on Tuesday the following week and feature Goldman Sachs. He also announced that he was "introducing into the record now four exhibits that we will be using during the Tuesday hearing to explore the role of investment banks during the financial crisis." He promised to post them on PSI's website by morning so they'd be available to the public.

Inserting the four Goldman documents into the credit rating hearing record turned out to be an important move. It was done to comply with a Senate rule that forbid the release of confidential subpoenaed documents except in connection with an official Senate action such as a hearing or report. By introducing the documents into the hearing record on Friday, Senator Levin gained the ability to release them publicly in advance of the Tuesday hearing on Goldman. Their public release was designed to counter an anticipated public relations effort by Goldman over the weekend to shape public perception of the upcoming hearing. Senator Levin wasn't about to let Goldman outflank PSI. And it turned out he was 100% right about Goldman's plans.

The credit rating hearing ended around 4:00 p.m. I made it back to my office about an hour later and immediately began work on the Goldman hearing. That's when I got a call from a Washington Post reporter who was following the PSI hearings. The reporter described receiving some documents related to the upcoming Goldman hearing. While unable to show them to me, the reporter offered to describe the documents in hopes of getting a comment from PSI.

The reporter said the documents seemed to indicate that Goldman wasn't sure that the mortgage market was losing value and raised questions about whether Goldman had made a deliberate decision to bet against the market or its clients. I laughed and said they sounded like documents supplied by Goldman. The reporter responded with the expected line about being unable to disclose a source. I said PSI had no comment and recommended waiting for the documents PSI was releasing in the morning. I also asked the reporter to make clear in the article that the documents cited by the Washington Post had not come from PSI. I repeated that the only documents PSI was releasing were the ones we'd put into the record at the credit rating hearing.

The next morning, Saturday, April 24, the Washington Post ran not one, but two stories on Goldman. The first described internal Goldman documents allegedly showing "the firm was unsure whether housing prices would rise or fall and did not take any action at odds with the interests of its clients." The second article described several startling emails sent by a Goldman mortgage trader, Fabrice Tourre, to a girlfriend describing his mortgage dealings in unflattering terms, including his joking reference to selling mortgage securities "to widows and orphans that I ran into at the airport." Neither article described how the paper had obtained the documents.

When I got to the office that morning—the whole crew was already in—I asked if we had copies of all the documents described in the Post articles; apparently we didn't. We wondered why Goldman had not given us copies of some of them and why it had released the Tourre emails to the press, speculating that perhaps the firm had already turned them over to the SEC and was scapegoating its own employee. I also frowned over the Washington Post's failure to state in either piece, as we'd requested, that the documents did not come from PSI. I called the Post reporter and left a message asking for that statement to be added to the stories.

A few minutes later, my telephone rang. This time it was a Wall Street Journal reporter I'd known for many years who was also covering our hearings. The reporter told me Goldman had just dropped off a collection of documents which it claimed PSI had given to the Washington Post the night before. Steam exploded from my ears. My first reaction was that Goldman's claim that we'd given documents to the Washington Post and not to the Wall Street Journal was likely to make the Wall Journal reporter feel snubbed. If taken as true, we would also be blamed for releasing the tawdry Tourre emails. Perhaps PSI might even be accused of violating Senate confidentiality rules by releasing documents outside the context of a hearing or report.

I took a deep breath and explained to the reporter that PSI had not given the documents to the Post, and the only ones we'd released were posted on our website. I also explained that Senator Levin would not have released the Tourre emails without redacting personal information unrelated to the investigation. Luckily, the reporter had dealt with PSI for many years, knew how we operated, and believed me. Goldman's attempt to cause trouble between the press and PSI didn't work, but it made me consider just how far the firm would go to try to undercut our investigation.

In the meantime, the four documents we'd posted on the PSI website were so surprising and powerful in their content that they quickly dominated the Saturday news cycle, overwhelming Goldman's competing narrative. All four were emails showing that Goldman's top brass had known about and discussed with each other Goldman's shorting activity in the mortgage market.

The first email was from Goldman CEO Lloyd Blankfein. In an exchange with other top Goldman executives, he described how the firm had come out ahead in the mortgage crisis by taking short positions. Mr. Blankfein wrote: "Of course we didn't dodge the mortgage mess. We lost money, then made more than we lost because of shorts."

In the second email, Goldman's chief financial officer David Viniar responded to a trading report indicating that—in one day—the firm had netted $50 million from mortgage-backed securities by taking short positions that increased in value as the mortgage market cratered. Mr. Viniar wrote: "Tells you what might be happening to people who don't have the big short." As Senator Levin put it in a PSI press release accompanying the four emails: "There it is, in their own words: Goldman Sachs taking 'the big short' against the mortgage market."

In the third email, Goldman employees discussed mortgage securities that had been underwritten and sold by Goldman and were tied to mortgages issued by Washington Mutual's subprime lender, Long Beach Mortgage Company. Reporting the "wipeout" of one Long Beach security and the "imminent" collapse of another as "bad news" that would cost the firm $2.5 million, a Goldman employee then reported the "good news"—that the failure would also bring the firm $5 million from a bet it had placed against the very securities it had assembled and sold.

The final email came from a senior Goldman manager reacting to news that the credit rating agencies had downgraded $32 billion in mortgage-related securities, causing massive investor losses. He noted Goldman had bet against the very same securities and wrote: "Sounds like we will make some serious money." A colleague replied: "Yes we are well positioned."

Together, the four documents demonstrated that senior Goldman personnel knew about and celebrated the firm's shorting activity, which had positioned the firm to make "serious money" from the mortgage market's downfall. Major papers carried detailed stories describing the emails.[4] The result was that, notwithstanding Goldman's hardball tactics, PSI won the first round in the press leading up to the Tuesday hearing.

Holding Goldman Accountable

Our final financial crisis hearing took place on April 27, 2010. Three panels of Goldman witnesses testified: a panel of mortgage traders, a panel composed of Goldman's chief financial officer and chief risk officer, and, finally, Goldman's CEO Lloyd Blankfein.

The Goldman hearing was by far the toughest of the four. First, we were already stumbling in exhaustion from the earlier hearings. Second, Goldman was taking an uncompromising hard-nosed stance, hotly disputing evidence showing it had knowingly packaged poor-quality mortgages into securities, sold those securities to clients, and profited from betting against those and other mortgage-related securities.

On top of that, we'd been surprised by an April 16 civil lawsuit filed by the SEC against Goldman for defrauding investors in connection with the Abacus CDO.[5] While we viewed the lawsuit as accurate and well-deserved, we'd been planning to feature Abacus at our hearing. Now, just ten days before the hearing date, the facts we'd intended to disclose were already detailed in the SEC complaint.

Senator Levin told us to alter course and feature some Goldman CDOs in addition to Abacus at the hearing. Everyone with an ounce of energy left rallied to help the team get it done. The result was that, instead of the hearing highlighting a single CDO where Goldman had favored one client over several others, it also detailed three other CDOs where Goldman had managed to benefit the firm itself at the expense of its clients. We came to view those three other CDOs, known as Hudson, Anderson, and Timberwolf, as even more troubling than Abacus.

All four CDOs were complex financial investments that were tricky to explain. Essentially, Goldman had designed them so that each "referenced" a basket of mortgage-related assets, and enabled investors to wager on whether the value of that basket would rise or fall. Investors holding the "long" side of the bet wagered the value would rise; investors holding the "short" side bet it would fall.

Unlike Abacus, where clients took both sides of the bet and wagered against each other on the basket's value, in Hudson, Anderson, and Timberwolf, Goldman quietly took all or a substantial portion of the short side of the bet. At the same time, Goldman advised its clients to take the long side. Goldman advised its clients to bet long, even though the firm was secretly betting short, having concluded internally that the mortgage market was about to crash and that the CDOs themselves referenced poor-quality mortgage assets that Goldman expected to lose value. In the case of Hudson, Goldman took 100% of the short side of the bet and ended up making a $1.7 billion profit, taking money right out of the pockets of its own clients.

During the investigation, our investment bank team had gathered data on Hudson, Anderson, and Timberwolf, but hadn't examined them to the same degree as Abacus which we knew up, down, and sideways. So the team called for a deeper dive into all three. Multiple staffers, from senior investigators to interns on both sides of the aisle, dove into the document ocean. One immediately hit gold: a Goldman email in which an executive called Timberwolf a "shitty deal" at the same time Goldman was selling it to investors. Another spotted a Goldman email in which Hudson was referred to as "junk." The team dove even deeper into the documents, following them back and forward in time, building a detailed chronology and document history for each CDO. The amount of information the team amassed in ten days and integrated into its written materials—at the same time our first three hearings were unfolding—was awe-inspiring. Senator Levin ingested the new information in between hearings and gave the green light to go with it.

On Monday, April 26, the day before the Goldman hearing, we held our usual press briefing. The Levin press shop informed us they'd switched to a bigger room. When we walked in, it was a zoo—over 70 reporters filling every chair, cameras lining the back wall, and our handouts disappearing in minutes. It was the first signal that our hearing was entering a perfect storm—a vortex of press obsession with Goldman, public outrage at the financial crisis, and an ongoing congressional struggle over whether to take up financial reform. We released a 13-page Levin-Coburn memorandum, document quotes, and a joint press release. The press briefing lasted over two hours.

The hearing started the next day at 10:00 a.m. When we entered the hearing room through the staff door behind the senators' dais, the press storm was bigger than anything I'd been in. Reporters, photographers, and cameras were swarming witnesses. The audience included protestors dressed in fake prison suits, some waving flat paper masks decorated with Mr. Blankfein's face. C-SPAN was filming. It was a scene.

As soon as we entered, one Goldman lawyer steamed up to the dais, gestured at the press and audience antics, and demanded, "What are you going to do about this?" Bob looked at him coolly: "Do about what?" Soon after, Senator Levin entered the room, took his seat, gaveled the hearing room quiet, and launched into his opening statement.

The hearing turned out to be the longest of the Levin PSI years: eleven hours. One reason was that every subcommittee member made an appearance, the only PSI hearing in years with that distinction. Senators from both parties expressed concern with the two central facts uncovered by the investigation: that Goldman had made billions of dollars from the mortgage market's downfall, and that it had bet against its own clients.

Goldman strenuously denied both facts. First, it insisted it had not shorted the mortgage market, despite a stack of evidence to the contrary. The hearing exhibits included the Blankfein email stating that Goldman had not dodged "the mortgage mess," but "made more than we lost because of shorts"; and the Viniar email speculating about "what might be happening to people who don't have the big short." Dozens of other exhibits made the same point, including an internal submission to Goldman's own board of directors stating: "Although broader weakness in the mortgage markets resulted in significant losses in cash positions, we were overall net short the mortgage market and thus had very strong results." Senator Levin marched the witnesses through document after document detailing Goldman's shorting activity.

Senator Levin also took them through the evidence that Goldman had bet against its own clients. He highlighted an exhibit indicating Goldman held 100% of the short side of the $2 billion Hudson CDO it had advised investors to buy. He asked almost every witness to comment on the Goldman email describing Timberwolf as a "shitty deal" at the same time the firm was marketing it to investors and shorting the CDO. Beforehand, we'd given Senator Levin several alternatives for describing that email's salty language, but when he'd asked Senator Collins about using the actual phrase, she'd smiled and indicated she saw no problem with using it. So he did. Repeatedly. Telephones in the Levin personal office lit up with calls from offended viewers, and I cringed at every utterance, but Senator Levin was completely untroubled. He later shrugged that he was merely quoting Goldman's own email.

At one point, Senator Levin asked Goldman's chief financial officer David Viniar how he felt when he heard that Goldman employees were selling Timberwolf to clients at the same time a senior Goldman executive was calling it a bad deal. Mr. Viniar replied: "I think that is very unfortunate to have on email." Journalists sitting behind him broke into laughter, and he turned red. I felt sorry for him; of all the Goldman executives we'd interviewed, he'd been the most straightforward. But what seemed to me to be a Freudian slip may have reflected what more than one Goldman representative may have been thinking at that moment.

Another dramatic hearing moment involved Senator Coburn. It concerned Fabrice Tourre, the Goldman mortgage trader who'd been named in the Abacus lawsuit and whose personal emails had been released by Goldman over the weekend. Senator Coburn asked Mr. Blankfein if he set the tone at Goldman; Mr. Blankfein replied, "I do, sir." The Senator then asked whether releasing the personal Tourre emails was fair to his employee, and if it constituted a deliberate political or defense "ploy." Mr. Blankfein's spluttered explanation was incoherent.

Moving Dodd-Frank

The next day, the Senate voted to end the filibuster delaying Senate consideration of what became the Dodd-Frank Wall Street Reform and Consumer Protection Act of 2010. Enacted into law three months after the Goldman hearing, the law imposed a sweeping set of financial reforms targeting many of the problems highlighted by PSI.[6]

The Act imposed limits, for example, on the trading that banks could conduct to earn profits for themselves versus their clients—the so-called Volcker Rule which was added to the bill by Senators Jeff Merkley and Levin. The law also incorporated a Levin provision imposing new conflict of interest prohibitions and high-risk limits on federally insured banks. It even achieved that Washington rarity of abolishing an agency: OTS.

Other Dodd-Frank provisions restricted high-risk mortgages, barred "liar loans" with unverified borrower incomes, and established an SEC office to regulate credit rating agencies. Another section of the law eliminated legal prohibitions on the federal regulation of swaps and credit derivatives. The law also authorized banking regulators to hike bank capital requirements related to high-risk activities.

Still another innovation was creation of the Consumer Financial Protection Bureau which, among other duties, was charged with protecting consumers from predatory mortgages and with regulating mortgage issuers that had previously escaped oversight. Another key reform was establishment of the Financial Stability Oversight Council which, for the first time, required federal financial regulators from multiple agencies to sit down at the same table and combine forces to identify and mitigate systemic risks in the U.S. financial system.

The Dodd-Frank Act was far from perfect. Important reforms that Senator Levin and others fought for never made it into the law due to intense lobbying by the financial industry. For example, Senator Levin and Senator Byron Dorgan from North Dakota sought to ban synthetic financial instruments enabling banks and others to make casino-like bets on the value of stocks, bonds, and other investments.[7] Allowing those bets diverted resources from the banks' socially useful function of investing capital in business ventures viewed as likely to succeed. The senators also tried to ban "naked" credit default swaps that enabled banks and others to make bets on financial instruments they didn't own. Senator Levin likened naked credit default swaps to taking out insurance on a neighbor's house and making money when the house burned down, contending that U.S. markets had no use for a financial strategy that encouraged folks to root for failure rather than the success of investments. Other worthy reforms aimed at curing credit rating agency conflicts of interest, limiting high-risk investments by banks, and reducing market distortions also bit the dust. But that was par for the course in most legislative efforts; it didn't undermine our support for the reforms that survived.

While the Dodd-Frank Act didn't fix all the problems that contributed to the financial crisis, it was a worthy response to many of the key causes of the crash. We were proud of PSI's role in contributing to reforms that could help prevent another devastating market downturn.

Writing It Up

While enactment of the Dodd-Frank Act addressed many of the ills targeted in our investigation, PSI's work wasn't over. Senator Levin decided we needed to issue a comprehensive report on the key causes of the financial crisis. He felt it was too important and PSI had invested too much time and energy to allow most of what we'd learned to fade away. Even four hearing records had failed to lay out the majority of the facts we'd gathered.

So we spent another full year producing a 750-page bipartisan report, with 2849 footnotes. It nearly killed us, but it was worth every word, because it preserved everything we'd learned about the mortgage market, mortgage-related securities, and those who'd contributed to the financial crisis. Its most important message was that "the crisis was not a natural disaster, but the result of high risk, complex financial products; undisclosed conflicts of interest; and the failure of regulators, the credit rating agencies, and the market itself to rein in the excesses of Wall Street."[8] In other words, the crisis had not been an unavoidable calamity, but the product of corrupt financial practices that could have been prevented.

Writing the report was a complex undertaking. On the positive side, we had a lot of experience drafting long reports, since we viewed educating the public and policymakers about complex issues as one of PSI's most important functions. So we knew what to do. On the negative side, knowing what to do didn't make it easy.

As a first step, we spent several months after the hearings on additional document analysis and interviews to deepen our understanding of the facts and issues. Early on, we met with Goldman and let the firm know that, while we were ready to finish the investigation, we would persist for as long as necessary to get the information Senator Levin wanted. In response, Goldman got us the additional data we needed, and we were able to accelerate our work. We also spent substantial time developing Deutsche Bank as a second investment bank case study to provide a broader view of the contributing role played by investment banks.

Finally, it was time to put pen to paper—actually fingers to the keyboard. Since the Democrats were in the majority, it was our responsibility to come up with the first draft. Due to the breadth of the topics to be covered, we planned to use multiple writers writing simultaneously. So we needed to take steps to coordinate and standardize everyone's efforts.

Our first step was to produce a detailed, multi-page outline. The objective was to lay out how the report would be organized, how each part would work with the others, and how the various parts would contribute to an overarching narrative. The outline needed to list every issue we intended to cover, so everyone could see what fit where and minimize duplication.

I took first crack at the outline. It wasn't hard, since we already had four bipartisan hearing memos addressing the major issues. It was a matter of turning those hearing memos into report chapters, adding background sections, and producing a coherent whole. Senior staff offered edits, comments, and ideas, and we quickly reached consensus on a final version. We then sent the outline to every Levin staffer working on the report to let them know where we were going and how. It enabled everyone to understand how the part they were working on fit into the whole and made it easier for everyone to work on all the sections simultaneously.

A second step in the process was circulating instructions on the format for footnotes. Footnotes played a prominent role in PSI reports; they were the key mechanism we used to identify the evidence supporting each of the facts recited in the text. We typically provided a footnote for almost every sentence, not only to identify the supporting evidence for the reader but also to remind ourselves what it was. After all, a long report contained so many facts and figures, it was practically impossible to recall where they came from without a written reminder.

We'd also learned that, unless a standard footnote format was provided upfront, everyone used a different approach which then required a tedious and time-consuming effort to correct the entries. So we circulated the one-pager early in the process and threatened anyone who ignored it that they'd have to correct their own footnotes.

PSI also had a standard approach to writing up the major points in the chapters. The ideal was to lay out the facts in chronological order, with heavy reliance on multiple, direct quotes from documents and interviews, and a minimal amount of interpretation or elaboration. We'd found that sticking closely to the documents and using a chronological description of what happened cut down on factual errors, ensured we followed the evidence, sped up the writing, and facilitated bipartisan consensus on the facts. We also instructed everyone to write the body of the chapter first and only then the chapter's introduction. The introduction itself was required to summarize what followed in the chapter, again hewing closely to the facts. The overall goal was a fact-heavy, evidence-based explanation of the key causes of the financial crisis.

Each of the four PSI teams was given a deadline to produce an initial draft of their chapter. Each team divvied up assignments among its team members, and everyone got started writing at the same time. Team leaders were responsible for assembling and editing the parts into a single narrative. Earlier chapters were given earlier deadlines so that the chapters were finished sooner and could be reviewed first. That approach also gave extra time for the investment bank chapter, which was the last of the four and the most difficult. Due to the issues' complexity, we devoted a lot of time and space to providing context—historical background, laws, regulations, markets, financial instruments—to help readers view the financial crisis in a broader setting.

As editor-in-chief, it was my responsibility to integrate the chapters and background sections to ensure they were consistent with each other, weren't overly repetitive, and used the same phrases and terminology. I also made sure the evidence cited in the footnotes actually supported the points made in the text, and worked to clarify and strengthen the analysis. I spent a lot of time on chapter and section headings, as well as a detailed table of contents, using them to lay out our argument, highlight salient points, and help readers navigate the report.

Once the chapters, background sections, and table of contents were done, we turned to the executive summary. The executive summary is always the most important part of a report, since most readers never get beyond it. We worked hard to make it clear, concise, and readable, but also technically correct and informative.

In writing the executive summary, we drew from the introductory sections of each chapter and, to facilitate bipartisan support, wove in the major points made by Senators Levin and Coburn during the hearings. The final version of the executive summary was 18 pages long, which we thought was pretty good compared to the more than 700 pages that followed.

Normally, the executive summary of a PSI report includes both findings of fact and policy recommendations. In this report, however, we included the dozen plus recommendations set out in the four hearing memos, but not the 35 findings of fact. We decided reciting so many factual findings in the executive summary would be too much. Instead, we put the relevant findings of fact at the beginning of each of the four key report chapters.

Writing the draft was only one milestone on the way to the finish line. The next step was getting Senator Levin's approval. Because the report was so long, we didn't wait until the whole thing was done, but presented individual chapters to Senator Levin as they were ready. He reviewed every word, made numberless edits, and met with us to go over his concerns and comments. After we revised each chapter to reflect his views, we gave the corrected draft to our Republican colleagues and essentially went through the same process with them.

Reaching consensus on the report with the Coburn staff was made easier by the fact that our bosses had already agreed on the four hearing memos, and the report was carefully drafted to reflect those memos. But even with that basis for agreement, Chris Barkley, Senator Coburn's staff director, spent hours going over the draft, screening the evidence, and rewording sections to reflect Senator Coburn's point of view and concerns. Numerous issues came up that required discussion and resolution. It took time. The last details required an in-person meeting between Senators Levin and Coburn to resolve. It was a wonderful moment when we finally reached agreement on the text of the report.

But even then, our work wasn't done. The next phase was probably the most painful part of the drafting process—a final round of fact-checking and footnote review. Everyone spent countless hours doublechecking the parts of the report assigned to them, ensuring that the facts in the text were supported by the evidence in the footnotes. Others doublechecked a range of technical and formatting issues to ensure consistent treatment across all 750 pages. Multiple passes by multiple staffers, law clerks, and interns caught fewer and fewer errors. At long last, we thought the report was ready.

The next step in the process was PSI's standard procedure of giving the parties negatively portrayed in the report 24 hours to review the text before we released it to the public. We contacted legal counsel for each of the affected parties, explaining that an advance copy would be provided to the client as a courtesy, on a confidential basis, before the press saw it. We also explained that, while the findings were not negotiable, if anyone spotted a factual error and could prove it, we would correct the error prior to the report's release.

After agreeing in writing to keep the report confidential, Washington Mutual, OTS, FDIC, OCC, Moody's, S&P, Goldman, and Deutsche Bank each got copies of the parts of the report that pertained to them. We were told later that Goldman's legal counsel had lined up 100 attorneys to review its portion of the report during the 24-hour period, dividing up the text and footnotes among the lawyers and instructing them to test every word for accuracy. Good thing we'd gone through the same exercise ourselves. While none of the parties who received early copies of the report agreed with its negative findings and overall conclusions, because the report hewed so closely to the evidence, their lawyers disputed only a few relatively minor points that we agreed to change before releasing the report publicly.

PSI issued the Levin-Coburn report on April 13, 2011, one year after the PSI financial crisis hearings of April 2010. The day before, Senators Levin and Coburn held a joint press briefing on its content and were rewarded with high-quality press coverage the following day.

But even then we weren't done. The final step was preparing the hearing record for publication. Led by our chief clerk Mary Robertson, we combined the four hearing transcripts, the hearing exhibits, the report, and thousands of documents, so everyone could see the evidence we relied on. We added a lengthy table of contents and individualized descriptions of the 400+ hearing exhibits, as well as a document locater chart, to help folks wend their way through the materials. We sent the final proofs to the Government Printing Office which, several months later, printed an eight-volume set of bound books containing the complete record of PSI's financial crisis investigation.

Following Up

The final stage in every PSI investigation is trying to fix the identified problems. In the case of the financial crisis investigation, the Dodd-Frank Act had been enacted into law three months after our hearings in 2010, putting into place a slew of promising new measures. We spent the next four years monitoring the regulatory process and writing comment letters urging agencies to issue strong regulations that faithfully implemented the law.

Many of the final regulations carried out the law effectively, including those preventing predatory mortgages, imposing risk-related capital requirements, and implementing the Volcker Rule. Others were disappointing, including rules related to the credit rating agencies, foreign currency swaps, and offshore swap transactions. Still others languished in regulatory limbo for years, including rules to prohibit conflicts of interest when selling asset-backed securities, impose position limits on commodity trades, and establish a fiduciary standard for financial advisors. It was hard to understand why so many rules were so delayed or weakened, given the importance of preventing a new financial crisis. We did all we could to get strong rules in place.

In addition, we did what we could to help hold some of the wrongdoers accountable. Congressional investigations are not prosecutions and cannot impose criminal or civil penalties on anyone. The Senate and House are, instead, constitutionally limited to conducting inquiries with a "legislative purpose." At the same time, if a congressional investigation uncovered possible criminal or civil misconduct, the relevant committee or subcommittee could refer the matter to appropriate executive branch agencies to determine what legal action to take, if any.

At PSI, under a subcommittee rule allowing bipartisan referrals of matters where "there is reasonable cause to believe that a violation of law may have occurred," we sent referral letters to the Department of Justice, SEC, and other law enforcement and regulatory agencies, along with a copy of our report.[9] Our referrals led to multiple meetings with law enforcement and regulatory personnel considering taking action in specific cases. One of the big disappointments of the financial crisis was how few wrongdoers were ever prosecuted, an outcome at odds with prior financial scandals like the savings and loan crisis of the 1980s. While criminal prosecutions were few and far between, numerous civil actions eventually collected billions of dollars from the investment banks, mortgage issuers, and others involved with the wrongdoing. Our investigative results contributed to some of those cases.

In the end, perhaps PSI's most important function was gathering, in a careful and comprehensive manner, the facts and evidence on the financial crisis for review by future analysts and policymakers. They say those who don't remember the past are doomed to repeat it. Here's hoping PSI's investigative work on the past financial crisis will help the country avoid a future financial catastrophe.

Notes

1. See "Financial Regulatory Reform: Financial Crisis Losses and Potential Impacts of the Dodd-Frank Act," Report No. GAO-13-180, Government Accountability Office (1/2013), http://www.gao.gov/assets/660/651322.pdf; "The Cost of the Crisis: $20 Trillion and Counting," Report by Better Markets (7/2015), http://bit.ly/1jIwRXV. See also "How Bad Was It? The Costs and Consequences of the 2007–09 Financial Crisis," Tyler Atkinson, David Luttrell

and Harvey Rosenblum, Federal Reserve Bank of Dallas Staff Paper (7/2013), https://dallasfed.org/assets/documents/research/staff/staff1301.pdf.

2. The information in this chapter is based on the eight-volume publication of the U.S. Senate Permanent Subcommittee on Investigations containing its financial crisis hearings, report, and supporting documents. See "Wall Street and the Financial Crisis: The Role of High Risk Home Loans," S. Hrg. 112-671 (4/13/2010), https://www.gpo.gov/fdsys/pkg/CHRG-111shrg57319/pdf/CHRG-111shrg57319.pdf; "Wall Street and the Financial Crisis: The Role of Bank Regulators," S. Hrg. 112-672 (4/16/2010), https://www.gpo.gov/fdsys/pkg/CHRG-111shrg57320/pdf/CHRG-111shrg57320.pdf; "Wall Street and the Financial Crisis: The Role of Credit Rating Agencies," S. Hrg. 112-673 (4/23/2010), https://www.gpo.gov/fdsys/pkg/CHRG-111shrg57321/pdf/CHRG-111shrg57321.pdf; "Wall Street and the Financial Crisis: The Role of Investment Banks," S. Hrg. 112-674 (4/27//2010), https://www.gpo.gov/fdsys/pkg/CHRG-111shrg57322/pdf/CHRG-111shrg57322.pdf; "Wall Street and the Financial Crisis: Anatomy of a Financial Collapse," S. Hrg. 112-675 (4/13/2011), Part I (report and documents supporting the Washington Mutual, OTS, and credit rating agency sections of the report), https://www.gpo.gov/fdsys/pkg/CHRG-112shrg57323/pdf/CHRG-112shrg57323.pdf; Part II (documents supporting the Deutsche Bank section of the report), https://www.gpo.gov/fdsys/pkg/CHRG-112shrg66050/pdf/CHRG-112shrg66050.pdf; Part III (documents supporting the Goldman Sachs section of the report), https://www.gpo.gov/fdsys/pkg/CHRG-112shrg66051/pdf/CHRG-112shrg66051.pdf; and Part IV (additional documents supporting the Goldman Sachs section of the report), https://www.gpo.gov/fdsys/pkg/CHRG-112shrg66052/pdf/CHRG-112shrg66052.pdf.

3. See, for example, "Berating the Raters," *New York Times*, Paul Krugman (4/25/2010), http://nyti.ms/2j6yTmx.

4. See, for example, "Goldman Cited 'Serious' Profit on Mortgages," *New York Times*, Louise Story, Sewell Chan and Gretchen Morgenson (4/24/2010), http://nyti.ms/2zOmcau; "Goldman's Tourre Foresaw Subprime Chaos, Emails Show," *Wall Street Journal*, Susanne Craig and John D. McKinnon (4/24/2010).

5. See "SEC Charges Goldman Sachs with Fraud in Structuring and Marketing of CDO Tied to Subprime Mortgages," SEC Press Release No. 2010-59 (4/16/2010), https://www.sec.gov/news/press/2010/2010-59.htm. On July 14, 2010, Goldman agreed to pay the SEC $550 million to settle the lawsuit. *SEC v. Goldman, Sachs & Co.*, Case No. 10-CV-3229 (BSJ), (USDC SDNY), Consent of Defendant Goldman, Sachs & Co. (7/14/2010), https://www.sec.gov/litigation/litreleases/2010/consent-pr2010-123.pdf.

6. H.R. 4173, Dodd-Frank Wall Street Reform and Consumer Protection Act, P.L. 111-203 (7/21/2010). The Senate version of the bill was S. 3217.

7. See Senate Amendment 4008, offered to Senate Amendment 3739 to S. 3217, CR S3728 (5/13/2010), cosponsored by Senators Dorgan, Levin, Cantwell, Feingold, Sanders, and Kaufman.
8. "Wall Street and the Financial Crisis: Anatomy of a Financial Collapse," S. Hrg. 112-675, Volume 5, Part I (4/13/2011), at 9, https://www.gpo.gov/fdsys/pkg/CHRG-112shrg57323/pdf/CHRG-112shrg57323.pdf.
9. "Rules of Procedure," U.S. Senate Permanent Subcommittee on Investigations, Rule 19.

10

Combating Money Laundering: Round Two

"Wrongdoers can use U.S. dollars and U.S. wire transfers to commit crimes, arm terror groups, produce and transport illegal drugs, loot government coffers, even pursue weapons of mass destruction. That's why our country has made combating money laundering and terrorist financing a national security imperative."
Senator Carl Levin, HSBC hearing (July 17, 2012)

PSI's investigations into the financial crisis, unfair credit card practices, and offshore tax abuses were important. But over the years, the Levin PSI crew rated money laundering as its hands-down favorite investigative topic due to the bipartisan satisfaction that came from battling dirty money that was fueling crime and empowering wrongdoers.

Senator Levin launched his PSI career by investigating money laundering via private banking accounts opened for corrupt officials and correspondent accounts opened for high-risk offshore banks. The criminality and terrorist vulnerabilities he exposed culminated in enactment of Levin-Sarbanes legislation revamping U.S. anti-money laundering (AML) laws in the 2001 Patriot Act. Those new laws were intended to herald a new era of stronger AML safeguards protecting the U.S. financial system from terrorists, drug lords, and dishonest officials.

But tough new laws don't do much good unless they are enforced. So Senator Levin decided he would also track how the new laws were being implemented. Over the next decade, he presided over three follow-up hearings, each with explosive findings.

A 2004 investigation into a bank in the nation's capital, Riggs Bank, specializing in serving embassies and foreign leaders, showed how the bank had

© The Author(s) 2018
E. J. Bean, *Financial Exposure*, https://doi.org/10.1007/978-3-319-94388-6_10

handled millions of dollars in suspect funds, while ignoring the new laws. A 2010 hearing exposed how some corrupt foreign dictators and their relatives were able to circumvent the stronger AML controls by using shell companies, sleazy lawyers, and other U.S. professionals to infiltrate our financial system. A third hearing, in 2012, disclosed how a major global bank, HSBC, had allowed its U.S. branch to be misused by Mexican drug traffickers, Russian fraudsters, and rogue regimes like Iran.

The eye-popping tales PSI uncovered included a U.S. bank transferring $1.6 million to an offshore shell company despite a court order freezing the funds; a daughter with $1 million in shrink-wrapped bills snuck across U.S. borders by her dictator father; a corrupt dictator's son circumventing AML controls by funneling suspect cash through his U.S. lawyers' bank accounts; a Washington lobbyist passing millions through his local accounts for a head of state; and a U.S. bank's accepting $7 billion in cash from Mexico with no questions asked, while also allowing a backlog of 17,000 suspicious transactions to pile up without review. Senator Levin used the shocking facts to compel U.S. regulators to stiffen America's AML defenses.

Helping Dictators Move Dirty Money—Riggs Bank

The first of the three follow-up investigations was triggered by a singular name—Simon Kareri. In early 2003, Bob read an article by journalist Ken Silverstein on how Teodoro Obiang Nguema Mbasogo, longtime dictator of Equatorial Guinea (EG), a small, oil-rich country in West Africa, was suspected of depositing hundreds of millions of dollars in oil revenues in secret accounts he controlled at Riggs Bank.[1] Three quarters of the way through, the article named Mr. Obiang's private banker at Riggs as Simon Kareri.

The prior year, Bob had interviewed Mr. Kareri in connection with another investigation. Bob's shady-dealings radar had immediately begun pinging. Bob had promised himself that, if the opportunity arose, he would look more carefully into Mr. Kareri's activities. The Silverstein article opened the door. Senator Levin had been contemplating an investigation to test bank implementation of the AML provisions in the 2001 Patriot Act. Those provisions obligated U.S. banks, among other measures, to exercise due diligence when handling accounts for foreign political figures and to refuse any funds suspected of arising from foreign corruption.

Bob proposed using Riggs as a test case. Senator Levin agreed. Since it was a natural follow-up to our earlier money laundering investigations, PSI's chair at the time, Senator Coleman, also green-lighted the inquiry. Because Bob and I were then submersed in a PSI tax shelter probe, Laura Stuber and Dan Berkovitz from our staff took the early lead on Riggs. Over time, as it gained steam, the Riggs inquiry consumed nearly every staffer on both sides of the aisle.

Catering to Foreign Political Elites

Riggs was a bank with a pedigree. Small by U.S. standards with only about $4 billion in deposits, it had a storied history as a bank used by past U.S. presidents, including Abraham Lincoln. Its headquarters sat across the street from the White House. Its history included such banking successes as financing Samuel Morse's invention of the telegraph and supplying $7.2 million in gold toward the U.S. purchase of Alaska.

By 2000, Riggs had developed a new line of business: providing banking services to foreign embassies operating in Washington, D.C. The bank catered to the banking needs of not only the embassy and its personnel but also foreign leaders, their families, and associates. Following the 9/11 terrorist attack in 2001, however, Riggs' embassy banking business drew a negative national spotlight when media stories disclosed that the bank was housing multimillion-dollar accounts for Saudi Arabia, then suspected of supporting terrorism.

Riggs' controlling shareholder and chief executive at the time was Joe Allbritton, a larger-than-life Washingtonian known to enjoy hobnobbing with world leaders.[2] When he retired from the bank's executive suite in 2002, he handed the reins over to his son, Robert Allbritton, while retaining a seat on the board of directors. Under the Allbrittons, Riggs had never reported large profits. But the Allbrittons had allegedly brushed off offers to buy the bank, supposedly due in part to the entré that Riggs provided into elite foreign circles.

Investigating the Bank

Laura and Dan launched our Riggs investigation by researching the bank's history and speaking with its primary regulator, the Office of the Comptroller of the Currency (OCC).[3] They also met with experts on Equatorial Guinea and Saudi Arabia, two countries with large accounts at the bank, as well as with U.S. oil companies producing EG oil.

They learned that Equatorial Guinea's people were among the poorest on earth, even though the country was a growing source of oil for the United States and was run by a well-heeled elite. President Obiang had become the country's leader in a 1979 coup in which he deposed and executed his uncle. Over the following decades, he'd become infamous for human right abuses, torture, and corruption. In addition, he'd stacked the EG government with his relatives, including appointing his eldest son, also named Teodoro, as Minister of Forestry in charge of timber, the country's second largest export after oil.

Laura and Dan contacted Riggs to get an overview of its embassy accounts and AML controls. While Riggs wasn't happy to hear from us, its lawyers said the bank would cooperate. Riggs insisted its operations were above board and by the book.

Those claims lost credibility, however, when, in July 2003, the OCC issued a consent order requiring Riggs, without admitting wrongdoing, to strengthen its AML controls in a major way, including by developing procedures to screen high-risk clients, monitor high-risk transactions, and identify and report suspicious cash and wire transfers.[4] The long list of needed improvements suggested Riggs had been operating without basic AML controls. It also suggested that the OCC had allowed the bank's AML problems to smolder for years.

Another development further broadened the investigation. While pouring over Riggs records, Laura noticed a reference to Augusto Pinochet, Chile's controversial former president who'd assumed power after a U.S.-backed coup in 1973. During his rule, according to reports, an estimated 3000 persons had been murdered or "disappeared," 30,000 tortured, and some 80,000 imprisoned. He stepped down from the presidency in 1990, but continued as commander of the Chilean Army until 1998, when he retired from that post as well and became a "senator for life" with immunity from prosecution. During a 1998 visit to London, Mr. Pinochet had been detained under an international arrest warrant on charges filed in Spain for human rights abuses. A legal battle ensued over Spain's request for his extradition. In 2000, a U.K. court denied extradition and allowed him to return to Chile due to ill health. It was surprising to learn that he'd been a Riggs customer during at least some of that history, so we decided to take a closer look.

To get more information, we sent a subpoena to Riggs and a document request to the OCC. We asked Riggs for documents related to the 2003 AML consent order, its AML program, its embassy accounts, and dealings with Equatorial Guinea, Saudi Arabia, and Augusto Pinochet. We asked the OCC for its Riggs examination reports and analytical memos, including materials related to the three accounts. In addition, we subpoenaed documents from the U.S. oil firms that sent payments to EG accounts at Riggs. We also sought materials from other banks and individuals whose names surfaced in connection with transactions of interest. Since the parties we contacted were fairly cooperative, after some negotiations and clarifications, a rich collection of documents began rolling in.

Separating Out Saudi Arabia

While PSI was intensifying its Riggs inquiry, our full committee initiated its own investigation into the issue of terrorist financing. In July 2003, the same month the Riggs AML consent order was issued, the full committee held a hearing focused on the role of Saudi Arabia in financing terrorism.[5] Among other matters, the committee noted that 15 of the 19 terrorists in the 9/11 attack had been Saudis, and a report was claiming a Saudi civil aviation agency employee had paid many expenses for two of the terrorists.

After the hearing, Senator Susan Collins, then full committee chair, expressed an interest in examining the Saudi accounts at Riggs Bank. She asked PSI if it would be willing to hand over the documents we'd collected on those accounts so the full committee could investigate. No investigator likes to surrender their documents to someone else, but Senator Coleman, PSI chair, wanted to cooperate with the full committee and so did Senator Levin. So we packed up the Saudi account documents and shipped them to our Collins colleagues.

We later learned it may have been a blessing in disguise. The Collins staff ended up spending significant time and resources trying to get the Bush administration to declassify information related to the Saudi accounts so the committee could hold a public hearing. The administration resisted, and the classification dispute slowed and complicated the committee's work. After about a year, the committee called it quits and discontinued its Riggs inquiry, which meant potentially important information about the Saudi accounts never got to the public.[6]

Closing the EG Accounts

Losing the Saudi accounts was only the opening act in the lengthy drama that was the Riggs investigation, which underwent multiple twists and turns. Another standout moment was an early morning call from the bank asking us to meet as soon as possible. At the meeting, Riggs disclosed that, without warning, Simon Kareri, the top Riggs banker handling the EG accounts, had fled the country.

The bank explained that, as a result of our inquiry, it had begun to closely monitor the EG accounts. In December 2003, Riggs noticed several suspicious transactions, including one in which $140,000 was withdrawn from an account belonging to the EG president's son, passed through a mysterious account for "Bolly Ba," and landed in an account controlled by Mr. Kareri's wife. When Riggs confronted Mr. Kareri about the transaction, he claimed the funds were for a low-income housing investment. When Riggs contacted the president's son, he said he'd given Mr. Kareri a partially filled out check for $40,000 to buy a car, but never authorized the check alteration that converted the amount to $140,000. A second suspicious transaction in the Kareri accounts involved a $4300 payment by a contractor who'd just completed an embassy renovation for about $48,000. It looked suspiciously like a kickback.

In January 2004, Riggs fired Mr. Kareri. He later surfaced in Equatorial Guinea which suggests that, despite the altered check, he wasn't really at odds with the ruling family.

There was more. In February 2004, EG President Obiang asked Riggs bankers to travel to Equatorial Guinea to discuss his accounts. After Riggs declined, apparently due to safety concerns, President Obiang traveled with a large entourage to Washington to meet with the bank. He convened a meeting at the luxurious Four Seasons Hotel in Georgetown. According to Riggs, during the meeting, the bank asked about wire transfers that'd sent millions of dollars in oil revenues from an EG government account to two unfamiliar offshore corporations. When President Obiang declined to explain the transactions, Riggs decided to close the EG accounts.

A fleeing banker, a hotel confrontation with a head of state, the shutdown of multi-million-dollar accounts—it was getting hard to keep up.

Tracking the Misconduct

In the meantime, the PSI team was plowing through documents, preparing chronologies, and analyzing the facts. The EG account documents told one troubling story after another.[7] Over ten years, from 1995 to 2004, Riggs had administered more than 60 EG accounts, including an official EG government account for oil revenues, an EG embassy account, and numerous personal accounts for EG officials and their family members, including President Obiang, his wife, and sons. By 2003, the EG accounts represented Riggs' largest banking relationship, with aggregate deposits peaking at around $700 million.

The bank records also disclosed Riggs had established an offshore shell cor-poration in the Bahamas called Otong Ltd. for EG President Obiang and opened a U.S. account in Otong's name. In addition, the bank had repeatedly accepted large cash deposits to the Otong account as well as other accounts held by President Obiang or his wife. In fact, on two occasions, Simon Kareri had shown up at Riggs with suitcases of cash, the dollars shrink-wrapped in plastic, and deposited $3 million into the Otong account. Overall, Riggs records attested to a total of $13 million in cash deposits into Obiang-related accounts over the years.

During the same period, Riggs also executed wire transfers sending mil-lions of dollars from the EG government's oil revenues account to unfamiliar offshore corporations. For example, a total of $26 million was wired to Kalunga Co., an EG company with a bank account in Spain, and $8 million to Apexside Trading, a company with accounts in Luxembourg. Still other bank records showed substantial payments made by U.S. oil companies to both the EG oil revenues account and to accounts held by EG officials, their family members, or entities they controlled. Riggs had apparently facilitated all of the transactions with no questions asked.

The Pinochet documents were equally troubling. Bank records showed that, from 1994 to 2002, Riggs opened nine accounts for Mr. Pinochet with aggregate deposits of up to $8 million, without ever asking how someone on a government salary had amassed that level of wealth. The bank also formed two Bahamas corporations for him, Ashburton and Althorp, and opened accounts in their names. More surprising still was when Mr. Pinochet was placed under house arrest in London in 1998, under a court order freezing his assets, and Riggs quietly transferred over $1.6 million from an Althorp account at its London branch to an Althorp account in the United States. In other words, Riggs had knowingly helped Mr. Pinochet violate a court-ordered worldwide freeze on his assets.

That's not all Riggs did for Mr. Pinochet. Over the next two years, the bank sent him a series of 38 cashier's checks, each made payable to cash for $50,000. Riggs sent the checks—totaling $1.9 million altogether—to Mr. Pinochet in Chile. The first set was hand delivered to him by a Riggs banker who flew to Chile for that purpose; the rest were transported to him by overnight mail. Mr. Pinochet then gradually cashed them at Chilean banks. The funds came from his accounts, but on their face, the cashier's checks identified only Riggs Bank as the payor; none made any reference to him. By supplying its cashier's checks, Riggs enabled Mr. Pinochet to access his Riggs funds without leaving Chile and without disclosing his secret U.S. accounts.

The secrecy didn't stop there. After a U.K. newspaper reported that Mr. Pinochet had an account at Riggs, the bank changed the name on his personal accounts from "Augusto Pinochet Ugarte & Lucia Hiriart de Pinochet" to "L. Hiriart &/or A. Ugarte," essentially disguising them in the event of a computer search. In addition, Riggs concealed the existence of the accounts from its federal bank examiners. It was only after an OCC anti-money laundering examination spotted references to the cashier's checks and inquired into their origin that Riggs finally disclosed it harbored Pinochet funds. In response, the OCC essentially pressured Riggs to close the Pinochet accounts, which it did in 2002. Even then, the bank initially refused to provide the OCC with any account documentation, raising additional red flags.

There's more. The OCC documents disclosed that the bank examiners who spotted the Pinochet cashier's checks were AML specialists who, for a five-year period from 1997 to 2003, had repeatedly dinged Riggs for major AML deficiencies. Year after year, the bank promised to correct those deficiencies, but never did. Yet when the AML specialists complained to the OCC's bank examination team headed by Examiner-in-Charge Ashley Lee, the OCC team essentially shrugged its shoulders and declined to compel Riggs to strengthen its AML controls.

More troubling yet, when Ashley Lee retired from the OCC after overseeing Riggs Bank from 1998 to 2002, the documents showed that he ordered the Pinochet examination workpapers to be stored in a paper file, rather than in the OCC's electronic system as they should have been. By making them harder to find, he effectively buried the information about the accounts. Then, days after leaving the OCC, Mr. Lee started a new job working at—wait for it—Riggs Bank. It was a jaw-dropping switch from bank examiner to bank employee at the very bank he'd been overseeing. Within a year, he became Riggs' chief risk officer.

Conducting Interviews

After digesting those and other head-turning Riggs documents, we began a series of interviews to make sure we understood exactly what was going on.

We focused first on Riggs to learn more about the EG accounts. Since Mr. Kareri had fled the country, we interviewed his colleagues and superiors, all of whom claimed to know little about the EG relationship. In contrast to the first few months of our inquiry in which Riggs had indignantly defended Mr. Kareri—denying he'd engaged in any wrongdoing—senior Riggs personnel began blaming the absent Mr. Kareri for all the problems we'd uncovered.

The trouble with that line of defense was that the Pinochet accounts had nothing to do with Mr. Kareri, but were equally problematic. The Pinochet accounts had been administered by a group of Riggs bankers focused on Latin America. When we interviewed the key private banker, Carol Thompson, she seemed proud of having assisted Mr. Pinochet with his banking needs. She expressed no remorse about the bank's providing him with offshore corporations, hidden wire transfers, and secret cashier's checks. At one point, she dismissed a question about whether Mr. Pinochet had ever spoken with Joseph Allbritton, the head of the bank, by stating Mr. Allbritton didn't speak Spanish. When Zack asked if she'd ever translated for Mr. Allbritton so that he could communicate with Mr. Pinochet, she begrudgingly admitted she had.

Toward the end, we interviewed Robert Allbritton, who'd become Riggs' chief executive in 2002, after his father stepped down. He professed to know little about any of the troubling facts. When asked about Riggs' creating secret offshore corporations for its foreign clients, accepting millions in cash deposits from them, and wiring funds in defiance of a court-ordered asset freeze, Mr. Allbritton explained that he hadn't been involved—he'd been skiing in France, on his honeymoon in Europe, or frolicking at some other exotic location. He left the impression that he was a social dilettante with little understanding of or involvement in the bank's day-to-day management. It may have even been true—the records suggested Lawrence Hebert, a confidant of the father, Joe Allbritton, may have been actually running the bank.

Our final Riggs interview was with Ashley Lee, who'd served as head of the OCC examination team for Riggs before becoming Riggs' chief risk officer. Unsurprisingly, he defended his work at both the OCC and the bank, denied any wrongdoing, and noted he'd broken no law by taking a job at the bank he'd supervised.

We conducted a second set of interviews at the OCC. The AML examiners confirmed they'd written up Riggs five years in a row for inadequate AML controls, but were unable to get their superiors to take any enforcement action against the bank. OCC higher-ups had a tough time explaining why they'd never compelled the bank to fix its AML deficiencies, other than noting the Examiner-In-Charge Ashley Lee had never recommended it. They had an even tougher time explaining Mr. Lee's jump from Riggs regulator to Riggs executive.

Our final set of interviews was with the U.S. oil companies operating in Equatorial Guinea. When confronted with bank records showing large payments to not only the EG oil revenues account, but also the personal accounts of EG officials, they explained that, in a developing country, the ruling elite often controlled much of the country's economy. They said they had to pay Obiang family members to obtain land, housing, and business services. One oil company admitted making $400,000 in rental payments to a 14-year-old Obiang relative. Several admitted paying millions of dollars in "student expenses," a supposedly humanitarian effort that actually involved paying college tuition for the children of senior EG officials. According to the oil companies, that was how business was done in Africa.

Altogether, it took us a year to complete the Riggs investigation, but by the end, the evidence of misdeeds was substantial. Problems included Riggs' knowingly facilitating millions of dollars in suspect EG and Pinochet transactions and lax OCC oversight that allowed years of dubious bank practices to fester.

Going Public

On July 15, 2004, PSI held a four-hour hearing exposing the tawdry tale of Riggs' involvement with corrupt foreign officials. It was a bipartisan effort led by Senator Levin and two Republican colleagues, PSI chair Senator Norm Coleman and PSI member Senator Pete Fitzgerald from Illinois.

In connection with the hearing, the subcommittee released an 83-page report detailing the bank's handling of the EG and Pinochet accounts, and the OCC's weak AML oversight. The report also put a spotlight on the hidden ways in which U.S. oil companies were supplying funds to EG officials and family members. Senator Coleman did not formally join the report, even though his staff had been full partners in its drafting. Instead, as was PSI's practice back then, the staff report was issued under the sole auspices of Senator Levin who'd led the Riggs inquiry.

The hearing was lively, taking testimony from four panels. First up was Simon Kareri who'd eventually returned to the United States and been arrested for money laundering and tax evasion.[8] He asserted his Fifth Amendment right not to answer questions and was excused.

Next up were three senior Riggs officials, including Lawrence Hebert who, by then, was officially serving as Riggs' chief executive officer, and Ashley Lee, the bank's chief risk officer. Senators Levin, Coleman, and Fitzgerald grilled the officials about the bank's actions. At one point, Senator Levin asked Mr. Hebert about a fawning letter sent by Riggs to Mr. Obiang after hosting a luncheon for him. The letter stated in part:

> Dear Mr. President, We hope this letter finds you well and rested after your trip to Washington. We would like to thank you for the opportunity you granted us in hosting a luncheon in your honor here at Riggs bank. We sincerely enjoyed

the discussions. We formed a committee of the most senior officers at Riggs that will meet regularly to discuss our relationship. We are confident we can be of great assistance to you by providing you access to the best financial expertise both at Riggs and within the entire financial services industry.

The letter ended: "With gratitude," and was signed by four Riggs officials, including Robert Allbritton.

After noting President Obiang's atrocious human rights record and inclusion in a list of the world's ten worst dictators, Senator Levin asked the Riggs officials: "How do you write that stuff to a man as abominable as this guy … how do you, basically, live with yourself?"[9] Mr. Hebert seemed puzzled by the question. He responded: "Senator, the lunch with the president was a request on my part to meet this person. They had a significant amount of money in the bank." In other words, President Obiang was a wealthy client, so bank practice was to meet and woo him, no matter how suspect his reputation or funds.

The third hearing panel consisted of three OCC officials who admitted fault right up front. They stated that "Riggs represent[ed] a failure of supervision," and the OCC "should have been more aggressive in our oversight" and "insisted on remedial steps much earlier and much more forcefully than we did." They also admitted being troubled by its lead bank examiner's taking a job with Riggs. In addition, the OCC admitted, three years after the 2001 Patriot Act, it had yet to update its AML handbook to reflect the new AML requirements, and the Treasury had yet to issue key implementing regulations. The OCC committed to strengthening its AML efforts.

The final panel consisted of representatives from three oil companies doing business in Equatorial Guinea, ExxonMobil, Amerada Hess, and Marathon. Two of the companies admitted to being in business with the country's dictator via partnerships with an EG company he controlled. All three admitted paying hundreds of thousands of dollars for the college expenses of the children of senior EG officials. All three also admitted doing business with Obiang's relatives. The fact that the oil companies' actions had not been known to the public until we publicized them just added to the miasma surrounding the Riggs transactions.

Making Improvements

The Riggs hearing generated extensive press coverage critical of both the bank and OCC. It also led to quick progress on several fronts.

Most satisfying was congressional action to address the conflict of interest inherent in the OCC's senior examiner taking a job with Riggs Bank. Two months after the Riggs hearing, Senators Levin and Coleman introduced the Bank Examiner Postemployment Protection Act to impose a one-year cooling off period before senior federal bank examiners could work for a financial institution they oversaw. In December 2004, the Levin-Coleman provision was enacted into law.[10] It was the first—and as of 2017, I believe the only—federal law to impose a cooling off period before a federal regulator can work for a business once supervised by that regulator.

Also satisfying was a wave of enforcement actions taken by the OCC against other banks with AML deficiencies. Those enforcement actions signaled the banking community that federal regulators were no longer willing to ignore sloppy, lax, or intentionally weak AML programs.

Broader changes took longer. In June 2005, the OCC and other federal bank regulators finally issued a revised AML examination handbook with the reforms mandated by the 2001 law. The Treasury dragged its feet until early 2006, before finally issuing new due diligence regulations implementing the Patriot Act's AML requirements. The Treasury regulations broke little new ground, but at least supported, rather than hindered, what the bank examiners were already requiring. On still a broader stage, the Riggs inquiry bolstered ongoing public interest group efforts to increase the transparency of oil company payments to governments.[11]

Supplementing the Record

As those legislative, enforcement, and regulatory advancements began to unfold, PSI found itself launching a second round of inquiry into the Pinochet accounts.

In the aftermath of the Riggs hearing in 2004, Mr. Pinochet's adult son, Marco Antonio Pinochet Hiriart, called the Levin report "mere lies" and claimed his father had no bank accounts outside of Chile.[12] That bugged us. The Riggs bank statements not only proved the Pinochet accounts existed, but were laced with tantalizing cash transfers suggesting Pinochet had still more accounts at other U.S. banks. We decided to follow the money a bit further.

Even we were taken aback by what we found. After tracing cash transfers through multiple financial institutions, we discovered that Riggs had actually opened—not nine—but 28 accounts for Mr. Pinochet, including many in the names of Chilean military officials acting as fronts for their commander. In addition, we uncovered nearly 100 Pinochet accounts at half a dozen other U.S. banks, including Citibank, Bank of America, and a U.S. branch of Banco de Chile. Some reported millions of dollars in deposits and wire transfers to non-U.S. accounts.

The documents also showed Mr. Pinochet had made an art of opening accounts in various forms of his name. His complete given name was Augusto Jose Ramon Pinochet Ugarte. Laura found accounts he'd opened in the name of Augusto Ugarte, Jose Pinochet, and J. Ramon Ugarte, among others. We also obtained documents showing Mr. Pinochet had used at least three different Chilean passports to open the accounts. One passport used his full name and displayed his typical patrician photo with white hair; a second used the name Augusto Ugarte and showed him with dark hair, glasses, and a thick mustache; a third used the name Jose Ramon Ugarte and showed him balding and clean-shaven, with thinner-framed glasses. Chile later located the actual physical passports—with the photos removed—and charged Mr. Pinochet with passport fraud (Image 10.1).

Another disturbing surprise was a cache of Riggs documents tracing a close relationship between the bank and Chilean military. Letters and memos referred to in-person meetings, often in Chile, between senior Riggs personnel, including Joe Allbritton, and military leaders, including lunches, teas, and horse races. They also described gift exchanges involving such items as cufflinks, an "elegant lapis lazuli box," and children's board games.[13] At one

Pinochet Account Identification

Riggs Bank Miami   Riggs Bank London   Citibank New York

Prepared by the Permanent Subcommittee on Investigations, Minority Staff

Image 10.1 Three Pinochet passport photos. Source: 2005 Levin-Coleman Report Exhibit 3

point, Mr. Allbritton wrote to the Chilean Army commander: "Where do I begin to thank you? ... There are so many priceless gifts you have given, but above all let me thank you for your friendship. ... On behalf of the Riggs, I wish to thank you and the Army for our longstanding and magnificent relationship. ... If you find yourself needing the sun or the snow, you are welcome to sun at our place in La Jolla or to ski in Aspen."[14] A 1997 Riggs memo to Mr. Allbritton counted over $65 million in Chilean military and embassy deposits and $600,000 in bank fees in one year alone.

On March 16, 2005, PSI issued a joint Levin-Coleman report with the new information on the Pinochet-related accounts. The large number of accounts, deceptive names, use of Chilean military officers as fronts, and multi-million-dollar transactions demonstrated that Mr. Pinochet had orchestrated a worldwide network of secret bank accounts. It also showed multiple banks in addition to Riggs had failed to implement strong U.S. anti-money laundering controls.

After the second report came out, at the request of several Chilean journalists, we held a meeting in the PSI conference room with over a dozen of the country's top reporters, almost all of whom had flown in for the session. One problem was that we didn't speak Spanish, none of them was fluent in English, and no one had brought an interpreter. But we muddled through, showing them the documents we'd collected and answering their questions as best we could.

It quickly became clear to the reporters that we were no experts on Chile; we didn't fully understand its history, were unaware of many actions taken by Mr. Pinochet, and didn't even know the names by which his family members were known in the Chilean press. But strangely enough, our ignorance increased our credibility. The reporters could see we had no particular view of Mr. Pinochet, his family, or Chilean politics; our real focus was on U.S. banks.

Over time, we began to learn of the impact that PSI's investigative work had on Chile. Mr. Pinochet had apparently portrayed himself as an incorruptible politician who made tough decisions. The disclosure that he'd hidden millions of dollars in scores of secret bank accounts destroyed that illusion. The Chilean courts ended up stripping him of his immunity from prosecution and allowing charges of tax evasion, human rights abuses, and other crimes. But before he stood trial on any of those charges, he died of a heart attack on December 10, 2006.

Here in the United States, a Pinochet expert told us that PSI had uncovered the first really new information about Mr. Pinochet in years and had irrevocably changed the country's perception of the former president. His intense gratitude for our work brought home for me, in a way nothing else had, what our investigation meant to Chile.

We also met Equatorial Guinea activists who'd risked their lives opposing President Obiang. They, too, were grateful for PSI's work—uncovering the president's offshore company, the EG accounts at Riggs, the siphoning of millions of dollars in EG oil revenues to suspect offshore companies, and the secret oil company payments to senior EG officials. They said the evidence we'd uncovered would have been impossible for them to secure. Their thanks brought home, again, how PSI's investigative work reverberated beyond U.S. borders.

Facing the Music

Here at home, Riggs Bank finally had to face the music over its own misconduct. It pleaded guilty to failing to report suspicious activity in connection with the EG, Pinochet, and other accounts, and paid a $16 million criminal fine and $25 million civil money penalty to the United States.[15] For violating the 1998 order by a Spanish court freezing Pinochet assets, the Allbrittons paid $1 million to the court, and Riggs paid another $8 million to a foundation assisting victims of the Pinochet regime.[16]

Ironically, around the same time, the Allbrittons sold Riggs Bank to PNC Financial Services Group for about $650 million.[17] The sale allegedly netted the family hundreds of millions of dollars in profits, erasing the costs they'd incurred from the Riggs scandal. With that sale, after more than 100 years in operation, the Riggs name disappeared from the U.S. financial world.

One last coda. About a year after the Riggs investigation concluded, a Levin staffer went to visit a family friend at a local hotel. In the lobby, he stopped at a desk to speak with the hotel concierge. Their eyes met, and both stopped short, recognizing each other but unable to place how. The Levin staffer turned away, suddenly realizing he'd spent hours in a face-to-face interview with her at PSI. She was the former Riggs banker for Augusto Pinochet, now working as a hotel concierge. It was a surreal moment.

Dodging U.S. AML Controls—New Tactics

The Riggs investigation convinced U.S. bank regulators that more had to be done to strengthen U.S. AML controls. As standards rose, bank examinations intensified, and more banks tightened their AML programs, PSI turned its attention to other issues. But in 2009, five years after the Riggs investigation, AML problems again began to dominate the PSI agenda.

By then, the AML game had shifted. Foreign dictators could no longer waltz into a U.S. bank with $3 million in a suitcase and make a deposit. Those days were finally gone. But that didn't mean corrupt foreign officials had given up on infiltrating the U.S. financial system.

Why did they bother? What was it that made corrupt foreign officials so intent on using U.S. banks? The short answer was that the United States offered just too much of a good thing. U.S. dollars maintained their value better than any other world currency and were accepted just about everywhere. U.S. banks were considered honest and secure. U.S. wire transfer systems were reliable, quick, and capable of sending cash to even the most remote locations. U.S. certificates of deposit and other investments produced good returns. And the United States was fun to visit. While London, Paris, Geneva, and a few other destinations were also favored, the fact is that U.S. cities— New York, Miami, Los Angeles—were wildly popular with the wealthy and corrupt. So keeping their money out of the U.S. financial system was an ongoing battle.

Laura Stuber, working mostly on her own with occasional assists from Bob and an ever-changing crew of detailees, interns, and law clerks, initiated a new investigation. Her objective was to find out how foreign officials were managing to sneak millions of dollars in suspect funds into the United States, despite greater AML vigilance by U.S. banks and their regulators. To get the answer, Laura identified troubling incidents, subpoenaed documents from banks and other sources, methodically traced suspect transactions, and interviewed key players. Slowly, she collected hair-raising stories exposing a host of new tactics.

I first became active in the investigation when Laura brought me the results of her many months of work. The case studies she'd developed involved politically powerful foreign officials or their family members, a group of persons often referred to internationally as "Politically Exposed Persons" or PEPs. Because PEPs perpetrated some of the worst corruption and money laundering abuses, international standards issued by the Financial Action Task Force on money laundering had long ago required banks opening accounts for PEPs to exercise enhanced due diligence and monitoring of those accounts. We'd incorporated those stronger PEP requirements in the AML law we'd enacted in 2001.[18]

The case studies developed by Laura showed, however, how foreign officials, their relatives, and associates were managing to circumvent even those stronger PEP controls. Most had sent suspect funds into the United States using the services of U.S. professionals, such as lawyers, real estate and escrow agents, who were generally exempt from AML obligations to know their customers, evaluate the source of their funds, and report suspicious activity to law enforcement. Instead, those U.S. professionals were free to deal with shady clients, dubious money, and suspicious transactions.

Laura realized—and got us to realize—how those foreign officials were stealthily spreading corruption across the face of the United States, tainting not only our financial system, but also multiple facets of American business and culture. It was time to fight back by exposing exactly what they were doing.[19] We presented the facts to Senator Levin and our ranking Republican at the time, Senator Tom Coburn, and both signaled their support for moving forward. We decided to feature four case studies.

Tracking Obiang

Perhaps the most notorious of the four case studies involved Teodoro Nguema Obiang Mangue, the 40-year-old son of the president of Equatorial Guinea whom we'd investigated in 2004 in connection with Riggs Bank.[20] The son was the EG Minister of Forestry, making him a foreign official and a PEP in his own right. He was also known as a playboy, spendthrift, and fearsome bully. He'd already attracted the attention of the U.S. Justice Department which was looking into rumors of extortion and other misconduct.

Due to the Patriot Act's tougher AML controls that made banks leery of dealing with foreign officials suspected of corruption, Mr. Obiang had experienced trouble opening U.S. bank accounts in his own name. So he'd turned to two California lawyers, Michael Jay Berger and George I. Nagler, for assistance. Although the two lawyers did not work together, they used similar tactics to help Mr. Obiang dodge the new AML controls.

First, each lawyer formed California corporations for Mr. Obiang, employing fanciful names like Beautiful Vision, Unlimited Horizon, and Sweetwater Malibu. Next, the lawyers opened bank accounts in the names of those corporations, identifying themselves as the corporations' officer or manager. They generally left out any mention of Mr. Obiang.

Once the corporate accounts were operational, Mr. Obiang supplied funds which the lawyers deposited and used to pay his bills. The funds supported a lavish lifestyle for Mr. Obiang that included designer clothes, high-end cars, extravagant travel arrangements, and all the other accouterments that go with being a rich jet-setter.

At first, Mr. Obiang wired the funds directly from Equatorial Guinea to the California corporate accounts his lawyers had opened, but when the banks began asking questions about money sent from that high-risk country, his lawyers switched tactics. Each allowed Mr. Obiang to wire money from Equatorial Guinea to the lawyer's own law office or attorney-client bank accounts, after which the lawyers wrote checks transferring the funds from their accounts to the corporate accounts. That two-step process broke the direct connection between Equatorial Guinea and the California companies, and avoided uncomfortable bank questions.

The documents showed that, even with that two-step funding process, the banks generally figured out the scam within a few months to a year. Their monitoring systems repeatedly flagged the huge sums going into and out of the corporate accounts, after which their AML analysts took a closer look. The analysts saw Mr. Obiang's name pop up on check references, credit card transactions, or bill payments. Once the analysts conducted an Internet search on Mr. Obiang and figured out who he was, the bank typically closed the account rather than do business with a high-risk foreign official notorious for corruption.

The account closures didn't seem to faze Mr. Obiang's lawyers; they simply stayed one step ahead, opening new accounts before the old ones closed. Our review found that, over a six-year period from 2001 to 2007, the lawyers managed to open 29 U.S. accounts on behalf of their client at seven different U.S. banks, both large and small. Altogether, those banks handled Obiang funds exceeding $90 million.[21]

The bulk of those funds went toward two luxury purchases which we examined in detail involving a $30 million mansion in Malibu, California and a $38 million Gulfstream jet built in Kansas. In both cases, Mr. Obiang's lawyers managed to complete the deals using suspect funds that U.S. real estate and escrow agents willingly accepted.

His lawyers shouldn't have been able to dodge U.S. AML safeguards so easily. For decades, U.S. laws had imposed AML obligations on real estate agents and on escrow agents who handle vehicle, ship, or aircraft sales, due to the large sums of money involved. In 2001, Title III of the Patriot Act went a step farther by explicitly requiring real estate and escrow professionals, among others, to set up AML programs.

But in 2002, the Treasury undermined the law by granting U.S. real estate and escrow agents a "temporary" exemption from the new AML program requirement.[22] The Treasury explained it first had to oversee the AML programs to be set up by banks, securities firms, and money service businesses and would get to the real estate and escrow agents later. But the Treasury never did. During the period in which Mr. Obiang made his purchases, from 2004 to 2006, the "temporary" exemption had already been on the books for years, with no signs of disappearing.

Mr. Obiang's lawyers took full advantage of that hole in the law. To purchase the Malibu mansion, one of the lawyers set up a shell company called Sweetwater Malibu Inc., and directed Mr. Obiang to wire transfer $30 million in the name of that company from Equatorial Guinea to a U.S. escrow account set up to handle the sale. Due to the Treasury exemption, neither the real estate agent nor its affiliated escrow firm had any legal obligation to look behind the shell company sending them money, so neither did.

The bank hosting the escrow account did have an AML program, but the law required the bank to evaluate only its own direct accountholder—the real estate company and its escrow affiliate, both of which were legitimate California businesses. The law did not require the bank to also evaluate the clients of its client. In the case of the Malibu mansion, the real estate company and its escrow affiliate accepted the funds sent from Equatorial Guinea, completed the sale, and pocketed the resulting lucrative commissions, with no questions asked.

Mr. Obiang's purchase of the $38 million Gulfstream jet was a little more complicated. To make that purchase, Mr. Obiang used a non-U.S. shell company called Ebony Shine International as the official buyer. The escrow agent responsible for completing the sale had a voluntary AML program in place and asked for information about who was behind the shell company and the source of its $38 million. When Ebony Shine declined to provide the information, the escrow agent pulled out of the deal and returned the money. But its action caused only a momentary glitch; another escrow agent quickly stepped in and completed the sale with no questions asked. As the second escrow agent later explained to PSI, it had no legal obligation to ask any questions, so it didn't. That the responsible escrow agent—the one with the voluntary AML program—lost out to a more reckless competitor was a deeper twist of the knife.

Between his lawyers, shell companies, and U.S. real estate and escrow agents willing to look the other way, Mr. Obiang managed to bring nearly $70 million in suspect funds into the United States to buy the Malibu mansion and jet. Along the way, he exerted a corrupting influence over the U.S. legal, real estate, and escrow professionals who facilitated his purchases. It was a dirty business.

Taking a Second Look at Bongo

The second case study involved Omar Bongo, Gabon's president, whom we'd investigated ten years earlier in connection with his accounts at Citibank private bank. Afterward, Citibank had closed his accounts and ceased doing business with him. But just like Mr. Obiang, that didn't mean Mr. Bongo was done with U.S. banks. Laura uncovered two startling instances of Mr. Bongo once more infiltrating the U.S. financial system, the first of which involved one of his daughters and the second a Washington lobbyist.[23]

The daughter, Yamilee Bongo-Astier, was then a student living in New York City, enrolled first at New York University and later at Parsons School of Design. We reviewed three bank accounts she'd opened during her student years at HSBC, Commerce Bank, and JPMorgan Chase, beginning in 2000. At the first two banks, records showed numerous high-dollar deposits, wire transfers, and withdrawals that made no sense for an unemployed student. Other records suggested Ms. Bongo-Astier was using funds sent to her from Gabon to purchase automobiles for senior Gabon officials, presumably at the direction of her father. Essentially, her father was using his daughter's bank accounts to circumvent AML controls that had made it hard for him to open his own U.S. accounts and transfer funds from Gabon into the United States.

Even more troubling was a 2007 incident that showed Mr. Bongo was also using his daughter's account to circumvent U.S. controls on cash brought across U.S. borders. In 2003, after a high-dollar transaction triggered closure of her bank account at HSBC, Ms. Bongo opened a new bank account at Commerce Bank in Manhattan. At the time of the account opening, she did not disclose her relationship to President Bongo. In 2005, however, a bank review of two large cash transactions affecting her account led to the bank's learning about her father. An internal bank memo noted that she had no job, "[h]er only source of income [was] from her father," the Gabon president, and the large deposits to her account "coincide[d] with the arrival of her father when he [came] to the United States for official purposes. On other occasions cash [was] sent by her father through Gabon emissaries."

The bank decided to treat Ms. Bongo-Astier as a PEP and enhance its monitoring of her account, but asked no questions about the source of Mr. Bongo's funds. For the next two years, the bank continued to allow her to deposit and withdraw large sums, including wire transfers depositing funds sent from high-risk countries.

In 2007, Ms. Bongo-Astier took steps to purchase a $2 million condominium in Manhattan. In October, she visited the bank, asked it to deposit funds stored in her two safe deposit boxes, and send a $200,000 cashier's check to a real estate escrow agent to secure the purchase. In response, bank personnel opened her safe deposit boxes and found a collection of $100 bills wrapped in plastic. When counted, they totaled $1 million. The bank told PSI it had been unaware of the cash until then. When the bank asked about the source of the funds, Ms. Bongo-Astier explained that her father had brought her the money when he'd visited the month before, and would wire additional funds to her account to complete the real estate purchase.

The bank issued the $200,000 cashier's check and deposited the remaining $800,000 as requested, but a flurry of internal bank meetings, emails, and memos followed. A senior AML officer noted that the $1 million was far in excess of the funds normally in her account, and observed that President Bongo had been accused of being "involved with buying property in France with embezzled funds." A few days later, the AML officer reported that law enforcement had informed him that Mr. Bongo had failed to declare the $1 million he'd brought into the United States as required by law. The AML officer nonetheless recommended keeping the account open, since despite "numerous accusations and allegations," no formal criminal charges had ever been levied against the father or daughter in any country.

A month later, Commerce Bank decided to close the account anyway, due to concerns about the source of Mr. Bongo's wealth. Around the same time, it blocked and returned a $1 million wire transfer from Mr. Bongo to his daughter. Although the bank documents didn't say so, the fact that Mr. Bongo's daughter was buying New York real estate with her father's funds may have created an uncomfortable parallel with the French allegations about his buying property in France using misappropriated money.

The closing of the Commerce account caused little inconvenience to Ms. Bongo-Astier, who opened a new account at a JPMorgan Chase branch down the street. When opening the account, she again failed to disclose her relationship with her father. She deposited the $800,000 into the new account, made no new deposits, and slowly drew down the funds over the following few years. JPMorgan told PSI that the bank had seen no suspicious transactions involving the account and only learned of her PEP status when the subcommittee disclosed it.

Ms. Bongo-Astier proved to be as uncommunicative with PSI as she was with her U.S. banks. At one point, Laura called a cell phone number identified in the bank records in an attempt to reach Ms. Bongo-Astier and get her side of the story. Ms. Bongo-Astier answered. When Laura explained why she was calling and that she'd like to set up an interview, Ms. Bongo-Astier responded angrily, "Do you know who I am?" A strange question, since that was exactly why Laura was calling her. Through her legal counsel, Ms. Bongo-Astier declined to answer any questions about her accounts.

The second incident Laura uncovered in connection with President Bongo was equally disturbing. It involved his managing to get a Washington lobbyist to funnel millions of dollars for him through the lobbyist's own U.S. bank accounts. Bob helped dig out the facts.

Jeffrey C. Birrell, a U.S. citizen living in the Washington, D.C. area, was a registered lobbyist for Gabon. From 2003 until at least 2007, he worked on at least two Gabon projects, one involving the purchase and transport of several U.S.-made armored vehicles to Gabon, and the other seeking U.S. government permission for Gabon to buy six C-130 military cargo aircraft from Saudi Arabia, aircraft that could not be purchased without U.S. consent.

The first project was successful; the second was not. In the course of working on both, Mr. Birrell accepted wire transfers from Gabon totaling more than $18 million. He deposited the funds at a small Maryland bank where Mr. Birrell had several accounts in the name of his lobbying business. Part of the money came from President Bongo's personal account in Gabon, but most of the $18 million came from an account opened in the name of a mysterious Gabon entity called "Ayira." We never learned whether Ayira was a Gabon corporation or some other legal entity. The Maryland bank told us it had accepted the wire transfers with no questions asked, because Mr. Birrell was a longstanding, trusted customer.

At President Bongo's direction, Mr. Birrell spent part of the Gabon funds on the armored car and aircraft projects, including wiring more than $1 million to various "consultants" around the world and $4 million to a Bongo advisor with accounts in Brussels and Paris. The documents did not indicate what the money was for, but raised obvious red flags about possible payoffs. Mr. Birrell told us he'd never asked about the purpose of the wire transfers he'd facilitated.

When the second project fell through, Mr. Birrell, at the Bongo regime's direction, wired the $9 million remaining in his account to an account in President Bongo's name located not in Gabon, but in Malta.

In short, Mr. Birrell's corporate bank accounts served as conduits for multi-million-dollar suspicious wire transfers directed by President Bongo without Mr. Bongo's having to undergo any U.S. AML reviews. Instead, Mr. Birrell had enabled Mr. Bongo to wire millions of dollars in suspect funds into and out of the United States and around the globe, with no questions asked.

Examining Angola

The third case study Laura developed was as wild as the first two. It involved bank accounts and transactions associated with Angola, another African country battling corruption.[24] The evidence portrayed three separate incidents showing how Angolan PEPs had managed to send millions of dollars in suspect funds into the United States.

The first involved a notorious international arms dealer, Pierre Falcone, who supplied weapons during Angola's civil war in violation of a U.N. arms embargo. What Laura discovered was that, for a period of 18 years from 1989 to 2007, a Bank of America branch in Scottsdale, Arizona had supplied Mr. Falcone with more than 30 accounts and allowed a torrent of suspicious transactions to fly through them without asking any questions about the transactions.

Bank records showed Mr. Falcone had never hidden his career as an arms dealer from the bank. Public records also showed he had a long history of run-ins with the law. For example, media articles showed he'd been incarcerated for a year in France in 2000, was a fugitive from a 2004 arrest warrant, and at the time of our inquiry, was serving a six-year prison term in France.

Despite those facts, Bank of America had failed to subject his accounts to any heightened scrutiny. In addition, the bank never treated him as a PEP despite his status as an Angolan ambassador, and never designated his accounts as high risk despite numerous suspicious transactions involving substantial sums of offshore money. When confronted, Bank of America did not try to defend its actions; it closed the accounts and apologized for giving Mr. Falcone unfettered access to the U.S. financial system for nearly two decades.

Bank of America wasn't the only bank to have accommodated Angolan-related accounts that raised red flags. For over a decade, HSBC provided U.S. accounts and services to Banco Africano de Investimentos (BAI), a $7 billion Angolan private bank that catered to Angola's state-owned oil company, senior Angolan officials, and their family members and associates. Despite multiple PEPs in BAI's management and clientele, and its association with a high-risk country known for corruption, HSBC never subjected the BAI account to enhanced scrutiny. Nor did HSBC boost its monitoring after BAI repeatedly declined to identify its owners or provide a copy of its AML procedures. Instead, HSBC continued to provide BAI and its clients with ready access to the U.S. financial system, facilitating transactions involving millions of dollars.

The third incident was the strangest of the three. It involved the head of the Central Bank of Angola, Dr. Aguinaldo Jaime, who twice attempted to transfer $50 million in Angolan funds from a Central Bank account at Citibank London to accounts in the United States. The funding transfer was characterized at the time as intended to support an investment to produce humanitarian aid for the people of Angola, but other documents indicated it was part of a fraudulent "prime bank" investment scheme that may have led to the funds being lost or stolen.

The first attempt to transfer the $50 million failed when Bank of America flagged the transfer as suspicious, returned the funds to the Central Bank's account in London, and closed the California account that was supposed to have received the funds. The second attempt successfully transferred the government funds to a new personal account at HSBC in New York City, opened by Dr. Jaime who served as the sole signatory. He then instructed HSBC to use the funds to purchase $50 million in U.S. Treasury bills, which HSBC did. Next, he instructed HSBC to transfer the Treasury bills to a Wells Fargo securities account in the name of Jan Morton Heger, a California attorney. When Wells Fargo blocked the transfer as suspicious, Dr. Jaime directed HSBC to instead transfer the Treasury bills to a Heger law office account at Comerica Bank. HSBC tried, but the transfer failed due to an incorrect account number.

After the two failed transfers, HSBC continued to house the $50 million in Angolan Central Bank Treasury bills in the personal account opened by Dr. Jaime. He then informed HSBC that he'd be willing to keep the Treasury bills in the account, if the bank were to provide him with a "receipt" that he could use to transfer their ownership to a third party. HSBC initially agreed, but after internal memos flagged the request as highly unusual and suspicious, HSBC did not actually provide the "receipt." Soon after, Dr. Jaime took a new post outside of the Angolan Central Bank. Upon his departure, other Angolan Central Bank officials liquidated the Treasury bills and returned the $50 million to the Central Bank's account at Citibank London.

This stunning series of events was riddled with signs of fraud and corruption. As a result, Citibank conducted an internal review and decided Angola, as a whole, was too high risk to handle. In 2003, Citibank closed all of its Angolan-related accounts, shut down its Angolan branch, and ended the entire relationship. HSBC, however, took no similar action.

As part of the PSI inquiry into the Angolan matters, we set up a meeting with the Angolan embassy to see if it had any information it wished to convey to us. After presenting what we'd found and sharing some of the key documents, we were met by a lengthy silence from the embassy personnel. The officials present then denied knowing anything about the incidents involving the former Central Bank head, BAI private bank, or the arms dealer Pierre Falcone. As so often happened in our investigations, we found ourselves providing information to parties that should have already known the facts we'd uncovered, but claimed they did not.

Examining Nigeria

The fourth and final case study compiled by Laura involved the former vice president of Nigeria, Atiku Abubakar, who held that office from 1999 to 2007, and his fourth wife, Jennifer Douglas.[25] Bank records showed that, from 2000 to 2008, Ms. Douglas helped her husband bring over $40 million in suspect funds into the United States, depositing some of the money in a succession of U.S. bank accounts and wiring the rest to a U.S. university fully cognizant of Nigeria's longstanding corruption problem.

Prior to becoming vice president of Nigeria, Mr. Abubakar traveled to the United States, settled for a few years in the Washington, D.C. area and, in 2003, married Jennifer ("Jamila") Douglas, a naturalized U.S. citizen who was born in Nigeria and knew Mr. Abubakar while there. At the time of marriage, Ms. Douglas was a graduate student at American University.

While in the United States, Mr. Abubakar became a supporter of American University, donating $1 million through his wife to the school. The source of his wealth, then and later, was unclear, but was allegedly tied to business activities he undertook during and after his 20-year career as a Nigerian customs official (prior to running for office). Mr. Abubakar also invited the university to open an affiliated branch in his hometown of Yola, Nigeria. Already operating branches in other countries, the university agreed if Mr. Abubakar were to provide the funds. The university made that offer despite frank internal discussions about Nigeria's corruption problems.

Mr. Abubakar agreed to provide the financing. Bank records showed Ms. Douglas using multiple U.S. bank accounts to pay the expenses associated with constructing the American University branch in Nigeria as well as to support her own lavish lifestyle. The funds she deposited into her accounts came from large wire transfers supplied by offshore corporations with unusual names including LetsGo Ltd. Inc., Guernsey Trust Company Nigeria Ltd., and Sima Holding Ltd. The banks accepted the wire transfers despite having no information about the corporations supplying the funds.

Over time, however, each bank began asking questions about those offshore entities. When Ms. Douglas professed to have no information about them, one bank after another began closing her accounts. In response, Ms. Douglas, with the help of her U.S. lawyer, opened new accounts. Altogether, she deposited nearly $25 million in a succession of 30 U.S. accounts at multiple banks. In addition, her lawyer accepted $3.4 million from the same offshore firms to pay various legal bills and help fund American University's Nigerian branch.

In 2008, the German firm Siemens AG pled guilty to violating the U.S. Foreign Corrupt Practices Act and paid fines totaling $1.6 billion. It admitted, among other matters, to sending $2.8 million in bribes to a U.S. account in the name of Ms. Douglas as part of a scheme to bribe Nigerian officials.[26] By then, Ms. Douglas had moved to the United Arab Emirates and was working as a professor at an American University branch there. She denied all wrongdoing. Our investigation located, however, Siemens wire transfers which had deposited a total of $1.7 million into one of her U.S. bank accounts. We also learned that Mr. Abubakar, during his term as vice president of Nigeria, had been the subject of other corruption allegations.

On top of that, we identified $14 million in offshore funds that had been wired to American University by LetsGo, Guernsey Trust Company, and Sima Holding from places like Chile and Panama. The funds had paid fees charged by the university to develop the Nigerian branch. The university had accepted the offshore payments despite having no information about the corporations sending the money or why the funds were being sent from Latin America.

With some digging, we discovered that all three offshore corporations were associated with Gabriele Volpi, an Italian billionaire who was also a business partner and friend of Mr. Abubakar. But the source of the corporate funds remained unclear. An unapologetic American University informed PSI that it had not inquired into either the offshore corporations or the source of the offshore funds, because it had no legal obligation to do so.

Altogether, the evidence suggested Mr. Abubakar had orchestrated the transfer of funds into the United States through accounts belonging to his wife and her lawyer, and through wire transfers to American University, none of whom questioned the offshore money they'd received. The source of the offshore funds, as well as Mr. Abubakar's wealth generally, remained unclear.

By the end of the PSI investigation into the four case studies, we'd reviewed millions of pages of documents, conducted more than 100 interviews, and traced millions of dollars in suspicious transactions. Senators Levin and Coburn were ready to take the information public.

Going Public

In February 2010, PSI held a hearing and released a 330-page bipartisan staff report entitled, "Keeping Corruption Out of the United States: Four Case Histories." The Levin-Coburn report used the case studies to illustrate how foreign officials from Equatorial Guinea, Gabon, Angola, and Nigeria had successfully brought suspect funds into the United States, bypassing stronger U.S. AML controls.

The report showed how most of the U.S. professionals who helped bring the suspect cash into the United States, including lawyers, real estate and escrow agents, lobbyists, and university development officers, were exempt from U.S. AML laws requiring U.S. persons to know who they are dealing with, evaluate the source of the funds sent to them, and report suspicious activity to law enforcement. The report offered a number of bipartisan recommendations to help keep foreign corruption out of the United States, including by revoking the 2002 AML exemption granted by the Treasury to otherwise covered persons, extending AML controls to more U.S. professions, stopping the formation of U.S. shell corporations with hidden owners, and tightening AML controls on shell company and law office accounts.

The hearing took testimony from three panels of witnesses. The first panel called the two lawyers who'd helped Teodoro Obiang set up shell corporations in California, open accounts at California banks, and purchase the Malibu mansion and Gulfstream jet with suspect funds. They were joined by the lobbyist who'd deposited $18 million from Gabon into his corporate bank accounts and then distributed the funds to accounts around the world at the direction of President Bongo. All three asserted their Fifth Amendment rights against self-incrimination.

When hearing witnesses informed PSI that they planned to assert their Fifth Amendment rights, we typically met with their legal counsel to discuss what would happen at the hearing when their clients were called. We told them that the PSI chair would ask each client two or three questions, and if the client asserted a Constitutional right not to answer each one, the client would be excused from the hearing. We were also very clear that if the client began testifying about any matters, then we would consider them to have waived their Constitutional rights. The point of laying out those ground rules ahead of time was to avoid the situation where a witness asserted a Fifth Amendment right not to testify, but then began testifying anyway, opening up a Pandora's box of legal issues that can quickly lead to a court battle.

Over the years, many individuals had asserted their Fifth Amendment rights at PSI hearings without incident, but Michael Berger, one of the Obiang attorneys, broke the pattern. After asserting his right not to answer questions, Mr. Berger began offering comments on various issues. Using a script we'd prepared beforehand in case the unexpected happened, Senator Levin immediately stopped him and said that if he were willing to testify, he'd first have to undergo a deposition directly after the hearing. We didn't, after all, want to hear what he had to say for the first time in a public setting. Mr. Berger stopped short, consulted his counsel, and stated that he wouldn't offer any further comments. Like the others, he was excused from the hearing and left.

The second panel took testimony from the U.S. real estate agent, Neal Baddin, who'd helped Mr. Obiang purchase the $30 million mansion in Malibu; the escrow agent, Insured Aircraft Title Services (IATS), who'd completed the jet purchase; and two banks that had facilitated other suspect transactions. Both Mr. Baddin and IATS testified that they were exempt from U.S. AML obligations and so had no legal duty to inquire into the funds supplied to them. Both also testified that, if the law had required their firms to take AML precautions, they would have complied with the law. The two banks were Bank of America and HSBC. Bank of America expressed regret for having provided banking services to Pierre Falcone, the arms dealer. In contrast, HSBC defended providing accounts to the Angolan private bank and the Angolan Central Bank head. It denied any wrongdoing, a denial we would remember later.

The final panel heard from three federal agencies, the Departments of the Treasury, State, and Homeland Security. All three expressed concern about foreign persons fostering corruption in the United States and expressed support for reforms to stop the wrongdoing.

Making Slow Progress

Although PSI's 2010 investigation generated widespread negative press about the ongoing vulnerability of the U.S. financial system to corruption and elicited commitments from U.S. regulators to do more, actually strengthening the country's AML defenses to stop the new round of abuses proved difficult.

American banks had already stepped up their efforts to detect and stop dirty money, and were in no mood to add AML controls to accounts opened by lawyers, real estate agents, or escrow firms. In addition, few in the law, real estate, lobbying, or university fields were willing to admit to an AML problem. While some U.S. groups initiated some half-hearted reforms, they fell far short of the progress being made in the rest of the world.

For example, after the February 2010 hearing, the American Bar Association took action at its annual 2010 conference in August to approve a voluntary set of AML "best practices" for U.S. lawyers.[27] In 2014, the ABA took another step by issuing AML guidance to its members.[28] While the resulting ABA best practice and guidance documents were well done, nothing was made mandatory, and U.S. lawyers remained free to ignore them both. In contrast, the

European Union issued a directive—first in 1991 and again in 2005—requiring all 28 of its member countries to impose legally binding AML obligations on lawyers.[29] Today, EU lawyers, when acting in an administrative capacity rather than dispensing legal advice, are required to know their customers and evaluate their funding sources. Nothing comparable is even being contemplated in the United States. That's true even after, in 2016, a dozen New York law firms were filmed in a money laundering sting showing them apparently ready and willing to facilitate schemes concocted by foreign officials to launder suspect funds.[30]

AML reforms in the real estate and escrow industries have been equally slow-moving. Despite widespread abuses, the Treasury has maintained the "temporary" exemption excusing real estate and escrow agents from the law requiring them to establish AML programs. After a parade of indictments and articles on money laundering through real estate cranked up pressure on the agency, in 2016, the Treasury issued some "geographic targeting orders" to gather more data about what was going on, but still made no concrete move to repeal the AML exemption.[31] In the meantime, in 2012, the National Association of Realtors issued its own voluntary AML guidance for real estate professionals, but like the guidance for lawyers, made nothing mandatory.[32]

The lobbying community turned in an even more dismal performance, failing to issue even voluntary AML guidance for its members. Instead, the key trade association, the American League of Lobbyists—later renamed the Association of Government Relations Professionals—issued a code of ethics that omitted any mention of AML concerns.[33] In the university world, while some U.K. universities—spurred by U.K. legal requirements—issued AML guidance, U.S. universities as a whole continued to avert their eyes from the issue and pretend it didn't exist.[34]

Worse than those professions was the reaction of many state officials. Our 50 states together form nearly two million corporations a year, more than the rest of the world put together, but currently obtain no information on who is behind the companies they form. The PSI investigation demonstrated how U.S. corporations with hidden owners were being used by corrupt foreign officials to open U.S. bank accounts, move suspect funds into the United States, and use dirty money to purchase real estate, aircraft, armored vehicles, and more. In other hearings, we'd showed how anonymous U.S. companies were also being misused to advance terrorist financing, drug trafficking, health care fraud, and other wrongdoing.[35]

To clamp down on those abuses, in 2008, Senator Levin introduced a bill with Senators Coleman and Obama to require U.S. states to ask those seeking to form U.S. companies to provide the names of the persons who would control or benefit from those corporations—the so-called beneficial owners.[36] The bill should have been a no-brainer given the track record of anonymous U.S. corporations fueling crime and law enforcement's strong support for the bill. But the National Association of the Secretaries of State—which represented states making millions from incorporation services—opposed the bill. So did the American Bar Association and Chamber of Commerce, so the bill went nowhere. Later, Senator Chuck Grassley became the bill's lead Republican cosponsor, but the Levin-Grassley bill continued to stall.

In contrast, the European Union tackled the issue head on, taking multiple steps to strengthen corporate transparency. In 2015, the EU issued a directive requiring its member states to begin collecting beneficial ownership information for the corporations they formed, placing that information in a central corporate registry, and making it available to persons with a "legitimate interest" such as law enforcement.[37] Some countries, like the United Kingdom, Norway, and Ukraine, took the next step and made the registry information available to the public, so that anyone could find out the names of a company's true owners. Those reforms not only unnerved the offshore world, dismayed the corrupt, and struck a powerful blow for corporate transparency, they also left the United States in the dust.

As more countries prohibit forming corporations with hidden owners, the danger is that terrorists, criminals, and other wrongdoers looking for a place to hide will increasingly turn to the United States where it is still easy to form a corporation without saying who is behind it. For that reason, members of Congress in both the House and Senate have continued a bipartisan effort to enact a U.S. corporate transparency bill.

Exposing Misconduct at a Global Bank—HSBC

The final AML investigation during the Levin years was perhaps the most explosive.[38] It featured a global bank, HSBC, and revealed a rat's nest of improper conduct at the bank that shocked even our cynical ranks and led to another major ratcheting up of U.S. AML efforts.

HSBC had already caught PSI's attention after HSBC accounts repeatedly surfaced in our AML investigations, and several sources suggested all was not right with the bank's AML program. Then, six months after our foreign corruption hearing, HSBC's primary U.S. regulator, the OCC, issued a blistering supervisory letter criticizing HSBC's AML program for a full 31 pages. A related OCC cease and desist order essentially demanded that HSBC revamp its entire AML program. When we asked Senator Levin if we could find out what prompted that blast at the bank, he agreed. Senator Coburn was equally supportive. Neither blinked an eye at taking on one of the most powerful financial institutions in the world.

Getting Started

To get started, we contacted HSBC and two of its U.S. regulators, the OCC and Federal Reserve, and asked about the basis for the consent order. We followed up with detailed document requests. The regulators, who knew us from prior investigations, agreed to provide copies of their HSBC examination reports, workpapers, and internal memos, as well as copies of internal HSBC documents they'd collected. They also turned over key emails involving their AML specialists, the larger examination teams, and the bank.

HSBC was equally cooperative, in part because HSBC was already in hot water with its regulators and couldn't afford to look like it was obstructing Congress. In response to a PSI subpoena, HSBC provided extensive documents, including internal audit reports, analytical memos, bank records, and certain email. HSBC also gave us access to an array of non-U.S. documents, some of which had been collected by outside legal counsel under an arrangement with the Justice Department. Those non-U.S. documents turned out to be critical to understanding the bank's AML track record.

We collected additional materials from HSBC clients and correspondent banks, court cases, and other U.S. and foreign regulators. We interviewed a broad spectrum of individuals with first-hand information about the bank including senior and mid-level HSBC managers, as well as multiple AML, banking, and other experts. By the end of the investigation, we'd compiled 1.4 million pages of relevant materials and conducted 75 interviews.

Getting to Know HSBC

As we dug deep into the facts, we learned just how big HSBC was. Often described as the fifth largest bank in the world, HSBC's stats included $2.5 trillion in assets, 89 million customers worldwide, 7200 offices in more than 80 countries, and 300,000 employees. Begun as a British bank in China in 1865, HSBC's initials once stood for Hong Kong Shanghai Banking Corporation. By 2011, HSBC had its headquarters in London, but located its chief executive officer on the opposite side of the world in Hong Kong.

We learned that HSBC first entered the U.S. market in the 1980s, when it purchased several mid-sized U.S. banks. By 2011, it had 470 U.S. branches across the country with four million U.S. customers. More than that, HSBC Bank USA—HBUS—had become the U.S. nexus for the entire HSBC worldwide network. For example, of the more than 600,000 wire transfers that HBUS processed each week, two-thirds of the U.S. dollar transfers involved HSBC affiliates in other countries. One HSBC executive told the subcommittee that the main reason HSBC entered the U.S. market was not to compete for U.S. customers, but to provide a gateway for its overseas clients into the U.S. financial system.

Those clients included hundreds of banks around the world, including high-risk banks in remote regions of Asia, Africa, and the Middle East. We learned that, by 2010, HBUS had a total of 2400 bank clients, including the 80 HSBC affiliates. We also learned that HBUS provided a wide array of services to its bank clients, including U.S. wire transfers, U.S. monetary instruments like travelers checks and money orders, U.S. investment options, U.S. currency exchange, and physical U.S. dollars—called banknotes—that could be shipped abroad.

The materials we reviewed on HBUS' AML program were downright scary. Its AML efforts included dealing with numerous high-risk countries, rife with terrorist and criminal threats, as well as myriad high-risk clients and transactions. Over a five-year period, HBUS had run through five AML directors trying to deal with the issues. As one AML director who quit after less than a year put it, HBUS had an "extremely high risk business model from [an] AML perspective," insufficient staff to manage the risk, and generally "[o]perate[d] under 'crisis' mode." In 2010, he wrote to a senior HBUS compliance official: "With every passing day I become more concerned … if that's even possible."

HBUS' AML deficiencies, as described in the OCC's 31-page supervisory letter, were longstanding and widespread. They included a backlog of 17,000 alerts of suspicious activity that no one had investigated, and a failure to monitor $60 trillion in supposedly low-risk wire transfers using a risk rating system flawed by inappropriate and inconsistently applied risk factors. The problems also included a three-year failure by the bank to monitor billions of dollars in bulk cash transactions with HSBC affiliates, troubling transactions in the bank's embassy banking and travelers check processing units, and a failure to conduct any due diligence reviews of HSBC affiliates with U.S. accounts. On top of that were inadequate AML staffing and resources and unqualified personnel in AML leadership positions. With so many deep-seated problems, a key initial question was where to focus our efforts.

Honing in on Five Issues

To figure that out, we dug into the documents, reviewing audits, bank exams, memos, and emails describing the bank's AML deficiencies. We followed up with day-long interviews of key AML bank examiners, their superiors, and enforcement lawyers, as well as HSBC bankers, auditors, and compliance personnel. As we gathered information, we began to hone in on five issues illustrating not only HBUS' AML shortfalls, but also key AML vulnerabilities that applied to all global banks with U.S. branches.

The first of the five issues focused on HBUS' practice of opening U.S. accounts for high-risk HSBC affiliates without any due diligence review of the affiliates' clients, products, or operations. HSBC's worldwide policy was that all HSBC affiliates were on the same team, so every affiliate had to service every other affiliate with no questions asked. But that approach didn't jibe with U.S. law which required U.S. banks to conduct an AML due diligence review of every foreign bank seeking to open a U.S. account and to monitor any high-risk accounts to detect and prevent money laundering.[39] U.S. law made no exception for foreign affiliates.

To illustrate the AML dangers inherent in HSBC's approach, we zeroed in on a U.S. account opened for an HSBC affiliate in Mexico known as HBMX. Documents showed that in 2002, when HSBC purchased the Mexican bank that became HBMX, it knew the Mexican bank had "no recognizable compliance or money laundering function." In addition, the documents showed, despite years of effort, HSBC had failed to strengthen HBMX's AML culture, and HBMX's workforce continued to disregard required AML controls.

The problems included HBMX's opening over 50,000 accounts at a Cayman Island branch (which had no physical existence) for clients who deposited $2 billion while providing, in many cases, no information on who owned the assets. Some accounts were later linked to drug trafficking. At one point, HSBC's top Mexican AML officer referred to allegations that "60%–70% of laundered proceeds" in Mexico by drug cartels went through HBMX.

High-risk HBMX clients included a casa de cambio caught with drug proceeds at another bank and a chemical company CEO whose house, when raided by Mexican law enforcement, had $225 million in cash in a secret room. Still another problem: HBMX sent $7 billion in physical U.S. dollars over a two-year period from Mexico to HBUS, a volume exceeding every other Mexican bank and HSBC affiliate in the world. Law enforcement warned HBUS the total likely included drug money, and HBUS later admitted handling $880 million in drug proceeds.[40]

Bank documents also showed that, for ten years, HSBC's compliance head-quarters in London knew all about HBMX's severe AML deficiencies, but failed to alert HBUS, even though HBUS was providing HBMX with free entry into the U.S. financial system. It was a classic case of a U.S. affiliate being abused by both its parent and a non-U.S. affiliate.

The second issue we highlighted revolved around U.S. efforts to stop U.S. banks from doing business with the worst of the worst—terrorists, drug king-pins, persons involved with weapons of mass destruction, and rogue regimes like Iran, North Korea, and Sudan. To block that activity, the Treasury Department's Office of Foreign Assets Control (OFAC) had developed a list of prohibited persons and required U.S. banks to install an "OFAC filter" to halt transactions involving them. Transactions stopped by an OFAC filter had to undergo individualized reviews to see if a prohibited person were involved and, if so, to block them.

We found HBUS had processed a slew of OFAC-sensitive transactions without doing the individualized reviews, primarily because HSBC affiliates had stripped out information indicating prohibited persons were involved. Two HSBC affiliates in Europe and the Middle East had been the worst, hiding the participation of Iranians in at least 25,000 transactions involving over $19 billion. Another 3000 transactions involved such prohibited countries as North Korea and Sudan. One set of transactions even involved the Afghan National Credit & Finance Ltd., a bank set up to serve the Taliban.

Another disturbing example involved a wealthy Syrian, Rami Makhlouf. In 2008, OFAC added him to the list of prohibited persons due to his involvement with corruption. When OFAC asked HBUS if it had any Makhlouf accounts, HBUS replied it didn't, even though it knew an HSBC affiliate in the Cayman Islands had a trust account whose beneficiary was Mr. Makhlouf. The Cayman affiliate had told HBUS it tried to close the account in 2007, but was overruled by HSBC headquarters. HBUS failed to disclose the account to OFAC, even though HBUS serviced the Cayman affiliate. Concealment of the account showed HBUS hadn't truly accepted its legal obligation to keep the worst of the worst out of the U.S. financial system.

The third issue we developed involved HBUS' servicing foreign banks which its own personnel viewed as having possible links to terrorist financing. An example was Al Rajhi Bank, Saudi Arabia's largest private bank. The bank was owned by a group of Saudi brothers, the most senior of whom gained notoriety when disclosed as a member of the "Golden Chain" of early contributors to Al Qaeda. That same brother also set up a charity, the SAAR Foundation, whose U.S. holdings were raided by U.S. law enforcement on suspicion of supporting terrorism. On another occasion, U.S. law enforcement indicted an individual who'd cashed $130,000 in U.S. travelers checks at Al Rajhi Bank and used the funds to support terrorists in Chechnya. When U.S. prosecutors asked the bank to provide authenticated records for the criminal trial, the bank refused. On top of that, a classified CIA report described in a New York Times article claimed the bank knew terrorists were using its accounts. All that, while U.S. terrorism experts described Saudi Arabia as providing more terrorist financing than any other country.

In 2005, because of its terrorist financing concerns, HBUS decided to stop doing business with Al Rajhi Bank. Other HSBC affiliates, however, continued servicing the bank and even began pressing HBUS to restore Al Rajhi's access to U.S. banknotes. Two years later, after Al Rajhi Bank threatened to cut off all business worldwide with HSBC unless its U.S. banknotes account was restored, HBUS re-opened that account. For the next four years from 2007 to 2010, HBUS supplied Al Rajhi Bank with $1 billion in physical U.S. dollars. HBUS stopped only after HSBC decided the entire bank would exit the U.S. banknotes business.

The fourth issue we identified involved HBUS' clearing $290 million in U.S. dollar travelers checks for Hokuriku Bank in Japan under suspicious circumstances. The problem came to light when OCC AML examiners visited an HBUS office in New York and stumbled across stacks of $500 and $1000 travelers checks with sequential numbers and the same illegible signature. HBUS admitted clearing up to $500,000 per day in travelers checks for Hokuriku Bank. When asked about them, Hokuriku claimed the checks were deposited by used car businesses in rural Japan, but also admitted having little to no information about the accountholders. A little sleuthing discovered that all of the checks were being issued by the same bank in Russia and sold to the same Russian who was signing and shipping them to Japan. The facts shouted money laundering, but HBUS closed the Hokuriku account only after pressure from the OCC.

The fifth and final issue involved HBUS' maintaining 2000 high-risk U.S. bearer-share corporate accounts with $2.6 billion in assets. Bearer-share corporations enable anyone who holds a company's physical shares to claim ownership of the company, without recording an ownership stake in any government registry. The result: no one knows who owns the company unless they know who has possession of its physical shares. Widely condemned for facilitating money laundering, tax evasion, and crime, most banks won't touch bearer-share corporations. Yet HBUS maintained 2000 bearer-share accounts at its New York, Miami, and Los Angeles branches. It was another blatant indicator of the bank's high-risk profile.

OCC Failings

HSBC's across-the-board AML deficiencies had built up for years without the OCC's forcing the bank to clean up its act. Records showed OCC AML examiners had repeatedly documented the AML problems at HBUS, but were unable to convince any OCC higher-up to take formal or informal enforcement action to compel the bank to change its ways. The OCC's enforcement failure at HSBC mirrored its inaction at Riggs Bank back in 2004, but this time exposed the U.S. financial system to billions of dollars in suspect transactions.

In 2010, when the OCC finally decided to clamp down on HBUS' AML deficiencies, one key enforcement action it took was to lower HBUS' consumer compliance rating instead of its safety and soundness rating. What does money laundering have to do with how a bank meets its obligations to consumers? Nothing. Which was why every bank regulator other than the OCC treated AML deficiencies as a management failure affecting a bank's safety and soundness rating, not its consumer compliance rating. The OCC's weaker approach failed to pack any punch.

Going Public

In July 2012, PSI held its HSBC hearing and released a 400-page Levin-Coburn report laying out what we'd found. Following our standard practice, we held a press briefing the day before the hearing. It led to worldwide negative press on the morning of the hearing describing HSBC's misconduct and the OCC's regulatory failures. At the hearing itself, the two senators grilled the witnesses about HSBC's AML fiasco.

Four panels of witnesses testified. The second panel was the big one. It consisted of a half dozen senior bank officials from HSBC headquarters in London and HBUS offices in New York. The witnesses included, among others, Stuart Levey, HSBC's chief legal officer; David Bagley, HSBC's compliance head; and Irene Dorner, HBUS' CEO. Essentially, the bank admitted fault, expressed regret for its AML shortcomings, and described actions it was taking to improve. In a surprise announcement, Mr. Bagley, longtime head of HSBC compliance in London, apologized and resigned from his leadership post (though not from the bank).

The third panel heard from OCC officials who apologized for taking so long to confront HSBC's AML deficiencies and outlined actions being taken to compel bank reforms. The new head of the OCC, Tom Curry, who had just taken office, went farther. He announced that, in line with the Levin-Coburn report recommendations, the OCC was revamping its AML procedures. Most importantly, the OCC would no longer treat AML deficiencies as a consumer compliance problem, but as a management failure affecting a bank's overall safety and soundness rating. In one dramatic stroke, Mr. Curry changed 20-plus years of OCC AML practice for the better.

Stopping the Abuses

After the hearing, both the OCC and HSBC instituted major reforms. The HSBC changes included boosting HBUS' compliance staff from 130 to over 1000 U.S. compliance officers, increasing the U.S. annual compliance budget ninefold to about $250 million, closing over 300 high-risk bank and embassy accounts, upgrading its risk assessment systems, strengthening its wire transfer monitoring, eliminating the 17,000 alerts backlog, and imposing AML due diligence and information-sharing requirements on all HSBC affiliates. In addition, HSBC strengthened its global compliance office by giving it hiring and management authority over all 3500 compliance officers worldwide, authorizing global AML and compliance standards, and empowering it to order the closure of specific accounts.

While important, those reforms did not excuse the bank's years of misconduct. In 2013, HSBC and HBUS entered into a deferred prosecution agreement with the Justice Department, admitted wrongdoing, and paid a criminal fine of $1.9 billion.[41] A House committee later discovered that DOJ line prosecutors had wanted to indict the bank.[42] U.S. bank regulators had signaled support, but the U.K. financial regulator had fought hard against it, claiming an indictment would disrupt financial markets worldwide. In the end, Attorney General Eric Holder and Criminal Division head Lanny Breuer went with the deferred prosecution instead of an indictment. They also chose not to indict any individual, despite HBUS' admitting to funneling through the United States at least $880 million in illegal drug proceeds.

On the positive side, the deferred prosecution agreement didn't conclude the criminal case. It required HBUS, before the criminal case could be dismissed, to undergo five years of supervision by a bank monitor charged with ensuring effective AML controls were put in place. When the five years concluded in 2017, HSBC claimed its AML controls were significantly stronger. Time will tell.

Conclusion

During his PSI years, Senator Levin devoted significant PSI resources to combating money laundering. From his first two investigations into private and correspondent banking, to the landmark AML reforms in the 2001 Patriot Act, to a decade of focused oversight into how those reforms were enforced, Senator Levin and his Republican partners successfully used PSI to strengthen U.S. AML defenses. As a result, terrorists, drug traffickers, corrupt officials, and other wrongdoers have had a tougher time laundering ill-gotten gains through the United States. There's still a lot to do—from combating shell companies with hidden owners, to extending AML requirements to real estate agents, escrow firms, and lawyers, to cleaning up dirty banks—but even so, notch one up for congressional oversight.

Notes

1. "Oil Boom Enriches African Ruler," *Los Angeles Times*, Ken Silverstein (1/20/2003), http://lat.ms/2zORsWm.
2. See, for example, "A Washington Bank in a Global Mess," *New York Times*, Timothy O'Brien (4/11/2004), http://nyti.ms/2isIEMg.
3. The information in this section is based on "Money Laundering & Foreign Corruption: Enforcement and Effectiveness of the Patriot Act," S. Hrg. 108-633 (7/15/2004) (hereinafter "2004 Riggs Hearing"), https://www.gpo.gov/fdsys/pkg/CHRG-108shrg95501/pdf/CHRG-108shrg95501.pdf; and "Supplemental Staff Report on U.S. Accounts Used by Augusto Pinochet," S. Prt. 109-25 (3/16/2005) (hereinafter "Supplemental Pinochet Report"), https://www.gpo.gov/fdsys/pkg/CPRT-109SPRT20278/pdf/CPRT-109SPRT20278.pdf.
4. *In re Riggs Bank National Association*, OCC No. 2003-79, Consent Order (7/16/2003), http://www.occ.gov/static/enforcement-actions/ea2003-79.pdf.
5. "Terrorism Financing: Origination, Organization, and Prevention," Senate Governmental Affairs Committee, S. Hrg. 108-245 (7/31/2003), https://www.gpo.gov/fdsys/pkg/CHRG-108shrg89039/pdf/CHRG-108shrg89039.pdf.
6. As part of that effort, the committee tried unsuccessfully to declassify 28 blanked-out pages in a 9/11 report related to Saudi Arabia. Those pages were finally declassified in 2016.
7. Information about the EG and Pinochet accounts is based on the 2004 Riggs Hearing, including the report entitled, "Money Laundering & Foreign Corruption: Enforcement and Effectiveness of the Patriot Act, Case Study Involving Riggs Bank," at 126–210.

8. See *United States v. Kareri*, Criminal Case No. 1:05-CR-00212-RMU (USDC DC), http://www.plainsite.org/dockets/1fvltqsr/district-of-columbia-district-court/usa-v-kareri-et-al/; "Former Riggs Executive, Wife, Charged with Fraud and Conspiracy," *Washington Post*, Terence O'Hara (5/28/2005), http://wapo.st/2hLe2bF.

9. Id., at 40. For the list of dictators, see "Who Would You Say is the World's Worst Dictator?" *Parade Magazine*, *Washington Post* (2/22/2004), reprinted at id., at 493.

10. The Levin-Coleman bill, S. 2814, was added through Senate Amendment No. 3867 to S. 2845, the National Intelligence Reform Act of 2004, and enacted into law on December 17, 2004 as Section 6303(b) of the Intelligence Reform and Terrorism Prevention Act, P.L. 108-458.

11. See, for example, the Extractive Industries Transparency Initiative, https://eiti.org/.

12. See, for example, "U.S. Bank Helped Dictator Hide Millions," (7/16/2004) (citing AP report),http://bit.ly/2j4rp3u.

13. See Supplemental Pinochet Report, at 127–228.

14. Id., at 228, Appendix #4—FN 75.

15. See *United States v. Riggs Bank*, Criminal Case No. 1:05-CR-00035-RMU-1 (USDC DC), Judgment (3/31/2005), http://lib.law.virginia.edu/Garrett/plea_agreements/dockets/RiggsBank.htm; *In re Riggs Bank*, FinCEN Case No. 2004-01 (5/13/2004), Assessment of Civil Money Penalty, https://www.fincen.gov/news_room/ea/files/riggsassessment3.pdf. See also "Riggs Bank Agrees to Guilty Plea and Fine," *Washington Post*, Terence O'Hara (1/28/2005), http://wapo.st/2yVmJDy.

16. See Spanish court order, English translation, Supplemental Pinochet Report, at 96–101, Appendix #4—FN 5; "Allbrittons, Riggs to Pay Victims of Pinochet," *Washington Post*, Terence O'Hara (2/26/2005),http://wapo.st/2zeTaBl.

17. See "Order Approving the Merger of Bank Holding Companies," Federal Reserve System (4/26/2005), http://www.federalreserve.gov/boarddocs/press/orders/2005/200504262/attachment.pdf; "Riggs, PNC Reach New Merger Agreement," *Washington Post*, Terence O'Hara (2/11/2005), http://wapo.st/2zTAbt3.

18. See, for example, 31 U.S.C. §5318(i)(3)(B) requiring financial institutions to conduct "enhanced scrutiny of any [private banking] account that is requested or maintained by, or on behalf of, a senior foreign political figure, or any immediate family member or close associate of a senior foreign political figure, that is reasonably designed to detect and report transactions that may involve the proceeds of foreign corruption."

19. The information in this section is based on "Keeping Foreign Corruption Out of the United States: Four Case Histories," S. Hrg. 111-540, Volumes

1–2 (2/4/2010) (hereinafter "2010 Foreign Corruption Hearing"), https://www.gpo.gov/fdsys/pkg/CHRG-111shrg56840/pdf/CHRG-111shrg56840.pdf (Volume 1), and https://www.gpo.gov/fdsys/pkg/CHRG-111shrg57734/pdf/CHRG-111shrg57734.pdf (Volume 2).

20. The information in this section is based on the 2010 Foreign Corruption Hearing, Volume 1, at 141–250.

21. Id., at 510, Hearing Exhibit 1a.

22. See "Exempted Anti-money Laundering Programs for Certain Financial Institutions," 31 CFR 103.170.

23. The information in this section is based on the 2010 Foreign Corruption Hearing, Volume 1, at 251–329.

24. The information in this section is based on id., at 412–509.

25. The information in this section is based on id., at 330–411.

26. *SEC v. Siemens*, (USDC DC), Case No. 1:08-cv-02167-RJL, Complaint (12/12/2008), at paragraph 50.

27. "Voluntary Good Practices Guidance for Lawyers to Detect and Combat Money Laundering and Terrorist Financing," American Bar Association (8/2010), http://bit.ly/1i19Wza.

28. "A Lawyer's Guide to Detecting and Preventing Money Laundering," American Bar Association and Others (10/2014), http://bit.ly/2AdbwCK.

29. See EU Third Money Laundering Directive, ¶¶ 19–23, 45 and Article 2(1)(3)(b) (10/26/2005), http://eur-lex.europa.eu/LexUriServ/LexUriServ.do?uri=OJ:L:2005:309:0015:0036:en:PDF.

30. See "Anonymous Inc.," *60 Minutes* (1/31/2016), http://cbsn.ws/1UBarEW. For another example of lawyers involved with potential corruption schemes, see "Mossack Fonseca: Inside the Firm That Helps the Super-Rich Hide Their Money," *The Guardian*, Luke Harding (4/8/2016), http://bit.ly/22hAFiq.

31. See, for example, "FinCEN Takes Aim at Real Estate Secrecy in Manhattan and Miami," FinCen Press Release (1/13/2016), https://www.fincen.gov/news_room/nr/html/20160113.html; "FinCEN Expands Reach of Real Estate 'Geographic Targeting Orders' Beyond Manhattan and Miami," FinCen Press Release (7/27/2016), https://www.fincen.gov/news_room/nr/pdf/20160727.pdf.

32. "Anti-Money Laundering Guidelines for Real Estate Professionals," National Association of Realtors (11/15/2012), http://bit.ly/2aanJaZ.

33. The American League of Lobbyists issued a code of ethics for its members in November 2010, nine months after the PSI hearing in February 2010, but it made no mention of AML issues. See "Code of Ethics," American League of Lobbyists (11/2010), http://bit.ly/2zOXoP0.

34. For an example of a university that has issued its own AML guidance, see "University of Nottingham Anti-Money Laundering Policy and Procedures," University of Nottingham, http://bit.ly/2zQc8h8.

35. See, for example, "State Business Incorporation—2008," two hearings before the Senate Committee on Homeland Security and Governmental Affairs, S. Hrg. 111-953 (6/18 and 11/5/2009), https://www.gpo.gov/fdsys/pkg/CHRG-111shrg51788/pdf/CHRG-111shrg51788.pdf.

36. Incorporation Transparency and Law Enforcement Assistance Act, S. 2956, introduced on May 1, 2008.

37. "Tougher Rules on Money Laundering to Fight Tax Evasion and Terrorist Financing," European Parliament Press Release (5/20/2015), http://www.europarl.europa.eu/news/en/news-room/20150513IPR55319/tougher-rules-on-money-laundering-to-fight-tax-evasion-and-terrorist-financing.

38. The information in this section is based on "U.S. Vulnerabilities to Money Laundering, Drugs, and Terrorist Financing: HSBC Case History," S.Hrg. 112-597, Volumes 1 and 2 (7/17/2012), (hereinafter "HSBC Hearing"), https://www.gpo.gov/fdsys/pkg/CHRG-112shrg76061/pdf/CHRG-112shrg76061.pdf (Volume 1) and https://www.gpo.gov/fdsys/pkg/CHRG-112shrg76646/pdf/CHRG-112shrg76646.pdf (Volume 2).

39. See 31 U.S.C. 5318(i)(1), enacted as Section 312 of the Patriot Act of 2001.

40. See "HSBC Holdings Plc. And HSBC Bank USA N.A. Admit to Anti-Money Laundering and Sanctions Violations, Forfeit $1.256 Billion in Deferred Prosecution Agreement," Department of Justice Press Release (12/11/2012), https://www.justice.gov/opa/pr/hsbc-holdings-plc-and-hsbc-bank-usa-na-admit-anti-money-laundering-and-sanctions-violations.

41. Id.

42. See "Too Big to Jail, Inside the Obama Justice Department's Decision Not to Hold Wall Street Accountable," Republican Staff Report, House Committee on Financial Services (7/11/2016), http://financialservices.house.gov/uploadedfiles/07072016_oi_tbtj_sr.pdf.

11

Exposing Corporate Tax Dodgers

"We pay all the taxes we owe."
Apple CEO Tim Cook, Senate hearing testimony (May 21, 2013)

As the Levin PSI staff matured as an investigative team, Senator Levin began ruminating about tackling what he saw as one of the great American injustices—profitable U.S. corporations paying little or no tax to Uncle Sam. To him, corporate tax dodgers were tearing at the very fabric of American society, hiding profits, robbing the U.S. treasury of revenues needed for the country to thrive, and fueling middle class anger at the feds' failure to hold wealthy corporations accountable for their greed and deception.

By 2011, the senator already had several high-stakes tax investigations under his belt: he'd helped halt the mass marketing of tax shelters by accounting firms; exposed bankers, lawyers, and tax professionals facilitating offshore tax evasion; and blasted tax haven banks aiding and abetting tax evasion by the wealthy and corrupt. But he had yet to take on the most ruthless offshore tax dodgers of them all—U.S. multinational corporations. So as our financial crisis investigation wound down, he decided the time had come. His assignment: find out how U.S. multinationals used offshore tax havens to ditch U.S. taxes. We started digging.

Over the next three years, Senator Levin led PSI in a series of groundbreaking inquiries into U.S. multinational corporate tax dodging. They focused on four iconic American companies: Microsoft, Hewlett-Packard, Apple, and Caterpillar. Each case study laid out the complex, deceptive offshore gimmicks being used to dodge payment of billions of dollars in tax. In each case, a profitable U.S. multinational claimed it had paid all the taxes it

© The Author(s) 2018
E. J. Bean, *Financial Exposure*, https://doi.org/10.1007/978-3-319-94388-6_11

owed, while secretly shifting profits offshore and pushing its share of the U.S. tax burden onto working American families, domestic competitors, and small business. Exposing the multinationals' unrelenting, devious, and secretive tax schemes became one of Senator Levin's oversight priorities.

Becoming Corporate Tax Detectives

When we started the new assignment, the PSI staff knew little about corporate tax issues. None of us were tax specialists; no one was savvy about corporate tax loopholes. At the outset, we worried that the tax schemes might be too complicated to unravel. But if there was one thing we'd learned over the years, it was that we knew how to learn.

That was one of the takeaways from our two-year investigation into the complex financial instruments behind the financial crisis. We'd started out neophytes and ended up derivative experts. The Levin and Coburn staffs had also learned how to work together to disentangle even the most stubborn of Gordian knots. We trusted them and they trusted us to get to the facts, no matter where they led. On top of that, Senator Coburn had a longstanding interest in tax matters and was as fearless as Senator Levin in taking on powerful interests. So when we told our Republican colleagues about our new investigative assignment, they were game.

We began by forming a core team of corporate tax detectives. Bob Roach, our chief investigator, was team leader. From our side, David Katz and Dan Goshorn were his primary partners, with Allison Murphy, me, and other Levin staffers brought in to work on discrete issues. The Coburn staff provided Keith Ashdown, their chief investigator, with backup from Chris Barkley, Senator Coburn's staff director. Supporting the core team was an evolving roster of PSI detailees, law clerks, and interns. The team spent the next three years on the corporate tax investigation, which continued until Senator Levin's last day in office.

Getting the Low Down

To get started, we called in IRS lawyers, tax professors, and other tax and accounting experts to educate us in the ways of corporate tax dodging. We endured hours of instruction on a litany of abusive tax practices, learning the nitty-gritty details of how U.S. corporations arranged their affairs to outwit Uncle Sam. It took time, but what once seemed impenetrable gibberish slowly began to clarify, as we immersed ourselves in a half dozen common corporate tax ploys, focusing in particular on tax dodges utilizing offshore tax havens.

Here's what we learned, in simplified terms. Picture a typical U.S. multinational. Let's say it conducts research and development in the United States to design and improve its products. It manufactures those products in China, and sells them around the world from Germany to Kenya to Vietnam. While our tax experts sometimes disagreed over how the resulting profits should be attributed to specific countries for tax purposes, one area of universal agreement was that the profits should not be attributed to a tax haven subsidiary that played little or no role in the company's research, manufacturing, or sales activities. Yet the ten-year trend showed exactly what the experts feared—the majority of U.S. corporate foreign profits were increasingly attributed to shadowy tax haven subsidiaries that often operated with no employees, no physical offices, and no real economic presence.

The statistics were troubling. One chart tracking U.S. corporate profits attributed to tax haven subsidiaries showed that, by 2011, U.S. multinationals were telling the IRS that over half of their foreign profits came from subsidiaries in six tax havens (Image 11.1).[1]

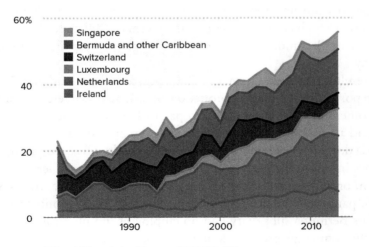

Image 11.1 EPI Chart—Over half of U.S. corporate profits are in tax haven countries. Source: Americans for Tax Reform & Economic Policy Institute (used with permission)

The statistics for the individual tax havens were equally mind-blowing. In 2010, for example, profits attributed by U.S. multinationals to subsidiaries in Bermuda totaled $94 billion, which was a figure 15 times larger than Bermuda's entire Gross Domestic Product (GDP) of $6 billion, a factual absurdity.[2] U.S. multinationals reported the same absurdity—profits in excess of a country's entire GDP—for the Cayman Islands, British Virgin Islands, Luxembourg, and Ireland.[3]

We asked tax experts how U.S. multinationals could justify claiming that so much of their foreign profits were earned in tax havens. We anticipated getting a complex or mysterious explanation, but we were wrong. The experts said that corporate profit-shifting was actually quick and easy, a function of U.S. multinationals using a variety of relatively simple mechanisms to transfer funds to themselves in the tax havens they wanted to exploit.

In one common scenario, a U.S. multinational parent formed a subsidiary in a tax haven. It then sold or assigned the so-called economic rights to use its patented products to that tax haven subsidiary. The subsidiary, as owner of the economic rights, could then charge a royalty fee to any other company affiliate seeking to sell the patented products. In fact, the tax haven subsidiary could set its royalty fee in an amount large enough to suck the profits from any affiliate operating in a jurisdiction attempting to tax those profits.

Consider, for example, a U.S. multinational that formed a subsidiary in Bermuda and gave it the right to sell its products worldwide. The U.S. parent could then instruct its sales office in Germany to pay a royalty fee to the Bermuda subsidiary in connection with each product sale. With some analysis and support from its parent corporation, the Bermuda subsidiary could set the royalty fee high enough to require the German affiliate to ship the bulk of its profits to Bermuda, retaining only enough to keep its doors open in Germany.

The result: even if the German affiliate posted billions of dollars in sales, it could report minimal taxable profits on its German tax return, blaming its low income on the royalties it had to pay to Bermuda. The German affiliate could end up paying little or no tax in Germany. At the same time, since Bermuda doesn't tax corporate profits, the Bermuda sub could pile up billions of dollars in untaxed royalty payments streaming in from Germany, Kenya, Vietnam, or anywhere else the U.S. parent had a sales office. And—voila!—the U.S. parent could end up attributing the bulk of its profits to Bermuda, even if its Bermuda subsidiary had no employees, no physical office, and no role in the company's product design, manufacture, or sales.

The profit-shifting trick, experts explained to PSI, wasn't confined to royalty payments. U.S. parents could arrange for their tax haven subs to charge their affiliates all kinds of fees or costs—for using the parent's brand name, buying raw materials like coffee beans, conducting research, or purchasing spare parts. The variations were endless. The only constant was that the tax haven subsidiary set its fees, costs, or prices high enough to shift profits from the higher-tax jurisdictions to its lower-tax venue. The beauty of the arrangement was that, because all the parties were related, no sales office complained, dragged its feet, or refused to pay even outrageous fees that beggared its in-country operations. Everyone knew paying the tax haven subsidiary was how the company moved its money offshore to a low-tax or tax-free venue.

We also learned that shifting profits to a tax haven did not trigger the payment of U.S. tax, under a longstanding U.S. corporate tax policy known as "deferral." Deferral generally allowed U.S. multinationals to postpone paying U.S. taxes owed on profits booked offshore until the U.S. company actually "repatriated" the funds to the United States. No other taxpayer has the same right to defer paying the taxes they owe for as long as they want; only multinationals. The ability to indefinitely defer paying U.S. tax on some foreign profits had created a powerful tax incentive for U.S. corporations to move operations offshore, keep the resulting profits out of the United States, and minimize their foreign taxes by shifting foreign earnings into tax havens.

Our research also showed that shifting corporate profits to tax havens wasn't a recent innovation. That type of profit-shifting went back decades. In fact, at one point in the 1960s, when corporate profit-shifting was hammering the U.S. treasury, President John F. Kennedy responded by proposing the immediate taxation of all offshore corporate profits—ending the deferral loophole.[4] Aghast, the multinationals fought back and, despite public condemnation of their tax-dodging ways, managed to win a significant compromise known as Subpart F.

Under the Subpart F compromise, the United States continued to allow U.S. corporations engaged in "active" businesses abroad—think McDonald's selling hamburgers in Paris—to defer paying U.S. tax on their foreign earnings until they brought those earnings home. But the new twist was that any corporation that played the profit-shifting game—sending profits to a tax haven subsidiary with no real business activity—was subject to an immediate tax on the movement of that so-called "passive" income to the tax haven subsidiary.

President Kennedy and Congress added Subpart F to the U.S. tax code in 1962.[5] For many years, by requiring the immediate taxation of passive foreign income, it successfully tamped down corporate profit-shifting to tax havens. But it didn't last. Thirty-five years later, in 1997, the IRS sabotaged the compromise by issuing a regulation known as "check-the-box."[6]

The IRS didn't intend to sabotage Subpart F; it was trying to fix a technical tax problem. The problem involved the different tax treatment given to corporations, partnerships, and other types of business entities like limited liability companies. While corporations were taxed directly on their income, partnerships and certain other business entities were not—the income was instead passed through to their partners or owners and taxed as income reported on personal tax returns. The problem was that the states, foreign jurisdictions, and courts used a variety of tests to determine when a business entity was subject to direct taxation versus when it qualified as a "pass-through," and businesses were tying the IRS in knots every time the issue came up.

The IRS decided the fights weren't worth the time and expense, and so issued a regulation permitting businesses to simply check a box on their tax returns indicating whether a subsidiary should be treated as a corporation, partnership, or some other type of business entity, and whether a lower-tier subsidiary should be "disregarded" for tax purposes and its income "passed through" or attributed to its owner.

When multinationals got wind of the new rule, their tax lawyers went wild, using the new check-the-box authority to launch a thousand different offshore tax dodges to get around Subpart F taxation. Many involved corporate structures in which lower-tier foreign subsidiaries were designated as "disregarded entities" for tax purposes, and their "active" sales income attributed to their owners, which just happened to be tax haven subsidiaries, thereby magically converting what was once taxable "passive" income into "active" income immune to Subpart F taxation.

Go back to the example of the U.S. multinational that owned a shell company in Bermuda and a sales office in Germany. To take advantage of the new rule, suppose the U.S. parent rearranged its corporate structure, so that that the direct owner of its German sales office was no longer the U.S. parent, but its Bermuda subsidiary. Suppose further that the German sales office continued to sell the company's products to customers, while paying a royalty fee on each product sale to its new owner, the Bermuda sub, resulting in the German sales office shipping most of its profits to Bermuda.

Under Subpart F, that scenario wouldn't have made much economic sense, because the German payments to the Bermuda sub would have been immediately taxed as "passive income" under Subpart F. The Subpart F tax removed any incentive to send the funds to the tax haven.

But under the new check-the-box rule, the tax outcome changed. The U.S. parent was suddenly able to designate its German sales office as a "disregarded" entity for tax purposes, and attribute its "active" sales income to its new direct owner, the Bermuda sub. The Bermuda company could, in turn, claim that because the funds it received from Germany retained their character as "active" sales income, the funds were immune to immediate taxation under Subpart F. In addition, under the doctrine of deferral, the Bermuda sub could defer paying any U.S. tax on that "active" income until it sent the funds to the United States. Which might be never.

In short, with the new check-the-box rule, income that for 30 plus years was taxable under Subpart F suddenly became non-taxable even when moved to a tax haven.

Within months of its issuance in 1997, as multinational check-the-box tax dodges proliferated and corporate tax revenue plummeted, the IRS tried to rescind the offending regulation.[7] But the multinationals smelled blood, loudly objected to any change in the check-the-box rule, and quickly enlisted Members of Congress in an effort to block the rule's rescission. In the face of the onslaught, the IRS gave up and left the regulation in place.[8] U.S. multinationals became even more emboldened and manufactured more tax schemes invoking the check-the-box rule, including arrangements never contemplated or intended by the regulation. The IRS challenged some of the schemes in court, but the cases were tough to explain to judges. The IRS won some, but lost others. Its litigation costs mounted.

The multinationals didn't stop there. Worried that the IRS might one day get up the gumption to revoke the check-the-box rule—which, after all, had no statutory basis—the multinationals convinced Congress to enact a 2004 statute that mimicked the contours of the regulation.[9] Referred to as the "CFC Look-Through Rule," the new statute essentially authorized multinationals to "look through" certain foreign subsidiaries (called "controlled foreign corporations" or CFCs) and attribute their active income to their owners, without triggering taxation under Subpart F. It was a second crippling blow against Subpart F. Together, the check-the-box rule and 2004 statute essentially gutted the Subpart F compromise that, for so many years, had defended the U.S. treasury against abusive offshore profit-shifting.

As the profit-shifting to tax havens accelerated, the IRS tried to stem the abuses by stressing that when a multinational's subs engaged in transactions with each other, they had to charge each other the same fees or prices that unrelated parties would have charged after engaging in an "arms-length" negotiation. The idea was that the arms-length principle would cut down on the false pricing used to shift income to tax havens.[10] But it was a losing battle. The companies executing transactions with each other weren't unrelated parties. The whole point of their transactions was to move company profits into tax havens, so no one had any incentive to abide by the arms-length standard. In addition, even establishing an arms-length price was arduous, since so few multinationals—in the real world—ever sold their patent rights or brand names to unrelated third parties.

U.S. multinationals, aided by an armada of tax lawyers and economists, invariably claimed their intra-company transactions used arms-length prices, even as the bulk of their profits continued to end up in tax havens. The IRS tried challenging the prices, but was stymied by a lack of real-world pricing examples to prove its point. In addition, litigation costs in even its successful cases ate up scarce IRS resources, limiting the agency's ability to stop abuses. There were simply too many corporations pushing the envelope, too many tax schemes proliferating, and too many battles over fact-specific evidence for the IRS to get ahead of the curve.

Instead, U.S. corporate offshore tax dodging continued to build. Reports began surfacing of profitable U.S. corporations paying little or no U.S. tax. A 2011 report by one public interest group identified 30 multinationals that, despite more than $160 billion in profits, paid no federal income tax at all over a three-year period.[11] A respected academic calculated that, by 2012, offshore profit-shifting had produced lost corporate tax revenues of over $100 billion per year (Image 11.2).[12]

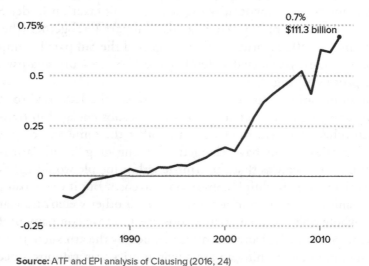

U.S. loses over $100 billion a year in revenue to corporations shifting their profits offshore

Revenue loss due to corporate income shifting, as a share of GDP, 1983–2012

Source: ATF and EPI analysis of Clausing (2016, 24)

Image 11.2 EPI Chart—U.S. loses over $100 billion a year in revenue. Source: Americans for Tax Reform & Economic Policy Institute (used with permission)

The collective blow to the U.S. fisc was massive. The share of corporate income taxes in the United States fell from a high of 32% of federal tax revenue in 1952 to about 10% in 2013.[13] That meant the share of federal tax dollars paid by corporations fell from 1 in 3 to 1 in 10. Meanwhile, payroll taxes—paid by almost every working American—skyrocketed from 10% of federal revenues to over 45%.[14] Profitable U.S. multinationals were offloading their tax burden right onto the backs of American workers.

Surveying Corporate Tax Practices

Once we grasped the history, common tactics, and statistics behind the dismal landscape of corporate tax dodging, we decided our next step was to develop specific case studies, not only to deepen our understanding but also to illustrate what was going on. But it wasn't obvious to us which corporations would make the best case studies.

When we sought help from the experts, we were told we'd have to rely on guesswork, because when it came to taxes, multinational corporations were masters of secrecy. To our surprise, we learned that no tax authority in the world, no agency, and no academic had country-by-country data showing where specific multinationals declared their profits and paid taxes. U.S. tax authorities didn't have systemic data, for example, on how much tax a specific U.S. company paid to other countries or how U.S. tax assessments for that company stacked up against tax assessments by other jurisdictions. Since no government required any multinational to disclose even basic information about its worldwide tax payments, it was all a deep dark mystery.

We brainstormed about how to get better information to identify good case studies. One alternative we considered was to subpoena tax returns from likely corporations, but we knew their tax returns would be so massive, complicated, and unique, that they probably wouldn't provide us with useful comparative data. We decided a better course of action was to send likely candidates a survey asking specific questions focused on what we really wanted to know.

Experience had taught us that surveys could be powerful oversight tools, but they took a lot of work to pull off, and succeeded only when they zeroed in on facts that couldn't be fudged. With assists from experts who'd helped us with prior surveys in the tax area, we designed a questionnaire focused on multinationals' use of tax haven subsidiaries. The questions asked the U.S. parent to provide, for example, a list of all of its foreign subsidiaries and, for each, to identify where it was formed, where it was a tax resident, what functions it performed, how many employees it had, how much income it reported, how much cash it held, and the amount of taxes it paid. We also asked the multinational to disclose the percentage of its profits reported by its U.S. versus non-U.S. subsidiaries. Every question was carefully designed to request factual information that couldn't be ducked.

We sent the survey to more than a dozen multinationals rumored to be playing offshore games. We got more than one groan in response, and some initially signaled they were too busy to reply any time soon. Our reaction was to establish a rigorous process to collect the survey responses. Our tax team called every survey recipient, obtained the name of a company contact responsible for the survey, and offered to address any questions or concerns. In other words, we got a dialogue going with each of the survey recipients. If a company failed to reply to our calls, we pressed its Washington representative for an in-person meeting. As time went on, we made repeated calls to each company, warning of the approaching deadline and requesting a date certain on which its survey response would be provided.

In the end, every corporation supplied us with a survey response, though the responses varied widely in clarity and detail. In most cases, the information raised multiple questions, which led us to the next phase of the process: setting up meetings with each corporation to go through its information. The follow-up meetings were a pain to schedule, because we needed personnel who were familiar with the corporation's offshore tax practices, foreign subsidiaries, and cash management practices, as well as its survey response. Usually that meant the corporation had to fly in multiple individuals for a day-long meeting. Every company dragged out the scheduling, citing difficulties with coordinating its personnel.

But we persisted, and step-by-step, we got the meetings scheduled. In each one, we made sure we understood the information that had been disclosed, identified data gaps, and got clarifications and additional information. We also integrated any data we'd acquired from our prior tax surveys. We soon realized we had a target-rich environment, with evidence of abusive offshore tax practices running in every direction.

We were still scheduling follow-up meetings when Senator Levin ran out of patience. He said it was time to select case studies for a hearing to be held before the Congress ended in 2012. We gave him some options, consulted our Republican colleagues, and reached a consensus.

Microsoft and Hewlett-Packard—2012

The decision was to focus the first hearing on two case studies involving Microsoft and Hewlett-Packard.[15] Both were very profitable U.S. corporations with suspicious offshore tax arrangements. We decided to use Microsoft to examine how U.S. profits were being moved offshore to avoid U.S. taxes, and HP to examine how some offshore profits were being returned to the United States, untaxed.

Microsoft

Taking on Microsoft was rough. A powerful corporation with an army of Washington lobbyists, it made the PSI tax team sweat to acquire every fact. The tax disclosures in its public filings were limited, and the IRS was banned by law from discussing any individual taxpayer, so detailed information on Microsoft's offshore tax practices could be obtained from only a limited set of players, primarily Microsoft itself.

The survey gave us a solid start. To dig deeper, we made a follow-up document request. We didn't request Microsoft's actual tax returns, because we knew they would be so lengthy and complex, they'd likely be of little real assistance. Instead, we concentrated on documents related to Microsoft's offshore subsidiaries, including their formation, activities, and relationship to tax havens. We also sent additional written questions, seeking specific facts.

To get a second source of information, we contacted Microsoft's accountant, Deloitte & Touche, who'd been auditing Microsoft's books for years and had a lot of information about its offshore arrangements. The accountant's materials, when added to Microsoft documents, survey, and other information, with multiple interviews all around, got us where we needed to go.

When it all shook out, the story went like this. Microsoft developed its software products primarily in the United States, reducing the cost by taking advantage of U.S. research and development tax credits. Microsoft kept its patents, brand name, and other intellectual property in the United States, taking advantage of the protections provided by U.S. patent law and U.S. courts. At the same time, Microsoft assigned the "economic rights" to market its patented products to foreign subsidiaries it controlled in Puerto Rico, Ireland, and Singapore. Using aggressive pricing arrangements, those foreign subsidiaries managed to shift the bulk of Microsoft's worldwide sales profits to their home countries, as well as to Bermuda. Microsoft benefited from the low or no taxes in those jurisdictions, while also ducking U.S. tax.

The facts were particularly stark when it came to Microsoft's U.S. product sales. We discovered that Microsoft's U.S. parent—call it Microsoft USA—sold the right to market its intellectual property in the Americas (including the United States) to a Puerto Rican subsidiary—call it Microsoft Puerto Rico. Microsoft USA then bought back from Microsoft Puerto Rico the U.S. distribution rights. In other words, the U.S. parent bought back a portion of the rights it had just sold, agreeing to pay a percentage of its U.S. sale income—in effect, a royalty payment—to Microsoft Puerto Rico for the privilege of selling its own products right here in the United States.

Under the intra-company agreements, from 2009 to 2011, Microsoft USA paid fees totaling nearly $21 billion, or almost half of its U.S. retail sales net revenue, to Microsoft Puerto Rico. Microsoft sent those billions of dollars offshore to Puerto Rico even though its products were developed, marketed, and sold to customers right here in the United States. By sending its U.S. funds offshore, Microsoft avoided paying any U.S. tax on nearly half its sales income. As a result, in 2011 alone, Microsoft's profit-shifting enabled it to avoid paying U.S. tax on 47% of its U.S. sales revenue. Altogether during the three years we studied, from 2009 to 2011, Microsoft dodged up to $4.5 billion in U.S. taxes on its U.S. sales income, an amount so large it worked out to nearly $4 million in U.S. taxes per day.

Not only that, but due to a special tax deal it had negotiated with the government of Puerto Rico, Microsoft paid an effective tax rate on its profits there of only about 2%.

Microsoft engaged in similar, aggressive profit-shifting tactics with its subsidiaries in Singapore and Ireland, two jurisdictions with low corporate tax rates. In 2011, those two subsidiaries paid Microsoft USA $4 billion for the right to market its patented products outside of the United States; Microsoft Singapore paid $1.2 billion, and Microsoft Ireland $2.8 billion. That sounded like a lot of money. But over the next year, the Microsoft Singapore group reported revenues totaling $3 billion, while Microsoft Ireland reported $9 billion. So Microsoft USA had sold the rights to its products for $4 billion, and then watched its offshore subs make a one-year killing of $12 billion. But Microsoft hadn't cut a dumb deal with its subsidiaries. What really happened is that Microsoft had arranged its corporate structure to enable it to shift billions in U.S. taxable income offshore to two low-tax jurisdictions.

While Subpart F normally would have required Microsoft to pay immediate taxes on any passive income sent to a tax haven subsidiary, Microsoft used the check-the-box rule and 2004 look-through law to defer paying U.S. taxes of $2 billion. With a straight face, Microsoft attributed billions of dollars in U.S. and non-U.S. sales income to its foreign subsidiaries, even though all three played a minimal role in the corporation's design, manufacturing, and sales activities. The cherry on top: Microsoft's foreign subsidiaries kept nearly 90% of their "offshore" income in U.S. cash or U.S. investments at U.S. financial institutions, benefiting from the security and efficiency of the U.S. financial system while dodging payment of the taxes needed to keep that system going.

Hewlett-Packard

The Microsoft case study painted the first half of the offshore tax picture—tracking how U.S. corporate profits that should have been attributed to the United States were instead sent to tax havens. The second half—tracking how untaxed offshore income made its way into the United States while remaining untaxed—came from Hewlett-Packard, another powerful U.S. corporation with extensive offshore tax activities.

HP won its spot as one of our first case studies due to a delicious mystery. One day, the head of the PSI tax team, Bob Roach, walked by the printer nearest his desk and, as he often did, idly picked up the latest printed document and glanced at it. He hadn't printed it; we never learned who did. But when Bob looked at it, he suddenly realized that it portrayed a blatant, abusive short-term loan scheme designed to bring billions of HP's offshore funds into the United States without paying any U.S. tax.

That moment of epiphany was followed by months of painstaking inquiry to see if the document really meant what it seemed to. To get the facts, we confronted HP with the document and asked whether the U.S. parent was, in fact, receiving large-scale loans from its foreign subsidiaries. When the answer came back yes, we forced the company to disclose, step-by-step, which HP subsidiaries provided the loans, what loan terms applied, how the loan proceeds were used, and how and when the loans were repaid. To doublecheck the information, we asked the same questions of HP's longtime accountant, Ernst & Young. Document requests to both HP and E&Y unearthed a mass of relevant documents, including E&Y memoranda discussing the offshore loans. Interviews with HP and E&Y personnel cemented the details.

The tax dodge centered on Section 956 of the tax code, a section which treats a loan to a U.S. corporation as taxable "property," if it meets certain requirements.[16] But Section 956 also contained exceptions, one of which has been interpreted by the IRS as allowing a U.S. corporation to bring any amount of offshore funds into the United States tax free, if structured as a loan that is repaid in less than 30 days and held during certain time periods.[17] Some tax experts told us that the short-term loan exception was intended to allow U.S. corporations facing a sudden need for cash to tap into their foreign funds on an emergency basis. Skeptics described it as a scheme that enabled U.S. corporations to bring back foreign funds to fortify their balance sheets just before the end of a quarter, report better financial results than they really had, and then return the cash offshore, all without paying any tax. After scouring the legislative history, we were unable to substantiate either rationale.

What we were able to establish was the extent and operational details of the HP loans. It turned out that the loans were issued by two offshore corporations controlled by HP, one in Belgium and the other in the Cayman Islands. For years, the two offshores had provided serial, alternating, short-term loans to HP's U.S. parent in alleged compliance with Section 956. When a short-term loan from one of the offshore corporations ended, it was immediately replaced by a short-term loan from the other. While the logistics might sound daunting, they weren't. That's because both corporations were shell entities with no employees or offices of their own. Their activities consisted solely of book entries in ledgers kept by HP at its U.S. headquarters.

HP used the short-term offshore "loans" to repatriate billions of dollars in foreign funds to the United States and, without paying any tax, use them to run its U.S. operations. HP records showed that, from March 2008 to September 2012, to finance the company's U.S. activities, the foreign "loans" provided HP with an average of $11 billion per day.[18] The records also showed that, without the offshore funds, HP had only about $500 million in U.S. funds on hand at any given time, which was insufficient cash to run its U.S. operations. The records were crystal clear that the offshore funds had been made continuously available to HP's U.S. operations for years at a time, in blatant disregard of Section 956's exception for "short-term" lending.

Despite the black-and-white facts documenting HP's years-long reliance on billions of dollars in offshore funds to run its U.S. operations, HP insisted it had fully complied with the law and that its loans met the requirements of Section 956. When asked about a court case that invalidated a similar set of serial offshore loans providing continuous funding to a U.S. corporation over a two-year period, HP claimed that the precedent didn't apply.[19] Its reasoning? That case had invalidated serial loans supplied by a single offshore corporation, while HP's loans were being supplied by two offshore corporations.

HP's weak explanation was made even less tenable by internal memoranda from its auditor, E&Y, which—even before PSI began asking questions—had raised concerns about the company's serial offshore loans, citing the very same court case.[20] When asked about those memos, HP pointed out that, despite expressing concerns, E&Y had supported the company's view that its offshore loans complied with Section 956. HP was correct that E&Y had ended up siding with the company but, to us, that only showed how pliable an auditor could become when pressed by a major client to approve a questionable tax dodge.

Once the fact-finding finished, the tax team—led by David Katz—wrote up a 25-page memo describing the Microsoft and HP case studies. The tax team spelled out both the law and the companies' offshore tax arrangements so that a lay reader could follow what happened.

2012 Hearing

In September 2012, PSI featured the Microsoft-HP case studies in its final hearing of the 112th Congress. It was an afternoon hearing that lasted nearly five hours.

Earlier in the day, Senator Levin had held a press briefing on the upcoming hearing. At it, we distributed to reporters the 25-page Levin-Coburn memo laying out the law and the facts. During the press briefing, Senator Levin was careful to make clear that the subcommittee had not reached a conclusion as to whether Microsoft or HP had violated the tax code; he noted that the Senate's job was to focus on policy issues, while the executive branch's job was to determine whether laws were broken. He spent time instead describing the facts—the convoluted, deceptive, and secretive arrangements that both companies claimed had enabled them to avoid paying billions of dollars in U.S. tax. After he left, PSI staff remained behind to answer questions about how the tax dodges worked. The early backgrounder gave reporters added time to digest the facts and evaluate the evidence prior to the hearing.

The hearing itself took testimony from three panels of witnesses. The first panel consisted of three tax and accounting experts who'd examined the evidence beforehand and concluded that Microsoft and HP's tax and accounting practices were abusive. The three experts summarized the complicated fact patterns, explained the relevant tax code provisions, and estimated the amount of U.S. taxes dodged. They set the table for the rest of the hearing.

The second panel got down to brass tacks. The witnesses were senior tax officials from Microsoft and HP, as well as HP's auditor E&Y. The senators grilled the witnesses about actions taken by Microsoft to shift billions of dollars in U.S. sales income offshore without paying U.S. tax, and by HP to shift billions of dollars into the United States through serial short-term offshore loans, again, without paying any tax. The witnesses claimed everything they did was allowed by law. But even if those claims were true—which was far from clear—the facts exposed how devious their actions were and how much tax they were dodging.

The final panel took testimony from the IRS and the Financial Accounting Standards Board which promulgates Generally Accepted Accounting Principles for corporate America. Representatives testified about the tax and accounting issues at stake in both case studies, while declining to express an opinion on the two companies in particular. Their testimony was subdued, with a weary air that suggested neither expected the government to prevail in its ongoing battle to end corporate tax abuses. It wasn't an encouraging performance.

Apple—2013

The 2012 Microsoft-Hewlett-Packard hearing generated a lot of press about corporate tax dodging, but it paled in comparison to our second hearing held eight months later. That's when we took on one of the most powerful and best-liked corporations in America, Apple Inc.[21]

At the time of the investigation, most folks on Capitol Hill and in the media loved their iPhones, iPads, and Macs. Many were awestruck by the artistry, ambition, and ability of Apple's former CEO Steve Jobs to produce world-altering products. Everyone seemed enchanted that Apple portrayed itself as a proud American company.

The widespread adulation made showing Apple's dark side on taxes a huge risk. It also came at a time of change when, in the 113th Congress, Senator Coburn left PSI to become ranking Republican for the full Homeland Security and Governmental Affairs Committee, and Senator John McCain became PSI's new ranking Republican. Lucky for us, Senator McCain had a long history of standing up to big corporations and a long history of working with Senator Levin on the Senate Armed Services Committee. He signaled that he was ready and willing to join Senator Levin in the battle to expose Apple's suspect tax practices.

Getting the Apple Facts

After the Microsoft-HP hearing concluded, Senator Levin told the tax team to take a deep breath and immediately begin preparing the next case study. To get started, the team pulled out the surveys from the year before and considered which company to profile next. Apple was a leading candidate, having turned in survey responses laced with indicia of offshore tax dodging. We hadn't had time to schedule a follow-up meeting with Apple before the Microsoft-HP inquiry intensified, but now we did.

The day-long meeting took place in early 2013. Our bipartisan tax team went through Apple's survey responses, working with Apple's tax professionals who'd flown in for the day. The survey had requested basic information about Apple's foreign subsidiaries, including where each was formed, where it did business, and where it was a tax resident. While Apple had supplied most of the requested information, for one Irish subsidiary, it had left a blank when asked to name the country where that subsidiary was a tax resident. The missing data caught the eye of one of our tax experts who alerted Bob. During the meeting, Bob asked Apple's representatives to fill in the blank. They tried ducking the question, but Bob persisted. After some hemming and hawing, looking up at the ceiling, down at their shoes, and then at each other, Apple's tax team finally admitted they'd left the question blank, because the Irish subsidiary wasn't a tax resident of any country.

Bob played it down during the interview, but afterward told me what Apple had admitted. He and I viewed it as a bombshell. Virtually every U.S. multinational we examined had subsidiaries that were tax residents of tax havens like Bermuda or the Cayman Islands. But Apple was the first to admit to forming a foreign subsidiary with no tax residency anywhere. Senator Levin later called Apple's claimed result the "Holy Grail" of offshore tax dodging.

How did Apple do it? It exploited a key difference between U.S. and Irish law. The United States based tax residency on where a corporation was formed; since the Apple subsidiary was incorporated in Ireland, it wasn't a tax resident of the United States. At the same time, Irish law based tax residency on where a company was managed and controlled; since Apple's Irish subsidiary had no employees and so was not managed or controlled in Ireland, it wasn't a tax resident of Ireland. So Apple had decided its Irish sub wasn't a tax resident anywhere.

Bob and I decided right then and there that Apple would be the focus of PSI's next tax hearing. We also knew that the story was so explosive, we needed to make sure we had the facts straight, that we understood the implications, and that we had the goods, so Apple couldn't take it back or twist it around during the hearing and damage the subcommittee's credibility.

It took another six months to lock down the facts. First, we went back to Apple to pry more information out of its tax office. We also sent document requests to Apple's accountant, which was none other than E&Y. Already exhausted from dealing with PSI over the HP loan scam, E&Y knew we meant business and didn't even try to stiff us. We ended up collecting key documents and data from both Apple and E&Y.

We also conducted multiple interviews. One of the most interesting involved Apple's tax director, Phillip Bullock. He was a clear tax expert, yet tended to give vague answers to our questions and veer away from uncomfortable topics into more favorable territory. We also discovered that if pressed to answer questions carefully phrased to elicit specific information, he'd eventually provide an answer. We pressed him and his colleagues for the facts.

In a nutshell, here's what we found out. We learned that Apple had established not one, but three Irish subsidiaries with no tax residency anywhere, ran those subsidiaries from the United States, and shifted more than $74 billion in profits to them over a four-year period, taking advantage of a special tax deal it had negotiated with the Irish government that, overall, gave Apple an effective tax rate of 2% or less. The $74 billion in profits and less than 2% effective tax rate were the most extreme figures we'd seen in both categories.

Apple's Irish Subsidiaries

The three Irish subsidiaries were Apple Operations International (AOI), Apple Operations Europe (AOE), and Apple Sales International (ASI) (Image 11.3). Apple established AOI in the 1980s, when Ireland was first trying to attract U.S. multinationals to set up operations within its borders. AOI had never had any employees or physical presence, yet functioned as a sort of phantom "head office" for Apple's Irish operations. In response to our questions, Apple disclosed that AOI had not filed a tax return with any country for five years.

AOI owned AOE which, in turn, owned ASI. When established, both AOE and ASI were shell operations with no employees of their own and no physical offices. They, like AOI, were run from the United States, where Apple employees kept their books. Apple employees in the United States also served as their officers and directors. One additional director was an Irish citizen, as required by Irish law. The board meetings of the three Irish subs were held in the United States, often by telephone. Of the 21 board meetings held over four years, the Irish director had participated by telephone in three and in-person only once.

The three Irish shell companies played pivotal roles in Apple's offshore profit-shifting. After their formation, Apple signed licensing agreements with AOE and ASI, giving them the right to sell Apple's patented products across Europe, the Middle East, Africa, and Asia. Apple retained the right to sell its products in North and South America. That meant that all profits earned from Apple products sold in Canada, Mexico, Central and South America— not to mention the United States—were attributed by Apple to its U.S. operations and paid U.S. tax. In contrast, Apple products sold in the rest of the world were not attributed to the United States, but instead were diverted to Apple's shell companies in Ireland.

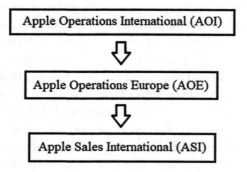

Image 11.3 Apple's Irish subsidiaries as of 2013. Source: 2013 Senate Hearing Exhibit 1b

The decision to send a huge portion of Apple sales income to Ireland was made at the most senior levels of the company. The 2008 version of the licensing agreement sending sales income to AOE and ASI in Ireland was signed, for example, by three senior Apple executives sitting in Apple's U.S. headquarters.[22] Peter Oppenheimer, then Apple's chief financial officer, signed the licensing agreement on behalf of Apple. Gary Wipfler, then Apple's treasurer, signed on behalf of AOE where he was a director. And who signed on behalf of ASI? An ASI director who was none other than Apple's then president, Tim Cook.

The 2008 licensing agreement with its triple signatures by senior U.S. Apple executives was proof, not only that the Irish subs were under the complete control of their U.S. parent, but also that their profit-splitting arrangement was not the result of an arms-length negotiation hammered out by unrelated parties, but an internal decision by Apple's corporate leaders about where to direct its income and where to pay tax.

Other documents showed that ASI entered into sublicensing agreements with Apple sales offices in various countries, enabling them to sell Apple products in exchange for royalty fees. The fees were set high enough to suck billions of dollars in Apple sales profits from stores throughout Europe, the Middle East, Africa, and Asia, and send the profits to ASI in Ireland.

In response to our questions, Apple disclosed that, over the four-year period from 2009 to 2012, ASI had received income from Apple sales offices totaling $74 billion. After those funds arrived in Ireland, ASI issued dividends to AOE which, in turn, issued dividends to AOI attributing a large portion of the funds to Apple's phantom Irish head office which had no employees or physical presence. As a result, of the $74 billion that made its way to Ireland, dividends totaling $30 billion went up the chain to AOI, which filed no tax return anywhere.

Which is not to say that Apple's Irish operations were 100% tax free. Apple did deign to pay a small amount of tax to its host government. Under a special, confidential tax deal that Apple negotiated with the Irish government in 1991 and renewed in 2007, ASI agreed to pay a certain amount of Irish tax, but the amount was so small that in 2011, for example, it resulted in an effective tax rate of only 0.05 or five hundredths of one percent. Not zero, but close.

Apple enjoyed that almost-zero effective tax rate despite Ireland's statutory corporate tax rate of 12.5%. Apple declined to explain to PSI exactly how its effective tax rate ended up so tiny, and since the tax payment involved Ireland rather than the United States, we decided not to go down that particular rabbit hole. Instead, we focused on several other U.S. tax dodges Apple used during the same four years, including check-the-box, which enabled Apple to avoid paying U.S. taxes on $44 billion of otherwise taxable offshore income.

Now, I've set out these facts as if we learned the whole sordid tale in one sitting with a coherent narrative, but it wasn't actually like that. Apple was cagey and slippery. Bits and pieces of the story surfaced in a disjointed, confusing roll out of various facts, documents, and interviews. Apple's tax professionals often tried to distract us by leading us on tangents unrelated to their Irish tax planning.

Apple didn't admit for months, for example, that all three of its Irish subsidiaries had no tax residency anywhere. Because of its survey response, we'd gotten lucky in getting Apple to admit early on that AOI had no tax residency, but once Apple realized we were homing in on that fact, it stalled on providing the tax status of AOI's subsidiaries. Apple finally admitted ASI's no-tax-residency status shortly before the PSI hearing in May 2013. Since AOE was lodged in between AOI and ASI, we demanded to know whether AOE had the same status. Apple finally admitted AOE did—orally—the night before the hearing. Too late to get it into our hearing memo, but not too late to disclose Apple's hat-trick of tax dodging Irish subs at the hearing itself.

At the same time it was stonewalling PSI staff, Apple tried every trick in the book to get Senators Levin and McCain to back off the entire investigation. Apple and its CEO Tim Cook were big Democratic contributors and apparently reached out to multiple Democratic senators, but none we know of actually spoke with Senator Levin; perhaps they knew it wouldn't have dissuaded him. Apple also met with most, if not all, of our subcommittee members to present its side of the story. That was fair game, but didn't seem to help much since the Democratic offices generally supported profitable corporations paying tax, and some of the Republican offices seemed to enjoy watching a Democratic-contributing company squirm. In the end, Apple's biggest champion on PSI turned out to be Senator Rand Paul, a Kentucky Republican known to oppose U.S. efforts to pierce tax haven secrecy laws to collect U.S. tax.

2013 Hearing

The Apple hearing took place in May 2013. It generated intense interest in both our subcommittee and the media. More PSI members made an appearance at the Apple hearing than any other hearing during the Levin years, other than the financial crisis hearing on Goldman Sachs. Media inquiries were massive.

To handle the press, we followed the pattern set in the Microsoft-Hewlett-Packard inquiry and held a press briefing, this one on the day before the hearing. We distributed a 49-page Levin-McCain memo laying out what we'd found. Senators Levin and McCain both spoke at the briefing. Both were careful to state that the subcommittee had not found a violation of law, since it was the job of the executive branch—not the Senate—to make that type of determination. Instead, the senators concentrated on conveying the facts we'd unearthed—that Apple owned three Irish subsidiaries which, from 2009 to 2012, had hauled in $74 billion in profits, yet were tax resident nowhere, paid virtually nothing in U.S. tax, and paid only a pittance to Ireland. The details of how a rich corporation used offshore subsidiaries and convoluted legal arrangements to outwit Uncle Sam riveted the press. The next morning, articles describing Apple's offshore tax dodging rocketed around the globe.

The hearing opened before a packed audience. Senator Levin spoke first, detailing the PSI investigation. Senator McCain followed with a strong supporting statement, describing Apple as "one of the biggest tax avoiders in America." Next up was Senator Rand Paul who delivered a quite different message. He announced that he was "offended by a $4 trillion government bullying, berating, and badgering one of American's greatest success stories." He called on PSI to apologize for dragging Apple before the Senate and said, "instead of Apple executives we should have brought in here today a giant mirror" because the problems at issue were the fault of an "awful Tax Code" devised by Congress. He, again, called for an apology.[23]

Senator Levin responded by saying anyone could offer an apology or hold up any mirror they wanted, but "no company should be able to determine how much it is going to pay in taxes." He said the subcommittee wasn't going to apologize to Apple for examining its tax practices.

Senator McCain later provided this striking defense of his Democratic colleague: "I have had the honor of serving with you for more than a quarter of a century. I know of no Member of the U.S. Senate that has ever accused you of bullying or harassing a witness in the thousands of hearings that you and I have been part of over many years. And, frankly, it is offensive to hear you accused of that behavior." Senator McCain also asked Apple's CEO Tim Cook if he felt he'd been bullied, harassed, or dragged before the subcommittee; Mr. Cook stated that he had not. Senator McCain's staunch defense of Senator Levin following Senator Paul's accusatory remarks was a moving illustration of PSI's bipartisan ethic.

The hearing ultimately took testimony from three panels of witnesses. As in the Microsoft-HP hearing, it started off with two tax experts who set the table for the hearing. Both were unequivocal in criticizing Apple's use of offshore tax gimmicks, especially its creation and use of shell Irish subsidiaries with no tax residency anywhere.

The second panel featured Apple itself, represented by three senior executives: Tim Cook, CEO; Peter Oppenheimer, chief financial officer; and Phillip A. Bullock, head of tax operations. Mr. Cook spoke on behalf of the company, claiming Apple had paid all the taxes it owed, "every single dollar," and did "not depend on tax gimmicks." Under fierce questioning, however, the witnesses did admit that the company had three Irish subsidiaries with no tax residency anywhere, that over $70 billion in Apple sales profits had been sent to Ireland, and that Apple's maximum effective tax rate in Ireland was 2%. Those facts were stubborn things.

Tim Cook later disclosed that, to prepare for the hearing, he'd consulted with Goldman Sachs CEO Lloyd Blankfein who'd been grilled by PSI three years earlier, as well as former President Bill Clinton who'd testified before Congress several times.[24] Supposedly, Mr. Cook was content with his performance. We were also content since, from our perspective, Apple had admitted the key facts we'd uncovered. Those facts would continue to reverberate around the world, showcasing a highly profitable corporation stiffing every country where it did business out of the taxes needed for that country to function.

The third and final hearing panel took testimony from the Treasury's most senior tax official and the head of the IRS' transfer pricing office. While neither commented on the Apple case in particular, both expressed weary frustration over the tax loopholes enabling so many U.S. multinationals to continue to avoid payment of U.S. taxes.

At the hearing, senators both praised Apple's products and criticized its tax practices. Because Apple was one of the best-known and most profitable companies in the world, bragged about its profitability, and had the chutzpah to set up companies with no tax residency anywhere, the Senate hearing on its profit-shifting Irish subsidiaries made news around the globe. Apple became the poster child for outrageous corporate tax dodging, elevating the issue worldwide.

One side note involves Ireland. After Senator Levin described Ireland as a "tax haven" during the hearing, a huge debate erupted across Europe over the country's status. Irish leaders insisted their country was not a tax haven, and the Irish government had not given Apple a favorable tax deal. But that stance contradicted the facts, especially Apple's admission that it paid an effective tax rate of five hundreds of one percent in 2011. Privately, we wondered whether Ireland had even known the extent to which Apple had been exploiting the country's loose tax laws to stockpile cash virtually tax free.

Caterpillar—2014

The third and final installment in the PSI series on corporate tax dodging featured still another American icon, Caterpillar Inc.[25] Unlike Microsoft, HP, and Apple, Caterpillar wasn't a darling of Silicon Valley; it was a Midwestern manufacturer of heavy equipment. We picked it for our final case study in part because we wanted to show that offshore corporate tax dodging wasn't confined to computer companies—any multinational could join the club.

In addition, while Caterpillar wasn't as glamorous as Apple, and its tax dodging wasn't as massive, the company still offered a fascinating story involving a $55 million tax shelter, Swiss skullduggery, and deceptive tax practices that dodged payment of billions of dollars in U.S. tax. It opened another window onto the offshore tax dodging practiced by U.S. multinationals.

Like Microsoft, HP, and Apple, Caterpillar didn't make the inquiry easy. We learned that Caterpillar's CEO, Doug Oberhelman, was a leader in the Republican party's anti-tax movement and had fought a long public battle against state taxes in Illinois.[26] He apparently believed corporations had a moral duty to pay as little tax as possible, in direct contrast to Senator Levin's view that corporations had a civic obligation to support the communities where they did business.

A second problem was that our Republican counterparts had taken an internal drubbing after the Apple hearing. The McCain staff let us know that multiple Republican offices had contacted them to complain about their boss' pro-tax stance and his working so closely with Senator Levin. That type of negative backlash from colleagues is never easy to take, but was made worse by the fact that the McCain staff was so new to PSI. We didn't have years of working together to reassure them that the tough stretches were worth the pain. While the McCain staff never buckled under the pressure, they did become noticeably less enthusiastic about investigating corporate tax dodging.

David Katz and Dan Goshorn from the Levin staff took the lead on the Caterpillar investigation which ended up taking nearly a year to complete. They doggedly gathered information using the survey responses, document requests, and interviews at both the company and its auditor, PricewaterhouseCoopers.

During the course of the year, one of the things we learned was what a remarkable company Caterpillar was. Its primary business was to design, build, and sell heavy-duty equipment like bulldozers, trucks, and mining equipment. Each of its machines—sporting the company's signature color of canary yellow—cost a lot to manufacture, and the documents indicated the company made a bare profit on each sale.

But that's when Caterpillar's secondary business kicked in—selling parts for its equipment. Caterpillar's machines were famous for lasting decades. But to continue in operation, each had key parts that needed to be replaced on schedule. Caterpillar made most of its profit from supplying those parts. Not only that, it had developed a worldwide parts logistics business that was so efficient, it enabled Caterpillar to promise to replace any needed part within 24 hours of a request. To meet that pledge, the company had developed sophisticated software that could not only predict what parts would be needed when, but also direct the manufacture of those parts in time for them to be shipped where needed.

We learned that Caterpillar manufactured about 70% of its parts in the United States, mostly using third party suppliers located within a few miles of its headquarters in Peoria, Illinois. It maintained ten U.S. parts warehouses worldwide, with the largest a mammoth building in Morton, Illinois housing millions of parts. The Morton warehouse also housed the logistics experts and parts software integral to the company's success. Caterpillar used independent sales offices—Caterpillar-approved dealers—in the United States and elsewhere to sell its machines and spare parts to customers around the world.

For much of its history, Caterpillar had reported 85% or more of the profits from the parts it sold outside of the United States as U.S. income subject to U.S. tax. It attributed the other 15% to several small Swiss affiliates that acted as liaisons with some of the non-U.S. dealers selling Caterpillar products. That all changed, however, after its auditor, PricewaterhouseCoopers (PwC), designed a "tax strategy" to save Caterpillar millions of dollars in U.S. tax. In 1999, Caterpillar paid PwC over $55 million for that customized tax shelter.

PwC helped Caterpillar implement the tax strategy over the next few years. The tax savings arose from one key change. Instead of Caterpillar's selling its parts worldwide from Peoria, the company issued a license to one of its Swiss affiliates, Caterpillar SARL (CSARL), handing over the right to make certain non-U.S. sales of Caterpillar's third-party-supplied parts. In exchange, the Swiss affiliate agreed to pay Caterpillar a royalty fee equal to about 15% of the parts profits generated under the license, while keeping the remaining profits—85% of the total—for itself in Switzerland. In addition, because the affiliate lacked the personnel, infrastructure, and expertise to actually conduct the parts operations, it paid Caterpillar the cost plus a small service fee for continuing to run the parts business.

Think about what an absurd deal that was for the U.S. parent company. Although Caterpillar had spent 90 years building its international parts business, Caterpillar handed over a license to sell its non-U.S. parts sales to its Swiss affiliate without requiring that affiliate to pay a penny for the business.

In an arm's length transaction, no company would hand over an established profitable business line to another party for zero compensation. Nor would a business relinquish 85% of the ongoing profits from that business in exchange for 15% of the profits. But that's exactly what Caterpillar did.

In addition, the new licensing arrangement changed almost nothing in the day-to-day functioning of Caterpillar's parts business, other than changing the name on the sales invoices from Caterpillar to CSARL. Caterpillar continued to run the parts business from the United States, controlling the design, manufacturing, warehousing, parts forecasting, distribution, and shipping components. All it got paid in return was its cost plus a small fee. Since Switzerland was a mountainous, landlocked country, its Swiss subsidiary never established a warehouse there or manufactured or shipped any parts from there. Caterpillar's 5000 parts employees remained in the United States, including its senior parts executives; CSARL hosted only 65 parts employees, including just one parts executive with limited authority.

Even though the U.S. parent company kept running the parts business, after the licensing agreement was signed Caterpillar switched from reporting 85% or more of its foreign parts profits on its U.S. tax return to reporting 85% of more of those same profits on CSARL's Swiss tax return. And surprise, surprise, due to a special deal negotiated with Swiss tax authorities, its Swiss affiliate ended up paying an effective Swiss tax rate in the range of 4%, a rate below the Swiss statutory rate. Sound familiar?

A final twist of the tax-dodging knife was that PwC, in its role as Caterpillar's independent auditor, approved Caterpillar's use of the very tax shelter that PwC itself had sold to the company in its role as a tax consultant. The result was that, from 2000 to 2012, Caterpillar used the Swiss tax strategy to shift $8 billion in foreign parts profits from the United States to Switzerland, cutting Caterpillar's U.S. tax bill by $2.4 billion.

The Caterpillar facts, to us, were as compelling as those in the Microsoft, HP, and Apple case studies, replete with offshore tax gimmicks, a secret tax deal, and billions in unpaid U.S. tax. But our McCain colleagues weren't so sure. They pointed to Caterpillar's claim that its Swiss affiliate played a key role in its parts business and so deserved 85% of the profits.

In response, David and Dan dug deeper into the facts, researching CSARL's role and comparing it to the U.S. role. The claim just didn't check out. The U.S. side of the parts business had substantially more parts employees, executives, third party suppliers, logistics software, warehouses, and shipping than the Swiss side. When evaluating CSARL's role in overseeing Caterpillar's independent foreign dealers, the Levin tax team found a media interview in which Caterpillar's top U.S. parts executive described how a new Caterpillar program was empowering him to assert greater control over those dealers, with no mention of Switzerland.[27] The Levin team also found an internal email exchange in which a tax partner at Caterpillar's accountant, PwC, joked that justifying the profit split between the U.S. and Swiss operations in light of all the parts product managers in the United States might require "some dancing." His PwC colleague responded: "What the heck. We'll all be retired when this comes up on audit."

The deeper dive into the facts built an even stronger case for challenging Caterpillar's decision to send 85% of its parts profits to Switzerland. Despite the new facts, the McCain staff expressed continued reluctance to join our analysis. In response, we sought guidance from Senator Levin. His faith in Senator McCain was rock-solid, and he told us to go ahead with the hearing as planned. He indicated that he would speak with Senator McCain, but was willing to go it alone if his colleague felt he couldn't join us in this particular matter at this particular time.

2014 Hearing

PSI held the Caterpillar hearing in April 2014, midway through Senator Levin's last year in office. In connection with the hearing, we issued a 95-page majority staff report laying out what we'd found. Senator McCain did not sign onto the report, but we gave it to his staff to review anyway and incorporated as many of their comments and concerns as we could. Twice as long as the memo from the Apple hearing, it was chock full of facts. The doubts expressed by the McCain staff had energized us to be as thorough and persuasive as we could—which is exactly the way bipartisan oversight ought to work.

As with the prior two hearings, we held a press briefing on the day before the hearing. We handed out the majority staff report, Senator Levin described what we'd uncovered, and after he left, we answered questions from reporters. Again, we didn't claim Caterpillar had broken the law; we just conveyed the facts—the $55 million price tag for the tax shelter, the profits diverted to Switzerland even though the parts business was still run out of Peoria, and the $2.4 billion in claimed U.S. tax "savings." While the Caterpillar case study didn't attract the same media buzz as Apple, the reporters who'd been following PSI's work for the past three years took it all in and, the next morning, press articles appeared nationwide describing how Caterpillar was skirting U.S. taxes and sending billions to Switzerland.

Following the same pattern as the earlier hearings, three panels of witnesses provided testimony at the Caterpillar hearing. The first panel presented two international corporate tax experts who summarized Caterpillar's actions and criticized its offshore tax strategy as one more set of tax-dodging gimmicks. They set the table for the rest of the hearing.

The second panel heard from three PwC accountants who'd helped develop and implement Caterpillar's Swiss tax shelter. All three defended the PwC-developed tax strategy and denied PwC had a conflict of interest in selling the tax shelter to Caterpillar and then auditing and approving its use by the company.

The final panel heard from Caterpillar itself. Three executives testified: the chief tax officer, a former tax manager who oversaw implementation of the Swiss tax shelter, and a financial executive who confirmed the $55 million payment to PwC as well as the billions of dollars in tax savings. All three stoutly defended Caterpillar's use of the Swiss tax strategy, including shifting $8 billion in parts profits from the United States to Switzerland, and deferring payment of $2.4 billion in U.S. taxes as of 2012.

The most surprising testimony during the hearing was Caterpillar's insistence that the IRS had never objected to its Swiss tax strategy and never proposed any tax "adjustments" as a result. When Senator Ron Johnson asked: "because they [the IRS] have proposed no adjustments, they have basically given their blessing to what you have done here from the standpoint of compliance with tax law, correct?" Caterpillar's chief tax officer Robin Beran responded: "That is the way I have taken it."[28] It was the company's strongest argument justifying its actions, and it seemed to have swayed both Senator Johnson and Senator McCain.

The problem: it wasn't true. About a month after the hearing, Caterpillar submitted a filing to the SEC and included a letter stating that the IRS had, in fact, proposed tax adjustments related to its Swiss tax strategy in December 2013—more than three months before the PSI hearing.[29] After learning of the letter, we demanded a copy of the "Notice of Proposed Adjustment" sent by the IRS to Caterpillar on December 23, 2013. In it, the IRS officially notified Caterpillar that the IRS strongly objected to its Swiss tax strategy, proposed tax adjustments for four tax years totaling more than $3 billion, and planned to impose substantial penalties on the company for using an "abusive corporate tax shelter."[30] Caterpillar's failure to disclose the IRS' objections to its tax strategy—while testifying that no such objections existed—was a shocking conclusion to PSI's investigation of the company's tax-dodging record.

Sparking Change

The Caterpillar hearing in mid-2014 brought the subcommittee's corporate tax-dodging investigation to a close. For more than three years, from 2011 to 2014, we'd dug into the details of how profitable U.S. multinational corporations were deceiving Uncle Sam, describing Irish shell companies that claimed to have no tax residency anywhere, a Puerto Rican subsidiary that claimed billions of dollars in untaxed U.S. sales income, Cayman and Belgian shell companies that provided billions of dollars in undisclosed and untaxed serial loans to their U.S. parent, and a Swiss subsidiary that claimed the lion's share of untaxed profits from a business actually run from the United States. We'd laid out the facts and explained the deceptive tax practices in ways that enabled policymakers and the public to understand what was happening.

Each of the subcommittee hearings had packed a wallop, but Senator Levin's oversight career drew to a close before we could do much to stop the abuses we'd uncovered. And yet, the PSI hearings did help spur change, sparking developments in the United States and elsewhere.

More Oversight in More Places

One welcome development was that legislatures in other countries began holding their own hearings on multinational corporate tax dodging. The U.K. Parliament went first, with the Public Accounts Committee led by Margaret Hodge holding a series of 2012 hearings asking why, despite billions of dollars in U.K. sales, Amazon, Starbucks, and Google paid so little U.K. tax.[31] The European Parliament in Brussels went one better, creating a new investigative committee referred to as TAXE which held multiple hearings on European corporate tax dodging, calling in Disney, Facebook, IKEA, and McDonald's, among others.[32] On the other side of the world in Australia, a legislative committee held hearings questioning the tax practices of Airbnb, Chevron, Microsoft, and Uber, among others.[33] It was a worldwide medley of oversight investigations that, together, built a record of corporate outrages and a factual foundation for change.

Tax Enforcement Actions

A second development was a wave of tax enforcement actions against the companies we'd profiled in our investigations.

First, the IRS breathed new life into its longstanding audit of Microsoft's offshore tax arrangements. Initiated in 2007, the agency had reportedly begun to bring the audit to a close with a preliminary tax assessment in 2011,[34] but then reportedly withdrew that assessment and, after the 2012 PSI hearing, started asking more questions. Microsoft fought back, refusing to make available certain documents and certain executives for interviews, objecting to the

IRS' use of a private firm to help analyze the company's offshore dealings, and filing Freedom of Information Act lawsuits to squeeze information out of the IRS.[35] After a year-long standoff, in November 2015, a federal district court ordered Microsoft to cough up the information requested by the IRS and dismissed its effort to stop the IRS from using an outside expert.[36] Since then, some U.S. tax experts have characterized the Microsoft case, described by the IRS as involving billions of dollars in unpaid tax, as one of the most important in the IRS' ongoing battle to stop corporate offshore tax abuse. At the same time, as of mid-2018, more than two years after the court ruling, the IRS has yet to announce the outcome of the Microsoft audit.

An IRS audit of Caterpillar progressed farther. As with Microsoft, the IRS initiated the audit prior to the PSI investigation, but intensified it after the PSI hearing. In early 2015, Caterpillar disclosed in a public filing that—for the years 2007–2009—the IRS had assessed the company about $1 billion related to its Swiss arrangements.[37] The company wrote that it planned to "vigorously contest" the IRS assessment. The filing also disclosed Caterpillar had received a federal grand jury subpoena seeking information in an ongoing criminal inquiry.

In February 2017, Caterpillar disclosed in another public filing that the IRS tax assessment had increased to $2 billion, after adding the years 2010–2012,[38] with more years yet to be reviewed. In March 2017, with no prior notice, three federal agencies, search warrants in tow, raided Caterpillar's Illinois headquarters and parts warehouse in connection with its Swiss tax arrangements and carted away boxes of materials.[39] The nature of the criminal investigation was unclear; one question was whether it included Caterpillar's false testimony to the Senate that, as of the 2014 PSI hearing, the IRS had not objected to its Swiss tax strategy.

In still another development, Caterpillar's auditor, PwC, apparently became the subject of an inquiry by the Public Company Accounting Oversight Board to determine the propriety of PwC's auditing the same offshore tax strategy that the firm sold to its audit client.

In contrast to Microsoft and Caterpillar, as of this writing, no public evidence has emerged of an IRS audit of Hewlett-Packard's short-term offshore loan activities. In 2013, the IRS did send the subcommittee a letter announcing that it was stepping up its review of Section 956 loan abuses. Two years later, in 2015, the IRS issued new guidance to its auditors requiring them to look at whether multiple loans claimed as tax-exempt under Section 956 should be "collapsed" into a single taxable loan obligation.[40] While welcome and important, both efforts targeting short-term loan abuses left us wondering whether the IRS ever took a hard look at HP.

Apple Confronted

Which leaves Apple. To date, the IRS has taken no public action questioning Apple's no-tax-resident-anywhere Irish subsidiaries. But that isn't the whole enforcement story. While U.S. authorities appeared disinterested, European authorities interceded. In August 2016, after a two-year inquiry, the European Commission ordered Ireland to collect taxes from Apple totaling $14.5 billion plus interest.

The 2016 Apple tax assessment was played by the media as a big surprise. But for those following international corporate tax issues, it was the culmination of a long process. The European Commission first announced its inquiry into Apple's Irish tax arrangements in 2013, later crediting the Senate's 2013 Apple hearing with bringing the company to the Commission's attention.[41] The Commission opened the Apple case in connection with a larger inquiry it had already undertaken into allegations that certain European governments, including Luxembourg, Ireland, and the Netherlands, were granting secret sweetheart tax deals to favored corporations.

That larger inquiry was the product of a European tax scandal known as LuxLeaks, involving the leak of thousands of documents from accounting firms and others disclosing how Luxembourg tax authorities, for a fee, had been approving arrangements designed to enable participating corporations to dodge taxes from other European governments. In other words, Luxembourg had been taking money to help multinationals dodge tax payments to other EU governments.

The Senate hearing on Apple's sweetheart tax deal with Ireland exploded onto the world stage at the same time the LuxLeaks scandal was generating widespread European outrage. After a lengthy inquiry, the Commission's head of competition, Margrethe Vestager, found that, instead of applying its normal 12.5% statutory tax rate, Ireland had given Apple a special tax deal that enabled it to pay an effective corporate tax rate of less than 1%, including a 2014 rate that dropped all the way to 0.005%.[42]

The Commission held that, by disadvantaging Apple's competitors, Ireland had granted Apple "illegal state aid" in violation of European law. It ordered Ireland to collect all the tax that Apple should have paid under its 12.5% statutory rate going back ten years, which was as far back as EU law allowed. The Commission also stated that, if a tax authority could show that some portion of the $14.5 billion should have been paid to the United States or some other tax authority, that amount could, in fact, be paid to that tax authority instead of Ireland.

Ireland and Apple claimed to be shocked—shocked—that they would be accused of engaging in inappropriate tax favoritism and announced they would appeal the Commission's decision, guaranteeing years of court battles. More surprising, the Obama Treasury Department also cried foul. President Obama's Treasury Secretary Jack Lew announced that 100% of Apple's worldwide profits, after credits were granted for any foreign taxes paid, were subject to U.S. tax. He noted that higher Irish taxes meant larger foreign tax credits and, thus, less tax money left over for the U.S. treasury. He complained that Europe had no right to impose Ireland's full statutory tax rate on Apple when Apple had been promised it could pay less.[43]

Secretary Lew's professed indignation over the Commission's tax assessment caught many in Europe and the United States by surprise. His alleged anger over the United States' being left with less tax revenue didn't explain why the European Commission was wrong to insist on Apple's paying the legal tax rate in Ireland, especially given how the lower tax rate disadvantaged Apple's competitors. In addition, his claim that the United States supported Ireland's lower tax rate in order to ensure the United States could collect its rightful share of Apple taxes fell flat given Apple's longstanding taunts that it had no intention of bringing any profits back to the United States until the United States lowered its corporate tax rate.[44]

The United States' position was further undercut by its failure to challenge Apple's blatant tax dodging through its Irish subsidiaries, despite the hit to the U.S. treasury. The facts were clear that Apple was directing tens of billions of dollars in worldwide profits to a phantom Irish company with no employees, no physical presence, and no real economic activity. The IRS could have—then or since—branded the phantom company as an instrumentality of Apple's U.S. parent company, and directed all of the phantom company's income to be attributed to Apple Inc. and taxed in the United States. But the IRS never took that stance, perhaps because it worried no one in the Treasury or the Justice Department had the political guts to back it up. Given U.S. reluctance to challenge Apple's tax dodging, U.S. indignation when Europe finally objected to what was clearly an abusive arrangement seemed less like a principled stance than an effort to protect a wealthy and powerful U.S. company.

For those of us who first uncovered Apple's Irish high jinx, the European Commission's enforcement action was both unexpected and welcome. We saw it as striking a massive blow against corporate tax dodging. After all, the Apple decision was one in a lengthening line of Commission orders invalidating sweetheart corporate tax deals handed out by Ireland, Luxembourg, the

Netherlands, and others. By invalidating those government-sponsored tax deals, the Commission was essentially shutting down EU tax havens. That meant no more secret tax deals for large U.S. multinationals directing worldwide profits to Europe.

Even before the Commission decision on Apple came down, the European Union had expressed its own determination to clamp down on multinational tax dodging by issuing a raft of directives increasing corporate tax transparency, closing loopholes, and requiring its member countries to share cross-border tax rulings.[45] While those directives had caveats and short-comings, they nevertheless placed a new chokehold on EU tax havens. And curbing European tax havens made it that much harder for U.S. multinationals to game the U.S. tax system.

Base Erosion and Profit Shifting (BEPS)

There's more. Fed up with multinationals conning governments out of needed tax revenue, in 2012, world leaders from the G20 group of countries, including the United States, endorsed a new international effort to clamp down on abuses. Called the Base Erosion and Profit Shifting (BEPS) Project, set up under the auspices of the Organization for Economic Cooperation and Development (OECD), the project assembled a group of international tax experts to figure out what steps could be taken to stop multinationals from playing governments off each other and fleecing everyone.

In 2013, the BEPS Project announced a consensus by its participating countries that: (1) multinational corporations ought to pay taxes—a proposition some U.S. multinationals had been fighting against for years; and (2) corporate income taxes ought to be imposed where value is created.[46] While both statements may seem straightforward, getting multiple countries to sign onto them, including the United States, was a monumental advance in international tax fairness.

The BEPS Project didn't stop there. In 2015, it announced consensus on 15 specific action plans to reduce multinational tax dodging.[47] The action plans proposed, for example, revamping international tax treaties to prohibit "non-taxation" of multinational corporate profits; stopping the use of corporate "hybrid mismatches" and certain other mechanisms used by multinationals to game tax authorities in multiple jurisdictions; and improving international standards indicating when a multinational corporation had a taxable presence in a jurisdiction.

Country-by-Country Reporting

While most of the BEPS action plans required additional steps to complete, one measure was put on a fast track—requiring greater corporate transparency. Action 13 of the BEPS Project called on all participating countries to require their large multinationals to disclose key financial data in each country where they did business, using an agreed-upon template.[48] The template, set up to serve as an annual report, required each corporation to identify, for each country where it operated, its profits or losses before taxes, number of employees, stated capital, net book value of tangible assets, and taxes accrued and paid. It also required each corporation to list its subsidiaries, including where they were formed and where they were tax resident. Mandatory disclosure of that basic information was aimed at ending the secrecy that enabled multinationals to play one country off another, with no one sure where corporations were doing business, declaring profits, or paying tax.

The United States was one of the first to implement the new country-by-country disclosure requirement. In 2016, the U.S. Treasury finalized a rule requiring U.S. multinationals, beginning in 2017, to file country-by-country reports on a confidential basis with the IRS.[49] The reports were limited to companies making at least $850 million in revenues per year, and they weren't available to anyone outside the IRS. But the reports still represented a sea change in corporate tax disclosure. The world is beginning to recognize there is simply no reason why multinationals should be able to continue to keep everyone in the dark about their tax practices.

Conclusion

Tougher enforcement actions, greater corporate transparency, and stronger tax regulations have put a crimp in multinational corporate tax dodging, but nonpayment of U.S. corporate taxes remains rampant. U.S. legislation is needed to close the abusive tax loopholes, stop the tax haven profit-shifting, and strengthen taxes on profitable multinationals with offshore income. But a lot more outrage at corporate tax dodging will be needed to fuel that effort.

In 2017, the Trump Administration went the other way and won passage of a tax bill that will further reduce corporate tax revenues through lower tax rates, new loopholes, and new tax incentives to shift U.S. corporate profits offshore. How far U.S. revenues will drop as a result, what lower revenues will mean for the country, and whether the public will demand new taxes on profitable multinationals, are policy issues that will require years to resolve.

In the meantime, when I look back on the Levin hearings, it seems to me their most important accomplishment was simply describing what some American corporations were doing to dodge their tax obligations. That truth-telling—disclosing the facts accurately and in detail—helped inform and energize a worldwide conversation on corporate tax dodging. That's the power of oversight.

Notes

1. *The Hidden Wealth of Nations: The Scourge of Tax Havens*, Gabriel Zucman (University of Chicago Press 2015), http://gabriel-zucman.eu/hidden-wealth/. The chart is used with permission from "Corporate Tax Chartbook: How Corporations Rig the Rules to Dodge the Taxes They Owe," Economic Policy Institute and Americans for Tax Fairness, Frank Clemente, Hunter Blair, and Nick Trokel (9/19/2016), Chart 7, at 10, http://bit.ly/2d0NRau.
2. See "American Corporations Tell IRS the Majority of Their Offshore Profits Are in 12 Tax Havens," Citizens for Tax Justice Report (5/27/2014), at 1, chart entitled, "The Dozen Most Obvious Corporate Tax Havens," citing data from the IRS and World Bank (hereinafter "CTJ Chart"), http://ctj.org/pdf/corporateoffshore-profitsirs.pdf. See also "The Effect of Profit Shifting on the Corporate Tax Base in the United States and Beyond," Professor Kimberly A. Clausing (6/17/2016), at 4, http://papers.ssrn.com/sol3/papers.cfm?abstract_id=2685442.
3. CTJ Chart.
4. In the debates leading up to enactment of Subpart F, President Kennedy stated in 1961:

> The undesirability of continuing deferral is underscored where deferral has served as a shelter for tax escape through the unjustifiable use of tax havens such as Switzerland. Recently more and more enterprises organized abroad by American firms have arranged their corporate structures aided by artificial arrangements between parent and subsidiary regarding intercompany pricing, the transfer of patent licensing rights, the shifting of management fees, and similar practices which maximize the accumulation of profits in the tax haven as to exploit the multiplicity of foreign tax systems and international agreements in order to reduce sharply or eliminate completely their tax liabilities both at home and abroad.

"President's Recommendations on Tax Revision: Hearings Before the House Ways and Means Committee," 87th Congress, Session 1 (1961), reprinted in *Tax Havens and Their Use by United States Taxpayers—An Overview*, report to the IRS Commissioner and others by Richard A. Gordon, IRS Special Counsel for International Taxation (1/12/1981), at 44, https://archive.org/details/taxhavenstheirus01gord.

5. See, for example, 26 U.S.C. § 952 (defining Subpart F income).

6. 26 C.F.R. 301.7701-1 through 301.7701-3 (1997).

7. See Notice 98-11 (2/9/1998) and proposed regulations (3/26/1998).

8. See Notice 98-35 (7/6/1998), withdrawing Notice 98-11 and the proposed regulations.

9. See 26 U.S.C. § 954(c)(6).

10. See 26 U.S.C. § 482.

11. "Corporate Taxpayers & Corporate Tax Dodgers 2008–10," Citizens for Tax Justice Report (11/2011), at 3–4, http://bit.ly/2jAVhZ7.

12. "The Effect of Profit Shifting on the Corporate Tax Base in the United States and Beyond," Professor Kimberly A. Clausing (6/17/2016), at Figure 4, papers.ssrn.com/sol3/papers.cfm?abstract_id=2685442. The chart is used with permission from "Corporate tax Chartbook: How Corporations Rig the Rules to Dodge the Taxes They Owe," Economic Policy Institute and Americans for Tax Fairness, Frank Clemente, Hunter Blair, and Nick Trokel (9/19/2016), Chart 16, at 19, http://bit.ly/2d0NRau.

13. "Revenue Statistics 2015—United States," OECD (12/3/2015), http://www.oecd.org/tax/revenue-statistics-united-states.pdf; "Reasons for the Decline in the Corporate Tax Revenues," Congressional Research Service, Mark P. Keightley, Report No. R42113 (12/8/2011), at 1, http://bit.ly/2zO3i3l; "The Corporate Income Tax System: Overview and Options for Reform," Congressional Research Service, Mark P. Keightley and Molly F. Sherlock, Report No. R42726 (12/1/2014), at 11, http://bit.ly/1behTOJ. See also *The Hidden Wealth of Nations: The Scourge of Tax Havens*, Gabriel Zucman, chart entitled, "The Effective Rate Paid by US Corporations has been Reduced by 1/3 since late 1990s," http://gabriel-zucman.eu/files/Zucman2015SlidesShort.pdf.

14. "The Corporate Income Tax System: Overview and Options for Reform," Congressional Research Service Report, at 11, http://bit.ly/1behTOJ.

15. The information in this section is based on "Offshore Profit Shifting and the U.S. Tax Code—Part 1 (Microsoft and Hewlett-Packard)," S. Hrg. 112-781 (9/20/2012) (hereinafter "2012 Microsoft-HP Hearing"), https://www.gpo.gov/fdsys/pkg/CHRG-112shrg76071/pdf/CHRG-112shrg76071.pdf.

16. Section 26 U.S.C. § 956(c)(1)(C); Treas. Reg. 1.956-2T(d)(2).

17. Section 26 U.S.C. § 956(c)(2); IRS Notice 88-108; General Legal Advisory Memorandum 2007-016. In addition, to be excluded from tax, all of the loans made by an offshore entity throughout the year must be outstanding for less than 60 days in total for that year.

18. 2012 Microsoft-HP Hearing, at 362, 615.

19. *Jacobs Engineering Group*, 79 AFTR 97-674 (C.C. Calif. 1997) (finding 12 serial short-term loans from a foreign controlled corporation to its U.S. parent should be treated as a single loan triggering tax under Section 956).

20. See 2012 Microsoft-HP Hearing, at 223.

21. The information in this section is based on "Offshore Profit Shifting and the U.S. Tax Code—Part 2 (Apple Inc.)," S. Hrg. 113-90 (5/21/2013) (hereinafter "2013 Apple Hearing"), https://www.gpo.gov/fdsys/pkg/CHRG-113shrg81657/pdf/CHRG-113shrg81657.pdf.

22. See 2013 Apple Hearing, at 203–204, "Amended & Restated Cost Sharing Agreement between Apple Inc., Apple Operations Europe & Apple Sales International" (5/2008).

23. Id. See also Paul statement, at 31–33.

24. See, for example, "Apple CEO Consulted Bill Clinton before Testimony," *The Hill*, David McCabe (8/15/2016), http://bit.ly/2ASFvfz.

25. The information in this section is based on "Caterpillar's Offshore Tax Strategy," S. Hrg. 113-408 (4/1/2014) (hereinafter "2014 Caterpillar Hearing"), https://www.gpo.gov/fdsys/pkg/CHRG-113shrg89523/pdf/CHRG-113shrg89523.pdf.

26. See, for example, "What State Needs to Do to Compete," opinion editorial by Doug Oberhelman, *The State Journal-Register* (2/14/2012), http://bit.ly/2mGumfo; "Caterpillar's Doug Oberhelman: Manufacturing's Mouthpiece," *Bloomberg Businessweek*, Mina Kimes (5/16/2013), https://bloom.bg/2jBKwG7.

27. See, for example, "Caterpillar Dealer Push May Drive Some Out, Levenick Says," Reuters, James B. Kelleher (3/6/2014), http://reut.rs/2ARj0HN.

28. 2014 Caterpillar Hearing, at 68.

29. See 5/30/2014 letter from Caterpillar to the SEC, reprinted in the 2014 Caterpillar Hearing, at 639–648, in particular the passage at 645.

30. 2014 Caterpillar Hearing, at 633–635.

31. See, for example, "Tax Avoidance—Google," London: House of Commons, Committee on Public Accounts, 9th Report 2013–2014, http://www.publications.parliament.uk/pa/cm201314/cmselect/cmpubacc/112/112.pdf; "Special Report: How Starbucks Avoids UK Taxes," UK Parliament Committee on Public Accounts, Minutes of Evidence, HC 716, Session 2012–2013, Tom Bergin, (10/15/2012), http://www.publications.parliament.uk/pa/cm201213/cmselect/cmpubacc/716/121112.htm.

32. See, for example, "Tough Debate with Multinational Companies on Corporate Tax Practices," European Parliament Committee on Tax Rulings and Other Measures Similar in Nature or Effect (TAXE) Press Release, (11/17/2015) (discussing committee's final hearing on tax dodging with witnesses that included 11 multinationals), http://bit.ly/2yXlMuC. The EU Parliament has since created two successor investigative committees, sometimes referred to as TAXE2 and TAXE3, to continue its examination of corporate tax dodging.

33. See, for example, "Corporate Tax Avoidance," Report by Australian Senate Committee on Economics References, No. ISBN 978-1-76010-274-6 (8/18/2015), http://bit.ly/1fFXLNX; "Chevron Hits Out at 'tax dodger' Claims at Fiery Senate Inquiry," *Sydney Morning Herald*, Heath Aston (11/18/2015), http://bit.ly/29LoKYL.

34. See, for example, "Judge Orders Microsoft to Give IRS What It Wants," *Seattle Times*, Matt Day (11/23/2015), http://bit.ly/2AZYmGa.

35. See, for example, *United States v. Microsoft*, Case No. 2:15-cv-00102-RSM (USDC WD Washington), Petition to Enforce IRS Summons (12/11/2014), http://bit.ly/2hAoqzh, and Order Granting Enforcement of Summons (11/20/2015), http://bit.ly/2zO3QpV; *Microsoft v. IRS*, Case No. 2:15-cv-00850-RSM (USDC WD Washington), Complaint for Declaratory and Injunctive Relief (5/29/2015), http://bit.ly/2hIg8Jv.

36. See, for example, "How Microsoft Moves Profits Offshore to Cut Its Tax Bill," *Seattle Times*, Matt Day (12/12/2015), http://bit.ly/1Z5qSfy. See also "Microsoft's Bermuda Subsidiaries Subject To Tax Inquiry, Documents Show," *Huffington Post*, Ryan Grim, Zach Carter, and Christina Wilkie (1/31/2014), http://bit.ly/2jBFtp4.

37. Caterpillar Form 10-K for the year ended December 31, 2014, filed with the SEC (2/17/2015), at 22 and A-30, http://www.caterpillar.com/en/investors/sec-filings.html.

38. Caterpillar Inc. 10-K filing with the SEC (2/15/2017), at 101, http://www.caterpillar.com/en/investors/sec-filings.html.

39. See, for example, Search and Seizure Warrants, Case Nos. 17-MJ-7038, 7039 and 7040 (C.D. IL 2/24/2017), http://bit.ly/2zVaU1B; "Caterpillar Goes from White House Kudos to Multi-Agency Raid," Bloomberg, Joe Deaux, Mario Parker, and David Voreacos (3/2/2017), https://bloom.bg/2mKc4Gd.

40. "Short Term Loan Exclusion from United States Property," IRS LB&I International Practice Service Transaction Unit, Document No. RPA/9414.01_01 (2015), at 8, https://www.irs.gov/pub/int_practice_units/RPA9414_01_01.pdf.

41. See, for example, "EU's Apple Tax Case Prompted by Senate Tip Off, Vestager Says," Bloomberg, Peter Chapman (9/9/2016), https://bloom.bg/2cuTnTa.

42. "State Aid: Ireland Gave Illegal Tax Benefits to Apple Worth Up to €13 billion," European Commission Press Release (8/30/2016), http://europa.eu/rapid/press-release_IP-16-2923_en.htm.

43. See, for example, "Europe's Bite Out of Apple Shows the Need for U.S. Tax Reform," *Wall Street Journal*, opinion editorial by Treasury Secretary Jacob Lew (9/12/2016), http://on.wsj.com/2ck7LMg.

44. See, for example, testimony of Apple CEO Tim Cook, 2013 Apple Hearing, at 60–61.

45. See, for example, "Communication on Further Measures to Enhance Transparency and the Fight Against Tax Evasion and Avoidance," Communication from European Commission to European Parliament and the Council, No. COM (2016) 451 Final (7/6/2016), http://data.consilium.europa.eu/doc/document/ST-10977-2016-INIT/en/pdf.

46. "Action Plan on Base Erosion and Profit Shifting," OECD (2013), http://bit.ly/1ecYiXB.

47. See, for example, "OECD/G20 Base Erosion and Profit Shifting Project Explanatory Statement: 2015 Final Reports," OECD, http://www.oecd.org/ctp/beps-explanatory-statement-2015.pdf.
48. See, for example, "OECD/G20 Base Erosion and Profit Shifting Project Action 13: Country-by-Country Reporting Implementation Package," OECD (2015), http://www.oecd.org/ctp/transfer-pricing/beps-action-13-country-by-country-reporting-implementation-package.pdf.
49. "Country-by-Country Reporting," Treasury Final Rule, 81 Fed.Reg. 126 (6/30/2016), at 42482.

12

Beaching the London Whale

"When Wall Street plays with fire, American families get burned."
Senator Carl Levin, London whale trades hearing (March 15, 2013)

The year 2012 was a hectic one for PSI. Our first corporate tax investigation was building to a crescendo, a Coburn investigation into social security disability fraud was intensifying, and a bank-related commodities investigation was picking up steam. That's why I thought PSI had to take a pass when a new bank scandal erupted in April involving a JPMorgan Chase trader dubbed the "London Whale." The whale had supposedly engaged in such massive, reckless credit derivatives trades that he lost the bank over $6.2 billion. After the story broke, JPMorgan cast him as a rogue trader, promised to absorb the losses without taxpayer help, and claimed there was nothing more to look at. Which, of course, made Senator Levin want to look.

When the Senate Banking Committee announced it intended to investigate, I thought PSI was off the hook—the Banking Committee would get the facts and let everyone know what happened. But Senator Levin didn't want to rely on another committee and called me in to see what PSI could do. As staff director, part of my job was to shield PSI staff from investigative demands that couldn't be met. I told Senator Levin that with the tax, social security disability, and commodity investigations underway, there was no one left to conduct a major new inquiry. Senator Levin knew we were already working flat out, so he sighed and didn't press me.

Instead, he turned to Ty Gellasch who handled banking, securities, and tax issues for him on his personal staff. Two years earlier, Ty had staffed the senator

© The Author(s) 2018
E. J. Bean, *Financial Exposure*, https://doi.org/10.1007/978-3-319-94388-6_12

in a successful effort to add a Merkley-Levin amendment to the Dodd-Frank Act codifying what was known as the "Volcker Rule." The Volcker Rule was designed to restrict certain high-risk activities by federally insured banks, but federal regulators had yet to finalize the implementing regulations. Senator Levin asked Ty to find out whether the whale trades would have been stopped by the Volcker Rule, if its regulations had been finalized. He also asked Ty to do his best to investigate the facts underlying the London whale trades, outside the confines of PSI.

Surprised but willing, Ty met with JPMorgan and bank regulators to get preliminary information, talked to the Banking Committee staff, requested documents, and began briefing Senator Levin on what he'd found. But Ty's inquiry kept raising more questions than answers. While the senator had initially focused on whether the trades would have violated the Volcker Rule, he began to have a range of concerns about the banking practices surrounding the trades. There was no way Ty could cover all the emerging issues or come close to replicating the full-court press of a PSI inquiry, which is what the boss really wanted.

Senator Levin's dissatisfaction grew when, in June 2012, Senate Banking members used a hearing on the whale trades to ask JPMorgan's CEO Jamie Dimon for advice on the economy instead of about what caused the derivatives disaster.[1] Senator Levin called me in and said PSI had to find a way to do the whale trades investigation on top of everything else. So we did.

I asked Allison Murphy, an efficient, cheerful, and fierce investigative counsel on our staff, to drop what she was doing and head up the new London whale inquiry. Given all the other inquiries underway, I warned her she'd have only limited help. Unfazed, she got a download from Ty, talked to our GOP colleagues, and put together an investigative plan. Given JPMorgan's strong reputation for risk management and the Banking Committee's seeming equanimity with what happened, I didn't expect her to find much. But I was wrong.

Among many unexpected revelations, the investigation found a massive JPMorgan derivatives portfolio, riddled with risk yet unknown to regulators.[2] The inquiry also uncovered a runaway train of high-stakes derivatives trading that had crashed through JPMorgan's risk limits while the risk managers shrugged or minimized the danger. It uncovered hidden losses, deliberate mispricing, and inaccurate financial statements. Bank executives downplaying bad bets while their traders doubled down on those bets, throwing good money after bad. Regulators both inattentive and misled. Worst of all, the investigation uncovered derivatives problems that stretched far beyond one bank and one trading fiasco.

The 2008 financial crisis had taught us, as Senator Levin once put it, that when Wall Street plays with fire, American families get burned. The whale trades opened a window onto a hidden world of high-risk derivatives trading posing billion-dollar threats to the U.S. financial system and, by extension, to U.S. taxpayers. They exposed a JPMorgan derivatives trading culture that piled on risk, misstated derivative values, disregarded risk limits, manipulated risk assessment models, disguised losses, dodged oversight, and misinformed regulators, investors, and the public. The facts were so compelling that, once disclosed, they forced federal bank regulators to re-evaluate the whole episode. The end result was not only a regulatory clampdown on abusive practices at JPMorgan, but a broader regulatory effort to limit derivatives risk.

Getting the Facts

Allison began the PSI London whale inquiry by assembling a small bipartisan team of investigators. The team included a senior Coburn staffer who, after our ranking member changed, was replaced by Stephanie Hall from Senator McCain's staff. It also included two detailees, Beth Baltzan from the Public Company Accounting Oversight Board and Eric Walker from the FDIC. Added firepower came from an evolving roster of fellows, interns, and law clerks. When the investigation intensified, Zack Schram and I also joined the team.

Learning About Credit Derivatives

Allison's next step was to line up a series of briefings to learn more about credit derivatives. The experts included academics as well as senior staff from the Office of the Comptroller of the Currency (OCC) which oversees large U.S. banks that trade derivatives. The experts gave the team the low down on derivatives generally, explaining they were complex financial instruments that derived their value from other assets. It was a subject we were familiar with from our financial crisis investigation.

The experts then bore down on credit derivatives—financial instruments that essentially enabled two parties to bet against each other on the creditworthiness of a specified financial instrument like a corporate bond, or a specified entity like a corporation. Typical bets were whether a bond would default or a company declare bankruptcy during a specified time period. Betting on creditworthiness turned out to be a tricky business. The experts explained how the financial status of bonds and corporations were evaluated over time, how credit derivatives were priced, how trades were structured, how the credit derivative markets worked as a whole, and how banks were supposed to monitor their trades and avoid outsized risks and losses.

To get a still broader perspective, someone on staff brought in a friend who, after graduating from college, had been trained for two years by a major bank on how to trade credit derivatives. In an amazing two-hour session, the ex-trader briefed us on his training regime—how a senior trader had explained the markets to him, let him trade with phantom money at first, and then gradually gave him more and more real cash to make trades, while critiquing his trading activity. He also explained how, under bank accounting and risk rules, he was required to report his profits and losses, and the value of his holdings, at the close of every business day.

He told us that, since credit derivative markets had relatively few players, most of the traders seemed to know each other and engage in never-ending cat and mouse games to gain trading advantages. He said the best credit derivative traders at his bank arrived early, traded with intensity all day, and then typically went to a bar at night to talk to other traders about the markets. He said that, due to the late nights at the bar, it wasn't unusual for traders to start their morning trading hung over. He warned us we were entering a strange world.

With that background, Allison set up a series of briefings with JPMorgan and the OCC to learn more about JPMorgan's credit derivatives trading activity in general and the London whale trades in particular. The briefings disclosed that only a handful of credit derivative traders had been involved with the whale trades, all of whom worked out of the bank's offices in London but reported to bank executives in New York. We also learned that the whale trades had lost their money over essentially a three-month period in the first quarter of 2012, before being shut down. Another interesting fact was that JPMorgan had financed the trades, in part, by using money from its federally insured bank deposits in the United States.

Those deposits had been made by clients at JPMorgan's many branches across the United States. JPMorgan's Chief Investment Office, or CIO, which was based in New York, was responsible for investing those deposits as well as other funds totaling, in 2012, about $350 billion. While the CIO placed the bulk of those funds in conservative, low-risk investments like U.S. treasuries and blue chip stocks, starting in 2006, it also sent a portion of the funds to the London credit traders for use in higher-risk credit trades. The hope was that those higher-risk trades would produce higher returns than the ultra-safe investments otherwise funded by the bank deposits. That U.S. federally insured deposits were used in the London credit trades was particularly striking, since it drew a direct line between the bank's higher-risk trading and a U.S. bank insurance program that, if all went wrong, could trigger a U.S. taxpayer bailout.

Requesting Documents

To dig deeper, Allison and the PSI team reviewed the documents Ty had collected and sent additional document requests to both JPMorgan and the OCC. Because the London whale trades had taken place over a recent, compressed period of time, both responded fairly quickly with a relatively limited set of highly relevant documents. They included trading records, memoranda, reports, and emails exchanged among the traders, their supervisors, and risk managers, and between the bank and its regulators.

In addition, because U.K. law required large banks to record nearly all telephone calls made by bank personnel involved with trading activities, we obtained records of hundreds of telephone calls made by the London traders. Our FDIC detailee Eric Walker took it upon himself to listen to virtually all of them and transcribe the most important conversations. When some turned out to be in French, one of our law clerks disclosed that he was fluent in the language and put in the hours needed to transcribe those calls as well.

Added information came from an internal investigation conducted by the bank itself. To evaluate the facts and develop remedial measures, JPMorgan had established a special management task force headed by a senior bank executive, Michael Cavanagh. For nearly a year, the task force gathered documents and conducted interviews. In response to PSI requests, the task force read aloud to PSI investigators portions of a few of its interview transcripts, including with the traders based in London, although it declined to provide transcript copies. In January 2013, the task force issued a 129-page public report.[3] While the task force report contained little that was new to the PSI team, it helped confirm many of the facts we'd already assembled.

Altogether, the PSI investigation compiled nearly 90,000 documents and audio files. The team used the information to develop detailed chronologies of events, identify key players, and locate evidence. It worked hard to develop an accurate picture of the London credit trading operations, how the bank managed its trading risks, and how the regulators oversaw the bank's activities. The team also developed theories about how the credit trades went wrong and why.

Interviewing the Players

The investigation moved into the next gear when Allison and Zack began scheduling interviews. They asked first to speak with the four London traders most immediately involved with the whale trades, but all four declined. Since all four resided outside the United States beyond our subpoena power, we couldn't compel their cooperation. Allison and Zack tried to convince the traders' legal counsel that it was in their clients' best interest to provide their side of the story, but the traders were unmoved. That meant the PSI team had to reconstruct the traders' actions based upon their emails, memos, and telephone conversations as well as the interviews they'd given to the JPMorgan task force.

To get as complete a picture of the facts as possible from other sources, Allison and Zack undertook a grueling set of interviews over the summer of 2012, scheduling them at least every other day and sometimes every day, including some Saturdays. They spoke with multiple bank employees as well as OCC regulators who'd overseen the bank or investigated the scandal. The interviews began with lower-level personnel and worked their way up the chain at both the bank and OCC. The PSI team also spoke with other regulators, banks, and traders who'd observed or acted as counterparties to JPMorgan's credit trades.

During the bank interviews, it became clear that the bank's outside legal counsel had spent significant time coaching bank personnel and attempting to limit the information they provided to PSI. In one session with JPMorgan's chief financial officer Douglas Braunstein, for example, when he was asked to explain a common bank term known as Value-At-Risk, he claimed he didn't know what the term meant. Allison and Zack paused in disbelief. Value-at-Risk was one of the key metrics used by the bank on a daily basis. Realizing his response was not credible, the bank's lawyers signaled to Mr. Braunstein that he could go ahead and explain the term, which he did.

Interviewing Jamie Dimon

One of the last interviews conducted by the PSI team was with Jamie Dimon, JPMorgan's CEO. It was critical to speak with him, since Mr. Dimon had personally waived some of the risk limits on the whale trades, approved financial reports that were later restated by the bank due to incorrect figures, and initially provided inaccurate descriptions of the whale trades to investors, analysts, and the public.

The bank wasn't pleased with the interview request, but after lengthy discussions agreed to a date. The week before, Allison received a call from one of the bank's outside lawyers who said a larger room would be needed, since the bank planned to bring an entourage of about 20 persons to accompany Mr. Dimon. After checking with our Republican colleagues to make sure they agreed, Allison called back to say the interview would take place in the same conference room as all other interviews, which meant the bank could bring 8–10 persons, but no more.

Another lawyer called Zack. The lawyer explained that, because Mr. Dimon was so well known, the bank needed to set up special arrangements to ensure his safe passage to the PSI conference room. It was the first security request we'd received in 13 years. After checking with me and the Senate Sergeant at Arms, Zack called back the lawyer. Zack explained that for the Sergeant of Arms to provide a special escort or other special security arrangement for Mr. Dimon, Senator Levin would have to make a written request. Zack noted that Senator Levin drove himself to work every day, walked to and from his office unescorted, and had never had any trouble. Zack asked whether the bank really wanted him to ask Senator Levin to send a written request to the Sergeant of Arms for special security arrangements for Mr. Dimon. A day later, the lawyer withdrew the request.

On the day of the interview, Mr. Dimon arrived at the Senate, went through the same security screening as the rest of the public, and walked to the PSI offices, apparently without anyone recognizing him. His entourage included lawyers, bank personnel, and two bodyguards.

The interview lasted most of the day. Zack and Allison took the lead in questioning him, using a list of questions developed beforehand by the bipartisan PSI team. Mr. Dimon answered all of the questions, although he couldn't remember some key documents and facts, and often paused for whispered assistance from his lawyers. Mr. Dimon also salted his answers with a number of expletives, including a few F-bombs that appeared to be part of his daily lexicon but were surprising in a Senate setting. At another point, Mr. Dimon began one of his answers by saying, "Zack, suppose you worked for me." It was a pugnacious, free-wheeling performance.

At the end of the day, Mr. Dimon left with his lawyers, staff, and bodyguards in tow. Apparently, no one bothered him on the way out. The press never got wind of his appearance, and nothing about the interview or his trip to Washington appeared in the media.

Altogether, PSI conducted over 50 interviews and briefings.

Writing It Up

Once the evidence collection, document analysis, and interviews were done, the next step was to write up what we'd learned. The final result was a 300-page bipartisan staff report supported by both Senator Levin and Senator McCain.

Writing up the results of a lengthy investigation isn't easy. It involves working through a lot of documents and evidence, and making a series of decisions about what really happened. To manage that task, Allison, working with Beth, had constructed a matrix of key facts and issues and, over the course of the inquiry, had diligently listed relevant documents and interview evidence addressing the central factual questions. Their matrix greatly simplified compiling the information needed to write the report. A second exercise in drafting the report was figuring out how to explain the complexities of the whale trades with an appropriate level of detail. We decided our goal was to remain technically accurate, but also to present the information in a way that would be comprehensible to policymakers and the public.

A third dimension of the drafting process was our desire to produce a bipartisan report. That goal required us to engage in a continuous dialogue with the McCain staff to reach a bipartisan consensus, not only on the facts, but also on how to describe those facts. A complicating factor was that Senator McCain had become the new ranking member on PSI in January 2013, well after most of the London whale document review and interviews were over. Luckily, the McCain staff was willing to put in the time and work needed to get up to speed.

To expedite the drafting, we assigned each chapter to a different person and required everyone to draft their chapters at the same time. I took on the role of editor-in-chief. My tasks included developing an outline showing how all of the issues would be addressed while minimizing duplication, ensuring everyone used consistent terms and footnotes, and keeping everyone moving. In addition, we knew that our readers would comprehend the whale trades best if they were presented as a story. So another key task was constructing an overarching narrative in a way that would also enable us to dig into the details of the particular issues.

We decided that the overarching narrative was a simple one: the JPMorgan whale trades lost billions of dollars, because the bank had a lousy risk management system that failed to curb the bank's appetite for high-risk bets. Since that explanation directly contradicted JPMorgan's self-portrait as a skilled risk manager, we knew we had to carefully marshal the evidence to support our version of events.

We broke down the narrative into five segments. The segments focused on how, during the first quarter of 2012, bank personnel had: (1) binged on high-risk derivatives trading; (2) mismarked the derivatives trading book to hide mounting losses; (3) disregarded multiple indicators of increasing risk; (4) dodged its regulators; and (5) misinformed regulators, investors, and the public about the nature, riskiness, and financial results of the whale trades. Together, the chapters wove a story laced with excessive risk and deceptive conduct. More than that, the whale trades exposed industry-wide flaws in derivative valuation and risk management systems that undermined the safety and soundness of U.S. banks heavily invested in derivatives.

Piling On Risk

The Levin-McCain report began by detailing JPMorgan's secretive, high-stakes credit derivatives trading.

The evidence showed that the derivatives that fueled the whale trades were conducted through a "Synthetic Credit Portfolio" sponsored by the bank's Chief Investment Office (CIO). The evidence indicated that, for years, the bank had failed to disclose the existence of the portfolio to its regulators, burying its activities and profit-loss numbers within the CIO's larger investment activities. The bank failed to disclose the portfolio even after the CIO traders went on a 2011 buying spree that increased the portfolio's size tenfold, from a net notional value of $4 billion to more than $50 billion. The OCC told PSI that, despite its status as JPMorgan's primary regulator, at the time the trading was occurring, it had no idea the CIO was wagering tens of billions of federally insured deposits on complex, high-risk credit derivatives.

Just the year before, the OCC had issued new regulations aimed at reducing risky bank investments. The new rules essentially required U.S. banks, over a transition period, to raise more capital from investors to offset any higher-risk activities. In other words, the riskier an activity or asset, the more capital a bank would have to raise to ensure that, in the event of a problem, it could cover its losses without requiring a taxpayer bailout. In addition—no surprise here—the rules generally treated derivatives as higher-risk assets requiring more capital.

The new capital requirements posed a quandary for JPMorgan, given its massive derivatives portfolios and other higher-risk assets. To reduce the new capital it would have to raise, the bank decided to reduce its risk profile—exactly the result the new rules were aimed at producing. So in early January 2012, the bank ordered the CIO and its other bank departments to reduce their risky assets and lower their capital requirements.

The CIO immediately targeted the Synthetic Credit Portfolio, which by then held over $51 billion in capital-intensive credit derivatives, and ordered the London credit traders to reduce its risky assets. But there was a problem. When the order came down, the demand for credit derivatives was already falling, their value was sinking, and the trading book had already begun to lose value. To sell the derivatives in those market conditions meant substantial losses.

The evidence indicated that the head of the CIO's international office, Achilles Macris, who was based in London, was dead-set against recording a big loss on the portfolio. He said as much to the head of credit trading, Javier Martin-Artajo, who relayed that message to the trader in charge of the Synthetic Credit Portfolio, Bruno Iksil. Rather than incur a loss, his immediate supervisors wanted Mr. Iksil and his colleague, a junior trader named Julien Grout, to reduce the portfolio's risk profile some other way.

Mr. Iksil and Mr. Grout tried, buying a growing mix of derivatives intended to offset the portfolio's existing risk. Due to their efforts, by the end of the first quarter in 2012, the portfolio contained over 100 different credit derivatives, some long, some short, some targeting U.S. credit risks and others European credit risks. But an internal bank analysis showed that the new holdings did not lower the portfolio's overall riskiness and did not lead to lower capital requirements. Worse yet, the overall market value of the portfolio was continuing to fall. To avoid recording losses, the traders responded by buying still more derivatives, essentially generating demand to prop up the prices.

At the end of January, Mr. Iksil urged his superiors to "take the pain fast" and "let it go." If they had taken his advice—selling the bulk of the credit derivatives right then despite the lower prices—the bank would have incurred limited losses, reduced the CIO's risk profile, and avoided higher capital charges. But his supervisors rejected his recommendation and again instructed him to find another way. The credit traders bought still more derivatives in February and March, trying to turn lead into gold, but it didn't work.

As the credit derivatives portfolio continued to lose value despite the purchase of additional assets, the traders began to panic. In a mid-March telephone call, Mr. Iksil told his colleague Julien Grout:

I don't want to overstate it but it's worse than before, there's nothing that can be done. This is the first time I've ever seen this, there's nothing that can be done, absolutely nothing that can be done, there's no hope. There is no solution, the book continues to grow more and more monstrous.

By then, the credit derivatives portfolio had tripled in size to $157 billion. Some holdings were so large that when the relevant derivative's value dropped by even a few pennies, it rolled into millions of dollars in losses. To counteract those falling values, the traders engaged in purchases so huge that the transactions began affecting global prices, roiling the $27 trillion worldwide credit derivatives market, and sparking a media hunt for who was behind the massive market-moving trades. On March 23, 2012, after being told the CIO credit traders were "defending" the bank's positions in the market, CIO head Ina Drew ordered the traders to "put phones down," stop trading, and undergo an intensive analysis of the portfolio.

A few weeks later, the press exposed JPMorgan as the bank behind the whale trades. When confronted publicly, the bank initially described the trades as part of a hedge designed to lower, not increase, the bank's overall risk. But that rosy description of the trades began to fall apart when its regulators discovered that JPMorgan was unable to identify the assets being hedged, how the credit derivative trades had lowered the bank's risk, and why the credit derivative paperwork differed from the paperwork for all other CIO hedges.

In an email sent to a colleague, an OCC examiner later scoffed at the bank's explanation, calling the Synthetic Credit Portfolio a "make believe voodoo magic 'Composite Hedge.'" At the Senate Banking hearing in June 2012, JPMorgan's CEO Jamie Dimon offered a different take, asserting that, while begun as a hedge, over time the "portfolio morphed into something that rather than protect the Firm, created new and potentially larger risks."[4] In fact, the Synthetic Credit Portfolio had piled on risk and exploded into losses that eventually exceeded $6.2 billion.

Hiding Losses

The second section of the Levin-McCain report discussed how, after the credit derivatives portfolio began losing serious money, the credit traders began mismarking the trading book to hide the losses. Our report exposed not only the mismarking at JPMorgan, but also the imprecise, malleable, and ultimately untrustworthy system being used industry-wide to record the market value of credit derivatives.

Under U.S. accounting rules, JPMorgan's credit traders were required to book the market value of their derivative holdings at the close of every business day. They did so by assigning a value, or "mark," to each of the credit derivatives in the Synthetic Credit Portfolio and then using those values to produce a profit-loss statement for the portfolio as a whole.

Julien Grout, as the junior-most credit trader, was responsible for assigning the marks to the individual credit derivatives at the close of each day and sending the portfolio's overall daily profit-loss statement to CIO headquarters in New York. The CIO then combined those figures with many others to produce the CIO's overall daily profit-loss statement. The CIO's data was, in turn, folded into JPMorgan's composite financial statement which presented the bank's daily profit-loss figures to its senior management and regulators. At each quarter's end, under Securities and Exchange Commission financial reporting rules, the bank was required to file a financial statement with the SEC and also make it available to the public.

To disguise the growing losses in the credit derivatives portfolio in early 2012, the credit traders in London began essentially overstating the value of some individual derivatives when calculating the daily profit-loss figures sent to New York. Their standard practice had been to value each credit derivative by using the midpoint in the daily range of prices offered to buy or sell that derivative in the marketplace. That's the typical way to value derivatives, and some commercial services, for a fee, regularly calculate the daily midpoint prices for a wide range of derivatives. Beginning in late January 2012, however, the JPMorgan traders stopped using the midpoint prices for some of its credit derivatives and started using more favorable prices within the daily price range in an effort to inflate the derivatives' value and minimize their losses.

The evidence indicated that the traders began using the inflated values, in part, at the insistence of their supervisor, Javier Martin-Artajo.[5] They weren't happy about it either. In one recorded telephone conversation referring to Mr. Martin-Artajo and the overstated prices, Mr. Iksil told Mr. Grout: "I don't know where he wants to stop, but it's getting idiotic." In another, Mr. Iksil tried to explain to his supervisor why, earlier that day, he had booked larger portfolio losses for some derivatives—"closer to where the market is"—despite repeated expressions of dismay by Mr. Martin-Artajo at reporting the losses.

At one point, Mr. Grout created a spreadsheet to track the difference between using the credit derivatives' midpoint prices versus the more favorable prices they'd been using when preparing the portfolio's profit-loss statements. Over just five days in March, the spreadsheet showed the difference exceeded $400 million. In other words, by overvaluing some individual credit derivatives, the traders had concealed over $400 million in portfolio losses. Mr. Grout stopped recording the differences after that.

In theory, the inflated values should have been caught and corrected when the CIO's books were reviewed each month by the bank's "Valuation Control Group" whose sole mission was to ensure that the derivative prices were accurate. JPMorgan later admitted, however, that its valuation "group" consisted of a single overworked individual who failed to perform any independent review of the derivative values appearing in the CIO books.[6] The marks also should have been questioned when, in March and April 2012, counterparties to the CIO's derivative trades began disputing the booked values, pointing out that the CIO was using much higher values for some derivatives than JPMorgan's own investment bank.

In fact, those disputes prompted a special one-time review of the CIO's derivative values in early April 2012, by JPMorgan's head controller, Shannon Warren. Documents from that special review showed that the controller's staff quickly realized that the CIO credit traders had stopped using midpoint prices when valuing some derivatives in the Synthetic Credit Portfolio, and replaced them with "aggressive" prices that minimized the portfolio's losses.

The controller's final report explicitly noted that change in the traders' pricing practices, detailing examples of pricing changes made to minimize losses. Nevertheless, the controller concluded that the CIO's actions were "consistent with industry practices." Her conclusion was based, in part, on U.S. accounting rules which did not require banks to use midpoint prices when valuing their derivatives, but allowed them to select any price within a market's price range. JPMorgan concurred in the controller's analysis, determining that the pricing discretion granted by U.S. accounting rules allowed the CIO traders to assign aggressive prices to the Synthetic Credit Portfolio's derivatives.

The problem with the position taken by the bank and its controller is, not only that the mismarked values contradicted the bank's standard pricing practice and the values used in other parts of the bank, but also that the traders had deliberately changed their pricing practice to conceal losses. While JPMorgan was correct that the accounting rules gave banks leeway in pricing their derivatives, the rules said nothing about banks using that leeway to make their financial results look better than they really were.

The deception didn't last. After the press unmasked JPMorgan as the bank behind the whale trades, pressure from regulators, investors, analysts, journalists, and the public forced the bank to admit the Synthetic Credit Portfolio had incurred substantial losses. As others began to ask questions about the nature and scope of those losses, JPMorgan re-examined its numbers.

In July 2012, the bank decided to restate its first quarter earnings report, erasing $660 million in profits attributed to the mismarked credit derivatives. The bank explained that, while the earlier derivative values did not violate bank policy or U.S. accounting rules, an internal investigation had uncovered telephone conversations in which the bank's traders had mocked the values they were assigning to some credit derivatives. For that reason, the bank decided that it had lost confidence in the "integrity" of the marks, replaced them with the midpoint prices it usually used, and restated the resulting earnings using the much lower values.

JPMorgan's cringe-worthy defense of its traders' dishonest valuations was bad enough. But the larger issue was that U.S. accounting rules apparently were so loose that they enabled derivative holders to pick almost any price in the marketplace when valuing their derivatives, whether those prices were outliers, varied within the bank, or were disputed by counterparties.

If derivative books could be cooked as blatantly as they were in the London whale case—enabling a bank to hide $660 million in losses without breaking the rules—then the system for pricing derivatives was a lousy one, generating prices that were overly subjective, open to manipulation, and inherently untrustworthy. The gravity of the problem was magnified by the fact that U.S. bank profits had become increasingly reliant on the valuing of their derivatives. It was a foundation-shaking realization.

Ignoring Risk Limits and Alerts

The third section of the Levin-McCain report focused on how the CIO's credit derivatives trading had triggered multiple risk alerts within JPMorgan's vaunted risk management system, but were allowed to continue unabated and unexamined. The evidence showed that, instead of sparking a careful review of the high-risk trading activity, the risk alerts had been disregarded, silenced by hiking the relevant risk limits, or resolved by re-engineering the risk assessment model to produce lower risk values for the investments at issue.

During the first quarter of 2012, the Synthetic Credit Portfolio had breached five different risk limits at the bank. The most well known was the "Value-at-Risk" or VaR limit. VaRs were intended to measure the total amount of loss that a particular investment activity could be expected to incur within a single day during ordinary market conditions. VaR limits were used to set ceilings, expressed in dollars, on the total amount of allowable losses to be incurred by a particular investment, portfolio, group, or department during the course of a single day.

JPMorgan had set VaR limits on various components of the bank's trading operations, including on particular portfolios, specific banking units like the CIO, and for the bank as a whole. It had also established an automated risk management system that tracked how close each portfolio or unit came to its VaR limit, issued alerts when a VaR limit was breached, and automatically forwarded those alerts to the relevant supervisors, risk managers, and bank executives. JPMorgan boasted that its sophisticated risk management system was efficient, effective, and guaranteed to protect the bank from significant loss.

In the case of the London whale trades, the system actually worked, providing multiple warnings of the losses threatened by the high-risk Synthetic Credit Portfolio. But there was another problem: bank personnel across the board ignored the warnings.

In January 2012, for example, due to its rapid growth and risky trades, the Synthetic Credit Portfolio breached the VaR limit, not just for the CIO, but for the bank as a whole. The breach continued for four days, meaning that on four consecutive days the credit derivatives portfolio risked losses in excess of what the bank had determined was safe. Alerts went up through bank channels all the way to the top, including CEO Jamie Dimon. In his interview with PSI, Mr. Dimon said he didn't recall seeing the alert, but admitted that the documents showed he'd been informed of the VaR breach and, on his staff's advice, had personally approved a temporary increase in the CIO's risk limit which technically ended the breach.

The documents also showed that Mr. Dimon had approved the temporary increase, in part, because he had been informed that a new VaR risk assessment model was just about to be approved that would show a much lower risk of loss from the Synthetic Credit Portfolio. And as promised, within days, the CIO won hurried approval of that new VaR assessment model. When applied to the Synthetic Credit Portfolio—surprise, surprise—the new model found it to be significantly less risky than the prior VaR model. In fact, in one fell swoop, it dropped the portfolio's risk rating by 50%. That lower risk rating meant that the portfolio no longer breached the CIO's VaR risk limit. It also meant that the CIO credit traders could resume trading, exacerbating the portfolio's risk and, ultimately, its losses.

During our investigation, we interviewed the CIO mathematician, Patrick Hagan, who designed the new VaR risk assessment model that produced the lower risk rating. He admitted he had no prior experience designing VaR assessment models and encountered stiff resistance from the bank's other modeling experts in validating his approach, but nevertheless won approval of his new model. He told the subcommittee that he and the CIO credit traders were convinced that the trades they conducted were significantly less risky than the prior model indicated. He explained both he and they viewed his new model as a more accurate reflection of the real risk.

Mr. Hagan also disclosed a number of operational problems that plagued the new model once it went into effect. He explained that, to produce an accurate risk analysis, the model required daily updates of numerous data elements from the credit derivatives marketplace. He said the bank had promised, but never actually delivered the funds needed, to set up automated electronic entry of those data elements into the model. Instead, Mr. Hagan said he was forced to enter the daily data himself, manually, using spreadsheets which frequently contained errors and often forced him to work late into the night. He also admitted that the model experienced a number of operational glitches which he had worked to resolve.

That a Ph.D. mathematician was doing manual data entry and software troubleshooting into the wee hours of the night, because JPMorgan refused to pay for an automated data entry system to support a VaR model analyzing $350 billion in risky assets, was a jaw-dropping revelation. So much for JPMorgan's nose-in-the-air, state-of-the-art risk management system.

Not only that, but the new VaR model turned out to be a bust. Within months, contrary to the model's predictions, the Synthetic Credit Portfolio was losing billions of dollars. In May 2012, the bank unceremoniously dumped the new VaR model and resurrected its predecessor.

The VaR limit wasn't the only risk limit breached by the credit derivatives portfolio. Four other risk limits also incurred sustained breaches, but did no better in getting a risk manager to take a closer look at the portfolio. For example, for months running, the portfolio exceeded established limits on what was known as Credit Spread 01, at times exceeding it by 1000%. When bank regulators asked about the breach, JPMorgan risk managers responded that the Credit Spread 01 wasn't a "sensible" limit so they were disregarding it and planned to allow the breach to continue. The regulators neither objected nor examined the trading activity.

When still another risk metric, called Comprehensive Risk Measure, projected that the Synthetic Credit Portfolio could lose as much as $6.3 billion in a year, the CIO's senior risk officer dismissed the projection as "garbage." But it wasn't garbage; it was a spot-on prediction, as that risk officer later acknowledged. But at the time, the credit derivatives traders and their risk managers thought they knew better and simply disregarded the warning.

Downplaying risk, ignoring one risk warning after another, waiving risk limits, and re-engineering a key risk assessment model to project a lower risk rating—all flatly contradicted JPMorgan's claim to prudent risk management. More broadly, the whale trades also demonstrated how easily any Wall Street bank could manipulate its risk controls.

The financial industry has repeatedly assured the American public that it can manage high-risk investment activities, because the attendant risks are measured, monitored, and limited. But the London whale trades showed how easily risk alerts could be disregarded, waived, challenged, or re-engineered. The London whale fiasco was a real-world example of the danger inherent in relying on Wall Street banks to prudently manage their own derivatives risks when bank personnel can so easily ignore or game a bank's own risk management systems.

Dodging Oversight

The fourth section of the Levin-McCain report asked the question: where were the regulators? Why didn't the regulators know about the bank's credit derivatives portfolio, uncover the mounting losses, inquire into the many risk alerts, or question the new risk assessment model? The evidence indicated that, while the regulators could and should have done more, they were wrestling with a belligerent bank that had failed to disclose key information, including about the gargantuan risk it had taken on.

JPMorgan's primary regulator was the OCC, which is charged with overseeing America's nationally chartered banks. Our investigation found that, for a period of more than five years ending in January 2012, the bank had failed to fully disclose to the OCC the existence of the Synthetic Credit Portfolio, much less its growing size, risk, and losses. The bank had essentially buried the portfolio within its larger investment activities. In addition, it had omitted overall CIO performance data from its regular reports to the OCC, failed to provide any separate CIO performance data during a critical four-month period in 2012, and omitted any mention of the portfolio's mounting losses during 2012's first quarter.

Even after the media exposed JPMorgan's role behind the London whale trades, the OCC had a hard time getting meaningful information out of the bank about the trades. In fact, when the media story broke in April 2012, the bank downplayed the trades so thoroughly that the OCC initially considered the matter closed. It was only in May, when the whale losses exploded and the bank realized it would have to report a $2 billion loss in its second quarter financial report, that JPMorgan finally informed the OCC about the portfolio's true status.

Depriving the OCC of data on its high-risk credit derivatives portfolio was just one example of the bank's sometimes combative attitude toward OCC oversight. Another example involved a 2010 OCC supervisory letter criticizing the CIO's failure to "document investment policies and portfolio decisions" to ensure they met the investment and risk expectations of senior bank management and the board of directors. The head of the CIO, Ina Drew, was less than gracious in responding to the criticisms. In an email sent to his supervisor, OCC Examiner-in-Charge at JPMorgan, Scott Waterhouse, described how Ms. Drew "'sternly' discussed [the OCC's] conclusions" with one of his examiners for 45 minutes, asserted that all CIO investments decisions were made "with the full understanding of executive management including Jamie Dimon," and warned how the OCC's proposed new controls would "destroy" the business by eliminating necessary flexibility. Mr. Waterhouse told PSI that level of resistance to an OCC recommendation on bank practice was both unusual and unwelcome.

During his PSI interview, Mr. Waterhouse also indicated that it was "very common" for JPMorgan executives to respond aggressively to OCC criticisms and recommendations. He recalled one instance in which bank executives yelled at OCC examiners and called them "stupid," and another occasion on which multiple bank risk managers essentially ganged up on a lone junior examiner and gave him a hard time.

Mr. Waterhouse also described an incident which suggested that the bank's belligerent tone went all the way to the top. He explained that, one day in August 2011, the daily profit-loss report for JPMorgan's investment bank stopped arriving in the OCC's email. No notice, no explanation, no report. Assuming it was a glitch, the OCC mentioned it to the bank only to be told that the bank had decided it would no longer deliver the bank's daily profit-loss statement, "because it was too much information to provide to the OCC."

Mr. Waterhouse explained that the OCC was forced to escalate the issue all the way to the chief financial officer, Doug Braunstein, to get delivery reinstated. At a subsequent meeting attended by Mr. Waterhouse, Mr. Braunstein, and CEO Jamie Dimon, when Mr. Braunstein disclosed that he'd restored delivery of the investment bank's daily profit-loss report to the OCC, Mr. Dimon raised his voice in anger at Mr. Braunstein. According to Mr. Waterhouse, Mr. Dimon revealed that he'd been the one who'd ordered the halt in delivery, because he didn't think the OCC needed the information.

It was a dismaying display of the bank's disregard for the OCC's oversight role and a graphic example of Jamie Dimon's getting on his high horse with the bank's chief regulator. We decided to include the incident in our report, because it illustrated the bank's sometimes disrespectful and combative approach to OCC oversight. When, pursuant to our standard practice, we provided a copy of the Levin-McCain report to the bank prior to its public release, we got immediate blowback about including the incident. The bank protested that, because the daily report involved the investment bank rather than the CIO, the confrontation was irrelevant.

In light of JPMorgan's aggressive reaction, we contacted Mr. Waterhouse to make sure he would stand by his description of the incident. He said that he would. We also contacted Senator Levin and Senator McCain's staff to inform them of the bank's objection. Both senators instructed us to keep the incident in the report, since it spoke volumes about the bank's at times inappropriate reaction to its regulator's oversight function.

Those and other incidents made it clear that JPMorgan didn't make life easy for the OCC. At the same time, the bank's intransigence didn't excuse the

OCC's own poor performance in curbing JPMorgan's high-risk credit derivatives trading before it blew up.

The OCC's primary job is to ensure that nationally chartered U.S. banks operate in a safe and sound manner. The OCC didn't do its job at JPMorgan. It failed for years to uncover a multi-billion-dollar, high-risk derivatives trading portfolio fueled with federally insured deposits; failed to investigate the CIO's multiple, monthlong breaches of the bank's risk limits; failed to challenge a new risk assessment model that, overnight, reduced the risk rating for the credit derivatives portfolio by nearly 50%; and passively accepted JPMorgan's claim that the London whale media reports were overblown. Worst of all, the OCC failed to establish an effective regulatory relationship with JPMorgan in which the bank accepted rather than fought the OCC's oversight efforts.

Misinforming Investors

The final section of the Levin-McCain report focused on what the bank said about the London whale trades once they became public knowledge.

To ensure fair and efficient markets, federal securities laws require market participants to refrain from making untrue statements or omitting material facts in connection with the sale or purchase of securities. Despite those legal requirements, JPMorgan initially misinformed regulators, investors, and the public about the nature, risk, and financial consequences of the whale trades.

The media first broke the story about the whale trades on Friday, April 6, 2012. JPMorgan's first public response came the next trading day, Tuesday, April 10, when its spokesperson, using prepared talking points approved by senior executives including Jamie Dimon, told reporters—incorrectly—that the whale trades were "for hedging purposes" and its regulators were "fully aware" of them. Not only were both characterizations inaccurate, but the bank also omitted the little fact that, during that same day, the portfolio was experiencing dramatic losses, eventually recording its largest daily loss to that date totaling $415 million.

More misinformation followed. On April 13, during a scheduled bank conference call with analysts, investors, and the media to discuss its first quarter earnings, the bank's chief financial officer Doug Braunstein volunteered a series of inaccurate statements about the whale trades. Despite receiving information beforehand raising multiple red flags about the portfolio, he said that the whale trades had been "put on" by the bank's risk managers and were fully transparent to regulators; the trades had been made on a "very long-term basis" and were essentially a hedge; and the bank believed the trades were consistent with the Volcker Rule which prohibits high-risk proprietary trading by banks. He also said the bank was "very comfortable" with the portfolio's investments. All of those public statements were untrue.

During the same call, CEO Jamie Dimon dismissed media reports raising questions about the whale trades as "a complete tempest in a teapot." He made that comment despite being in possession of significant negative information about the credit derivatives portfolio, including that it contained billions of dollars in assets rapidly losing value, the losses had escalated for three months straight, and selling the losing assets would be difficult.

In addition, both JPMorgan executives left out key negative information about the portfolio. They neglected to mention, for example, that the portfolio had breached multiple risk limits at the bank, had recently tripled in size to $157 billion, had seen its losses exceed $1 billion, and the CIO traders and managers had already moved into what one described as a "crisis mode." When asked why the bank downplayed the portfolio's negatives in April, multiple executives indicated that they thought the portfolio would improve. Essentially, they were gambling that the portfolio's bad bets would recover before anyone took a closer look.

Instead, the losses quickened. At the end of May 2012, faced with finalizing its first quarter financial reports at the SEC, the bank finally disclosed negative information. During a business update call, Jamie Dimon admitted publicly for the first time that the CIO's credit derivative bets had gone south, the losses exceeded $2 billion, more losses were expected, and the portfolio was much riskier than "previously believed." He said that the credit derivatives portfolio had been designed as a hedge but was "flawed, complex, poorly reviewed, poorly executed and poorly monitored." Over the next few months, the losses continued to skyrocket until, in July, JPMorgan dismantled the portfolio and distributed its deteriorating assets around the bank. In September, the bank stopped counting the portfolio's losses at $6.2 billion.

Recommending Changes

The London whale investigation provided raw evidence that the American public couldn't rely on a major bank to resist risky bets, honestly report derivative losses, or disclose bad news. In addition, it showed that complex derivatives posed financial threats to even large financial institutions with experienced traders. To address the problems, the Levin-McCain report offered a number of bipartisan recommendations for change. They included the following.

- Bank regulators should require large U.S. banks to identify all internal investment portfolios with derivatives over a specified size, require periodic reporting on the derivatives' performance, and conduct regular reviews of bank activities to detect undisclosed derivatives trading.
- When banks claim to be trading derivatives to hedge risks, regulators should require them to identify the assets being hedged and how the trades reduced the risks.
- Regulators should encourage banks to use independent pricing services to ensure accurate derivative valuations; require disclosure of any large valuation disputes with counterparties; and require disclosure and justification when derivative values start deviating from midpoint prices.
- When risk alarms go off, banks and their regulators should investigate the breaches, analyze the activity that triggered the alarms, and take action to reduce risks.
- Regulators should require banks to disclose any new risk models that materially lower purported risk, and look for evidence of model manipulation.
- Regulators should impose adequate capital charges for derivatives trading so that banks suffering losses don't require a taxpayer bailout.
- Regulators should finalize regulations implementing the Volcker Rule and thereby clamp down on high-risk proprietary activities at federally insured banks.

Going Public

In March 2013, the subcommittee held its hearing on the London whale trades and released the Levin-McCain report describing our investigative findings.

One key question in getting ready for the hearing was whether to invite Jamie Dimon to testify. Reasons to invite him included his personal participation in the facts and ongoing leadership role at the bank. Plus he would attract a lot of media attention. On the other hand, if he did testify, the media would likely portray the hearing as a battle between two titans: Senator Levin and Jamie Dimon. Their exchanges would likely dominate hearing coverage, and relegate the substantive issues to a dusty corner. Another drawback was that Mr. Dimon had already testified before the Senate Banking Committee, and it wasn't clear he had anything new to offer. After weighing the pros and cons, Senator Levin decided it was more important to focus attention on the issues raised by the London whale trades. That meant no Mr. Dimon.

With that decision out of the way, the subcommittee settled on two hearing panels, featuring senior executives from both the bank and OCC. We started with the bank panel, which Senator Levin used to walk through what happened and why. At the hearing, it soon became clear that JPMorgan had decided not to fight the facts, but to acknowledge its missteps and misconduct, which its witnesses did in response to hearing questions. The one fact they resisted was admitting that the bank's senior executives had misrepresented the whale trades when first disclosed to the public. The OCC panel focused on discussing the difficulties the OCC had encountered when trying to oversee a behemoth bank that resisted oversight and failed to see that its regulators were trying to protect the bank from its own worst impulses.

Perhaps the most fascinating witness of the day was Ina Drew, former head of the CIO. Until she left the bank after the London whale fiasco, Ms. Drew had spent 30 years at JPMorgan, rising to become one of its highest-ranking executives. She was a confidant of Jamie Dimon, oversaw the investment of $350 billion in bank deposits, and had been widely admired for her risk management skills. Her ending annual pay was in the range of $15 million.

The PSI hearing was Ms. Drew's first public appearance in connection with the whale trades. She showed up in a demure, blue-gray outfit with a fitted jacket, a gentle frill, and peter pan collar. Her blonde hair fell in soft curves. No power suit, no bright colors—no physical hint of her past executive rank. Her clothes whispered she was an innocent bystander to a tragedy. We shook our heads in cynical admiration of her sartorial choices. After the hearing, when a PSI staffer approached one of the bank's outside lawyers, he admitted to helping select her clothes.

During her PSI interview, Ms. Drew had indicated she didn't know until after the fact that the CIO traders under her command had been hiding losses by mismarking the trading book. She'd seemed shaken by the blatant mispricing. But our investigation also uncovered evidence that raised questions about just how innocent Ms. Drew really was.

At the hearing, Senator Levin asked her about one particular telephone call. The call took place in April 2012, soon after the whale trades had become public. The conversation was between Ms. Drew in New York, and Javier Martin-Artajo, head of credit trading in London, later indicted for pressuring the CIO traders to misstate the value of the credit derivatives.

During the call, Mr. Martin-Artajo told Ms. Drew that, for the first time in months, the credit derivatives portfolio appeared to have increased in value, rather than suffered more losses. He said he hoped to record an increase that day of between $20 and $100 million, depending upon how the market closed. In response, Ms. Drew gave him the following guidance:

Here's my guidance. It's absolutely fine to stay conservative, but it would be helpful, if appropriate, to get, to start getting a little bit of that mark back. If appropriate, so you know, an extra basis point you can tweak at whatever it is I'm trying to show, with demonstrable data ....[7]

At the hearing, Senator Levin read the transcript to Ms. Drew and asked about her suggestion that Mr. Martin-Artajo "tweak" the "mark" valuing the portfolio. She responded she'd made that suggestion, because she'd understood the traders were using very conservative values and noted she'd cautioned him to ensure any value was based on "demonstrable data." I didn't buy it. Aside from the lack of evidence that anyone at the CIO was using conservative marks to value the credit derivatives, there was no getting around the fact that Ms. Drew had used the word "tweak." And that she said tweaking the mark would be "helpful." That was a boss talking to a subordinate under huge pressure to minimize losses from a deepening financial disaster. Requesting a "tweak" didn't exactly signal an interest in accuracy.

By the end of the hearing, Senators Levin and McCain had raised disturbing questions about how U.S. banks were valuing their derivatives, managing their trading risks, and disclosing key information to regulators, investors, and the public. The hearing also questioned whether the American public could rely upon federal regulators to protect them from risk-driven banks dealing in derivatives.

Fixing the Problems

Media coverage of the London whale investigation was extensive and worldwide. More importantly, the media storm was followed by a series of developments aimed at holding JPMorgan accountable for its actions and addressing industry-wide problems related to the valuation, risk management, disclosure, and oversight of credit derivatives.

Bank Penalties

In 2013, after our hearing concluded, regulators imposed two civil monetary penalties on JPMorgan in connection with the London whale trades. The first, from U.S. and U.K. bank and securities regulators, sought to penalize JPMorgan's failure to supervise its traders, use of faulty risk controls, and assignment of inflated values to its credit derivatives portfolio. To settle the charges, the bank agreed to pay civil fines totaling $920 million.[8]

Commenting on the settlement, JPMorgan CEO Jamie Dimon expressed contrition: "We have accepted responsibility and acknowledged our mistakes from the start, and we have learned from them and worked to fix them. … Since these losses occurred, we have made numerous changes that have made us a stronger, smarter, better Company."[9] In his 2013 annual letter to shareholders, Mr. Dimon was even more blunt, calling the London whale trade losses "a real kick in the teeth" and one of the ways in which the bank had "let our regulators down."[10]

The second penalty was imposed by the U.S. Commodity Futures Trading Commission (CFTC) which fined JPMorgan $100 million for manipulating credit derivative prices through "reckless" massive trades. The CFTC wrote:

> [B]y selling a staggering volume of these [credit derivative] swaps in a concentrated period, the Bank, acting through its traders, recklessly disregarded the fundamental precept on which market participants rely, that prices are established based on legitimate forces of supply and demand.[11]

JPMorgan, again, admitted wrongdoing, including that its traders had acted recklessly in initiating massive trades intended to affect market prices, and paid the fine.

Together, the civil fines assessed against JPMorgan exceeded $1 billion. The settlements also required JPMorgan to undertake revisions of its internal controls and procedures.[12]

In London, in addition to the civil fine on JPMorgan, U.K. authorities imposed a $1.1 million fine on the senior-most U.K. executive involved in the whale trades, Achilles Macris, for failing to fully disclose the trades to U.K. regulators.[13] U.K. authorities did not fine any of the other three Londoners involved with the whale trades.

London Whale Indictments

In contrast to the civil cases, criminal proceedings were unsuccessful. The U.S. Department of Justice initially indicted the two London-based JPMorgan employees most closely linked to hiding the whale trade losses, Javier Martin-Artajo, who pushed the credit traders to cook the books, and Julien Grout, the junior trader who actually submitted the inaccurate figures. The charges against them included falsifying books and records and committing wire fraud.[14] Neither proceeding named Bruno Iksil, the original so-called "London Whale." When he was asked why, he pointed to his warning the bank against the trading strategy, his opposition to hiding the losses, and his cooperation with U.S. prosecutors.

To avoid standing trial on the criminal charges, the two JPMorgan employees fled to countries that generally oppose extradition of their nationals to the United States. Mr. Martin-Artajo went to Spain, while Mr. Grout went to France. Both were fugitives for more than three years. In 2017, the Trump Justice Department dismissed the indictments against both traders, stating it had determined, in part, that the Department could no longer "rely on the testimony of Iksil in prosecuting" the case.[15]

The Justice Department never took criminal action against any JPMorgan employee based in the United States, including the bank executives who made misleading statements about the whale trades to investors and the public. The same was true in the United Kingdom, where U.K. authorities took no criminal action against any individual involved with the whale trades. Despite the bank's admission of wrongdoing, no one went to jail or even to trial.

Bank Reforms

JPMorgan did express public remorse for its actions and promise reforms. In his 2013 annual letter to JPMorgan shareholders, Jamie Dimon wrote the following:

> Let me be perfectly clear: These problems were our fault, and it is our job to fix them. In fact, I feel terrible that we let our regulators down. We are devoted to ensuring that our systems, practices, controls, technology and, above all, culture meet the highest standards. We want to be considered one of the best banks— across all measures—by our shareholders, our customers *and* our regulators. … Our control agenda is now priority #1—we are organizing and staffing up to meet our regulatory obligations. …
>
> The London Whale was the stupidest and most embarrassing situation I have ever been a part of. But it is critical that we learn from the experience—otherwise, it truly was nothing but a loss. I also want our shareholders to know that I take personal responsibility for what happened. I deeply apologize to you, our shareholders, and to others, including our regulators, who were affected by this mistake.[16]

Gone was the bank's belligerent, dismissive attitude toward its regulators. In its place were a very public apology and a commitment to do better. While to some extent JPMorgan had little choice but to admit fault, the bank still said all the right things to recalibrate its relationship with its regulators.

The bank also made a raft of personnel, administrative, and procedural changes to remedy the weaknesses uncovered by the whale trades. One early action was to clean house, firing all four of the Londoners involved with the whale trades: Achilles Macris, Javier Martin-Artajo, Bruno Iksil, and Julien Grout, while also accepting the retirement of Ina Drew. The bank also clawed back some of the millions of dollars in compensation paid to those employees. In addition, the bank cut in half the 2012 pay of both Mr. Dimon and Mr. Braunstein, an action that sounds tougher than it was, since Mr. Dimon still took home about $11.5 million, while Mr. Braunstein took home about $5 million.[17]

In addition to personnel actions, the bank established a new Firmwide Oversight & Control Group that reported directly to the bank's chief operating officers, authorized that group to make decisions on compliance and control issues, and required every business line to appoint a business control officer to report to the group. The bank also increased its compliance budget and staff, and instituted new risk management measures.

The JPMorgan reforms were welcomed by the investigators at PSI, despite skepticism about some of them. The one we disliked the most was an increase in the number of risk measurements applied to credit derivatives from five to over 200 factors, purportedly to ensure the bank's risk analysts had adequate information to detect and prevent problems. Our reaction was that, during the whale trades, the risk managers disregarded data from five risk limits, so why would those same managers pay attention to data pouring in from 200 risk measurements? The problem wasn't the data; it was risk managers who failed to act on the data they had.

Still, we knew that strengthening JPMorgan's derivatives practices was a big deal, since JPMorgan was the largest derivatives dealer in the world and the largest single participant in world credit derivatives markets. Better derivatives practices at JPMorgan strengthened the entire derivatives industry, which felt good.

Volcker Rule Implementation

What also felt good was evidence that the whale trades investigation spurred changes that went beyond a single bank. One prominent example was the investigation's impact on the Volcker Rule.

The Volcker Rule had been enacted into law as part of the Dodd-Frank Act of 2010, through the efforts of Senator Jeff Merkley and Senator Levin. But three years later, its legally required safeguards were not being enforced. In simplified terms, the Volcker Rule prohibited federally insured banks from engaging in high-risk activities geared to profit the bank itself instead of its clients—so-called proprietary trading.[18] The reasoning was that, when a bank traded on its own behalf, it tended to engage in increasingly risky transactions that could lead to conflicts of interest with its customers and to taxpayer bailouts. The Volcker Rule was designed to stop high-risk, conflicts-ridden bank activities by reinstating a statutory prohibition on proprietary trading that had been part of U.S. banking law for more than sixty years, until its repeal in 1999.[19] Due to ferocious opposition from the banks, however, the final Volcker Rule wasn't as strong as it should have been and, worse yet, its implementing regulations had stalled.

In 2013, President Obama instructed the Treasury to work with the other federal financial regulators to get the Volcker Rule regulations finalized. As the regulators dug in, the London whale trades began to figure prominently in their deliberations, offering a recent case of a bank engaging in high-risk proprietary trading leading to billions of dollars in losses. As Daniel Tarullo, then head of the Federal Reserve's regulatory effort, put it: "One of the key mandates to the staff from all the five agencies working on the final rule has been to ensure that London Whale, in substantive and procedural terms, couldn't happen again."[20] According to the press, "he called the JPMorgan losses 'a real-world case' that allow[ed] them to backtest the Volcker rule, which bans proprietary trading at banks."

Volcker Rule regulations were finalized that same year. They faithfully implemented the law's prohibition on banks engaging in high-risk derivatives trading for the bank's own profit. One set of the provisions seemed designed especially to address the London whale trades: they required banks to identify each hedge at the time the hedge was entered into, specify the precise risks being hedged, explain how the hedge would lower rather than raise those risks, and lay out how the hedge's effectiveness would be measured.[21] The required documentation seemed geared to stop banks from attempting to disguise proprietary trading as risk-reducing hedges.

Even More Regulatory Fallout

The whale trades prompted other regulatory safeguards as well. U.S. regulations increased bank capital requirements for high-risk derivatives trading.[22] To prevent concealment of derivatives portfolios, the OCC instructed banks to disclose all "significant derivatives exposures, anywhere in the bank," and instructed bank examiners to check with third party data repositories to find undisclosed trading activity.[23] To clamp down on pricing misconduct, the OCC clarified that banks were prohibited under U.S. accounting rules from changing derivatives valuation procedures to hide losses.[24] To catch high-risk activities, the OCC required its bank examiners to investigate large or sustained breaches of risk limits.[25] The OCC also tightened controls over risk assessment models.[26] Concerns about suspect risk assessment models even reached bank regulators in Basel, Switzerland who provide guidance to bank regulators around the world.[27]

Conclusion

The London whale trades confronted Americans, already weary from the financial crisis, with another example of a bank behaving badly. The whale trades revealed how a U.S. bank had engaged in a little known, high-stakes, high-risk financial activity, while concealing its actions from regulators, investors, and analysts. The whale trades' hidden risks, sudden huge losses, shoddy risk management, and misleading financial reporting shook public confidence that Wall Street was back under control. Through its fact-based, bipartisan, in-depth investigation, PSI was able to disclose what really happened and spur government action to force a powerful bank to admit wrongdoing, penalize the abusive conduct, and put stronger preventative measures in place. It was one more demonstration of the value of congressional oversight.

Notes

1. See, for example, "The Senate's Muckraker," *New York Times*, Joe Nocera (3/19/2013), http://nyti.ms/2j4IXfL.
2. The information in this chapter is based on "JPMorgan Chase Whale Trades: A Case History of Derivatives Risks and Abuses," S. Hrg. 113-96 (3/15/2013), Volumes 1–2 (hereinafter "PSI London Whale Hearing"), https://www.gpo.gov/fdsys/pkg/CHRG-113shrg80222/pdf/CHRG-113shrg80222.pdf (Volume 1) and https://www.gpo.gov/fdsys/pkg/CHRG-113shrg85162/pdf/CHRG-113shrg85162.pdf (Volume 2).
3. "Report of JPMorgan Chase & Co. Management Task Force Regarding 2012 CIO Losses," reprinted in PSI London Whale Hearing, Volume 1, Exhibit 98, at 963.
4. PSI London Whale Hearing, Volume 1, Exhibit 3, at 528.
5. Id., at 288–289, 293–297; see also *United States v. Javier Martin-Artajo*, Case No. 13-MAG-1975 (USDC SDNY) Sealed Complaint (8/9/2013), ¶¶ 34, 38–39.
6. See *In re JPMorgan Chase & Co.*, "Order Instituting Cease-and-Desist Proceedings Pursuant to Section 21C of the Securities Exchange Act of 1934,

Making Findings, and Imposing a Cease-and-Desist Order," (9/19/2013), at ¶¶ III-4, 5, 7, https://www.sec.gov/litigation/admin/2013/34-70458.pdf.

7. PSI London Whale Hearing, Volume 1, at 659, Exhibit 32c; see also hearing testimony, at 43–44.

8. The bank paid $200 million to the SEC, and the remaining $720 million to the Federal Reserve, OCC, and U.K. Financial Conduct Authority. "JPMorgan Chase Agrees to Pay $200 Million and Admits Wrongdoing to Settle SEC Charges; Firm Must Pay $920 Million in Total Penalties in Global Settlement," SEC Press Release No. 2013-187 (9/19/2013), https://www.sec.gov/news/press-release/2013-187.

9. "JPMorgan Chase Reaches Settlements with SEC, FCA, OCC and Federal Reserve on CIO Trading Matter," Statement by JPMorgan Chase & Co. (9/19/2013), http://bit.ly/2AbAxy7.

10. Jamie Dimon 2013 letter to JPMorgan Chase & Co. shareholders, at 6–10, http://bit.ly/2AbouRn.

11. "CFTC Files and Settles Charges Against JPMorgan Chase Bank, N.A., for Violating Prohibition on Manipulative Conduct in Connection with 'London Whale' Swaps Trades," CFTC Press Release, No. PR6737-13 (10/16/2013), http://www.cftc.gov/PressRoom/PressReleases/pr6737-13.

12. See, for example, *In re JPMorgan Chase & Co.*, "Order Instituting Cease-and-Desist Proceedings Pursuant to Section 21C of the Securities Exchange Act of 1934, Making Findings, and Imposing a Cease-and-Desist Order," (9/19/2013), https://www.sec.gov/litigation/admin/2013/34-70458.pdf; *In re JPMorgan Chase Bank, N.A.*, CFTC Docket No. 14-1, Order Instituting Proceedings Pursuant to Sections 6(c) and 6(d) of the Commodity Exchange Act, Making Findings and Imposing Remedial Sanctions (10/16/2013), http://bit.ly/2AZHYpp.

13. See, for example, "Ex-JPMorgan Executive Fined $1.1 Million Over 'London Whale'," Bloomberg, Suzi Ring (2/9/2016), https://bloom.bg/1oo8dPa.

14. "Attorney General, Manhattan U.S. Attorney, and FBI Assistant Director-in-Charge Announce Charges Against Two Derivatives Traders in Connection with Multi-Billion Dollar Trading Loss at JPMorgan Chase & Company; Defendants Hid More than Half-a-Billion Dollars in Losses Resulting from Derivatives Trading in JPMorgan's Chief Investment Office; a Third Trader, Bruno Iksil, Entered a Non-Prosecution Cooperation Agreement," DOJ Press Release No. 13-272 (8/14/2013), https://www.justice.gov/usao-sdny/pr/attorney-general-manhattan-us-attorney-and-fbi-assistant-director-charge-announce. The SEC also filed parallel civil charges. See "Securities and Exchange Commission v. Javier Martin-Artajo and Julien G. Grout, Civil Action No. 13-CV-5677 (S.D.N.Y.)," SEC Press Release No. 22779 (8/14/2013), http://www.sec.gov/litigation/litreleases/2013/lr22779.htm.

15. "Acting U.S. Attorney Announces Filing of Motion to Dismiss Pending Charges in United States V. Javier Martin-Artajo and Julien Grout," DOJ Press Release No. 17-228 (7/21/2017), https://www.justice.gov/usao-sdny/pr/

acting-us-attorney-announces-filing-motion-dismiss-pending-charges-united-states-v.

16. Jamie Dimon 2013 letter to JPMorgan Chase & Co. shareholders, at 7–9, http://bit.ly/2AbouRn.

17. See, for example, PSI London Whale Hearing, at 35; "JPMorgan Halves Dimon's Bonus to $10.5 Million after London Whale Fiasco," *Forbes*, Steve Schaefer (1/16/2013), http://bit.ly/2zP8fbE.

18. Dodd-Frank Wall Street Reform and Consumer Protection Act, Section 619, P.L. 111-203 (7/21/2010).

19. Proprietary trading was banned by Section 16 of the Glass-Steagall Act of 1933, P.L. 73-66, but that ban was dissolved by the Gramm-Leach-Bliley Act of 1999, also known as the Financial Services Modernization Act, P.L. 106-102, which repealed the Glass-Steagall Act.

20. "Fed's Tarullo Says Volcker Rule Will Prevent More London Whales," Bloomberg, Jeff Kearns and Jesse Hamilton (11/23/2013), https://bloom.bg/2hAXJui.

21. See also steps taken by the OCC with respect to the banks it regulates, PSI London Whale Hearing, OCC Responses to Questions for the Record, Exhibit 101, at 1126.

22. See, for example, id., at 1127.

23. See, for example, id., at 1116–1117.

24. See, for example, id., at 1121; see also "OCC Accounting Guidance to Banks That File Call Reports—On Derivatives Valuation," (7/1/2013), http://www.fdic.gov/news/news/financial/2013/fil13029a.pdf ("[I]t would be inappropriate for an entity to alter its valuation methodology or policies to achieve a desired financial reporting outcome. An example of an inappropriate change in valuation methodology that would result in a fair value estimate that would not be representative of a derivative position's exit price would be for an entity to migrate from a mid-market pricing convention to using a price within the bid-ask spread that is more advantageous to the entity to offset the impact of adverse changes in market prices or otherwise mask losses.").

25. See, for example, PSI London Whale Hearing, OCC Responses to Questions for the Record, Exhibit 101, at 1119–1121.

26. See, for example, id., at 1123–1126.

27. See, for example, "Reducing Excessive Variability in Banks' Regulatory Capital Ratios: A Report to the G20," Basel Committee on Banking Supervision (11/2014), http://www.bis.org/bcbs/publ/d298.pdf; "The Manipulation of Basel Risk-Weights," Mike Mariathasan, Ouarda Merrouche, *Journal of Financial Intermediation*, Volume 23, Issue 3 (2014), at 300–321, http://econpapers.repec.org/article/eeejfinin/v_3a23_3ay_3a2014_3ai_3a3_3ap_3a300-321.htm.

13

Targeting Commodity Speculation

"But to tell the truth, Sam, I had sort of made up my mind to keep out of speculation since my last little deal. A man gets into this game, and into it, and into it, and before you know he can't pull out—and he don't want to."
Frank Norris, The Pit: A Story of Chicago *(1903)*

Tax cheats made Senator Levin see red. So did money laundering, corruption, and corporations behaving badly. But another topic rang his outrage bell so incessantly that it became a constant on the PSI calendar—commodity speculation. While most members' eyes glazed over at just the mention of the topic, Senator Levin saw deeper. We ended up with more hearings on commodity speculation than any other, and it even starred in our last Senate hearing.

"Commodities" are commercial goods traded in bulk on specialized markets for trillions of dollars. They include staples like oil, natural gas, wheat, coffee, and copper. The problem that transfixed Senator Levin: price manipulation and excessive speculation that distorted prices and often forced American families and businesses to pay more than they should for basic necessities like electricity, fuel, and food.

In theory, commodity prices are set by the marketplace—the invisible hand of capitalism using numerous individual transactions to set prevailing market prices. But pricing theory and reality don't always jibe. One reason is price manipulation, caused by traders who secretly corner or squeeze a market by buying up goods (or financial instruments representing those goods) and then force everyone to pay inflated prices. Another is "excessive speculation," caused by traders who engage in such massive commodity transactions that they distort market prices that way. The federal Commodity Exchange Act

© The Author(s) 2018
E. J. Bean, *Financial Exposure*, https://doi.org/10.1007/978-3-319-94388-6_13

outlaws both price manipulation and excessive speculation, but outlawing them isn't the same as preventing them.

Over the years, Senator Levin had repeatedly witnessed commodity prices that made no economic sense—prices that spiked or crashed out of sync with market forces of supply and demand, generating windfall profits for crafty traders and harming American families and businesses forced to ride the roller coaster price changes. He wanted to stop the abuses.

He held his first in-depth investigation in 2001, after Michigan gasoline prices drove consumers crazy with seemingly irrational and costly price swings. That investigation led to a second one focused on crude oil prices. Which led, in turn, to a whole series of PSI inquiries that, along the way, required us to confront financial heavyweights, inept bureaucrats, arrogant bankers, and multiple victims paying through the nose for overpriced necessities.

The investigations also forced us to wade through the complexities of modern commodity markets, which included an exploding array of trading tools like futures, options, forwards, and swaps, and nonsense legal barriers that crippled market oversight. We uncovered complex games by commodity traders playing one market off another to manipulate prices, timid or indifferent exchange officials, and the federal agency responsible for policing commodity markets, the Commodity Futures Trading Commission, disabled by inadequate funding and limited authority.

Together, the PSI investigations exposed multiple problems and threats besetting the pricing of some of the most vital components of a healthy economy—energy, food, and raw materials. PSI's work also helped fuel reforms. They included closing a regulatory gap known as the "Enron Loophole" barring oversight of key energy markets; imposing safeguards on novel trading tools like commodity swaps; increasing market transparency; clamping down on excessive speculation; and reducing bank involvement with physical commodities. It was a grinding battle worth fighting; it is also a battle far from won.

Pricing Gasoline

Senator Levin's years-long journey into the commodities world began in 2001, when he initiated an investigation into spiking Michigan gasoline prices.[1] At the time, Democrats were the majority party in the Senate by a slim margin, and he was in his first tour of duty as PSI chair. Since he'd already ordered everyone on his PSI staff to investigate Enron's 2001 bankruptcy, he decided to hire a new staffer to lead the inquiry into gasoline pricing.

The new hire was Dan Berkovitz, an energetic Washington professional with a black mustache, curly black hair, a big smile, and an earnest, professorial demeanor. He was an expert on energy markets, having worked at the Department of Energy, Nuclear Regulatory Commission, and a Senate energy subcommittee. He wasn't then an expert on commodity markets but, over the next eight years, by sheer force of will and intellect, he became one.

Because I was assigned to the Enron team, I played no part in the gasoline pricing investigation. But I did watch it from afar. Working with Linda Gustitus, then Senator Levin's PSI staff director, with assists from Laura Stuber and Bob Roach, Dan produced a 400-page report pulling back the curtain on how gasoline prices were set in three different regions of the country. The 2002 report detailed how, over the prior three years, retail gasoline prices had risen faster than at any time in 50 years, producing higher prices overall, "extraordinary" price spikes, and unprecedented price volatility. The report also disclosed that, for every one-cent increase per gallon of gas, the income to oil companies rose by $1 billion per year. Pennies mattered.

The report explained how gasoline prices were influenced by multiple factors including crude oil costs and refining expenses. It also disclosed that the closing of over 100 U.S. oil refineries, followed by a flurry of oil industry mergers, had dramatically reduced competition and increased concentration in the oil industry. The result was, in many states, that four firms or fewer essentially controlled gasoline production. And because there were so few firms, actions by any one of them could have a disproportionate impact on local gasoline supplies and prices.

The report explained further that, in many states, oil refineries had chosen to maintain low gasoline inventories that restricted local supplies and maintained pressure on prices. In most cases, the inventories provided no more than a three-day supply to meet an area's gasoline needs. As Senator Levin later explained, with supplies so tight and the market so concentrated, "the market responds wildly to the slightest problem or potential problem."

The report's most powerful evidence was an array of internal oil company documents, unearthed by PSI subpoenas, showing how oil industry executives plotted to hike prices by limiting gasoline production, supplies, or imports. A Mobil oil memo, for example, discussed blocking the start-up of a refinery called Powerine that would produce more gasoline: "Needless to say, we would all like to see Powerine stay down." A Texaco memo discussed changing gasoline specifications "to assist in reducing supplies." An Exxon memo advised against deals that would lead to "importing barrels to the West Coast." A Mobil memo counseled against importing gasoline, because it would depress profit margins. Another company, ARCO, advised: "Export to keep the market tight." Still another proposed exporting gasoline to the Gulf Coast even at a loss, because the losses "would be more than offset by an incremental improvement in the market price" of the remaining gasoline.

An internal document from BP—formerly known as British Petroleum— was perhaps the most dramatic. It presented a long list of ideas discussed during a "brainstorming" session among senior BP executives on ways to reduce Midwestern gasoline supplies and thereby hike Midwestern gas prices by 1–3 cents per gallon. Options included shutting down some refining capacity, exporting gasoline to Canada, convincing cities outside of the Midwest to request reformulated gas pulled from Midwestern supplies, lobbying for environmental regulations to ban chemicals that made gasoline flow faster in pipelines; and offering incentives to discourage a specific company from shipping gasoline to Chicago. Together, the documents provided shocking first-hand evidence of oil company efforts to reduce gasoline supplies and hike gasoline prices paid by American consumers.

Adding insult to injury was an internal Marathon oil company document that praised Hurricane Georges for providing a "helping hand" to "oil producers," noting that the hurricane had "caused some major refinery closures, threatened offshore oil production and imports, and generally lent some bullishness to the oil futures market." That an oil company was cynically celebrating a hurricane for restricting gasoline production and hiking prices would never have come to light without the PSI inquiry.

In April 2002, Senator Levin held two days of hearings on the investigative findings. A bipartisan mix of Senators attended, all of whom were troubled by spiking gasoline prices. Senator Susan Collins, PSI's then ranking Republican, for example, provided a strong opening statement at the hearing that reaffirmed the report's fact-finding about higher gasoline prices, reduced oil company competition, and tighter gasoline inventories.

On the hearing's first day, the opening panel was a lineup of executives from five major oil companies: BP, ChevronTexaco, ExxonMobil, Marathon, and Shell Oil. All five executives essentially claimed their companies were reliable, good faith producers of gasoline, whose pricing was buffeted by crude oil costs, refining limitations, regulatory requirements, and other market forces beyond their control. While Senator Levin acknowledged many of those factors did impact gasoline prices, he explained that, for purposes of the hearing, "what we want to focus on is what our staff investigation disclosed, which is strong evidence that you don't simply respond to market factors, but that you actively help to create and maintain a tight market."

Senator Levin went through the oil company documents and pressed the oil executives to explain them. He started off with the BP memo listing options for restricting gasoline supplies and hiking prices. In response, the BP executive disavowed all of the discussed options and agreed they were "outrageous" and "inappropriate." Senator Levin also pressed the oil executives about the practice of "parallel pricing" in which retail gasoline stations were compelled by their suppliers to look to their competitors when setting gasoline prices, resulting in price increases that rose and fell in tandem among local outlets, with little or no pricing competition among them. The oil companies defended the practice.

Senator Levin's Republican colleagues asked more tough questions. Senator Collins pressed the witnesses about why their companies didn't make the investments needed to avoid the refinery disruptions blamed for causing gasoline price spikes. Senator Bunning from Kentucky asked about local gasoline pricing differences that made no economic sense. Senator Voinovich from Ohio asked whether the companies planned to expand their refining operations to increase capacity and competition, only to be informed by most that they were content with the refineries as is. The oil executives made no apologies and offered no solutions for the rising, volatile gasoline prices raging across the country.

By the end of the hearings, the PSI investigation had disclosed to the public a wealth of new factual information related to why gasoline prices were spiking, the role played by oil companies, and why gasoline price competition was so often missing in local communities. To curb future pricing abuses, among other steps, Senator Levin urged the Federal Trade Commission to oppose new oil industry mergers that would further concentrate the market and give individual oil companies even more market power over U.S. gasoline prices.

Pricing Crude Oil

Senator Levin was so energized by the gasoline pricing hearing that he immediately ordered a new investigation to dig deeper into the facts. After consulting with Dan and Linda, he decided the focus should be on crude oil prices, which were a major factor in gasoline prices. Crude oil was also used to manufacture home heating oil, jet fuel, diesel, and other fuels, making crude oil prices even more important to consumers and businesses. In addition, industry insiders had tipped Dan that some oil companies might be trying to manipulate crude oil market prices. Senator Levin asked Dan to lead the new investigation. Senator Levin asked me to assist.

I have to admit, at first, I wasn't thrilled with my new assignment. Investigating commodity markets generally, and crude oil in particular, struck me as dull and difficult. But Dan began to turn me around. The more he taught me about commodity markets, the more I began to understand that fairly-priced commodities were the lifeblood of a thriving economy and a critical affordability issue for average Americans.

Learning the Basics

Since I knew virtually nothing about commodities, I told Dan that, if he wanted me to help with the investigation, he'd have to start with the basics. So he did.

His first step in my education was to get me to grasp the rich diversity of goods that made up commodity markets. The crude oil market was the single largest commodities market in the world, trading hundreds of millions of barrels each day. Another huge market involved natural gas, which was used to power electricity and manufacturing plants around the globe. Copper markets allocated goods critical to computers, cable wiring, and plumbing. Aluminum markets supported the construction of aircraft, vessels, cars, and industrial machines. Gold and silver markets traded ingots supporting public treasuries, banks, and private billionaires, as well as the jewelry industry and certain medical procedures. Cotton clothed billions. Wheat and corn fed billions more. Coffee, sugar, cocoa, and orange juice met consumer needs spanning the globe. Even cattle and pork bellies played critical roles in feeding the hungry. "Commodity" was, in fact, a poor gray word for all the vital economic activity fueled by a myriad of agricultural, industrial, and energy-based products.

Dan's next step was to teach me about commodity "markets," the places where bulk commodities are bought and sold. His big message was that every commodity had its own peculiar market, with rules, contracts, trading rhythms, and pricing parameters specific to that product. Oil markets were nothing like wheat markets which were nothing like gold markets. Each had to be studied and understood on its own terms.

He also taught me that it was important to keep in mind that every commodity was sold in two very different types of markets—physical and financial—which interacted in complex ways. Both affected a commodity's price.

The "physical" market was where the commodity was sold to buyers interested in taking possession of the physical goods. Buyers often wanted the physical goods to produce another product, such as using wheat to make bread, crude oil to refine gasoline, or natural gas to produce electricity. Physical markets that facilitated immediate delivery of the goods were typically referred to as "spot" markets.

In other physical markets, rather than take immediate delivery of the goods, a buyer took possession of a document, such as a warehouse certificate, signaling ownership of physical goods being held in storage, such as copper or aluminum. Stored goods could be held for later use or resale. Dan explained that the amount of commodities held in storage—inventory levels—also affected prices. High inventory levels generally meant more supply and lower prices; low inventories generally meant less supply and higher prices. He noted that the prices fetched by commodities on physical spot markets, as well as their inventory levels, also impacted commodity prices on "financial" markets.

"Financial" markets referred to places where financial instruments representing physical commodities were bought and sold. The most well known were the highly regulated "futures exchanges" where registered "future merchants" sold standardized futures contracts promising delivery of a standard amount of a physical commodity at a specified price on a specified date in the future. On the specified "closing" date, the futures contract typically arranged for delivery of the physical commodity even though, in the vast majority of cases, neither the buyer nor seller wanted to take actual possession of the goods. They were focused instead on the profits to be made from buying or selling the futures contracts prior to their closing dates.

Dan taught me that each commodity had its own standardized futures contract with rules for pricing, storing, and delivering the commodity. Again, a crude oil futures contract was nothing like a wheat contract which was nothing like a gold contract. For example, while standard futures contracts sold commodities in industrial-sized lots, the volumes differed—crude oil sold in batches of 1000 barrels each, soft red winter wheat in units of 5000 bushels, and Grade A copper in units of 25 metric tons. The contracts also used different time periods and closing dates on which the specified commodity had to be delivered or the contract settled in a cash transaction. And each contract could be sold multiple times at multiple prices prior to its closing date. Dan explained that the transactions could be executed in person on a trading floor, by brokers doing deals over the telephone, or by traders interacting electronically by computer.

Dan explained further that futures markets, which have been around for more than 100 years, were used to set worldwide commodity prices. At the time of our investigation in 2003, the major futures exchanges were the New York Mercantile Exchange (NYMEX); Chicago Mercantile Exchange (CME); Chicago Board of Trade (CBT); London Metal Exchange (LME); and the International Petroleum Exchange (IPE) in London. Each exchange oversaw the trading of a variety of futures contracts covering dozens of different commodities.

In the United States, futures exchanges were policed by the Commodity Futures Exchange Commission (CFTC), an independent federal agency charged with ensuring orderly futures markets and preventing trading abuses like price manipulation and excessive speculation. Because the markets were so large and complex, trading abuses were tough to detect and even tougher to prove or punish. So federal law and the CFTC favored prevention over punishment. As a result, the CFTC and the futures exchanges it oversaw had developed a variety of preventative measures, including requiring traders to file large trading reports, placing limits on the total futures held by any one trader, enabling regulators to quiz traders about transactions raising pricing concerns, and even forcing individual traders to reduce their futures holdings.

While regulated futures exchanges once held a monopoly over the trading of financial instruments based on commodity prices, by 2003, other types of financial markets had also emerged. Traders used the phrase "over-the-counter" or "OTC" to refer to commodity-related financial instruments that were traded outside of the regulated futures exchanges. One common scenario involved parties whose trading needs couldn't be met by a standard futures contract and wanted a customized OTC contract instead. Dan indicated customized OTC contracts were a longstanding and useful, if nontransparent and largely unregulated, supplement to the regulated futures markets. Historical data also suggested they played a relatively small role in the trading.

Trading commodities through unregulated electronic markets was something else again. Back then, using computer programs to trade commodities was still relatively new. In addition, the new electronic markets often used a new financial instrument called "commodity swaps" to conduct their trading. Dan explained that, beginning around 2000, swaps began competing with futures as a tool used by speculators to profit from commodity price changes. Commodity swap contracts were worded differently than futures contracts, but the two types of contracts functioned in such similar ways that some swaps were referred to as future "look-alikes." While some swaps were traded on regulated futures exchanges, others traded on the unregulated electronic exchanges that increasingly resembled futures exchanges, but claimed to be able to operate outside of CFTC oversight due to loopholes in the law.

Some critics charged that commodity swaps were futures parading under another name and cast them as unlawful attempts to circumvent regulation of the futures markets. Legal disputes had erupted over whether commodity swaps should be treated like futures subject to CFTC oversight, and cases were then making their way through the courts. Dan warned that, at the moment, the law was a mess, and the increasing use of unregulated electronic markets to trade commodity-related swap contracts threatened to disrupt commodity markets worldwide.

Differentiating Commodity Markets from Stock Markets

A final nugget of wisdom from Dan involved teaching me the difference between commodity markets and stock markets. He explained that many market participants—even regulators—thought the two should be treated the same, even though they had very different goals, constituencies, and rules.

Dan explained that, from their inception, commodity markets had been designed to be used primarily by commodity producers and users to set market-based prices for their goods, using actual transactions executed by individual buyers and sellers. The resulting commodity prices were intended to reflect fundamental market forces of supply and demand. A second key goal was to help commodity producers and users "hedge" against price changes, by enabling them to enter into a contract that locked in the price that would be paid for the goods at a particular date in the future. Think of farmers who want to sell their crops and grocers who want to buy them. Locking in the price enabled both the producer and user to plan for their costs and returns, without continuing to be at the mercy of an unpredictable market. Hedging through the commodity markets was vital to both sets of market participants.

In addition, Dan explained that, while the needs of commodity producers and users were viewed as paramount, commodity markets also accommodated trading by "speculators." Speculators were defined by U.S. commodities law as traders who did not plan to use the physical commodities being traded, but sought simply to profit from the changes in commodity prices over time. Dan explained that speculators were viewed as market participants who helped grease the wheels of commerce, but whose profit-making aims were subordinate to the primary market goals of price discovery and hedging. As evidence, he noted that, for many commodities, the CFTC imposed limits on the number of futures contracts that an individual speculator was permitted to hold at any one time. Those "position limits"—which applied only to speculators and not to commodity producers or users—were designed to prevent speculators from dominating the trading, or cornering or squeezing the market, and thereby distorting commodity prices.

Stock markets, in contrast, had completely different goals. They had no stake in pricing physical commodities. Instead, stock markets were designed to attract investors who, by buying or selling shares of stock, contributed to the market value of specific businesses. The primary function of the stock market was to attract investment, allocate capital among competing businesses, and produce capital returns for savvy investors. Another way to look at it was that investors who bought and sold stock were essentially placing bets on the success of particular business ventures. In contrast, commodity traders who bought or sold futures were not investing in a business; they were simply placing bets on whether a particular commodity price would go up or down. The first type of investment was at the heart of U.S. market capitalism; the second was more akin to betting on the ponies.

To further illustrate the difference between the two markets, Dan highlighted two of their contrasting practices. First, he pointed out that while futures exchanges typically placed position limits on market speculators to prevent them from distorting commodity prices, no comparable limits were placed on the number of shares held by a stock investor. Placing a numerical limit on an investor's stock holdings made no sense, since the point of a stock exchange was not to constrain speculators or set fair prices, but to attract as much investment as possible.

A second contrasting practice involved insider trading. Dan noted that, in commodity markets, traders were not subject to any prohibition on insider trading. It was perfectly lawful for a farmer, for example, to use information that only the farmer knew about the size and quality of the farmer's crop when entering into a futures contract with another party. In contrast, in the stock market, buyers and sellers were explicitly prohibited from making trading decisions about their own companies using information unavailable to the rest of the investing public, because the law deemed such nonpublic information to convey an unfair trading advantage. Using or sharing inside information was prohibited, because all investors were supposed to have access to the same information when trading stocks. As a result, commodity markets and stock markets had almost diametrically opposed rules on insider trading.

It took me awhile to wrap my mind around the differences between the two markets, but I gradually got it. One was geared to help commodity producers and users figure out prices for their products and protect them against price changes; the other was geared to attract as many investors and as much investment as possible. Those two different sets of goals and constituencies led to critical differences in how the two markets operated.

Investigating Crude Oil

With that basic grounding in commodity markets, I proceeded to play backup to Dan as he led a year-long investigation into U.S. crude oil prices.[2] The work was performed in our usual bipartisan fashion with help from the staff of our then ranking Republican Senator Susan Collins.

The first step was a deep dive into the specifics of crude oil—how it was produced, transported, stored, used, and priced—and how crude oil markets functioned. We learned there were hundreds of different types of crude oil produced around the world, but only a few—Brent oil produced in the North Sea and West Texas Intermediate (WTI) oil produced in the United States— that were used to set "benchmark" prices for the oil market as a whole. We also learned that, in 2002, the worldwide crude oil market was finely balanced between the amount of oil produced each year and the amount of oil used each year. The United States was the world's biggest crude oil consumer, but not its biggest producer, which meant it had to import oil. In 2002, the United States consumed about 18 million barrels of crude oil each day and had to import 10 million barrels per day to meet its needs. Most of the imported crude oil, about 90%, was refined into various types of fuel like gasoline, home heating oil, and diesel.

The data also showed that, in 2002, U.S. crude oil inventories were usually tight, and demand for oil was fairly inelastic. That meant if demand increased or supplies dropped by even a small amount, crude oil prices could skyrocket. The data also showed a recent trend of climbing U.S. crude oil prices which, in turn, increased fuel costs for American families and businesses across the country. Dan dug into the reasons for those rising prices.

One factor that immediately grabbed his attention was a new player on the market—the U.S. Strategic Petroleum Reserve or SPR. Established in 1975, after U.S. oil shortages in the early 1970s, the purpose of the Reserve was to "store petroleum to reduce the adverse economic impact of a major petroleum supply interruption to the United States." By 2001, the SPR contained about 560 million barrels of crude oil, a stockpile that could theoretically cover U.S. oil needs for a month. The SPR had managed to build that stockpile with minimal impact on U.S. oil prices, because it bought oil only when supplies were plentiful and prices low. After the 9/11 terrorist attack, President George W. Bush ordered the Department of Energy (DOE) to fill the SPR to its full capacity of 700 million barrels "in a deliberate and cost effective manner." DOE chose to interpret that order as requiring it to step up its crude oil purchasing in a big way.

In the past, when buying oil for the SPR, DOE had bought crude oil when market prices were low and allowed oil companies to defer promised deliveries if market conditions turned difficult. But in early 2002, DOE began relentlessly filling the SPR without regard to price, buying three to four million barrels of crude oil every month, even when prices surged from under $20 to over $30 per barrel. Dan saw DOE's cost-blind buying spree as a major change in the market, taking tens of millions of barrels of oil off the market for indefinite storage, reducing commercial oil supplies, and, as a result, pushing up crude oil prices.

In addition to the SPR, Dan attempted to evaluate allegations that rising oil prices were due, in part, to oil companies' manipulating oil prices on the New York and London exchanges, but he was stymied by a lack of data. For example, neither DOE nor the CFTC collected data on crude oil transactions in the over-the-counter and swap markets, creating a huge gap in pricing records. Without more data, Dan was unable to analyze the price manipulation claims. He was, however, able to identify several technical problems with the NYMEX futures contract for U.S. crude oil that also appeared to be contributing to U.S. price increases.

As Dan was working through those issues, politics intervened. In November 2002, national elections flipped the Senate majority by giving Republicans a 51-49 lead. As a result, in January 2003, Senator Collins became chair of our full committee, while Senator Norm Coleman, a freshman Republican from Minnesota, became chair of PSI. Senator Levin reverted to PSI's ranking minority member. Despite his change in status, under PSI rules allowing minority-led investigations, Senator Levin was able to continue his crude oil pricing investigation into the new 108th Congress.

In March 2003, nearly a year after the investigation began, Dan completed a 285-page staff report entitled, "U.S. Strategic Petroleum Reserve: Recent Policy Has Increased Costs to Consumers But Not Overall U.S. Energy Security." The report showed how crude oil prices had nearly doubled in 2002, climbing from a low of around $18 per barrel in January to a high of $34 per barrel in December, with increases as high as $40 in early 2003. The report identified several contributing factors, but highlighted crude oil purchases by the SPR as a major reason why U.S. crude oil supplies had tightened and prices jumped.

The report concluded, because DOE had bought 40 million barrels of high-cost oil and took it off the market in 2002, it forced taxpayers to pay more than they should have to fill the Reserve. The report also showed how, in a one-month period in 2002, higher crude oil prices had spiked U.S. spot prices for home heating oil by 13%, jet fuel by 10%, and diesel fuel by 8%, imposing on U.S. consumers additional total fuel costs of between $500 million and $1 billion.

On top of that, the report showed that, while the SPR's oil storage level increased during 2002, U.S. commercial crude oil inventories plummeted due to the costs associated with buying and storing higher-priced oil. That meant when the SPR and commercial supplies were added together, the United States saw no net increase in its overall oil supplies. In other words, despite its much higher cost, the new SPR policy had failed to increase U.S. energy security overall. As a result, the report called on DOE to abandon its policy of filling the SPR without regard to cost.

It was a powerful report with strong policy recommendations. The problem: our new PSI chair, Senator Coleman, wasn't in the Senate when the original investigative work was done. His staff had no first-hand exposure to the crude oil data or to the DOE and SPR interviews, which made it hard for them to recommend that their boss sign onto the Levin report. So they didn't.

Because Senator Coleman declined to sign onto the crude oil report and because he'd been on PSI for only a few months, Senator Levin decided against asking him to hold a hearing on the report's findings. Instead, Senator Levin simply issued the report, together with a press release. As a result, it received a lot less attention than if DOE and SPR officials had been called in to testify. We were disappointed, but we all knew that elections had consequences, and one of them was that Senator Levin no longer set PSI's agenda.

Battling for Reforms

After we issued the report, we followed our usual protocol and worked to correct the problems we'd uncovered. We knew that Senator Dianne Feinstein, a Democrat from California, had already introduced legislation to strengthen energy market oversight and clamp down on price manipulation. Dan analyzed her bill and, based upon PSI's work, identified ways it could be improved. Senator Levin approached Senator Feinstein, and together they offered a revised, bipartisan Feinstein-Lugar-Levin amendment to an energy bill then making its way through the Senate.[3] While the amendment wasn't successful in 2003, by persevering over time, much of what they recommended back then eventually became law.[4]

We also worked to stop DOE from continuing to fill the SPR with high-cost crude oil that put upward pressure on fuel prices and imposed excessive costs on taxpayers. Luckily, because Senator Collins' staff worked with us on the first part of the SPR investigation, we had a Republican partner. Over the next five years, Senators Levin and Collins made four joint attempts to change DOE policy and practice, while DOE continued to thumb its nose at us by filling the SPR with high-cost oil and watching the oil companies bank record profits year after year. Finally, in 2008, Senators Dorgan, Levin, Collins, and others enacted legislation that prohibited DOE from depositing any oil into the SPR, until oil prices fell below a specified price per barrel.[5] The "stop-the-fill" law finally put a halt to DOE's cost-blind SPR policy, five years after PSI first identified it. It was an expensive lesson in how inflated commodity prices weighed down average American families and businesses with billions of dollars in excess costs.

Pricing Natural Gas

While Dan continued to be Senator Levin's go-to staffer on commodity issues, he was increasingly assigned to work on other PSI investigations as well. But in 2006, scandal brought both Dan and me back to the commodities world on a full-time basis.[6]

The scandal was the financial implosion of an obscure hedge fund called Amaranth Advisors which, in November 2006, lost $6.6 billion betting on natural gas prices. Six months earlier, Amaranth's top trader, Brian Hunter, had been named as one of 2005's most profitable energy traders in an article cited in a 2006 Levin-Coleman report on how market speculators were driving up U.S. fuel prices.[7] The report, which Dan and I had put together at Senator Levin's request, cited estimates that speculators had contributed $20–$25 to the then $70 price for a barrel of crude oil, and that, over three years, $100–$120 billion in new speculative money had infiltrated crude oil markets and affected energy trading.

Amaranth's massive loss was almost unheard of in the natural gas market. Rumors flew about price manipulation or speculation schemes that must have backfired. Dan proposed a full-blown investigation, and Senator Levin agreed. By then, the 2006 elections had put the Democrats back in the Senate majority, and Senator Levin was once more setting PSI's agenda.

Dan assembled a bipartisan team from the Levin and Coleman staffs and dove into the facts. The PSI team talked first to commodity experts who described the key role natural gas played in the U.S. economy powering electrical plants and manufacturing. They explained that, due to its impact on electricity, heating, and manufacturing costs, natural gas pricing affected the finances of millions of American families and businesses. They also explained that natural gas was typically sold directly by producers to consumers like utilities and industry plants, but, in 1990, natural gas futures had also began trading on regulated exchanges, primarily NYMEX.

In 2000, Congress also opened the door to natural gas trading on unregulated financial markets. Pushed by Senator Phil Gramm of Texas, that change was made in the Commodity Futures Modernization Act, at the behest of Enron and others. It created what soon became known as the Enron Loophole.

The Enron Loophole exempted from CFTC oversight any financial commodity market with the following three characteristics: trading was done electronically, the only traders allowed were large firms, and the only commodities traded involved energy or metal products. The exemption's supposed justification was that large traders could take care of themselves and didn't need government oversight when trading with each other on electronic markets. But government oversight was never intended just to protect large traders from each other; it was also intended to protect the public from commodity traders engaged in price manipulation and excessive speculation. Nevertheless, Enron and its buddies won the new exemption.

Once on the books, the Enron Loophole fueled the rise of a new type of energy trading that operated outside government safeguards by using electronic trading venues available only to big firms. To avoid government oversight, the new electronic exchanges relied mainly on swaps rather than futures for trading. Doing so enabled them not only to avoid the futures regulations, but also to take advantage of a second loophole in the Commodity Futures Modernization Act of 2000, which essentially barred government oversight of swaps.

The new swaps loophole was so sweeping that it barred federal agencies from not only regulating swaps, but also gathering any information on swap transactions. So when it came to swaps involving energy and metal commodities, by law, the CFTC and the rest of the federal government were rendered completely blind. They weren't allowed to look at what was happening. The crazy result was that commodities like pork bellies and cocoa were subject to full regulatory oversight, while commodities involving such important energy and raw materials as crude oil, natural gas, copper, and aluminum were stripped of key public protections.

In 2006, the leading unregulated exchange for energy swaps was the InterContinental Exchange or ICE, which was headquartered in Atlanta, Georgia. It offered several natural gas swap contracts whose settlement prices were explicitly linked to the settlement prices of the equivalent natural gas futures traded on NYMEX. In other words, when a NYMEX natural gas futures contract reached its closing date and settled on a final price for the natural gas sold through that contract, that final settlement price applied to not only the natural gas sold through the NYMEX futures contract, but also to the natural gas sold through the equivalent ICE swap. At the same time, due to the Enron Loophole and the statutory bar on regulating swaps, the CFTC had no authority to police the ICE exchange and no information about the swaps it traded.

At the time of the Amaranth disaster, rumors abounded about commodity traders trading simultaneously on the NYMEX and ICE exchanges, and using complex trades to play one venue off the other. But when Dan asked leading commodity experts about the rumors, they sniffed that the volume of swaps trading on ICE wasn't significant enough to have impacted 2006 natural gas prices or to have caused Amaranth's $6.6 billion loss. The experts dismissed the rumors despite the total lack of public data on the role played by swaps or ICE in the Amaranth fiasco. Dan decided to use the Amaranth case study to go beyond the rumors and get to the facts.

Uncovering Amaranth's Hidden Trades

Dan's first step was to subpoena Amaranth's 2006 trading records from both NYMEX and ICE. It was apparently the first time anyone had ever subpoenaed trading records from both exchanges for the same trader. The resulting data dump was so huge I couldn't imagine how Dan would sift through it. His solution was to enroll in several courses offered to congressional staff on how to handle large data sets on Microsoft Access and Excel spreadsheets. As he told me later, the training enabled him to produce in minutes a variety of detailed analytical charts based upon Amaranth's trading records. It was a striking lesson on how a single determined staffer could produce a break-through analysis.

Over the next month, Dan translated the 2006 trading records into a series of charts that laid bare Amaranth's day-to-day natural gas trading on both exchanges. He tried various formats until he came up with one so simple that, at a glance, it conveyed undeniable proof that Amaranth had been trading on both NYMEX and ICE in a coordinated fashion. By coloring the NYMEX trades one way and the ICE trades another way in a combined bar chart, the graphics showed, for example, how on a single day Amaranth bought and sold multiple natural gas contracts in both markets (Image 13.1).

The combined trading data had another surprise. It showed that Amaranth had not only traded natural gas on both markets in a coordinated fashion, it had also engaged in massive natural gas transactions throughout 2006. The data disclosed that Amaranth had traded thousands of natural gas contracts daily—sometimes tens of thousands in a single day. On some days, Amaranth had held as many as 100,000 contracts at a time, representing between 60% and 70% of the entire U.S. natural gas market. In short, one mysterious hedge fund had been essentially dominating the U.S. natural gas market, without any regulator realizing it.

On top of that, on several occasions, the trading records disclosed highly suspicious trading patterns. On those occasions, the trading took place on the day that a specific natural gas futures contract closed, and the exchange assigned a final "settlement" price to the natural gas sold through that contract. Under the contract's standard terms, trading was required to end on the closing day at 2:30 p.m. The final settlement price would then be determined

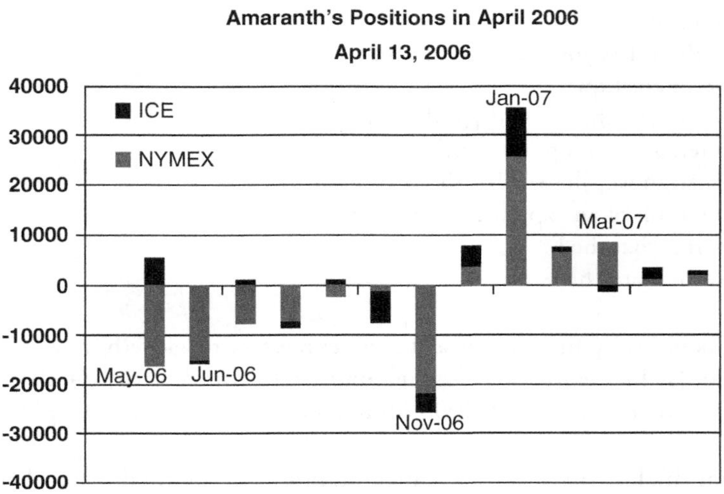

Amaranth's Positions in April 2006
April 13, 2006

Image 13.1 Amaranth natural gas trading positions in April 2006. Source: 2007 Senate Hearing at 271

by the prices bid during the last 30 minutes of trading. Amaranth trading records showed that, on several days during the final few minutes of the closing periods, Amaranth had suddenly bought or sold thousands of natural gas futures contracts, causing the settlement price to suddenly spike or crash. The tactic was called "banging the close" or "smashing" the price.

To examine the suspicious trades more closely, Dan subpoenaed Amaranth's emails and instant messages on those trading days. In addition to the materials he unearthed, even more dramatic messages surfaced later in regulatory enforcement actions. One example is a series of instant messages between Amaranth's lead trader, Brian Hunter, and a colleague talking about the hedge fund's planned trades during the last few minutes of trading on a futures contract that closed on February 24, 2006. A later court opinion described the messages as follows:

At about 12:15 p.m. on February 24, Hunter sent an instant message to Amaranth trader Matthew Calhoun, stating that the March 2006 contracts needed 'to get smashed on settle then 4 day is done.' Less than half an hour before the closing range, Hunter disclosed his trading strategy to another trader, who expressed astonishment that Hunter had so many March 2006 contracts left to sell:

Hunter: We have 4000 to sell MoC
Hunter: shhhh
gloverb: come on

Hunter: y
gloverb: unless you are huge bearish
gloverb: position
gloverb: why the f would y[ou] do that
Hunter: all from options yest[e]rday
Hunter: so we[']ll see what the floor has
Hunter: bit of an exp[e]riment mainly
gloverb: what the f
gloverb: that is huge

At about 2:11 p.m., Hunter sent another message to 'gloverb,' stating that he had 'alot [sic] more to sell … waiting until 2:20.' On February 24, defendants sold more than 3000 March 2006 contracts during the closing range."[8]

Amaranth's last-minute trades affected not only the final price of the natural gas sold through the futures contract on NYMEX, but also the natural gas sold through the equivalent swap contract on ICE, since the ICE swap used the same settlement price as the NYMEX futures contract.

To understand what the regulators knew and did, Dan also obtained the communications between Amaranth and NYMEX. NYMEX was required by the CFTC to ensure that commodity prices on its exchange were protected against price manipulation and excessive speculation. After Amaranth's large holdings triggered internal NYMEX alerts, followed by Amaranth's banging the close on several occasions, emails showed NYMEX officials expressing increasing concern about Amaranth's trading practices. NYMEX quizzed the hedge fund about the size of its positions and the purpose of its large, last-minute trades. Finally, in August 2006, NYMEX ordered Amaranth to reduce its natural gas futures holdings and to stop trading during the final 30 minutes on August 29, which would determine the settlement price for the September futures contracts. NYMEX was trying to protect U.S. natural gas futures prices from Amaranth trading practices that smacked of price manipulation and excessive speculation.

NYMEX trading records suggested that Amaranth had bowed to NYMEX's demands. Amaranth had immediately reduced its natural gas holdings on the exchange and conducted no trades during the final hour of trading on August 29. But it turned out that wasn't the whole story. ICE trading records disclosed that, after Amaranth reduced its natural gas futures holdings on NYMEX, Amaranth increased its natural gas swap holdings on ICE by an even bigger margin. By August 29, Amaranth's combined NYMEX-ICE holdings were just as big—or bigger—than they had been when NYMEX ordered

Amaranth to reduce its position. But NYMEX didn't know it, because it was barred by law from policing the ICE exchange, and didn't ask Amaranth about its swap holdings. The trading records were crystal clear, however, that Amaranth had used its ICE holdings to circumvent the NYMEX limit on its natural gas trading.

The data painted a larger picture as well. It showed that, during the summer of 2006, Amaranth had used its NYMEX-ICE trades to build massive natural gas positions in several contracts with closing dates during the fall and winter season. Amaranth's large purchases had essentially pushed up the prices for 2006 winter gas. Municipalities planning their natural gas purchases were taken by surprise at the higher winter prices. But they were forced to pay the inflated prices, because they had to secure natural gas supplies for the winter and couldn't, as one municipality put it, just wait, roll the dice, and see if prices came down later. Amaranth profited off the backs of municipalities buying natural gas to provide heat and electricity for their towns.

But that wasn't the end of the story. Because natural gas supplies were plentiful and demand was steady, most speculators in the natural gas market refused to buy the overpriced winter contracts, thereby reducing demand for them. Reduced demand, in turn, caused the winter prices to begin to fall. To prop up the prices, Amaranth increased its buying and built up even larger natural gas positions. Its rivals began trying to figure out exactly who was buying all the natural gas contracts and pushing up the winter prices to excessive levels.

On August 29, 2006, the same day Amaranth quit the futures market early in compliance with NYMEX's demand that it stop banging the close, one of its rivals—a hedge fund called Centaurus Energy—gave Amaranth a dose of its own medicine. In the last 45 minutes of the trading day, Centaurus acquired such massive numbers of short natural gas positions that the winter gas prices plunged during the closing, sinking the final September settlement price as well as various price spreads.

When markets opened the next morning, the value of Amaranth's natural gas holdings had fallen by $2 billion. In response, both NYMEX and ICE required the hedge fund to post additional cash collateral to cover its potential losses. But Amaranth didn't have the cash. To raise it, Amaranth sold some of its holdings at the lower prices, even though it incurred losses doing so. The sales triggered more price drops, more collateral calls, more forced sales, and more losses. Within weeks, the resulting downward spiral left Amaranth staggering under losses totaling $6.6 billion. It was the worst hedge fund loss in U.S. commodity market history.[9]

Dan's meticulous charts, laying out Amaranth's combined NYMEX and ICE trades, not only exposed Amaranth's trading strategy and how it backfired, they also shattered multiple myths about the state of the U.S. natural gas market. Traders were clearly trading in the futures and swap markets in a coordinated fashion, playing one venue off the other. The volume of swaps trading on ICE roughly equaled or exceeded the volume of futures trading on NYMEX. An individual speculator not only could, but did surreptitiously dominate the U.S. natural gas market in 2006, affecting nationwide gas prices through massive trades.

When NYMEX tried to stop Amaranth's abusive trading, Amaranth foiled the effort by moving the bulk of its natural gas trading from NYMEX to the unregulated ICE exchange. Amaranth's successful circumvention of NYMEX's trading limit revealed that the U.S. natural gas market was functioning like a town that prohibited excessive drinking in saloons on one side of the street, but not the other. The drunks just crossed the street, and the carousing continued.

Going Public

In June 2007, nearly a year after the Amaranth implosion, Senator Levin released a Levin-Coleman report explaining what had happened. It included 169 pages of text and 344 pages of charts. He also held two days of hearings on Amaranth's trading catastrophe and the new reality in U.S. energy markets.

The bipartisan Levin-Coleman report concluded that Amaranth had distorted 2006 U.S. natural gas prices through large speculative trades in the NYMEX and ICE markets. It also concluded that U.S. energy markets were dangerously vulnerable to price manipulation and excessive speculation due to commodity rules that regulated some energy markets but not others. It recommended multiple reforms, including closing the Enron Loophole that enabled large traders to trade on electronic energy markets free of government oversight.

In minority views added at the end of the report, Senator Coleman's staff praised the investigation and joined the report's recommendations, while also expressing less "certitude" about whether Amaranth was always driving, rather than sometimes reacting to, higher U.S. natural gas prices. The Coleman staff wrote: "[F]actual findings regarding the degree to which Amaranth affected prices are not necessary to justify the recommendations articulated in this Report. We make these recommendations because they will better preserve the integrity of U.S. energy markets." The Coleman additional views were a great example of how the two parties in a bipartisan investigation can express their differences, while still acting in concert.

At the hearings, the subcommittee heard first from angry municipalities and businesses who'd been forced to pay higher winter prices for natural gas, despite ample gas supplies. The witnesses estimated that the inflated prices caused by Amaranth's trading had loaded billions of dollars in unjustified costs onto the backs of American consumers. They condemned the lack of government authority to detect and stop the abusive trading in U.S. energy swap markets.

Next up was an Amaranth trader who worked for Brian Hunter. Mr. Hunter was himself unwilling to testify given that he was then under investigation for price manipulation and excessive speculation. His colleague essentially denied all wrongdoing, claiming that, while Amaranth's trades were large, he couldn't agree they were excessive since the only reliable trading data was confined to NYMEX and failed to encompass all the other commodity markets and large traders. He also claimed Amaranth was responding to rather than driving the higher natural gas prices, and denied that any trader could dominate the U.S. natural gas market. He freely admitted that Amaranth had traded in both the futures and swap markets at the same time, and that both markets ought to be regulated the same way.

The final panel consisted of the heads of NYMEX, ICE, and the CFTC. All three condemned Amaranth's actions and agreed U.S. commodity markets needed to be protected against price manipulation and excessive speculation. All three also acknowledged that the Amaranth facts proved the futures and swap markets affected each other's prices and should be regulated in an integrated way. ICE surprised everyone by expressing a willingness to take on the same responsibilities as NYMEX to prevent price manipulation and excessive speculation within its exchange, including by imposing reporting and trading limits on speculators. CFTC Chair Walter Lukken seemed taken aback by ICE's position. His remarks suggested he was leery of extending oversight responsibilities to ICE specifically and to swap markets generally.

Following the Hearing

The hearing received widespread press attention and seemed to shake up how regulators, experts, and even the energy industry viewed U.S. energy markets. For the first time, conventional wisdom began to acknowledge the folly of regulating futures exchanges but not swap markets, when the same energy traders were trading in both.

The hearing also boosted ongoing enforcement efforts by the CFTC and the Federal Energy Regulatory Commission (FERC) against Amaranth and its lead trader Brian Hunter. In July 2007, a month after the PSI hearing, both agencies filed civil charges against Amaranth and Mr. Hunter for manipulating natural gas prices on NYMEX.[10] In 2009, Amaranth settled both cases, paying a civil penalty of $7.5 million.[11] Mr. Hunter, however, continued to fight both cases in court. In 2013, he won a major victory when the D.C. Circuit Court of Appeals overruled the district court, and held the CFTC had exclusive jurisdiction to penalize manipulative trading activity on futures exchanges and, so, FERC lacked jurisdiction to penalize Mr. Hunter for trades made on NYMEX.[12] By dismissing the FERC charges, the court imposed a major new limitation on FERC's authority to combat the manipulation of electricity prices. In 2014, Mr. Hunter settled the remaining CFTC charges, paying a $750,000 fine and accepting a permanent ban on his trading during any settlement period on a futures exchange.[13]

Over the same time period, the Amaranth investigation began to spur regulatory and legislative reforms. In the regulatory arena, the CFTC started demanding more information about the trades undertaken by natural gas traders on all types of commodity markets, not just futures exchanges. Legislatively, a key victory came in 2008, when Senator Levin helped win enactment of legislation that closed the Enron Loophole and abolished the statutory prohibition against CFTC oversight of electronic markets used by large traders to trade energy and metal commodities.[14] The new law finally gave the CFTC clear authority to oversee ICE as well as NYMEX, so that traders could no longer use one to circumvent trading limits set by the other. It was a fitting culmination to the Amaranth investigation.

What we didn't know then was that even stronger legislation combating commodity price manipulation and excessive speculation would be enacted as part of the Dodd-Frank Wall Street Reform and Consumer Protection Act of 2010. But that was still in the future.

Navigating Changes

Senator Levin savored the Amaranth investigation's success in spurring regulatory and legislative reforms. At the same time, he knew, even after the Enron Loophole was closed, that price manipulation and excessive speculation remained potent threats. To build the case for stronger safeguards, Senator Levin continued to produce investigations, reports, and hearings exposing dark corners of the commodities world.[15]

In 2008, the financial crisis hit, devastating American families and businesses, roiling financial markets, and fueling popular anger against large financial institutions engaged in high-risk transactions. In November 2008, the American people elected the first president from the Democratic Party in eight years, Barack Obama. His new administration promised to rescue the economy and curb high-risk financial activities.

In 2009, as part of that effort, President Obama nominated Gary Gensler to lead the CFTC. Senator Levin interviewed him as part of the confirmation process. When in response to a question, Mr. Gensler stated that commodity speculation contributed to higher commodity prices and excessive speculation needed to be curbed—expressing none of the doubt or reticence that characterized prior CFTC leadership—we knew a corner had been turned.

Another corner was turned when Mr. Gensler asked Senator Levin if he could hire Dan Berkovitz to serve as the CFTC's general counsel, and help him close the Enron Loophole, extend CFTC oversight to energy commodity markets, and implement other reforms. Senator Levin gave his blessing and, in 2009, Dan left PSI for the CFTC. It was hard to see him go, but his new position provided an invaluable opportunity to help strengthen commodity safeguards.

Another big change came in 2010, when Congress enacted the Dodd-Frank Act which, among other provisions, included the biggest revamping of federal commodity laws in decades.[16] For the first time, the law gave the CFTC clear, sweeping authority to oversee and regulate all commodity-related swap markets and financial instruments. The CFTC's new duties included registering swap exchanges, requiring more transparent reporting of OTC and swap transactions, and imposing position limits on a wider range of commodities. The law also strengthened the CFTC's authority to combat price manipulation and excessive speculation. As CFTC general counsel, Dan Berkovitz was suddenly at the center of a whirlwind effort to implement the brave new world of Dodd-Frank commodity safeguards.

Senator Levin worked hard to support the new law, combating efforts by the financial industry to thwart restrictions on high-risk trading and increased transparency requirements for commodity markets. He continued to use PSI hearings to expose the commodity underworld, relying largely on David Katz, his PSI staffer who'd been assigned the commodities portfolio.

One huge battle involved a new CFTC rule, required by the Dodd-Frank Act, imposing stronger position limits on speculators to curb speculative trading. The financial industry challenged the rule in court. To support the CFTC, Senator Levin honchoed the filing of an amicus brief signed by multiple Members of Congress in support of the rule. But industry won that round, and the court sent the rule back to the CFTC drawing board. By then, both Gary Gensler and Dan Berkovitz had left the agency, and the will to oppose industry had weakened. As of 2018, the CFTC had yet to find the backbone to issue a replacement rule as required by law. The knife fight to rein in speculative commodity traders continues.

Banks Investing in Physical Commodities

The final Levin foray into the commodities world focused on Wall Street banking conglomerates that, over time, had become major players in physical commodities, meaning buying and selling, not financial instruments, but actual physical goods like oil, coal, and gas.[17] Their physical commodity activities incurred new types of risks generally unknown in modern U.S. banking, including exposure to such catastrophic events as oil spills, gas line explosions, nuclear incidents, and coal mining disasters, as well as allegations of unfair trading, conflicts of interest, undue economic concentration, and, if it all went wrong, taxpayer bailouts.

The investigation's origins lay in our discovering, during the course of other PSI inquiries, that U.S. banks and their holding companies had become ever bigger players in energy and metals markets. Three financial institutions, in particular, had caught our attention: Goldman Sachs, JPMorgan Chase, and Morgan Stanley.

In 2012, a new law review article not only decried the same banking risks we'd become concerned about, but also provided the first comprehensive legal analysis we'd seen of the key federal statutes and regulations. Titled "The Merchants of Wall Street" by Professor Saule Omarova, it crystalized the practical and legal risks inherent in banks taking control of physical commodities.[18] We gave the law review article to Senator Levin and asked for permission to launch an in-depth investigation. He agreed. When we reached out to our Republican colleagues, then led by Senator Coburn, he also gave a thumbs-up to the inquiry.

Getting the Facts

I assigned myself lead responsibility for the investigation and made David Katz my second in command. Since PSI was already conducting several other inquiries, this one evolved slowly over time. As the pace picked up, we involved more and more staff until, by the end, the investigation absorbed pretty much everyone on both sides of the aisle.

To get started, David set up meetings with the three banks to get preliminary information about their commodity activities. We also met with the Federal Reserve and OCC, the two main banking regulators, to find out what they knew. In addition, we met with the CFTC, FERC, and a variety of commodity experts, including Professor Omarova. Based upon our preliminary research, David sent out a dozen formal document requests seeking more specific information.

It was the document request to the Federal Reserve that struck gold. In the aftermath of the 2008 financial crisis, the Federal Reserve had revamped its efforts to detect hidden risks to the U.S. financial system. Among other actions, it had set up a "Risk Secretariat" charged with uncovering those hidden risks.

In 2009, the Risk Secretariat had identified financial holding company involvement with physical commodities as a major emerging risk area warranting immediate investigation. The Secretariat ordered formation of a Commodities Team at the Federal Reserve Bank of New York and directed it to conduct a special review. Three years later, the Commodities Team provided its conclusions in a 2012 summary analysis. Just in time for PSI to make good use of all that work.

But the Federal Reserve didn't make it easy. Fed officials didn't like outsiders reviewing their work or getting internal Fed documents. We reminded them that the Federal Reserve had allowed PSI to do just that several times over the years—for example, in connection with our private banking and Riggs investigations—and PSI had never broken a confidence or leaked a Fed document. Despite those precedents, the Fed continued to give us the runaround, promising but never actually producing the requested documents. Finally, David telephoned the head of the congressional liaison office and said that if the documents were not produced the following week, PSI would be sending a subpoena.

In response, Federal Reserve Chairman Ben Bernanke telephoned Senator Levin to discuss the PSI document request. We weren't privy to the conversation, but the upshot was that the documents were on their way.

When they arrived, however, the documents were stippled in black. Someone had spent hours redacting them, blacking out dates, names, and whole paragraphs. It was impossible even to put the documents in chronological order, much less understand their content. In a tense conversation, David informed the Fed that there was no legal basis for the redactions, and it needed to send us a new set of unredacted documents. After several more conversations and our actually preparing a subpoena, the Federal Reserve finally agreed to send a clean set.

The final documents turned out to be worth the months-long battle. They laid out in detail the Fed's own extensive findings, worries, and recommendations. They disclosed that, from 2009 to 2012, the Commodities Team had examined physical commodity activities at multiple financial institutions and found an unprecedented level of financial holding company involvement with the energy, metal, and agricultural commodity sectors. The three banks we'd been eyeing turned out to be the biggest players in the physical commodities arena. The Fed documents not only spelled out the commodity activities at each one, they identified and analyzed numerous related risks, including operational and environmental vulnerabilities, inadequate risk management procedures, legal liability risks, insufficient capital and insurance, and ineffective regulatory safeguards. A 2012 summary document laid out the Commodity Team's findings and recommendations to reduce the risks to the U.S. financial system.[19] In essence, the Fed documents validated all of PSI's concerns.

Meanwhile, we were making steady progress in obtaining information directly from JPMorgan, Goldman, and Morgan Stanley, perhaps because all three had already given the same information to the Fed examiners. David had designed and sent all three a questionnaire requesting basic facts about their commodity activities, including the types of physical commodities they handled, the size of their holdings, and the commodity-related businesses they conducted. We were staggered by what the three had disclosed. Each one handled dozens of physical commodities, maintained holdings worth billions of dollars, and engaged in multiple related businesses posing a variety of operational risks.

To make the investigation manageable, we decided to confine ourselves to three case studies at each of the three banks—nine case studies in all. We chose them to illustrate the variety of physical commodity activities underway at the banks and the risks they raised. We informed each bank of the activities we intended to examine and requested more information about them. We skipped a number of technical topics, including the banks' capital, insurance and risk management systems, since those issues were already covered in the Fed documents.

In the end, PSI collected over 90,000 pages of documents and conducted 78 interviews and briefings. On top of that, we spoke with multiple academic, agency, and industry analysts with expertise in such fields as banking law, commodities trading, environmental and catastrophic risk management, and in markets involving aluminum, coal, copper, electricity, jet fuel, natural gas, oil, and uranium. To handle all the work, we used not only PSI's regular staff and our usual collection of detailees, law clerks, and interns, but also hired Ty Gellasch, a former Levin banking and securities expert who was willing to help out. We got more help from Joe Bryan on Senator Levin's Armed Services Committee staff, since so many of the issues had implications for the defense world. Due to the broad reach of the banks' physical commodity activities, it turned out to be one of our most sprawling and complex investigative efforts.

Building the Case Studies

To develop the nine case studies, we formed nine teams. Given our limited personnel, every staffer was assigned to more than one team. Each team dug into the specifics of their assigned commodity activities, gathering background, collecting documents, and conducting interviews. The teams were able to assemble an astonishing array of materials and information. Together, they addressed such activities as trading uranium, operating a coal mine, warehousing aluminum, building a compressed natural gas facility, running oil and gas storage and pipeline facilities, selling jet fuel to airlines, operating electrical power plants, and stockpiling copper. Each case study was more surprising than the next in terms of what each financial firm had gotten itself into and the risks it carried.

The three Goldman case studies were particularly striking. The first case study involved Goldman's purchase of a company that dealt in physical uranium. After Goldman bought the firm, its employees left, so Goldman's own personnel began running what had become a shell company, making operational decisions about buying and selling different types of uranium, arranging its storage, and supplying uranium fuel components to nuclear power plants. Whoever heard of a bank-related financial holding company running a uranium business?

The second case history examined Goldman's purchase of two open-pit coal mines in Colombia. Goldman used Colombian subsidiaries to mine, market, and transport the coal. A financial statement filed by the lead Goldman subsidiary described a raft of operational risks, including mining mishaps, railroad incidents, and air and water pollution. The mines also experienced severe labor unrest which, at one point, led Goldman's subsidiary to request help from the Colombian police and military to remove a human blockade—mainly miners' wives and children—barring entry to the mines. Breaking the blockade risked physical injuries, a political backlash, and international condemnation. Together, the many mining-related environmental, safety, and workforce risks raised liabilities normally far afield from banking.

The third case study scrutinized Goldman's involvement with physical aluminum. In 2010, Goldman acquired a warehouse company, Metro International, which, among other assets, owned nearly 30 warehouses in

Detroit, Michigan, storing various types of metal. During Goldman's ownership, Metro aggressively sought to attract and retain an increasing volume of physical aluminum certified for trade on the London Metal Exchange, eventually compiling the largest LME aluminum stockpiles in the world. At the same time, Goldman increased its own aluminum holdings and trading, amping up the total value of the bank's aluminum portfolio from less than $100 million in 2009, to more than $3 billion in 2012.

Over the same period, Goldman became the subject of worldwide complaints that its warehousing practices were slowing down aluminum deliveries and driving up prices. When we dug into the facts, we unearthed documents related to Metro's engaging in so-called "merry-go-round" transactions, first disclosed by the New York Times, in which Metro paid cash incentives to some warehouse clients to unload their aluminum from one Metro warehouse and load it right back into another—sometimes around the corner. Taking advantage of imprecise LME rules, Goldman had used those unloading and loading activities to fill up the warehouse's "exit queue," and delay the ability of other warehouse clients to remove their aluminum from storage.

The time it took to remove aluminum from the Goldman warehouse complex ballooned from a few weeks to nearly two years, an unprecedented delay. Over a dozen industrial users of aluminum eventually sued Goldman, claiming its warehouses had artificially slowed the release of aluminum from storage in order to restrict supplies and boost prices. Additional concerns were raised about unfair trading as Goldman oversaw warehouse practices that affected aluminum prices, while simultaneously buying and selling billions of dollars worth of aluminum in financial and physical markets.

The next three case studies revolved around Morgan Stanley's extensive involvement with energy commodities. The first case study focused on its growing natural gas activities. The investigation disclosed to the public for the first time that, in 2013, Morgan Stanley had established two shell companies—later adding a third—to construct a $355 million compressed natural gas facility in Texas. Since none of the shell companies had any employees, Morgan Stanley's own personnel were directing the construction project, an activity wholly unconnected to the business of banking. The investigation also disclosed that Morgan Stanley had used an infrastructure fund it controlled—Morgan Stanley Infrastructure Partners—to take ownership of a U.S. company named Southern Star which operated a sprawling network of natural gas pipelines across the Midwest. Together, those natural gas activities exposed Morgan Stanley to a raft of environmental, safety, and operational risks, including pipeline leaks and explosions, compressed gas construction mishaps, and multiple potential pollution problems.

The second case study examined Morgan Stanley's extensive array of businesses handling oil products, including trading, storing, transporting, and supplying oil. Morgan Stanley had built up those businesses over many years, prior to becoming a bank holding company, and continued operating them under special statutory authority allowing it to "grandfather" certain activities. One of its businesses managed nearly 50 oil storage sites across the United States and Canada; another oversaw a fleet of 100 vessels that transported liquid fuels; and a third blended and stored oils, and at one point ran about 200 retail gasoline stations in Canada. A bank running gas stations? At another point, Morgan Stanley's top oil trader controlled such a vast network of East Coast oil storage facilities that he was dubbed "King of New York Harbor." Its oil activities exposed Morgan Stanley to a vast array of low-probability but high-cost risks including fires, explosions, and catastrophic pollution events.

The third Morgan Stanley case study detailed its role as a long-term supplier of jet fuel to several airlines. Under one set of contracts that spanned a ten-year period from 2003 to 2013, Morgan Stanley had served as the primary jet fuel supplier for United Airlines, locating, purchasing, storing, and transporting jet fuel worth $1–$3 billion per year to United Airline hubs across the country. In addition, Morgan Stanley provided a range of hedging services to several airlines to help them manage their fuel price risks. To meet its fueling and hedging commitments, Morgan Stanley maintained extensive jet fuel inventories at multiple locations. The attendant risks included flash fires and explosions; storage, pipeline, and transportation leaks; and volatile prices with potentially severe financial consequences.

Building a natural gas compression plant, running oil pipelines, and supplying jet fuel to airlines—none of those activities was remotely within the normal business of banking.

Our final three case studies involved JPMorgan Chase which seemed to engage in a greater volume of commodity activities than any other U.S. financial holding company. We focused our review on activities involving electricity, copper, and—in a twist—JPMorgan's efforts to circumvent regulatory limits on the very size of its physical commodity holdings.

The first case study focused on JPMorgan's acquisition and control of over 30 electrical power plants across the United States, while also trading in electricity markets. Its risks included such industrial worksite problems as mechanical and electrical equipment failures, fires, explosions, and workforce injuries. In addition, since the plants used coal or natural gas as fuel, they incurred a variety of catastrophic event risks related to environmental or safety lapses. On top of that, in 2013, JPMorgan paid $410 million to settle charges by federal energy regulators that it'd used multiple pricing schemes to manipulate electricity payments to certain power plants it controlled in California and Michigan, leading consumers to pay excessive electricity charges.

The second case study examined JPMorgan's involvement with physical copper. Its activities included massive copper trades in the physical and financial markets and maintenance of physical copper inventories that sometimes exceeded a value of $2 billion. Most of the copper was held in the name of JPMorgan's federally-insured bank, exposing the bank not only to unpredictable copper prices, but also to allegations that JPMorgan's copper activities could be linked to price manipulation or excessive speculation. In addition, in 2012, JPMorgan submitted a proposal to the SEC to establish the first exchange traded fund (ETF) backed by physical copper. After its ETF proposal was attacked by some industrial copper users as enabling JPMorgan to create artificial copper shortages and price increases, raising conflicts of interest and market manipulation concerns, JPMorgan postponed its plans.

The final JPMorgan case study focused not on a specific commodity, but on a major regulatory safeguard to reduce risk—a Federal Reserve limit on the size of physical commodities that may be held by a financial holding company at any one time. The investigation disclosed that JPMorgan had used aggressive interpretations, unintended loopholes, and questionable valuation methodologies to claim it had stayed under the size limit when, in fact, it hadn't. Its tactics included excluding the value of its physical copper stockpiles, oil and gas leases, and power plants as well as billions of dollars in physical commodities held in the name of its bank.

The result was that JPMorgan had amassed physical commodity holdings far in excess of the applicable limit, without informing the Federal Reserve. In September 2012, for example, JPMorgan held physical commodity assets with a combined estimated market value of $17.4 billion, which at the time equaled nearly 12% of its Tier 1 capital of $148 billion, while telling the Federal Reserve that its holdings totaled only $6.6 billion, well below the applicable limit of 5% of its Tier 1 capital. In addition, PSI released email traffic among federal bank regulators expressing surprise and dismay over the true size of JPMorgan's holdings, which their bank examiners had discovered by happenstance.

Deviating from the Business of Banking

Together, the physical commodity activities at the three financial holding companies demonstrated how far the firms had deviated from the traditional business of banking. For over 150 years, the United States had discouraged the mixing of banking and commerce, but that longstanding principle was being steadily eroded at some of the biggest banks in America. As a consequence of the banks' actions, the investigation identified three sets of serious risks.

First were the grave environmental, safety, and operational risks normally not present in the banking sector—the possibility of a major U.S. bank being held responsible for a devastating oil spill, natural gas explosion, railway crash, coal mine collapse, or nuclear incident. A second set of risks involved issues of unfair trading, including market manipulation, excessive speculation, and misuse of insider information, issues that came up in some of the case studies we examined. The third set of risks revolved around competitiveness concerns: banks competing against non-bank businesses—natural gas utilities, jet fuel suppliers, coal companies—while enjoying unfair business advantages, including lower borrowing costs, lower capital requirements, and greater control over credit. Still another problem was what regulators called the threat of "undue economic concentration." Since banks already exercised significant control over U.S. credit markets, giving them added control over energy markets, industrial raw materials, and agricultural markets would extend their influence over the U.S. economy to an unhealthy degree. Preventing that type of economic concentration was a primary motivation for the traditional U.S. ban on the mixing of banking with commerce.

Going Public

In November 2014, PSI released a 467-page Levin-McCain bipartisan report and held two days of hearings entitled "Wall Street Bank Involvement with Physical Commodities." They constituted the final investigative effort of Senator Levin's PSI career.

Using our standard procedures, we held a press briefing the day before the hearings. Senators Levin and McCain both spoke, summarizing the facts we'd uncovered. After they left, the staff went through all nine case studies in detail and answered questions. Many of the reporters seemed bowled over by the breadth of the banks' activities, although we were careful to stress that the Federal Reserve had already began to curb them.

Since the hearings couldn't begin to cover all the ground plowed by the investigation, Senator Levin decided to highlight one case study in detail: Goldman's involvement with aluminum. For him, that case study encapsulated all the dangers at hand. It not only involved aluminum stored at warehouses located in his hometown of Detroit, it also illustrated the broad range of issues troubling him—from concerns about a bank taking over a commercial business; to that bank's exercising control over a key raw material important to U.S. defense, the auto industry, and American consumers; to Goldman's disrupting commodity markets and driving up commodity prices through questionable practices; to concerns about whether Goldman was using inside information from its warehouse activities to line its own pockets in financial markets. It rang all his outrage bells at once.

Senator Levin opened the hearings by observing: "If you like what Wall Street did for the housing market, you will love what Wall Street is doing for commodities." After generally describing the nine case studies at Goldman, JPMorgan, and Morgan Stanley, he launched into detail about Goldman's physical aluminum activities.

The first two hearing witnesses were the president of the Detroit warehousing company purchased by Goldman and the head of Goldman's commodities group. Both denied wrongdoing and defended the warehouse's actions, but were hard pressed to explain the merry-go-round transactions in which clients were paid millions of dollars to move their aluminum from one Goldman warehouse to another. Both admitted Goldman itself had engaged in a massive aluminum transaction that contributed to the warehouse's already lengthy exit queue. Yet both denied that any of those transactions contributed to the steadily climbing U.S. aluminum prices. In addition, under questioning, both acknowledged that at least 50 Goldman employees got regular reports on confidential warehousing activities, while denying Goldman ever used any of that inside information for its own trading purposes.

The next panel heard from two more witnesses, one a leading aluminum market analyst and the other the largest purchaser of aluminum in the world, Novelis, which supplies aluminum used to make beer and soda cans, auto parts, and consumer electronics. Both blasted Goldman's warehouse activities for artificially restricting aluminum supplies, driving up prices, and costing consumers billions of dollars. They expressed outrage about the nearly two-year delay to get aluminum out of the Goldman warehouse, and strenuously disputed the claim that the warehouse's actions had no effect on overall aluminum prices. Novelis' representative testified point blank: "[B]anks and trading companies should not be allowed to own warehouses."

The second day of hearings took testimony from experts and federal regulators who, rather than comment on the Goldman case study, testified more broadly about the negative impacts of bank involvement with physical commodities. One key moment came when Law Professor Saule Omarova and industrial risk analyst Chiara Trabucchi were shown a chart depicting 31 U.S. power plants and related facilities located across the country that, in 2011, were all controlled by JPMorgan Chase (Image 13.2).[20]

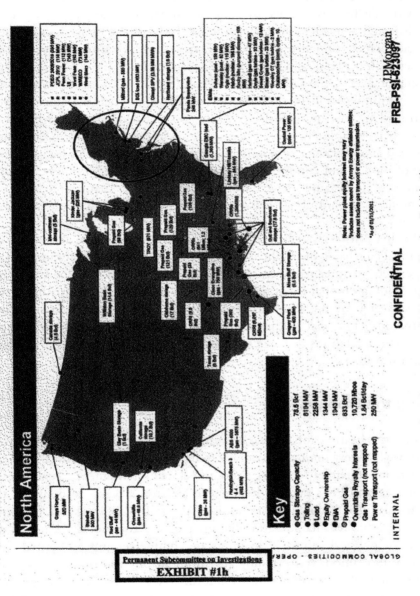

Image 13.2 JPMorgan's electrical power plant chart. Source: 2014 Senate Hearing Exhibit 1h

Professor Omarova described it as a "terrifying picture" which "the law did not mean to happen at all. ... [B]anks should not be doing this stuff." Ms. Trabucchi described it as "a very dangerous proposition" to have so many industrial facilities controlled by bank personnel "who are not necessarily as sophisticated about how to manage those risks as they are in their inherent industry, which is finance." She warned how a single catastrophic event could impact both the bank and the power plant industry.

Senator McCain interjected: "[A]m I exaggerating too much when I say this is reminiscent of the days of the robber barons when the railroads were controlled by one individual? ... Am I too alarmed?" Professor Omarova responded: "Absolutely not." She said it is "precisely" what "back almost 100 years ago, this country was up in arms against: This kind of seamless wedding of money and control over raw materials and transportation and pure commerce. ... Because we were worried about the fact that people who control money and control raw materials can control too much of our society in general."

The final witness was Federal Reserve Governor Daniel Tarullo who oversaw the Fed's bank oversight efforts. While he avoided the dramatic language used by other witnesses, it was clear that he, too, saw the banks and their holding companies as having incurred serious risks normally outside the field of banking. He indicated that the Fed wanted it to stop, had informed the financial holding companies of the Fed's concerns, and would be issuing regulations to make sure those hidden risks to the U.S. banking system would end.

Fixing the Problem

Because the hearing took place only months before Senator Levin's retirement, we had very limited time to try to fix the problems we'd uncovered.

First, on December 12, 2014, a month before his retirement, Senator Levin introduced and PSI's ranking Republican Senator McCain cosponsored the "Ending Insider Trading in Commodities Act."[21] The bill was short, but powerful. It prohibited manipulating the price of any commodity-related swap, future, or physical shipment in interstate commerce, and prohibited large financial institutions from trading any future or physical commodity "while in possession of material, nonpublic information related to the storage, shipment, or use of the commodity arising from" the firm's owning a related business. It was too late to seek any action on the bill, but its introduction made the text available to others interested in taking up the challenge.

Second, Senator Levin instructed the PSI crew to track the physical commodity activities at the three institutions we'd examined. To our relief, within months of the hearing, under pressure from the Fed and OCC, all three financial institutions substantially reduced their physical commodity footprint, although none exited the business entirely.

By the end of 2016, two years after the PSI hearing, according to news reports Goldman had shut down its uranium business and sold its Columbian coal mines and the Metro warehouses. Morgan Stanley had sold its oil storage and pipeline facilities, ended its jet fuel business, and sold its ownership interests in the construction of the natural gas compression facility and Southern Star pipeline company. JPMorgan no longer owned any power plants, its bank had eliminated its metal holdings, and it had installed new controls to ensure its physical commodity holdings complied with the Fed's size limit. The dangers we'd highlighted in the nine case studies had been mitigated.

The third and final Levin strategy, pushing regulatory reforms, saw mixed success. In 2016, both the OCC and Fed proposed new rules to tamp down on the risks to the financial system caused by bank involvement with physical commodities. The OCC finalized its rule by the end of the year, essentially banning physical commodities at national banks.[22] The Fed proposed an equally tough rule which included higher capital requirements for more risky physical commodity activities, a more effective size limit, and other safeguards to reduce the risks to the financial system.[23] But the Fed failed to finalize the proposed rule before Dan Tarullo, its driving force, retired in 2017. The new Trump Administration has expressed little interest in following through.

Another disappointment was the CFTC's ongoing failure to strengthen position limits on commodity speculators to deter price manipulation and excessive speculation in U.S. commodity markets. The Dodd-Frank Act of 2010 required the CFTC to strengthen U.S. position limits, including by applying them to all energy commodities, but as of 2018, those limits still were not in place. The CFTC had proposed a rule with a weak set of position limits, but it was struck down by a court and, despite pressure from Congress, the CFTC has so far failed to finalize a new version. The Trump Administration, with its heavy influx of former Goldman Sachs officials, seems unlikely to take up the fight.

Today, despite the economic and financial dangers connected to bank involvement with physical commodities, none of the three financial institutions we'd examined completely left the physical commodities field. It is possible in the Trump de-regulatory era that all the risks associated with banks engaging in physical commodity activities could return.

Conclusion

For 13 years, from 2001 to 2014, Senator Levin fought abusive commodity pricing using all the investigative tools he had. He used hearings and reports to expose oil company gimmicks to push up gasoline prices; government missteps in taming crude oil prices, natural gas price manipulation, and excessive speculation; the growing, negative impact of hedge funds and other speculators on U.S. commodity prices; and bank attempts to gain control over U.S. energy and raw materials. He pushed hard for greater transparency, more effective government policing of commodity markets, and better safeguards to protect American businesses and consumers from roller coaster commodity prices. The battle was complicated, it was exhausting, and it won him few plaudits from the media or voting public. That didn't matter. To Senator Levin, it was a battle worth fighting, offering exactly the type of bipartisan, fact-based, in-depth issues that congressional oversight was meant to tackle.

Notes

1. The information in this section is based on "Gas Prices: How Are They Really Set?" S. Hrg. 107-509 (4/30 and 5/2/2002), including the majority staff report at 322, https://www.gpo.gov/fdsys/pkg/CHRG-107shrg80298/pdf/CHRG-107shrg80298.pdf.
2. The information in this section is based on "U.S. Strategic Petroleum Reserve: Recent Policy Has Increased Costs to Consumers but Not Overall U.S. Energy Security," Minority Staff Report, S. Prt. 108-18 (3/5/2003), https://www.gpo.gov/fdsys/pkg/CPRT-108SPRT85551/pdf/CPRT-108SPRT85551.pdf.
3. See Feinstein-Lugar-Levin Senate Amendment 2083 to the FY2004 agricultural appropriations bill, H.R. 2673. The amendment failed 41-56. Senate Roll Call Vote 436 (11/5/2003).
4. See S. 2058, Close the Enron Loophole Act, introduced by Senator Levin in 2007; and Harkin-Chambliss-Feinstein-Snowe-Levin Senate Amendment No. 3851 to Senate Amendment No. 3500 to H.R. 2419, the 2008 farm bill, also known as the Food, Conservation, and Energy Act. The Senate amendment was agreed to by voice vote (12/13/2007), and retained in the final bill, Public Law No. 110-234, as Section 13201 et seq.
5. Their first attempt to stop the high-cost filling of the SPR was in 2003: Levin-Collins Senate Amendment No. 1750 to H.R. 2691, FY2004 Interior appropriations bill (9/23/2003), https://www.congress.gov/amendment/108th-congress/senate-amendment/1750. The amendment passed the Senate, but was dropped in conference. The second attempt was in 2004: Levin-Collins

Senate Amendment No. 2817 to S. Con. Res. 95, FY2005 budget resolution, Senate Roll Call Vote No. 54 (3/11/2004). The amendment passed the Senate, but the underlying bill was never enacted into law. The third attempt was in 2005: Frist (for Senators Levin and Collins) Senate Amendment No. 864 to H.R. 6, Energy Policy Act of 2005, adding Section 301 (6/22/2005), Public Law No. 109-58 (8/8/2005), https://www.congress.gov/amendment/109th-congress/senate-amendment/864. The amendment was enacted into law, but DOE ignored the required balancing test. The successful fourth attempt was in 2008: S. 2598, Strategic Petroleum Reserve Fill Suspension and Consumer Protection Act (2/6/2008), was incorporated into Reid Amendment No. 4737 to Senate Amendment No. 4707 to S. 2284, Flood Insurance Reform and Modernization Act (5/13/2008), https://www.congress.gov/amendment/110th-congress/senate-amendment/4737; and enacted into law in H.R. 6022, Strategic Petroleum Reserve Fill Suspension and Consumer Protection Act (5/14/2008), Public Law No. 110-232 (05/19/2008). For more information on oil company profits, see, for example, "Money Guzzlers: Big Oil Prepares to Announce Profits," Center for American Progress, Daniel J. Weiss and Anne Wingate (7/23/2007), chart entitled, "Big Five Oil Company Profits 2001–2007," http://ampr.gs/2jEEJQ5; "Global 500: The World's Largest Corporations," *Fortune*, Telis Demos (7/11/2007) (in 2006, due to high oil prices, oil companies were among the most profitable corporations in the United States), http://for.tn/2zfBZj7.

6. The information in this section is based on "Excessive Speculation in the Natural Gas Market," S. Hrg. 110-235 (6/25 and 7/9/2007) (hereinafter "2007 Natural Gas Hearing"), https://www.gpo.gov/fdsys/pkg/CHRG-110shrg36616/pdf/CHRG-110shrg36616.pdf.

7. See "The Role of Market Speculation in Rising Oil and Gas Prices: A Need to Put the Cop Back on the Beat," Staff Report by the U.S. Senate Permanent Subcommittee on Investigations, S. Prt. 109-65 (6/27/2006), at 24, https://www.gpo.gov/fdsys/pkg/CPRT-109SPRT28640/pdf/CPRT-109SPRT28640.pdf.

8. *CFTC v. Amaranth Advisors LLC*, Case No. 1-07-cv-06682-DC (SDNY 5/21/2008), Court Opinion, at 6.

9. "The Amaranth Collapse: What Happened and What Have We Learned Thus Far?" EDHEC Risk and Asset Management Research Centre, Hilary Till (8/2007), http://bit.ly/2ARGXyX.

10. *CFTC v. Amaranth Advisors LLC*, Case No. 1-07-cv-06682-DC (SDNY), CFTC Complaint (7/25/2007); *In re Amaranth Advisers LLC*, 128 FERC ¶ 61,085, Order to Show Cause and Notice of Proposed Penalties (7/26/2007).

11. "Amaranth Entities Ordered to Pay a $7.5 Million Civil Fine in CFTC Action Alleging Attempted Manipulation of Natural Gas Futures Prices," CFTC Press Release No. 5692-09 (8/12/2009), http://www.cftc.gov/PressRoom/PressReleases/pr5692-09; *In re Amaranth Advisers LLC*, 128 FERC ¶ 61,154 Order Approving Uncontested Settlement (8/12/2009), https://www.ferc.gov/enforcement/market-manipulation/amaranth.pdf.

12. *Hunter v. FERC*, 711 F.3d 155, 157 (D.C. Cir. 2013).

13. "Federal Court Orders Brian Hunter of Calgary, Alberta to Pay a $750,000 Civil Fine in CFTC Action Alleging Attempted Manipulation of Natural Gas Futures Prices during the Expiry on Two Trading Days," CFTC Press Release No. pr7000-14 (9/15/2014), http://www.cftc.gov/PressRoom/PressReleases/pr7000-14.

14. See 2008 farm bill, Public Law No. 110-234, Title XIII, Commodity Futures, Section 13201 et seq.

15. See, for example, "Excessive Speculation in the Wheat Market," S. Hrg. 111-155 (7/21/2009), https://www.gpo.gov/fdsys/pkg/CHRG-111shrg53114/pdf/CHRG-111shrg53114.pdf; Levin letter filed with the SEC (3/19/2012) in response to a concept release, "Use of Derivatives by Investment Companies under the Investment Company Act of 1940," SEC Release No. IC 29776, RIN: 3235-AL22 (8/31/2011), https://www.sec.gov/comments/s7-33-11/s73311-54.pdf; "Compliance with Tax Limits on Mutual Fund Commodity Speculation," S. Hrg. 112-343 (1/26/2012), https://www.gpo.gov/fdsys/pkg/CHRG-112shrg73671/pdf/CHRG-112shrg73671.pdf; "Excessive Speculation and Compliance with the Dodd-Frank Act," S. Hrg. 112-313 (11/3/2011), https://www.gpo.gov/fdsys/pkg/CHRG-112shrg72487/pdf/CHRG-112shrg72487.pdf.

16. Public Law 111-203 (7/21/2010).

17. The information in this section is based on "Wall Street Bank Involvement with Physical Commodities," S. Hrg. 113-501 (11/20–21/2014), Volumes 1–2 (hereinafter "2014 Senate Commodities Hearing"), https://www.gpo.gov/fdsys/pkg/CHRG-113shrg91522/pdf/CHRG-113shrg91522.pdf.

18. "The Merchants of Wall Street: Banking, Commerce, and Commodities," *Minnesota Law Review*, Professor Saule T. Omarova (11/24/2012), Volume 98, Issue 265 (2013), https://papers.ssrn.com/sol3/papers.cfm?abstract_id=2180647.

19. 2014 Senate Commodities Hearing, "Physical Commodity Activities at SIFIs," Prepared by the Federal Reserve Bank of New York Commodities Team (10/3/2012), FRB-PSI-200477-510 (sealed exhibit).

20. 2014 Senate Commodities Hearing, Hearing Exhibit 1h, at 823; discussed at 103–105.

21. S. 3013.

22. "Industrial and Commercial Metals," Rule Promulgated by the OCC, 81 Fed. Reg. 251, at 96353 (12/30/2016).

23. "Regulations Q and Y; Risk-Based Capital and Other Regulatory Requirements for Activities of Financial Holding Companies Related to Physical Commodities and Risk-Based Capital Requirements for Merchant Banking Investments," Rule Proposed by the Federal Reserve, 81 Fed. Reg. 190, at 67220 (9/30/2016).

14

Pursuing Oversight

"Not everything that is faced can be changed; but nothing can be changed until it is faced."
James Baldwin, The Cross of Redemption: Uncollected Writings *(Vintage International 2011)* ©

In January 2015, Senator Levin hung up his public service hat. After 36 years in the Senate—Michigan's longest serving Senator—he moved back home to Detroit. The Levin PSI crew disbursed. Some of us went to other Senate jobs, some to the executive branch, some to law firms, and some of us retired.

The Levin legacy at PSI lives on. New PSI leadership has taken up the subcommittee's traditions of bipartisan, fact-based, in-depth investigations. In 2015, for example, PSI chair Rob Portman and then ranking minority member Claire McCaskill launched a bipartisan investigation into sex trafficking on the Internet, targeting a U.S. company called Backpage.com. A protracted battle to obtain documents from Backpage.com led to a 2016 court decision upholding PSI's right to subpoena the information.[1] Backpage.com eventually produced the documents, and PSI wrote up its investigative results. Backpage owners and officers were later indicted for profiting from prostitution, money laundering, and other crimes.[2] In another example, in 2018, PSI chair Portman and then ranking minority member Tom Carper joined forces on an investigation to stop illegal opioids from being shipped into the United States.[3]

As important as inspiring a new generation of bipartisan PSI investigations, the Levin legacy furnishes proof of a series of propositions that might otherwise be discounted as improbable or even impossible. First, Senator Levin's

© The Author(s) 2018
E. J. Bean, *Financial Exposure*, https://doi.org/10.1007/978-3-319-94388-6_14

15 years on PSI offer incontrovertible evidence that fact-based, bipartisan, in-depth oversight is not only possible in Congress, it can happen even when partisan gales are blowing. Effective bipartisan oversight is not a matter of pie-in-the-sky, wishful thinking, but a feasible undertaking by determined members of Congress. Second, the Levin years demonstrate that congressional investigators, when given resources and member backing, have the investigative tools needed to unravel complex issues and hidden misconduct. Finally, the Levin years prove that effective congressional oversight can lead to useful, even profound policy reforms. Congressional fact-finding can effect positive change.

Those are important messages for an American public wondering if Congress has the wherewithal to meet its Constitutional obligations: to act as a check on executive branch excesses and to champion the public interest against private sector wrongdoing. Conventional wisdom paints a dismal picture of Congress—riven by partisan warfare, seeped in unpleasantness, politically paralyzed. It says partisan politics have choked the life out of Congress, and we should all give up and go home.

But the Levin oversight record offers a powerful counterpoint to that gloomy assessment. It offers hope to those willing to take up the call of good government despite the dire analysis of Congress. Contrary to the conventional view of Washington, my days working for the Senate were filled with purpose, bipartisan teamwork, and the exhilaration of meeting the challenges inherent in that most favored of American political pursuits: to form a more perfect Union.

The truth is that oversight offers a satisfying avenue of work even when Congress as a whole is experiencing division and dysfunction. When legislation is elusive, oversight offers immediate opportunities to attack problems in a useful way. When partisanship is roaring, oversight staffs can disappear behind closed doors, cross party lines, and join forces on an investigative project. All they need is direction from their bosses. More, nothing about a congressional investigation is wasted effort when the objectives are to develop a bipartisan understanding of a problem, write it up so others can comprehend it, hold a public hearing to air concerns, and initiate a sustained effort to remedy the disorder.

What surprised me the most about congressional oversight was the power of simply bearing witness to the facts. In every investigation, one of our driving goals was to educate policymakers and the public about a complex problem. We started with what happened, then dove deeper to examine why and how, seeking the larger context needed to understand the significance and consequences of the events and issues. Conveying that complex web of information in a fair and intelligible way was the key challenge behind every inquiry. And the pleasant surprise was how often conveying the facts with accuracy and sensitivity led to meaningful reforms.

Of course, it helped having a leader like Senator Levin and the power to issue Senate subpoenas, not to mention the bipartisan traditions that shielded us from so much of the rancor that reined outside the PSI realm.

Today, as I look back over the Levin years, I've concluded that our most important accomplishment was taking up the PSI mantle of bipartisanship and doggedly working with our Republican partners to complete every investigation. Together, from money laundering to offshore tax abuse to banks behaving badly to commodity speculation, we bridged our political divides, exposed wrongdoing, and sparked change. While colleagues in other offices bemoaned the deterioration of Congress and spent years circling the same mulberry bushes to no effect, PSI built a record of bipartisan trust and effective oversight—proving it could be done.

At the same time, our investigations weren't quick or easy. Bipartisanship can't be rushed. The necessary precursor was a joint decision by the PSI chair and ranking member to work together. Both sides then needed to join forces to seek the documents, interviews, and other evidence they viewed as relevant to the inquiry. After gathering the information, both sides needed to lower their guards, recognize their ideological biases, and marinate in the facts. Consensus on what happened had to be built slowly, using specific evidence and reasoned analysis. Reports took months to produce. Compromise was mandatory.

The consequence was that most of PSI's investigations required a year or longer. That meant PSI had only a few hearings each year, instead of the weekly or monthly hearings that some in Congress viewed as an objective marker of effectiveness. We saw less as more—fewer investigations, in greater depth with more bipartisan interactions, led to more accurate fact-finding, greater consensus, better ideas for reforms, and stronger commitments to change. Our go-slow, go-deep approach stood in marked contrast to the go-quick, go-wide approach taken by many other congressional committees, but we saw ourselves as equally or even more productive. We measured our success by the bipartisan nature of our hearings, the degree of consensus in our reports, and our progress in achieving reforms.

Congressional investigations aren't rocket science. They are a matter of common-sense planning, persistence, patience, and commitment to the facts. They require the realization that the best fact-finding is done by parties who bring different perspectives to the task, ask different questions, and notice different details and connections. It is the interaction of disparate views that leads an investigative team to a broader, deeper, and more accurate under-standing of what happened and why. And when differing sides set aside their differences to work together in good faith to find the facts, it can be a deeply satisfying experience.

More than that, constructive congressional oversight lies at the heart of good government. It is all about identifying and solving problems to protect and strengthen our communities. When the target is problematic government programs or agencies, congressional oversight contributes to the system of checks and balances envisioned by our Constitution as vital to a well-functioning government. When the target is the private sector, congressional oversight can expose and address a wide range of abusive conduct, from finan-cial wrongdoing to workplace dangers, environmental misdeeds, tax dodging, price gouging, and many of the other ills plaguing modern society. When done well, congressional oversight can not only identify and repair problems but also help restore public confidence in Congress.

Of course, many investigations fall short of what congressional oversight ought to be. Too many inquiries are marred by partisan distrust or incivility, disregard for facts, or unethical or ineffective investigative tactics. Some com-mittees select investigative topics guaranteed to produce partisan dogfights, or design inquiries that attack individuals rather than policy problems. Others deliberately exclude or limit the participation of the minority party in the investigative work. Still others use hearings or reports to railroad an ideologi-cal viewpoint through committee instead of generating a bipartisan dialogue. Those failed efforts should be condemned, and pressure put on the partici-pants to adopt the bipartisan, cooperative norms that mark successful con-gressional investigations.

History shows, of course, that those investigative norms don't always prevail. Some members of Congress simply don't value bipartisanship and view working with the opposing party—with all the negotiations and compromises required—as a betrayal of their values. Others value bipartisanship, but don't engage in it, because of pressure from peers or congressional leaders. Some committee mem-bers have gone so far as to forbid their staffs to sign letters with the other party, conduct joint interviews, or share an investigative report before it goes public. I've seen that type of hyper-partisanship on both sides of the aisle.

When faced with that kind of partisan hostility, bipartisan congressional investigations can become virtually impossible. But that doesn't mean the snubbed party ought to give up investigating or start conducting one-sided inquiries likely to make party relationships even worse. A better approach is to undertake fact-based, nonpartisan inquiries that raise issues of such impor-tance to the public that the other party has to take notice.

If the party making the effort conducts a solid, fair-minded investigation with interesting results, it may even begin to break down the political divides. One example of how that can work involves Congressman Henry Waxman from California. He became known for conducting influential investigations, even when in the minority party and even when facing partisan hostility.[4] For example, a Waxman-led investigation into the tobacco industry, conducted despite Republican opposition, uncovered such powerful facts that it helped alter the public perception of tobacco products, while helping spur changes in federal tobacco policy. Another Waxman investigation began as a solo effort, but garnered Republic support after discovering that, in response to Hurricane Katrina, FEMA provided hurricane victims with trailers contaminated by toxic chemicals. The facts were too powerful to ignore.

Single-party investigations can be effective, especially when an inquiry is fact-based, intellectually honest, and of interest to the public. At the same time, single-party investigations are inherently harder to conduct and less trusted by the public and policymakers. They have to jump hurdle after hurdle just to win respect. That's why bipartisan inquiries remain the gold standard. They make it easier for Congress to get information and harder for opponents to stop an investigation. They are inherently more trustworthy. They produce better reforms. They are worth the hard work they require.

It is perhaps also worth noting that bipartisan, fact-based congressional investigations are an American innovation almost unique in the world. Few other countries enable their elected legislators to conduct the type of intensive investigations for which the U.S. Congress is world famous—from Watergate to the 9/11 Commission to the financial crisis. Some non-U.S. legislatures have begun to adopt the U.S. model. Legislatures in the United Kingdom, European Union, and Australia have increasingly held oversight hearings in the U.S. mold, exposing wrongdoing, identifying problems, and advocating policy reforms. Those oversight efforts should be acknowledged for promoting hallmark American principles, including the importance of checks and balances, effective self-government, and sustainable democracy.

Given U.S. world leadership and the need to solve our own political problems, it is more important than ever to strengthen congressional oversight. We need to build up the norms that favor bipartisan, fact-based investigations and reject efforts to portray partisan squabbles or sloppy research as equivalent to a congressional inquiry. We need to provide training for members of Congress and their staffs on how to conduct effective oversight, including how to find the facts, write up the results, conduct public hearings, and pursue policy reforms. We need to support the legislators who take the time needed to conduct bipartisan inquiries and the congressional leaders who encourage bipartisan efforts. In addition, we need to encourage research into the factors that lead to effective investigations.

The Levin era on PSI provides a template for productive congressional oversight investigations. It demonstrates that bipartisan, effective congressional oversight is not only possible, but a tool within the reach of every member of Congress. It champions robust, bipartisan congressional investigations as a precious American heritage that should be respected, nurtured, and celebrated.

Notes

1. *Senate Permanent Subcommittee on Investigations v. Ferrer*, 199 F.Supp.3d 125 (D.D.C. 2016), *appeal vacated as moot*, 856 F.3d 1080 (D.C. Cir. 2017).
2. See, for example, "Justice Department Leads Effort to Seize Backpage.Com, the Internet's Leading Forum for Prostitution Ads, and Obtains 93-Count Federal Indictment," DOJ Press Release (4/9/2018), https://www.justice.gov/opa/pr/justice-department-leads-effort-seize-backpagecom-internet-s-leading-forum-prostitution-ads; "Attorney General Kamala D. Harris Announces Criminal Charges Against Senior Corporate Officers of Backpage.com for Profiting from Prostitution and Arrest of Carl Ferrer, CEO," State of California Attorney General Press Release (10/6/2016), https://oag.ca.gov/news/press-releases/attorney-general-kamala-d-harris-announces-criminal-charges-against-senior.
3. "Combatting The Opioid Crisis: Exploiting Vulnerabilities In International Mail," Bipartisan Staff Report, U.S. Senate Permanent Subcommittee on Investigations (1/24/2018), https://www.hsgac.senate.gov/imo/media/doc/Combatting%20the%20Opioid%20Crisis%20-%20Exploiting%20Vulnerabilities%20in%20International%20Mail1.pdf.
4. See, for example, *The Waxman Report: How Congress Really Works*, Henry Waxman (Twelve 2009).

Index[1]

---

[1] Note: Page numbers followed by 'n' refer to notes.

© The Author(s) 2018
E. J. Bean, *Financial Exposure*, https://doi.org/10.1007/978-3-319-94388-6